Systems

Programming

for **Windows® 95**

Walter
Oney

PUBLISHED BY
Microsoft Press
A Division of Microsoft Corporation
One Microsoft Way
Redmond, Washington 98052-6399

Library of Congress Cataloging-in-Publication Data pending.

Printed and bound in the United States of America.

1 2 3 4 5 6 7 8 9   MLML   1 0 9 8 7 6

Distributed to the book trade in Canada by Macmillan of Canada, a division of Canada Publishing Corporation.

A CIP catalogue record for this book is available from the British Library.

Microsoft Press books are available through booksellers and distributors worldwide. For further information about international editions, contact your local Microsoft Corporation office. Or contact Microsoft Press International directly at fax (206) 936-7329.

Acquisitions Editor: Eric Stroo
Project Editor: Katherine A. Krause
Technical Editors: Kurt Meyer, Jim Fuchs

*To my wife, Marty, who's the second happiest person
in the world that this is done.*

Contents

Preface

A NOTE ABOUT NEW TECHNOLOGY

Microsoft announced the Win32 Driver Model (WDM) at the 1996 Windows Hardware Engineering Conference (WinHEC) in San Jose, California, while this book was in production. WDM will someday let you write a single device driver that will work equally well in Windows NT and in the successor to Windows 95. WDM drivers will look more like today's kernel-mode drivers in Windows NT than like today's virtual device drivers (VxDs) in Windows 95. Microsoft's announcement was sufficiently terse that more than one WinHEC attendee misunderstood and complained about having to unlearn VxD programming just when it was finally becoming clear.

To understand the significance of the WDM announcement, you have to understand what motivated it. In my opinion, the purpose of WDM is twofold: to provide a way to extend Plug and Play functionality to Windows NT and to enable hardware manufacturers to build drivers for consumer electronics devices destined for connection to USB and 1394 buses. The fact that the drivers will look more like Windows NT drivers than like VxDs is probably just an expression of Microsoft's internal political processes.

I believe that WDM will only be incrementally important over the next few years. Anybody's current investment in VxD technology will still be valuable for as long as there is a product called "Windows" in addition to one called "Windows NT." Windows 95 and its immediate successors will continue to run VxDs. Devices for which you currently write VxDs will continue to *require* VxDs until Microsoft gets around to extending WDM to all classes of devices. That may not happen soon. Furthermore, Microsoft has already announced that WDM will initially be available only in OEM releases of Windows 95. In particular, there won't be an upgrade generally available for end users for a while.

Consequently, if you want to extend Windows 95, or if you want to write a driver that will work on the installed base of Windows 95 machines in the immediate future, you need to know the things that this book talks about. A fortiori, if you want compatibility with Windows 3.1 as well, the techniques in this book are the ones to learn.

REFERENCES TO THE DDK

References in this book to the Windows 95 Device Driver Kit (the DDK) are based on the April 1996 version. Later versions of the DDK may not contain the specific section titles referred to in this book. In addition, please note that all references to subject hierarchies in the DDK are based on the DDK as presented by the MSDN viewer, rather than as presented by the DDK help file (DDPR.HLP) or the DDK Word (.DOC) files.

A MICROSOFT VISUAL C++ 4.1 BUG

As this book was going to press, Microsoft released version 4.1 of Visual C++. The new version has an unfortunate bug in its handling of enumerated constants in inline assembly statements. Consequently, you can't use this new version for building VxDs with the DDK. (You can, however, use Visual C++ version 4.0.) A fix is planned for a later version.

THE COMPANION CD

Real-mode CD-ROM drivers under Windows 95 truncate all long filenames on a CD. If your CD-ROM drive uses a real-mode driver, you will not be able to see all of the directories or files on this disc. (If this is the case, you should contact your CD-ROM drive manufacturer for an updated Windows 95 driver.) You can still use the companion disc, however, by following the installation instructions below; files will be copied from a special SETUP directory on the companion CD to your hard disk, being renamed with the appropriate long filename in the process. You can then browse the files on your hard disk. Alternatively, you can browse the files using their 8.3 aliases from within the SETUP directory on the CD.

Installing the Companion CD Files on Your Hard Disk

To install the program files on your hard disk, run SETUP.EXE in the root directory of the CD. Then follow the onscreen instructions. The DDK help file and annotation file will *not* be copied to your hard disk.

The Help File on the Companion Disc

The companion disc contains a copy of the help file that accompanies the DDK, along with my annotations for that help file. The help file is from the April 1996 version of the DDK. More current versions are available quarterly from MSDN, but the annotations file may not be useable for versions other than the one on this disc. When the help file is updated on the DDK, new versions of the annotations file will be made available through the World Wide Web at the following address:

http://www.tiac.net/users/waltoney

See the README.TXT file in the root directory of the companion disc for more information about the help and annotation files and for additional information about the rest of the contents of the disc.

SUPPORT

Every effort has been made to ensure the accuracy of this book and the contents of the companion disc. Microsoft Press provides corrections for books through the World Wide Web at the following address:

http://www.microsoft.com/mspress/support/

If you have comments, questions, or ideas regarding this book or the companion disc, please send them to Microsoft Press using either of the following methods:

Postal Mail:
Microsoft Press
Attn: *Systems Programing for Windows 95* Editor
One Microsoft Way
Redmond, WA 98052-6399

Email:
MSPINPUT@MICROSOFT.COM

Please note that product support is not offered through the above mail addresses. For support information on Visual C++ you can call C/C++ Standard Support at (206) 635-7007 on weekdays between 6 a.m. and 6 p.m. Pacific time. For support information on MASM you can call Macro Assembler Standard Support at (206) 646-5109 during the same hours. If you need additional support for VxD programming in general, contact Microsoft Support Network Sales at (800) 936-3500.

ACKNOWLEDGMENTS

Most things in our highly dependent society are team efforts nowadays. This book certainly was. It needed Dean Holmes and Eric Stroo to believe in the need for it, and Lee Fisher and Jonathan Kagle to read the outlines and proposals. It needed the considerable input of technical reviewers, including Raymond Chen, Rich Pletcher,

Sriram Rajagopalan, Harish Naidu, Bill Parry, Ron Radko, Pierre-Yves Santerre, Ray Pedrizetti, Matt Squires, Martin Borve, Doug Howe, Bill Ingle, and Sandeep Sahas-rabudhe. *They* all needed management from David Cole, Dennis Adler, Jon Thoma-son, Brad Hastings, Jan Robbins, and Teri Schiele. It needed Kathy Krause's and Kurt Meyer's editorial eyes. It needed Jamey Kirby to shed light on some of the nuances of the Input/Output Supervisor. It also needed all of the people who asked or answered questions on the CompuServe WINSDK forum and thereby forced me to research issues I hadn't even realized were there to be researched, and it needed my seminar students looking perplexed so I could better understand what trips up beginners at systems-level programming for Windows 95. And, like computer books from *real* authors, it needed Claudette Moore to bring an author and a publisher together so that it might be created.

Part I

Introduction

Chapter 1

Overview

I needed this book desperately six years ago when I wrote my first virtual device driver. Windows 3.0 had just come out, and I had the task of keeping TSR programs built on top of a DOS extender working as Windows started up and shut down. The solution to that problem required me to write a virtual device driver (VxD), but the only documentation available was a photocopy of a beta draft of the *Virtual Device Adaptation Guide.* As an instruction on how to design, build, and debug a VxD, that document wasn't very helpful. Somehow I struggled through that project, and through many projects since, but I always wished someone had already written down all of the things I kept learning the hard way.

I know other programmers don't understand the system interfaces of Windows 95 well enough to get their jobs done, either. I've spent a lot of time in the WINSDK forum on CompuServe during the past year, and I've seen people constantly ask the same basic questions that I've asked somewhere along the line. Larry Niven and Jerry Pournelle wrote in *The Mote in God's Eye* (Simon and Schuster, 1974) about an alien species with an Engineer subtype that's exceptionally good at practical problem solving and exceptionally bad at communication. I sometimes feel that Microsoft has published the DDK for use by Motie Engineers, who could probably figure it out.

I think users suffer when programmers can't do their jobs well. Microsoft and Windows end up taking the blame, because users can't tell the difference between a bad operating system (it's not), bad third-party programmers (they're not), and sketchy or elliptical documentation (well, yes it is) that leads to bugs. I've done my best not to be sketchy in this book and to tell you what *to* do, instead of merely what *not* to do, and *why* to do it. Having Microsoft Press for a publisher didn't give me any special access to inside information, though. I especially wanted to look at the Windows 95 source code so I could report accurately the information that

Microsoft probably wants you to know about how to use its operating system, but I couldn't even get to the plate to make my case, much less to first base. Despite my best care and that of many developers who looked at this material, therefore, you are certain to find occasional mistakes here.

WHO SHOULD READ THIS BOOK

You should read this book if you want to learn how to use the lowest-level operating system facilities of Windows 95 to get your job done. These are some of the jobs that this book will help you do:

- Write a device driver for a new piece of hardware. Windows 95 works better when hardware manufacturers supply 32-bit protected-mode drivers instead of MS-DOS real-mode drivers or 16-bit Windows DLL drivers. This book will tell you all about writing a driver that fits well into the system architecture of Windows 95.

- Upgrade a device driver. If you're starting with a Windows 3.x virtual device driver, you may not have far to go; try reading the chapters on Plug and Play (Chapters 11 and 12) and see whether (maybe) all you have to do is add a veneer of Plug-and-Playness to your existing code. If you're starting with a 16-bit driver, however, you're in the same boat as a programmer who needs to write a brand new driver.

- Provide support services for a system tool. Debuggers, system monitors, troubleshooting tools, and the like all benefit from (and sometimes require) help from the operating system that Microsoft doesn't provide. Writing a virtual device driver lets you plug into the lowest level of the operating system *using documented interfaces rather than undocumented hacks.*

- Understand how Windows 95 works on the inside. You've probably read about the fact that Windows 95 relies to some extent on the INT 21h interface to perform file operations. But did you know (for example) that INT 21h file system calls on one system can end up being serviced by a virtual device driver on another computer elsewhere on the network? This book will explain the magic underneath that process and other Windows 95 processes.

Systems programming necessarily involves knowing many details about hardware and about assembly language. I've tried to minimize the amount of that knowledge you'll need to make use of this book. You should (obviously) already understand thoroughly the area in which you're working—such as the quirks of your particular serial board or the application you're trying to enhance. Beyond that, you should be able to *read* fragments of assembly-language programs for the Intel x86 processor, although you don't necessarily need to be able to write such programs. And you should be fluent in the C or C++ programming languages; most of the examples in this book use C or C++.

HOW THIS BOOK IS ORGANIZED

This book has four parts. Part I, comprising Chapters 1 through 5, presents an overview of the Windows 95 system architecture and of crucial concepts involved in systems programming for Windows 95.

- Chapter 1 (this chapter) describes the overall organization of the book and tells you how to find your way around the book and the companion CD.

- Chapter 2 places Windows 95 in the context of all of Microsoft's operating systems and explains the roles of various kinds of device drivers.

- Chapter 3 summarizes the architecture of Windows 95 from the perspective of a systems programmer.

- Chapter 4 describes the programming interfaces used to interact with the Virtual Machine Manager and other core components of the Windows 95 operating system.

- Chapter 5 summarizes the special features of the Intel 32-bit processor chips that run Windows 95. This chapter assumes that you already know a lot about 16-bit programming for Intel chips. If you don't, you might want to skip the chapter, because the rest of the book makes perfect sense without it.

Part II of the book covers the essentials of virtual device driver programming. No matter what systems programming project you have in mind, you'll need to know about these topics.

- Chapter 6 describes how the Virtual Machine Manager manages memory and processor time.

- Chapter 7 explains the details of how to build a virtual device driver in assembly language, in C, or in C++. Microsoft and third-party tools have finally reached a level of integration that lets you easily write drivers in the language of your choice, and this chapter explains the nitty-gritty.

■ Chapter 8 discusses loading and initializing device drivers. Gone are the days when you could just add a device= statement to the CONFIG.SYS file and know that everything would be taken care of by MS-DOS. Read this chapter to learn how to load a Windows 95 virtual device driver statically or dynamically and what to do to initialize the driver.

■ Chapter 9 contains a grab bag of useful programming techniques for virtual device driver authors. This chapter explains how a driver can call (and be called by) other drivers, how to allocate memory, how to provide for asynchronous callbacks, and how to synchronize execution with other drivers and with applications.

■ Chapter 10 explains how to *virtualize* hardware and software for the benefit of programs running in virtual machines. In previous versions of Windows, virtualization was the main reason you wrote a *virtual* device driver, and the techniques explained in this chapter remain important even now.

Building on these basics, Part III of the book discusses input/output programming. These are the chapters that programmers writing hardware drivers will be most interested in.

■ Chapters 11 and 12 collectively describe the Configuration Manager and the Plug and Play architecture of Windows 95. Read these chapters to learn how Windows 95 identifies hardware, assigns resources, and loads and initializes drivers.

■ Chapter 13 explains what a driver should do with the hardware once the driver is loaded and once it has identified the interrupts, direct memory access (DMA) channels, and the other resources that the hardware uses. This chapter explains how to handle hardware interrupts, how to "trap" I/O ports to manage contention or to simulate devices, how to access memory-mapped hardware, and how to deal with DMA.

■ Chapter 14 describes communications drivers, which work together with Microsoft's VCOMM driver to handle serial and parallel ports. This chapter presents an extended example of a serial port driver written in C++, showing you how to craft your own customized port driver.

■ Chapter 15 discusses the Input/Output Supervisor (IOS), which handles disk devices and other "block" devices. This chapter features a working RAM-disk driver and an IOS request monitor that illustrate how to write port and vendor-supplied drivers, which are the two kinds of block device drivers most people are likely to write.

Finally, Part IV describes some additional features of Windows 95 that allow you to extend the functionality of the system.

■ Chapter 16 covers the Installable File System Manager, which is the eventual target for those INT 21h calls I mentioned earlier. This chapter explains how to write a driver that supports a new file system on a local disk device.

■ Chapter 17, the last chapter in the book, describes the DOS Protected Mode Interface (DPMI). Although new programs don't need the features of DPMI anymore, so-called "legacy" applications and 16-bit applications that must be portable to Windows 3.1 sometimes do need them.

ABOUT THE CODE SAMPLES

A sample is not the same thing as an explanation. That's why you'll find very few complete program listings in this book. Instead, I've tried to use fragments of code to illustrate general points. And there are a *lot* of code fragments because this is a book for programmers who think in computer languages.

Another reason I haven't included long listings in the book is that, frankly, I think there are already enough books in the series *My Code and Welcome to It.* You know the kind of book I mean: the author, who's primarily a programmer rather than a writer, has written a bunch of code that he or she thinks is really neat, so he or she writes a book that reprints the code so we can all appreciate it. Well, I'm primarily a programmer too, and I often think my code is pretty neat. But I think you're more interested in making your own programs work than in admiring mine.

Notwithstanding all that I just said, you'd feel cheated if you didn't have the surrounding context for the many code fragments in the text. That's why there's a companion CD. The CD contains a few working programs and a great many examples that either compile or work only on my particular computer. A README file on the CD explains how to tell the difference and how to experiment with them on your own. The samples are suitable for use with Microsoft's MASM 6.11 [the special version on the Microsoft Windows 95 Device Driver Kit (DDK), that is] and with Microsoft Visual C++ version 4.0. Most of the samples rely on the DDK, although some of them illustrate how to use VTOOLSD from Vireo Software. The samples were compiled and tested on a Pentium 90 with 64 MB of memory, an ISA bus and a PCI local bus, and a 3.5-inch floppy disk drive.

Another thing you'll find on the CD is a copy of the official Microsoft WinHelp files from the Windows 95 DDK *and* my own annotation file with notes about the official entries. I created the annotations based on my own observations and those of other programmers who sent me email on CompuServe. (If you'd like to add your own input to the next edition of this book, my email address is waltoney@oneysoft.com.)

NOTE   For more detailed information about the companion CD, please see the Preface.

ABOUT ALL THE UNDOCUMENTED HACKS

ABOUT ALL THE DOCUMENTED HACKS

I left the preceding section blank to make a point: this is *not* a book about undocumented secrets. It *is* a book about how to get your job done using system interfaces that Microsoft wanted you to know about. All of those interfaces are documented (or would have been if someone hadn't overlooked them). The only side effects I mention are the ones that will bite you if you don't know about them. The only time I mention disassemblies or undocumented fields in control blocks is when there is no other way to explain how to use an interface that you're supposed to be able to use.

Don't imagine that I'm toeing a line drawn by Microsoft just because Microsoft Press is publishing this book. I happen to think that everyone is best served by coloring within the lines. Microsoft has some sort of obligation to preserve the functionality of a documented interface as Windows evolves. Besides, you and I read the documentation that Microsoft prepared to guide its *own* programmers in writing portions of the system. If Windows 95 itself relies heavily on a feature, such as the way the Virtual Communications Device manages contention for serial ports, you can be pretty sure that the feature will be fairly stable over time. On the other hand, if you rely on devious ways of tricking the system into doing your bidding (like calling the *VxDCall* interface in the KERNEL32 module despite the lengths to which Microsoft has gone to make it hard for you to do so), you pretty much deserve what happens when that interface changes unexpectedly, especially if there's a documented way to accomplish the same result, and there always is.

Another reason I prefer not to rely on undocumented features of the system is heuristic. I've learned to recognize roadblocks and extreme complexity as a signal that I'm trying to solve a problem in an inappropriate way. So if I find myself fuming that (for example) I can't easily create a hidden virtual machine from within my driver so that I can run a real-mode program to do something or other, I've learned to ask myself if maybe there might be an easier and less fragile way.

But, of course, every aspect of virtual device driver programming seems full of roadblocks and complexity when you're starting out. I hope that this book will clear up a lot of the confusion that has plagued Windows systems programmers over the years. I hope it saves you weeks and months of wasted effort.

Chapter 2

Flavors of Windows and Drivers

As a longtime systems programmer, I love being immersed in the practical details of getting programs to work. I find that I am most effective at my chosen trade when I understand where the systems I work on fit into the scheme of operating systems, both past and present. In this chapter, I review some things that you probably already know.

Windows 95 takes one more step along a path that Microsoft hopes will end with Windows NT being the standard desktop operating system. To date, systems programming in Windows versions other than Windows NT has increasingly meant writing a 32-bit, ring-zero module known as a virtual device driver (VxD). VxDs originally had the job of *virtualizing* hardware for ring-three modules such as

---

ring-zero software   Software that runs with the highest level of privilege available on an Intel processor.

ring-three software   Software that runs with the lowest level of privilege available on an Intel processor.

MS-DOS drivers and Windows DLL drivers. In Windows 95, VxDs provide the primary interface to hardware, and they also serve diverse application needs for software services.

In my opinion, Windows 3.0 was the first version of Windows that was solid and capable enough to be worthy of serious attention as an application platform. Windows 3.0 made its debut in 1990 after a lengthy and much publicized (but supposedly secret) beta program. At this stage, Intel 80386 machines were still at the high end of desktop computing, and running in enhanced mode (introduced with the 80386 processor) was more the exception than the rule. Windows 3.0 ran best (even on 80386 machines) in standard mode, and it provided continued support for the hoary old real mode, the only mode available on Intel's original 8086 processor. To no one's surprise, and probably to no one's regret, Microsoft dropped support for real mode in the Windows 3.1 release. And Windows 95 drops support for standard mode as well. Windows 95 now runs only in enhanced mode and therefore requires at least an Intel 80386 processor.

---

real mode   The default operating mode of Intel 80x86 processors that provides applications with an environment that provides one task at a time with free access to system memory and input/output devices.

A TAXONOMY OF WINDOWS SYSTEMS

Windows 95 occupies a particular niche in the ecology of operating systems. The Windows architecture itself spans a variety of microprocessor designs at many levels of capability. Windows NT targets high-end systems. Windows 3.x ran well on 80386 systems. Windows 95 aims at today's midrange desktop systems—systems with an Intel i486 processor and about 8 MB of memory. Microsoft would like you to believe, however, that an 80386 processor with only 4 MB of memory will do.

Windows NT

Windows NT is the most powerful operating system you can buy for an Intel-based desktop computer, but you need a powerful platform for it to run well. (I don't intend to wade into the fray about whether OS/2 might really be the wave of the future. Personally, I don't think so. One look at the graphics in the OS/2 Solitaire game made my mind up for me long ago.) Windows NT distinguishes itself from other species of Windows in several ways. First and foremost, Windows NT is a secure system; it prevents unauthorized access to programs and data if you place your hard disk in the care of Windows NT's native file system. Windows NT is also the only Microsoft operating system that spans different microprocessor architectures.

Windows NT introduced the 32-bit Win32 Applications Programming Interface (API). If the developer takes reasonable care, an application written for this API will run on any of the microprocessors supported by Windows NT after a simple recompilation. The Win32 API supports graphical Windows applications as well as character-mode applications, the latter of which are indistinguishable by the end user from stodgy old MS-DOS applications that don't use graphics. The key difference between the Win32 API and other Windows APIs is that it is for 32-bit programs.

NOTE Of course, an API is an abstract concept that is technically distinct from any concrete implementation of the API. Thus, someone with a lot of talent and too much spare time could create a quixotic 16-bit implementation of the Win32 API.

The Win32 API is incredibly rich and diverse. The first two books in the 1993 edition of the *Microsoft Win32 Programmer's Reference* (Microsoft Press, 1993) contain 85 chapters, with each chapter devoted to summarizing a separate aspect of the API. Twenty-seven of those chapters fit under the heading "System Services." Among the classes of system services available to the Win32 programmer are several ways of managing virtual memory, functions for creating and managing new processes and threads, four different flavors of synchronization primitives, three different file systems, at least three different methods for interprocess communication across networks, and so on.

Windows NT was first introduced about five years ago and has been slow to catch on. Two factors seem to be responsible for the slow adoption of this otherwise first-class operating system. First of all, performance is a bit of a problem. Windows NT 3.5 runs much better than the initial 3.1 version did, but you still need a very powerful computer to get the most out of it. Yesterday's high-end machine is today's midrange and tomorrow's boat anchor, though, so the importance of the performance factor will diminish over time.

The second factor in Windows NT's slow start is that there haven't been very many 32-bit applications that need it. Most Windows applications have been 16-bit, and Windows NT frankly does not run many of them as well as Windows 3.1 does. Microsoft invented the rather lame Win32s subsystem for Windows 3.1 to tempt application vendors to build 32-bit applications. The idea behind Win32s was that you could use it to develop a Win32 application to be deployed both on Windows NT and on Windows 3.1. Restrictions, incompatibilities, and outright bugs made Win32s unappealing to software vendors. Lacking a viable mass-market platform for 32-bit applications, therefore, vendors were reluctant to develop any 32-bit applications.

Windows 3.1

Windows 3.1 lies slightly below Windows NT in a ranking of capability. Designed for what are today's low-end 80386 computers, Windows 3.1 is a 32-bit operating system that runs 16-bit Windows applications, MS-DOS applications, and extended DOS applications.

---

extended DOS application   A 16-bit or 32-bit program that is built on top of a DOS extender so that it can run in protected mode while still relying on MS-DOS and the BIOS for system services. Windows itself—the KERNEL, USER, and GDI modules that applications use, rather than the operating system—is really a 16-bit extended DOS application in this sense.

protected mode   An operating mode of Intel 80286 and higher processors that supports multitasking, data security, and virtual memory.

Windows 3.1 applications use a 16-bit API to interface with the windowing system, and software interrupts to interface with MS-DOS and the BIOS. Programmers build 16-bit applications using much of the same runtime library used for regular MS-DOS applications, in fact. A major purpose of the 32-bit operating system that supervises Windows 3.1 applications is to field the software interrupts that occur in protected mode and turn them into real-mode interrupts intelligible to real-mode MS-DOS and BIOS components.

Systems programming in Windows 3.1 means working with MS-DOS device drivers, terminate-and-stay-resident (TSR) utilities, and the DOS Protected Mode Interface (DPMI). The adventurous few have also built virtual device drivers to support advanced systems programming requirements.

There are many problems with Windows 3.1. The most aggravating one is probably the requirement that Windows applications periodically yield control of the computer back to the windowing system to support cooperative multitasking. A poorly behaved application can stall the machine. Certain kinds of applications—computationally intensive programs and programs that rely on interprocess communication, to name just two—are very hard to write without violating the rule about yielding. Another problem with Windows 3.1 is that core system components such as the USER and GDI modules have limited heap space. Many users complain of an inability to launch applications because of heap limits.

At the systems level, Windows 3.1 constantly bumps up against the facts that MS-DOS isn't reentrant, that it runs only in real or *virtual 8086* (V86) mode, and that it can access only about 1 MB of memory. These facts are important because Windows 3.1 relies on MS-DOS and the BIOS for access to disk drives and the file system. Among the limitations that this reliance on real-mode software creates are the following:

- Unless the end user sets aside a region of a hard disk for a permanent swap file, Windows 3.1 needs to single-thread through MS-DOS or the BIOS to perform paging I/O.

- Access to CD-ROMs requires the MSCDEX TSR, which interferes with some peer networking software.

- Peer networking servers interfere with Windows' ability to access disk drives, with the result that server machines can't use permanent swap files and the smart paging that a permanent swap file enables.

- File system I/O requires a mode switch from protected mode to V86 mode and requires the allocation of buffers in the first megabyte of address space.

- The population of real-mode drivers, especially the ones that manage network connections, sometimes uses so much of the first megabyte of memory that the user can't run any applications.

---

reentrant code   Program code that can be interrupted and executed by another thread.

Windows 95

Windows 95 addresses many of the problems posed by Windows 3.1 and makes an independent contribution to the evolution of user-friendly computing. On the end-user front, Windows 95 adds many convenience features, including long filenames, a dockable taskbar, and a more fully integrated, document-centric interface shell. Although it is based on the same virtual-machine technology as Windows 3.1, Windows 95 includes a 32-bit file system, 32-bit disk drivers, and 32-bit network interfaces. It supports preemptive multitasking of Win32 applications using the same process and thread model as Windows NT. Its Plug and Play subsystem makes it easy for end users (and ten-thumbed systems programmers like me) to add new hardware.

One of the aspects of Windows 95 that I find especially striking is the extent to which it's compatible with older software. One of my all-time favorite cartoons illustrates the point nicely. In the first panel of the cartoon, U.S. Army Private Sack pauses to read the company bulletin board, which is nearly covered by memos. In successive panels, we watch Sack dig through layers of paper that eventually block out the sun. Evidently, nothing has ever been discarded from this bulletin board. In

Figure 2-1. *Compatibility in Windows 95.*

the last panel (see Figure 2-1), Sack holds a match in order to read General George Washington's order for the Delaware River crossing.[1]

Well, Windows 95 is like that. The software equivalent of the Delaware crossing might be the Program Segment Prefix (PSP) data area that MS-DOS uses to distinguish one application (and, most importantly, one set of file handles) from another. Even a Win32 application has a PSP in Windows 95, and it's in the first megabyte of memory, where MS-DOS can get at it.[2] Just about any feature of MS-DOS, the BIOS, or Windows itself that was important to "legacy" applications is still alive and well in Windows 95. For example:

■ Windows 95 will handle all networking tasks using brand-new 32-bit drivers if it can, but it will use your existing real-mode network if that's all you have.

■ Windows 95 will use brand-new 32-bit drivers to access all your hardware or it will use left-over real-mode drivers if necessary. To cite one of many possible examples, my system has a CD-ROM and a hard disk for which

---

1. George Baker, "The Bulletin Board," in *The Sad Sack, By Sergeant George Baker,* Simon & Schuster, 1944. Cartoon panel reprinted with the permission of Simon & Schuster from THE SAD SACK by Sergeant George Baker. Copyright © 1944 by George Baker. Copyright renewed 1972 by George Baker.

2. Andrew Schulman, *Unauthorized Windows 95: A Developer's Guide to Exploring the Foundations of Windows "Chicago,"* IDG Books, 1995.

I never bothered to install real-mode drivers. I can't access these disks at all until I start Windows 95, whereupon I start using 32-bit drivers that I never explicitly asked for—Windows 95 Setup detected the hardware and automatically configured my system to match.

■ Because 16-bit Windows applications sometimes depend both on the ability to share memory with each other and on the cooperative multi-tasking model of previous releases of Windows, Windows 95 runs 16-bit applications in essentially the same way as Windows 3.1 does.

■ Commercially important 16-bit Windows applications incorrectly test the Windows version number, so Windows 95 lies to them so that they will run.

All of this compatibility poses special problems for those of us who want to write systems programs. On one hand, it's relatively easy (or would be if you had enough of an explanation beforehand) to write a straightforward 32-bit extension to the operating system in the form of a virtual device driver. On the other hand, it can be very difficult to make your system extension work equally well on behalf of real-mode MS-DOS, extended DOS, 16-bit Windows, and 32-bit Windows applications. For example, if you're supporting a disk device, it may be sufficient to provide a layer driver that fits neatly into the Input/Output Supervisor architecture, but in general, hardware support sometimes requires you to trap and simulate access from V86-mode programs, and that task is a little bit complicated.

A BRIEF HISTORY OF DEVICE DRIVERS FOR WINDOWS

Many of the tasks that systems programmers perform revolve around writing device drivers for particular hardware. Generally speaking, I think those tasks are easier in Windows 95 than they were in previous versions of Windows. In programming a device driver, it helps to understand some history.

Real-Mode Windows

MS-DOS and the system BIOS have supplied drivers for many hardware devices since the beginning. The BIOS exports driver services by means of a few well-known software interrupts, such as INT 10h for the video subsystem, INT 13h for the disk subsystem, and INT 16h for the keyboard. The BIOS also handles hardware interrupts and assumes responsibility for managing the Programmable Interrupt Controller. MS-DOS also exports system services by means of software interrupts like 21h, 25h, 26h, and so on, and it provides a mechanism (the device= statement in

CONFIG.SYS) whereby new or improved drivers can be loaded at startup time. Ralf Brown and Jim Kyle's *PC Interrupts* (Addison-Wesley, 1994) contains a comprehensive discussion of these MS-DOS and BIOS interfaces, which have been familiar to many PC programmers for years.

Standard-Mode Windows

MS-DOS and the BIOS had paramount importance in the early days of Windows. Windows was originally a real-mode "operating environment" that provided a graphical overlay to MS-DOS. At the system level, Windows was nothing more than a large graphics application. The advent of the Intel 80286 processor made it possible for Windows to run in protected mode and to thereby gain access to up to 16 MB of physical memory. By switching the processor in and out of protected mode, Windows continued to use MS-DOS and the BIOS for all its system needs. This mode of operation eventually became known as *standard mode*.

Switching between real and protected modes was horribly expensive on the Intel 80286 processor. Intel provided a single, relatively fast instruction for switching from real to protected mode, but apparently assumed that no one would ever need to switch back. Consequently, the only way for a protected-mode program like standard-mode Windows to access real-mode software like MS-DOS was to reset the processor. Among the popular ways people developed to trigger the reset were to goose the keyboard controller to supply the same external signal that normally occurs when Ctrl-Alt-Delete is pressed, and causing a so-called "triple fault" that the processor is inherently incapable of handling. All methods were expensive, because they required at least a short detour through the BIOS bootstrap code. Mode switches on some 80286 machines consumed whole milliseconds, in fact.

Windows plainly needed a way to avoid switching to real mode every time input events like keystrokes or mouse motion occurred. The solution was to write protected-mode device drivers that could handle I/O interrupts entirely in protected mode. These drivers are still with us; you'll find them in the SYSTEM directory with the file extension .DRV. There was (and still is) a MOUSE.DRV, a COMM.DRV, and so on. We can refer to these drivers as *ring-three DLL drivers* to describe the fact that they all look like Windows 16-bit dynamic-link libraries (DLLs) internally and run in the least-trusted protection ring of the Intel chip. Their purpose is to interface between the hardware and the standard Windows KERNEL, USER, and GDI modules without ever leaving protected mode.

Enhanced-Mode Windows

The Intel 80386 processor made possible a third mode of operation, dubbed *enhanced mode*, in which Windows used the paging and V86 features to create virtual machines (VMs). To an application, a VM looks like a regular personal computer, complete with its own keyboard, mouse, display, and so on. In reality, several different VMs share a single physical machine through a process called *virtualization*. From the end user's perspective, the main advantage of enhanced mode over standard-mode and real-mode Windows was the ability to have MS-DOS sessions running in windows on the graphical desktop.

Supporting virtualization is the job of a virtual device driver (VxD). The name VxD comes from "virtual *x* device," meaning the driver that virtualizes some generic device, which is represented by the *x*. A driver named VKD virtualizes the keyboard so that Windows and multiple MS-DOS sessions can all act as though they were interacting with their own keyboards. Another driver named VMD performs similar magic for the mouse. Some VxDs don't virtualize any particular hardware at all, but serve instead as convenient repositories for various low-level system services. The PAGESWAP and PAGEFILE drivers are examples of this sort of "deviceless" VxD; together they manage the swap file that enhanced-mode Windows uses to augment the physical RAM on the computer in order to provide a large virtual address space.

Despite its impressive technical underpinnings, though, enhanced-mode Windows continued to use MS-DOS and the BIOS for disk and file I/O. So, for example, when Windows 3.0 needed to swap a page, it switched the processor to V86 mode in order to let plain old MS-DOS and the BIOS handle the I/O operations.

All of the mode switching between protected mode and real or V86 mode slowed Windows down. A further slowdown resulted from the fact that neither MS-DOS nor the BIOS is reentrant. Windows therefore had to force all applications to wait in a single line for real-mode services. Among other things, the fact that there was only one line made it impractical to overlap paging or file system I/O with program execution.

Windows 95

A description of Windows 95 rounds out this historical discussion. Windows 95 uses several different models for hardware device drivers, most of which are oriented toward using 32-bit, ring-zero virtual device drivers instead of ring-three components. The general model for device handling in Windows 95 is that a VxD handles all interrupts and performs all data transfers, and applications use function calls to communicate their needs to the VxD.

One good example of the VxD-oriented approach to device programming in Windows 95 is serial communications. Windows communications formerly used a ring-three driver (COMM.DRV) that contained hardware interrupt handlers and all the logic needed to drive a standard universal asynchronous receiver-transmitter (UART) chip. Unbeknownst to this driver, two VxDs (VCD and COMBUFF) intercepted the hardware interrupts and the software IN and OUT instructions in order to virtualize each port and ameliorate the problems posed by multitasking. Windows

95 also has a ring-three component named COMM.DRV, but the component has become a thin shell around a new VxD named VCOMM, and simply provides an interface between 16-bit applications and VCOMM. VCOMM sits at the center of a web that attaches to applications, to VxD client programs, and to VxD port drivers. The port drivers now handle all interrupts and perform the actual IN and OUT instructions that talk to the hardware.

The Windows 95 file system is another good example of the shift to VxDs. Formerly, file system requests originated as INT 21h calls in 16-bit protected-mode programs. A VxD handled the INT 21h calls and turned them into V86-mode calls to be processed by MS-DOS. MS-DOS issued INT 13h requests to use BIOS functions for hard disk I/O and INT 2Fh requests to allow network redirector modules to transmit requests over networks. Windows 95 presents a compatible interface to the application world, in that INT 21h requests still result in file system operations, but its underpinnings are vastly different.

In Windows 95, an Installable File System (IFS) Manager handles all INT 21h requests, even those that start out in V86 mode, and routes control to a file system driver (FSD). There's an FSD named VFAT that understands the MS-DOS file allocation table file system, another FSD named CDFSD that understands the format of a CD-ROM, and still other FSDs that understand how to communicate over various networks. Disk operations for local file system drivers like VFAT go through a stack of VxD drivers under the overall supervision of the Input/Output Supervisor (IOS). Even V86-mode INT 13h calls end up inside the IOS. In other words, it's possible for both real-mode and protected-mode programs to issue file system requests for both local and remote disk drives that get serviced entirely (or almost entirely) by VxDs.

A major benefit of the Windows 95 VxD-centric model of device driver is that the Windows 95 systems programmer no longer has to be an expert about MS-DOS and the BIOS to program a device driver. Programmers who provide system extensions for particular applications are similarly lucky. Whereas you previously needed to know DPMI and many arcane or undocumented features of the Windows core modules, you now need only to understand the Win32 *DeviceIo-Control* API function and the Win32 APIs that support so-called "alertable" waits. These two interfaces let you use a VxD as an extension of a 32-bit application.

Notwithstanding the frank emphasis on VxD programming as a way to extend Windows 95 at the system level; Windows 95 still preserves impressive compatibility with Windows 3.1 and earlier versions. DPMI is still present for those 16-bit applications that need to use it, and you can still run real-mode network or file system drivers if you really want to. In fact, you can often take a working set of device and network drivers, 16-bit applications, and their supporting VxDs from a Windows 3.1 system and run them under the umbrella of Windows 95 without encountering major problems.

Chapter 3

Windows 95 System Architecture

Windows 95 is a 32-bit protected-mode operating system designed to run 16-bit and 32-bit application programs on midrange Intel-based personal computers. Windows 95 provides virtual memory (up to 4 gigabytes, depending on the physical memory and swap space available to the particular PC) and supports preemptive multitasking of Windows-based and MS-DOS–based applications. Like Windows 3.x, Windows 95 runs *only* on PCs based on Intel processor chips. Unlike the earlier versions, however, Windows 95 requires an 80386 or more advanced processor and runs only in what used to be called "386 enhanced mode." Unlike Windows NT, which supports

---

virtual memory   A technique that allows an operating system to provide applications with more memory than is physically available by temporarily storing data on a hard disk.

---

privilege level   The level in which a program runs that determines what data can be accessed, what code in memory can be executed, and what machine instructions can be executed by that program. Ring zero is the most privileged level on an Intel processor. Ring three is the least privileged level.

memory model   The approach used by a program to address code and data. In the flat memory model, a single segment maps all of the virtual memory in a process's address space. Sixteen-bit applications often use the *large* memory model, in which available virtual memory is subdivided into segments of up to 64 KB.

---

the same basic set of application programs, Windows 95 does not attempt to provide a secure environment wherein programs and data can be insulated from another program's inadvertent or intentional misbehavior.

The operating system components of Windows 95 run at the most trusted level of privilege, *ring zero*, of the Intel processor and use the 32-bit *flat memory model*. Application programs run at the least trusted level of privilege, *ring three*. Applications can use either the 32-bit flat model or any of the memory models (large, medium, compact, or small) traditionally available to 16-bit programs.

Programmers of Windows-based applications learn that three modules—KERNEL, USER, and GDI—underlie the Windows operating environment. While this is a correct picture insofar as applications programming is concerned, it doesn't describe the operating system at all. In fact, the Windows KERNEL, USER, and GDI modules are actually ring-three applications with no greater privileges than, say, the Solitaire game. The *real* operating system in Windows 95 (and in earlier Windows 3.x versions too) is the *Virtual Machine Manager* (VMM).

Much of this book talks in detail about the VMM and the APIs it makes available to systems programmers. This chapter presents an overview of the VMM to explain the architecture of Windows 95. The concept of the *virtual machine* is central to the way Windows 95 operates internally. There is a "system" virtual machine (the System VM) that contains all Windows-based application programs, and there can be other virtual machines that contain MS-DOS–based applications. Not only does the System VM run 16-bit and 32-bit Windows-based applications, but it also harbors multiple 32-bit execution threads that all share the processor under the overall control of a preemptive multitasking scheduler. MS-DOS virtual machines are important for compatibility, but the role of MS-DOS is much diminished in Windows 95 from what it used to be in earlier versions of Windows.

VIRTUAL MACHINES

Virtual machines grew from the need in Windows 3.0 to support multiple MS-DOS–based and Windows-based applications at the same time. Windows programmers knew they were working in a cooperatively multitasked environment, wherein they were responsible for giving up control to the operating environment periodically to let other applications run. Windows-based programs are well behaved in their use of input devices, since the core Windows components (KERNEL, USER, and GDI) act as intermediaries between applications and device drivers. MS-DOS–based programs, on the other hand, are notoriously ill behaved: they think they own the keyboard, the mouse, the display screen, the processor, and the user's attention. And to compound the problem, MS-DOS itself is a single-threaded, real-mode, non-reentrant system that doesn't readily support multiple applications.

To permit several applications to share the processor and other resources that have only one real incarnation, Windows 95 uses *virtual machines*. A virtual machine (VM), a fiction created solely by software, reacts to application programs the same way a real computer would react. In a weird sort of way, you can look at the standard PC architecture as defining an API. The elements of this "API" include the hardware I/O system and the interrupt-based interfaces to the system BIOS and MS-DOS. Windows 95 often substitutes its own software for these traditional "API" elements in order to multiplex scarce real hardware. But by presenting the same standard interface that MS-DOS programmers have been using for over a decade, Windows 95 makes possible an unprecedented level of application compatibility. Not only will Windows-based applications built for earlier versions of Windows run success-fully, but so will most MS-DOS–based applications.

What Is a Virtual Machine?

In the 1960s, IBM developed an operating system named VM/370. VM/370 provided preemptive multitasking among disparate applications by simulating the existence of multiple virtual machines within the confines of a single real machine. In a typical VM/370 session, a user seated at a remote telecommunications terminal simulated the operation of a real-machine Initial Program Load push button by means of a control program IPL command. Thereupon, a complete operating system booted into the virtual machine and commenced a session with the user. The simulation was eventually so complete that systems programmers could run virtual copies of VM/370 itself to debug new versions.

The problem VM/370 solved for IBM is very similar to the problem Microsoft needed to solve for Windows 3.0: allowing applications to multitask when they think they are alone on the machine. And the virtual machine concept once again provided the solution. Running within a virtual machine, an application or an operating system can believe that it acquires input from a real keyboard and mouse and displays output on a real video monitor. Within limits, it can even believe that it owns the processor and all the memory that is physically present. Hardware and software *virtualization* is the key to this magic.

Virtual Hardware

As I indicated earlier, a virtual hardware component acts, as far as the software can tell, the same way the corresponding piece of real hardware would act. For example, suppose an MS-DOS–based application needs to read input from the keyboard. The application code itself might use runtime library calls like *fgets* and *_kbhit*, but the runtime library will eventually issue software interrupt 21h to call MS-DOS or interrupt 16h to call the BIOS directly. MS-DOS contains a keyboard driver that talks to the BIOS via interrupt 16h. The BIOS uses port I/O operations (IN and OUT instructions) to talk to the keyboard and interrupt controller chips, and it handles hardware interrupts that originate in the keyboard controller to interpret the user's individual keystrokes. Figure 3-1 illustrates the typical layering of application and system calls for this interaction.

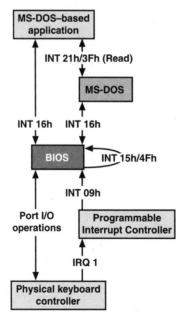

Figure 3-1. *How an MS-DOS–based application reads from the keyboard.*

The earliest versions of Windows ran—not very well—in real mode under MS-DOS, and they used the keyboard in pretty much the same way I just outlined. When Windows moved to protected mode, an immediate complication arose. The complication was that a protected-mode program cannot directly call the real-mode MS-DOS INT 21h handler, nor can it directly participate in the real-mode BIOS handling of keyboard interrupts. Microsoft could have taken the high road by writing a completely new protected-mode operating system in which all the details of keyboard handling were performed in protected mode, without any reliance on the real-mode BIOS or on MS-DOS. Or they could have taken a middle road by crafting a way for protected-mode code to reach real-mode, and vice versa. In fact, Microsoft adopted both solutions simultaneously. The high road culminated in both OS/2 version 2 and in Windows NT. The middle road has ended (so far, anyway) with Windows 95 and has included stops for the several releases of Windows 3.x. (The low road would have been to do nothing at all and leave owners of multimegabyte PCs at the mercy of MS-DOS and the 640-KB barrier imposed by a 16-bit, real-mode operating system.)

You could use the term *software virtualization* to describe the mechanisms that allow protected-mode Windows components to interoperate with real-mode MS-DOS and BIOS components. Software virtualization basically requires the operating system to intercept calls that attempt to cross the boundary between protected and real modes and to change the processor's operating mode after suitably adjusting parameter registers. An additional software component called a *virtual device driver,* or VxD, translates the protected-mode interrupt call into a call (or series of calls) through the real-mode Interrupt Vector Table. As part of the translation process, the VxD uses parameters in protected-mode extended memory to create appropriate real-mode parameters in memory accessible by the real-mode operating system. The real-mode operating system, however, runs in *virtual 8086* (V86) *mode,* rather than real mode. The VxD then translates the results of the real-mode calls back into the extended memory of the protected-mode caller. The entire process is illustrated in Figure 3-2 on the following page. Doing this translation well creates "virtual" versions of MS-DOS and the BIOS that appear to run in protected mode.

Hardware virtualization goes much further than software virtualization. Virtual hardware *appears* to generate interrupts on hardware interrupt request lines. And virtual hardware *appears* to respond to IN and OUT instructions, changes in special mapped memory locations, and so on. But the actuality may differ greatly from

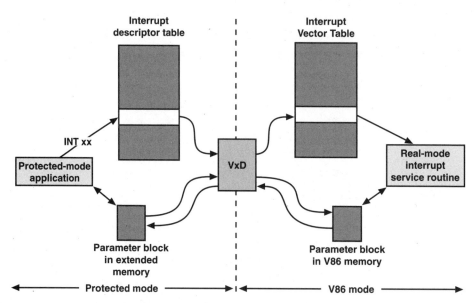

Figure 3-2. *Software virtualization of MS-DOS and the BIOS.*

the appearance. Figure 3-3 illustrates how two different MS-DOS–based programs might simultaneously access virtual keyboards. The important thing to note is that these programs execute exactly the same machine instructions—from the application all the way down through the BIOS—as the simple MS-DOS program that was shown in Figure 3-1. We've added some virtual device drivers that provide the necessary hardware virtualization. Since we're virtualizing a keyboard and a Programmable Interrupt Controller (PIC), we might call these drivers VKD (short for virtual keyboard device) and VPICD (short for virtual PIC device). A virtual device driver for the mouse might be VMD, and so on. The Virtual Machine Manager itself is a VxD.

Hardware virtualization depends on several features of the Intel 80386 chip and its successors. One of these features, the *I/O permission mask*, makes it possible for the operating system to trap all IN and OUT instructions for particular I/O ports. Since some of the crucial parts of handling hardware interrupts involve I/O to and from the Programmable Interrupt Controller, this "port trapping" capability also makes it easier for software to simulate the interrupt subsystem. Another feature, hardware-assisted *paging*, allows the operating system to provide virtual memory and, if desired, intercept accesses to memory locations. Virtualizing the video RAM is one of the many things paging makes possible. Finally, the V86 mode of the processor allows an MS-DOS–based application to run as if the processor were in

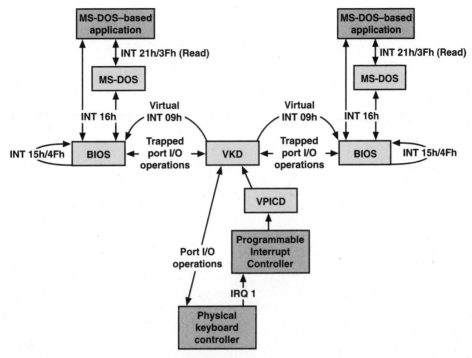

Figure 3-3. *Hardware virtualization of keyboard operations.*

real mode when the processor is really in protected mode. V86 mode allows the operating system to "map" blocks of extended memory into the real-mode address space inhabited by MS-DOS and the BIOS, trap I/O accesses, and field hardware and software interrupts.

Virtual Device Drivers

The VMM and a possibly large collection of VxDs are the keys that unlock the potential of hardware virtualization. There are two types of VxDs, *static VxDs* and *dynamic VxDs*. In Windows 95, the VMM uses the system registry, the SYSTEM.INI configuration file, and a software scheme based around INT 2Fh, function 1605h, to collect a list of static VxD names. The VMM loads static VxDs while erecting the scaffolding to support virtual machines, and the static VxDs stay loaded for the duration of the Windows session.

Windows 95 also makes it possible to load and unload VxDs dynamically in response to changing demands. The primary users of this capability are the Windows

95 *Configuration Manager* and *Input/Output Supervisor*, which are themselves static VxDs. Using the registry and various protocols that allow hardware to identify itself, the Configuration Manager selects and loads just the right collection of dynamic VxDs for the actual hardware. The Input/Output Supervisor uses a simpler scheme, based on the physical location of VxD program files, to load drivers for physical disk drives.

PROCESSES AND THREADS

Windows 95 uses the *process* and *thread* concepts in a way similar to the way Windows NT uses them. That is, each Windows-based application occupies a process that consists of a dedicated address space and one or more threads of execution. Each thread corresponds to a sequence of program steps and the evolving state of processor registers and system objects associated with that sequence. Windows 95 uses a priority-based scheme to preemptively multitask threads.

In a fully general system based on virtual machines, processes, and threads, each virtual machine could contain multiple processes, and each process could contain multiple threads. Windows 95 doesn't implement this fully general model, however. One of the virtual machines in a Windows 95 system—the System VM—is special because it is where all Win16 and Win32 applications run. The VMM always creates the System VM, and it does so very early in the process of starting a Windows 95 session. The System VM has one process for each application, and each Win32 process can also consist of more than one thread. There can be additional VMs besides the System VM. These additional virtual machines are for MS-DOS–based applications, and each contains exactly one process and exactly one thread.

Win16 application   A 16-bit Windows application.

Win32 application   A 32-bit Windows application.

Although Windows 95 circumscribes MS-DOS virtual machines in the way I just described, the command shell creates a somewhat different appearance. You can normally launch 16-bit and 32-bit Windows applications from an MS-DOS prompt in Windows 95. You can't tell the difference between an application launched in this way and one launched graphically from the desktop. In fact, once Windows 95 launches a GUI application from an MS-DOS prompt, the MS-DOS VM regains control to present another command prompt. Furthermore, a Win32 application is free to create new threads no matter how it was launched. So does this mean that MS-DOS has suddenly grown a graphical front end, or perhaps that an MS-DOS VM can really have more than one process or more than one thread per process?

If you think the answer is "No," you're correct, but you should hear the confusing results of another experiment before sticking your neck out. You can create so-called *console-mode* Win32 applications that use all of the Win32 API except the parts that relate to the Windows graphical interface. Try launching a console-mode application that does multithreading, such as THREAD.EXE, included on the companion disc in the \CHAP03\THREAD directory. THREAD.C (also on the companion disc) is shown here:

THREAD.C

```c
#include  <windows.h>
#include  <stdio.h>

DWORD WINAPI mythread(LPVOID junk)
    {                              // mythread
    puts("Hello from the thread!");
    return 0;
    }                              // mythread

int main(int argc, char *argv[])
    {                              // main
    DWORD tid;
    HANDLE hThread;

    hThread = CreateThread(NULL, 0, mythread, NULL, 0, &tid);
    if (hThread)
        {                          // thread has been started
        puts("Hello from the main program!");
        WaitForSingleObject(hThread, INFINITE);
        }                          // thread has been started
    return 0;
    }                              // main
```

When you launch this application from a Windows 95 MS-DOS prompt, it correctly creates and runs the *mythread* thread. You'll see the output in the MS-DOS window, just as if you were running Windows NT. And you won't return to the MS-DOS prompt until the application exits. It looks for all the world like this Win32 application is running as an MS-DOS–based application and spawning new threads in apparent violation of what I said about the limitations of MS-DOS virtual machines.

The command shell uses some sleight of hand to deal with this sample program. When you issue an MS-DOS command, the MS-DOS COMMAND.COM command shell issues an MS-DOS interrupt (INT 21h, function 4Bh) to load and execute the executable file you specified. The VMM intercepts the interrupt and notices that you're trying to run a Win32 application. The VMM launches it in the System VM rather than in the MS-DOS VM from which you typed the command. If you start a GUI application, MS-DOS regains control right away, and the application continues on its own independent way. If you start a console-mode application, the VMM simply doesn't return from the INT 21h, function 4Bh, handler until the application terminates. But in either case the application actually runs as a new process in the System VM.

WINDOWS-BASED APPLICATIONS

Windows-based applications come in two flavors: 16-bit and 32-bit. Win16 applications use the time-tested (and rather shopworn) 16-bit Windows API that evolved from Windows 1.0 through Windows 3.11. Win32 applications use a very extensive subset of the Win32 API developed originally for Windows NT version 3.1. Both flavors of application use the protected mode of Intel 80386 and higher processor chips, thereby gaining access to the full extent of virtual memory provided by the Virtual Machine Manager. A Win32 application can contain multiple threads, whereas a Win16 application can contain only the one thread it starts out with. Win32 applications participate in preemptive multitasking under the overall control of the scheduling subsystems of the VMM, whereas Win16 applications must cooperatively multitask amongst themselves.

As a general rule, 32-bit applications run faster and use memory more effectively than their 16-bit cousins. This is because 32-bit programs use the flat memory model, wherein all code and data can be addressed in a single segment covering all of virtual memory. Sixteen-bit programs must constantly load segment *selectors* into the processor's segment registers to access more than 64 KB of memory. Loading protected-mode selectors can be as much as seven times more expensive than simply loading a 32-bit flat pointer. Because the basic Windows APIs contained in the KERNEL, USER, and GDI modules occupy significantly more than 64 KB of memory and are frequently used by all applications, and because the cooperative multitasking imposed by the 16-bit Windows multitasking model guarantees frequent switches from one application to another, it's pretty likely that frequent selector loads will occur.

Win32 Applications

Not only do 32-bit applications usually perform better than 16-bit applications, they also have other advantages. The Win32 API is portable among all the platforms on which Windows NT runs, so a well-crafted Win32 application can probably be ported to other hardware platforms simply by being recompiled and relinked. The Win32 API is also richer and more logical than the Win16 API, making it easier for the programmer to interact with the system and with other applications. To cite only one example, Win32 applications can readily create virtual file mappings that allow them to address disk files as virtual memory, thereby tremendously simplifying tasks as diverse as managing a database or loading an executable file for execution.

Only Windows NT supports all the features of the full Win32 API. Windows 95 supports a substantial subset that omits security, event logging, and Unicode support. Windows 95 also implements a small number of Win32 functions differently than Windows NT does, primarily because in Windows 95 these functions squeeze through a 16-bit program somewhere along the way. You can find additional details about the Windows 95 implementation of the Win32 API in Article 3 of the *Programmer's Guide to Microsoft Windows 95* (Microsoft Press, 1995).

Despite their advantages for applications programmers, Win32 applications pose a problem to the Virtual Machine Manager. Believe it or not, the VMM believes in its innermost heart that the System VM is running 16-bit code. As a result, most of the systems programming interfaces for talking to the VMM and other VxDs are only available from 16-bit programs. When a Win32 application issues a software interrupt to invoke such an interface, a crash ensues fairly quickly. Microsoft has no wish to change the underlying design decisions that cause this surprising result for fear that too many nonportable Win32 applications would be produced.

A Win32 application that wants to work directly with MS-DOS or the BIOS is therefore limited to what can be sent through the Win32 API. The API is pretty powerful, of course. An application has at its disposal a rich set of API calls for manipulating and synchronizing processes and threads. The system registry, which controls many aspects of Windows 95, is very easy to access and modify using Win32 calls. One application can supervise and control another by using the debugging primitives, and there's an extensive performance-metering API too.

When the Win32 API doesn't suffice, an application can fall back on *DeviceIo-Control* to send and receive information to and from a VxD. For example, a Win32 application can do low-level disk I/O by sending IOCTL codes to the VWIN32 device. VxDs themselves can use an *asynchronous procedure call* to initiate calls back to Win32 programs as well. Mind you, applications that rely on these mechanisms probably won't work on any operating platform but Windows 95 and its direct successors. It's not obvious to me that these two methods create *better* nonportable applications than the ones you could create using traditional interfaces, but I'm doing my job if I explain how things really work, even if I don't necessarily approve.

Win16 Applications

Even though Windows 95 makes 32-bit programming significantly more attractive than it's ever been on the Intel chip, 16-bit programs continue to play an important part in Windows 95. From the standpoint of compatibility alone, it's obvious that Windows 95 has to support much of the existing base of Win16 applications or else fail commercially. Windows 95 gives compatibility more than mere lip service, too. For example, some commercially important Win16 applications contain code like the following to determine which version of Windows they are using:

```
BOOL bAtLeast_3_10 = ((WORD)GetVersion() >= 0x0A03); // wrong!
```

The *GetVersion* API call returns the major version of Windows in the low-order byte and the minor version in the high-order byte. To compare for anything but equality, an application really ought to compare the major and minor version numbers separately or else reverse the bytes first so that the major version is in the high-order byte, as shown in this example:

```
WORD wVersion = (WORD)GetVersion();
wVersion = (LOBYTE(wVersion) << 8) | HIBYTE(wVersion);
BOOL bAtLeast_3_10 = wVersion >= 0x030A; // correct!
```

Microsoft originally wanted to use 4.00 as the internal designation for Windows 95. In fact, Win32 callers of the *GetVersion* function will get 0x0004, and VxD callers of *Get_VMM_Version* will also learn that version 4.00 is running. But because of the prevalence of incorrect version tests in existing 16-bit applications, Microsoft ended up changing the 16-bit *GetVersion* API call to return 0x5F03 (that is, 3.95) instead of 0x0004! Thus, the following sample program produces different results depending on whether it is built as a Win16 application or as a Win32 application:

GETVER.C

```
#include <windows.h>

int WINAPI WinMain(HINSTANCE hInstance, HINSTANCE hPrev,
    LPSTR lpCmd, int nShow)
    {                                // WinMain
    char msg[128];
    wsprintf(msg, "Windows version is %4.4X", (WORD)GetVersion());
    MessageBox(GetFocus(), msg, "GetVersion Value",
        MB_OK | MB_ICONINFORMATION);
    return 0;
    }                                // WinMain
```

GETVER.C and 16-bit and 32-bit versions of GETVER.EXE are included on the companion disc in the \CHAP03\GETVER16 and \CHAP03\GETVER32 directories.

Compatibility also manifests itself in the way Windows 95 manages memory for Win16 applications and in the way it handles multitasking between them. In Windows 3.x, the linear addresses of memory blocks were pretty much a matter of indifference because all Windows-based and MS-DOS–based applications shared a single 4-GB virtual address space. In Windows 95, however, each Win32 process owns its own area of virtual memory occupying the linear addresses from 00400000h to 80000000h. Just as in Windows NT, therefore, Win32 applications don't directly share memory except by means of named file mappings. But Win16 applications are used to sharing memory indiscriminately with each other and with extended DOS applications that use DOS Protected Mode Interface (DPMI) services to allocate memory. For this reason, Windows 95 places all Win16 applications, the memory blocks they allocate via *GlobalAlloc*, and all DPMI-allocated memory in the linear address range 80000000h to C0000000h. This range is shared among all processes.

Win16 applications must still voluntarily yield control to allow cooperative multitasking to work. Some applications actually *depend* on not losing control to other applications except at defined yield points. For compatibility, therefore, Windows 95 provides the same cooperative multitasking model for Win16 applications that earlier versions of Windows did. In actual fact, each Win16 application is part of a distinct process and thread (although there's no way to find this out except from within a debugger like Soft-Ice/W that lets you examine ring-zero control structures). A Win16 thread runs only after it has claimed the *Win16Mutex* mutual exclusion (mutex) semaphore, however. Using the mutex simulates the behavior of earlier versions of Windows by allowing only one Win16 program at a time to be eligible for scheduling by the preemptive multitasker within the VMM.

Mixing 32-bit and 16-bit Code

With Win32 and Win16 programs all running more or less simultaneously in the System VM, you might hope that it would be possible for them to work together easily. However, mixed-bitness programming is difficult in the Windows environment for many reasons. The new executable (NE) file format used by Win16 programs accommodates only 16-bit segments, and the portable executable (PE) format used by Win32 programs accommodates only 32-bit segments. Win32 programs run with the CS, DS, ES, and SS segment registers all pointing to a 32-bit flat segment, and they use 32-bit registers and offsets for data and code addressing. Win16 programs use a combination of a segment register and a 16-bit register or offset instead. For a Win32 program to successfully call a Win16 program, therefore, a *thunk* is required. A thunk, among many other things, switches from 32-bit to 16-bit code and stack addressing and truncates integers from 32 bits to 16 bits. Calls in the other direction require similar work. There are many, many additional complications associated with switching bitness that I can't go into here.

You can read in the *Programmer's Guide to Microsoft Windows 95* about the *thunk compiler* that allows programmers to easily create their own interfaces between 16-bit and 32-bit components in Windows 95. The thunk compiler is a vast improvement over the so-called *universal thunk* that allowed Win32 programs running under the Win32s subsystem in Windows 3.1 to call Win16 DLLs. It's also an improvement over the *generic thunk* that allowed Win16 programs in Windows NT to call Win32 functions. Both of these earlier thunking mechanisms were idiosyncratic and primarily unidirectional. The Windows 95 thunking mechanism, in contrast, is robust and bidirectional (but, unfortunately, incompatible with both universal and generic thunks).

Thunking between 16-bit and 32-bit code works so well in Windows 95 that Microsoft relies on it heavily to run Windows programs. I tossed around the terms KERNEL, USER, and GDI earlier as though there was only one each of these components. In fact, there are 16-bit and 32-bit versions of these system components, and they are connected together with thunks. For example, KERNEL32.DLL calls KRNL386.EXE to do some of the work, and vice versa. Most of the work associated with managing window objects is done in the (16-bit) USER.EXE component, with a little help from USER32.DLL. Similarly, the 32-bit version of the GDI (GDI32.DLL) shares the load with the 16-bit version (GDI.EXE).

But since the 16-bit system components are essentially left over from Windows 3.1 and aren't reentrant, Windows 95 needs to synchronize their execution. The *Win16Mutex* semaphore serves this purpose in addition to synchronizing Win16 applications. Whenever a 32-bit system component like GDI32 needs to call a function in one of the 16-bit modules, it claims the *Win16Mutex* semaphore. The result is that only one thread (16-bit *or* 32-bit) at a time can execute 16-bit code in the System VM. Multiple threads can be running 32-bit code, however. See *Windows 95 System Programming Secrets*, by Matt Pietrek (IDG Books, 1995), for a full discussion of many aspects of how the Windows 95 KERNEL, USER, and GDI subsystems operate.

MS-DOS AND MS-DOS–BASED APPLICATIONS

Windows was originally a mere operating "environment" built atop MS-DOS. In effect, the earliest versions of Windows were just fancy command shells that were easier to use than a command prompt. As Windows has grown up over the years, it has subsumed more and more of the core operating system functionality once provided by MS-DOS. Architectural pictures of earlier versions of Windows would have shown MS-DOS and a large collection of real-mode device drivers nearest the hardware at the bottom. (See Figure 3-4.) In Windows 95, it would be more accurate to show the Virtual Machine Manager and a large collection of VxDs nearest the hardware at the bottom, with MS-DOS and a smaller collection of real-mode drivers appearing as clients of the VMM. (See Figure 3-5.)

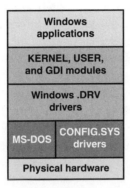

Figure 3-4. *The role of MS-DOS in versions of Windows before Windows 95.*

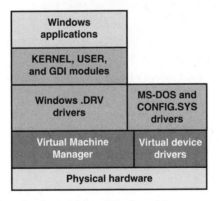

Figure 3-5. *The role of MS-DOS in Windows 95.*

The shift in orientation from MS-DOS to the VMM reflects the evolution of the PC hardware and software marketplaces. In the past, less capable computers based on the 8086 and 80286 chips occupied a significant number of desktops, and these computers ran MS-DOS much better than they did Windows. Application builders also found it much easier to write programs for MS-DOS, perhaps using a DOS extender or a commercial library to achieve adequate memory performance and user friendliness. The computers sold today contain much more powerful processors that run Windows in 386 enhanced mode so well that there's no longer any good reason to stay with MS-DOS. Furthermore, with some help from Microsoft in the form of documentation and training, and as a result of considerable pressure from end users, application vendors now routinely produce excellent graphically oriented applications for Windows.

With most new applications being aimed at Windows, and with most new computers able to run 32-bit protected-mode programs, why even worry about MS-DOS? I guess the answer is just compatibility and familiarity. As I write this chapter, I'm using Windows 95 on a state-of-the-art computer. But I'm running a network with real-mode drivers because my network vendor hasn't gotten around to porting its drivers to protected mode, even after the two-year beta program for Windows 95. I have an MS-DOS box open on the desktop so I can type commands like DIR and GREP, among others. I also run some game programs (gasp!) from time to time that run only under MS-DOS. Perhaps the strongest lesson Microsoft learned from its experience with OS/2 and Windows NT is that an operating system simply won't penetrate the market if there isn't a large body of compelling applications that will run under it. Windows 95 will succeed because it's better than MS-DOS and Windows 3.1 *and* it runs all the same programs. Windows 95 will also foster development of 32-bit applications because it will provide the first mass-market platform for them to run on. (I discount the Win32s subsystem in Windows 3.1, which most vendors seem to have classified as a toy.)

Windows 95's coexistence with MS-DOS starts when you boot your computer. The bootstrap loader on your hard disk loads and runs an IO.SYS file that contains MS-DOS version 7.0. At least, that's the version that DOS function 21h/30h will report, as shown in the following output. (The version number is returned in register AX in minor version/major version order.)

```
C:\>debug
-a 100
2E01:0100 mov ah,30
2E01:0102 int 21
2E01:0104 int 3
2E01:0105
-g

AX=0007  BX=FF00  ...
DS=2E01  ES=2E01  ...
2E01:0104 CC            INT    3
-q
```

MS-DOS 7.0 processes CONFIG.SYS and AUTOEXEC.BAT in more or less the way you're used to from previous versions of MS-DOS, and then it automatically issues the WIN command to run the WIN.COM program in the Windows 95 directory.

This launches the Windows 95 Virtual Machine Manager, which takes over the machine and runs the graphical operating environment. There are several ways to short-circuit this process and remain in MS-DOS. For a long time, I had a dummy WIN.BAT file in my path ahead of WIN.COM. This BAT file got control instead of WIN.COM when MS-DOS did its automatic WIN command. You can also press F8 during the boot sequence and specify that you want to stop at a command prompt. Nowadays, I just run with the following setting in the (normally hidden) MSDOS.SYS file:

```
[Options]
BootGUI=0
```

You can do all the normal DOS-like things you're used to at this command prompt, including running an earlier version of Windows, if you still have it around. I often use the opportunity to configure and start a debugger. There's not really much point to stopping at MS-DOS except for odd situations like this, however. To start Windows 95 from MS-DOS, simply execute WIN.COM from the Windows 95 directory.

A more interesting picture emerges when you closely examine how the VMM and other parts of Windows 95 use MS-DOS once the graphical shell is up and running. Andrew Schulman explored this topic in great depth in *Unauthorized Windows 95* (IDG Books, 1994). Among the tidbits of information Andrew discovered was that Windows 95 *still* creates a more-or-less normal program segment prefix (PSP) for every application and that it relies on MS-DOS to do this. But MS-DOS has very much receded into the background insofar as most system services are concerned: interrupt handling and I/O operations now happen in 32-bit protected mode as much as possible. Even the MS-DOS file system is now (usually) implemented by VxD code.

Compatibility requires that MS-DOS drivers and terminate-and-stay-resident (TSR) utilities continue to work, however. Compatibility also requires that Win16 programs still be able to use software interrupts, including INT 21h, to request operating system services. The VMM and the collection of VxDs that work with it ensure compatibility by virtualizing MS-DOS itself. In other words, when *any* program, even a real-mode MS-DOS application, uses INT 21h to request a file system service, VxDs will service the request and perform the disk I/O. When a real-mode device driver tries to do I/O to the port it thinks it's managing, VxDs will intercept and supervise the access. In effect, therefore, Windows 95 treats MS-DOS like an application.

Chapter 4

Interfaces for Systems Programming

Every operating system I've ever worked with has provided a set of interfaces for applications to use to request system services. I cut my teeth on IBM's OS/360 operating system, which controlled the room-sized mainframe computers that represented the limits of technology in the sixties and seventies. OS/360 provided a single pipeline to its services—the Supervisor Call (SVC) machine instruction—and an incredibly elaborate set of assembly-language macro instructions for inserting requests into this pipeline. IBM also provided unbelievably complete and accurate documentation describing how to use the interfaces. It's no exaggeration to say that an experienced programmer could code calls to unfamiliar interfaces according to the documentation and be reasonably sure that the resulting program would work as expected. And if, perchance, something unexpected were to occur, a systems programmer could consult program logic manuals and microfiche containing the complete source code for the system. One of IBM's operating systems (VM/370) even came with machine-readable source code that systems programmers routinely modified to suit the needs of their local user community, and IBM offered formal instruction in how to make the modifications.

Contrast the order and precision of an OS/360 systems programmer's life with the chaos and bewilderment that characterizes the life of a Windows 95 systems programmer, if you will. While it's true that the Intel INT instruction underlies every request for a system service, there are several families of services, each with its own rules about how to invoke them. For example, learning how to use INT 21h to request file system services tells you nothing about how to use the INT 31h DOS Protected Mode Interface (DPMI). You can use INT 21h in situations for which DPMI is unavailable (in other words, in real-mode programs). Using either of these formerly universal interfaces in a 32-bit Windows program will crash your program, however. And there are situations in which the "normal" INT 21h service won't work and you must use DPMI either to force real-mode MS-DOS to perform the function (as you would with the case translation function that's part of MS-DOS's international language support, for example) or to perform the function a different way (for example, when you need to allocate real-mode memory).

If the sheer number of different system interfaces isn't complication enough, the state of the documentation for these interfaces will defeat all but the most determined attempt of a new systems programmer to learn his or her trade. To continue the example of the previous paragraph, the INT 21h interface is now documented in reasonable detail, but only because a group of diligent reverse engineers figured out and documented much of that detail. To learn MS-DOS programming, the new programmer has to buy books written by third parties that talk, more or less episodically and anecdotally, about the results of experiments or of heroic disassembly. As one example of the many I could cite, there are situations in which a programmer needs to write code to examine the chain of MS-DOS memory blocks. One such situation is when a TSR needs to check to see if an earlier copy of itself is already loaded. The structure of the MS-DOS memory blocks is well known, as is the INT 21h, function 52h, interface you use as a first step to find the head of the linked list of memory blocks. (See, for example, Ralf Brown and Jim Kyle's *PC Interrupts* [Addison-Wesley, 1991], page 8-45.) But Microsoft never published any of this information: curious and frantic programmers figured it out on their own and risked lawsuits to publicize it.

Some parts of the operating system are exhaustively documented, of course. In this book, I'll talk at length about how to write virtual device drivers (VxDs). The Microsoft Windows 95 DDK explains in detail *how* to call the system interfaces used by a VxD, but not *why*. It doesn't explain side effects, and it doesn't explain how to put all of the different interfaces together to form a coherent program. Unlike my experience with OS/360, in other words, my experience with Windows is that I can't write a working VxD just by reading the official documentation. Many are the times I've struggled to make a program work only to learn too late that I'm misusing or overlooking some VxD service.

Now that I've explained by implication why I wrote this book, it's time to begin exploring how one extends and uses the Windows 95 operating system. I'll summarize here the various interfaces one uses in a systems programming project. These include the VxD service API and the several structured API sets defined for specific classes of devices like serial and parallel port drivers, network file systems, and so on. These also include a set of older Windows system interfaces like DPMI that Windows 95 preserves for compatibility.

VIRTUAL DEVICE DRIVERS

The core of the Windows 95 operating system is a collection of virtual device drivers operating under the umbrella of the Virtual Machine Manager (VMM), which is itself a VxD. VxDs communicate with each other using three basic methods: system control messages, service API calls, and callback functions.

A VxD can also easily export an API entry point for use by real-mode and protected-mode application programs. To access the API, an application uses INT 2Fh, function 1684h, to obtain the function entry point. When the application calls that entry point, the VMM gains control and routes control to the VxD. The VxD then manipulates an image of the virtual machine's ring-three registers (the so-called *client register structure*) to respond to the application's request. This application mechanism is available to 16-bit Windows programs, 16-bit MS-DOS programs, and either 16-bit or 32-bit programs running under a DOS extender. Win32 programs instead use the *DeviceIoControl* function to request services from VxDs.

Reference documentation covering all possible VxD service calls is included in the Windows 95 DDK. Most of this book provides additional detail about how and when to use the mechanisms summarized in this chapter.

System Control Messages

The VMM sends system control messages to all loaded VxDs in a predefined order. Each VxD exports a *device control procedure* to receive these messages. This procedure examines a message code and either dispatches a handler function within the VxD or returns with the carry flag clear to indicate successful handling of the message. Roughly 50 system control messages are currently defined. Some messages describe various stages in the startup and shutdown of Windows 95 and in the creation and destruction of virtual machines and threads. Other messages relate to various other events having global significance to many device drivers.

Because there are often many VxDs loaded and because each one gets a crack at most system control messages, it's important to restrict messages to truly important events that will likely be of interest to many VxDs. Thus, you don't see system control messages that are as fine-grained as, say, the application-level Windows message WM_MOUSEMOVE.

Windows 95 introduces a few new system control messages that pertain only to a single VxD. They're defined as system control messages because the device control procedure is the only entry point that the VMM can initially locate. And there's also now a scheme whereby VxDs can define their own control messages and send them to other VxDs that understand their meaning.

Where's the Device Control Procedure?   As mentioned in the text, the only entry point to a VxD that the VMM can initially find is the device control procedure that handles system control messages. A static *device description block* (DDB) structure points to this procedure. The DDB is in turn the one and only symbol exported from the executable file that contains the VxD.

Startup and Shutdown Messages

The VMM communicates the important events during Windows 95 startup and shutdown by means of the system control messages listed in Table 4-1.

Message	*Description*
Sys_Critical_Init	Notifies the VxD that this is the first stage of initialization; interrupts are disabled.
Device_Init	Notifies the VxD that this is the second stage of initialization; interrupts are enabled.
Init_Complete	Notifies the VxD that this is the third stage of initialization.
System_Exit	Notifies the VxD that this is the first stage of shutdown; interrupts are still enabled.
System_Exit2	Same as System_Exit, but message is sent in reverse initialization order.
Sys_Critical_Exit	Notifies the VxD that this is the second stage of shutdown; interrupts are disabled.
Sys_Critical_Exit2	Same as Sys_Critical_Exit, but the message is sent in reverse initialization order.
Reboot_Processor	Instructs the VxD that if it knows how to reboot the processor, it should do so.

Table 4-1. *Startup and shutdown system control messages.*   *(continued)*

continued

Message	Description
Device_Reboot_Notify	Notifies the VxD that the VMM is about to restart the system; interrupts are enabled.
Device_Reboot_Notify2	Same as Device_Reboot_Notify, but the message is sent in reverse initialization order.
Crit_Reboot_Notify	Notifies the VxD that the VMM is about to restart the system; interrupts are disabled.
Crit_Reboot_Notify2	Same as Crit_Reboot_Notify, but the message is sent in reverse initialization order.

The important things to note about these messages are listed here:

■ There are three initialization messages. Sys_Critical_Init occurs immediately after the switch to protected mode but before interrupts are enabled. Device_Init occurs after interrupts are enabled, and Init_Complete occurs after all devices have had their chance to initialize during Device_Init.

■ There are two shutdown messages. System_Exit amounts to an announcement that Windows is about to shut down. Sys_Critical_Exit occurs after interrupts are disabled but before the processor is halted. In Windows 3.1 and earlier, Windows returned the processor to real mode after sending this message, whereupon DOS would regain control. In Windows 95, DOS usually never regains control after Windows shuts down. (True power users—in which category I couldn't count myself until I read the following tip in Spencer Katt's column—will know that if you started Windows 95 from an MS-DOS prompt, you can often just type the command *mode co80* to get from the graphics screen reading "It's now safe to shut down your computer" back to the MS-DOS prompt. Microsoft expects most users to shut their computers off at this point, of course.)

■ The Device_Reboot_Notify and Crit_Reboot_Notify messages are similar to System_Exit and Sys_Critical_Exit, respectively. They occur when Windows 95 is shutting down in order to reboot the processor.

■ The shutdown-type messages have two variants—for example, System_Exit and System_Exit2. The VMM maintains an *initialization order* ordinal for each VxD that governs the order in which it sends system control messages to the loaded VxDs. The VMM sends the "2" variants in *reverse* of the initialization order. This is the way the shutdown messages should probably have worked from the beginning, of course: any given VxD is allowed to rely on services provided by VxDs that initialize before it, and this reliance should be able to continue through shutdown.

Virtual Machine Messages

Table 4-2 lists the system control messages that concern the important events in the life of a virtual machine.

Message	Description
Create_VM	Notifies the VxD that this is the first stage of creating a VM (other than the System VM).
VM_Critical_Init	Notifies the VxD that this is the second stage of creating a VM (other than the System VM).
Sys_VM_Init	Notifies the VxD that this is the initialization of the System VM.
VM_Init	Notifies the VxD that this is the third stage of creating a VM (other than the System VM).
Begin_PM_App	Notifies the VxD that a DPMI client has switched to protected mode.
Kernel32_Initialized	Notifies the VxD that KERNEL32.DLL has initialized.
VM_Suspend	Notifies the VxD that the VM temporarily cannot run.
VM_Suspend2	Same as VM_Suspend, but the message is sent in reverse initialization order.
VM_Resume	Notifies the VxD that the VM can run once again.
Kernel32_Shutdown	Notifies the VxD that KERNEL32.DLL is about to shut down.
End_PM_App	Notifies the VxD that the protected-mode DPMI client has exited.
End_PM_App2	Same as End_PM_App, but the message is sent in reverse initialization order.
Query_Destroy	Queries the VxD as to whether it is okay to destroy a particular VM.
Close_VM_Notify	Notifies the VxD that a VM is about to be terminated because of a call to the *Close_VM* service.
Close_VM_Notify2	Same as Close_VM_Notify, but the message is sent in reverse initialization order.

Table 4-2. *Virtual machine control messages.* *(continued)*

continued

Message	Description
Sys_VM_Terminate	Notifies the VxD that this is a normal shutdown of the System VM.
Sys_VM_Terminate2	Same as Sys_VM_Terminate, but the message is sent in reverse initialization order.
VM_Terminate	Notifies the VxD that this is a normal shutdown of a VM (other than the System VM).
VM_Terminate2	Same as VM_Terminate, but the message is sent in reverse initialization order.
VM_Not_Executeable	Notifies the VxD that this is the next-to-last phase of destroying a VM.
VM_Not_Executeable2	Same as VM_Not_Executeable, but the message is sent in reverse initialization order.
Destroy_VM	Notifies the VxD that this is the last phase of destroying a VM.
Destroy_VM2	Same as Destroy_VM, but the message is sent in reverse initialization order.

The important things to note about these messages are listed here:

■   Reflecting its privileged position in the Windows hierarchy, the System VM has its own initialization and shutdown messages.

■   When creating a new virtual machine, Windows sends three control messages: Create_VM, VM_Critical_Init, and VM_Init. Only the last of these has a System-VM counterpart (the Sys_VM_Init control message), because creating the System VM is one of the things the VMM does automatically before calling any VxDs.

■   If a VM terminates normally, Windows sends a VM_Terminate message. VxDs can destroy virtual machines in abnormal ways, such as by calling the *Nuke_VM* service or the *Crash_Cur_VM* service. No matter how a VM terminates, VM_Not_Executeable *[sic]* and Destroy_VM messages accompany its demise.

■   The shutdown-type messages have two variants, just as the system startup and shutdown messages described in the previous section do. That is, the VMM sends the "2" variants of each message to VxDs in reverse of the normal initialization order.

Other System Control Messages

Table 4-3 lists the other system control messages.

Message	Description
Set_Device_Focus	Instructs the VxD to reassign ownership of a device or of all devices.
Begin_Message_Mode	Notifies the VxD that SHELL is about to display a message.
End_Message_Mode	Notifies the VxD that SHELL is done displaying a message.
End_Message_Mode2	Same as End_Message_Mode, but the message is sent in reverse initialization order.
Debug_Query	Instructs the VxD to generate debugging output.
Power_Event	Instructs the VxD to handle a change in the system's electrical power.
Sys_Dynamic_Device_Init	Instructs the VxD to initialize a dynamically loaded VxD.
Sys_Dynamic_Device_Exit	Instructs the VxD to prepare to unload a dynamically loaded VxD.
Create_Thread	Notifies the VxD that this is the first stage of creating a new thread.
Thread_Init	Notifies the VxD that this is the second stage of creating a new thread.
Terminate_Thread	Notifies the VxD that this is the first stage of destroying a thread.
Thread_Not_Executeable	Notifies the VxD that this is the second stage of destroying a thread.
Destroy_Thread	Notifies the VxD that this is the third stage of destroying a thread.
PNP_New_Devnode	Notifies the VxD that a new device node has been created.
W32_DeviceIoControl	Notifies the VxD that a Win32 program has issued a *DeviceIoControl* call.
Get_Contention_Handler	Notifies the VxD that VCOMM wants the address of a contention handler.

Table 4-3. *Other system control messages.*

The important things to note about these messages are listed here:

■ Set_Device_Focus is the basic way Windows changes the ownership of a device such as the mouse. One can issue this message for a specific device, in which case each VxD still gets to look at the message to see if the message pertains to its device. Alternatively, one can issue this message for all devices, in which case multiple VxDs will respond.

■ Begin_Message_Mode and End_Message_Mode bracket the presentation of a system modal message by the SHELL device. These messages often have the familiar "blue screen message box" appearance. While such a message is visible, device drivers shouldn't do anything that might interfere with the message or the user's obligation to respond to it.

■ Debug_Query occurs when a programmer uses a special dot command in the debugger. For example, the *.V86MMGR* command causes this message to be sent to the V86MMGR device. Servicing this message helps you debug your own code.

■ Power_Event notifies interested VxDs that a change is about to occur in the electrical power supplying this computer. In my experience with laptops on airplanes, this change is usually for the worse.

■ Sys_Dynamic_Device_Init and Sys_Dynamic_Device_Exit are used by Windows to initialize and shut down dynamically loaded VxDs.

■ The five thread-lifetime messages Create_Thread, Thread_Init, Terminate_Thread, Thread_Not_Executeable *[sic]*, and Destroy_Thread bracket the existence of Win32 threads.

■ PNP_New_Devnode informs a VxD that the Configuration Manager has created a new device node, the control block representing a physical device.

■ A Win32 program can use the *CreateFile* function to obtain a device driver handle, which it can then supply as an argument to *DeviceIoControl*. The *DeviceIoControl* calls turn into W32_DeviceIoControl control messages.

■ VCOMM, the VxD that manages serial and parallel ports, uses Get_Contention_Handler to get the address of a callback function for handling device contention.

Private Control Messages

VxDs designed to work together can use the *Directed_Sys_Control* API call to send private messages to each other. The system control message codes for this protocol range from 70000000h through 7FFFFFFFh (BEGIN_RESERVED_PRIVATE_-SYSTEM_CONTROL through END_RESERVED_PRIVATE_SYSTEM_CONTROL). The VMM doesn't provide any registry for these private messages. Instead, the VxDs that communicate in this way must all understand what the message codes mean.

The VxD Service API

VxDs communicate with the VMM and other VxDs using the *VxD service API*. This API provides dynamic linkage between VxDs using software interrupt 20h and a set of VxD service ordinals. Service ordinals uniquely identify a particular VxD and a service function within that VxD. The VMM provides roughly 400 services that have general utility to many VxD clients. Other VxDs export more limited service APIs for special purposes.

Each VxD that exports service entry points has a unique 16-bit identifying integer (its VxD ID) and a branch table whose address appears in the driver's device description block. Each entry in the branch table points to a function that implements an externally callable service. The driver's author provides a header file that defines a series of 32-bit service table constants with mnemonic names like *VKD_Define_Hot_Key* and values like 000D0001h. The high-order half of each constant is the VxD ID, while the low-order half is the zero-based index of the branch-table entry for a particular service (see Figure 4-1). Thus, 000D0001h represents service number 1 (*Define_Hot_Key*) within the Virtual Keyboard Device (VKD), whose ID is 000Dh.

A VxD that wants to call a service function issues an INT 20h instruction that's immediately followed in memory by an inline data value specifying the appropriate service table constant. The VMM uses the device ID part of the constant to locate

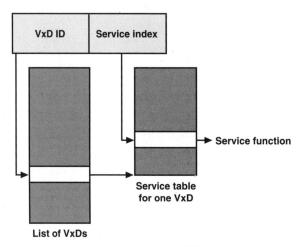

Figure 4-1. *A VxD service identifier.*

the VxD that contains the service function, and it uses the index part of the constant to locate the branch table entry within that VxD's service table. The VMM then calls the service function and arranges to return control to the calling VxD immediately after the inline data value. Assembly-language drivers use the VMMCall and VxDCall macros to automate the generation of the INT 20h instruction and the subsequent data value. For example:

```
include vkd.inc
...
mov      al, scancode
mov      ah, scantype
mov      ebx, shiftstate
mov      cl, operationflags
mov      esi, offset32 callback
mov      edi, delay
VxDCall VKD_Define_Hot_Key
```

It's obviously relatively expensive to look up the VxD's service table and index into it. Therefore, the VMM *snaps* service linkages the first time it encounters them. Thus, the VxDCall macro will initially expand to:

```
CD 20           INT   20h
01 00 0D 00     DD    VKD_Define_Hot_Key
```

After these instructions are executed for the first time, the VMM will replace these six bytes with an indirect CALL instruction that points directly to the service entry, as shown below (the x's represent the address of the service entry):

```
FF 15 xx xx xx xx    CALL [$VKD_Define_Hot_Key]
```

The snapped link will obviously run much faster than the original, unsnapped link. Some snapped service calls are even more efficient. For example, the VMM replaces a *Get_Cur_VM_Handle* service call with a MOV instruction that directly references the memory location where it keeps the current VM handle. This works because the MOV instruction occupies six bytes, just like the INT 20h instruction plus the service identifier.

This method of function linkage offers several important advantages. First of all, it's possible to overstore an entry in a service branch table and thereby intercept all the calls made by other VxDs. There's a VMM service named *Hook_Device_Service* that does just that. Another advantage is that the VMM can dynamically resolve one VxD's references to entry points in another VxD. This is similar to the dynamic linkage of DLLs within Windows applications. But, since the linkage occurs when the caller actually makes a VxD service call, no penalty accrues to having code that merely references nonexistent symbols without actually calling them. That is, you can build a VxD that conditionally calls certain services based on facts discovered at runtime without worrying about not being able to load the VxD. To accomplish the analogous dynamic linkage with a Windows DLL, you have to laboriously resolve references yourself using *GetProcAddress*.

A final advantage to the service linkage scheme is that you can easily tell whether a particular driver is loaded by calling one of its services. By convention, every VxD that exports services provides a *Get_Version* service at index 0, so that's the one you usually call. If this call fails, you conclude that the driver in question isn't loaded:

```
VxDCall FOO_Get_Version
jc      not_loaded
...
```

The reason you call the *Get_Version* service for this purpose is that it can't normally fail, so failure must mean something unusual—namely, that there's no VxD at the other end to answer the service call.

Services in Dynamic VxDs   The *Get_Version* test works just fine for statically loaded VxDs. They're either loaded the first time you ask, or they never will be. Although (strictly speaking, that is) you're not supposed to export services from dynamically loaded VxDs, it's possible to do so. It's then possible to have a scenario in which the *Get_Version* service isn't present the first time someone tries to call it. Even if the VxD eventually appears, the caller will always get the same "Nobody home" answer because the VMM snaps the dynamic link once and for all. To avoid this confusion, use the *Get_DDB* service to inquire about the existence of a dynamically loaded device, and use the *Directed_Sys_Control* service plus some sort of cross-registration protocol to communicate with it.

Callback Functions

VxDs also communicate by means of callback functions. In this context, a "callback" function is a procedure in one VxD that some other VxD calls through a pointer supplied originally by the first VxD. In one typical scenario, the VMM calls a VxD's device control procedure to process some system control message like Sys_Dynamic_Device_Init. The VxD's message handler uses a VxD service call such as *_VCOMM_Register_Port_Driver* to register a callback function address with some other central service provider. Thereafter, the central provider calls the registered function to perform other activities.

In another typical scenario involving callbacks, a VxD "hooks" an interrupt (that is, it installs the address of a new handler for the interrupt) while handling a system control message. The VMM or some other first-level interrupt handler calls the hook procedure, which then processes the interrupt.

THE WIN32 API

The Win32 API created for 32-bit programs running under Windows NT is now easily and freely available to applications running under Windows 95. Just as you would do in Windows NT, you create a 32-bit program using the Win32 API. You can create 32-bit Windows applications and DLLs, and you can also create 32-bit "console" applications that work like regular command-line utilities. Several classes of Win32 APIs are useful in systems programming, and I'll summarize them here.

Process and Thread Management

Windows 95 supports the same process and thread model for Win32 programs as Windows NT does. In this model, each application owns a *process* that contains one or more *threads* of execution. All threads in the system compete with each other for processor time on the basis of priority and other algorithmic factors that ensure fair allocation. Each process owns a distinct *memory context* that occupies linear addresses in the range 00400000h to 80000000h; the threads within the process share the physical memory mapped by these linear addresses, but threads in other processes are unable to access this memory.

You create a new thread by calling *CreateThread*. One of the parameters to *CreateThread* is the address of a function that the new thread will execute; the thread terminates when this function returns or when the thread calls *ExitThread*. Another argument specifies whether the thread should be created in the suspended state or not; you can use *ResumeThread* to release a suspended thread for execution. *CreateThread* returns a thread handle that you can use for various purposes. For example, you can call *TerminateThread* to forcibly terminate the thread, *GetExit-CodeThread* to obtain its termination code, or a synchronization primitive such as *WaitForSingleObject* to wait for the thread to terminate of its own accord.

All threads within one process share the same virtual memory context, including the static storage belonging to program modules. In order for a function within one thread to create persistent data that differs from data owned by another thread, the function uses the *thread local storage* mechanism. Using the Microsoft Visual C++ compiler, you can declare thread local objects by using the *__declspec(thread)* directive. At runtime, a master thread can use *TlsAlloc* to allocate a *TLS index* for use by itself and other threads. Typically, you would save this index in a global variable to make it accessible to the subroutines that will use it in calls to *TlsGetValue* and *TlsSetValue*.

The Virtual Machine Manager contains a so-called "secondary scheduler" VxD that implements the Win32 thread priority model. This scheduler is one of the clients of the "primary scheduler," which operates on a strict priority basis. You can control the base priority values of a thread by calling *GetThreadPriority* and *SetThreadPriority*.

The secondary scheduler applies "priority boosts" to the base priorities you establish in order to influence the primary scheduler's choice. Other VxDs also add and subtract priority boosts to threads, and these boosts are usually much larger numerically than the boosts used by the secondary scheduler. Accordingly, the priority values you set with Win32 API calls are just one factor in determining which threads receive execution time.

You can find additional details about process and thread management in Chapter 43 of the *Microsoft Win32 Programmer's Reference*, Vol. 2 (Microsoft Press, 1993) and in Chapter 6 of this book, which describes thread scheduling in more detail.

Thread Synchronization

Windows 95 implements several kinds of synchronization objects to allow threads to sequence their operations: mutex objects, semaphore objects, and event objects. You use a type-specific API call to create any one of these objects and to obtain a handle for the object. You destroy the object by calling *CloseHandle*. You use any of the *WaitForSingleObject*, *WaitForSingleObjectEx*, *WaitForMultipleObjects*, and *WaitForMultipleObjectsEx* API calls to cause a thread to wait until one or more synchronization objects reaches the "signalled" state. (You can also use other types of handles in these calls. For example, a thread handle is considered "signalled" when the associated thread terminates.)

A *mutex object* ("mutex" stands for "mutual exclusion") can be owned by only one thread at a time. You create a mutex with *CreateMutex*. A mutex is considered "signalled" when no thread owns it and "unsignalled" when some thread does own it. Thus, to enter a mutual exclusion region, a thread uses one of the wait primitives previously listed. Normal completion of the wait primitive means that the mutex is now owned by the waiting thread and that any other thread will block if it waits on the mutex. To exit the mutual exclusion region and return the mutex to the signalled state, the thread calls *ReleaseMutex*. Other threads waiting for the mutex will then have the opportunity to gain control and execute.

A *semaphore object* is essentially an unsigned integer with associated synchronization semantics. A semaphore is "signalled" when its count is greater than 0 and "unsignalled" when the count is 0. You create a semaphore by calling *CreateSemaphore*. You wait for a semaphore to have a nonzero count by calling one of the wait primitives previously listed. Any thread, not just one that has successfully waited on the semaphore, can call *ReleaseSemaphore* to increment the semaphore's counter. This feature allows you to use a semaphore to synchronize access to an object that supports several simultaneous users subject to some maximum limit.

An *event object* is a simple gate. You create an event by calling *CreateEvent*. You use one of the wait primitives listed earlier to wait for the event to reach the signalled state. Whether an event is considered "signalled" or "unsignalled," and for how long, depends both on whether you use *SetEvent* or *PulseEvent* to signal it and on whether the event has the manual or automatic reset attribute. An argument to *CreateEvent* specifies the manual or automatic reset attribute. The *SetEvent* API call places a manual-reset event into the "signalled" state, where it stays until someone calls *ResetEvent*. Any thread that waits while the manual-reset event is signalled is then immediately released. The *SetEvent* API call also puts an automatic-reset event into the "signalled" state, but the event reverts back to "unsignalled" as soon as one thread gets released. (The release may happen immediately if some thread is already waiting. Otherwise, it will occur the next time a thread waits.) The *PulseEvent* API call has no effect if no threads are currently waiting on the event. Calling *PulseEvent* for a manual-reset event releases all threads that are currently waiting; calling it for an automatic-reset event releases just one thread. In any case, the event is still "unsignalled" when *PulseEvent* completes.

The extended forms of the wait primitives (*WaitForSingleObjectEx* and *WaitForMultipleObjectsEx*) allow for what is called an *alertable wait state*. In Windows NT, you use an alertable wait state to permit the system to call an asynchronous I/O completion routine in the same thread. In Windows 95, you can use an alertable wait state to wait for an *asynchronous procedure call* scheduled by a VxD.

Windows 95 implements a function named *OpenVxDHandle* that creates a ring-zero handle for a Win32 event object. You can pass this handle to a VxD using the *DeviceIoControl* function, and the VxD can then use ring-zero analogues of several Win32 functions in conjunction with the handle. For example, a VxD can use the *_VWIN32_SetWin32Event* service to perform the equivalent of a ring-three *SetEvent* call.

You can find additional details about thread synchronization in Chapter 44 of the *Microsoft Win32 Programmer's Reference*, Vol. 2 and in Chapters 9 and 10 of this book, which describe how VxDs use ring-zero synchronization calls and asynchronous procedure calls.

The System Registry

The Windows 95 registry is a hierarchical database composed of keys and values. Every key can have subkeys ad infinitum. Each key can also have a single unnamed value and any number of named values. System components and applications alike use the registry to store persistent data about the installed hardware and software.

Two top-level branches of the system registry have particular importance for systems programming: the HKEY_LOCAL_MACHINE (abbreviated HKLM) branch and the HKEY_DYN_DATA branch. The Windows 95 Configuration Manager VxD uses HKLM entries to configure the system and to select device drivers. The Configuration Manager also records runtime information in dynamic keys within the HKEY_DYN_DATA branch.

Win32 programs can use the regular Win32 API to access and modify the registry. Typically, you open a handle to a named subkey of one of the top-level keys (such as HKLM) by calling *RegOpenKey* or you create a new subkey by calling *RegCreateKey*. You interrogate the single unnamed value associated with a key by calling *RegQueryValue*, and you examine named values by calling *RegQueryValueEx*. You use the analogous *RegSetValue* and *RegSetValueEx* calls to modify values within an open key. To learn which subkeys or values exist below an open key, you call *RegEnumKey* and *RegEnumValue*, respectively.

Win16 programs can also access the registry using functions declared in the Windows 95 version of the 16-bit WINDOWS.H header file (a part of the DDK and, eventually, of 16-bit compiler products).

You can find additional details about the registry in Chapter 52 of the *Microsoft Win32 Programmer's Reference*, Vol. 2 and in Chapters 11 and 12 of this book, which describe the Plug and Play subsystem of Windows 95, whose Configuration Manager component makes heavy use of the registry.

COMPATIBILITY INTERFACES

Several system interfaces were important in previous versions of Windows. These include the DOS Protected Mode Interface (DPMI), the XMS and EMS standards for managing extended and expanded memory, and virtual DMA services. Windows 95 supports these interfaces in order to provide upward compatibility for applications.

DPMI

DPMI gives protected-mode programs access to a subset of Windows 95 system services. The original purpose of DPMI was to make it possible for commercial DOS extender products to operate within Windows 3.0's MS-DOS virtual machines. Windows application programmers discovered uses for DPMI transcending this original purpose. Windows 95 continues to support DPMI to avoid breaking the applications that still rely on it.

DPMI addresses the needs of a DOS extender running in a virtual machine. The program begins life in V86 mode and issues an INT 2Fh, function 1687h, call to obtain the address of a *mode-switch* function. Calling this function switches the processor from V86 to protected mode. The program then uses INT 31h to request additional services from the so-called DPMI "host" system. When done, the program executes INT 21h, function 4Ch, to simultaneously leave protected mode and return to an MS-DOS prompt. Of some interest is the fact that the Windows 95 KERNEL component itself uses this same mechanism to begin running Windows components in the System VM.

Using DPMI is practical only from assembly language. DPMI calls use a function code in the AX register to specify one of several dozen services. Some calls require additional parameters in other general and segment registers. Results are always returned in general registers, and the carry flag indicates success (carry flag clear on return) or failure (carry flag set on return). Registers not specifically documented as holding return values are unchanged on return.

The DPMI function codes use the high-order byte to designate a broad class of services and the low-order byte to designate a particular service within that class. In Table 4-4 I've listed the functional groups provided in version 0.9 of the DPMI specification plus one more, 0Exxh. The DPMI Committee intended version 0.9 to be an interim specification pending development of a real specification, denominated 1.0. The 1.0 specification did eventuate, but Microsoft never implemented any of its additional provisions except the 0Exxh class of functions for coprocessor management. Windows 95 therefore continues to support DPMI level 0.9, just as Windows 3.0 and 3.1 did before it and just as Windows NT does today.

Function Class	Description
00xxh	Selector and descriptor management services
01xxh	V86 memory management (first megabyte) services
02xxh	Interrupt hooking services
03xxh	Protected-to-real-mode and real-to-protected-mode calls
04xxh	Get version service (only one provided: 0400h)
05xxh	Extended memory management services
06xxh	Page locking services
07xxh	Paging performance-tuning services
08xxh	Physical memory mapping service (only one provided: 0800h)
09xxh	Virtual interrupt state management services
0Axxh	Obsolete function (0A00h) for locating a vendor-provided entry point
0Bxxh	Debug register management services
0Exxh	Floating-point coprocessor management services

Table 4-4. *Classes of DPMI services.*

If you look closely at the kinds of services DPMI provides, you'll notice a narrow focus on functions needed by DOS extenders. I'll give a quick sketch of a DOS extender to illustrate this. The several DOS extenders I'm familiar with are basically program loaders with runtime libraries to support standard MS-DOS and BIOS software interrupt interfaces. After switching to protected mode, the extender needs to open and read an executable file. Economy of coding effort suggests using the standard INT 21h API for this purpose, but the extender needs to hook the protected-mode version of this interrupt using DPMI function 0205h in order to pass it down to real-mode DOS:

```
mov    ax, 0205h            ; function 0205: set PM interrupt vector
mov    bl, 21h              ; BL = interrupt number
mov    cx, cs               ; CX:DX -> interrupt handler
mov    dx, offset int21     ; ..
int    31h                  ; hook interrupt in protected mode
```

Assistance from the DPMI host is required in this instance because the interrupt descriptor table isn't easily accessible by the DOS extender. Now, when the DOS extender issues an INT 21h call, the program named *int21* gains control (still in protected mode). It will likely use DPMI function 0300h (Simulate Real Mode Interrupt) to pass the interrupt down to real mode. Assistance from system software is needed once more because the switch from protected to real mode and back requires changing processor registers that are accessible only from a ring-zero supervisory program. Part of the DOS extender's work will also be to translate pointer parameters from the selector:offset form used by a protected-mode program into the segment:offset form used in real mode. Translation may also require copying data from extended memory locations to locations in the first megabyte of virtual memory, since V86 programs can't access data anywhere else. The copy operation might require the use of DPMI functions 0100h to allocate memory in the first megabyte, 0000h to allocate a selector for addressing that memory, 0007h to set the base address of the selector to the address of the real-mode memory, and so on.

Although the fact isn't widely known, it turns out that Windows 3.0 already contained, and Windows 95 still contains, a fairly complete DOS extender. If you can load a program and relocate it so that it uses protected-mode selectors, Windows will handle all of the software interrupts that it's likely to use. Thus, it isn't really necessary for a DOS extender to hook INT 21h, because Windows' default handling of INT 21h is to translate pointer arguments and pass the interrupt down to real mode. Windows provides reasonable handling for mouse driver calls (INT 33h), video BIOS calls (INT 10h), and so on. Thus, one could have written a DOS extender for Windows 3.0 that simply used DPMI to switch into protected mode and loaded the client program into extended memory using regular file system calls. (It turns out that a few functions in standard runtime libraries were ill behaved in protected mode and needed to be replaced as well, but most commercial DOS extenders went much further than this.)

Given that DPMI is mostly useful for extended DOS programs, its main purpose in Windows 95 is to preserve compatibility for them. Since you can now write 32-bit console applications using the Win32 API, there's not much reason to also buy a commercial DOS extender. If you're responsible for an extended DOS application, you should see if you can rebuild it as a Win32 console application instead, thereby freeing yourself from your DOS extender and simultaneously paving the way for portability to other 32-bit platforms.

There still remain some limited uses for DPMI within 16-bit Windows programs. (For technical reasons, a 32-bit Windows program cannot use DPMI calls or any other interface based on software interrupts.) Whenever your application needs to call a nonstandard real-mode program—that is, one for which the built-in DOS extender won't handle the necessary pointer translation—you may need to use one of the DPMI 03xxh functions. In addition, the DPMI 09xxh functions allow you to control the virtual interrupt flag that gates whether the VMM will reflect interrupts into the VM.

DPMI function 0800h can be useful to a Windows application as a way of developing a virtual address by which to access memory, such as that on an expansion card, whose physical address in extended memory is known. Building the necessary selector for use in a pointer could be done using various DPMI calls, but the Windows *AllocSelector*, *SetSelectorBase*, and *SetSelectorLimit* API functions are just as convenient. Before Microsoft documented these selector management functions in the Windows 3.1 SDK, many programmers relied on the DPMI services because they didn't know that there might be another way.

Finally, DPMI calls still provide a way for legacy applications—that is, applications written for MS-DOS or for earlier versions of Windows—to share memory with each other. An extended DOS program running in one virtual machine can use function 0501h to allocate a block of extended memory whose linear address will be in the shared region of the address space from 80000000h to C0000000h. Extended DOS programs running in other virtual machines can access the same memory at the same linear address, as can Win16 programs running in the System VM. Microsoft would prefer applications that still work this way to be recast as Win32 programs that communicate by means of named file mappings.

The ultimate source of information about DPMI is the official specification, which is available from several sources, including Intel Corporation. Chapter 17 of this book discusses DPMI in more detail as well.

Extended Memory Management (XMS)

The Extended Memory Specification (XMS) governs how MS-DOS programs access and use extended memory—that is, memory beyond the first megabyte of physical address space. Every Windows 95 system includes an XMS provider, usually the Windows 95 version of HIMEM.SYS. A real-mode program obtains the address of an XMS service routine by issuing interrupt 2Fh, function 4310h. This interrupt returns the address of a real-mode function that performs a variety of memory allocation functions, depending on the function code in the AH register. Note that XMS isn't directly usable in protected mode; programs such as DOS extenders that need to make XMS calls first switch to real mode in order to call the XMS service function.

XMS services permit the caller to reserve and release portions of the "high memory area" that begins at linear address 00100000h, to allocate and release blocks of extended memory, and to control the A20 hardware line. (The A20 hardware line carries the 21st bit of a physical address. Because the 8086 processor only provided for 20-bit physical addresses, 80286 and later processors allow programmers to disable the A20 hardware line to provide backward compatibility.) MS-DOS applications only rarely use XMS services directly. It's much more usual for applications to rely on an underlying program like a DOS extender to interface with the XMS provider.

XMS affects Windows 95 in two ways. First of all, Windows 95 uses XMS during system startup to obtain control over all the free extended memory in the system. Second, Windows 95 simulates XMS services in order to preserve compatibility for real-mode software that happens to rely on it. For example, the following DEBUG session obtains the XMS entry point and uses XMS function 0h to query the version number of the provider:

```
C:\>debug
-a 100
2DBE:0100 mov ax, 4310
2DBE:0103 int 2f
2DBE:0105 mov [200], bx
2DBE:0109 mov [202], es
2DBE:010D mov ah, 0
2DBE:010F call far [200]
2DBE:0113 int 3
2DBE:0114
-g

AX=0300  BX=035F  CX=0000  DX=0001 ...
...
2DBE:0113 CC              INT     3
-q
```

The return value in the AX register indicates that the provider supports XMS version 3.00. The value in the BX register indicates an internal provider revision level of 3.95.

More information about XMS is provided by the *Extended Memory Specification (XMS) 3.0*, available in the "Specifications" section of the Microsoft Developer Network disk.

Expanded Memory Management (EMS)

So-called "expanded" memory has a history that neatly mirrors the almost biological growth of PC hardware and software standards. Serious MS-DOS applications had hard going in the early days because, at most, 640 KB of memory was available to them. An early solution to "RAM cram" was the Lotus-Intel-Microsoft Expanded Memory scheme. One added to the PC an expansion card that contained a few megabytes of additional memory. The card also implemented what appeared to be normal random access memory at a configurable segment address (the *page frame*) within the option ROM area of memory (between A000h:0000h and the start of the BIOS at F000h:0000h). Software could program the card to make different 16-KB pages of expansion memory available through addresses within that page frame. Rather than directly programming the hardware through I/O ports, applications used software interrupt 67h to access a driver specific to the particular expansion card purchased by the end user.

With the advent of the 80386 processor, it became possible to simulate the existence of expanded memory in software. Expanded memory managers like EMM386, QEMM, and 386Max rely on the processor's V86 mode and paging capabilities to do this. In brief, the memory manager switches the computer to V86 mode and enables paging with a set of page tables that maps most of the first megabyte of virtual memory to the identical physical locations. The manager honors expanded memory requests by mapping pages of extended memory into the designated V86 page frame address.

Modern expanded memory managers also fill in holes in the physical address space from extended memory. A typical PC has RAM at addresses 00000h to A0000h, corresponding to segment addresses 0000:0000h to A000:0000h. Expansion cards and the BIOS provide additional ROM and RAM at various locations within the remaining 384 KB, but there are usually sizeable holes where no memory exists. The memory manager can create so-called *upper memory blocks* in these holes to allow MS-DOS to use the memory for device drivers and TSR utilities.

An unfortunate side effect of running the PC in V86 mode is that some instructions that are normally okay in a real-mode program are suddenly privileged and generate general protection faults. The first programs to run into this problem were DOS extenders. The vendors of the then-leading 32-bit DOS extender and memory manager (Phar Lap Software and Quarterdeck Office Systems) teamed up to define the Virtual Control Program Interface (VCPI) standard, which prescribes how a DOS extender can coexist with a memory manager. VCPI also uses software interrupt 67h and provides functions for entering and leaving protected mode, for managing physical pages, and for accessing otherwise privileged processor registers.

Windows 95 cannot coexist with a VCPI memory manager. In fact, if you use interrupt 67h, function DE00h, in a Windows 95 MS-DOS box to detect VCPI, you'll be told that VCPI isn't present, even if you loaded a VCPI memory manager before starting Windows. During startup, Windows 95 issues interrupt 2Fh, function 1605h, to alert all resident software that Windows 95 is about to take over the machine. A VCPI memory manager is supposed to provide the address of a mode-switch routine that Windows 95 can later call to switch the processor from V86 to real mode. An undocumented interface allows the memory manager to supply information about its page mappings to Windows 95. The mapping information in turn allows the V86 memory management VxD to duplicate the upper memory blocks that were already in use when Windows 95 started. Any extended DOS TSR that happens to be present will be unable to run without the assistance of a VxD while Windows 95 is active.

A good source of additional information about VCPI is Chapter 10 in Ralf Brown and Jim Kyle's *PC Interrupts* (Addison-Wesley, 1991).

Virtual DMA Services

Direct memory access (DMA) provides a way for hardware devices to transfer data at high speed to and from memory. To our considerable misfortune, the hardware DMA controller has three severe limitations: it only deals with *physical* addresses, it prohibits certain memory boundary crossings, and it might (depending on what hardware bus it's attached to) only deal with physical memory in the first 16 megabytes. Programs running under Windows 95 use virtual memory, whose linear addresses are meaningless to the DMA controller, and the computers they run on might have considerably more than 16 megabytes of memory.

As it happens, real-mode programs can continue to program DMA transfers as they always have, in blithe ignorance of the possibility for problems posed by the Windows 95 environment. This is because the Virtual DMA Device (VDMAD) virtualizes the DMA controller ports in a way that makes everything work. Thus, a real-mode floppy disk driver can initiate a transfer to a given V86-mode address without worrying that the V86 memory manager might have mapped two discontiguous physical pages from beyond the first 16 megabytes into the V86 address space at the specified location.

Virtual device driver writers who want to program DMA transfers can also avoid many of the details of controller capability by calling VDMAD services instead of directly accessing the controller ports.

Protected-mode applications (including ring-three Windows device drivers) form a class of program that isn't covered by VDMAD's virtualization or its VxD service interface. For whatever reason, VDMAD does not virtualize DMA transfers initiated directly by ring-three protected-mode programs. These programs are instead required to use a little-known system interface called Virtual DMA Services (or VDS for short). The basic purpose of VDS is to provide a way for a protected-mode application to access VDMAD by means of software interrupt 4Bh.

More detail about Virtual DMA Services is provided by the *Virtual DMA Services (VDS) Specification 1.0*, available in the "Specifications" section of the Microsoft Developer Network disk, among other places.

Chapter 5

Systems Programming in Assembly Language

You're probably already familiar with some form of PC assembly-language programming and with the basic architecture of Intel processors. Your expertise in manipulating machine registers, keeping track of the values you've pushed onto the stack, and so on, has undoubtedly stood you in good stead. But, like most programmers I meet, you've probably been hoping you could work more with high-level languages such as C and concentrate on the logic of your programs instead of on their mechanics. The good news on this front is that you can implement most Windows 95 systems programs in C or C++ using either the Microsoft Windows 95 DDK or the VTOOLSD package from Vireo Software. In fact, we'll be working with examples written in C as much as possible in this book.

The bad news on the language front is that you'll still need to at least *understand* assembly language in order to read about systems programming tasks. Sometimes you'll even need to write large or small portions of a project in assembly language. To do this, you'll need to understand several arcane features of the Intel 80386 and later processors, including the following:

- The difference between real, protected, and virtual 8086 (V86) addressing modes

- How to use 16-bit and 32-bit registers

- How the Intel processors handle interrupts

- How Windows 95 uses various kinds of systems-level registers and data structures, such as descriptor tables and task state segments

Explaining everything there is to know about machine-level systems programming in assembly language would take up a lot of space—more than we have in this book. This chapter is a primer on the important features of 32-bit protected-mode programming for Intel processors, with emphasis on the way Windows 95 uses the processor's features. The ultimate reference source on this subject is one of the Intel programmer's reference manuals; I highly recommend the i486 manual, which seems to be better organized and to have fewer obvious errors than equivalent manuals for earlier or later processors. A good tutorial book is Igor Chebotko's *Assembly Language Master Class* (WROX Press, 1995), which also explains a number of systems programming topics not specifically related to the Windows environment.

ADDRESSING MODES

As you know, many of the instructions in any assembly program refer to memory operands. An Intel processor generates the address of a memory operand by combining a segment register with offset values held in one or two general registers and/or in the instruction itself. Processors compatible with the Intel 80386 offer real, protected, and V86 addressing modes, and the all-important detail of how the processor interprets the segment portion of a memory address depends on which of these modes happens to be in effect.

Real-Address Mode

In *real-address mode* (or just *real mode*), the processor forms addresses the same way the original 8086 and 8088 chips did—by adding a physical paragraph address held in a segment register to an offset derived from the instruction operands (see Figure 5-1). The resulting physical address theoretically spans somewhat more than one megabyte of physical memory. In practice, reserved regions reduce that potential megabyte of physical address space to 640 KB plus whatever memory happens to be present on option cards and in the BIOS module.

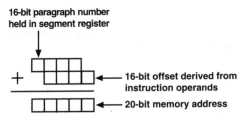

Figure 5-1. *Address computation in real mode.*

Your computer operates in real mode from the time you turn it on until Windows 95 or some other protected-mode program starts. Memory managers such as EMM386 are protected-mode programs, so the switch out of real mode might happen pretty quickly, but the fact remains that activities such as the BIOS's power-on self test and MS-DOS's initialization occur in real mode.

Application programmers, especially game developers, sometimes prefer real mode as a platform because there are no restrictions on what their programs can do. A real-mode program can access any register or any address in the first megabyte of memory without constraint, and it can execute nearly any instruction. This freedom makes it possible, for example, to achieve the best possible performance for a graphically oriented game. But even game developers need memory to work their magic, and the real-mode limitation of 640 KB is a powerful inducement to create software that runs under protected mode.

Protected Mode

In *protected mode,* the processor forms addresses in a substantially different way than in real mode (see Figure 5-2 on the following page). A segment register contains a *selector,* so called because it selects a *descriptor* in a *descriptor table.* There are two descriptor tables: the *global descriptor table* (GDT) and the *local descriptor table* (LDT). The selector includes a field that specifies which table it is indexing. The GDT contains descriptors belonging to the operating system or to all virtual machines. The LDT contains descriptors belonging to the current virtual machine.

A descriptor contains a base address, a segment limit, and access control flags that govern allowable types of memory access (see Figure 5-3 on the following page). Instruction execution includes forming a *virtual address* (sometimes also called a *linear address*) by adding the descriptor's base address to an offset derived from instruction operands. Because the base address is a 32-bit quantity, a protected-mode program can access up to 4 GB (2^{32} bytes) of memory. Since practical computers

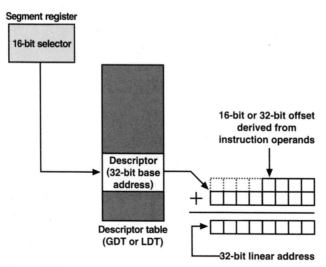

Figure 5-2. *Address computation in protected mode.*

can't (yet) contain 4 GB of physical memory, the operating system uses a disk swap file to temporarily hold sections of memory for which there's no room in the computer's physical memory. So although a computer may have only 8 MB or 16 MB of physical memory, an application can access up to 4 GB of virtual memory. This, however, requires the operating system to be able to relocate a *page* of virtual memory anywhere in physical memory. The virtual address, an address that may

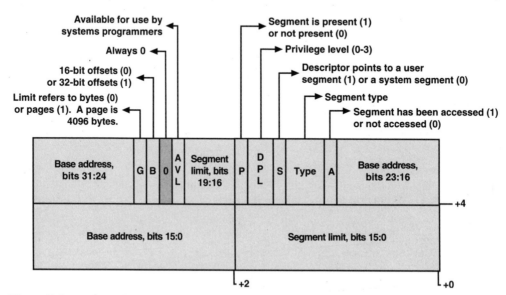

Figure 5-3. *Segment descriptor format.*

remain constant for the application, is translated by the processor—using *page tables*—into a physical address, which varies depending on where the page is located in physical memory. The translation process is illustrated in Figure 5-4.

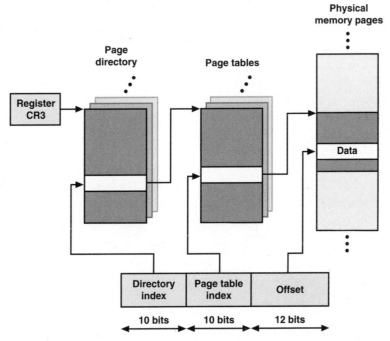

Figure 5-4. *Translation of virtual to physical addresses.*

Note on Terminology When you work a great deal with protected-mode assembly-language programs, you tend to get sloppy about terminology. Strictly speaking, a *segment register* holds a *segment selector* that refers to a *segment descriptor* in either the GDT or the LDT. To be completely accurate, therefore, one should never use a phrase like "a selector's limit" because the limit is an attribute of the segment recorded in its descriptor. I'm happy to report that you haven't stumbled into a nest of pedants by buying this book, however. I'll be as sloppy as I can get away with except when precision is called for. In any case, there's a one-to-one correspondence between selectors and descriptors, and I learned in my youth that the isomorphism defined by a one-to-one mapping could be considered identity for most purposes. So it may not be that far off base to confuse selectors and descriptors after all.

Segment Access Controls

The "protected" part of protected mode comes from several validation steps the processor automatically performs while executing instructions. The validation revolves around segment attributes contained in the descriptor. The S-bit and the Type field of a descriptor (see Figure 5-3 on page 64) provide the first level of control. Only so-called "user" segments (S-bit = 1) are directly accessible to software; the other kind of segment is a "system" segment, but you don't need to know about system segments in detail unless you're building the inner core of an operating system. User segments include *code segments,* which contain program instructions, and *data segments,* which contain the data used by a program (see Figure 5-5). No program can alter the contents of a code segment, just as no program can execute an instruction contained in a data segment. A program can read data from a code segment only if the segment has the *readable* attribute. A program can write to a data segment only if the segment has the *writeable* attribute. Windows 95 normally creates code segments with the *readable* attribute and data segments with the *writeable* attribute, although applications and VxDs can omit these attributes if they want. The other attributes of the Type field, *Conforming* and *Expand-down,* will be explained later in this chapter.

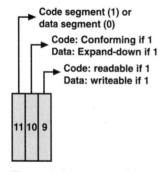

Figure 5-5. *The Type field for a user segment descriptor.*

In addition to verifying that the type of access (read, write, or execute) an instruction is attempting is appropriate for the target segment, the processor also ensures that the access is within the virtual memory occupied by the segment. The Segment Limit field of a descriptor (see Figure 5-3 on page 64) is a 20-bit number that usually equals one less than the number of bytes in the segment. For example, a 64-KB segment would have a limit of 0FFFFh. The processor wouldn't allow a program to access data in this segment using an offset beyond the 64-KB limit. To provide for segments larger than 1 MB (2^{20} bytes), Intel implemented a page granularity bit (or *G-bit*) in the descriptor (see Figure 5-3 on page 64). If set, the G-bit indicates that the segment limit is in units of 4096-byte pages; if clear, it indicates that the segment limit is in units of bytes. Thus, a limit of FFFFFh describes a 4-GB segment if the G-bit is set and a 1-MB segment if the G-bit is clear.

Segment limit checking usually ensures that a memory operand lies between offset 0 and the end of a segment. A data segment can, however, have the *Expand-down* attribute set (see Figure 5-5). An Expand-down segment's limit is 1 less than the *lowest* allowable offset rather than equal to the highest allowable offset. Windows 95 uses this concept in a very clever way to trap the use of NULL and nearly NULL pointers from 32-bit programs. These programs use a data selector with a base address of 0, with a limit of 00FFFh, and with the *Expand-down* attribute set. Consequently, the processor won't allow the program to dereference a data pointer that is numerically smaller than 4096. This trapping protects a programmer from directly dereferencing a NULL pointer, or from trying to access a field in a structure whose address is a NULL pointer, so long as the offset to the field is smaller than 4096 bytes.

Note on NULL Pointers   The Win32s subsystem of Windows 3.1 protects against NULL pointer references in a different way than Windows 95 does. Under Win32s, 32-bit programs use code and data selectors whose base address is FFFF0000h and whose limit is FFFFFFFFh. By arranging that no page tables map linear addresses in the last 64 KB of the address space, Win32s guarantees that NULL pointer references will generate page faults. References with a 32-bit pointer value of 1000h or higher wrap around to the legal linear addresses beginning at 0h. Unfortunately, handling the page faults hasn't always gone smoothly, with the result that some early Win32s implementations crashed instead of correctly interpreting the page fault as a NULL pointer reference. Furthermore, you need to be aware of the different segment base addresses if your VxD supplies linear addresses to a 32-bit client and has to be compatible with both Windows 95 and earlier versions of Windows.

NULL pointer references also cause faults in 16-bit programs, but Windows 95 relies on a different protection feature to trap them. You cannot reference a memory operand using a 0 selector. A 16:16 NULL pointer is 0000:0000h, so you can see that trying to dereference NULL or a field putatively in a structure whose address is NULL will cause a fault. (The 16:16 notation indicates a 16-bit paragraph or selector component and a 16-bit offset component.)

The General Protection Fault

I have been deliberately vague until now about how the processor enforces the access restrictions it places on protected-mode programs. The usual penalty for a violation of the access rules is a *general protection fault* (GP fault). The general protection fault is the Swiss Army exception of the Intel processor. The circumstances in which the processor will generate a GP fault are incredibly diverse. Many of them indicate a program bug, but many occur in the normal course of running a Windows program. Here's an abbreviated list of common causes for GP faults:

■ Any attempt to load into segment registers DS, ES, FS, or GS a selector that is not a valid data selector or whose descriptor privilege level makes it more privileged than the current program.

■ Any attempt to reference through a 16:16 NULL pointer, whose selector is 0. You're allowed to *load* a NULL selector into a segment register; you just can't use it to reference data.

■ Any attempt to call a program at a different privilege level.

■ Any attempt to reference code or data beyond the limit of the segment as recorded in its descriptor.

■ Any attempt to write to a read-only data segment, to read an execute-only code segment, to execute a data segment, or to write to a code segment.

■ Any attempt to signal an interrupt beyond the limit of the interrupt descriptor table (IDT). This GP fault happens all the time when programs issue software interrupts 60h and above, so it's not necessarily a program error.

■ Any attempt by a protected-mode application to execute the CLI or STI machine instructions. This fault also happens constantly. Windows traps the fault and sets the virtual interrupt flag for the affected virtual machine appropriately.

Numerologic Note   It's interesting, albeit pretty irrelevant, to note that the general protection fault is processor exception 0Dh. This culturally sinister number is the same number IBM chose as the abnormal-termination supervisor call (ABEND, or SVC 13) for OS/360. Of similar importance is the observation that regional system-programmer slang where I live and work includes the notion that a program "Oh Dees" when it dies on a GP fault.

Privilege Rings

The processor provides for four levels of privilege, often called *privilege rings,* to partition software according to the degree of control it requires over system resources. Windows uses only two of the privilege levels. The operating system supervisor runs in *ring zero,* at the highest level of trust. Ring-zero code can alter any location in memory and any processor register. Application software runs in *ring three,* which is the least trusted. Ring-three programs cannot access system control registers, nor can they read or write to memory areas the operating system designates as protected. The processor also traps certain operations from ring-three programs (such as the CLI and STI instructions mentioned above) to allow the supervisor to emulate those operations or to control how and when applications perform them.

To make sense of some of the discussions you will see about privilege levels, I have to introduce some apparently complex terminology. Let me first mention that Windows 95 uses the processor's privilege features in such a way that you can mostly ignore the complexity. The low-order two bits of a selector (see Figure 5-6) contain a *requested privilege level* (RPL). The descriptor for a segment contains a *descriptor privilege level* (DPL) that can theoretically be different from the corresponding selector's RPL. The RPL of the selector in the CS segment register is slightly special: it's called the *current privilege level,* or *CPL* for short, and it equals the privilege ring within which the program is executing.

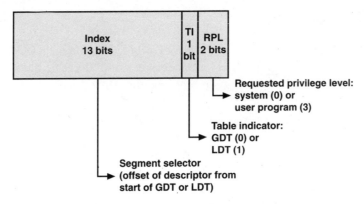

Figure 5-6. *The layout of fields in a selector.*

There are elaborate rules governing how a program running with a given CPL can load selectors with the same or different RPLs and DPLs. (Remember what I said earlier about being sloppy about the difference between a selector and a descriptor? You and I both know that the RPL is an attribute of a selector and that the DPL is an attribute of a descriptor. But I couldn't stomach the sentence that was going to result from being exact about this.) As I said, you can ignore most of these rules in Windows 95 because a ring-zero program always executes with a CPL of 0 using selectors whose RPL and DPL are also 0; applications always execute (in ring three) with a CPL of 3 using selectors whose RPL and DPL are also 3. Ring-zero programs also usually use GDT selectors, while applications usually use LDT selectors. Thus, you'll find that system software uses code selector 28h (a ring-zero GDT selector) and data selector 30h (also a ring-zero GDT selector) and that applications use code and data selectors of the form *xxx*7h or *xxx*Fh (ring-three LDT selectors).

The processor restricts a program's access to code and data belonging to another program that is executing in a different ring. Ring-three code cannot access ring-zero data, and it cannot directly call a ring-zero program. To communicate with the operating system, therefore, a ring-three program has to trigger a ring transition by causing an interrupt. The Intel architecture provides for *gate descriptors* (a kind of system segment) and for *conforming code segments* (distinguished from regular code segments by having their *Conforming* attributes set in their descriptors' Type fields), either of which can be directly called by outer-ring code. Windows doesn't use either of these features, however.

A ring-zero program can access data belonging to any ring, but it cannot directly execute code in any other ring. To execute user-mode code, therefore, the ring-zero supervisor must execute an IRET machine instruction on a specially formatted stack containing the complete context of the outer-ring program.

Virtual 8086 Mode

Virtual 8086 Mode (*V86 mode*) is a kind of protected mode for DOS and other real-mode programs. In V86 mode, the processor forms addresses the same way as in real mode: by combining a paragraph number held in a segment register with the offset specified by the instruction. In contrast to real-mode addresses, however, the resulting 20-bit address is a virtual address rather than a physical address. Therefore, a V86 address undergoes the same page translation as every other protected-mode address. This fact allows Windows and other system software to map the megabyte of address space accessible to real-mode programs into extended memory. Using paging to let programs access extended memory with first-megabyte addresses was the basic trick used by QEMM, 386Max, and other 80386 memory managers, and it underlies the concept of MS-DOS virtual machines in Windows 95.

An operating system can closely supervise a V86 program if it wants to. The V86 program acts in most respects as if it's running in ring three. This means that attempts to use privileged instructions or to reference privileged registers or data areas result in general protection faults. It's also possible for the supervisor to set the I/O privilege level (IOPL) bits in the EFLAGS register to a value less than 3, thereby causing certain normally innocuous instructions (including INT, PUSHF, POPF, IRET, CLI, and STI) to generate general protection faults. Intel's intent was to allow the operating system to use this feature to virtualize the interrupt flag. (You'll note that the thing these instructions have in common is that they save or restore the interrupt flag.) Microsoft discovered that MS-DOS programs ran about 15 percent slower if this was done, however. Therefore, Windows 95 normally sets the IOPL to 3 while running a V86 program unless it's specifically trying to trap a virtual-machine IRET instruction. An MS-DOS program can therefore halt the computer by executing a tight loop with interrupts disabled. The PS/2 architecture supports a watchdog timer that can generate an interrupt even in a case like this, but the standard PC architecture leaves the computer open to this kind of programming mistake.

DETECTING V86 MODE

If you know your program can run only under MS-DOS, you can tell the difference between real mode and V86 mode by using the obscure SMSW instruction. This was an 80286 instruction that still works on 80386 and later processors. It stores the low-order half of the CR0 register, whose low-order bit indicates protected-mode operation:

```
pe_mask equ 1        ; protected-execution bit in CR0

smsw    ax           ; capture low-order part of CR0
test    ax, pe_mask  ; test PE-bit
jnz     InV86Mode    ; branch if in protected mode
```

For compatibility reasons, the SMSW instruction isn't privileged, which means that ring-three programs can execute it. The logic behind this fragment is this: we've assumed that the program only runs under MS-DOS, which implies that it runs either in real mode or in V86 mode. If the PE-bit is set, the processor can't be in real mode and must therefore be in V86 mode.

If you know your program will run under Windows and you want to tell the difference between V86 mode and protected mode, you can't use this trick: the SMSW instruction will tell you that you're in protected mode in both cases. To distinguish between these cases, use INT 2Fh, function 1686h:

```
mov  ax, 1686h      ; function 1686h
int  2Fh            ; detect mode
test ax, ax         ; any bits set?
jz   ProtectedMode  ; if no, program is in protected mode
```

Intel designed V86 mode to be as transparent as possible to a program. There is, in fact, no direct way for a program to know that it's running in V86 mode. This is true even though a bit (the VM bit) in the EFLAGS register controls whether the processor is in V86 mode or not (see Figure 5-8 on page 74, in the subsequent discussion of 32-bit programming). For better or worse, Intel implemented the PUSHFD instruction, which pushes the EFLAGS register onto the stack, so that it masks the VM bit to 0. Accordingly, the following naïve code won't work. If you're a little rusty on using 32-bit registers in a 16-bit program, refer to the next section in this chapter.

```
pushfd              ; push EFLAGS register onto stack
pop     eax         ; pop EFLAGS image into EAX
bt      eax, 17     ; test VM bit in EFLAGS image
jc      InV86Mode   ; branch never taken!
```

Although V86 mode is supposed to be transparent to applications, there are times when you don't *want* transparency, namely when you specifically want to invoke a service provided by the Windows 95 operating system. You do this from a V86 program by executing the ARPL (Adjust Requested Privilege Level) instruction, which causes an invalid operation processor exception. The Virtual Machine Manager examines the segment:offset address of the resulting exception and routes control to some VxD service routine. IBM used essentially the same trick in CP-67 and VM/370, wherein virtual machine code executed the privileged Diagnose instruction to communicate with the control program.

THIRTY-TWO–BIT PROGRAMMING

The main point of using an Intel 80386 or later processor and an advanced operating system like Windows 95 is to gain the considerable benefits that accrue from writing 32-bit programs. These include improved performance (a direct benefit to the end user) and programmer convenience (an indirect benefit to the end user, who receives better applications in a more timely manner). The basic difference between 32-bit programming and the 16-bit programming you did on earlier processors or under earlier operating systems is the use of *extended registers* to hold 32-bit instruction operands and addresses. In addition, the 16-bit programs you're used to writing used one of four memory models (small, compact, medium, or large) depending on whether you had more than 64 KB of code or data (or both or neither). Thirty-two–bit programs normally use the *flat address model* (the added "dimension" of multiple segments is eliminated), which gives easy access to 4 GB of code and data without ever reloading a segment register.

Extended Registers

On 80386 and later processors, a program can access eight general-purpose registers (sometimes called just *general registers*) and six segment registers (see Figure 5-7) as well as a flags register (see Figure 5-8 on the following page) no matter what addressing mode it's using. The general-purpose and flags registers are 32 bits wide, which an assembly-language programmer indicates by putting an *E* (for *extended*)

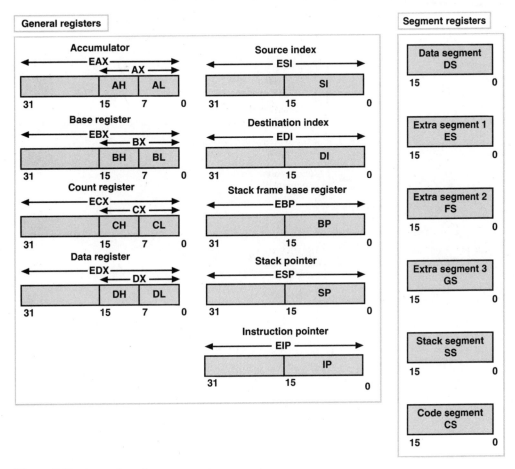

Figure 5-7. *General and segment registers.*

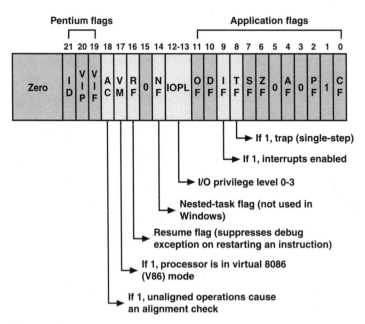

Figure 5-8. *The flags register.*

in front of the name of the register. For example, to access the 32-bit EAX register, a programmer codes something like this:

```
xor eax, eax        ; clears 32-bit extended AX register
```

The 16-bit registers you're used to using in 16-bit programs are just the low-order halves of the corresponding extended registers. Thus, the AX register holds the low-order 16 bits of EAX. Similarly, the 8-bit registers such as AH and AL occupy portions of the extended registers too. Instructions that move quantities between 8-bit, 16-bit, and 32-bit registers abound in 32-bit code. Here are three examples:

```
movzx ecx, al       ; zero-extend 8 bits from AL to ECX

cdq                 ; sign-extend EAX into EDX:EAX

rol   eax, 16       ; interchange high and low halves of EAX
```

It's probably obvious why you might want to use 32-bit operands in instructions: it's easier to do arithmetic on 32-bit quantities using 32-bit instructions. For example, adding two 32-bit numbers requires the following more-or-less ungainly combination of 16-bit instructions:

```
mov ax, word ptr a          ; low-order part of "a"
mov dx, word ptr a + 2      ; high-order part of "a"
add ax, word ptr b          ; accumulate 32-bit result
adc dx, word ptr b + 2      ;   (including carry from low-order)
mov word ptr c, ax          ; low-order part of sum
mov word ptr c+2, dx        ; high-order part of sum
```

The equivalent code using 32-bit operands is appreciably simpler:

```
mov eax, a
add eax, b                  ; add a + b
mov c, eax                  ; store the result
```

If you're limited to 16-bit registers, you have to write a very involved software simulation of a repeated-subtraction hardware algorithm to perform 32-bit division, but dividing two long integers is essentially trivial using 32-bit instructions:

```
mov eax, dividend
cdq                         ; sign-extend the dividend
idiv divisor                ; divide it by the divisor
mov quotient, eax           ; store the result
```

Thirty-two–bit addressing makes your life simpler too, because it eliminates the need to constantly reload segment registers as operands cross 64-KB boundaries. For example, a few data structures in Windows (notably graphical bitmaps) can be larger than 64 KB. You can deal with such structures in a 16-bit program by declaring a "huge" pointer. The Windows *GlobalAlloc* function will assign contiguous selectors (that is, selectors that are 8 apart, such as 7E7h, 7EFh, etc.) to cover the entire memory block, and your program's arithmetic to generate the selector for a data access will work as expected. Suppose you wanted for some totally unknown (and probably unknowable) reason to count the number of black pixels in a 256-color bitmap and were willing to assume that a 0 byte in the bitmap denoted a black pixel (it probably would, actually). You could use the following C code to count them:

```
LONG CountBlack(BYTE __huge * lpBits, LONG nbits)
    {                               // CountBlack
    LONG result = 0;
    LONG i;
    for (i = 0; i < nbits; ++i)
        if (!lpBits[i])
            ++result;
    return result;
    }                               // CountBlack
```

If you don't already know what sort of assembly code the C compiler will generate for the reference to *lpBits[i]* on a 16-bit platform, you will probably be horrified:

```
mov     ax, WORD PTR i
mov     dx, WORD PTR i+2
mov     cx, WORD PTR lpBits
mov     bx, WORD PTR lpBits+2
add     ax, cx
adc     dx, 0
mov     cx, OFFSET __AHSHIFT
shl     dx, cl
add     dx, bx
mov     bx, ax
mov     es, dx
mov     al, BYTE PTR es:[bx]
```

In this fragment, *__AHSHIFT* is an external constant (actually an imported symbol) equal to 3. The net effect of this code is to add the quantity $(i/65536) \times 8$ to the first selector for the *lpBits* memory block and to use the quantity i % 65536 as an offset from that selector. If you ever wondered why *BitBlt* calls were so slow in previous versions of Windows, now you know!

A 32-bit version of the same program generates this obviously smaller and faster code for the same access:

```
mov     eax, DWORD PTR i
mov     ecx, DWORD PTR lpBits
xor     edx, edx
mov     dl, BYTE PTR [eax+ecx]
```

Not only does 32-bit addressing make your life easier when it comes to managing large blocks of data, but it also helps you manage arrays. The original 808*x* processor architecture severely restricted the ways you could form addresses by combining base and index registers with the offset data in an instruction. In contrast, you can use *any* register as a base register in a 32-bit address and any register but ESP as an additional index register. Furthermore, you can multiply the index value by 1, 2, 4, or 8. The preceding code fragment shows one example of combining registers to form an address; here's an example that illustrates this kind of multiplication to index an array of long (4-byte) elements:

```
mov ecx, array         ; ECX points to base of long[] array
mov edx, i             ; EDX = loop index (0 to n)
mov eax, [ecx + 4*edx] ; EAX <- i'th element of array
```

USE32 and USE16 Segments

Even though the general registers are 32 bits wide, programs don't necessarily access the full width. Bits within the descriptor for the current code segment determine whether operand values and instruction addresses are 32 bits or 16 bits wide by default. Instructions in a so-called USE32 segment use 16:32 addresses (a 16-bit selector and a 32-bit offset) and deal with 32-bit operands. Conversely, instructions in a USE16 segment use 16:16 addresses (a 16-bit selector and a 16-bit offset) and deal with 16-bit operands. In either case, the virtual address generated for an instruction is 32 bits wide, 32 bits being the size of the base address in the segment descriptor. The only difference between 32-bit and 16-bit addressing in protected mode on 80386 and higher processors is how many bits of additional address data (the offset) get added to the base address to form the final virtual address.

To illustrate the importance of the *bitness* of the code segment, consider the machine instruction whose hexadecimal representation is 8B 07. Even if you've committed the encoding of Intel instructions to memory, you can't tell just from looking at this what it does. In a USE16 segment, this particular instruction would be:

```
mov ax, [bx]     ; 16-bit address, 16-bit operand
```

In a USE32 segment, however, the same encoding would yield a substantially different instruction:

```
mov eax, [edi]   ; 32-bit address, 32-bit operand
```

Address and Operand Size Override Prefixes

Instruction prefix operations allow the programmer to override the default operand and/or address width for the duration of a single instruction. Thus, inserting the operand-override prefix 66h into the instruction stream makes the next instruction use the opposite operand width, and inserting the address-size override 67h makes it use the opposite address width. Within a USE16 segment, the basic 8B 07 instruction I just mentioned can mean any of four things, depending on the presence or absence of override prefixes:

```
8B 07        mov ax, [bx]    ; no overrides
66 8B 07     mov eax, [bx]   ; operand-size override
67 8B 07     mov ax, [edi]   ; address-size override
67 66 8B 07  mov eax, [edi]  ; both overrides
```

Within a USE32 segment, conversely, you could have these four possibilities:

```
8B 07       mov eax, [edi]  ; no overrides
66 8B 07    mov ax, [edi]   ; operand-size override
67 8B 07    mov eax, [bx]   ; address-size override
66 67 8B 07 mov ax, [bx]    ; both overrides
```

Does this mean that you need to explicitly insert override prefixes into your programs when you want something other than the default address and operand sizes? No. Luckily, the assembler you use to compile an assembly-language program knows how to use the override prefixes to make your life relatively simple. You first declare the bitness of your code segment by using either the *USE16* or *USE32* directive:

```
_TEXT   SEGMENT BYTE PUBLIC USE16 'CODE'
```

or

```
_TEXT   SEGMENT BYTE PUBLIC USE32 'CODE'
```

32-BIT OPERANDS AND ADDRESSES IN 16-BIT CODE

Using 32-bit registers from a 16-bit program can be very useful, and you might have been surprised to learn that you can do it. Some 16-bit C compilers will generate 32-bit integer arithmetic for "long" operands, for example, if they know the program will run on a 32-bit processor. And using a 32-bit address in a protected-mode Windows-based program is also very useful as a high-performance way to handle *__huge* data arrays such as bitmaps.

Using a 32-bit address in a real-mode program (what some people call "big real mode") probably seems like nonsense, but it actually isn't. The processor caches the descriptor of each segment. When you're running in real mode, these caches normally indicate a limit of 64 KB and a base address equal to the 20-bit physical paragraph address of the segment. If you switch to protected mode, load a selector into some segment register and then switch back to real mode without first restoring that segment register, the processor's descriptor cache will continue to hold the new descriptor with a base address that can point to any location in physical memory (including locations outside the first megabyte). You can then access whatever memory the protected-mode selector pointed to, and this includes being able to access more than 64 KB by using a 32-bit address. As soon as something, such as a random interrupt handler, modifies the segment register, however, the cached base address gets reloaded and you lose your temporary freedom of access.

From then on, simply code references to operands and addresses using the symbols for extended or nonextended registers, as appropriate, as shown in the preceding examples. The assembler will insert the necessary prefixes to make things work out right at runtime.

One important caution is in order here. A few instructions—including PUSHF, PUSHA, MOVS, and so on—have implicit register operands. If you want the assembler to generate the 32-bit version of these instructions, you must explicitly add the letter *D* to the opcode (PUSHFD, PUSHAD, MOVSD, and so on), even if you're coding a USE32 segment. I once saw a released commercial VxD with the egregious mistake of a PUSHA/POPA where PUSHAD/POPAD had presumably been intended. Don't make this kind of rookie mistake yourself!

NOTE   Microsoft's MASM assembler assigns the default bitness of a segment based on the processor type you declare with directives like *.286*, *.386*, and so forth. If you specify *.286*, the assembler lets you use 16-bit general registers and the segment registers and instructions that were supported by Intel 80286 processors; all segments will be USE16 because that's the only kind you could have on an 80286. If you specify *.386*, the assembler lets you use 32-bit general registers and the additional segment registers and instructions supported by 80386 processors. In addition, specifying *.386* implies a default segment bitness of USE32, because that's probably what you want. This default choice is normally convenient, but it can get you into unexpected trouble. Say you start a program with the *.386* directive because you want to use extended registers as operands. Then you code the directive *model large, c* because you're writing part of a large-model Windows-based program. Your segments incorrectly end up as USE32. To avoid this, put the *model* directive before the *.386* directive.

The Flat Memory Model

Thirty-two bit programs normally use the *flat memory model*. In the flat model, the CS register holds a code selector having a 0 base address and a 4-GB limit. The DS, ES, and SS registers hold a different selector (different because it claims to be a data selector rather than a code selector) that also has a 0 base address and a 4-GB limit. (I didn't forget that Windows 95 uses an Expand-down data segment with a 4-KB limit for ring-three programs, I just didn't want to overly complicate this particular discussion.) A 32-bit offset therefore provides enough information by itself to address any location in the 4-GB virtual address space. The offsets in 32-bit flat-model address calculations are sometimes called 0:32 pointers to emphasize the minimal role of the segment selector, or sometimes simply *flat* or *linear* pointers. Flat-model programs therefore don't need to change the contents of segment registers. Sixteen-bit programs, however, need to constantly reload segment registers to access scattered pieces of memory. The cost of loading a segment descriptor and performing all of the validation steps associated with protected mode is very high, up to seven times more than just loading a flat pointer, and large-model 16-bit programs are therefore often much slower than flat-model 32-bit programs.

SYSTEMS PROGRAMMING FEATURES

Several features of the Intel 80386 and later processors are for the exclusive use of the operating system supervisor. These features include the control registers and the debugging registers, as well as system tables like the global and local descriptor tables and the interrupt descriptor table. You're probably at least a little bit familiar with how an Intel processor handles interrupts in real mode and with how a real-mode interrupt service routine uses the IRET instruction to resume execution, but there are some important differences between real-mode and protected-mode interrupt programming. You can probably go the whole rest of your life without knowing any of the details I'm about to describe, but you will understand the Windows 95 Virtual Machine Manager much better if you do know them.

Control Registers

The processor includes at least four control registers, which are designated CR0 through CR3. The control registers are accessible only to ring-zero programs. Bits within control register zero (CR0; see Figure 5-9) govern the operating mode of the processor (real or protected), whether paging is enabled or not, whether math coprocessor instructions are to be trapped and emulated or not, and so on.

Control register three (CR3) contains the physical address of the page directory, from whence the processor locates all active page tables while translating virtual addresses to physical addresses (see Figure 5-4 on page 65). Control register two (CR2) receives the linear address responsible for any page fault. (A page fault occurs when a requested page of virtual memory is not present in physical memory.) The number and purpose of other control registers depends on the CPU model, and Windows makes no particular use of them. Variants of the MOV instruction allow access to and from the control registers. Here are two examples:

```
mov    cr0, eax        ; copy eax to cr0
mov    eax, cr2        ; copy cr2 to eax
```

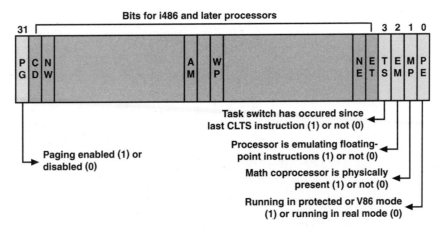

Figure 5-9. *Control register zero.*

If you want to code these and other ring-zero instructions in a Microsoft Macro Assembler (MASM) program, you must tell the assembler that you're using privileged instructions by appending a *P* to the processor-type directive:

```
.386p
mov     eax, cr0
```

A general protection fault ensues if a ring-three program tries to read or write one of the control registers. Forbidding a ring-three program to *read* CR0 is a bit silly, since the unprivileged SMSW instruction will store the low-order 16 bits of CR0.

Even though the processor prevents a ring-three program from changing CR0, Windows allows certain benign changes anyway by trapping and emulating them. For example, the only way for a V86-mode program to enable coprocessor emulation on a computer that has a real coprocessor is to force the EM bit on in CR0:

```
em_mask equ 4              ; emulate coprocessor bit

mov     eax, cr0           ; normally privileged, but OK
or      eax, em_mask       ; enable coprocessor emulation
mov     cr0, eax           ; normally privileged, but OK
```

The reason this works in Windows 95 is that the VMM analyzes the general protection faults that the two MOV instructions generate. The MOV from CR0 to EAX is safe, so Windows emulates it for the ring-three program. Turning on the EM bit is also safe, so Windows emulates that portion of the MOV into CR0 as well.

Debugging Registers

The processor also includes eight debugging registers. Four of them (DR0 through DR3) hold breakpoint addresses. The remaining registers control how the processor generates debugging exceptions when the program accesses memory at a breakpoint location. The registers allow you to halt execution on loads, stores, or executes at as many as four addresses. The Pentium lets you also trap port I/O operations in this way, which you can use to advantage by coding OUT instructions to bogus ports. System software uses special forms of the MOV instruction to access the debug registers, two of which are shown here:

```
mov     eax, dr0        ; copy DR0 to EAX
mov     dr7, eax        ; copy EAX to DR7
```

Windows makes these registers available to debuggers via DPMI calls. Kernel debuggers such as WDEB386 and Soft-Ice/W also use the debugging registers to assist systems programmers such as you and I.

The Global Descriptor Table

The GDT register contains the length and virtual location of the *global descriptor table* (GDT), one of the two descriptor tables I mentioned earlier. The GDT contains segment descriptors (see Figure 5-3 on page 64) that describe the starting address and length of each segment in use by any task, along with the type and access rights. Windows creates the GDT during the initial boot process and populates it with ring-zero selectors for system segments. Except for the special case of selector 40h (which references the BIOS data area at physical address 0400h), GDT selectors usually have a DPL equal to 0. Therefore, application programs cannot normally access segments described by GDT descriptors. Only ring-zero or real-mode programs can use the LGDT instruction to alter the GDT register. Software at any privilege level can use SGDT to discover the contents of this register, however:

```
gdtlimit    dw      ?           ; GDT's length - 1
gdtaddr     dd      ?           ; linear base addr of GDT
...
sgdt        fword ptr gdtlimit  ; any ring
lgdt        fword ptr gdtlimit  ; ring zero only
```

Note that SGDT and LGDT deal with 6-byte memory operands. That is, the SGDT in this code fragment stores the limit of the GDT in the *gdtlimit* variable and the virtual address of the GDT in the neighboring *gdtaddr* variable, and LGDT loads the 6-byte GDT register from both variables.

The Interrupt Descriptor Table

The IDT register contains the length and virtual location of the *interrupt descriptor table*. The IDT contains *gates* that specify handlers for processor interrupts (see Figure 5-10 on the following page). The Windows IDT contains entries only for interrupts 0 through 5Fh; interrupts 60h through FFh can be generated only by software executing an INT instruction and actually cause a general protection fault because of the IDT segment's limit. Access to the IDT register is similar to access to the GDT register: ring-zero and real-mode code can use the LIDT instruction to alter the register, but code in any ring can use the SIDT instruction to learn the contents of the IDT register:

```
idtlimit    dw    ?          ; length - 1 of IDT
idtaddr     dd    ?          ; linear base addr of IDT

...
sidt        fword ptr idtlimit    ; any ring
lidt        fword ptr idtlimit    ; ring zero only
```

Like SGDT and LGDT, the SIDT and LIDT instructions use 6-byte operands.

SUBVERTING PROTECTION

A little knowledge can be a dangerous thing. Some readers are now planning experiments along the lines of, "How can I use the nonprivileged instructions SGDT and SIDT to take over the machine?" I want to take the challenge out of these experiments by describing the results of the most obvious of them: SGDT and SIDT will indeed give you the linear addresses and lengths of the GDT and IDT system tables, and you can easily modify the tables to your heart's content. It's so easy, it's not even fun. (Beware that the IDT address you get with SIDT may belong to a debugger instead of to Windows, however.) If you want to, you can build a gate descriptor that will transport you magically to ring zero, whereupon you will probably crash and burn because you won't handle interrupts correctly. Well, it's your computer.

Windows could have protected the pages that contain these critical tables, since the processor's protection facilities forbid ring-three access to pages marked as belonging to the supervisor. Windows doesn't even try to protect its pages, though. After all, you're dealing with a *personal* computer. If you buy a car, you're free to drain the oil and see how well the engine runs, but you'll pay the price for your curiosity later on. The same thing is true of Windows. I'll admit to doing my share of reverse engineering to get programs to work, but I'd rather leave the gory details of managing the machine up to the system software that already knows how to do it.

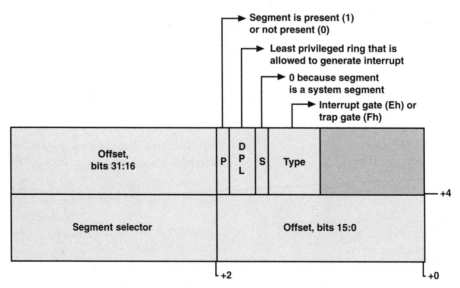

Figure 5-10. *Gate entries in the interrupt descriptor table.*

The Local Descriptor Table

The LDT register contains the selector of a *local descriptor table*. Windows 95 creates a separate LDT for each virtual machine. The LLDT instruction for loading the LDT register is privileged, but the SLDT instruction for storing it is not. The Type field in the descriptor of an LDT segment indicates that the LDT is a "system" segment. You can't load the selector for an LDT into a segment register, in other words—you can load it (if you have the privilege) only into the LDT register. (The address and length of the descriptor table in memory are in the LDT's segment descriptor. You would need a different selector—one marked as being a regular user data segment—to access the table itself.) An LDT contains descriptors that look the same as the descriptors in the GDT. As mentioned previously, bit 2 of a selector determines whether it selects an LDT descriptor (bit 2 set) or a GDT descriptor (bit 2 clear).

Interrupts

Three kinds of events interrupt the normal flow of an application program and transfer control to the operating system: hardware interrupts, software interrupts, and processor exceptions.

- A hardware interrupt originates in an I/O device that presents an interrupt request (an IRQ) to the Programmable Interrupt Controller chip (PIC) in the computer.

- Software interrupts occur when a program executes the INT *n* instruction on purpose to communicate with system software.

- Processor exceptions occur when the processor recognizes a problem or other exceptional condition (such as a page fault or a general protection fault) that requires operating system intervention.

These three kinds of interrupts happen all the time. We could also add the non-maskable interrupt (NMI) to this list, but it's not generally supposed to occur on a working system.

Regardless of their source, all interrupts save the context of the currently running program on a stack and switch execution to a handler specified by the gate entry in the IDT. The precise way in which the processor saves the context depends on the relative privilege levels of the interrupted program and the handler.

Interrupts from the Same Privilege Level In many cases, the handler is located at the same privilege level as the interrupted program. In these cases, the processor pushes the flags and the current instruction counter onto the current stack and transfers control to the handler. The handler later executes an IRET or IRETD instruction to return to the point of interrupt. (IRET is for 16-bit interrupt service routines, and IRETD is for 32-bit interrupt service routines.) This sequence is very similar to what happens in real mode, except that real-mode interrupts vector through the interrupt vector (located in physical memory at address 0:0) instead of through gate entries in the IDT.

Interrupts from an Outer (Lesser) Privilege Level More interesting things happen when the handler specified by the IDT gate is at ring zero and the interrupt is coming from ring three. The processor first examines a special system segment called the *task state segment* (TSS). (Intel intended every different thread to have its own TSS, which could be the basic structure involved in multitasking. Task switching by means of different TSSs is very expensive, however, and Windows doesn't use this method. Instead, Windows maintains a single TSS and uses more brute-force instructions to accomplish context switches.) The processor needs to look at the TSS to handle a ring-crossing interrupt because the TSS contains a pointer to the top of a ring-zero stack on which to save the old context. This is a static pointer that's the same every time an interrupt triggers a switch to ring zero.

After switching to the ring-zero stack, the processor pushes the old (ring-three) stack pointer (SS:ESP) and a standard interrupt frame containing the EFLAGS register and the CS:EIP instruction pointer (see Figure 5-11). When the supervisor later executes an IRETD instruction, the processor pops the standard interrupt frame, then notices that the RPL of the new code selector requires a switch back to outer privilege, so it also pops the stack pointer.

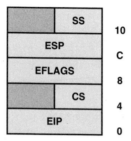

Figure 5-11. *The stack frame generated by an interrupt to inner privilege.*

Interrupts from V86 Mode A somewhat more complicated process occurs when an interrupt happens in V86 mode. At the time of the interrupt, the segment registers contain real-mode paragraph numbers that will be meaningless in protected mode. After switching to the ring-zero stack, the processor saves GS, FS, DS, and ES and then sets them to 0. Zeroing the segment registers might forestall an unrepeatable general protection fault by forcing the interrupt handler to load valid selectors before trying to access any data. Then the processor pushes the old SS:ESP, EFLAGS, and CS:EIP as described earlier. Figure 5-12 diagrams this stack frame. The eventual IRETD restores the segment registers along with everything else. When we eventually discuss the client register structure used in VxD programming, I'll remind you to look at Figure 5-12 again because the two structures are very similar.

Handling Interrupts

There are four other details about interrupt handling in Windows 95 that you ought to know about. When we're done with these details, we'll be done discussing what most systems programmers need to know about the assembly-language internals of Windows 95.

The first detail has to do with *disambiguating* hardware interrupts. Real-mode BIOSs program the PIC so that interrupt requests (IRQs) 0h through 7h interrupt on interrupts 8h through Fh and IRQs 8h through Fh interrupt on 70h through 77h. An interrupt handler for, say, IRQ 5 has to worry about the fact that it might be reached because of a hardware-generated INT 0Dh, a processor-generated general protection

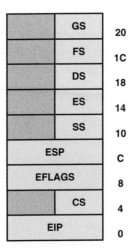

GS	20
FS	1C
DS	18
ES	14
SS	10
ESP	C
EFLAGS	8
CS	4
EIP	0

Figure 5-12. *The stack frame generated by an interrupt from V86 mode.*

fault, or an INT 0Dh instruction executed by an incontinent user program. This last case (software INT 0Dh) is an aberration, and the issuing program probably deserves the confusion it will generate. The first two cases might, however, occur in a normally working system. The interrupt handler generally has to examine the PIC's in-service register to determine why it was entered.

Windows avoids the necessity for disambiguating hardware interrupts by moving them out of the normal ranges. IRQs 0h through Fh interrupt on interrupts 50h through 5Fh under Windows, and therefore there's no possibility of confusing hardware interrupts with processor exceptions. (Don't worry that all of your real-mode drivers and TSRs suddenly need to hook to new interrupts. The VPICD presents hardware interrupts *to virtual machines* in the accustomed places.)

Even with the PIC reprogrammed, there's still a residual confusion between IRQ 0Ch (usually a bus mouse interrupt) and the NetBIOS interrupt, because both appear on INT 5Ch. The second interesting detail about interrupt handling explains how Windows handles this confusion. There are actually *two* different privilege levels associated with an IDT gate. We've only talked so far about the privilege level of the handler itself, which determines the need for a ring transition as the processor fields the interrupt. There's also a Descriptor Privilege Level (DPL) field in the gate descriptor, and this determines whether the processor will allow an INT *n* instruction to occur. The gate entry for interrupt 5Ch has a DPL of 0. If a ring-three program tries to issue INT 5Ch, the processor generates a GP fault instead because of the privilege mismatch. The GP fault handler can then route control to NetBIOS.

The third detail you should know is that some (but not all) processor exceptions also push an error code onto the stack in addition to everything else. The code actually turns out to be pretty useless to Windows, since the amount of information conveyed by the error code is very small. The fact that exceptions sometimes push error codes is another reason why one must accurately code first-level exception handlers. For example, the first-level handlers for interrupts and exceptions that *don't* push error codes generally have to push a dummy value so that all handlers can deal with a uniform stack layout. And the system must skip over the error code as part of restoring registers preparatory to returning to the interrupted program.

Finally, IDT gates come in several flavors. *Interrupt gates* are the usual kind, and they cause the interrupt handler to gain control with interrupts disabled. You can also have *trap gates* that differ from interrupt gates only by leaving interrupts enabled. Windows uses trap gates for software interrupts like INT 21h that vector directly to user-privilege code. Doing so allows the handler to dispense with the otherwise obligatory step of re-enabling interrupts by means of the STI instruction, which would generate an expensive GP fault. Gates are further subdivided into 16-bit and 32-bit varieties. The bitness of the gate controls how wide the context saved on the stack will be and has nothing to do with whether the handler runs in a USE16 or USE32 segment. Hardware interrupts always vector through 32-bit gates in Windows because one can't tell in advance whether 16-bit or 32-bit code will be running. Many software interrupts in the System VM vector through 16-bit gates, however, and this fact precludes their use by Win32 programs.

Part II

Virtual Device Driver Basics

Chapter 6

The Virtual Machine Manager

The Virtual Machine Manager (VMM) is the core of the Windows 95 operating system. The VMM erects and maintains the framework for managing virtual machines (VMs). Virtual device drivers (VxDs) work with the VMM to "virtualize" hardware devices and to provide system services to applications and to each other. If you like, you can think of the VMM as the virtual driver for the whole computer, because it allows multiple programs to operate simultaneously as though each of them was alone on a real machine. The VMM has more responsibility than the typical VxD, however, in that it also provides utility functions that are called by nearly all VxDs and it supervises all the other VxDs.

This chapter describes three aspects of the VMM's operation that underlie practically everything that happens in Windows 95: memory management, interrupt handling, and thread scheduling. The basic thing you need to know about memory management is how the VMM partitions the address space; later chapters will talk about the service calls you make from a VxD to allocate or control memory. You need to understand how the VMM handles interrupts because without this knowledge it's hard to know how to hook the several kinds of interrupts that can occur. Finally, you need to understand how the VMM selects threads for execution because that's the basic mechanism through which application programs are permitted to run.

MANAGING MEMORY

All of the resources on a computer are scarce in one way or another: There are never enough processor cycles to go around. The screen never seems big enough to hold all the windows we'd like to open, or the video card isn't fast enough or doesn't have high enough resolution to support whatever images are currently in vogue. Modems don't satisfy the increasing demand for bandwidth on the Information Superhighway. Of all of a computer's resources, however, the one that has seemed most consistently scarce is memory. Small wonder, then, that Windows 95 continues the trend toward more sophisticated management of system memory.

The System Memory Map

The VMM uses the paging functionality of the Intel 80386 and later processors to implement a 32-bit virtual address space. To simplify memory management, the VMM subdivides the available address space into five regions, as shown in Figure 6-1. The four significant regions are

■ **The V86 region**, extending from linear address 0h through 10FFEFh, belongs to the currently executing virtual machine. (As explained in the sidebar on page 94, the addresses from 10FFF0h through 003FFFFFh aren't used.) This region encompasses all of the memory addressable by a 16:16 pointer in the range 0000h:0000h through FFFFh:FFFFh.

■ **The private application region** begins at 00400000h and extends through 7FFFFFFFh. This portion of virtual memory is private to a specific *memory context,* which essentially corresponds to a Win32 process. Each virtual machine and each Win32 application belongs to a distinct process, and therefore each has its own context.

■ **The shared application region** follows at addresses 80000000h through BFFFFFFFh. Windows loads some of the system's own ring-three DLLs, such as KERNEL32.DLL and USER32.DLL, and all Win16 applications into this region of the address space. Windows also uses this range of linear addresses to satisfy file-mapping requests (created by *CreateFileMapping*) from Win32 programs running in the System VM and to field memory allocation requests from DPMI clients in virtual machines.

■ **The shared system region** from C0000000h to the top of virtual memory holds system data and programs that are shared among all processes and VMs. This is where the VMM and all the other VxDs live. The pages of each VM's V86 region are also mapped to addresses in this range of the address space. This so-called *high-linear* mapping allows a VxD to access a particular VM's V86 memory even if the VM isn't current (in which case some other VM's memory would occupy the first megabyte of address space).

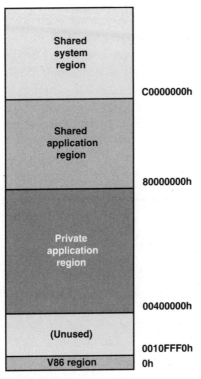

Figure 6-1. *A map of the Windows 95 virtual address space.*

Memory Sharing

Differentiating between context-specific memory and shared memory has several important implications for systems programmers. Placing all Win16 applications into the shared application region is an ugly but necessary choice that allows Windows 95 to maintain compatibility with earlier versions of Windows, in which applications could freely access each other's memory. Satisfying DPMI allocation requests from this region allows Win16 programs and extended DOS programs to continue sharing linear addresses too.

Win32 programs are subject to different compatibility constraints, however. The only legal way for two Win32 applications to share memory is for them to create a named file mapping. (Despite its appealing name, the *GMEM_SHARE* option of *GlobalAlloc* does *not* create shared memory. It allocates memory within the per-process private application region instead. This will be no surprise to experienced Windows NT programmers.) And, if memory is shareable by Win32 applications, it's automatically available to Win16 and extended DOS applications as well.

Compatibility Note   You shouldn't rely on sharing memory between Win32 applications on the one hand and Win16 and DOS applications on the other without checking the version of Windows under which you're running. Microsoft might change the address assignments in the future. In addition, Windows 95 currently places both shared (named) and unshared (unnamed) memory-mapped file allocations into the shared application region, but Microsoft considers this a bug. Eventually, unshared mappings will go into the private application region of the address space to prevent them from being shared.

THE FIRST FOUR MEGABYTES

You might be wondering what Windows 95 does with the approximately 3 MB of address space between the end of the V86 region and the start of the private application region (addresses 0010FFF0h through 003FFFFFh). The answer is, nothing. The reason Windows 95 abandons this addressing capability has to do with the way the Intel chip organizes page tables. One of the system's control registers (CR3) points to a 4096-byte page table directory. Each 4-byte entry in the page table directory is the physical address of a 4096-byte page table. Each 4-byte entry in a page table is in turn either the address of a 4096-byte page in physical memory or a 32-bit value that the VMM can use to initialize the page or to fetch it from the swap file.

Notice how much memory a single entry in the page table directory controls: 1024 page table entries × 4096 bytes per page, or 4 MB. That is, one DWORD in the page table directory describes 00400000h bytes of virtual memory, which is exactly the size that the VMM effectively reserves for the V86 region of a virtual machine. In Windows 3.0 and 3.1 (where there was no per-process memory region), the VMM was able to switch the memory context from one VM to another simply by replacing the first page table pointer in the page directory. Because V86 memory occupies only the first 1 MB or so, the remaining 3 MB referred to by that page table directory entry are simply lost. (Windows 95 still uses one entry in the page table directory to refer to V86 memory, but Windows 95 needs to swap *many* page directory pointers on each context switch.)

VxDs must take care not to make out-of-context memory references at awkward times. During a hardware interrupt, for example, a VxD should not reference the memory of a process other than the one that was interrupted. Disobeying this rule can generate a page fault at a time when the VMM can't tolerate a page fault, thereby crashing the system. A variant of the _LinPageLock service allows a VxD programmer to lock a private page into memory and to obtain a shared-region alias that will be valid no matter what the current context.

Memory Management APIs

VxDs use three classes of VMM services to allocate and release virtual memory. The paging subsystem provides services, including _PageAllocate and _PageFree, for allocating large areas of virtual memory in multiples of the system page size of 4096 bytes. The heap manager offers the _HeapAllocate and _HeapFree services for allocating smaller blocks of memory from one of several heaps. There are three separate heaps: one for pageable memory, one for page-locked memory, and one for memory that's discarded at the end of device initialization (after the Init_Complete system control message has been processed, in other words). The linked-list manager allows a VxD to create a pool of fixed-size memory blocks upon which to draw by calling List_Allocate.

VxDs use the heap and linked-list services for memory that will be used only by ring-zero code. In contrast, VxDs use _PageAllocate primarily to allocate memory areas for use by applications. The large block of V86 memory that's local to a single VM and that usually appears as free space between the end of MS-DOS memory and paragraph A000h comes from _PageAllocate, for example, as does the collection of pages that lies behind the video RAM addresses in each VM. Application calls to VirtualAlloc or to the DPMI memory allocation functions also lead to _PageAllocate calls. And the memory blocks which the heap and linked-list managers suballocate start out as pages assigned by _PageAllocate.

HANDLING INTERRUPTS

A computer can be considered to be in its "normal" state when it is performing a computation whose result benefits the end user. Interrupts are the fundamental mechanism for suspending execution of a beneficial computation so the operating system can handle an exceptional condition or supply an operating system service to the application. The executive summary of what the VMM does is therefore as follows: the VMM wakes up when an interrupt happens; it processes the interrupt and then executes an IRETD instruction to resume what was going on before the interrupt (see Figure 6-2 on the following page).

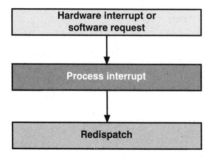

Figure 6-2. *The Virtual Machine Manager's main loop.*

First-Level and Second-Level Interrupt Handlers

The VMM contains a large collection of first-level interrupt handlers, one for each possible interrupt. The prosaic job of a first-level handler is to save the state of the interrupted program and transfer control to a second-level handler that will actually service the interrupt. State saving amounts to using the processor's PUSHAD and MOV instructions to save all the general and segment registers on the stack. The second-level interrupt handler does whatever it needs to do to service the interrupt and then transfers control to a redispatch routine. The redispatcher restores the saved state and executes an IRETD instruction to resume execution at the point of interrupt.

Saving the Coprocessor Context When you read that the VMM uses the PUSHAD and MOV instructions to save the state of the current program, did you wonder what happens to the math coprocessor? The FSAVE and FRSTOR instructions save and restore the complete state of the coprocessor. They're incredibly expensive compared to other instructions, however. Therefore, Windows doesn't automatically save the coprocessor state during an interrupt. In fact, it doesn't even automatically save this state when it switches from one thread to another. Instead, it relies on the obscure Task Switched flag in register CR0. Setting this flag during a thread switch causes the next coprocessor instruction to fault, whereupon Windows switches coprocessor contexts. This is "just in time" programming with a vengeance!

Redispatching after an interrupt is actually more complicated than this. The second-level handler might schedule an event to perform work that cannot be processed at the time. If so, the redispatcher must call the associated event callback function before completing the current interrupt. In addition, there might be some good reason for the redispatcher to run a thread other than the interrupted one. For example, the interrupted thread's time slice might have expired, or the second-level interrupt handler might have blocked the thread. Therefore, the *scheduler* gets a chance to decide who should run next.

Interrupt Descriptor Tables

Each VM has its own interrupt descriptor table (IDT). Because Windows 95 always runs the computer in protected mode (if you leave aside the peculiar case of Single MS-DOS Application Mode, which is "real" real mode), all interrupts in a given VM initially vector through its own IDT to the first-level handler within the VMM.

The VMM initializes a VM's IDT when it first creates the VM. The initial values come from a default table that the VMM and other VxDs create during system initialization. VxDs use the *Set_PM_Int_Vector* and *Set_PM_Int_Type* services to specify any initial values for IDT entries that differ from the VMM's defaults.

How Many IDTs? The *Set_PM_Int_Vector* service specifies the first-level handler for an interrupt coming from a protected-mode application. This handler isn't appropriate for a V86-mode application, however. Each VM therefore actually has *two* IDTs: one for V86 programs and another one for protected-mode programs. V86 interrupts vector to first-level handlers whose default action is to *reflect* the interrupt through the Interrupt Vector Table at 0000h:0000h.

Flavors of Interrupts

Windows 95 differentiates between hardware interrupts, software interrupts, and processor exceptions. Hardware interrupts indicate an I/O device's need for service. Programs generate software interrupts by using the INT *n* instruction. The processor itself generates exception interrupts when it determines that the operating system needs to handle some exceptional condition.

The classification of interrupts governs how VxDs and protected-mode applications hook them and how the VMM services them. Applications use DPMI services to hook interrupts and exceptions. VxDs, including the ones that service DPMI calls, use several different VMM services to hook hardware interrupts, software interrupts, and processor exceptions:

■   *Set_PM_Int_Vector* and *Set_PM_Int_Type* alter the gate entry in the IDT and thereby change the first-level handler for interrupts coming from protected-mode applications. A VxD would normally use these two functions only to install a ring-three handler (because a ring-zero first-level handler needs to do a lot of state-saving and stack-switching work). However, the ring-three handler is often actually an INT 30h operation created by calling *Allocate_PM_Call_Back*. When the interrupt occurs, the associated ring-zero callback routine gets control after the VMM sets up the normal VxD execution environment.

■ *Set_V86_Int_Vector* alters a far function address in the 0000h:0000h Interrupt Vector Table. This changes the address of the V86-mode service routine for a given virtual interrupt.

■ *Hook_PM_Fault* establishes the second-level handler for a processor exception or software interrupt that occurs in a protected-mode application. The default first-level handler reached from the IDT calls this handler after saving the context. (Any nonstandard first-level handler installed by *Set_PM_Int_Vector* gets control first. If it chains to the default handler, VxDs that used *Hook_PM_Fault* get their chance at the interrupt.)

■ *Hook_V86_Fault* establishes the second-level handler for a processor exception that occurs in a V86-mode program. The default handler reflects the interrupt to the 0000h:0000h Interrupt Vector Table.

■ *Hook_V86_Int_Chain* adds a VxD to the list of second-level handlers that get first crack at software interrupts coming from V86 mode.

■ *Hook_VMM_Fault* establishes the second-level handler for a processor exception that occurs while ring-zero code is running. It's very unusual for a VxD to need this service, because the VMM already contains appropriate handlers for ring-zero faults. You can use *Install_Exception_Handler* to trap errant pointer references in a VxD (and you can use the VMM service *_Assert_Range* to prevent your VxD from generating bad pointers in the first place).

Default Handling

The original purpose of the VMM was to virtualize the computer so that Windows and multiple MS-DOS sessions could operate simultaneously. You already know that MS-DOS contains an extensive set of interrupt handlers. The Windows KERNEL, USER, and GDI modules, together with the ring-three device drivers those modules use, also handle interrupts. To make the virtualization work out right, therefore, the VMM's default handling for nearly every interrupt is to *reflect* it to one or another VM so that a ring-three handler can deal with it. Reflecting an interrupt amounts to altering the saved register images that belong to the VM in question so that the appropriate interrupt service routine gains control when the VMM next dispatches that VM.

Immediately reflecting an interrupt isn't always the right thing to do, however. When a hardware interrupt occurs, the correct hardware interrupt handler may reside in a different VM than the one that was active at the time of the interrupt. Many processor faults, especially page faults, require handling by the VMM rather than by software running in any VM. The VMM and other VxDs might need to at least examine software interrupts in order to virtualize the resources that those interrupts are concerned with.

Hardware Interrupts

A system component named the VPICD (Virtual Programmable Interrupt Controller Device) contains the first-level handler for interrupts 50h through 5Fh. The VPICD reprograms the real interrupt controller so that interrupt requests 0h through Fh interrupt on these numbers (50h through 5Fh) instead of on the real-mode BIOS defaults (08h through 0Fh and 70h through 77h). The IDT gates for these interrupts indicate a DPL of 0, so ring-three programs that try to issue them as software interrupts cause a GP fault instead. Ring-zero code, of course, will not try to issue them as software interrupts in the first place.

By default, the VPICD reflects a hardware interrupt to the ring-three handler in whichever VM seems most appropriate. Which VM gets the interrupt depends on several things, including whether the IRQ was masked or not when Windows 95 started up. Chapter 13 discusses the routing of virtual interrupts in more detail.

VxDs can override the default handling of an IRQ by calling *VPICD_Virtualize_IRQ*. (It would be a very bad idea for a VxD to directly alter the IDT entry for a hardware interrupt.) Sometimes a VxD merely wants to choose a different VM to service the interrupt than the VPICD would have chosen. An especially good reason to virtualize an IRQ is to provide complete handling for a hardware device in ring zero, in which case the VxD arranges *not* to reflect the interrupt to any VM at all.

Processor Exceptions

Intel attempted to reserve interrupts 0h through 1Fh for its own use to describe processor exceptions. The story goes that IBM read the word "reserved" in Intel's documentation as meaning "reserved for IBM" and assigned some of the numbers that weren't used on the 8088 for use as hardware and BIOS software interrupts. Thus, a real-mode operating system or standalone DOS extender can't immediately distinguish, for example, between an INT 0Eh caused by a page fault or one caused by a floppy disk controller on IRQ 6. Windows 95 manages to avoid ambiguity by moving hardware interrupts to the 50h through 5Fh range and by judiciously using DPL = 0 gate entries to block the INT *n* instruction.

VxDs can override the default handling for protected-mode exceptions by calling *Hook_PM_Fault*. This is what happens when code like the Windows 95 kernel uses DPMI function 0203h to hook an exception. You shouldn't change the IDT gate for an exception interrupt via *Set_PM_Int_Vector* because this would disrupt the normal chain of fault handlers. VxDs can override the default handling of V86-mode exceptions by calling *Hook_V86_Fault*. Because standard VxDs hook some of the exceptions, it's helpful to know how they're likely to be handled before you add your own VxD to the mix:

Exception 00h (Divide Error)   The default action is to reflect the interrupt back to the VM, whereupon a handler installed by the application's runtime environment will probably crash the application.

Exception 01h (Debugger Call)   The default action is to reflect the interrupt back to the VM, which will often ignore the interrupt. Application-level debuggers hook this interrupt to single-step an application and to handle address breakpoints contained in the debugging registers.

Exception 02h (NonMaskable Interrupt)   The default action is to ignore the interrupt.

Exception 03h (Breakpoint)   The default action is to reflect the interrupt back to the VM, which will often ignore the interrupt. Application-level debuggers hook this interrupt to set single-byte breakpoints.

Exception 04h (INTO-Detected Overflow)   The default action is to reflect the interrupt back to the VM.

Exception 05h (BOUND Range Exceeded)   The default action is to reflect the interrupt back to the VM.

Exception 06h (Invalid Opcode)   This occurs normally when V86 code executes the ARPL instruction that Windows 95 uses as a breakpoint. In this case, the default action is to call the breakpoint callback routine in some VxD, which will rearrange the VM registers in some appropriate way. In other cases, the default action is to crash the VM. The Windows 95 kernel always hooks this fault for the System VM, however, to prevent the crash.

Exception 07h (Coprocessor Not Present)   The default action would be to reflect the exception to the VM, but the Virtual Coprocessor Device (VCPD) hooks this exception. The VCPD uses the Task Switched flag in register CR0 to trigger this exception in order to virtualize the real coprocessor (if there is one), and it also arranges for VWIN32 (a VxD that performs low-level functions for the KERNEL) to emulate a nonexistent coprocessor on behalf of Win32 applications.

Exception 08h (Double Fault) This exception indicates a serious problem with the system control tables and is the only interrupt that vectors through a task gate to guarantee a safe, consistent set of registers. The handler for this interrupt doesn't do anything, however, which means that whatever caused the fault is doomed to repeat until the user gets tired and shuts the machine off.

Exception 0Ah (Invalid Task State Segment) This fault should not occur. If it does, Windows 95 should crash, but it actually reflects the interrupt back to the VM anyway.

Exception 0Bh (Segment Not Present) This exception cannot occur from V86 mode. The default action for a protected-mode fault would be to crash the VM. The Windows 95 kernel always hooks this fault for the System VM because it relies on not-present exceptions to load LOADONCALL segments in 16-bit programs.

Exception 0Ch (Stack Exception) The default action for a protected-mode stack fault is to crash the VM, but the Windows 95 kernel always hooks this fault for the System VM to prevent the crash. You really have to work at it to generate this fault from a V86 program, whereupon you'll be rewarded by an infinite loop of faults because the default handler simply restarts the faulting instruction.

Exception 0Dh (General Protection) There is no single default action because so many different things, many of them normal, cause GP faults. If neither the VMM nor any VxD anticipated the fault, the only thing left to do is crash the VM. The Windows 95 kernel always hooks this fault for the System VM to prevent the crash.

Exception 0Eh (Page Fault) The default action is to read the faulting virtual address from register CR2 and assign a physical memory page

Exception 10h (Floating-Point Error) This exception does not occur in Windows 95 because Windows 95 doesn't alter the enabling bit in register CR0.

Exception 11h (Alignment Check) This exception does not occur in Windows 95 because Windows 95 doesn't alter the enabling bit in register CR0.

Exception 12h (Machine Check) The VMM reflects this Pentium exception to the current VM instead of crashing.

V86-Mode Software Interrupts

The default action for a software interrupt in V86 mode is to reflect the interrupt back to the VM through the 0000h:0000h Interrupt Vector Table. A VxD can intervene by using *Hook_V86_Int_Chain*. For example, the VMM and other standard VxDs normally hook INT 2Fh to filter out 16*xx*h functions. The SHELL virtual device also hooks INT 2Fh to filter out 17*xx*h functions for clipboard access, and any VxD can pile onto INT 2Fh to look for function 168Ah (Get Vendor-Specific API Entry Point).

Protected-Mode Software Interrupts

The default action for a software interrupt in protected mode is to reflect the interrupt to the VM in V86 mode. That is, this *used* to be the default in Windows 3.0 and 3.1, where MS-DOS and the BIOS handled most of the software interrupts that applications used. Strictly speaking, it's still the default in Windows 95, but VxDs hook most of them in order to perform as many functions as possible in protected mode. One important example of this is INT 21h, which MS-DOS and Win16 programs use to request system services. In previous versions of Windows, the VMM sent most INT 21h requests, especially the ones related to file access, along to MS-DOS in V86 mode, perhaps after suitably altering pointer parameters to describe V86 memory. In Windows 95, the Installable File System Manager grabs the file system requests and implements them entirely in ring zero.

Events

Like most operating systems, the VMM needs an internal mechanism to generate and then service a queue of events. An *event* in this context really refers to a unit of work that the VMM couldn't safely or conveniently perform when the need first became apparent. As a simple example, a hardware interrupt that indicates completion of an operation that some VM is waiting for might occur while another VM is running. In such a case, the interrupt handler might schedule an event callback to execute in the context of the other VM.

The usual reason why a VxD needs to enqueue an event, however, has to do with paging. Hardware interrupts can occur whenever the processor is enabled for interrupts, which is most of the time. To avoid losing interrupts, the VMM keeps interrupts enabled while it manipulates the data structures associated with paging. (In fact, the VMM and other VxDs normally leave interrupts enabled except for very brief critical sections of code, but we're only concerned with paging in this paragraph.) Since the paging system isn't reentrant, even in Windows 95 in which ring-zero programs instead of MS-DOS handle paging I/O, it's important that hardware interrupts not trigger recursion. Accordingly, hardware interrupt handlers are allowed to use only those VxD services that are specifically designated as *asynchronous*. Asynchronous services are guaranteed not to cause any paging operations, which means that they occupy locked memory pages and refer only to locked memory structures. Furthermore, they only use asynchronous VxD services (if they use any at all).

Most hardware interrupt handlers need to perform operations that aren't asynchronous. For example, many handlers need to notify ring-three code that an operation has completed, but the services that must be used to do so are emphatically not safe to use in a hardware interrupt handler. The event queuing mechanism provides the escape valve that allows hardware interrupt handlers to schedule deferred work items that the VMM will perform when it's safe to do so.

The basic idea behind the event queue is that a VxD can create an event object at any time, especially while servicing a hardware interrupt. When the VMM reaches the point of stability when it can tolerate a page fault, it scans the event queue and calls the callback routines associated with the queued events. The callback routines can call *any* VxD services at this point, so whatever needs to take place can finally occur. Once all the events have been serviced, the VMM executes an IRETD instruction to finally redispatch some application. The application that regains control might be the one that was originally interrupted, or it might be one that the scheduler has decided should now run.

The VMM classifies events according to the context in which they must execute:

- **Global events** apply to the system as a whole rather than to any particular VM, process, or thread. The VMM processes queued global events first.

- **Local events** apply to a particular VM, process, or thread, and must run in that context. After processing global events, the VMM processes any queued local events for the current VM, process, and thread. One of the event callbacks might trigger a VM or thread switch, whereupon the VMM will process a new queue of events for the new local context.

Nested Execution

Events are one way in which the VMM's mainline path of execution differs from a simple "service and IRETD" paradigm. *Nested execution* is another way. Nested execution occurs when the VMM redispatches code that is different than the code that was interrupted. The "nesting" in this situation arises because the specially dispatched code returns to the VMM (by generating another interrupt), which can then resume its original mainline and eventually return from the outermost interrupt. For technical reasons, nested execution blocks usually occur within the confines of an event callback routine.

The nested execution concept will make you dizzy without an example. Figure 6-3 on the next page and the following explanation should help to clarify this concept. Suppose a Windows application issues an INT 5Ch to perform a

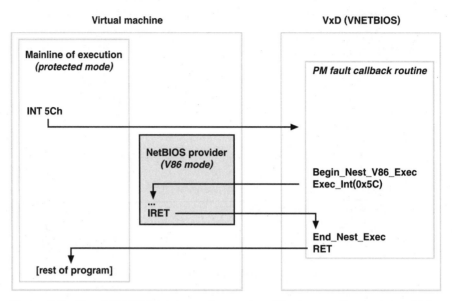

Figure 6-3. *How VNETBIOS uses nested execution. (The intermediate steps in which the VMM gains control are not shown.)*

NetBIOS request, but suppose that the only NetBIOS provider is a stodgy old network driver that lives in real mode. You'll recall that the INT 5Ch instruction will actually cause a GP fault because of a DPL mismatch. The VNETBIOS driver will eventually gain control because it hooked INT 5Ch. It will enter a nested-execution block in order to run the real-mode INT 5Ch handler. When the real-mode handler eventually performs an IRET to return from what it thinks is a real-mode NetBIOS call, it will actually reach an ARPL instruction that causes an Invalid Opcode exception (interrupt 06h). The VMM knows that this signifies the return from the VM and returns control to VNETBIOS, which exits from the nested execution block and returns control to the VMM. Sooner or later, the VMM redispatches the original protected-mode caller of INT 5Ch.

SCHEDULING THREADS

The VMM uses two scheduler components to implement preemptive multitasking among multiple threads and VMs. The so-called *primary* scheduler is responsible for selecting the next thread for execution. Basically, the primary scheduler just selects the thread having the highest execution priority from a list of eligible threads. This selection occurs while the VMM is in control (servicing an interrupt), and its outcome determines the register context that the VMM will restore when it eventually redispatches user code. VxDs use primary scheduler services to adjust the execution priority of threads to control the selection, and they use various synchronization primitives to make threads eligible or ineligible for scheduling.

One of the primary scheduler's clients is the *time-slicing,* or *secondary,* scheduler. The time-slicing scheduler uses primary scheduler services to conduct round-robin allocation of the processor to threads based on a complex priority scheme. It also responds to application-level API calls such as *SetThreadPriority* and *SetPriorityClass* with the help of an internal interface between KERNEL32.DLL and the VWIN32 VxD.

Execution and Win32 Priorities

The primary and time-slicing schedulers use different priority schemes. The *execution priority* of a thread determines whether the primary scheduler will give it control next. This decision is all-or-nothing: the highest priority thread gets to run. Since Windows 95 is a uniprocessor operating system, no other thread can run at all while that thread is running. So far, I've described an operating system that will just run a single thread until that thread terminates—not a very useful multitasking system. Execution priorities are constantly changing, however, as various VxDs apply and remove *priority boosts*. Suppose, for example, a thread having a base priority of 8h enters a critical section. In order to let this thread finish its operation and release the critical section, the VMM boosts the thread's priority by adding the CRITICAL_SEC-TION_BOOST value (00100000h). With a new execution priority of 00100008h, the thread is much more likely to run than it used to be. The time-slicing scheduler also applies priority boosts to single out a thread for execution.

Table 6-1 on the following page lists the execution priority boosts in Windows 95. You're allowed to boost execution priorities by amounts other than those listed in Table 6-1, but it's not common to do so. The primary scheduler uses the *RESERVED_LOW_BOOST* and *RESERVED_HIGH_BOOST* values for its internal validation; you and I aren't supposed to try to boost a thread priority by either of these amounts. The time-slicing scheduler uses the *CUR_RUN_VM_BOOST* value to temporarily boost whichever thread it has selected to run next in its round-robin scheme. The *Begin_Critical_Section* service automatically boosts thread priority by the *CRITICAL_SECTION_BOOST* value, and *End_Critical_Section* automatically removes the boost. Similarly, the VPICD temporarily applies the *TIME_CRITICAL_BOOST* while running a hardware interrupt handler in a VM in order the clear the interrupt as quickly as possible. The time-critical boost is numerically larger than the critical-section boost, which means that handling hardware interrupts takes precedence over completing an operation protected by a critical section.

Symbolic Name	Numeric Value
RESERVED_LOW_BOOST	00000001h
CUR_RUN_VM_BOOST	00000004h
LOW_PRI_DEVICE_BOOST	00000010h
HIGH_PRI_DEVICE_BOOST	00001000h
CRITICAL_SECTION_BOOST	00100000h
TIME_CRITICAL_BOOST	00400000h
RESERVED_HIGH_BOOST	40000000h

Table 6-1. *Execution priority boost values.*

Making sense of the other two priority boosts (*LOW_PRI_DEVICE_BOOST* and *HIGH_PRI_DEVICE_BOOST*) requires exploration of the time-slicing scheduler's priority model. The time-slicing scheduler uses the *Win32 priority* model created for Windows NT. In this model, a thread occupies one of five priority classes, each of which contains a range of priority levels (see Table 6-2). The priority ranges partially overlap, so a high-priority thread in the *IDLE_PRIORITY_CLASS* class might have a higher absolute priority than a low-priority thread in the *NORMAL_PRIORITY_CLASS* class, for example. An application (including ring-three code like KERNEL32) uses the Win32 API function *SetPriorityClass* to change a thread's class from the default value, and it uses *SetThreadPriority* to alter a thread's priority within the range available to that class.

Thread Priority (THREAD_- PRIORITY_xxx)	Priority Class (xxx_PRIORITY_CLASS)				
	IDLE	NORMAL (Background)	NORMAL (Foreground)	HIGH	REALTIME
IDLE	01h	01h	01h	01h	10h
LOWEST	02h	05h	07h	0Bh	11h–16h
BELOW_NORMAL	03h	06h	08h	0Ch	17h
NORMAL	04h	07h	09h	0Dh	18h
ABOVE_NORMAL	05h	08h	0Ah	0Eh	19h
HIGHEST	06h	09h	0Bh	0Fh	1Ah
TIME_CRITICAL	0Fh	0Fh	0Fh	0Fh	1Bh–1Fh

Table 6-2. *Win32 priority classes. The absolute priority is given within the grid.*

For example, the following Win32 calls would set a thread's Win32 priority to 10h:

```
SetPriorityClass(hThread, REALTIME_PRIORITY_CLASS);
SetThreadPriority(hThread, THREAD_PRIORITY_IDLE);
```

The time-slicing scheduler partitions the CPU among all the threads that share the highest Win32 priority by giving each thread a *time slice* in turn. The basic algorithm is to build a list of the top-priority threads and give the first thread a priority boost. At the same time, the time slicer schedules a timer interrupt to preempt the current thread when its time slice expires, whereupon the scheduler will boost the next thread for a while, and so on. The time-slicing scheduler also applies some additional algorithms to keep the system running smoothly. For example:

■   If a thread doesn't run within a "reasonable" length of time, the scheduler boosts it to prevent *starvation*. What constitutes a "reasonable" length of time depends on the length of an average time slice, on how many threads are eligible for execution, and on an internal algorithmic constant.

■   If a thread owns a resource (such as a semaphore) on which a higher priority thread blocks, the scheduler raises the owning thread's priority to the same level as the blocked thread. This *priority inheritance* allows the low-priority owner of the resource to get out of the way of the high-priority thread that needs the resource.

■   If a thread blocks, the scheduler boosts its priority when it later unblocks. This has the effect of giving a thread that competes for resources the same average amount of processor time as a thread that doesn't compete for resources.

■   The scheduler often makes priorities *decay* from a boosted value back to the base value as time slices expire. In other cases, the scheduler simply unboosts the thread after completion of the task that caused the boost in the first place.

To summarize, the time-slicing scheduler obeys the instructions Win32 applications give it as well as its own algorithmic rules to generate absolute priorities in the range 0h through 1Fh. It establishes a thread's execution priority by calling the primary scheduler's *Adjust_Thread_Priority* service, and it applies execution priority boosts to persuade the primary scheduler to run the most appropriate thread next.

Hardware interrupts and critical section boosts modify execution priorities so substantially that they effectively override the Win32 priority scheme (although you could conceivably have two threads with the same Win32 priority that both have a time-critical boost, and they would share the processor because of time slicing).

A VxD can use the *LOW_PRI_DEVICE_BOOST* value to increase the likelihood that a thread will be able to perform an operation in a timely fashion. This boost value is only 10h, however. Thus, applying this boost to a *THREAD_PRIORITY_IDLE* thread in the priority class *NORMAL_PRIORITY_CLASS* raises its absolute priority from 1h to 11h, placing it ahead of all but *REALTIME_PRIORITY_CLASS* threads. Boosting by *HIGH_PRI_DEVICE_BOOST*, however, raises this same thread's priority from 1h to 1001h, which moves it ahead of *REALTIME_PRIORITY_CLASS* threads too. In either case, the thread remains behind threads that have higher boosts.

Chapter 7

Virtual Device Driver Mechanics

It's safe to say that virtual device driver programming can be pretty mysterious. Not only do VxDs run in ring zero, where they often use privileged features of the processor that most programmers only read about, but they also use API calls that perform strange tasks in apparently inexplicable ways. As if the programming mysteries weren't enough, VxD programming also relies on tools that are out of the mainstream with which most developers are familiar. Don't walk into a computer superstore, in other words, and expect to buy a shrink-wrapped Visual VxD integrated development environment (IDE). There's no such thing. The closest thing you'll find to a warm-and-friendly IDE is the VTOOLSD package from Vireo Software, which I describe later in this chapter. Unless you are using this package, VxD programming currently involves writing assembly-language or C code, which you then process with tools from the Microsoft Device Driver Kit (DDK).

In this chapter, I discuss the mechanics of building a VxD. As you'll see, this involves creating an executable file in an otherwise obsolete file format. I also discuss the mechanical aspects of writing a VxD program in assembly language, C, or C++. Even if you're planning to use a higher-level language, you'll want to read the discussion of assembly-language drivers because two crucial concepts—the device description block (DDB) and the device control procedure—make sense only when you understand the assembly-language underpinnings. When you're done reading this chapter, you'll know how to build a VxD. You'll find out in later chapters what to put into your source files to accomplish a useful result.

EXECUTABLE FILE FORMAT

No matter what programming language you plan to use, you'll need to build an executable file to contain your driver. Windows uses a *sui generis* form of executable file for virtual device drivers. The *linear executable,* or *LE-format,* file pioneered for OS/2 version 2.0 can contain both 16-bit and 32-bit code. This turns out to be one of the requirements for a VxD because such a file accommodates the optional real-mode initialization section that some VxDs contain. Even though no other software anywhere uses LE-format files anymore, Windows continues to use them for VxDs. For a long time, developers used the aging LINK386 linker from early beta releases of OS/2 version 2.0 to create VxD files. Microsoft's language products now ship with a LINK program that can also build LE files. Linkage editors from other

---

LINKERS AND EXECUTABLE FILE FORMATS

I guess I'm one of the people who "live and breathe object file format issues."[1] Therefore, I think it's useful to understand the taxonomy of executable files so as to better understand the features and restrictions of various tool sets.

■   A COM file contains the binary image of a 16-bit program but no relocation information. DOS can load and execute a COM file anywhere, but the file runs only because it needs no relocation.

■   The MZ format is the relocatable format DOS understands. An MZ-format executable file contains 16-bit code and data all smooshed together with relocation information so that DOS can put the program wherever it needs to. Each of the more complicated file formats in this list begins with an MZ-format stub. The stub often serves only to print a cautionary message, but it can be a more complicated program. A field in the MZ header points to the *real* file header elsewhere in the file.

---

1. See Adrian King's *Inside Windows 95* (Microsoft Press, 1994), p. 143, n. 26.

language tool vendors (notably WLINK, included with Powersoft's Watcom C/C++ product) can also handle the LE format.

SEGMENTATION OF VXDS

Not only does Windows use a nonstandard file format for VxDs, but it also uses these files in a nonstandard way. Normally, a protected-mode executable file contains code and data in separate sections. Attribute flags in the file header instruct the loader about various details concerning these sections. VxDs, on the other hand, intermix code and data in segments whose attributes reflect the desired runtime permanence of the code and data they contain. (Mixing code and data works because

---

■ A file in NE format (for *new executable*) contains 16-bit Windows or OS/2 programs. The key feature of the NE format is that it isolates code, data, and resource objects into separately loadable pieces. It also sports runtime dynamic linkage by means of symbolic imports and exports.

■ A file in LX format (for *linear executable*) contains either 16-bit or 32-bit code and data, or a mixture, along with resources. OS/2 version 2.x uses this format. LE was the original version of linear executable, but it became obsolete (except for VxDs) when IBM took over sole development of OS/2.

■ A file in PE format (for *portable executable*) contains 32-bit code and data in a highly idiosyncratic variation of the UNIX Common Object File Format (COFF). Microsoft's 32-bit systems (Windows NT, Windows 95, and Win32s) use this format. The key advances of PE over other file formats are an alphabetically sorted list of exports and an orientation toward direct page mapping of the image into virtual memory.

Given the age and history of the LE file format, you can bet that Microsoft is just looking for a chance to dump it in favor of PE. If it weren't for (a) the occasional need to run 16-bit initialization code in real mode, (b) the slight difficulty of writing a new runtime loader, and (c) all the VxDs that are already out in the field, I'm sure they would have done so for Windows 95. I'm told that the transition is under way as I write this, with Microsoft's own SCSI and network miniport drivers having mutated already.

---

the flat code and data selectors used by a VxD have the same base address and limit, thereby allowing a VxD to access its code or data using whichever segment register is most appropriate for the kind of reference.) Table 7-1 lists the segments that a Windows 95 VxD might contain and the segment attributes that distinguish those segments in an LE file. Each segment's attributes are declared in the VxD's definition (.DEF) file. I'll show you a sample .DEF file later in this chapter. As you look at the table, be aware that segment attributes, in this context, do not mean what you expect them to mean. The CONFORMING attribute on the DBOCODE segment, for example, doesn't create a conforming code segment: it's just a flag to the VxD loader indicating that the segment contains debug-only code and data.

Segment Class	*Description*	*.DEF File Attributes*
LCODE	Page-locked code and data	PRELOAD NONDISCARDABLE
PCODE	Pageable code	NONDISCARDABLE
PDATA	Pageable data	NONDISCARDABLE SHARED
ICODE	Initialization-only code and data	DISCARDABLE
DBOCODE	Debug-only code and data	PRELOAD NONDISCARDABLE CONFORMING
SCODE	Static code and data	RESIDENT
RCODE	Real-mode initialization code and data	None—this is normally the only 16-bit segment in a VxD.
16ICODE	USE16 protected-mode initialization data	PRELOAD DISCARDABLE
MCODE	Locked message strings	PRELOAD NONDISCARDABLE IOPL

Table 7-1. *Segmentation of a virtual device driver.*

The LCODE, PCODE, and PDATA segments contain most of the code and data in a VxD. The LCODE segment contains code and data that must always be present in memory, whereas the PCODE and PDATA segments contain code and data, respectively, that Windows can page in and out as necessary. For example, code that handles a hardware interrupt must occupy locked pages (in the LCODE segment) because Windows can't deal with a page fault while trying to service a hardware interrupt. Similarly, the data used by a hardware interrupt handler must also be page locked. Windows, however, has no trouble paging code that handles application time events (for example), which occur at times when paged application code might also run. As a VxD author, you decide whether your code and data can safely be paged or whether it must instead be locked into physical memory.

The VxD loader also accommodates several special-purpose segments. The ICODE segment contains initialization code and data that the VMM can discard once all drivers complete their initialization. Discarding initialization-only code and data saves virtual memory, which ultimately helps performance by freeing up physical memory and swap-file space. The DBOCODE segment contains code and data that is useful only if you're running under control of a debugger. In particular, the handler for a Debug_Query system control message belongs in this segment. The RCODE segment contains the 16-bit code and data for real-mode initialization and is the *raison d'être* for LE-format files. MCODE segments, despite the inclusion of the word CODE, contain message strings that are compiled with the help of the macros in MSGMACRO.INC. (See the section titled "Message Macros" in the "Kernel Services Guide" section of the Windows 95 DDK for information about the message macros, which help you create international versions of your drivers.)

The 16ICODE segment gives you an easy way to statically define program code that you will copy from protected mode to V86 mode during initialization. This segment is a USE16 segment that is discarded after initialization. Despite the name, you don't execute code from this segment. Rather, you access the contents of this segment *as data* from the 32-bit protected-mode initialization code in your VxD. Suppose, for example, that you want to create a small real-mode code fragment as part of a more elaborate scheme to modify the behavior of a real-mode driver or TSR. The fragment you want to create merely loads the AX register with the word located at DS:BX and returns. You might try placing the following code in a regular USE32 code or data segment:

```
VxD_INIT_DATA_SEG
fragment: mov ax, [bx]   ; don't do this in a USE32 data segment!
          ret
VxD_INIT_DATA_ENDS
```

You wouldn't get the results you expect, however. When you copy the *fragment* code from a USE32 segment to a USE16 real-mode segment, the meaning of the first instruction changes subtly to become MOV EAX, [EDI]. Instead, place the *fragment* code in a 16ICODE segment. Then, because a 16ICODE segment is a USE16 segment, the assembler will generate the correct bit pattern for the 16-bit instruction you intend.

Finally, a VxD can contain static code and data in the SCODE segment. Dynamically loaded drivers might need to use this segment to solve a peculiar problem. Sometimes, the same VxD gets dynamically loaded and unloaded more than once during a Windows session but needs to remember certain state information from one instance to the next. The VMM can't destroy application callback objects, for example, so a dynamically loaded driver that creates a callback must provide a static callback function and remember the callback address in static data.

NOTE Windows 3.1 provided for only LCODE and ICODE segments. Even though the Windows 3.1 DDK provided segmentation macros that distinguished between locked and pageable segments, these macros nonetheless generated LCODE segments.

LINK SCRIPTS FOR VXDS

Since you're going to be using command-line tools for VxD development, you'll also be manually creating or adapting a MAKE script. A typical rule for linking a VxD using the Microsoft Visual C++ linker would read as follows in a Microsoft NMAKE file:

```
myvxd.vxd: $*.obj $*.def
    link /vxd /nod /map:$*.map /def:$*.def $*.obj
```

(If you're a little shaky on MAKE-file syntax, one good place to look for more information is the *Environment and Tools* manual that accompanies MASM.)

The linker that comes with Microsoft Visual C++ (even version 4.0) does not work for building VxDs. You need to use a replacement linker (version 2.60.5046) that comes on the Windows 95 DDK disc instead. You will still get a large number of linker warnings with assembly-language drivers. Since the warnings don't affect the operation of the drivers, you can ignore them.

The analogous MAKE-file rule for the LINK386 linker, which needs to be version 1.02.004 or later, is

```
myvxd.vxd: $*.obj $*.def
    link386 /noi /nod /map /li $*,$@,$*,,$*;
```

In either case, you need to supply a module definition file. You can adapt the standard one that's part of the GENERIC sample in the \BASE\SAMPLES\GENERIC directory on the Windows 95 DDK disc. For example:

```
VXD MYVXD

DESCRIPTION 'MYVXD VxD for Microsoft Windows'

SEGMENTS
    _LPTEXT      CLASS 'LCODE'    PRELOAD NONDISCARDABLE
    _LTEXT       CLASS 'LCODE'    PRELOAD NONDISCARDABLE
    _LDATA       CLASS 'LCODE'    PRELOAD NONDISCARDABLE
    _TEXT        CLASS 'LCODE'    PRELOAD NONDISCARDABLE
    _DATA        CLASS 'LCODE'    PRELOAD NONDISCARDABLE
    CONST        CLASS 'LCODE'    PRELOAD NONDISCARDABLE
    _TLS         CLASS 'LCODE'    PRELOAD NONDISCARDABLE
    _BSS         CLASS 'LCODE'    PRELOAD NONDISCARDABLE
    _LMSGTABLE   CLASS 'MCODE'    PRELOAD NONDISCARDABLE IOPL
    _LMSGDATA    CLASS 'MCODE'    PRELOAD NONDISCARDABLE IOPL
    _IMSGTABLE   CLASS 'MCODE'    PRELOAD DISCARDABLE IOPL
    _IMSGDATA    CLASS 'MCODE'    PRELOAD DISCARDABLE IOPL
    _ITEXT       CLASS 'ICODE'    DISCARDABLE
    _IDATA       CLASS 'ICODE'    DISCARDABLE
    _PTEXT       CLASS 'PCODE'    NONDISCARDABLE
    _PMSGTABLE   CLASS 'MCODE'    NONDISCARDABLE IOPL
    _PMSGDATA    CLASS 'MCODE'    NONDISCARDABLE IOPL
    _PDATA       CLASS 'PDATA'    NONDISCARDABLE SHARED
    _STEXT       CLASS 'SCODE'    RESIDENT
    _SDATA       CLASS 'SCODE'    RESIDENT
    _DBOSTART    CLASS 'DBOCODE'  PRELOAD NONDISCARDABLE CONFORMING
    _DBOCODE     CLASS 'DBOCODE'  PRELOAD NONDISCARDABLE CONFORMING
    _DBODATA     CLASS 'DBOCODE'  PRELOAD NONDISCARDABLE CONFORMING
    _16ICODE     CLASS '16ICODE'  PRELOAD DISCARDABLE
    _RCODE       CLASS 'RCODE'

EXPORTS
    MYVXD_DDB @1
```

The file shown above is included on the companion disc in the \CHAP07\ASM directory. The name of your own VxD appears in three places here, but nowhere is it actually crucial. The things that matter about the .DEF file are two:

■ You must specify the correct attributes for each of the segments that your object code will contain. This sample is appropriate for C or C++ programs. It's overkill for assembly-language programs, but it will work for them too.

■ You must export the *device description block* (DDB). There's no point in using any ordinal but 1.

> **NOTE** I did some experiments to verify the true minimum requirements for driver naming. The VMM knows a driver by the name recorded in its DDB. It finds the DDB by looking for the first export from the module. (Another author wrote that the DDB has to be at a constant offset in the VxD, but that's not correct. You just need to export it, and it doesn't matter what name you give the exported symbol.) Soft-Ice/W, however, uses the name you specify in the VXD statement of the .DEF file. The linker issues a warning if the name on the VXD statement differs from the output filename, but both the VMM and the debugger are happy to load the driver under whatever name it ends up having. If you use the same 8-byte name in the Declare_Virtual_Device macro (which turns into the DDB, after all), in the VXD statement, and in the name of the driver file, and if the only symbol you export is the DDB, you will have no problems.

WRITING VXDS IN ASSEMBLY LANGUAGE

The archetypal method of building a VxD is to combine one or more assembly-language modules and headers into an executable file using tools provided with the DDK. The tools for doing this include a 32-bit assembler. Version 6 and later of Microsoft's MASM assembler and other third-party assemblers will now suffice for both 16-bit and 32-bit programs. In earlier times, Microsoft shipped version 5.10B of MASM in the DDK because 32-bit assemblers were harder to find.

Let's suppose you want to create MYVXD.VXD in assembly language (see Figure 7-1). Begin by writing MYVXD.ASM, which will look something like this:

```
    .386p
    include vmm.inc        ; required
    include debug.inc      ; optional but usual
Declare_Virtual_Device ... ; see page 118

Begin_Control_Dispatch myvxd
    [Control_Dispatch macros]
End_Control_Dispatch myvxd

VxD_IDATA_SEG
    [Initialization-only data]
VxD_IDATA_ENDS

VxD_ICODE_SEG
    [Initialization-only code]
VxD_ICODE_ENDS
```

```
VxD_LOCKED_DATA_SEG
    [Page-locked data]
VxD_LOCKED_DATA_ENDS

VxD_LOCKED_CODE_SEG
    [Page-locked code]
VxD_LOCKED_CODE_ENDS

end
```

After fleshing out this skeleton, you'll assemble MYVXD.ASM to produce an object file in the Common Object File Format (COFF). Then you run the object file through the linkage editor to produce an executable file in the LE format. Lastly, you run some utility or another to generate a symbol file for the debugger of your choice. The final output of the whole process is a file containing your driver, which usually has the extension .VXD.

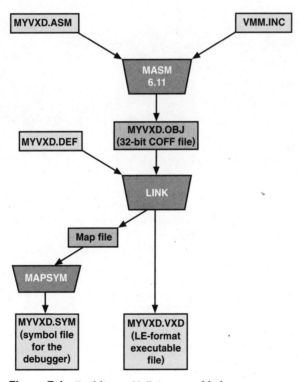

Figure 7-1. *Building a VxD in assembly language.*

> **NOTE** Actually, COFF is a UNIX standard to which Microsoft has applied a very considerable gloss of *ad hoc* and frequently undocumented extensions. Calling this format COFF is about as descriptive as calling the end user a "mammal": it's technically true, but it doesn't give you much information. ·

The Declare_Virtual_Device Macro

The VMM learns everything it needs to know about a VxD by inspecting the VxD's device description block (DDB) (see Figure 7-2). You use the Declare_Virtual_Device macro to create a DDB for your device driver, and you export the symbol that labels the DDB in your .DEF file. Declare_Virtual_Device accepts several positional parameters:

```
Declare_Virtual_Device Name, MajorVer, MinorVer, CtrlProc, DeviceNum,
        InitOrder, V86Proc, PMProc, RefData
```

```
struct VxD_Desc_Block {
    ULONG   DDB_Next;                    // 00h chain to next DDB (reserved)
    USHORT  DDB_SDK_Version;             // 04h DDK version used to build driver
    USHORT  DDB_Req_Device_Number;       // 06h unique device ID
    UCHAR   DDB_Dev_Major_Version;       // 08h major version number
    UCHAR   DDB_Dev_Minor_Version;       // 09h minor version number
    USHORT  DDB_Flags;                   // 0Ah flags used by VMM
    UCHAR   DDB_Name[8]                  // 0Ch 8-byte name of driver
    ULONG   DDB_Init_Order;              // 14h initialization ordinal
    ULONG   DDB_Control_Proc;            // 18h control procedure address
    ULONG   DDB_V86_API_Proc;            // 1Ch V86 API entry (if any)
    ULONG   DDB_PM_API_Proc;             // 20h PM API entry (if any)
    ULONG   DDB_V86_API_CSIP;            // 24h V86 version of API entry addr
    ULONG   DDB_PM_API_CSIP;             // 28h ring-3 version of API entry addr
    ULONG   DDB_Reference_Data;          // 2Ch reference data from RM init
    ULONG   DDB_Service_Table_Ptr;       // 30h address of service table (if any)
    ULONG   DDB_Service_Table_Size;      // 34h number of services
    ULONG   DDB_Win32_Service_Table;     // 38h address of VWIN32 service table
    ULONG   DDB_Prev;                    // 3Ch chain to previous DDB (reserved)
    ULONG   DDB_Size;                    // 40h size of this block (reserved)
    ULONG   DDB_Reserved1;               // 44h reserved
    ULONG   DDB_Reserved2;               // 48h reserved
    ULONG   DDB_Reserved3;               // 4Ch reserved
                                         // 50h
};
```

Figure 7-2. *Layout of the device description block.*

The *Name* parameter is an 8-byte device name that should be unique among all the VxDs running on a system. This name is ordinarily the same as both the filename of the driver file and the name you specify in the .DEF file VXD statement. The macro generates an external label for the DDB by appending _DDB to this name, too. Thus, the MYVXD driver has a DDB identified as *MYVXD_DDB*.

The *MajorVer* and *MinorVer* parameters specify version information about the driver. You can choose whatever values you want for these fields. Often, you'll pick values that correspond to the version of Windows for which you developed your driver. Note that the DDB fields that contain these two values are in *big-endian* order, so that code to access them as a unit must first reverse the order, as shown below:

```
mov     ax, word ptr MYVXD_DDB.DDB_Dev_Major_Version
xchg    ah, al          ; AH = major, AL = minor
```

big-endian order   A method of organizing data in memory so that the most significant byte in a multibyte value is stored first in memory, rather than last. Intel processors store data in little-endian order, in which the most significant byte is stored last.

The *CtrlProc* parameter names the *device control procedure* that processes system control messages on behalf of your driver. I discuss this important procedure on page 125. If you follow normal conventions, you would specify a name like *MYVXD_Control* for this parameter.

Some drivers need a unique identifier by which other software can address them, and you specify this identifier in the *DeviceNum* field. The identifier is a 16-bit integer that Microsoft assigns on the basis of need. If you don't need one of your own, use the constant *UNDEFINED_DEVICE_ID* in this field. You will need a unique identifier only if one of the following situations exists:

- Some TSR will use the INT 2Fh, function 1605h, interface to load your driver. In this case, the driver will need to have a real-mode initialization section to prevent duplication, and the driver will also need a unique identifier so that Windows can determine whether duplication is occurring.

- Your driver uses INT 2Fh, function 1607h, to broadcast its existence to real-mode software during initialization. In this case, programs looking for your broadcast will be comparing register BX with your known identifier.

■ Your driver exports VxD services for use by other drivers. The INT 20h service API relies on driver identifiers in the high-order half of service identifiers.

If you need an identifier for one of these reasons, you can ask Microsoft to provide one by following the instructions you'll find in VXDID.TXT in the \BASE\SAMPLES directory on the Windows 95 DDK disc. I've already made a bigger deal of this than I need to, because very few drivers nowadays need their own identifiers. The major reason for needing an identifier in previous versions of Windows was to support the INT 2Fh, function 1684h, interface for finding a driver's V86 or protected-mode API. In Windows 95, you can locate a driver's API if you know its 8-byte DDB name. You can also use the INT 2Fh, function 168Ah, protocol mentioned in the DPMI specification to export "vendor-specific" services to 16-bit applications; in this protocol, applications issue INT 2Fh, function 168Ah, with DS:[E]SI pointing to a null-terminated string that you define. The string takes the place of the unique identifier, which is therefore superfluous. The only way you can export services to 32-bit applications is by means of the *DeviceIoControl* function, which requires the application to know your driver's filename rather than its unique ID.

CAUTION In the original Windows 3.0 DDK, Microsoft established a convention that as many as 2048 software vendors could obtain an 11-bit identifier, which they could then use for as many as 32 VxD identifiers each. Microsoft soon realized that it would run out, so it abandoned the idea of giving out 32 identifiers to anyone who asked. You must now document your case for needing an identifier, and you can only get one number at a time. *It would be really unfriendly to everybody else in the industry to just appropriate an ID for your own use: you run the risk of breaking other people's code!*

Each driver also has an *initialization order* that places it in a sequential relationship with all the other drivers in the system. The *InitOrder* parameter of the Declare_Virtual_Device macro is where you specify this value. Use the *UNDEFINED_INIT_ORDER* constant if you don't care.

A driver can export an API for use by V86-mode programs, protected-mode programs, or both. The seventh and eighth parameters to Declare_Virtual_Device specify the addresses of these functions. Since you don't have to provide API entries, you can omit either or both of these fields.

Finally, you can specify reference data using the last argument to the Declare_Virtual_Device macro. The only reason to do so is when you're building a layer driver for use with the I/O Supervisor (IOS). In that case, you declare your virtual device with a reference data field pointing to a special driver registration packet so that the IOS can quickly ascertain key facts about your driver before calling any of your subroutines.

Common Coding Conventions

VxD programming in assembly language includes its own set of arbitrary conventions. Thankfully, there are many fewer conventions for this situation than for writing Windows applications, but you should still know about some of them.

Register and Flag Usage

Most of the time, a VxD is free to use any of the general registers and the FS and GS segment registers. Many VxD-level routines assume that the direction flag is clear, so that string operations like MOVS, CMPS, and the like, increment their operand addresses. You can temporarily change the direction flag, but you should always restore it before returning or calling another VxD. You can also disable interrupts for brief periods, but you should take care to *restore* the previous state of the interrupt flag rather than simply doing an STI:

```
pushfd              ; save current interrupt-enable state
cli                 ; disable interrupts BRIEFLY
...
popfd               ; restore interrupt flag
```

Conventional wisdom holds that a VxD should never alter the CS, DS, ES, or SS register. Without going into all the details of why this is so, I will only tell you that you should certainly not alter CS (by doing a far call, for example) or SS except in very unusual circumstances in which you're positive that no interrupts or page faults can occur. (And beware that touching a supposedly locked V86 page that contains instanced data can cause a page fault.) Beyond that, you *could* safely change DS and ES if you restore them before calling any VMM or VxD services. Rather than altering these registers, however, you can probably find a safer alternative. For example, *Map_Flat* is the approved way to generate a flat address from a virtual machine selector and offset, and it has the advantage of working in situations in which a naïve LDS or LES instruction would not. If you simply must change stacks, use *_Call_On_My_Stack* to preserve the bookkeeping that the VMM normally performs during context switches.

Service Calling Conventions

When you write your own VxD service entry points (a subject discussed in more detail in Chapter 9), you need to publish and adhere to a statement about what registers you preserve. Every function must perforce restore the ESP register or else it wouldn't be able to return to its caller. Register-oriented services typically preserve all registers except those that need to contain output parameters. C-oriented services must preserve the EBX, ESI, EDI, and EBP registers.

Segmentation Macros

Instead of directly specifying segment names, use the various macros, defined in VMM.INC and VMM.H and shown in Table 7-2.

Segment	VMM.INC or VMM.H Macro
_LTEXT	VxD_LOCKED_CODE_SEG
_LDATA	VxD_LOCKED_DATA_SEG
_PTEXT	VxD_PAGEABLE_CODE_SEG
_PDATA	VxD_PAGEABLE_DATA_SEG
_DBOCODE	VxD_DEBUG_ONLY_CODE_SEG
_DBODATA	VxD_DEBUG_ONLY_DATA_SEG
_ITEXT	VxD_INIT_CODE_SEG
_IDATA	VxD_INIT_DATA_SEG
_STEXT	VxD_STATIC_CODE_SEG
_SDATA	VxD_STATIC_DATA_SEG
_RCODE	VxD_REAL_INIT_SEG

Table 7-2. *Segmentation macros (assembly-language or C).*

This will allow you to adapt to changes in segment naming or grouping conventions by simply recompiling your source code, which should look something like this:

```
VxD_LOCKED_CODE_SEG
...
VxD_LOCKED_CODE_ENDS
```

Flat Addresses

Use the OFFSET32 macro to specify flat addresses. This expands into *offset flat:*, but it requires less typing. With earlier tool sets, you had to be careful to avoid simply saying *offset* without the *flat:* qualifier because the assembler and linker conspired to generate incorrect relocation information. Here's some sample code that shows how you would use the OFFSET32 macro:

```
functbl label    dword
        dd       offset32 function0
        dd       offset32 function1
        ...
        jmp    [functbl + 4*eax]
```

Delimiting Procedures

Instead of the *proc* and *endp* assembler directives, use the BeginProc and EndProc macros to bracket procedures:

```
BeginProc    OnDeviceInit, init
...
EndProc      OnDeviceInit

BeginProc    MYVXD_Get_Version, SERVICE, HIGH_FREQ
...
EndProc      MYVXD_Get_Version
```

When assembled for debugging, these macros generate useful logging information.

Table 7-3 lists the optional arguments that you can use with BeginProc. Some of these make your life simpler. Specifying the segment that contains the procedure, for example, lets you avoid explicitly using the segmentation macros and gives you more flexibility to arrange your source code in a logical way.

Argument	*Description*
HIGH_FREQ	Specifies that the procedure is called often, and instructs the assembler to DWORD-align the function.
PUBLIC LOCAL	Indicates scope of the procedure name.
PCALL SCALL CCALL ICALL	Specifies that the procedure uses a particular calling convention (Pascal, Standard, C, or default).
ESP	Instructs the assembler to use the ESP register for the stack frame when accessing ArgVar and LocalVar variables.
HOOK_PROC, *label*	Indicates that the procedure can be installed via Hook_xxx_*Fault* or *Hook_Device_Service*. Use *label* variable for chaining.
LOCKED PAGEABLE INIT etc.	Instructs the assembler to place the function in the VxD_*xxx*_CODE_SEG segment.
SERVICE ASYNC_SERVICE	Indicates that procedure is called via VxDCall.

Table 7-3. *Optional arguments for BeginProc.* (continued)

continued

Argument	Description
NO_LOG NO_PROFILE NO_TEST_CLD NO_PROLOG	Disables various checks that would otherwise be made in a debug build.
TEST_BLOCK TEST_REENTER NEVER_REENTER NOT SWAPPING	Specifies various characteristics of the calling environment in a debug build.
W32SVC	Specifies that procedure is a Win32 service.

Functions Called from C

When you write an assembly-language procedure that will be called by a C program, you can use ArgVar and LocalVar macros to define symbolic equivalents for argument and local variables. You also use EnterProc, LeaveProc, and return macros to generate prolog and epilog code. For example, here's how Microsoft's SERIAL.VXD defines its *PortSetState* procedure (one of the port driver functions called by VCOMM):

```
BeginProc PortSetState, CCALL, PUBLIC

ArgVar   hPort,DWORD
ArgVar   pDcb,DWORD
ArgVar   ActionMask,DWORD

LocalVar BaudRateChange,DWORD

        EnterProc
        [body of procedure]
        LeaveProc
        return

EndProc PortSetState
```

The *CCALL* argument to BeginProc indicates that this function will be called from a C program. *PUBLIC* indicates that the name of the function should be visible outside the assembly-language module in which this definition appears.

The three ArgVar macros declare the arguments to this function, and the LocalVar macro defines a local variable stored on the stack. With these macros, you can specify *BYTE*, *WORD*, or *DWORD* as the second argument to indicate the size of the argument or variable. Alternatively, you can specify some other expression giving the length of the variable.

For regular Windows programming, these macros are redundant with functionality that MASM 6.x builds into the *proc* directive. You don't use *proc* directives in VxDs, though, because BeginProc contains some needed additional functionality.

Device Control Procedures

Every VxD needs a device control procedure to respond to system control messages. Think of this as a switch or an MFC-like message map. Typically, your code would look like this:

```
Begin_Control_Dispatch vxdname

Control_Dispatch message, function
...
End_Control_Dispatch vxdname
```

The Begin_Control_Dispatch macro forces assembly into the locked code segment and declares a function named vxdname_*Control*. Each Control_Dispatch macro specifies a function to handle a specific system control message. End_Control_Dispatch closes off the control procedure by clearing the carry flag (to indicate success of any message you didn't process) and returning. This combination of macros also chooses automatically between an if-then-else network and a branch table, depending on which makes the most sense.

A Complete Assembly-Language Skeleton

It's difficult to provide a meaningful example of a complete VxD without using concepts that appear in later chapters, so I won't try. Putting together all the ideas in this section will yield the following skeleton (included on the companion disc in the \CHAP07\ASM directory) for an assembly-language VxD:

MYVXD.MAK

```
# MYVXD.MAK -- MAKE file for MYVXD.VXD

all: myvxd.vxd

myvxd.obj: $*.asm
    ml -coff -DBLD_COFF -DIS_32 -W2 -c -Cx -DMASM6 -Zd -DDEBUG $*.asm

myvxd.vxd: $*.obj $*.def
    link @<<
/vxd /nod
/map:$*.map
```

(continued)

continued

```
/def:$*.def
$*.obj
<<
```

MYVXD.ASM

```
; MYVXD.ASM -- Simple assembly-language skeleton
    name  myvxd
    .386p
    include vmm.inc
    include debug.inc

Declare_Virtual_Device MYVXD, 1, 0, MYVXD_Control, \
    Undefined_Device_ID, Undefined_Init_Order

Begin_Control_Dispatch MYVXD
    Control_Dispatch Device_Init, OnDeviceInit
End_Control_Dispatch   MYVXD

BeginProc OnDeviceInit, init
    clc                 ; indicate no error
    ret                 ; return to VMM
EndProc   OnDeviceInit

    end
```

Assembling the Sample Code To assemble and link the code sample, you must install the Windows 95 DDK and set the environment variables according to the directions in the README.TXT file included in the root directory of the companion disc. Enter the following command line at an MS-DOS prompt:

C:\projectfolder> *nmake -F myvxd.mak*

The linker will generate several warnings, which you can ignore.

I already showed you the module definition (.DEF) file you need to use with this skeleton (see page 115).

This driver does absolutely nothing, of course. Its only purpose in the scheme of this book is to show a syntactically complete example on which you can elaborate to suit your needs.

Windows 3.1 Compatibility   If you need to build a VxD that must run under Windows 3.1 as well as Windows 95, define the symbol *WIN31COM-PAT* before including VMM.INC. For example:

```
name myvxd
.386p
win31compat = 1
include vmm.inc
...
```

WIN31COMPAT marks your VxD as being Windows 3.1 compatible, and it also suppresses all declarations in DDK include files that pertain to Windows 95 but not Windows 3.1.

WRITING VxDs IN C OR C++

Most programmers would prefer to write VxDs in a higher-level language. C or C++ is easier to read and maintain than assembly language, and the logic of a high-level language program (usually) takes precedence over the mechanics of expressing it. Until quite recently, however, writing drivers in C or C++ has been very hard because

■ DDK components such as header files and documentation used to be exclusively oriented toward assembly-language programming.

■ It used to be hard to find a 32-bit C or C++ compiler.

■ C compilers from some vendors made it unreasonably hard to use inline assembly language.

■ Most VxD services need parameters in registers, and all of them depend on the inline INT 20h interface I described in Chapter 4.

■ Available debuggers for operating system code didn't (and still don't) handle high-level languages and their complex debugging information as well as application debuggers do.

There are now two reasonably good solutions to these problems: the Windows 95 DDK and the VTOOLSD package from Vireo Software. I'll describe both approaches in this section. To summarize the discussion, the DDK provides fairly good support for C programmers who understand what's going on beneath the covers. VTOOLSD is easier to use than the DDK for C programming, but its real strength is its C++ class library. Unfortunately, there's still no wonderful source-level debugger for VxDs, although Soft-Ice/W from Nu-Mega Technologies, Inc., comes close.

The Windows 95 DDK

In contrast to previous versions of the DDK, the Windows 95 DDK frankly encourages development in C. C header files specify all of the service APIs and data structures, and they contain all the commentary that you're going to find. While there are assembly-language .INC files in the kit, Microsoft generated them automatically from the C-language .H header files using an internal tool similar to H2INC that discards comments and destroys readability.

To use the DDK to build a C-language VxD, you will need to do the following:

■ Write C functions to handle system control messages and to participate in whatever layered device architectures (VCOMM, Plug and Play, or whatever) are appropriate.

■ Write your own wrappers for any VxD services that you need to call but for which Microsoft didn't provide wrappers. Be forewarned: this can be a major annoyance.

■ Package your Declare_Virtual_Device macro call and your device control procedure in a small assembly-language module. (The DDK contains no C-language equivalents for these pieces.) You'll need to use some additional parameters of the Control_Dispatch macro to route control to C-language handlers.

■ Write assembly-language wrappers for callback functions that receive parameters in registers. (Most do; this can end up being a major pain in the neck.)

Header Files for C

When you code a VxD in C, you always use two header files from the DDK, and you may wish to use many others. The two required header files are

■ BASEDEF.H, which defines basic typedef symbols and manifest constants such as *BOOL*, *TRUE*, and the like, and

■ VMM.H, which defines data structures and constants that nearly every VxD needs to use.

I've listed these and other DDK header files useful to VxD programmers in Table 7-4. Among the most useful is DEBUG.H, which allows you to use various debugging functions and macros to help you debug your VxD.

Header File	Purpose
BASEDEF.H	Provides basic typedefs for all VxDs
BLOCKDEV.H	Defines block device interface
CONFIGMG.H	Defines Configuration Manager interface
DBT.H	Defines constants for the WM_DEVICECHANGE message and *BroadcastSystemMessage*
DEBUG.H	Provides debugging services useful to most VxDs
DOSMGR.H	Defines DOS virtualization manager interface
INT2FAPI.H	Defines constants for Windows INT 2Fh interface
IOS.H	Defines I/O Supervisor interface (one of many headers needed for IOS components)
NETVXD.H	Provides VxD identifiers and initialization order constants for network VxD modules
PCCARD.H	Defines PCMCIA card manager interface
SHELL.H	Defines SHELL device interface
VCOMM.H	Defines Virtual Communications Driver interface
VFBACKUP.H	Defines backup device interface
VMCPD.H	Defines math coprocessor device interface
VMM.H	Defines interfaces to the VMM for use by all VxDs
VMMREG.H	Defines registry interface for VxDs
VPICD.H	Defines Programmable Interrupt Controller interface
VPOWERD.H	Defines power management interface
VTD.H	Defines timer chip interface
VWIN32.H	Defines Win32 application manager interface
VXDLDR.H	Defines VxD loader interface
VXDWRAPS.H	Provides function wrapper prototypes

Table 7-4. *VxD header files in the DDK.*

Segmenting a C Driver

You control the segmentation of a C-language driver built with the DDK by using pragma statements in association with preprocessor macros. For example:

```
#pragma VxD_LOCKED_CODE_SEG
#pragma VxD_LOCKED_DATA_SEG
```

This turns into:

```
#pragma code_seg("_LTEXT", "LCODE")
#pragma data_seg("_LDATA", "LDATA")
```

Students of Microsoft C compilers will recognize these pragma statements as controlling the segments within which succeeding functions and data definitions will appear. Table 7-2 on page 122 lists the symbols you can use in a pragma statement to specify common segments. Note that you use the same symbol in both C and assembly to specify a given segment.

The DDK header VMM.H also defines pragma statements for several additional segments, such as *VxD_VMCREATE_CODE_SEG*, *VxD_VMDESTROY_CODE_SEG*, and so on. These segments allow Microsoft to group related pieces of large VxDs such as the VMM together, thereby reducing the working set of those VxDs. You and I probably don't need to worry about this fine point.

Function Wrappers

One of the most important and commonly used headers is VXDWRAPS.H. In order to explain what it does, I need to talk about how a program invokes VxD services. In assembly language, you use the VMMCall macro or the VxDCall macro:

```
VMMCall Get_VMM_Version
VxDCall SHELL_Get_Version
```

Each of these macros generates an INT 20h instruction followed by inline data values to specify a particular VxD and an index within that VxD's table of service function pointers. A C-language VxD still needs to issue INT 20h instructions, but the DDK provides some components to make this less ugly than it might otherwise be. The first such component is the *VxDCall* preprocessor macro defined in VMM.H. This macro is part of an interlocking scheme that allows you to code things like this in a C-language driver:

```
WORD version;
VxDCall(Get_VMM_Version)
_asm mov version, ax
```

It's understandable if you are reluctant to litter your program with inline assembly language to load and store register values around calls to VxD services. The DDK provides a set of *wrapper* functions that allow you to code more naturally:

```
WORD version = Get_VMM_Version();
```

Function prototypes for many of these wrapper functions appear in the VXDWRAPS.H file; the code itself is either inline within your program or in a wrapper library such as VXDWRAPS.CLB that you link with your program. You might hope that you only need to include VXDWRAPS.H as an additional header file, whereupon you'd have immediate access to all of the service calls and data structures you need. The DDK doesn't make your life nearly so easy, though. I believe Microsoft tailored the DDK for programmers building hardware device drivers, and especially for programmers writing within the constraints of specific architectures like Plug and

Play or VCOMM. If you depart from this model, I think you will end up very frustrated unless you understand more of the details about how the DDK headers are put together.

The first thing you need to know about the Microsoft scheme for VxD function wrappers is the importance of the inclusion order and of the magic symbol *WANTVXDWRAPS*. If you need to include VXDWRAPS.H, define *WANTVXDWRAPS* before including any of the DDK headers, and be sure to include VXDWRAPS.H last:

```
#define WANTVXDWRAPS      // suppress inline declarations
#include <basedef.h>
#include <vmm.h>
...                       // other DDK includes
#include <vxdwraps.h>     // should be last DDK include
```

The #define statement above suppresses duplicate definitions of functions that are in other header files as well as VXDWRAPS.H. For example, both VMM.H and VXDWRAPS.H declare *Get_VMM_Version*. You include VXDWRAPS.H last because it declares only those functions for which you previously included the relevant header. For example, you get prototypes for VCOMM function wrappers only if you've previously included VCOMM.H.

The next fact about the DDK function wrappers that will bite you has to do with segmentation. Clever use of preprocessor macros within VXDWRAPS.H contrives to declare six different wrapper functions for each function that actually has a wrapper. The *Begin_Critical_Section* service, for example, has the six wrapper functions listed in Table 7-5.

Wrapper Name	Contained in Segment
LCODE_Begin_Critical_Section	LCODE (locked code)
ICODE_Begin_Critical_Section	ICODE (initialization code)
PCODE_Begin_Critical_Section	PCODE (pageable code)
SCODE_Begin_Critical_Section	SCODE (static code)
DCODE_Begin_Critical_Section	DCODE (debugging code)
CCODE_Begin_Critical_Section	CCODE (Configuration Manager)

Table 7-5. *Function wrappers for the* Begin_Critical_Section *service.*

I didn't discuss the CCODE segment in the earlier description of VxD segmentation. CCODE contains programs that interoperate with the Configuration Manager as part of the Plug and Play architecture of Windows 95. As we'll see when we study the Configuration Manager in Chapters 11 and 12, this area of the system is pretty much a law unto itself. I hereby give you permission to defer trying to understand this topic until you reach those chapters.

The point of having all of these function wrappers is to make it easy for you to call one of them from any code segment. If you're writing code that will appear in the initialization segment, you can call *ICODE_Begin_Critical_Section*, whereas in your locked code you can call *LCODE_Begin_Critical_Section* instead. Clearly, supplying all these segment-name prefixes is going to make your code harder to type and read, so VXDWRAPS.H attempts to simplify your life by defining only a simple name like *Begin_Critical_Section*. It defines these simple names in terms of whatever segment is returned by the preprocessor CURSEG macro. By default, this is LCODE. You can override the default by redefining the macro. For example:

```
#include <vxdwraps.h>
...
// code that uses wrappers in LCODE
...
#pragma VxD_INIT_CODE_SEG
#pragma VxD_INIT_DATA_SEG
#undef CURSEG
#define CURSEG() ICODE
```

Now the symbol *Begin_Critical_Section* turns into *ICODE_Begin_Critical_Section*. If you're going to be doing a lot of segment changing, you might want to follow the model of Vireo's VTOOLSD product and create some include files that contain the four-statement sequences needed to switch segments.

Another thing to know about VXDWRAPS.H is that it contains some inline function declarations in addition to prototypes for wrapper functions. For example, the *End_Critical_Section* function (the opposite of *Begin_Critical_Section*) is declared as follows:

```
VOID VXDINLINE End_Critical_Section(VOID)
    {
    VMMCall(End_Critical_Section);
    }
```

VXDINLINE expands to *static __inline*, which basically means that you'll get your own copy of the function instead of fetching it from an object library. The *VMMCall* macro is like its assembly-language counterpart: it generates an inline INT 20h instruction followed by the data values that specify a particular VxD service.

Finally, VXDWRAPS.H is maddeningly incomplete. It contains wrappers for only a few of the standard VxDs. Thus, if you want to call the Virtual Keyboard Driver (VKD), to name one example, you will need to write your own set of wrapper functions. In addition, even for those drivers it supports, the header defines prototypes only for selected services. The VMM, for example, has roughly 400 service entries, but VXDWRAPS.H supports only about 80 of them. You might not want to call the *Call_When_Thread_Switched* service, for instance, but then again you might, in which case you'll once again have to write your own wrapper. I also noticed some odd inconsistency and silliness. Although there's a wrapper for the *Get_Profile_Hex_Int* service, there's none for the *Get_Profile_Decimal_Int* service. Not only that, but each segment purports to contain a wrapper for this function even though it's available only at initialization time. You might have supposed there'd only be an *ICODE_Get_Profile_Hex_Int* wrapper.

I've gone into all of this detail about this one header file because I think you need to know what to expect before you embark on a serious VxD development project using C with the DDK. Any driver I've ever written required me to call services for which the DDK doesn't provide a C-language wrapper. An hour's study of the \DDK\BASE\VXDWRAPS directory on the DDK disc will show you how to build your own wrappers from simple assembly-language files. But I thought the idea was to avoid assembly language altogether, wasn't it?

Device Control Procedures for C

An assembly-language driver contains a device control procedure with one Control_Dispatch macro call for each system control message that the driver handles. A C-language driver also has an assembly-language control procedure, but its Control_Dispatch macros specify C-language handlers:

Control_Dispatch *message, function, type, <arguments>*

The third parameter can be *sCall* to indicate a *__stdcall* function call, *cCall* to indicate a *__cdecl* call, or *pCall* to indicate a *__pascal* call. The fourth argument is a list of function arguments surrounded by angle brackets.

You're theoretically free to choose the arguments to pass to your message handler, since both the device control procedure and the handler are programs you write. You'll obviously be guided by the assembly-language specification for the control message in question. With the Device_Init message, for example, the EBX register points to the VM control block for the System VM and the EDX register contains the reference data (if any) supplied by your real-mode initialization function. The control procedure, written in assembly, might therefore look like this:

```
Begin_Control_Dispatch myvxd
    Control_Dispatch Device_Init, OnDeviceInit, sCall, <ebx, edx>
End_Control_Dispatch myvxd
```

The C-language handler specified in the second argument of the Control_Dispatch macro above would then look like this:

```
BOOL __stdcall OnDeviceInit(PVMMCB hVM, DWORD refdata)
    {               //OnDeviceInit
    ...
    return TRUE;
    }               //OnDeviceInit
```

You'll notice that I declared a Boolean C function to handle the Device_Init system control message, whereas you'll recall that the device control procedure is supposed to indicate success or failure by setting or clearing the carry flag. The Control_Dispatch macro makes the translation between a Boolean return value and the required carry flag setting by executing the following instruction:

```
cmp  eax, 1
```

This instruction clears the carry flag if EAX, treated as an unsigned 32-bit integer, is greater than or equal to 1. In other words, if the C-language function returns any nonzero value, the control procedure will return with the carry flag clear to indicate success. Conversely, if the C-language function returns 0, the control procedure returns with the carry flag set to indicate failure.

NOTE The real truth is that Control_Dispatch only *usually* tests EAX. In the case of the PNP_NEW_DEVNODE message, it *always* sets the carry flag before returning. This is because returning from this message with the carry flag set is how the handler informs the caller that it actually processed the message. This in turn triggers calls to functions you presumably registered inside the handler.

The Device_Init message also arrives with the ESI register pointing to the command tail that accompanied the original call to WIN.COM. This isn't of much use in Windows 95, where the call to WIN.COM occurs as an automatic afterthought to processing AUTOEXEC.BAT. Therefore, I left this parameter out of the sample. I think this flexibility poses a problem, however, in that different programmers might decide to implement their message handlers in different, incompatible, ways.

Global Variables

I'm used to defining global variables without initializers if their initial value is 0. For example, if I have a global counter called *counter,* I usually define it like so:

```
int counter;          // don't do this in a VxD
```

Don't omit the initializer in a C-language VxD, though, because no one will initialize the variable to 0. Always include an explicit initializer:

```
int counter = 0;      // the right way
```

The reason you need an explicit initializer has to do with the way the C compiler, the linker, and the runtime library normally work together to initialize data that you don't explicitly initialize. The compiler places such uninitialized global data in the block-started-by-symbol (BSS) segment. To save space in the executable file image on disk, the linker doesn't generate any data records for BSS data.

The standard startup routine supplied by the runtime library uses a block-store instruction to zero the BSS segment before it calls your main procedure. When you build a VxD from a C program, however, you don't include any of the standard runtime library. Consequently, no one will ever execute the code needed to zero the BSS segment. You can either write such code yourself or use explicit initializers where they matter.

Runtime Library Calls

One of the advantages that normally accrues from writing a program in a high-level language such as C is that you gain access to a large library of utility functions. I'm sure there will be a time when I'll want to call an exotic function like *strxfrm* from a VxD. (The *strxfrm* function transforms a string based on locale-specific information.) Unfortunately, the runtime library usually comes with a good deal of extra baggage in the form of error-reporting and exception-handling code, and it usually also requires extensive initialization to make it work right. The standard *crt0* routine that wraps most C executable programs has no chance of working in a VxD. (For starters, one of the first things that program does is call a Win32 API to obtain the command line, which is a concept utterly without meaning to a VxD. But there are other, more subtle reasons, too.) Therefore, you don't link VxDs with the standard runtime library at all.

Even though you can't use most of the standard runtime library in a VxD, you *can* use any function for which the compiler provides an intrinsic implementation. An intrinsic function is one for which the compiler can generate inline code. A good example of an intrinsic function is *memcpy*. The compiler knows how to generate a block-move instruction to implement a *memcpy* call. It even knows how to generate simple MOV instructions for *memcpy* calls that involve just a few bytes of data. When you compile a release version of a program, you normally use optimization options that force the use of intrinsics whenever possible. Even when you compile a debug version of a program (which you often do when developing a VxD), you can use the pragma statement to the same purpose. For example, in my C-language drivers, I normally include the following two statements so that I can freely use string and byte functions:

```
#include <string.h>
#pragma intrinsic(memcmp, memcpy, memset, strcat, strcmp,\
    strcpy, strlen)
```

Callback Wrappers

I have to jump the gun a little bit in order to explain one of the harder problems you'll face when you write a VxD in C. There are a great many situations in which you supply the address of a *callback function* to the VMM or to another VxD. Some component or another then calls your callback function at a later time when some event occurs. I'll discuss callback functions in more detail in later chapters, but I'll give one example here to motivate the current discussion.

You can arrange to have a function called after a specific time period elapses by calling the *Set_Global_Time_Out* service. In assembly language, you'd code something like this to set up a 1-second interval:

```
mov     eax, 1000            ; 1000 milliseconds
mov     edx, refdata         ; "reference" data
mov     esi, offset32 timeout ; address of callback routine
VMMCall Set_Global_Time_Out
```

The equivalent code in C is

```
Set_Global_Time_Out(timeout, 1000, refdata);
```

When the timer expires, the VMM calls the callback routine with the register images shown in Table 7-6. Note in particular that the EBP register points to an image of the current virtual machine's registers. Note also that the EDX register contains some arbitrary "reference" data that (presumably) means something to the callback function. You often use the EDX register as a pointer to some small control block containing parameters, for example.

Register	Contents
EBX	Handle of current virtual machine
ECX	Number of "extra" milliseconds that have elapsed since the requested timeout occurred
EDX	Reference data supplied to *Set_Global_Time_Out*
EBP	Address of "client" (virtual machine) register images

Table 7-6. *The contents of registers at entry to a timer callback routine.*

If you code the callback routine in assembly language, you can see that it's a snap to use the register parameters supplied to the callback. But what do you do in C? The C compiler uses the EBP register as a pointer to a function's stack frame, assumes the ECX and EDX registers are volatile and usable for any purpose, and treats the EBX register as a working register that it will restore before returning. There isn't any obvious, safe way to get access to these registers before compiled code changes them.

Because of these problems with registers, you must write callback functions in assembly language. There are two basic approaches. The first approach is to write the function entirely in assembly language. You can either place it in a separate ASM file, or you can use an obscure Microsoft language extension together with inline assembly language to leave it within a C file:

```
void __declspec(naked) timeout()
    {
    _asm
        {
        ...                 ; assembly code
        ret                 ; return to caller
        }
    }
```

The *__declspec(naked)* directive causes the compiler to omit all of its normal prolog and epilog instructions. All register saving and restoring, and even the final RET instruction, are entirely up to you. The code within the inline *_asm* block is normal 32-bit assembly language with some restrictions. You can't, for example, use privileged instructions because the Microsoft compiler's inline assembler doesn't understand them.

The second approach to writing a callback function is to provide an assembly-language wrapper that calls a C function. To continue the timeout example, you could code something like this:

```
void __declspec(naked) timeout()
    {
    _asm
        {
        push    ecx         ; extra time since timeout
        push    edx         ; ref data from Set_ call
        push    ebp         ; client register pointer
        push    ebx         ; current VM handle
        call    OnTimeout   ; call C-language handler
        ret                 ; return to caller
        }
    }

void __stdcall OnTimeout(PVMMCB hVM, PCRS pRegs,
    PVOID refdata, DWORD extra)
    {
    ...
    }
```

You choose which of these approaches to use based on the tradeoff between your own productivity and the importance of high performance. The wrapper approach is obviously slower, but it lets you write more of your code in C.

A Complete C Skeleton

With the same caveats I expressed earlier about the difficulty of providing a meaningful example, here are the pieces of a basic VxD written in C using the DDK (these files are provided on the companion disc in the \CHAP07\C-DDK directory):

MYVXD.MAK

```
# MYVXD.MAK -- MAKE file for sample VxD

all: myvxd.vxd

devdcl.obj: $*.asm
    ml -coff -DBLD_COFF -DIS_32 -W2 -c -Cx -DMASM6 -Zd -DDEBUG $*.asm

myvxd.obj: $*.c
    cl -c -Zdp -Gs -Zl $*.c

myvxd.vxd: devdcl.obj $*.obj $*.def
    link @<<
-machine:i386 -debug:none -pdb:none -def:$*.def -out:$@
-map:$*.map -vxd vxdwraps.clb
devdcl.obj myvxd.obj
<<
```

DEVDCL.ASM

```
; DEVDCL.ASM -- Required assembly-language part of C driver
    .386p
    include vmm.inc
    include debug.inc

Declare_Virtual_Device MYVXD, 1, 0, MYVXD_control,\
    Undefined_Device_ID, Undefined_Init_Order

Begin_Control_Dispatch MYVXD
    Control_Dispatch Device_Init, OnDeviceInit, sCall, <ebx, edx>
End_Control_Dispatch   MYVXD

    end
```

(continued)

continued

MYVXD.C

```
// MYVXD.C -- C-language skeleton using DDK tools
#define WANTVXDWRAPS
#include <basedef.h>
#include <vmm.h>
#include <debug.h>
#include <vxdwraps.h>

#pragma VxD_ICODE_SEG
#pragma VxD_IDATA_SEG

BOOL __stdcall OnDeviceInit(PVMMCB hVM, DWORD refdata)
    {                          // OnDeviceInit
    return TRUE;
    }                          // OnDeviceInit
```

Using C++ with the Windows 95 DDK

Before being forced by necessity to discover otherwise, I uncritically assumed for a long time that it would be unreasonably hard to write a VxD in C++. After all, at first blush it looks like you need an extensive runtime library to make the average C++ program work. You certainly do if you're building an MFC application, at any rate.

It turns out to be much easier than I expected to write a C++ VxD using nothing but a regular old C++ compiler such as Microsoft Visual C++ version 4.0 and the headers in the DDK. I present an extensive example of a C++ driver in Chapter 14 when I talk about how to build a VCOMM port driver. In this chapter, I simply present the mechanics of building a C++ driver. There are two problems that need to be solved in addition to all the problems that are associated with a C-language driver: how to handle static initializers and how to deal with the *new* operator. You also need to bracket the DDK include files with the *extern "C"* directive to avoid generating demands for VxD service wrapper functions under strangely decorated names.

WARNING   Version 4.1 of Microsoft Visual C++ cannot be used for building VxDs. It contains a bug that causes incorrect code to be generated for inline assembler references to enumerated constants. This bug causes every *VxDCall* macro or variant to generate bad code that will cause a runtime crash.

Handling Static Initializers

You really must handle static initializers if you want to support reasonably useful C++ drivers. A *static initializer* is a fragment of code that initializes a static or global variable, often by calling the constructor for a static instance of a class. As a simple example, suppose your driver uses a CPort object declared as follows:

```
class CPort
    {
public:
    CPort(DWORD address);
    CPort*        m_next;
    DWORD         m_address;
    static CPort* First;
    };
```

Further suppose that the logic of your driver requires it to build a linked list of CPort objects in static memory. You would want to write code like the following:

```
CPort::First = NULL;

CPort::CPort(DWORD address)
    {                                        //CPort::CPort
    m_next    = First;
    First     = this;
    m_address = address;
    }                                        //CPort::CPort

CPort(0x3F0);
CPort(0x3F1);
[etc.]
```

(This is an exceptionally contrived example, not least because you'd never hardcode an I/O port address in a Windows 95 driver; you'd work within the Plug and Play architecture and learn dynamically what ports you were using. But this contrived example shows how to implement static initializers rather than floppy disk drivers, so bear with me.)

Normally, the runtime library initialization program locates and executes the static initializers for you. It finds them because the compiler places them into a particular segment (.crt$xcu). Since you don't link a VxD with the startup routine that knows how to run the static initialization code, though, you have to provide your own substitute. For a number of boring technical reasons, you must first persuade the compiler to put the initializers into a different segment whose COFF and OMF names are the same. You do this by means of the following pragma statements:

```
#pragma warning(disable:4075) // nonstandard init seg
#pragma init_seg("INITCODE")
#pragma warning(default:4075)
```

(The name "INITCODE" isn't magic; it simply needs to match the name you use in the assembly-language module that does the initialization.)

Next, you add the following code to the assembly-language program that contains your device control procedure:

```
VxD_LOCKED_DATA_SEG
didinit  dd     0
VxD_LOCKED_DATA_ENDS

initcode segment dword public flat 'code'
beginit  dd     0
initcode ends
...
initend  segment dword public flat 'code'
endinit  dd     0
initend  ends

_bss     segment dword public flat 'lcode'
startbss dd     0
_bss     ends
...
_ebss    segment dword public flat 'lcode'
endbss   dd     0
_ebss ends
```

(I'm including the _BSS segment in the scheme I'm about to describe to provide for uninitialized global variables in addition to static initializers.)

You must also insert some initialization code into your device control procedure:

```
Begin_Control_Dispatch MYVXD

            bts    didinit, 0           ; been here before?
            jc     skipinit             ; if yes, skip init
            pushad                      ; save all registers
            mov    esi, offset32 beginit+4 ; point to first entry
@@:
            cmp    esi, offset32 endinit ; reached end of list?
            jae    @F                   ; if yes, leave the loop
            call   dword ptr [esi]      ; call init function
            add    esi, 4               ; process all of them
            jmp    @B                   ;    ..
@@:
```

```
        cld
        mov     edi, offset32 startbss    ; point to start of BSS
        mov     ecx, offset32 endbss      ; compute length
        sub     ecx, edi                  ;  ..
        shr     ecx, 2                    ; convert to DWORDs
        xor     eax, eax                  ; get const zero
        rep     stosd                     ; zero-fill BSS area

        popad                             ; restore registers

skipinit:

Control_Dispatch ...
[etc.]
End_Control_Dispatch MYVXD
```

This additional code begins by testing a flag bit to see if we've already done the extra initialization. (The BTS instruction tests a bit, sets the bit, and sets the carry flag if the bit was originally set.) The *initcode* segment contains pointers to all the initialization functions that need to be called. The arrangement of segment directives guarantees that the *beginit* and *endinit* symbols will neatly bracket the *initcode* pointers. I use an analogous trick to find the beginning and end of the *_BSS* area. (It should not, by the way, be necessary to actually define data objects within the extra bracketing segments. I encountered linker crashes when I attempted to locate the beginning and end of the *initcode* and BSS areas without doing so, though.)

Finally, you need to add some segment definitions to the module definition (.DEF) file for the VxD so that the linker will group all of the segments properly:

```
VXD MYVXD

SEGMENTS
        ...
        _EBSS          CLASS 'LCODE'      PRELOAD NONDISCARDABLE
        INITCODE       CLASS 'ICODE'      DISCARDABLE
        INITEND        CLASS 'ICODE'      DISCARDABLE
        ...
```

Overriding the *new* and *delete* Operators

The standard runtime library implementation of the *new* and *delete* operators relies on an extensive heap management subsystem that can't (and shouldn't) be reproduced in a VxD. If you use these operators sparingly, you can get by simply by providing your own functions that use the regular VMM heap manager:

```
void* ::operator new(unsigned int size)
    {                          //operator new
    return _HeapAllocate(size, 0);
    }                          //operator new
```

```
void ::operator delete(void* p)
    {                           //operator delete
    if (p)
        _HeapFree(p, 0);
    }                           //operator delete
```

But be careful not to allocate and release objects all over the place. Not only do you risk fragmenting the heap, but you might inadvertently try to call the heap manager at a time when you can't safely do so. For example, it would be very bad to implicitly call _HeapAllocate_ while handling a hardware interrupt, but you could easily do so without precisely meaning to with code like the following:

```
CPort CPort::GetPort(DWORD address)
    {                            // CPort::GetPort
    return CPort(address); // oops! calls new CPort
    }                            // CPort::GetPort
```

VTOOLSD

If using the Microsoft DDK to write a VxD in C seems like forcing a size 11 foot into a size 9 shoe, the VTOOLSD package will seem made-to-order. This is especially true if you use VTOOLSD for its apparent purpose of developing a C++ driver using its extensive class library. VTOOLSD is the brainchild of two former DOS extender developers who started a tiny company called Vireo Software, Inc., to elaborate on their idea of how to bring VxD programming to a wider group of programmers. VTOOLSD contains three basic components:

- The QuickVxd applet, which gathers the specification of a new VxD and generates a skeleton you can then flesh out. It's similar in concept to Microsoft's AppWizard, but it's also much less ambitious and leaves more of the details up to you.

- Headers and libraries that allow you to develop a VxD entirely in C—no assembly required (except for the occasional bit of inline assembly code, that is).

- Headers and libraries for a C++ class library that allow you to develop a VxD in C++.

On one hand, Vireo's playing David to Microsoft's Goliath (or dancing in toe shoes instead of galoshes, to continue the pedestrian flavor of the earlier metaphor) has one important advantage to developers: Vireo has to support and respond to all of its customers. In my experience, this means I can get my questions answered and my bug reports addressed. Another advantage is that you can use language tools from vendors other than Microsoft if you want.

On the other hand, Vireo's size prevents it from bringing VTOOLSD to a uniformly high state of polish. I've run into annoying problems like finding that the class members that I desperately need to access from a derived class have been declared private. Mind you, it would be hard to call the DDK "polished," too.

Using QuickVxd

I've got only enough space in this book to give you a taste of what it's like to use VTOOLSD. You begin with the QuickVxd applet (see Figure 7-3). The first tab of the QuickVxd dialog box allows you specify basic information about your driver, such as its name, ID, initialization order, and so on.

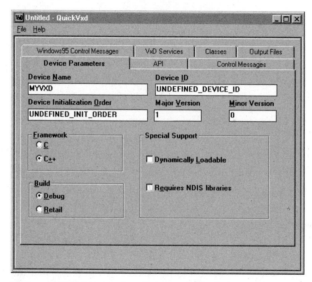

Figure 7-3. *The QuickVxd applet for defining a VxD.*

VTOOLSD immediately shows its greater simplicity over the DDK when you use the two Control Messages tabs in the QuickVxd dialog box (see Figure 7-4 and Figure 7-5). These two tabs let you indicate with a check mark which of the many system control messages your VxD will handle. QuickVxd also does a small amount of common-sense checking. If you indicate that you're building a dynamically loadable device driver, for example, QuickVxd will warn you if you don't also specify that you want to handle the Sys_Dynamic_Device_Init and Sys_Dynamic_Device_Exit messages, which nearly all dynamic device drivers need to handle.

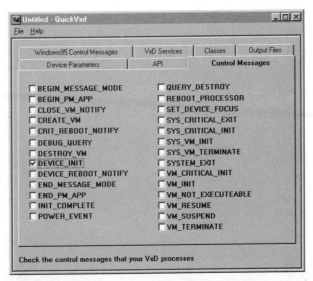

Figure 7-4. *The QuickVxd Control Messages tab.*

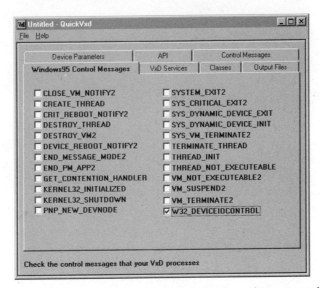

Figure 7-5. *The QuickVxd Windows95 Control Messages tab.*

A Skeleton in C

QuickVxd will generate a MAKE file, a header file, and a C-language source file if you specify the C framework (these files are included on the companion disc in the \CHAP07\C-VTOOLSD directory):

MYVXD.MAK

```
# MYVXD.mak - makefile for VxD MYVXD

DEVICENAME = MYVXD
FRAMEWORK = C
DEBUG = 1
OBJECTS = myvxd.OBJ

!include $(VTOOLSD)\include\vtoolsd.mak
!include $(VTOOLSD)\include\vxdtarg.mak

myvxd.OBJ:  myvxd.c myvxd.h
```

MYVXD.H

```
// MYVXD.h - include file for VxD MYVXD

#include <vtoolsc.h>

#define MYVXD_Major         1
#define MYVXD_Minor         0
#define MYVXD_DeviceID      UNDEFINED_DEVICE_ID
#define MYVXD_Init_Order    UNDEFINED_INIT_ORDER
```

MYVXD.C

```
// MYVXD.c - main module for VxD MYVXD

#define   DEVICE_MAIN
#include  "myvxd.h"
#undef    DEVICE_MAIN

Declare_Virtual_Device(MYVXD)

DefineControlHandler(DEVICE_INIT, OnDeviceInit);
DefineControlHandler(W32_DEVICEIOCONTROL, OnW32Deviceiocontrol);

BOOL __cdecl ControlDispatcher(
    DWORD dwControlMessage,
    DWORD EBX,
```

(continued)

continued

```
    DWORD EDX,
    DWORD ESI,
    DWORD EDI,
    DWORD ECX)
{
    START_CONTROL_DISPATCH

        ON_DEVICE_INIT(OnDeviceInit);
        ON_W32_DEVICEIOCONTROL(OnW32Deviceiocontrol);

    END_CONTROL_DISPATCH

    return TRUE;
}


BOOL OnDeviceInit(VMHANDLE hVM, PCHAR CommandTail)
{
    return TRUE;
}

DWORD OnW32Deviceiocontrol(PIOCTLPARAMS p)
{
    return 0;
}
```

It's apparent from this small sample that QuickVxd and the VTOOLSD framework take care of the details of defining your DDB and device control procedure without your needing to write any assembly language or even needing to be specifically aware of the register conventions associated with system control messages. To gain the maximum benefit from this built-in knowledge, however, you'll want to completely specify the interfaces to your VxD at the beginning to avoid the minimal difficulty of adding new control messages to the *ControlDispatcher* routine later on.

This sample also shows two potential problems you'll encounter with VTOOLSD. The first is disagreements in structure naming between VTOOLSD and the DDK. For example, Vireo uses the typedef *VMHANDLE* to describe a pointer to a virtual machine control block, whereas the DDK header VXDWRAPS.H uses *PVMMCB* to describe a pointer to the same structure. And Vireo calls the parameter structure for OnW32Deviceiocontrol an *IOCTLPARAMS*, whereas Microsoft calls it a *DIOCPA-RAMETERS*; each toolkit has its own name for the members of the structure, too. While disagreements like this persist, it will be hard to port code from one set of tools to another.

The second problem illustrated by this brief example is the way Vireo's framework calls the *OnDeviceInit* handler for the Device_Init system control message. As I mentioned earlier in this chapter, this message uses the EDX register to point to reference data supplied by the real-mode initializer. In the example I gave earlier, I ignored the command-tail pointer and included the reference data. It's not easy to tailor the Vireo framework in the same way, unfortunately.

NOTE The fact that the EDX register holds the real-mode initializer's reference data is documented only for Sys_Critical_Init, not for Device_Init or Init_Complete, which are the other two driver initialization messages in which this reference data might be useful. This is an oversight in the Microsoft documentation that VxD writers have already come to terms with. It's only slightly better documented that you can obtain this reference data from the *DDB_Reference_Data* field of the DDB. In a VTOOLSD driver, you'd reference the DDB under the external name *The_DDB*.

Callbacks Within the VTOOLSD Framework

Another area in which VTOOLSD may make your life a little simpler than the DDK does is when it comes to callback functions. I showed you earlier how to wrap the callback for a timer event when you use the DDK's C-language interfaces. VTOOLSD makes this easier by having you define a *callback thunk*, which it fills in with the necessary machine language to call your callback routine in C. Your code looks something like this:

```
static TIMEOUT_THUNK thunk;      // in locked data
TIMEOUT_HANDLER OnTimeout;       // forward declaration
...
Set_Global_Time_Out(1000, refdata, OnTimeout, &thunk);
...
void __stdcall OnTimeout(VMHANDLE hVM, PCLIENT_STRUCT pRegs,
    PVOID refdata, DWORD extra)
    {                            // OnTimeout
    ...
    }                            // OnTimeout
```

Many programmers will find this thunk-based approach simpler than using *__declspec(naked)*, but this is one area in which Vireo's documentation was inconsistent with the header files, at least in its earliest versions. The C++ framework, however, is much easier to use for callback functions, as I'll illustrate in the next section.

Segments and Wrappers

You don't need to specifically include any special header files to call VxD services; VTOOLSD automatically declares practically all of them for you. Although there are some gaps in VTOOLSD's coverage, VTOOLSD is much better than the DDK on this score.

As with the DDK, you can very simply control the segmentation of your own code:

```
#include LOCKED_CODE_SEGMENT
#include LOCKED_DATA_SEGMENT
```

The manifest constants represent the names of header files that accomplish the necessary change of segment names.

Not only does VTOOLSD include wrappers for all the VxD services you'll ever want to call, it actually includes five versions for each wrapper—one for each segment in which your calling function might live. Thus, there's an *INIT_Get_VMM_Version*, a *LOCK_Get_VMM_Version*, and so on. When you establish a particular code segment by referencing, say, *LOCKED_CODE_SEGMENT*, you also compile a bunch of #define statements that equate symbols like *Get_VMM_Version* to *LOCK_Get_VMM_Version*. The VTOOLSD runtime library contains wrappers under each of the five possible names. Each wrapper contains identical code to invoke the correct INT 20h call.

The inclusion of multiple wrappers means that your driver might end up containing multiple copies of each wrapper, one for each segment in which your code calls the wrapper. If space is important, just use the full name of a wrapper in a segment that has the most stringent of all necessary persistence constraints. For example:

```
#include INIT_CODE_SEGMENT
...
DWORD version = LOCK_Get_VMM_Version();
...
#include LOCKED_CODE_SEGMENT
...
DWORD version = LOCK_Get_VMM_Version();
```

But be careful! You obviously don't want to try to call the *INIT* or *PAGEABLE* wrapper from the locked code segment, for example.

Runtime Library Calls

Another important contrast between VTOOLSD and the DDK is that VTOOLSD allows you to use more runtime library functions. Both VTOOLSD and the DDK support functions that have compiler intrinsics (functions that the compiler can generate inline code to implement). For example, *strcmp* and *memcpy* (to name two such functions) are available with either tool set. But VTOOLSD also allows you to use nonintrinsic functions such as *atol*, *sprintf* and *malloc*, to name a few.

A Skeleton in C++

When you use the C++ framework, QuickVxd builds the following skeleton for you:

MYVXD.MAK

```
# MYVXD.mak - makefile for VxD MYVXD

DEVICENAME = MYVXD
FRAMEWORK = CPP
DEBUG = 1
OBJECTS = myvxd.OBJ


!include $(VTOOLSD)\include\vtoolsd.mak
!include $(VTOOLSD)\include\vxdtarg.mak


Myvxd.OBJ:  Myvxd.cpp Myvxd.h
```

MYVXD.H

```
// MYVXD.h - include file for VxD MYVXD

#include <vtoolscp.h>

#define DEVICE_CLASS        MyvxdDevice
#define MYVXD_DeviceID      UNDEFINED_DEVICE_ID
#define MYVXD_Init_Order    UNDEFINED_INIT_ORDER
#define MYVXD_Major         1
#define MYVXD_Minor         0

class MyvxdDevice : public VDevice
{
public:
    virtual BOOL OnDeviceInit(VMHANDLE hSysVM, PCHAR
        pszCmdTail);
    virtual DWORD OnW32DeviceIoControl(PIOCTLPARAMS
        pDIOCParams);
};

class MyvxdVM : public VVirtualMachine
{
public:
    MyvxdVM(VMHANDLE hVM);
```

(continued)

continued

```
};

class MyvxdThread : public VThread
{
public:
    MyvxdThread(THREADHANDLE hThread);
};
```

MYVXD.CPP

```
// MYVXD.cpp - main module for VxD MYVXD

#define DEVICE_MAIN
#include "myvxd.h"
Declare_Virtual_Device(MYVXD)
#undef DEVICE_MAIN

MyvxdVM::MyvxdVM(VMHANDLE hVM) : VVirtualMachine(hVM) {}

MyvxdThread::MyvxdThread(THREADHANDLE hThread) :
    VThread(hThread) {}

BOOL MyvxdDevice::OnDeviceInit(VMHANDLE hSysVM,
    PCHAR           pszCmdTail)
{
    return TRUE;
}

DWORD MyvxdDevice::OnW32DeviceIoControl(PIOCTLPARAMS
    pDIOCParams)
{
    return 0;
}
```

In summary, in the VTOOLSD C++ framework, you derive three classes from base classes in the VTOOLSD library:

■ *MyvxdDevice*, derived from the base class *VDevice*, implements your virtual device driver. Many system control messages have corresponding member functions in this class. Thus, you override base-class member functions like *OnDeviceInit* or *OnW32DeviceIoControl* to provide specialized message handling.

- *MyvxdVM*, derived from *VVirtualMachine*, implements any special handling you need for virtual machines. The VTOOLSD framework routes most of the system control messages that pertain to virtual machines to members of this class. (The exception is the Create_VM message, which your *MyvxdDevice* class handles in order to create a *MyvxdVM* object in the first place.)

- *MyvxdThread*, derived from *VThread*, handles any thread-specific messages for your VxD. Just as with the virtual machine class, your *MyvxdThread* class handles all the system control messages related to threads except Create_Thread, which your *MyvxdDevice* class handles in order to create an instance of *MyvxdThread*.

In many cases, you'll only really need the *VDevice*-derivative class. The classes that represent virtual machines and threads aren't necessarily useful in every VxD. Still, even if you never create instances of these latter two classes, their presence in your program won't do much harm.

Callbacks in C++

The VTOOLSD scheme for callbacks revolves around other base classes in the framework. You'd handle the timeout problem we've been using as an example by deriving your own class from *VGlobalTimeOut*:

```
class MyTimeOut : public VGlobalTimeOut
    {
public:
    MyTimeOut(DWORD msec) : VGlobalTimeOut(msec){}
    virtual VOID handler(VMHANDLE, PVOID, CLIENT_STRUCT*,
        DWORD);
    };
```

To schedule the timeout, you would write the following code:

```
(new MyTimeOut(1000))->Set();
```

To handle the timeout when it eventually occurs, you would write the following callback function:

```
VOID MyTimeOut::handler(VMHANDLE hVM, PVOID junk,
    CLIENT_STRUCT* pRegs, DWORD extra)
    {                                    // MyTimeOut::handler
    ...
    }                                    // MyTimeOut::handler
```

Chapter 8

Initializing and Terminating Virtual Device Drivers

Windows 95 classifies virtual device drivers as either static or dynamic, depending on when it loads them. The VMM loads static VxDs as Windows 95 starts up, and it keeps them present in virtual memory for the duration of the Windows 95 session. It loads dynamic VxDs dynamically (what else?) when an application or a VxD asks it to. Dynamic VxDs can be unloaded and reloaded many times during a Windows 95 session. As a general rule, VxDs that pertain to particular pieces of hardware or to an application are dynamic, whereas core components of the Virtual Machine Manager (including the VMM itself) are static.

The life cycle of a static VxD can be characterized as follows. The VMM finds static drivers to load by looking in the registry database or in the SYSTEM.INI file. Real-mode resident programs, such as TSR utilities and MS-DOS device drivers, can also hook an interrupt to ask the VMM to load specific static drivers. Static drivers receive three initialization messages as the system starts up—Sys_Critical_Init, Device_Init, and Init_Complete—corresponding to the important milestones the VMM reaches during startup. Static drivers can include initialization code that runs in real mode before the VMM switches to protected mode. Finally, static drivers receive a series of shutdown messages as the VMM prepares to exit from Windows 95 and return to real mode.

The VMM doesn't find dynamic drivers on its own. An application or another VxD such as the Configuration Manager or the Input/Output Supervisor determines that one or more additional VxDs are required and calls VXDLDR (itself a static VxD) to load them. In contrast to static drivers, dynamic VxDs receive just one initialization and one shutdown message. Despite these differences from static VxDs, both varieties of VxD are developed using the same tools and the same APIs. The only mechanical difference between a static and a dynamic VxD, in fact, is that a dynamic VxD advertises itself as dynamic in the VXD statement of its module definition file, whereas a static VxD does not.

STATIC VXDS

There are three ways to cause the VMM to load a static VxD. Most of the time, you (or your installation program) will modify the registry database or the SYSTEM.INI file located in the Windows 95 directory. In some cases, however, you will have a TSR utility or other resident program that can't function without a VxD; in this case, your TSR utility will hook software interrupt 2Fh and look for the 1605h startup broadcast.

Using the System Registry

The preferred method for loading a static VxD in Windows 95 is to add an entry to the system registry database within the local machine branch:

```
HKEY_LOCAL_MACHINE
    System
        CurrentControlSet
            Services
                VxD
                    key
                        StaticVxD=pathname
```

In this diagram of a part of the registry hierarchy, *key* is any registry key and *pathname* is the name of a virtual device driver that needs to be statically loaded. The VMM will enumerate all of the subkeys of the VxD key looking for *StaticVxD* named values, each of which specifies a driver file to be loaded statically.

For example, the Configuration Manager has the registry entry shown in Figure 8-1. In this example, the * preceding the name of the CONFIGMG device indicates that the driver is physically located within VMM32.VXD instead of in a separate disk file; you won't use this convention for your own drivers, of course. The various named values such as *Detect* exemplify how the registry can contain device-specific parameters. I'll describe later in this chapter how you can interrogate parameters such as *Detect* to configure your driver during initialization.

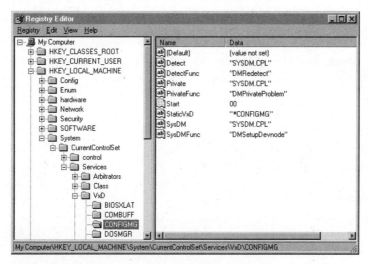

Figure 8-1. *Registry entries for the CONFIGMG device.*

Using the SYSTEM.INI File

In Windows 3.1 and earlier, the [386enh] section of the system configuration file SYSTEM.INI controlled many of the low-level system functions of Windows. Among other things, you could direct Windows to load virtual device drivers by using statements of the form

```
device=pathname
```

For example, if your VxD was named MYVXD.VXD and was installed in the MYAPP directory on the C drive, your SYSTEM.INI file would have contained the statement

```
device=c:\MYAPP\MYVXD.VXD
```

You can also use a SYSTEM.INI file in Windows 95, but it's preferable to modify the registry as described in the previous section. Nonetheless, I find it much easier during development of a static VxD to change the SYSTEM.INI file. The practical

BOOTING INTO MS-DOS

As it comes to you out of the box, Windows 95 boots into the graphical Windows environment when you boot your computer. You probably already know at least one way to short-circuit the boot process in order to start out at an MS-DOS prompt. Pressing F8 during the boot process, for example, gives you a menu that allows you to choose a command prompt instead of the graphical Windows environment. Useful things you can do at an MS-DOS prompt include configuring a real-mode network, installing debug or retail binaries from the DDK, or starting a debugger like Soft-Ice/W. You can also issue a WIN command to get into Windows 95, of course.

I find that I almost always want to pause in MS-DOS before starting Windows 95, so I learned a couple of additional ways to halt the boot process at MS-DOS. One way depends on the fact that Windows 95 receives control at startup because MS-DOS simply issues a WIN command when it finishes processing AUTOEXEC.BAT. If you place a WIN.BAT file in the path ahead of the WIN.COM file in the Windows directory, your .BAT file gets executed instead of Windows 95.

A more elegant way to get an MS-DOS prompt is to modify MSDOS.SYS. *Sacre bleu!* Isn't MSDOS.SYS one of the two hidden files (the other being IO.SYS) that contains MS-DOS? In earlier releases of MS-DOS, MSDOS.SYS was in fact a large binary file containing program code you wouldn't dream of modifying. (Well, maybe one or two readers would have, but most of us wouldn't.) In the Windows 95 release of MS-DOS, however, this file is a short ASCII text file in the root directory of your boot disk. It contains startup options for Windows 95 in approximately the same form as a standard Windows .INI file. The BootGUI option controls whether MS-DOS issues the implicit WIN command automatically or not. So you can just change this option to read as follows:

```
[Options]
BootGUI=0
```

To accomplish the edit, you'll need to remove the *Hidden, Read-Only,* and *System* attributes from the MSDOS.SYS file. You can restore them after the edit or not, as you please, because neither MS-DOS nor Windows 95 cares whether those attributes are set or not.

> By the way, don't try to edit the file named MSDOS.SYS if you've used the dual boot feature (controlled by the BootMulti=1 setting in the Options section of this same file) to boot an earlier version of MS-DOS. MSDOS.SYS will then really contain MS-DOS; Windows 95 renames certain files when you use the BootMulti feature, so the file you want to edit will be lurking under the name MSDOS.W40.

reason for using the SYSTEM.INI file is that a broken VxD can keep Windows 95 from starting up, but you can't modify the registry unless you have a working Windows 95 session. You can always edit your SYSTEM.INI file from real mode before starting Windows 95.

Using the INT 2Fh, Function 1605h, Startup Broadcast

Real-mode software is very much alive in Windows 95, even though its importance has diminished and will continue to diminish over time. For compatibility (if nothing else), Windows 95 continues to support several interfaces that allow real-mode drivers and TSR utilities to coexist with it. The interrupt 2Fh, function 1605h, broadcast I describe here is one of the most important of these interfaces.

The VMM issues software interrupt 2Fh with register AX set to 1605h while it's starting up. Resident software can hook interrupt 2Fh to receive this broadcast. Your handler will chain to other interrupt 2Fh handlers and return with the ES:BX register pair pointing to a linked list of startup information structures. The code will probably look something like this:

```
sis       db    3, 0          ; SIS_Version
          dd    0             ; SIS_Next_Dev_Ptr
          dd    vxdname       ; SIS_Virt_Dev_File_Ptr
          dd    refdata       ; SIS_Reference_Data
          dd    0             ; SIS_Instance_Data_Ptr
vxdname   db    'pathname', 0

          assume ds:nothing, cs:@curseg

          align 4
org2f     dd    ?
int2f:    cmp   ax, 1605h
          je    @F
```

```
        jmp    [org2f]
@@:     pushf
        call   [org2f]
        mov    word ptr sis+2, bx
        mov    word ptr sis+4, es
        mov    bx, cs
        mov    es, bx
        mov    bx, offset sis
        iret
```

In this code fragment, *pathname* represents the name of a virtual device driver and *refdata* represents a 32-bit data item that will be passed to the real-mode initialization function of that driver.

WHERE'S MY DRIVER?

If a TSR needs a VxD, you can provide end-user flexibility and simultaneously simplify your code by giving the VxD a name that differs from the TSR's only in the file extension, and by always keeping the VxD in the same directory as the TSR. The TSR can determine its own full pathname by scanning to the end of the environment block using code like this:

```
        mov    es, es:[2Ch]   ; ES:DI -> environment block
        xor    di, di         ;  ..
        cld                   ; force forward direction
        xor    al, al         ; AL = 0 to compare against
        xor    cx, cx         ; CX = essentially infinite count
        dec    cx             ;  ..
@@:  repne scasb             ; find end of current variable
        scasb                 ; is next byte 0?
        jne    @B             ; if not, skip next variable
        add    di, 2          ; ES:DI now points to our name
```

The name of the required VxD is then the name of the TSR file—you just need to change the file extension. For example, you might replace .COM with .VXD.

An even fancier trick is to code the real-mode TSR as an .EXE file and use it as the linker stub when you build the VxD. (That is, specify your TSR executable file in the *STUB* statement of your VxD's .DEF file, as illustrated in the MSDN article "Binding a TSR to a VxD.") This allows you to provide just *one* file. You'd still scan the environment to learn your own name, as shown in the code sample above, but you wouldn't need to replace the file extension.

Usually you will specify the full pathname of your driver. For example, if your driver were named MYVXD.VXD and were located in the MYAPP directory of the C drive, you'd specify:

```
vxdname db      'C:\MYAPP\MYVXD.VXD', 0
```

If your driver is stored in the Windows 95 or system directory, however, or if its directory is in the current path, you can just supply the name and extension.

It might happen that your resident program needs two or more virtual device drivers. In this situation, just create additional startup information structures before returning from your INT 2Fh handler.

Load Order and Duplication

The VMM shouldn't load the same driver twice. It identifies drivers by the identifier number in the device description block you build with the Declare_Virtual_Device macro. Thus, two drivers might be considered duplicates even if they are in different disk files, have different NAME statements in their .DEF files, and use different names in their Declare_Virtual_Device macro calls. The one exception to this is that two drivers with 0 identifiers (*Undefined_Device_ID*) are never considered to be the same, even if they are identical; it's not an error to load a duplicate of an undefined-ID driver.

Because it is possible—and very easy, in fact—to request the loading of the same device driver more than once, you might need to understand the order in which the VMM tries to load drivers:

1. The VMM loads drivers requested in INT 2Fh, function 1605h, Startup Information Structures first, in the order in which the structures appear in the linked list. This order is the reverse of the order in which resident programs hooked INT 2Fh, so the last program to hook the interrupt ends up having priority.

2. The VMM then searches the registry database for *StaticVxD* named values as described earlier.

3. Finally, the VMM loads drivers named in device statements in the SYSTEM.INI file, in the order in which the statements appear.

INITIALIZING AND TERMINATING A STATIC VXD

Windows 95 initializes a statically loaded driver in four steps. Before it switches the processor to protected mode, the VMM calls the *real-mode initialization* function if the VxD contains one. After switching to protected mode, but while the processor is disabled for interrupts, the VMM sends the driver a Sys_Critical_Init message. After enabling the processor, it sends the driver a Device_Init message. Most drivers perform their initialization at this time. After initializing all virtual devices with Device_Init, the VMM sends the driver an Init_Complete message.

Real-Mode Initialization

When you boot your computer, the processor starts out in real mode. It stays in real mode while MS-DOS initializes, while MS-DOS loads the drivers specified in CONFIG.SYS, and while MS-DOS processes the AUTOEXEC.BAT file. When AUTO-EXEC.BAT is finished, MS-DOS automatically issues a WIN command to load Windows 95. Windows 95 therefore commences operation in real mode. Windows 95 switches to protected mode only after it determines which static virtual device drivers to load.

NOTE It's almost pedantic to note this, but I'll mention it anyway: if you happen to load an expanded memory manager such as EMM386 during the processing of your AUTOEXEC.BAT file, the computer will actually be in V86 mode when Windows 95 starts. This could affect your ability to access memory in the first megabyte of linear address space during initialization, because the Windows V86MMGR device needs to take over management of upper memory blocks from the memory manager first. This occurs during the operation of V86MMGR's Sys_Critical_Init handler.

After the initial startup but before the switch to protected mode, the VMM performs real-mode initialization. Part of this phase of initialization is the INT 2Fh, function 1605h, startup broadcast, which gives resident programs the opportunity to specify the drivers they need. During this phase, the VMM also reads the registry and the device statements in the [386enh] section of SYSTEM.INI. The VMM examines each driver file to call the optional real-mode initialization function.

A real-mode initialization function can do any or all of the following things:

■   Check for multiple requests to load the same driver and select which copy to load.

■   Provide for instancing data areas.

■   Identify conventional memory pages as belonging to the virtual device.

■   Communicate with other real-mode programs.

■   Prevent Windows 95 from starting up.

instance data Data that occupies identical virtual addresses in every virtual machine but that can have distinct values in each virtual machine. In Windows 95, this term always refers to data that's initially located in the first megabyte of address space that doesn't belong to a hardware device. For example, the recall buffer for DOSKEY would be considered instanced, but the video RAM would not, even though both areas have the same address but different contents in different VMs.

Not every virtual device driver needs a real-mode initialization function, by the way. The usual reason that you'd provide one is to determine information that requires you to call real-mode code but that is needed in the Sys_Critical_Init phase of initialization (when real mode is temporarily inaccessible). Another reason is to detect duplicate load requests.

Program Structure

You will want to package your real-mode initialization function, together with all the data it will use, in a single 16-bit segment within your VxD:

```
VxD_REAL_INIT_SEG        ; starts _RCODE segment
...
VxD_REAL_INIT_ENDS       ; ends _RCODE segment
```

That is, you use the VxD_REAL_INIT_*xxx* segment macros to delimit the real-mode initialization segment. If you are using LINK386 with the Windows 3.1 DDK tools, you must also specify the starting point of your real-mode initialization function as the main entry point of your VxD by naming it on the END statement. You don't need or want anything on the END statement if you're using the Visual C++ or Windows 95 DDK linker.

Entry and Exit Conditions

At entry to your real-mode initialization function, the registers contain the values shown in Table 8-1 on the following page. The version number in register AX is 0400h for Windows 95, 030Ah for Windows 3.1, and so on. You can call the service routine whose address is in register ECX to examine entries in the registry or in the SYSTEM.INI file or to communicate with the real-mode loader. The reference data in register EDX will be 0 if the driver was loaded because of a device= statement in the SYSTEM.INI file or because of a registry entry. Otherwise it will be the value specified by the *SIS_Reference_Data* field in the particular INT 2Fh, function 1605h, startup information structure that caused the driver to be loaded.

Register	Contents
AX	VMM version number (for example, 0400h or 030Ah).
BX	Flags, as follows: Bit 0: *Duplicate_Device_ID*—If set, another driver with the same ID was already loaded. Bit 1: *Duplicate_From_INT2F*—If set, the earlier driver was loaded because it was specified in an INT 2Fh, function 1605h, response. Bit 2: *Loading_From_INT2F*—If set, this driver is being loaded because of an INT 2Fh, function 1605h, response.
ECX	Segment:offset address of initialization service entry point (Windows 3.1 and later).
EDX	0 or reference data from INT 2Fh, function 1605h, startup information structure.
SI	Segment containing the MS-DOS environment.
CS, DS, ES	Paragraph containing the _RCODE segment.

Table 8-1. *The contents of registers on entry to real-mode initialization.*

Version Numbers   Windows 95 reports 0004h (in other words, version 4.00) as its version number to Win32 programs and 0400h to VxDs. A Win16 application will obtain 5F03h (in other words, version 3.95) by calling *GetVersion*. The reason Windows 95 lies to Win16 programs is that too many of them incorrectly use *GetVersion*. Some programs ask, "Is this version 3?" when they really mean, "Is this version later than version 2?" Other programs fail to reverse the byte order of *GetVersion*'s return value before comparison, so they would incorrectly conclude that 0004h (4.00) is less than 0A03h (3.10).

The duplicate-driver flags (bits 0 and 1) in register BX indicate that this driver has the same driver identifier as a driver that is already loaded. Note that bit 1 (*Duplicate_From_INT2F*) refers to the *first* driver that has the same ID as this one. You discover that your driver was loaded via INT 2Fh, function 1605h, by examining bit 2 (*Loading_From_INT2F*).

Your real-mode initialization function should exit by performing a *near* return instruction with the register contents shown in Table 8-2. You indicate a normal return from your initialization function by setting AX to 0 (*Device_Load_Ok*).

Register	Contents
AX	Return code, composed from the following bits:
	Bit 0: *Abort_Device_Load*—If set, tells the VMM not to load this particular VxD (but a VxD with the same ID can still be loaded in response to a different request).
	Bit 1: *Abort_Win386_Load*—If set, tells the VMM not to start Windows 95 at all.
	Bit 15: *No_Fail_Message*—If set, tells the VMM not to display an error message about not loading this driver.
BX	Pointer to list of owned pages.
EDX	Reference data for protected-mode initialization.
SI	Pointer to list of instance data items.

Table 8-2. *The contents of registers on exit from real-mode initialization.*

I found it surprising that you need to use a *near* return instruction. It seems that the VMM places some additional code into the real-mode initialization segment at runtime. It then does a far call to the additional code, which does a near call to your initialization function. Your near return thus reaches a far return instruction that gives control back to the VMM.

The owned pages list is a vector of short integers ending in 0. The instance data item list is a vector of *Instance_Item_Struc* structures ending with a 32-bit zero fence (see Figure 8-2). Both the owned-pages and instance-item vectors are located in the _RCODE segment along with the code and data for your real-mode initialization function. I'll discuss the owned pages concept later in this section. I'll talk about instance data in Chapter 10.

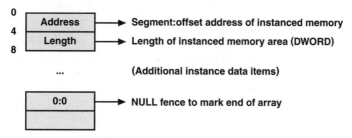

Figure 8-2. *Instance item structure list.*

Checking for Duplication

If you suspect that duplicate requests to load your device driver will be made, you can provide a real-mode initialization function to detect the duplication. For example:

```
rminit: test    bx, Duplicate_Device_ID   ; duplicate?
        setnz   al                        ; yes, set code
        cbw                               ;  ..
        xor     bx, bx                    ; no owned pages
        xor     si, si                    ; no inst data
        ret                               ; return
```

The SETNZ instruction sets the AL register to 1 if the result of the previous TEST instruction is nonzero. This value in register AL corresponds to the *Abort_Device_Load* flag.

You might wonder why Windows 95 doesn't just automatically detect driver duplication and load the first driver specified. Why does it call your real-mode initialization function and make you decide? The reason is that each request for the driver might indicate the need to claim an owned page or to mark some area of conventional memory for instancing. Windows 95 calls your initialization function to accommodate this possibility. But this also means that you must set the owned-page and instance-data return values in BX and SI even if you set the *Abort_Device_Load* flag on return.

Owned Pages

Windows 95 builds a page table for the conventional memory region of each new virtual machine. Each such page table maps some virtual addresses directly to the corresponding physical addresses and maps other virtual addresses to pages of extended memory. Very occasionally, you need to override the default choice for mapping a virtual address, and the *owned page list* permits you to do this.

I can best explain the concept of an owned page by describing the Windows 95 EBIOS driver. On a PS/2 machine, the BIOS allocates an *extended BIOS data area,* or *EBIOS area,* for temporary use as read-write storage. Compatibility constrains the size and use of the EBIOS area at 0040h:0000h, and the PS/2 BIOS therefore needs to use this additional region of physical memory. Each virtual machine needs to address the EBIOS area with a virtual-equals-real address or the BIOS won't work correctly in that virtual machine.

Other Windows 95 components might not realize that the EBIOS area is present, because the BIOS may report (via software interrupt 12h) that physical memory ends before the start of the EBIOS area. The default mapping behavior would therefore be to assign extended memory pages to the EBIOS address range. Since this behavior is incorrect, the EBIOS driver needs to override it.

The EBIOS driver's real-mode initialization function determines whether the EBIOS area is located within the last 40 KB of the 640-KB conventional memory region and, if so, claims the addresses beginning with the EBIOS area up to A000h:0000h as its own. It does so by returning with register BX pointing to an array of 16-bit integers, the last of which is 0. For example, if the EBIOS area starts at 9E80h:0000h, the array would contain three entries:

```
exc_bios_page dw 9Eh, 9Fh, 0
```

Later on, each time a new virtual machine is created, the EBIOS driver uses the _PhysIntoV86_ service to map physical pages 9Eh and 9Fh into the virtual machine's virtual pages 9Eh and 9Fh, respectively.

Device Callout Protocol

Within the real-mode initialization function, you can use BIOS and MS-DOS functions in a normal way. If you want to communicate with resident programs like MS-DOS device drivers or TSRs, you can use pretty much any method you please. Microsoft has defined a *device callout* convention based on software interrupt 2Fh to standardize this communication.

To use the device callout, load the general registers as follows: set register AX equal to 1607h and register BX equal to the unique identifier of your VxD. Then issue software interrupt 2Fh. Resident software that expects the callout will have hooked the interrupt and will be looking for function 1607h with the BX register equal to your device ID. The contents of any other registers, and the contents of the registers on return from the INT 2Fh call, are entirely up to you.

Real-Mode Initialization Services

Upon entry to the real-mode initialization function, the ECX register holds the paragraph:offset address of a service routine that provides several utility functions for decoding entries in the registry and in the SYSTEM.INI file. To use one of these services, you first save the address of the service routine in a memory DWORD:

```
rminit:  mov   _ServiceEntry, ecx
...
_ServiceEntry dd   0
```

Calling the variable in which you save the address _ServiceEntry_ will make it easier to use the registry access macros in VMMREG.H.

To invoke a particular service, load the AX register with a function index and execute a far call through the saved pointer:

```
mov   ax, n          ; AX = function index
call  [_ServiceEntry] ; call service routine
```

The available service routines are shown in Table 8-3. I found it hard to locate the reference documentation for these routines. The first six (0h through 6h) are documented in the Windows 95 DDK under "Programmer's Guide," in the section titled "Real-Mode Initialization," in the portion of the document titled "Reference." Search for the keyword *LDRSRV_COPY_EXTENDED_MEMORY* to find them on MSDN. The registry services are documented in the Windows 95 DDK under "Kernel Services Guide," in the section titled "Registry Services Reference," under the heading "Real-Mode Functions." Find them by searching MSDN under the keyword *LDR_RegCloseKey*.

AX Contents	Function Name
0h	LDRSRV_GET_PROFILE_STRING
01h	LDRSRV_GET_NEXT_PROFILE_STRING
03h	LDRSRV_GET_PROFILE_BOOLEAN
04h	LDRSRV_GET_PROFILE_DECIMAL_INT
05h	LDRSRV_GET_PROFILE_HEX_INT
06h	LDRSRV_COPY_EXTENDED_MEMORY
100h	LDR_RegOpenKey
102h	LDR_RegCloseKey
105h	LDR_RegQueryValue
106h	LDR_RegEnumKey
108h	LDR_RegEnumValue
109h	LDR_RegQueryValueEx

Table 8-3. *Real-mode initialization service calls.*

For example, suppose that you have added a [myvxd] section to your SYSTEM.INI file that specifies the I/O port address of your device:

```
[myvxd]
port=1234h
```

Your code to read this value might look like this:

```
rminit: mov    _ServiceEntry, ecx ; save service return address
        ...
        mov    ax, LDRSRV_GET_PROFILE_HEX_INT ; i.e., 05h
        mov    ecx, -1           ; ECX = default value
        mov    si, offset secname ; DS:SI -> section name
        mov    di, offset varname ; DS:DI -> setting name
        call   [_ServiceEntry]    ; get SYSTEM.INI setting
        mov    ioaddr, ecx        ; (returns in ECX)
        ...
_ServiceEntry dd 0
```

```
secname  db     'myvxd', 0
varname  db     'port', 0
ioaddr   dd     0
```

The code for accessing the registry is more complicated, partly because you have to know a great deal about the structure of the registry keys that cause your driver to be loaded. Here's an equivalent sample for retrieving a port address from the registry during real-mode initialization (this code is included on the companion disc in the \CHAP08\REALMODEINIT directory):

```
;RMREG.ASM -- Test of real-mode registry access

    .386p
    include vmm.inc
    include vmmreg.inc
    include regstr.inc

Declare_Virtual_Device RMREG, 1, 0, rmreg_control,\
    Undefined_Device_Id, Undefined_Init_Order

Begin_Control_Dispatch RMREG
End_Control_Dispatch RMREG

VxD_REAL_INIT_SEG
    mov    _ServiceEntry, ecx

    LDR_RegOpenKey HKEY_LOCAL_MACHINE, <offset namevxd>, ds,\
        <offset hvxd>, ds

    test   ax, ax
    jnz    fail1

    LDR_RegOpenKey hvxd, <offset myname>, ds, <offset hme>, ds

    test   ax, ax
    jnz    fail2

    Ldr_RegQueryValueEx hme, <offset portname>, ds, 0, 0, 0,\
        <offset port>, ds, <offset portsize>, ds

    test   ax, ax
    jnz    fail3

    ...              ; do something with "port" value

fail3:
    LDR_RegCloseKey hme
```

```
fail2:
    LDR_RegCloseKey hvxd
fail1:

alldone:
    xor    ax, ax
    xor    bx, bx
    xor    si, si
    ret


_ServiceEntry dd 0

namevxd  db    REGSTR_PATH_VXD, 0
hvxd     dd    0
myname   db    'RMREG', 0
hme      dd    0
portname db    'port', 0
port     dd    0
portsize dd    size port
VxD_REAL_INIT_ENDS

        end
```

I used several VMMREG.INC macros in this sample, and they all expect to find a DWORD named _ServiceEntry holding the address of the initialization services function.

To open the registry key governing a given device, you must first determine the name of the key. The manifest constant REGSTR_PATH_VXD (which is defined in REGSTR.INC) is \System\CurrentControlSet\Services\VxD. The easiest way to open RMREG's own key is to first open a key to this path and then open a subkey named RMREG below it. That's what the two calls to LDR_RegOpenKey accomplish. You use LDR_RegQueryValueEx to obtain a specific setting within an open key.

A major potential problem with the real-mode example I just showed you is that it depends on a compile-time decision about where you will put registry entries. As you'll see later on, it's slightly easier and more robust to access the appropriate registry key from within the protected-mode initialization functions of a VxD. This is because the _GetRegistryPath service will calculate the registry path that caused your VxD to be loaded, thereby reducing the amount of registry knowledge you need to have.

Communicating with Protected-Mode Initializers

The real-mode initialization function can communicate information to the protected-mode part of the driver by setting the EDX register to an arbitrary 32-bit *reference data* value before returning. This value occupies the EDX register when Windows

95 sends the protected-mode initialization messages to the driver. Windows 95 also stores this value in the *DDB_Reference_Data* field of the device descriptor block you create with the Declare_Virtual_Device macro.

In Windows 95, you can use the *LDRSRV_Copy_Extended_Memory* service to allocate and initialize a block of extended memory, whose address you would then pass back in register EDX for eventual use by the protected-mode parts of your driver. For example, the real-mode initializer for the Windows 95 Configuration Manager uses this service to pass a rather lengthy data area to its own protected-mode initialization functions. The data area contains information about the current hardware profile. In previous versions of Windows, before *LDRSRV_Copy_Extended_Memory* existed, you would have allocated real-mode memory and passed its address to your protected-mode initializer via register EDX. Since no one released that memory until Windows exited, it created a permanent blot on every MS-DOS virtual machine. Not only does *LDRSRV_Copy_Extended_Memory* avoid fragmenting real-mode memory, but you *must* use it because Windows 95 frees any memory allocated by real-mode initializers before switching to protected mode.

Protected-Mode Initialization

After determining which drivers to load, the VMM switches the processor from real mode to protected mode. The switch occurs while the processor is disabled for interrupts. The VMM then sends each device driver's control procedure a Sys_Critical_Init message. When all drivers have processed the message, the VMM enables the processor for interrupts and sends each driver a Device_Init message. Then it sends each driver an Init_Complete message to finish off the initialization process.

The VMM sends these messages to drivers in ascending initialization order, as specified in the respective Declare_Virtual_Device macros. Each of the drivers supplied by Microsoft has an initialization order constant defined in the VMM.H file. Here is a brief excerpt from the list of constants:

```
#define VMPOLL_INIT_ORDER      0x064000000
#define UNDEFINED_INIT_ORDER   0x080000000
#define WINDEBUG_INIT_ORDER    0x081000000
#define VDMAD_INIT_ORDER       0x090000000
```

In other words, WINDEBUG initializes after VMPOLL and before VDMAD.

Initialization order sometimes matters for the same reason that the order of loading MS-DOS drivers or TSRs often matters: the last program to hook an interrupt has priority in handling it. Or you may need to rely on services provided by another VxD, in which case you must initialize after it. If you don't care what order your driver is initialized in, choose *Undefined_Init_Order*. If you want to initialize just before or just after a particular device, choose a value somewhat smaller or larger than that device's initialization order. There's a lot of room between adjacent initialization order constants so that you can leave room for other people to get between you and your neighbors. Therefore, allow a gap of about 1000h between your device and the device you care about.

Calling Sequences

The VMM uses the same calling sequence for each of the three protected-mode initialization messages. Table 8-4 shows the contents of the general registers for these messages.

Register	Contents
EAX	0 (Sys_Critical_Init), 1 (Device_Init), or 2 (Init_Complete).
EBX	Handle (VM control block address) of System VM.
EDX	Reference data from real-mode initializer, or 0 if no real-mode initializer defined.
ESI	Address of command tail for VMM386.EXE. This is the address of the command tail in the Program Segment Prefix (PSP), which has a leading count byte, the command-line argument string, and a trailing 0Dh.

Table 8-4. *Register contents for protected-mode initialization control messages.*

If your VxD returns with the carry flag set (or with a C-language return value of FALSE) from any one of these three control messages, the VMM aborts loading this particular device driver. Your VxD should clear the carry flag (or return TRUE) to signify normal completion.

A skeleton VxD—written in C with an assembly-language control procedure—that handles all three of the initialization messages looks like this (this code is on the companion disc in the \CHAP08\C-DDK directory):

DEVDCL.ASM

```
;DEVDCL.ASM -- Assembly-language interfaces for sample VxD

    .386p
    include vmm.inc
    include debug.inc

Declare_Virtual_Device MYVXD, 1, 0, MYVXD_control,\
    Undefined_Device_ID, Undefined_Init_Order

Begin_Control_Dispatch MYVXD
```

(continued)

continued

```
Control_Dispatch Sys_Critical_Init, OnDeviceInit, sCall,<ebx, edx>
Control_Dispatch Device_Init, OnSysCriticalInit, sCall,<ebx, edx>
Control_Dispatch Init_Complete, OnInitComplete, sCall,<ebx, edx>

End_Control_Dispatch    MYVXD

    end
```

MYVXD.C

```c
// MYVXD.C -- Sample virtual device driver

#define WANTVXDWRAPS

#include <basedef.h>
#include <vmm.h>
#include <debug.h>
#include <vxdwraps.h>

#pragma VxD_ICODE_SEG
#pragma VxD_IDATA_SEG

BOOL _stdcall OnDeviceInit(PVMMCB hVM, DWORD refdata)
{
    return TRUE;
}

BOOL _stdcall OnSysCriticalInit(PVMMCB hVM, DWORD refdata)
{
    return TRUE;
}

BOOL _stdcall OnInitComplete(PVMMCB hVM, DWORD refdata)
{
    return TRUE;
}
```

Sys_Critical_Init

The VMM sends device drivers the Sys_Critical_Init message after switching to protected mode but before enabling interrupts. Most device drivers don't need to handle this message. Reasons why you might need to handle it include the following:

■   Your driver is acting as the DOS extender for a software interrupt. That is, your driver is responsible for fielding protected-mode calls to an MS-DOS or BIOS software interrupt and executing the interrupt in

V86 mode, probably after translating pointer arguments from protected-mode to real-mode format. You should hook your interrupt (using *Set_PM_Int_Vector*) during Sys_Critical_Init so that all other VxDs are free to call your interrupt via *Exec_VxD_Int* when they get their Device_Init call.

■ Your driver is responsible for some other service that VxDs will be calling during Device_Init. For example, the V86MMGR device takes over management of upper memory blocks during Sys_Critical_Init, which makes it possible for other VxDs to access all of the memory that real-mode programs were using before Windows 95 started up.

■ You want to provide a default interrupt handler that will be called last. By hooking the interrupt during Sys_Critical_Init, your driver takes precedence over the default handler that the VMM installs (because the VMM initializes ahead of your driver) but defers to device drivers that hook the interrupt during Device_Init or later.

■ Your driver exports VxD services to a driver whose initialization occurs earlier than yours. You might, therefore, need to initialize some data in order to respond to service calls during Device_Init.

It should go without saying that your driver must not enable interrupts while processing this message. Don't use services (such as *Exec_Int*) that execute real-mode code either. Finally, do the minimum possible amount of work during this message to avoid losing hardware interrupts due to excessive latency.

Device_Init

Windows 95 sends the Device_Init message after it enables interrupts. Most device drivers perform the bulk of their initialization in response to this message. Because interrupts are enabled, you can perform time-consuming operations without adversely affecting the system, and you can execute real-mode code. I'm being deliberately vague about what you should do during Device_Init because it all depends on the purpose of your VxD.

Init_Complete

After it initializes all device drivers, but before it releases initialization segments and takes the instance snapshot described in Chapter 10, the VMM sends the Init_Complete message.

Few device drivers need to process the Init_Complete message. One reason for doing so originates in the DOSMGR device, as follows: It's usually necessary for a real-mode MS-DOS device driver to instance all or part of its own memory. Modern drivers hook INT 2Fh and use the INT 2Fh, function 1605h, broadcast to do this, but a VxD may need to take care of this housekeeping detail for a real-mode driver that isn't Windows 95–aware. The *DOSMGR_Instance_Device* service does this, but it's only available during Init_Complete.

Services That Can Be Useful During Initialization

Your driver might need to interrogate entries in the registry or in the SYSTEM.INI file during initialization. You can use several groups of services for this purpose:

■ The registry services (such as *_RegQueryValue*) provide access to the registry database.

■ The get profile services (such as *Get_Profile_Decimal_Int*) read values from the SYSTEM.INI file.

■ The convert services (such as *Convert_Boolean_String*) convert strings to numeric values. Usually, you read the strings from the SYSTEM.INI file via *Get_Profile_String*.

There are other operations that you can do only during device initialization— *Get_Name_Of_Ugly_TSR*, for example, allows a device driver to see if an "uncooperative" TSR might prevent the driver from operating correctly but is only useful while the driver is initializing (if then).

All of the services described here except the registry services are physically located in the initialization code segment and therefore become unavailable after Init_Complete.

Using Registry Services The following paragraphs illustrate the use of initialization services to configure a driver. Suppose that you've written a driver named MYVXD.VXD that virtualizes an I/O port. For the sake of argument, let's assume that MYVXD is a "legacy" device for which none of the Plug and Play architecture of Windows 95 is relevant. Suppose further that you've followed the preferred practice and used the system registry to load the driver. Under the key \\HKLM\System\CurrentControlSet\Services\VxD\MYVXD you would have these values:

```
StaticVxD=c:\MyProd\Myvxd.vxd
Port=1234h
```

The StaticVxD entry causes your driver to be loaded. The Port entry, which should contain binary data, provides the crucial piece of configuration data to your driver by means of registry services:

```
extern VxD_Desc_Block MYVXD_DDB;

BOOL __stdcall OnDeviceInit(PVMMCB hVM, DWORD refdata)
    {                                    //OnDeviceInit
    char regpath[256];
    char *p;
```

```
HKEY hkey;
DWORD port;
DWORD cbdata = sizeof(port);

_GetRegistryPath(&MYVXD_DDB, regpath, sizeof(regpath));

p = regpath + strlen(regpath);
while (p > regpath && p[-1] == ' ')
    --p;   // trim trailing blanks from name
*p = 0;

_RegOpenKey(HKEY_LOCAL_MACHINE, regpath, &hkey);
_RegQueryValueEx(hkey, "Port", NULL, NULL, (PBYTE) &port,
    &cbdata);
_RegCloseKey(hkey);
return TRUE;
}                                   //OnDeviceInit
```

_GetRegistryPath retrieves the registry path responsible for MYVXD being loaded in the first place. In the case we're discussing, this will be the string

```
System\CurrentControlSet\Services\VxD\Myvxd
```

It turns out that the path returned by *_GetRegistryPath* ends in the 8-byte, blank-padded name of your device, taken directly from the DDB. Before you can use it in a call to *_RegOpenKey*, you must remove the trailing blanks. After you open the key, you can then interrogate configuration values like Port by calling *_RegQuery-ValueEx*. When you're done, you must close the registry key by calling *_RegCloseKey*.

During initialization, you only have access to the HKEY_LOCAL_MACHINE branch of the registry. After Device_Init, you can access the entire registry.

Using Profile Services The old-fashioned way to load a driver is by means of a device= statement in the SYSTEM.INI file. An equally old-fashioned way to record configuration data is to use traditional .INI file settings. You might, for example, expect a SYSTEM.INI file to contain entries like these:

```
[386enh]
device=c:\MyProd\myvxd.vxd
...
[myvxd]
port=1234h
```

Code equivalent to the earlier registry example would be as follows:

```
BOOL __stdcall OnDeviceInit(PVMMCB hVM, DWORD refdata)
    {                               //OnDeviceInit
    DWORD port = Get_Profile_Hex_Int(-1, "myvxd", "port");
    return TRUE;
    }                               //OnDeviceInit
```

Although this is simpler, it won't be as durable, and it won't fit as well into standard user interfaces for configuring devices. It will, however, also work in Windows 3.1.

Termination

Having been present at the Big Bang of system startup, static VxDs also have the honor of attending the Big Crunch when Windows 95 implodes back to real-mode MS-DOS. The VMM sends four system control messages to any VxD that happens to still be loaded at shutdown time:

- System_Exit announces that Windows 95 is about to shut down. The processor is still in protected mode, and it's still safe to execute real-mode code in the System VM. All other VMs have been destroyed by this time, however, and the Windows KERNEL module has exited.

- System_Exit2 follows on the heels of System_Exit. The two messages mean the same thing. The VMM sends System_Exit2 in reverse initialization order, however, to allow VxDs to rely, if necessary, on services provided by VxDs having earlier initialization orders. You should handle System_Exit2 instead of System_Exit in any new VxD.

- After all VxDs have handled the two system exit messages, the VMM disables interrupts and sends each VxD a Sys_Critical_Exit message.

- Finally, the VMM sends each VxD a Sys_Critical_Exit2 message. Like System_Exit2, this message arrives in reverse initialization order.

Most VxDs don't need to handle any of these system shutdown messages. However, you might need to handle one of them if you've done anything to the real-mode image that will make it unusable. For example, the V86MMGR device overstores the entry point to the XMS server with a breakpoint when Windows 95 starts up. It needs to restore the entry point to normal functioning when Windows 95 shuts down.

DYNAMIC VXDS

Windows 95 can dynamically load and unload device drivers. The primary motivation for this feature is to support dynamic hardware reconfiguration, but you can also use this feature to load and unload drivers whose only purpose is to support your own application.

To make your device driver capable of being dynamically loaded, you must do two things:

- Build the driver as a Windows 95–only file. Windows 3.1 drivers can't be dynamically loaded. (This step amounts to not defining the preprocessor macro WIN31COMPAT in your assemblies and compilations.)

- Add the keyword DYNAMIC to the VXD statement in your driver's module definition file:

```
VXD MYVXD DYNAMIC
```

In the remainder of this section, I'll describe how an application can load and unload a driver dynamically and how Windows 95 initializes and terminates a dynamically loaded driver.

Thirty-Two–bit Applications

The dynamic loading interface for a 32-bit application revolves around the regular Win32 API call named *CreateFile*. To load the driver, call *CreateFile* with the following peculiar set of parameters:

```
HANDLE hDevice = CreateFile("\\\\.\\pathname", 0, 0,
    NULL, 0, FILE_FLAG_DELETE_ON_CLOSE, NULL);
```

Most of the parameters don't matter when you use *CreateFile* this way, so you can leave them as 0. The curious name prefix \\.\ (recall that C undoubles the backslashes) indicates that you want Windows 95 to load a device driver and give you back a special device handle. Usually, of course, *CreateFile* opens a file for reading and/or writing. I don't want to offend whoever designed this interface for driver loading, but I think it's very surprising to overload a common API in this way. Sample code to implement and load a dynamic VxD is included on the companion disc in the \CHAP08\DYNALOAD-DDK and \CHAP08\DYNALOAD-VTOOLSD directories.

The next-to-last argument in this call to *CreateFile* is the attributes-and-flags argument. Using *FILE_FLAG_DELETE_ON_CLOSE* causes Windows 95 to automatically unload the driver when you later call *CloseHandle*:

```
CloseHandle(hDevice);
```

As usual, *CreateFile* returns *INVALID_HANDLE_VALUE* (in other words, -1) if it can't load the driver.

You must do one other thing to dynamically load a driver with this interface: you must handle the W32_DEVICEIOCONTROL control message in your VxD. The

VWIN32 VxD uses this control message to handle *DeviceIoControl* calls from Win32 applications. It also sends the message to a VxD when it dynamically loads the driver because of an application call to *CreateFile*. The minimal handler would be as follows:

```
#include <vwin32.h>
DWORD __stdcall OnW32DeviceIoControl(PDIOCPARAMETERS p)
    {                              // OnW32DeviceIoControl
    switch (p->dwIoControlCode)
        {                          // process control call
        case DIOC_GETVERSION:
        return 0;
        }                          // process control call
    }                              // OnW32DeviceIoControl
```

I can think of no good reason *why* sending a W32_DEVICEIOCONTROL message has to be part of implementing *CreateFile*; like so many things in Windows, it just *is*.

Sixteen-bit Applications

Sixteen-bit applications (in both real mode and protected mode) load a virtual device driver dynamically by calling the VXDLDR driver's API. This is very different, and much more complicated, than what a 32-bit application does. The first step is to locate the API entry point using the INT 2Fh, function 1684h, interface. (I'll describe this important interface in more general detail in Chapter 10.) Here's what the code looks like:

```
include vmm.inc  ; for VXDLDR_DEVICE_ID
...
vxdldr dd 0      ; address of VXDLDR API entry point
...
mov   ax, 1684h  ; function 1684h: find VxD API entry point
xor   di, di     ; clear ES:DI first to detect failure
mov   es, di     ;  ..
mov   bx, VXDLDR_DEVICE_ID ;
int   2Fh        ; locate loader's API entry point
mov   ax, es     ; was entry point found?
or    ax, di     ;  ..
jz    fail       ; if not, can't dynamically load drivers

mov   word ptr vxdldr, di
mov   word ptr vxdldr+2, es
```

Once you've located and saved the API address for VXDLDR, you can set register AX to a function code and call the entry point to load or unload virtual device drivers. To load a driver, include VXDLDR.H or VXDLDR.INC and code the following:

```
include vxdldr.inc          ; for VXDLDR services
...
mov     ax, VXDLDR_APIFUNC_LOADDEVICE ; i.e., 1
mov     dx, offset filename  ; DS:DX -> filename + 0
call    [vxdldr]             ; try to load driver
jc      fail                 ; CF set if unable to load
```

In this code sample, *filename* identifies a null-terminated string containing the pathname of the driver file you want to load. If your driver is named MYVXD.VXD, you would code

```
filename db    'myvxd.vxd', 0
```

To unload a driver, you would code

```
mov     ax, VXDLDR_APIFUNC_UNLOADDEVICE ; i.e., 2
mov     dx, offset name      ; DS:DX -> driver name + 0
call    [vxdldr]             ; try to unload driver
jc      fail                 ; CF set if unable to unload
```

In this case, *name* identifies a null-terminated string containing the internal name of the driver. If you named your driver MYVXD in the Declare_Virtual_Device macro, you would code:

```
name    db     'MYVXD', 0
```

Note that you use two *different* formats for the name you pass to the load and unload services. The *LOADDEVICE* function wants a pathname. The *UNLOADDEVICE* function, on the other hand, wants just the name of the device—namely, the string that appears in the VxD's Declare_Virtual_Device macro.

INITIALIZING AND TERMINATING A DYNAMIC VXD

Windows 95 initializes a dynamically loaded device driver by sending it a Sys_Dynamic_Device_Init message. Prior to unloading a dynamically loaded driver, it sends a Sys_Dynamic_Device_Exit message.

Because Windows 95 discarded the initialization segments and took the instance snapshot long ago, a dynamically loaded driver can't use any of the following initialization-only services.

_Add_Global_V86_Data_Area	Get_Next_Arena
_AddFreePhysPage	Get_Next_Profile_String
_AddInstanceItem	Get_Profile_Boolean
_Allocate_Global_V86_Data_Area	Get_Profile_Decimal_Int
_Allocate_Temp_V86_Data_Area	Get_Profile_Fixed_Point
_Free_Temp_V86_Data_Area	Get_Profile_Hex_Int
_GetGlblRng0V86IntBase	Get_Profile_String
_SetFreePhysRegCalBk	GetDOSVectors
_SetLastV86Page	Locate_Byte_In_ROM
Allocate_PM_App_CB_Area	MMGR_SetNULPageAddr
Convert_Boolean_String	OpenFile
Convert_Decimal_String	PageFile_Init_File
Convert_Fixed_Point_String	Set_Physical_HMA_Alias
Convert_Hex_String	V86MMGR_NoUMBInitCalls
DOSMGR_BackFill_Allowed	V86MMGR_Set_Mapping_Info
DOSMGR_Enable_Indos_Polling	V86MMGR_SetAvailMapPgs
DOSMGR_Instance_Device	V86MMGR_SetLocalA20
Get_Name_Of_Ugly_TSR	VDMAD_Reserve_Buffer_Space

A dynamically loaded device should obviously take care to unhook any interrupts it hooked and, in general, to undo any other operations whose continued effect would be inappropriate.

One exception to the injunction that a dynamically loaded device should clean up completely has to do with V86-mode and protected-mode callbacks allocated via the *Allocate_V86_Call_Back* and *Allocate_PM_Call_Back* services, respectively. There is no service for releasing these objects. If a device driver were to reallocate a callback each time it was dynamically loaded, therefore, it would waste resources. You deal with this problem by using the static code and data segments:

```
VxD_STATIC_DATA_SEG
mycallback dd    0
loaded    dd    0
VxD_STATIC_DATA_ENDS

BeginProc myfunction, static
          cmp    loaded, 1    ; is VxD really loaded?
```

```
            je     @f               ; if yes, good
            [failsafe code that doesn't leave static segment]
@@:         jmp    realcallback  ; transfer to real callback
            ...
EndProc myfunction

BeginProc OnSysDynamicDeviceInit, init
            mov    loaded, 1
            cmp    mycallback, 0
            jne    @f
            mov    esi, offset32 myfunction
            VMMCall Allocate_PM_Call_Back
            mov    mycallback, eax
@@:         ...
EndProc   OnSysDynamicDeviceInit

BeginProc OnSysDynamicDeviceExit, locked
            mov    loaded, 0
            ...
EndProc   OnSysDynamicDeviceExit

BeginProc realcallback, locked
            ...
EndProc   realcallback
```

(I've used assembly language for this sample because it's such a pain in the neck to code callbacks purely in C.)

One final thing to emphasize is that dynamic VxDs are not really very different from static VxDs, despite the differing treatment I gave them in this chapter. Dynamic VxDs receive two system control messages (Sys_Dynamic_Device_Init and Sys_Dynamic_Device_Exit) that static VxDs never see. Other than that, and other than the restrictions noted about services that can't be called after Init_Complete, any code you could put in a static VxD could also appear in a dynamic VxD, and vice versa. Moreover, while it's loaded, a dynamic VxD receives all the system control messages that occur. Most dynamic VxDs pay no attention to these messages, of course, but they could if they wanted to.

Chapter 9

Basic VxD Programming Techniques

The previous chapters have brought you to the point where you now know enough about VxD programming to be able to write meaningful drivers. The application programming interface you use when you write VxDs revolves around what Microsoft calls *VxD services*. In this chapter, I talk first about the mechanics of using this API from assembly language and C. Then I discuss the three major data structures you need to deal with as a VxD writer: the VM control block, the client register structure, and the thread control block. With these basics out of the way, I describe some of the API services that are common to most VxDs. These include services for memory management, event management, and thread synchronization.

THE VxD SERVICE INTERFACE

In this section, you'll learn how to call the service entry points in other VxDs and how to export a service API of your own. We've already been over some of this ground in earlier chapters. In particular, you already know that an assembly-language driver uses the VMMCall and VxDCall macros to generate INT 20h instructions for dynamically linking to service functions. This section describes the mechanics of using these macros. You also know that frameworks for C or C++ VxD programming provide wrappers for the INT 20h interface, but you will need to know how to write your own wrappers to cover omissions and mistakes in your framework. Finally, you'll learn how to define and implement a service API in your own driver.

The VMMCall and VxDCall Macros

Assembly-language drivers use the VMMCall and VxDCall macros to invoke services. VMMCall is for the services exported by the VMM itself; VxDCall is for services exported by other VxDs. Both macros have exactly the same syntax:

```
VMMCall service            ; assembly-language services
VMMCall _service, <args>   ; C-convention services
```

or

```
VxDCall service
VxDCall _service, <args>
```

VxD services use two calling conventions. The assembly-language convention applies to most of the services left over from the days of Windows 3.0 and Windows 3.1 and relies on registers and flags for parameter passing and return values. For example, *Get_Cur_VM_Handle* is a register-oriented service whose return value is in the EBX register and that specifically doesn't change any other register:

```
VMMCall Get_Cur_VM_Handle
[code that references VM control block via EBX]
```

The C-language convention passes parameters on the stack and returns results in the EAX register. C-convention services preserve the EBX, ESI, and EDI registers; they might modify the other registers and the flags. All C-convention services have names beginning with a leading underscore. Conversely, except for a few VWIN32 services, any service whose name begins with an underscore uses the C convention. For example, the *_HeapAllocate* service allocates memory from a ring-zero heap for use by a VxD:

```
VMMCall _HeapAllocate, <<size somestruc>, HeapZeroInit>
test    eax, eax
jz      failure
mov     address, eax
```

When you call a C-convention service using the VMMCall macro, you use angle brackets to delimit the arguments. To specify an individual argument that the assembler's macro processor would normally parse as more than one token, use an additional pair of angle brackets. The return value from the service appears in the EAX register. So, in this example, we specify two arguments to the *_HeapAllocate* service: the first argument is *size somestruc* and gives the number of bytes we want to allocate; the second argument is the manifest constant *HeapZeroInit*, which indicates that we want *_HeapAllocate* to zero the memory it allocates.

When you want to call the services exported by a VxD other than the VMM, you usually need to include a special header file that defines them. These services always include the name of the VxD as a prefix; the leading underscore for a C-convention service appears before this name prefix. You then use the VxDCall macro (instead of VMMCall). For example, the SHELL device exports a service you can use to determine its version number:

```
include shell.inc
...
VxDCall SHELL_Get_Version
...
```

I want to explain one more variation on VMMCall and VxDCall. Sometimes a VxD function ends in a call to some other VxD service. In their quest for ultimate performance, Microsoft provided the VMMJmp and VxDJmp macros. As you might expect, these macros jump to the target without pushing a return address onto the stack. When the called service returns, it bypasses its immediate caller and thereby saves one RET instruction. For example, the I/O service routine for a trapped port conventionally ends in a jump to *Simulate_IO*:

```
BeginProc IOCallback
    ...
    VMMJmp Simulate_IO       ; doesn't return
EndProc   IOCallback
```

NOTE Recall that BeginProc and EndProc contain call logging code in a debug build. To avoid screwing this up, VMMJmp and VxDJmp contain conditional assembly so that, in a debug build, they do a call followed by a return. In a retail build, they just do a jump.

Wrappers for C-Language Callers

Chapter 7 talked at length about how and why the DDK and third-party toolkits such as VTOOLSD from Vireo Software offer C-language wrappers for VxD services. In general, you don't explicitly reference the VMMCall or VxDCall macros in a C program. Instead, you call the wrapper function. For example, this is a typical call using the Microsoft DDK:

```
#define WANTVXDWRAPS
#include <basedef.h>
#include <vmm.h>
```

```
#include <shell.h>
#include <vxdwraps.h>
...
PVOID address = _HeapAllocate(sizeof(somestruc), HEAPZEROINIT);
if (!address)
    // handle error
...
WORD wShellVer = SHELL_Get_Version();
```

In this example, I'm showing a call to *_HeapAllocate*, a C-convention service for which the VMMCall macro would be appropriate in assembly language; and a call to *SHELL_Get_Version*, a register-convention service (that is, a service that accepts parameters in registers and returns results in registers) for which the VxDCall macro would be appropriate. You'll notice that the differences between the various ways of calling VxD services disappear when you program in C. The VTOOLSD C framework approach is similar, but you include fewer header files. You also take into account a difference in the declared return value from *SHELL_Get_Version*:

```
#include <vtoolsc.h>
...
PVOID address = _HeapAllocate(sizeof(somestruc), HEAPZEROINIT);
if (!address)
    // handle error
...
DWORD dwShellVer = SHELL_Get_Version();
```

NOTE One of the annoying inconsistencies between VTOOLSD and the DDK is the spelling of the VMMCall macro. Vireo spells it VMMcall (with a small *c*), whereas Microsoft spells it VMMCall (with a capital *C*). Both companies agree on VxDCall, however. Only Microsoft defined the VxDJmp and VMMJmp macros, though.

You sometimes need to write your own wrappers for service functions. This need can arise frequently when you use the DDK, but it can also arise when you use VTOOLSD. Most of the time, you can rely on inline assembly language to do the job. For example, if you're using the DDK and need to retrieve an entry in the SYSTEM.INI file using a call to *Get_Profile_Decimal_Int* (one of the functions for which there's no predefined wrapper), you could place the following declaration in a C file:

```
#pragma warning(disable:4035)
DWORD VXDINLINE Get_Profile_Decimal_Int(PCHAR pszProfile,
    PCHAR pszKeyName, DWORD dwDefault)
    {
    _asm mov eax, dwDefault
    _asm mov esi, pszProfile
    _asm mov edi, pszKeyName
    VMMCall(Get_Profile_Decimal_Int);
    }
#pragma warning(default:4035)
```

VXDINLINE expands to *static __inline*, causing the compiler to generate inline code whenever you call the function. Since this wrapper doesn't appear to return a value, the Microsoft C compiler would ordinarily generate a warning (#4035). You can overcome the annoyance of the warning by disabling it as shown here or by storing register EAX into a dummy variable that you then explicitly return.

When you define your own inline function wrappers, you sometimes also need to instruct the compiler about registers that the service entry will modify. Otherwise, the compiler's optimization logic might mistakenly think that it can reuse the contents of those registers. VMM.H contains a *Touch_Register* macro to make the possible modification manifest; the macro simply generates an XOR instruction to clear the specified register. Here's a sample wrapper for a C-convention service that might destroy registers ECX and EDX:

```
DWORD VXDINLINE _TestGlobalV86Mem(DWORD VMLinAddr,
    DWORD nBytes, DWORD flags)
    {
    DWORD result;
    Touch_Register(ECX)
    Touch_Register(EDX)
    _asm push flags
    _asm push nBytes
    _asm push VMLinAddr
    VMMCall(_TestGlobalV86Mem)
    _asm add esp, 12
    _asm mov result, eax
    return result;
    }
```

In this example, I used the technique of a dummy return variable to avoid warning #4035. The XOR instructions generated by *Touch_Register* are unnecessary, but calling this macro does serve the purpose of avoiding optimization-induced failures.

BUILDING A WRAPPER FOR A VxD SERVICE CALL

I can't describe a purely mechanical process whereby you can transform documentation for an assembly-language VxD service into a C-language wrapper, but I can present a few hints that will help you perform this often necessary task.

If you're trying to wrap a C-convention service, there's a very simple procedure that you can reliably follow. Recall that C-convention services usually have names that begin with an underscore and that they expect their arguments on the stack. For these services, simply declare an inline function that demands the same arguments in the same order as the documentation specifies. Use *DWORD* as the type for any argument that's specified as a mask or an integer. Whenever possible, use a specific *typedef* name for a pointer argument (pointer arguments often have an *offset32* directive in the documentation) to gain the maximum advantage from the compiler's error checking; use *PVOID* or *PFN* for nonspecific pointers to data or functions, respectively. Define the function using the *__declspec(naked)* directive and provide a body containing just a *VMMJmp* or *VxDJmp* (they are equivalent in a C program) to the appropriate service name.

For example, if you needed to write a wrapper for the *_HeapAllocate* service (you don't—the standard DDK already provides a wrapper for this commonly used function), you would consult the online documentation and discover this assembly-language prototype:

```
include vmm.inc
VMMcall _HeapAllocate, <nbytes, flags>

or      eax, eax          ; zero if error
jz      not_allocated
mov     [Address], eax    ; address of memory block
```

Using the method outlined above, you'd end up with this function declaration in one of your header files:

```
PVOID VXDINLINE __declspec(naked) _HeapAllocate(DWORD nbytes,
    DWORD flags)
    {                       // _HeapAllocate
    VMMJmp(_HeapAllocate)
    }                       // _HeapAllocate
```

For register-convention services, you can follow a more-or-less obvious procedure to transform the argument specification into a function prototype.

For example, the documentation for the *Get_Profile_Decimal_Int* service described in the text is as follows:

```
mov     eax, Default           ; default value
mov     esi, OFFSET32 Profile  ; points to section name
mov     edi, OFFSET32 Keyname  ; points to entry name
VMMcall Get_Profile_Decimal_Int

jc      not_found              ; carry set if entry not found
jz      no_value               ; zero set if entry has no value

mov     [Value], eax           ; entry value
```

The documentation goes on to specify that the *Profile* and *Keyname* arguments are null-terminated character strings. This much of the documentation therefore leads to the following (incomplete) function prototype:

```
DWORD VXDINLINE Get_Profile_Decimal_Int(PCHAR pszProfile,
    PCHAR pszKeyName, DWORD dwDefault
```

I haven't added the closing right parenthesis to this prototype yet because this particular service has more than one output. In particular, the flags returned by this service indicate two error and near-error conditions. If the carry flag is set, either the entry doesn't exist or its value isn't a valid decimal integer. If the carry flag is clear but the zero flag is set, the section and keyword exist but have no value (this can happen if the SYSTEM.INI file includes a Keyname= statement with nothing on the righthand side of the equal sign). If both the carry and zero flags are clear, the value exists, and register EAX holds the converted value. In either of the error cases, EAX holds the default value.

Given the complexity of the error cases, you might decide to add a store argument to hold an error code, yielding the following complete prototype:

```
DWORD VXDINLINE Get_Profile_Decimal_Int(PCHAR pszProfile,
    PCHAR pszKeyName, DWORD dwDefault, PDWORD pError);
```

Or you might decide that your purposes require only that you obtain *a* value, which can just as well be the default as one read from SYSTEM.INI. In that case, you wouldn't add a store argument at all.

Once you know the prototype for the function, it's usually a simple matter to code the inline assembly language to implement it. In the example I showed on page 185, I basically transcribed the documentation of the function into my program.

The centerpiece of these function wrapper examples is the VMMCall macro. VMMCall is a preprocessor macro that expands into an INT 20h instruction with the necessary inline data. For example, *VMMCall(Get_Profile_Decimal_Int)* generates the following code (*Get_Profile_Decimal_Int* has service identifier 000100ABh):

```
_asm
    {
    int 20h
    _emit 0abh
    _emit 0
    _emit 1
    _emit 0
    }
```

Microsoft could have included (but didn't include) a large number of #define statements for constants like *Get_Profile_Decimal_Int*. Instead, the DDK headers contrive to define this and other service identifiers as values of an enumerated type. The headers contain the following:

```
Begin_Service_Table(VMM, VMM)
VMM_Service(Get_VMM_Version, LOCAL)
...
VMM_Service(Get_Profile_Decimal_Int, VMM_ICODE)
VMM_Service(Convert_Decimal_String, VMM_ICODE)
...
End_Service_Table(VMM, VMM)
```

This code expands into the following enumeration:

```
enum VMM_SERVICES {
VMM_dummy = (VMM_DEVICE_ID << 16) - 1, // i.e., 0000FFFF
__Get_VMM_Version,          // i.e., 00010000
...
__Get_Profile_Decimal_Int, // i.e., 000100AB
__Convert_Decimal_String,  // i.e., 000100AC

...
Num_VMM_Services};
```

This technique cleverly relies on the fact that C automatically adds 1 to the value of an enumeration constant to get the next constant value unless you specify some other starting point.

Notice that the symbol that the *VMM_Service* macro actually defines is the same as the service name but with two leading underscores. This difference in names lets you define a function with the same name as the service. (If the name of the enumeration constant weren't decorated, you would get a complaint about multiple definitions of the symbol.)

Although I cast the preceding discussion in terms of the Microsoft DDK, you can do exactly the same things with VTOOLSD because Vireo Software distributes a number of DDK-like headers. There's one awkward situation that arises with VTOOLSD that you need to know about, however. If you want to make an inline call to a VxD service for which VTOOLSD *already contains* a wrapper, you must do an apparently strange thing:

```
#undef Get_VMM_Version
VMMcall(Get_VMM_Version)
...
```

The reason for the inexplicable #undef statement is that the VTOOLSD headers actually include #define statements that define each wrapped function in terms of the current code segment. Thus, when you switch to, say, the locked code segment, you'll end up getting the benefit of a definition like this one:

```
#define Get_VMM_Version LOCK_Get_VMM_Version
```

Normally convenient, this definition prevents you from using the normal symbol in the *VMMcall* macro, because the compiler expands it to *LOCK_Get_VMM_Version*. *VMMcall* then generates errors when it tries to use the undefined symbol *__LOCK_Get_VMM_Version* in its own expansion.

Defining Your Own Services

So far, I've talked about how you can call the services exported by other VxDs. It's also possible for you to define your own services in a static VxD that other VxDs can call. Once again, you have to dust off your assembly-language skills unless you're using VTOOLSD. To keep things as simple as possible, let's assume that your MYVXD device needs to export a service that will return its own version number. The conventional way to export services consists of two steps: creating a header or include file for potential callers, and defining a service table in the module where your Declare_Virtual_Device macro is. The include file (MYVXD.INC) would look something like this fragment:

```
MYVXD_DEVICE_ID equ 4242h
Begin_Service_Table MYVXD
MYVXD_Service  MYVXD_Get_Version, LOCAL
End_Service_Table MYVXD
```

In general, you create an include file that defines your device identifier (a unique ID that you have to ask Microsoft to assign to your device) and lists the services you're exporting. In this example, the Begin_Service_Table macro defines a new macro named MYVXD_Service that you call one or more times to specify your services. That macro in turn defines a manifest constant that identifies a service by device ID and service ordinal. In this example, the one and only call to MYVXD_Service would define the symbol *@@MYVXD_Get_Version* as equal to 42420000h.

By convention, you should include a *Get_Version* service as the first service. You should also name each service with a leading underscore if it must be called using the C convention, or *without* a leading underscore if it must be called with parameters in registers. There are no other rules or suggestions about what additional services (if any) you define. But changing the order of the services in the list requires all users of your VxD services to recompile. For this reason, you can't change this order once you distribute your VxD to the field unless you have control of all potential callers.

Applications that want to call one of your services do so in a way that should now look familiar:

```
include myvxd.inc
...
VxDCall MYVXD_Get_Version
```

You define a service table and the functions that implement the services in your own source code. The service table contains pointers to the service functions. Your device description block (DDB) in turn points to the service table, which is how the VMM finds it in the first place. The easiest way to create the service table is to define the enabling symbol *Create_xxx_Service_Table* and then include your own header file. Then define your DDB by calling Declare_Virtual_Device:

```
.386p
.xlist
include vmm.inc
.list

Create_MYVXD_Service_Table = 1
include myvxd.inc

Declare_Virtual_Device MYVXD, 1, 0, MYVXD_Control, \
            MYVXD_Device_ID, Undefined_Init_Order

Begin_Control_Dispatch MYVXD
End_Control_Dispatch MYVXD

BeginProc MYVXD_Get_Version, service, locked
        mov   ax, word ptr MYVXD_DDB.DDB_Dev_Major_Version
        xchg  ah, al
        clc
        ret
EndProc MYVXD_Get_Version

        end
```

You define the functions that implement your services with the help of the BeginProc and EndProc macros. The *service* parameter indicates that the device service table contains a pointer to the function. The details of the interface to your service function and what it does are pretty much up to you. Your *Get_Version* service, at least, should return with the carry flag clear to indicate success. This return fits into the convention I described in Chapter 4, whereby applications that want to find out if your device driver is loaded will call your *Get_Version* service. If your driver is not loaded, the VMM will fail the call by setting the carry flag. If you don't clear the carry flag, you'll confuse callers into thinking your VxD is not really there.

Where you physically put your service functions is up to you, but your choice has an effect on how you declare the services in your header file. Use the *LOCAL* keyword in the *xxx*_Service macro if you'll define the service function in the same source file that contains the service table. Otherwise, declare the service with no keyword at all to gain the benefit of an automatic *EXTRN* declaration.

At the very start of this section, I said that *static* VxDs could export services to other VxDs. Dynamic VxDs normally don't. The reason is that the two critical data structures associated with services—the DDB and the service table—are both in segments that don't persist when the VxD unloads. Since the VMM snaps the dynamic links to service functions, many other VxDs could have direct pointers through the service table after the VxD is unloaded, and there's no mechanism for unsnapping these links. As if the existence of these pointers weren't trouble enough, other drivers might have done *Hook_Device_Service* calls and thereby patched the service table.

Making Your Services Accessible in C

To allow other VxDs written in C or C++ to call your services, you'll need to provide a C-language header file in addition to an assembly-language include file. You will also want to provide appropriate wrapper functions. Continuing with the previous example, you might create the following MYVXD.H file:

```
#define MYVXD_DEVICE_ID 0x4242

#define MYVXD_Service Declare_Service
#pragma warning(disable:4003) // not enough parameters is okay

Begin_Service_Table(MYVXD)
MYVXD_Service(MYVXD_Get_Version)
End_Service_Table(MYVXD)

WORD VXDINLINE MYVXD_Get_Version(void)
    {
    WORD ver;
    VxDCall(MYVXD_Get_Version)
    _asm mov ver, ax
```

```
    return ver;
    }
```

If you peruse the DDK, you'll notice that Microsoft provides C-language headers (files with an .H extension) and assembly-language include files (files with an .INC extension) for many components of the operating system. It's obvious that Microsoft used an automated process to generate the .INC files from the .H files, but they didn't use the standard H2INC utility that comes with MASM 6.11. Faced with a large project, you might want to create your own tool to translate .H files into .INC files.

Services in VTOOLSD Drivers

When you work with VTOOLSD, you can avoid some of the details I just explained about service entries. First of all, you can declare your service entry points while you're running QuickVxd. (See Figure 9-1.) QuickVxd then generates the necessary service table in your header file and the necessary function skeletons in your source code:

MYVXD.H

```
// MYVXD.h - include file for VxD MYVXD

#include <vtoolsc.h>

#define MYVXD_Major        1
#define MYVXD_Minor        0
#define MYVXD_DeviceID     0x4242
#define MYVXD_Init_Order  UNDEFINED_INIT_ORDER

DWORD __cdecl MYVXD_Get_Version();

Begin_VxD_Service_Table(MYVXD)
    VxD_Service(MYVXD_Get_Version)
End_VxD_Service_Table
```

MYVXD.C

```
// MYVXD.c - main module for VxD MYVXD

#define   DEVICE_MAIN
#include  "myvxd.h"
#undef    DEVICE_MAIN

Declare_Virtual_Device(MYVXD)
DWORD __cdecl MYVXD_Get_Version()
{
    return (MYVXD_Major << 8) | MYVXD_Minor;
}
```

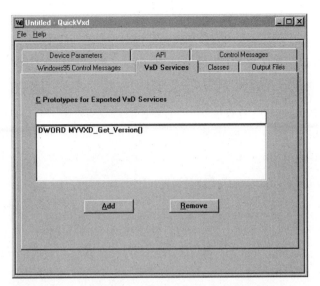

Figure 9-1. *Service functions generated by QuickVxd.*

The trouble is, this code isn't right as it stands. You might notice that *MYVXD_Get_Version* uses the C calling convention, so it should (strictly speaking) have a leading underscore in its name. Yet QuickVxd automatically generated this definition without the underscore. Because this service has no parameters and generates code that alters only the EAX register, the difference between calling sequences doesn't actually matter very much. What *does* matter is that the function doesn't clear the carry flag before returning. You can correct the problem by recoding *MYVXD_Get_Version* as follows:

```
DWORD __declspec(naked) MYVXD_Get_Version()
    {
    _asm
        {
        mov  ax, (MYVXD_Major shl 8) or MYVXD_Minor
        clc
        ret
        }
    }
```

Using *__declspec(naked)* ensures that the compiler won't generate any instructions that might change the carry flag before returning. If you're writing a driver in C, chances are that most of the services you export will use the C calling convention, so you won't need to worry about the carry flag, but you should change the service names to include a leading underscore.

Hooking Service Entry Points

DOS programmers are familiar with the idea of *hooking* an interrupt in order to alter the behavior of the system. A similar kind of redirection is possible with respect to VxD services. By calling *Hook_Device_Service*, one VxD can take over a service entry point belonging to another VxD. For example, the following code (included on the the companion disc in the \CHAP09\SERVICEHOOK-ASM directory) hooks calls to the *DOSMGR_Begin_V86_App* service:

```
VxD_LOCKED_DATA_SEG
next_begin dd 0
VxD_LOCKED_DATA_ENDS
...
BeginProc OnSysDynamicDeviceInit, locked
        GetVxDServiceOrdinal eax, DOSMGR_Begin_V86_App
        mov    esi, offset32 BeginHook
        VMMCall Hook_Device_Service
        jc     initfail
        ...
        clc
        ret

initfail:
        stc
        ret
EndProc  OnSysDynamicDeviceInit...

BeginProc BeginHook, service, hook_proc, next_begin, locked
        ...
        jmp    [next_begin]    ; chain to next hooker
EndProc  BeginHook
```

This sample uses a call to *Hook_Device_Service* to redirect calls to the *DOSMGR_ Begin_V86_App* service to your own *BeginHook* routine. The GetVxDServiceOrdinal macro loads the EAX register with the 32-bit identifier for the service, including the device identifier and the service table index. If the containing device uses *Undefined_Device_ID*, it's still possible to hook one of its services by also loading register EDI with the address of the 8-byte, blank-padded, case-sensitive name of the target device.

You declare the hook function itself with the *Hook_Proc* attribute, which must immediately be followed by the name of a page-locked DWORD (*next_begin* in the sample) in which the VMM saves the address of the previous service entry. The existence of this DWORD is what allows the VMM to implement the

> **NOTE** The GetVxDServiceOrdinal macro simply prefixes the service name with @@. Rather than manually encoding this particular naming convention, you should use the macro, because Microsoft may change the convention in later releases. The purpose of decorating the service names in the first place is to let you give service functions the same names as the services without getting duplicate symbol errors.

Unhook_Device_Service function. Within the hook routine, you do whatever it is that prompted you to intercept this particular service call. Then you chain to the real service entry (or to some previous service hook) by jumping indirectly through the *next_begin* variable.

If you hook a service in a dynamic VxD, you must also take care to unhook it before you unload, as shown in this example:

```
BeginProc OnSysDynamicDeviceExit, locked
        GetVxDServiceOrdinal eax, DOSMGR_Begin_V86_App
        mov    esi, offset32 BeginHook
        VMMCall Unhook_Device_Service
        ...
        clc
        ret
EndProc OnSysDynamicDeviceExit
```

Hooking *DOSMGR_Begin_V86_App* is the official way to learn when applications start in virtual machines. You might hook other services either to monitor them or to substitute your own code. In one project I worked on, a pre-Windows extended DOS TSR needed to perform direct memory access (DMA) transfers. The VDMAD device assumed that any transfer coming from a virtual machine had to be using low-memory addresses, and it therefore automatically added *CB_High_Linear* to each address. The addition produced the wrong result in our situation, since we were already working with physical addresses provided by the DOS extender that supported the TSR. Hooking *VDMAD_Lock_DMA_Region* made it possible to avoid the incorrect address adjustment so that DMA transfers worked correctly.

Besides the provision for unhooking, the Windows 95 implementation of *Hook_Device_Service* provides another advantage in that it avoids a possible problem in hooking an asynchronous service. In Windows 3.1, the following scenario might occur unless you were careful: you call *Hook_Device_Service*, and it successfully hooks the service by modifying the service table entry. Before you can store the previous function address in your chaining variable, however, an interrupt occurs and your hook function gets called. It then tries to chain through the uninitialized variable and crashes the system. Windows 95 closes this hole by disabling interrupts around the code that stores the new and old handler addresses. Thus, only a nonmaskable interrupt (NMI) could possibly lead to any problem.

Your hook procedure gets control with the same entry conditions as the original service and must return with the same exit conditions. You must preserve all registers (including flags) that the original service preserves. You might want to chain to the previous service entry from within your hook procedure. You chain by calling through the DWORD that records the previous entry address, as shown in the fragment on page 194. When you chain to another service handler, you must be sure to duplicate the entry conditions it is expecting. In the case of a register-based service, you must reload *all* registers, not just the ones that are advertised as being used for parameters. In practice, this requirement means that you must use an assembly-language function to hook a register-oriented service so that you can insert PUSHAD and POPAD instructions in the appropriate places.

Hooking device services was mechanically somewhat different in Windows 3.1. First of all, there was no *Unhook_Device_Service* because there were no dynamically loadable VxDs to need it. Furthermore, *Hook_Device_Service* returned the address of the previous service entry in register ESI; you would normally have saved this value so you could chain to the original handler from within your own hook procedure. Previous versions of the DDK defined service identifiers using the documented symbols, so you simply coded

```
MOV EAX, DOSMGR_Begin_V86_App
```

instead of using the GetVxDServiceOrdinal macro. Finally, BeginProc didn't have the *Hook_Proc* option because the details of hooking and chaining were managed totally by the VxDs involved.

Windows 95 can deal with a Windows 3.1 VxD that hooks a service, although it can't remove a Windows 3.1 hook procedure from the chain. The reason that Windows 3.1 VxDs with service hooks work is that the VMM can tell the difference between the new and the old styles of hooking services. The *Hook_Proc* attribute causes BeginProc to generate two extra JMP instructions before the service entry point. The first instruction jumps to the hook procedure; the second jumps indirectly through the previous-function pointer you've provided. These two instructions uniquely identify a hook function to Windows 95. The signature, or its absence, tells the VMM whether it has encountered a new-style hook or an old-style hook.

BASIC DATA STRUCTURES

In this section, I'll describe three basic data structures that pervade VxD programming: the VM control block, the client register structure, and the thread control block.

The VM Control Block

The VMM keeps track of a virtual machine by maintaining a *virtual machine control block*. There's no accepted official acronym for this control block, so I'll use VMCB to simplify discussion. Figure 9-2 shows the very few basic fields Microsoft has chosen to document in the VMCB.

```
struct cb_s {
    ULONG CB_VM_Status;          // 00 status flags
    ULONG CB_High_Linear;        // 04 unique address of V86 memory map
    ULONG CB_Client_Pointer;     // 08 address of client register structure
    ULONG CB_VMID;               // 0C virtual machine ID
    ULONG CB_Signature;          // 10 'VMcb' = 0x62634D56
};
```

Figure 9-2. *Documented fields in the virtual machine control block.*

To explain the *CB_High_Linear* field of the VMCB, I need to digress briefly and describe how Windows 95 provides addressability to the V86 memory area of a virtual machine. While the VM is running, linear addresses 000000h through 10FFEFh (formed from segment:offset addresses ranging from 0000h:0000h through FFFFh:FFFFh) map to the pages that contain that VM's V86 memory. A VxD can also access the very same set of pages by adding *CB_High_Linear* to a V86 linear address. Suppose a particular VM has a high-linear address of C1C00000h. That VM's video RAM is simultaneously accessible with linear addresses 000B8000h and C1CB8000h because the VMM copies the page directory entry describing the 4 MB at C1C00000h into the page table, so it also describes the 4 MB beginning at zero.

CB_Client_Pointer contains the address of the so-called client register structure, which contains images of the general and segment registers pertaining to the V86-mode and protected-mode applications running in the VM.

CB_VMID contains the numeric identifier for this VM. The identifier is a small integer. The System VM always has an ID of 1. The VMM assigns this ID when it creates a virtual machine, and the ID doesn't change thereafter. Once you close a VM, however, the ID becomes available for use by a new VM.

CB_Signature contains the eye-catcher string "VMcb". The signature can be useful to you when you're debugging a driver. The debugging macro Assert_VM_Handle—which generates code only if the *DEBUG* symbol is defined—also checks for this signature.

The VM Control Block Status Flags

Table 9-1 lists the various VM_Status flags. You should treat these flags and all the other fields in the VMCB as read-only.

Name	Mask	Description
VMSTAT_EXCLUSIVE	00000001	Exclusive execution required
VMSTAT_BACKGROUND	00000002	Background execution allowed
VMSTAT_CREATING	00000004	VM is being created
VMSTAT_SUSPENDED	00000008	VM is suspended
VMSTAT_NOT_EXECUTEABLE	00000010	VM has reached non-executable stage of shutdown
VMSTAT_PM_EXEC	00000020	VM is currently executing protected-mode code
VMSTAT_PM_APP	00000040	Protected-mode application is present
VMSTAT_PM_USE32	00000080	Protected-mode application is USE32
VMSTAT_VXD_EXEC	00000100	*Exec_VxD_Int* or *Exec_PM_Int* is active
VMSTAT_HIGH_PRI_BACK	00000200	VM is a high-priority background task
VMSTAT_BLOCKED	00000400	VM is blocked on a semaphore
VMSTAT_AWAKENING	00000800	VM is waking up after being blocked
VMSTAT_PAGEABLEV86	00001000	Part of V86 memory has been marked pageable by DPMI function 0602h
VMSTAT_V86INTSLOCKED	00002000	Nonpageable V86 memory is locked regardless of pager type
VMSTAT_IDLE_TIMEOUT	00004000	VM is scheduled by time slicing scheduler
VMSTAT_IDLE	00008000	VM has released its time slice
VMSTAT_CLOSING	00010000	VM is closing due to Close_VM message

Table 9-1. *Bits within the VM status field.*

The *VMSTAT_PM_APP* flag will be set if code executing in the VM used the DPMI mode-switch routine to switch into protected mode; the *VMSTAT_PM_USE32* flag will be set if the DPMI client indicated that it was a 32-bit program. In this connection, note that Windows 95 itself is a USE16 DPMI client. Of these two bits, therefore, only the *VMSTAT_PM_APP* flag is set for the System VM. The *VMSTAT_PM_EXEC* flag indicates that the VM is currently executing protected-mode code; the alternative is that the VM is executing V86 code.

The *VMSTAT_BACKGROUND* flag corresponds to one of the settings on the Misc tab of an MS-DOS Prompt Properties sheet. A TRUE setting indicates that the VM can continue to operate while another VM has the focus. Previous versions of Windows also honored a *VMSTAT_EXCLUSIVE* setting that gave all cycles to the VM whenever it had the focus. You can change these settings in a relatively nonobvious way:

```
VMMCall Get_Time_Slice_Priority
mov     eax, statusflags
VMMCall Set_Time_Slice_Priority
```

In this code fragment, *statusflags* is the desired new combination of *VMSTAT-_EXCLUSIVE*, *VMSTAT_BACKGROUND*, and *VMSTAT_HIGH_PRI_BACK*. Since changing a VM's background property may have unexpected side effects that only the VMM understands, you should use this method rather than directly changing the flag bits.

The *VMSTAT_VXD_EXEC* flag is 1 while the VM is processing an *Exec_VxD_Int* or *Exec_PM_Int* service call. If you've hooked a protected-mode interrupt, it's possible (though unlikely) that you'd need to inspect this flag within your interrupt handler to distinguish these cases from the more common case of a protected-mode application issuing the interrupt.

The *VMSTAT_PAGEABLEV86* flag indicates that a protected-mode application in the VM has used DPMI function 0602h to make part of the V86 region pageable. Unless this flag is set, it doesn't make much sense to call *_GetV86PageableArray*, because all the bits will be 0. This flag and the associated logic are so obscure that I'm almost sorry I mentioned them.

I'll discuss the *VMSTAT_V86INTSLOCKED* flag later on, in connection with the *Begin_Critical_Section* service. Trust me that you don't need to know anything about this flag.

Many of the remaining flag bits seem clearly to be for internal use by the VMM and by other components you and I don't need to understand in detail.

BITS AND MASKS

The DDK header files are sometimes hard to read because they define both a bit number and a mask for flag bits. For example, VMM.H defines a symbol called *VMSTAT_EXCLUSIVE_BIT* as 0 and then defines *VMSTAT_EXCLUSIVE* as *1L << VMSTAT_EXCLUSIVE_BIT*. The two definitions make more sense in assembly language, where you can test the bit by coding either of these instructions:

```
bt      [ebx+CB_VM_Status], VMSTAT_EXCLUSIVE_BIT
jc      is_exclusive
```

or

```
test    [ebx+CB_VM_Status], VMSTAT_EXCLUSIVE
jnz     is_exclusive
```

The first example uses the BT instruction to test a numbered bit within a bit string and to set the carry flag if the bit is 1. The second example uses the regular TEST instruction to set the condition code based on ANDing a memory DWORD and an immediate mask. Both methods accomplish the same result. The TEST instruction is faster than BT, but it occupies more space in the program if its immediate operand requires more than one byte.

Testing a flag field using a bit number rather than a mask makes it easier to simultaneously test a bit and then alter its state. For example, BTS sets the carry flag based on the current setting of a bit and then sets the bit to 1. Conversely, BTR tests the bit and then resets it to 0.

Finding the VM Control Block

Much of the time, the VMM maintains the EBX register as a pointer to the VMCB for the current VM. If you're writing in assembly language, therefore, you can nearly always access fields in the current VM's control block via the EBX register. If you're writing in C or C++, you'll want to use one of the following two services to get a VMCB address if you don't already have one as a function argument:

```
PVMMCB hCurrentVM = Get_Cur_VM_Handle();
PVMMCB hSystemVM  = Get_Sys_VM_Handle();
```

Table 9-2 lists the services you use for locating and enumerating VM control blocks. For example, you'll occasionally want to verify that you're performing an operation on behalf of a particular VM. For this purpose, use one of these two test services:

```
if (Test_Cur_VM_Handle(hVM))
    ...                             // is it the current VM?
if (Test_Sys_VM_Handle(hVM))
    ...                             // is it the system VM?
```

Service	Description
_Allocate_Device_CB_Area	Reserves device space in each VMCB
_Deallocate_Device_CB_Area	Releases device space in each VMCB
Get_Cur_VM_Handle	Gets current VMCB address into register EBX
Test_Cur_VM_Handle	Tests whether register EBX points to current VMCB
Get_Sys_VM_Handle	Gets system VMCB address into register EBX
Test_Sys_VM_Handle	Tests whether register EBX points to system VMCB
Get_Next_VM_Handle	Chains from register EBX to next VMCB

Table 9-2. *Services for locating and enumerating VM control blocks.*

Per-Device Space in the VM Control Block

Each VxD has the opportunity to enlarge the VMCB by reserving space for its own use via the *_Allocate_Device_CB_Area* service. When you call this service, you specify the size of the area you want to reserve in bytes. The return value is an offset that you can later add to the address of a particular VMCB to locate the area reserved for your use. Because of the way you use this offset, you normally save it in a global variable. In a static driver, you would normally reserve VMCB space while processing the Device_Init message.

The following example reserves sufficient space to hold a private *MYSTUFF* control block in the VMCB during Device_Init. The example also shows how to access the *MYSTUFF* structure at a later time:

```
typedef struct tagMYSTUFF
    {...} MYSTUFF, *PMYSTUFF;
DWORD cboffset;

BOOL __stdcall OnDeviceInit(PVMMCB hVM, DWORD refdata)
    {                               // OnDeviceInit
    cboffset = _Allocate_Device_CB_Area(sizeof(MYSTUFF), 0);
    ...
    return TRUE;
    }                               // OnDeviceInit

somefunction()
    {                               // somefunction
```

```
        PMYSTUFF p = (PMYSTUFF) ((DWORD) Get_Cur_VM_Handle() + cboffset);
        ...
        }                           // somefunction
```

Here, _Allocate_Device_CB_Area reserves sizeof(MYSTUFF) bytes of memory in every VM control block and returns the offset of the reserved area so you can save it in the cboffset variable. The somefunction fragment shows how you can add this offset to the address of the current VM's control block (determined by calling Get_Cur_VM_Handle) to locate your embedded MYSTUFF block.

The previous example is appropriate for a static driver. A dynamic driver can also allocate space for itself within the VMCB. But, since the VMM never sends a Device_Init message to a dynamic driver, the appropriate time to allocate space is in response to the Sys_Dynamic_Device_Init message. In addition, the driver should be sure to release the space before it unloads by calling the _Deallocate_Device_CB_Area service:

```
        _Deallocate_Device_CB_Area(cboffset, 0);
```

The VMM initializes your private space to 0, both in every new VMCB and in every VMCB that exists when you first allocate the space. As you will see later, the same thing isn't true of private space within thread control blocks.

The Client Register Structure

The client register structure (see Figure 9-3) exposes one of the facets of VxD programming that's hardest to grasp. The code in a VxD isn't really part of the world inhabited by application programs. Rather, it's a kind of metaprogram that watches over the shoulder of the real program running in ring three and occasionally applies corrections to that program's path. Recall that the VMM gains control only in response to an interrupt of some kind and that it immediately saves the processor registers. The only way the VMM can affect the interrupted program is by modifying the saved register images. When the VMM eventually redispatches the interrupted program, it loads the altered images into the real processor registers. The effect in ring three is as if execution were suddenly and inexplicably diverted to another place with another state.

The client register structure maps the images of the general and segment registers as the VMM's first-level interrupt handler saves them. Much of this structure exactly matches the layout of the stack following an interrupt from V86 mode to ring zero. (See Figure 5-12 on page 87.) In effect, the processor's own interrupt cycle plus a PUSHAD instruction builds the client register structure.

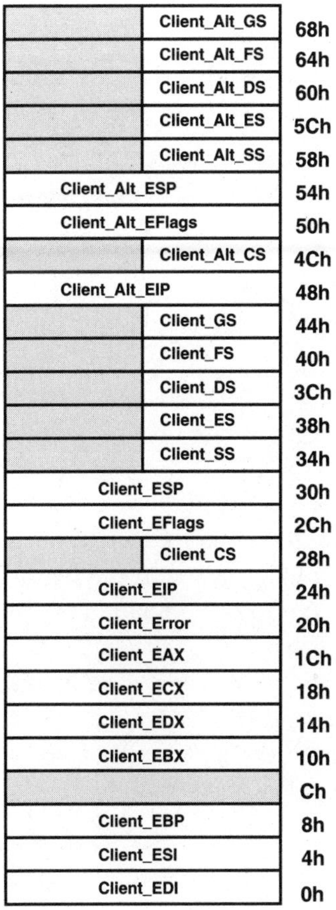

	Client_Alt_GS	68h
	Client_Alt_FS	64h
	Client_Alt_DS	60h
	Client_Alt_ES	5Ch
	Client_Alt_SS	58h
Client_Alt_ESP		54h
Client_Alt_EFlags		50h
	Client_Alt_CS	4Ch
Client_Alt_EIP		48h
	Client_GS	44h
	Client_FS	40h
	Client_DS	3Ch
	Client_ES	38h
	Client_SS	34h
Client_ESP		30h
Client_EFlags		2Ch
	Client_CS	28h
Client_EIP		24h
Client_Error		20h
Client_EAX		1Ch
Client_ECX		18h
Client_EDX		14h
Client_EBX		10h
		Ch
Client_EBP		8h
Client_ESI		4h
Client_EDI		0h

Figure 9-3. *The client register structure.*

The "alternate" set of registers in the client register structure contains the segment registers, the stack pointer, and the instruction pointer for the "other" mode of execution. If the VM is running a protected-mode program, its alternate register set describes the state of the V86 program. Conversely, if the VM is running a V86-mode program, its alternate register set describes the state of the protected-mode program. Just describing these alternate register images should make it clear that a VM has both a V86 and a protected-mode thread of execution, either of which can be active at a given time. The segment registers from one thread are inappropriate to the other, as are the stack and instruction pointers.

Accessing Client Registers

An assembly-language VxD normally uses the EBP register to point to the current VM's register images. The VMM arranges things so that the EBP register points to the register images for most calls into a VxD, and you can always use the following code to accomplish the same thing:

```
VMMCall Get_Cur_VM_Handle              ; sets EBX = current VMCB
mov     ebp, [ebx+CB_Client_Pointer]   ; EBP -> client regs
```

Thereafter, you access the registers belonging to the virtual machine by referencing fields in the client register structure:

```
mov     eax, [ebp + Client_ECX]    ; EAX = VM's ECX
movzx   ecx, [ebp + Client_AX]     ; ECX = VM's AX, 0-extended
lar     edx, dword ptr [ebp + Client_DS]
[etc.]
```

In this sample, I deliberately loaded the VxD's own registers with the contents of *different* virtual machine registers to make the point that whatever is currently in the VxD's registers has nothing to do with whatever was in the registers when the VM interrupted or with whatever will be in the registers when the VMM eventually redispatches the VM.

A C-language driver normally uses a pointer variable to address these register images. The DDK headers define a union called a *CLIENT_STRUCT*. The union contains the members *CRS* for the 32-bit registers, *CWRS* for the 16-bit registers, and *CBRS* for the 8-bit registers. Accessing individual registers therefore involves relatively verbose code like this:

```
CLIENT_STRUCT* pRegs;
DWORD a = pRegs->CRS.Client_EAX;
WORD  b = pRegs->CWRS.Client_BX;
BYTE  c = pRegs->CBRS.Client_CH;
```

Since the Microsoft VC++ compiler allows you to define union members without names, you can simplify your own code with a definition like this:

```
typedef union tagMYCLIENT_STRUC {
    struct Client_Reg_Struc;
    struct Client_Word_Reg_Struc;
    struct Client_Byte_Reg_Struc;
} MYCLIENT_STRUC, MYCRS, *PMYCRS;
```

This definition allows you to code more tersely:

```
PMYCRS pRegs;
DWORD a = pRegs->Client_EAX;
WORD  b = pRegs->Client_BX;
BYTE  c = pRegs->Client_CH;
```

If you're using VTOOLSD or if you write a set of #defines such as I use in the CRS.H file in the sample programs for Chapters 13, 14, and 16 (you can find it on the companion disc in the \CHAP13\RING0DMA directory), you can code yet more economically by always declaring a variable named *pRegs* to be a pointer to a *CLIENT_STRUCT* and by using one of the many macros VTOOLSD provides for client register access:

```
CLIENT_STRUCT* pRegs;
DWORD a = _ClientEAX;
WORD  b = _ClientBX;
BYTE  c = _ClientCH;
```

Addressing Client Data

Sometimes you need to access data belonging to the program in the virtual machine. Suppose, for example, that you've provided an API in which the DS:DX register pair points to a character string. Here's a plausible but very naïve fragment for addressing the string from within your VxD:

```
char __far *p = MAKELP(_ClientDS, _ClientDX);    // WRONG!
```

This code is what you'd probably write in a Win16 application. It hasn't a prayer in a VxD, though. First of all, you're probably hoping that the compiler will load your far pointer into the DS or ES register along with some general register. Well, doing so might crash Windows 95 because any VxD service routines you call thereafter will assume that DS and ES hold the ring-zero flat data selector. In addition, many 32-bit C compilers just won't let you use far pointers at all, not to mention 16:16 pointers involving a selector and a 16-bit offset. (Some compilers do understand 16:32 far pointers, but this code fragment still won't work because of the potential for crashing the system.) Another problem is that the header files you'll use probably don't have a MAKELP macro like WINDOWS.H does, mostly because you're not supposed to be using far pointers.

Well, suppose you elect to code in assembly language. Could you now just code something like this?

```
mov    dx, [ebp+Client_DX]     ; WRONG!
mov    gs, [ebp+Client_DS]
[access string via GS:DX]
```

This code would actually work some of the time because no one else in VxD-land depends on the setting of GS, which this code fails to save and restore. It's still not right, however. Here's why:

■ Suppose the VM is executing V86 code when it calls your driver. The *Client_DS* value is then a paragraph number rather than a selector. You'll probably generate a GP fault when you try to load it into a segment register.

- Suppose the VM is executing a 32-bit protected-mode program under a DOS extender. The API in this case should demand that the DS:EDX register pair point to the string, but you're only loading 16 bits of the pointer in the client's EDX register.

- Suppose the selector in *Client_DS* is invalid or null. You'll generate a GP fault when you access it, and Windows 95 will crash.

The right way to access the client string in this case is to use the *Map_Flat* service. In assembly language, this service uses register AH to encode the client-structure offset of the segment register and register AL to encode the client-structure offset of the offset register. It returns the linear address formed by adding the segment base to the specified offset, or -1 if the selector is invalid. For example:

```
mov     ah, Client_DS
mov     al, Client_DX
VMMCall Map_Flat
cmp     eax, -1
je      error
```

Map_Flat uses the *Client_DS* and *Client_DX* symbols in an unusual way. The AX register will end up containing 3C14h because 3Ch is the offset of *Client_DS* in the client structure and 14h is the offset of *Client_DX*.

What makes *Map_Flat* so useful is that it correctly interprets the segment register according to whether the VM is running V86-mode or protected-mode code, and it uses either the 16-bit or the 32-bit general register depending on whether the protected-mode client is 16-bit or 32-bit. If *Map_Flat* is given a valid selector, it always returns a 32-bit linear address that's directly usable by the VxD, which need not load any segment register at all.

Code like this call to *Map_Flat* is so common that Microsoft provided the Client_Ptr_Flat macro to make it even more painless:

```
Client_Ptr_Flat eax, DS, DX
```

If you're coding with the Microsoft DDK, you'll have to make your own C-language wrapper or macro to use *Map_Flat*. (I defined one in my CRS.H file.) VTOOLSD includes a wrapper for *Map_Flat* and a *MAPFLAT* macro. (Why couldn't it have been named *Client_Ptr_Flat*, inquiring minds want to know?) Here's how you might use the wrapper or my macro:

```
char *p = (char *) Map_Flat(CLIENT_DS, CLIENT_DX);
```

or

```
char *p = (char *) Client_Ptr_Flat(DS, DX);
```

Note that you use *DX* even if you suspect you're dealing with a 32-bit program. The *Client_Ptr_Flat* macro turns your reference into a structure offset, and both register DX and register EDX have the same offset (as does register DL, for that matter).

WIN32S-COMPATIBLE DATA REFERENCING

If your VxD must retain Windows 3.1 compatibility and must work with Win32s programs, you can't just use linear addresses supplied by the application because Win32s uses flat selectors with a base address of FFFF0000h instead of 0h. You might be tempted, therefore, to always call *Map_Flat* to try to linearize the address of Win32 data. Unfortunately, *Map_Flat* won't work: the VMM believes that the System VM contains a 16-bit DPMI client. It therefore will add only 16 bits of offset from the client DX register. The following code will do the trick:

```
VMMCall _SelectorMapFlat, <ebx, <dword ptr [ebp+Client_DS]>, 0>
mov     edx, [ebp+Client_EDX]
lar     ecx, dword ptr [ebp+Client_CS]
test    ecx, 00400000h
jnz     @F
and     edx, 0000FFFFh
@@:
add     eax, edx
```

This example uses *_SelectorMapFlat* to obtain the segment base address for the client's data segment. It then adds either the client DX or EDX register, depending on whether the client program is running in a USE16 or a USE32 segment.

What I've just shown you should be irrelevant, because you won't be passing linear addresses back and forth between Win32s applications and VxDs in the first place. Microsoft frankly hopes that people will stop pushing Win32s's envelope, too.

Accessing data supplied by Win32 programs in Windows 95 is much easier. Normally, you'll be responding to a *DeviceIoControl* call and you'll only be interested in the input, output, and output-length pointers passed to you by VWIN32. If there are pointers embedded in the data, you can just use the same linear addresses as the Win32 program uses. (But be careful to make copies of any VM data you need to access asynchronously because your caller's address context is valid only while it is the current process.)

The Thread Control Block

Windows 95 introduces another ubiquitous control block, the *thread control block (TCB)*, for keeping track of information about each of the execution threads in the system (see Figure 9-4). Table 9-3 indicates the individual bits within the *TCB_Flags* member of this structure. Unlike the client register structure, but like the virtual machine control block, the TCB is essentially read-only for most drivers.

Conventionally, assembly-language drivers pass the address of the current TCB around in the EDI register. There's a set of services for locating and scanning TCBs that's completely analogous to the set for VMCBs, and these are listed in Table 9-4.

```
struct tcb_s {
    ULONG    TCB_Flags;            // 00 thread status flags
    ULONG    TCB_Reserved1;        // 04 used internally by VMM
    ULONG    TCB_Reserved2;        // 08 used internally by VMM
    ULONG    TCB_Signature;        // 0C 'THCB' (0x42434854)
    ULONG    TCB_ClientPtr;        // 10 register images for this thread
    ULONG    TCB_VMHandle;         // 14 VM that contains this thread
    USHORT   TCB_ThreadId;         // 18 unique thread ID
    USHORT   TCB_PMLockOrigSS;     // 1A original SS before stack lock
    ULONG    TCB_PMLockOrigESP;    // 1C original ESP before stack lock
    ULONG    TCB_PMLockOrigEIP;    // 20 original EIP before stack lock
    ULONG    TCB_PMLockStackCount; // 24 count of stack locks for this thread
    USHORT   TCB_PMLockOrigCS;     // 28 original CS before stack lock
    USHORT   TCB_PMPSPSelector;    // 2A PSP selector
    ULONG    TCB_ThreadType;       // 2C DWORD passed to VMMCreateThread
    USHORT   TCB_pad1;             // 30 padding
    UCHAR    TCB_pad2;             // 32 padding
    UCHAR    TCB_extErrLocus;      // 33 extended error locus
    USHORT   TCB_extErr;           // 34 extended error code
    UCHAR    TCB_extErrAction;     // 36 extended error action
    UCHAR    TCB_extErrClass;      // 37 extended error class
    ULONG    TCB_extErrPtr;        // 38 extended error pointer
};                                 // 3C
```

Figure 9-4. *Layout of the thread control block.*

Name	Mask	Description
THFLAG_SUSPENDED	00000008	Thread has been suspended
THFLAG_NOT_EXECUTEABLE	00000010	Thread has been partially destroyed
THFLAG_THREAD_CREATION	00000100	Thread is in the process of being created
THFLAG_THREAD_BLOCKED	00000400	Thread is blocked on a semaphore
THFLAG_CHARSET_MASK	00030000	Default character set:

Name	Value	Description
THFLAG_ANSI	0	ANSI
THFLAG_OEM	1	OEM
THFLAG_UNICODE	2	Unicode

Name	Mask	Description
THFLAG_EXTENDED_HANDLES	00040000	Thread uses extended file handles
THFLAG_OPEN_AS_IMMOVABLE_FILE	00080000	Flag to disk defragmenter not to move files yet
THFLAG_RING0_THREAD	10000000	Thread runs only at ring zero

Table 9-3. *Flag bits in a thread control block.*

Service	Description
_AllocateThreadDataSlot	Reserves 4 bytes in each TCB for device use
_FreeThreadDataSlot	Releases device space in TCB
Get_Cur_Thread_Handle	Returns current TCB address in register EDI
Test_Cur_Thread_Handle	Tests whether register EDI points to current TCB
Get_Sys_Thread_Handle	Gets system thread's TCB
Test_Sys_Thread_Handle	Tests whether register EDI points to system TCB
Validate_Thread_Handle	Tests whether register EDI points to a valid TCB
Get_Initial_Thread_Handle	Gets initial thread for the register EBX VM
Test_Initial_Thread_Handle	Tests whether register EDI points to a VM's initial thread
Get_Next_Thread_Handle	Chains from register EDI to next TCB

Table 9-4. *Services for locating and enumerating thread control blocks.*

Just as you can use *_Allocate_Device_CB_Area* to reserve per-device space in a VM control block, you can use *_AllocateThreadDataSlot* to allocate a DWORD for your private use in each TCB:

```
DWORD tcboffset = _AllocateThreadDataSlot();
...
PDWORD p = (PDWORD) ((DWORD) Get_Cur_Thread_Handle()) + tcboffset);
```

Although thread data slots are analogous to the thread local storage used by Win32 applications, they occupy different physical memory locations. Thus, you can't give a Win32 application your slot offset for use in, say, a *TlsGetValue* call. Conversely, you can't take the result of a Win32 *TlsAlloc* call and use it as you would a ring-zero thread data slot.

There's an important complication associated with thread data slots—namely, the VMM doesn't initialize these slots in any way. Thus, when you allocate a thread data slot, you must initialize your slot in all existing and future TCBs. Additionally, since you're likely to use a slot to hold a pointer to a piece of heap memory, you'll want to be sure to avoid a possible memory leak by freeing the pointer before a thread terminates. So, you'll want to handle the Thread_Init and Destroy_Thread system control messages, and you might want to write your own helper routine for allocating thread data slots. The next section shows an example.

ALLOCATING MEMORY

Device drivers often need to allocate small blocks of memory for various purposes. The VMM provides a memory heap to satisfy this need, and it provides two sets of service calls for managing this heap. In general, you can use the *_HeapAllocate* function as a basic memory utility. To improve performance when you need to use many blocks of a small, fixed size, and to permit interrupt routines to acquire memory, the VMM also provides a set of *linked list* services.

The Heap Manager

Table 9-5 lists the heap manager services you use to manage small blocks of memory. You use *_HeapAllocate* to reserve storage for your use, and you later release this storage by calling *_HeapFree*:

```
PVOID p = _HeapAllocate(nbytes, flags);
...
_HeapFree(p, 0);
```

The return value is a flat pointer to a memory block at least as large as the number of bytes you requested. It should go without saying that you must take care not to overflow the boundaries of a memory block, because there's no protection for the memory manager or for other drivers if you do. You must also be sure to release memory blocks when they're no longer needed. Unlike Windows-based application programming, in which the kernel automatically releases global memory blocks when their owners terminate, in VxD programming there is no one to keep track of memory allocated by VxDs.

Service	Description
_HeapAllocate	Allocates a block of memory
_HeapFree	Releases a block of memory
_HeapGetSize	Determines size of a memory block
_HeapReAllocate	Reallocates a memory block

Table 9-5. *Heap management services.*

The *flags* argument is a combination of *HEAPZEROINIT* (which means what you think it means) and a flag specifying the desired location of the memory. The flag can be one of the following:

- *HEAPINIT,* which you can use only during device initialization, indicates that you want memory in the initialization data segment. The VMM will automatically release the memory after initialization through the simple expedient of deleting the segment that contains it.

- *HEAPSWAP* indicates that you want pageable memory. Use this flag with care, because it can lead to a deadlock under the circumstances described in the "Pageable Data Areas" sidebar.

- *HEAPLOCKEDIFDP* (*LOCKEDIFDP* stands for "locked if DOS paging"), indicates that you want pageable memory if Windows 95 is doing paging I/O in ring zero and locked memory if MS-DOS or the BIOS handles paging I/O.

PAGEABLE DATA AREAS

The ability to page VxD code and data in Windows 95 requires you to take extra care in allocating data objects. Even though Windows 95 contains full ring-zero support for disk I/O, the end user can force the system to page through MS-DOS and the BIOS. In this case, the VMM automatically locks otherwise pageable code and data segments to avoid reentering MS-DOS while executing VxD code. It doesn't automatically lock dynamically allocated data objects, however. If a VxD attempts to access pageable data at a time when MS-DOS or the BIOS is being used for paging, therefore, a deadlock will occur. You can avoid this problem by always using the *HEAPLOCKEDIFDP* flag when calling *_HeapAllocate* and the *PAGELOCKEDIFDP* flag when calling *_PageAllocate*.

If you specify none of these three location flags, _HeapAllocate_ allocates page-locked memory. In all cases, the memory comes from the shared system area above C0000000h.

As an example of using the heap, suppose your driver virtualizes a resource for each thread by saving various important per-thread data in a _MYSTUFF_ structure you define. The strategy for implementing the required virtualization is therefore something like this:

■ Each time the VMM creates a new thread, allocate a _MYSTUFF_ structure from free storage. Save the pointer to this per-thread memory in a slot within the thread control block.

■ Each time the VMM terminates a thread, release the memory you previously allocated.

The first step is to allocate a thread data slot for your own use. If your driver is a static driver, you'd allocate the slot while processing the Device_Init message. The code's a little more interesting if your driver is dynamically loaded, however, because you must provide for releasing the data slot when you unload. Also, as mentioned in the previous section, the VMM doesn't initialize thread data slots. Your initialization code would therefore look something like this fragment (included on the companion disc in the \CHAP09\HEAPMANAGEMENT-DDK directory):

```
DWORD tcboffset;

BOOL OnSysDynamicDeviceInit()
    {                                   // OnSysDynamicDeviceInit
    PTCB first, thread;
    tcboffset = AllocateSlot();
    if (!tcboffset)
        return FALSE;

    first = thread = Get_Sys_Thread_Handle();
    do {    // allocate stuff for each thread
        if (!(*(PMYSTUFF*)((DWORD) thread + tcboffset) =
            _HeapAllocate(sizeof(MYSTUFF), HEAPZEROINIT)))
            {    // can't allocate
            OnSysDynamicDeviceExit(); // cleanup
            return FALSE;            // fail device load
            }    // can't allocate
        thread = Get_Next_Thread_Handle(thread);
        } while (thread != first);
    return TRUE;
    }                                   // OnSysDynamicDeviceInit
```

```
DWORD AllocateSlot()
    {                                   // AllocateSlot
    PTCB first, thread;
    DWORD offset = _AllocateThreadDataSlot();
    if (!offset)
        return 0;
    first = thread = Get_Sys_Thread_Handle();
    do {     // initialize slot in each thread
        *(PDWORD) ((DWORD) thread + offset) = 0;
        thread = Get_Next_Thread_Handle(thread);
        } while (thread != first);
    return offset;
    }                                   // AllocateSlot
```

OnSysDynamicDeviceInit, which handles the Sys_Dynamic_Device_Init message to initialize this dynamic VxD, uses the *AllocateSlot* helper routine to obtain the offset of a thread data slot. It then loops over all the threads that are currently running to allocate a *MYSTUFF* block for each thread. The loop begins with the "system" thread, whose handle you obtain by calling *Get_Sys_Thread_Handle*. Because the thread control blocks form a ring, the loop proceeds by calling *Get_Next _Thread_Handle* over and over until you return to the system thread. *AllocateSlot* uses *_AllocateThreadDataSlot* to obtain a thread data slot. It then performs its own loop over all thread control blocks to initialize that data slot to 0. The way the code in this example is organized, if we succeed in allocating a thread data slot in the first place, its contents in every TCB will either be 0 or the address of a *MYSTUFF* block. You can rely on this fact to help prove the correctness of your VxD.

The second step is to allocate a *MYSTUFF* structure each time a new thread comes into existence and release it when the thread terminates. You'd accomplish this portion of the task as follows:

```
BOOL OnCreateThread(PTCB thread)
    {     // OnCreateThread
    PMYSTUFF* pcell = (PMYSTUFF*) ((DWORD) thread + tcboffset);
    PMYSTUFF pstuff = _HeapAllocate(sizeof(MYSTUFF),
        HEAPZEROINIT);
    if (!stuff)
        return FALSE;     // fail thread creation
    *pcell = pstuff;
    return TRUE;
    }     // OnCreateThread
```

```
VOID OnDestroyThread(PTCB thread)
    {    // OnDestroyThread
    PMYSTUFF* pcell = (PMYSTUFF*)((DWORD) thread + tcboffset);
    PMYSTUFF pstuff = *pcell;
    *pcell = NULL;
    if (pstuff)
        _HeapFree(pstuff, 0);
    }    // OnDestroyThread
```

OnCreateThread handles the Create_Thread system control message, which signifies creation of a new thread. You initialize your thread data slot to point to this thread's own *MYSTUFF* block. If you're unable to allocate the memory for the block, you fail creation of the thread by returning FALSE. In your released software, you should use a SHELL device service to generate a message explaining to the end user why you won't allow the new thread to be created.

OnDestroyThread handles the Destroy_Thread system control message, which signifies that the VMM is about to destroy a thread that has terminated. Here you release the memory allocated for the *MYSTUFF* block. Out of an excess of caution, I suggest also setting your thread data slot to NULL before calling *_HeapFree*. That way, if *_HeapFree* encounters some kind of problem, your thread data slot will be NULL and your driver can never again be the cause of that particular problem for this particular thread.[1]

You also need to clean up all the *MYSTUFF*-sized memory blocks when your device driver unloads. In this example, you can clean up relatively simply:

```
BOOL OnSysDynamicDeviceExit()
    {                            // OnSysDynamicDeviceExit
    PTCB first, thread;
    if (!tcboffset)
        return TRUE;    // shouldn't be possible
    first = thread = Get_Sys_Thread_Handle();
    do {    // clean up existing threads
        OnDestroyThread(thread);
        thread = Get_Next_Thread_Handle(thread);
        } while (thread != first);
    _FreeThreadDataSlot(tcboffset);
    return TRUE;    // i.e., okay to unload
    }                            // OnSysDynamicDeviceExit
```

---

1. Setting a pointer to NULL before freeing the memory to which it points is a fail-safe technique for avoiding an infinite loop of memory errors. Suppose something goes wrong inside *_HeapFree*. Since our thread hasn't yet been completely terminated, it might happen that the Destroy_Thread handler will be called again—maybe even recursively—whereupon it would trigger the same failure if we hadn't already taken the described precaution.

This code takes advantage of the fact that *OnDestroyThread* releases a thread's *MYSTUFF* block and nulls your driver's thread data slot. This function also shows another example of the loop over all threads that we used twice before in this sample.

Is It Thread-Safe? You can see an apparent hole in the preceding code if you look hard enough. Each of the three loops over thread control blocks would break if a new thread were to come or go while the loop is going on. As discussed later in this chapter, however, every system control message handler is protected by the Windows critical section. Therefore, it's not possible for threads to start or stop while one of the functions shown in the example is running, so the preceding code is safe after all.

Linked-List Services

The *linked-list* category of services comprises a collection of services for managing fixed-size blocks of memory that may or may not be linked together into a list (see Table 9-6). The first step in using these APIs is to create a new list object by calling *List_Create*. When you're all done, you'll call *List_Destroy* to clean up:

```
VMMLIST list = List_Create(flags, nodesize);
...
List_Destroy(list);
```

Service	Description
List_Allocate	Allocates a new element of a list
List_Attach	Adds a new element to the head of a list
List_Attach_Tail	Adds a new element to the end of a list
List_Create	Creates a new list object
List_Deallocate	Releases an element of a list
List_Destroy	Destroys a list object
List_Get_First	Retrieves the first element in a list
List_Get_Next	Gets the next element from a list
List_Insert	Inserts a new element into a list
List_Remove	Removes an element from a list
List_Remove_First	Removes the first element from a list

Table 9-6. *Linked-list services.*

List_Create allocates a pool of storage from which to satisfy later allocation requests. The *nodesize* argument specifies the fixed size of the elements that you'll later allocate from this pool. The *flags* argument specifies options to control how the list object will later behave. The *flags* argument is 0 or a combination of the following:

- **LF_USE_HEAP** specifies that list elements should be allocated from the system heap using *_HeapAllocate* calls. There's not much point in allocating a list with this option unless you're reluctant to implement your own doubly linked chaining logic.

- **LF_ASYNC** indicates that you'll be allocating list elements while processing interrupts. Creating a list with this option is the only way you can allow an interrupt handler to allocate memory on the fly.

- **LF_ALLOC_ERROR** instructs the list manager to indicate failure of subsequent element allocation by setting the carry flag and returning. The alternative is to crash Windows 95.

- **LF_SWAP** indicates that you want list elements allocated from the swappable heap.

Once you create the list object, you then use *List_Allocate* and *List_Deallocate* to obtain and release elements of the fixed size you previously specified:

```
VMMLISTNODE node = List_Allocate(list);
...
List_Deallocate(list, node);
```

If you want, you can use only the list management services I've already described as a simple and fast way to allocate memory of a convenient, fixed size. A list with the *LF_ASYNC* option also affords the only way an interrupt handler or other asynchronous service can allocate memory. If your data structure demands it, however, you can also use the other linked-list services shown in Table 9-6 to maintain a doubly linked list structure. For example, a FIFO queue of service requests might be implemented by having an interrupt handler add an element to the tail of a list:

```
VMMLIST stufflist;  // created with LF_Async
...
void SomeInterruptHandler()
    {
    PMYSTUFF p = (PMYSTUFF) List_Allocate(stufflist);
    List_Attach_Tail(stufflist, p);
    }
```

In this example, I'm assuming that the *SomeInterruptHandler* function is in a locked code segment and gets called during processing of a hardware interrupt at a time when interrupts are disabled. (Having interrupts disabled is a requirement when you call list manager services for an *LF_ASYNC* list.) *List_Allocate* allocates a new block of size *sizeMYSTUFF* from a pool in page-locked memory. If you specified the *LF_ALLOC_ERROR* flag when you created the list, the assembly-language *List_Allocate* service would return with the carry flag set if it were unable to allocate the new block; otherwise, *List_Allocate* would crash Windows 95 immediately if allocation failed. A C-framework wrapper for *List_Allocate* should turn a carry-set return into a NULL pointer return for inspection by your C program.

All that *List_Allocate* does is allocate memory. It's up to you to do something with that memory. In this code fragment, I used *List_Attach_Tail* to add the new element to the end of a linked list. A callback routine would run through the list at some later time:

```
void SomeCallback()
    {
    PMYSTUFF p;
    while ((p = (PMYSTUFF) List_Remove_First(stufflist)))
        {
        ...
        List_Deallocate(stufflist, p);
        }
    }
```

At each iteration of the loop in this function, you use *List_Remove_First* to detach the first element from the linked list. After somehow processing the information in the list element, you call *List_Deallocate* to return the element's memory to the free pool.

PROCESSING EVENTS

In common with other operating systems, Windows 95 provides a method whereby a VxD can request that the VMM call it back at a later, more convenient time to perform an item of work that can't be performed immediately. In Windows, such deferred work items are called *events*. There are two common situations in which you might need to schedule an event callback:

■ If you're performing an operation on behalf of a particular VM or a particular thread, you may need to do something in the context of a different one. You can't directly trigger the task or thread switch that would let you do so. You can, however, schedule an event callback for the next time that particular VM or thread becomes active.

■ If you're handling a hardware interrupt, you labor under two restrictions: your code must occupy locked pages, and it can call only those VxD services designated as *asynchronous*. This second requirement simply means (circularly) that the services you call are safe for use during interrupt processing because they don't violate these rules either. Very few services are asynchronous, though (see Table 9-7). In order to completely handle the interrupt, therefore, you schedule an event callback to occur when the VMM reaches the point of stability where it can relax these restrictions.

Event services	Get_Next_Thread_Handle
Linked-list memory allocation*	Get_Next_VM_Handle
Most VPICD services**	Get_Sys_Thread_Handle
Various debugging services†	Get_Sys_VM_Handle
Call_When_Idle	Get_System_Time
Crash_Cur_VM	_GetThreadExecTime
Disable_Touch_1st_Meg	Get_Time_Slice_Info
DOSMGR_Get_DOS_Crit_Status	Get_VM_Exec_Time
Enable_Touch_1st_Meg	Get_VMM_Reenter_Count
Fatal_Error_Handler	Get_VMM_Version
Fatal_Memory_Error	GetSetDetailedVMError
Get_Crit_Status_No_Block‡	_lmemcpy
Get_Crit_Status_Thread	_lstrcpyn
Get_Cur_Thread_Handle	_lstrlen
Get_Cur_VM_Handle	Set_Async_Time_Out
Get_Execution_Focus	Set_Global_Time_Out
Get_Initial_Thread_Handle	Set_Thread_Time_Out
Get_Last_Updated_System_Time	Set_VM_Time_Out
_GetLastUpdatedThreadExecTime	_SHELL_CallAtAppyTime††
Get_Last_Updated_VM_Exec_Time	_SHELL_QueryAppyTimeAvailable

* Use the *LF_Async* flag in the call to *List_Create*.

** *VPICD_Virtualize_IRQ* is not asynchronous.

† Consult the Windows 95 DDK online help for descriptions of various _Debug_ and Debug_ services. _Debug_Flags_Service is especially useful as an assertion about the execution environment.

‡ *Get_Crit_Status_No_Block* is the asynchronous version of *Get_Crit_Status*.

†† Note that _SHELL_CancelAppyTimeEvent is *not* asynchronous.

Table 9-7. *Asynchronous services.* *(continued)*

continued

SHELL_Update_User_Activity	Test_Sys_Thread_Handle
Signal_Semaphore	Test_Sys_VM_Handle
Signal_Semaphore_No_Switch	Update_System_Clock
Test_Cur_VM_Handle	Validate_Thread_Handle
Test_Initial_Thread_Handle	Validate_VM_Handle

The way event scheduling works mechanically is that you call a VMM service that schedules the event callback. There are several kinds of events, and you pick the one that's appropriate to the task at hand (see Table 9-8). Depending on what you say in the scheduling API call, the VMM may process the event immediately; immediate processing is possible if you use a *Call_xxx_Event* function. The VMM may instead queue the event for later processing; queueing always occurs if you use a *Schedule_xxx_Event* function and might occur even if you use *Call_xxx_Event*. At any rate, the VMM calls your event procedure sometime later, and the procedure does its thing and returns to the VMM. Note that an event is a one-time concept. That is, once the VMM calls the event procedure, it destroys the event object you created earlier. You can also cancel the event yourself at any time before the VMM calls the event procedure; the scheduling and cancellation functions are paired—you use a specific function to cancel a particular kind of event.

Kind of Event	*Services*
Global	Call_Global_Event, Cancel_Global_Event, Schedule_Global_Event
Virtual machine	Call_VM_Event, Cancel_VM_Event, Schedule_VM_Event
Thread	Cancel_Thread_Event, Schedule_Thread_Event
Priority VM	Call_Priority_VM_Event, Cancel_Priority_VM_Event
Restricted	Call_Restricted_Event, Cancel_Restricted_Event

Table 9-8. *Kinds of events and their services.*

The VMM processes events when it's just about to transfer control from ring zero to ring three. This transfer happens when the handler for the outermost interrupt returns to the VMM. Event processing also occurs when any VxD calls *Resume_Exec* or *Exec_Int*. *Resume_Exec*, in particular, acts something like the Windows *PeekMessage* function with the *PM_NOYIELD* flag set in that it allows event procedures to run without performing a context switch.

Kinds of Events

These are the different kinds of events in Windows:

- **Global events** are events whose callback routines can run in any VM and thread context. A hardware interrupt routine might use a global event to finish its operation as soon as possible without waiting for a task or thread switch.

- **VM events** have callbacks that must run in the context of a particular VM. You would normally use a VM event as part of an operation affecting an MS-DOS prompt box or the collection of all Windows applications as a whole. Calling into the System VM to post a message, for example, might most logically be done via a VM event except that a priority VM event (discussed below) fits the bill better by providing some conditions on when it will run.

- The VMM services a **thread event** in the context of a specific thread. You most often use a thread event when you're operating in cooperation with a Win32 application.

- A **priority VM event** is a VM event that carries a set of optional restrictions about when the associated callback occurs and that specifies a priority boost to be applied while the callback runs. The possible restrictions include a timeout period (the expiration of which automatically fires the event) and the requirements that all of the VM's threads have virtual interrupts enabled, that no VM own the single Windows critical section, that no VM be performing a time-critical operation as indicated by its execution priority, and that the VM not be in the middle of handling a simulated hardware interrupt. In Windows 3.1, this kind of event was the most frequently used because of the ease with which you could specify restrictions and a priority boost.

- **Restricted events** are new in Windows 95 and provide some additional ways of restricting the timing of callbacks beyond the features of priority VM events. You can specify that a restricted event run in a particular thread context (thereby creating a kind of priority thread event) and that restrictions such as critical-section and virtual-interrupt status be met for the thread alone. You can also specify that the callback not occur while the VM is executing a V86-mode program. Finally, you can create global events of this type too. There are additional possible restrictions that

Microsoft claims most of us will never need to use but that it documents in the DDK "for completeness." Most of us will now be creating restricted events because they solve some annoying problems related to deadlock prevention.

When the VMM gets around to processing events, it handles global events first, then VM events for the current VM (that is, the one with the highest execution priority), and then thread events for the current thread. The order in which the VMM processes events isn't otherwise specified. Notice too that a VM or thread event procedure might alter execution priorities or release blocked threads, thereby making some other VM or thread current. The VMM would then switch its attention to any pending events for the new VM or thread.

Coding Event Callbacks

When you initially create an event, you specify the address of an event callback procedure. For example:

```
BeginProc hwIntProc, locked
...
mov  esi, offset32 OnMyEvent
VMMCall Schedule_Global_Event
...
EndProc hwIntProc
```

The VMM will eventually call your event handler with the register contents shown in Table 9-9. The direction flag will be clear (the usual state for C programs), and the processor will be enabled for interrupts. Your callback must preserve registers EBP and ESP as well as the interrupt and direction flags. In common with other parts of the system, it must not alter the DS, ES, or SS registers, but it can use (and restore) the FS or GS register if necessary.

Register	*Contents*
EBX	Current VMCB address
EDX	Pass-through "reference" data from the *Call_xxx_Event* or *Schedule_xxx_Event* call
EDI	Current thread control block (TCB) address
EBP	Client register structure for current thread

Table 9-9. *Register contents at entry to an event callback.*

In general, an event callback can use any VxD service. The ability to make these calls is, after all, why you use the event mechanism in the first place. There are nonetheless some restrictions on what you can do. Because a global event callback runs in any VM and thread context, it probably won't have any use for the VMCB and TCB addresses it receives as arguments. Even a VM or thread callback isn't synchronized with the VM or the thread, with the result that the client registers are unpredictable. The callback routine therefore shouldn't alter the client registers unless it first saves and later restores them. Chapter 10 illustrates this kind of programming, which is most often used when you want to execute ring-three code during the event callback.

Another major set of restrictions on event callbacks derives from the need to prevent resource deadlocks. These problems ultimately arise from the fact that, if the *BLOCK_SVC_INTS* flag is specified in a call to a synchronization service, a thread can block on the requested resource in such a way that event callbacks can still occur in that thread. The following list explains the circumstances under which a deadlock can occur and how to avoid them:

■   In general, an event callback shouldn't block on a semaphore or other synchronization primitive. It might be called in the context of the thread that owns the same resource, whereupon that thread promptly deadlocks. Even if no deadlock occurs, blocking may adversely affect smooth multitasking because of the likelihood that the event-handling thread might own resources that other threads need.

■   A deadlock can occur during registry access. Suppose an event callback receives control in a particular thread, but that the same thread's ring-three program happens to be accessing the registry. If the event callback also tries to access the registry, it will deadlock the thread. You can avoid the deadlock by only accessing the registry from restricted event callbacks in which you specify the *PEF_Wait_Not_Nested_Exec* flag.

■   If MS-DOS is being used for paging, an event procedure can inadvertently cause a deadlock by accessing a dynamically allocated data area that's pageable or by calling a memory allocation function. The deadlock would arise if your thread were already blocked waiting for paging but needed to (recursively) page some data. To prevent a problem with your own code, always use the *HEAPLOCKEDIFDP* flag when calling *_HeapAllocate* and the *PAGELOCKEDIFDP* flag when calling *_PageAllocate* instead of allocating always-pageable data. In addition, avoid memory allocation calls within event callbacks. If you're not sure of the origin of a data pointer, you can call *PAGESWAP_Test_IO_Valid* and reschedule your event if the result shows that MS-DOS paging can't be performed, or you can schedule a restricted event with the *PEF_Wait_Not_Crit* flag. Note that the restriction applies only to dynamically allocated data: the VMM page-locks VxD code and data segments automatically if MS-DOS or the BIOS is being used for paging.

Canceling Events

Each of the services that creates an event returns an *event handle* in the ESI register. The event handle is NULL if the VMM has already called the event procedure. If you want to preserve the possibility of canceling the event before the callback eventually happens, you save the handle somewhere:

```
hEvent   dd    0
...
mov      esi, offset32 OnSomeEvent
VMMCall  Call_xxx_Event
mov      hEvent, esi
```

To cancel the event later, you call the matching *Cancel_xxx_Event* service. You need to cancel the event very carefully to avoid the possibility of preemption. In fact, the event callback and the mainline code that cancels the event need to cooperate to make the operation completely safe:

Mainline Code

```
xor      esi, esi
xchg     esi, hEvent
VMMCall  Cancel_xxx_Event
```

Callback Routine

```
BeginProc OnSomeEvent
xor       eax, eax
xchg      eax, hEvent
test      eax, eax
jnz       @F
ret
@@:
...
EndProc OnSomeEvent
```

In looking at this code fragment, it helps to know that the cancellation function tolerates a NULL event handle without complaining. The event callback routine uses the atomic XCHG instruction to fetch the value of *hEvent* while simultaneously setting *hEvent* to NULL. If *hEvent* is already NULL, it means that the mainline code canceled the event, whereupon the event callback routine returns without doing anything. Conversely, if the mainline program reaches its XCHG instruction and finds *hEvent* nonzero, it means that the callback hasn't run yet, whereupon it will cancel the event.

Events in VTOOLSD

The VTOOLSD C++ class library provides several classes that simplify the creation and handling of events in a high-level language. For example, you can schedule a global event by deriving your own class from Vireo's *VGlobalEvent* class:

```
class MyEvent : public VGlobalEvent
    {
public:
    MyEvent(PVOID refData = 0) : VGlobalEvent(refData){}
    virtual void handler(VMHANDLE hVM, CLIENT_STRUCT* pRegs,
        PVOID refData);
    };
```

The *VGlobalEvent* base class has *call* and *schedule* member functions that issue *Call_Global_Event* and *Schedule_Global_Event* calls aimed at an assembly-language thunk. The thunk in turn calls your handler. An object self-destructs after calling its handler function. Therefore, normal coding involving an event like this one is relatively painless:

```
// mainline code
(new MyEvent)->call();    // schedule or call event
...
void MyEvent::Handler(VMHANDLE hVM, CLIENT_STRUCT* pRegs, PVOID refData)
    {
    ... // operations not requiring you to delete this
    }
```

Because you derive your own class, you're free to create data members with wild abandon and, in general, to do all the wonderful things that you can do with a C++ class.

The Vireo event classes also contain *cancel* member functions. You won't want to use them, because they don't use thread-safe code for deciding whether to cancel the event on the one hand or to proceed with the callback on the other. If you want to be able to cancel an event, you must write the appropriate assembly-language code yourself. And the *cancel* member function is unfortunately not a virtual function, so you must also have control over all the places that might cancel the event so you can code a call to your own thread-safe routine, as shown in the following example (this code is included on the companion disc in the \CHAP09\EVENTHANDLING-VTOOLSD directory):

Header File

```
class MyEvent : public VGlobalEvent
    {
    ...
public:
    BOOL CancelSafely();
    }
```

Mainline Code

```
MyEvent* pEvent = new MyEvent;
pEvent->call();
...
pEvent->CancelSafely();
```

Callback Routine

```
BOOL MyEvent::CancelSafely()
    { MyEvent::CancelSafely
    _asm  mov  edx, this
    _asm  xor  esi, esi
    _asm  xchg esi, [edx]VEvent.m_handle
    #ifdef Cancel_Global_Event
        #undef Cancel_Global_Event
    #endif
    VMMcall(Cancel_Global_Event);
    BOOL result;
    _asm  mov result, eax
    if (result)
        delete this;
    return result != 0; // TRUE means actually cancelled
    }                    // MyEvent::CancelSafely

void MyEvent::handler(VMHANDLE hVM, CLIENT_STRUCT* pRegs, PVOID refData)
    {                    // MyEvent::handler
    _asm  mov  edx, this
    _asm  xor  eax, eax
    _asm  xchg eax, [edx]VEvent.m_handle
    BOOL not_cancelled;
    _asm  mov not_cancelled, eax
    if (!not_cancelled)
        return;          // event was cancelled, so abort callback
    ...
    }                    // MyEvent::handler
```

Well, I guess the cancellation logic is a lot of work after all!

SYNCHRONIZING EXECUTION

The VMM can preempt a VxD at practically any time in Windows 95. Therefore, VxDs frequently need to protect shareable data objects by means of a synchronization primitive. This section discusses when a VxD might lose control because of preemption, and then it describes the various ways that a VxD can synchronize its execution with other VxDs and with other instances of itself in other threads.

The reason a VxD can be so easily preempted has to do with paging. If VxD code causes a page fault, the current thread might block waiting for the paging subsystem to fetch a page. Or, if a VxD calls a nonasynchronous service—that is, a service that isn't designed to be used during interrupt servicing—it might reach pageable code. Such a call can trigger a page fault—resulting in preemption—even if the VxD's code is page-locked. Because page faults can occur whether hardware interrupts are enabled or not, preceding a sensitive section of code with a CLI instruction isn't sufficient to protect you.

There are some more prosaic situations in which you might expect to be preempted. If your VxD does one of the following things, it can be preempted:

■ Adjusting the execution priority of another thread can cause the primary scheduler to give control immediately to the other thread.

■ Allocating memory might require paging I/O or changes to the swap file that in turn trigger preemption.

■ Calling *Resume_Exec* will allow queued events to be processed and could generate a thread switch for any number of reasons.

■ Most obviously, calling one of the synchronization services described later in this section can block the calling thread.

Once it is past the initial stages of handling a hardware interrupt, a VxD normally runs with interrupts enabled. Hardware interrupts that preempt a running VxD can't cause a context switch, however, because the rules governing hardware interrupt handlers prescribe that they run in locked code using locked data and that they not call any nonasynchronous services. Furthermore, when a hardware interrupt handler completes its operation and returns to the VMM, the VMM redispatches the VxD that was previously interrupted. The most that can happen as a result of a hardware interrupt, therefore, is that a VxD temporarily loses control while the handler runs.

Suspending and Resuming a Virtual Machine

In Windows 3.0, the only sort of preemptive multitasking was between virtual machines. The VMM provided only rudimentary methods of synchronizing virtual machines in those days: you could suspend a virtual machine completely, thereby making it ineligible for scheduling, and you could wake it up later. Code written by individual VxD writers decided whether to suspend a VM. Windows 3.1 added support for semaphore objects, and Windows 95 adds support for a much richer set of synchronization primitives that I'll discuss presently. The original mechanisms for suspending and resuming tasks at the coarse level of a virtual machine remain in Windows 95, however, even though there's no particular reason to use them in new code.

Sometimes the VMM needs to suspend a VM to prevent it from running while some task occurs. For example, a windowed MS-DOS VM gets suspended while the user does a clipboard copy. Allowing the VM to run might let the screen change in the middle of the operation, thereby frustrating the user. I'm talking about a different use of suspension here, however—namely suspension as a way of synchronizing threads.

Because you might read code from older VxDs that use this obsolete method to synchronize tasks, you should understand what the services do. *Suspend_VM* increments a suspension counter associated with a particular VM:

```
BOOL okay = Suspend_VM(PVMMCB hVM);
```

The return value indicates whether the VM was successfully suspended or not. The VMM does not allow you to suspend the System VM or the critical section owner. If the VM isn't already suspended, the VMM sends a VM_Suspend system control message to all devices before returning from *Suspend_VM*. In response to the message, a device driver might unlock resources (such as V86 memory) that were being held in readiness for the VM.

A suspended VM receives no processor time. Moreover, the V86-mode memory for a suspended VM might be swapped out, which means that a VxD should not try to touch this memory (even at the high-linear address) unless the VxD knows that the memory was page-locked or that paging I/O will be safe.

To restore a VM to eligibility, you call *Resume_VM*:

```
BOOL okay = Resume_VM(PVMMCB hVM);
```

Resume_VM decrements the suspension count for the virtual machine. If that count reaches 0, the VMM sends a VM_Resume system control message to every device. Any VxD receiving this message can fail the *Resume_VM* call by returning with the carry flag set. Failing the call would be the right thing to do if, for example, it were impossible at that time to lock a resource required by the program running in the VM. There's another service you can use—*No_Fail_Resume_VM*—if you're unwilling to tolerate a failure. Because *Resume_VM* can cause a task switch if the newly released VM has the highest execution priority, *Resume_VM* might not return immediately. (The return would happen when the current VM next moves to the front of the execution queue.)

Execution focus is another concept that you need to understand here. The term refers to the foreground virtual machine. The end user ultimately controls which VM has the execution focus by selecting from among the current collection via the mouse, the taskbar, or the Alt-Tab shortcut. In response, the VMM issues a *Set_Execution_Focus* call, which has the effect of suspending all other VMs that aren't enabled for background execution.

The time-slicing scheduler understands another VM state known as *idle* that's similar in some respects to suspension. Idle in this context means that the VM has no useful work to perform, even though it remains theoretically available for execution. A VxD can force a VM into the idle state by calling the *Release_Time_Slice* service. Code running in the VM can also release its own time slice by issuing INT 2Fh, function 1680h. Windows-aware DOS applications should release their time slices rather than continuously polling for some expected event that will take time to complete. Once the expected event occurs, a cooperating VxD should boost the VM's priority and issue a *Wake_Up_VM* call to take the VM out of the idle state. If no one does these two things, the VM won't necessarily receive processor time for a while.

By calling the *Time_Slice_Sleep* service, a VxD can also idle the VM for a long period of time; the VM wakes up if the timeout expires or if someone calls *Wake_Up_VM*. In principle, the VM can wake up early for other reasons, too. In other words, the sleep period is just a maximum; the VxD caller must be prepared for an earlier wakeup.

Critical Sections

The VMM implements a single *critical section* that gates sensitive operations for a large number of system components. You use the *Begin_Critical_Section* service to enter the section. If a thread tries to enter the section when some other thread owns the section, it blocks until the section becomes free. If a thread tries to enter the critical section at a time when it already owns the section, the VMM increments the *claim counter*. Calling *End_Critical_Section* decrements the claim counter. When there have been as many calls to *End_Critical_Section* as to *Begin_Critical_Section*, the section becomes free. See Table 9-10 for a list of all the services that relate to critical sections.

Service(s)	Description
Begin_Critical_Section End_Critical_Section	Enters or leaves the single critical section
Call_When_Not_Critical Cancel_Call_When_Not_Critical	Creates or cancels a callback to be executed when the critical section is not owned
Claim_Critical_Section Release_Critical_Section	Increments or decrements the critical section claim counter by specified values
End_Crit_And_Suspend	Blocks until another VM processes an event (obsolete)
Get_Crit_Section_Status Get_Crit_Status_No_Block Get_Crit_Status_Thread	Determines the current owner of the critical section

Table 9-10. *Services for managing a critical section.*

When you enter the critical section, you specify some flag bits that control when and whether the thread can still be scheduled even while it is blocked waiting for the section:

```
Begin_Critical_Section(flags);
```

The *flags* argument is a combination of the following bits:

■ *BLOCK_THREAD_IDLE* means that the thread should be considered idle for scheduling purposes.

■ *BLOCK_SVC_INTS* allows events and simulated interrupts to be serviced.

■ *BLOCK_ENABLE_INTS* causes the VMM to reflect interrupts into the VM even if the VM is (virtually) disabled. This flag makes sense only if *BLOCK_SVC_INTS* is also set.

The only synchronization primitive Windows 3.0 provided was this single critical section. Accordingly, a great many VxDs did (and still do!) protect whatever they need to protect by claiming it. This excessive use of the critical section is clearly overkill, because there's no particular reason to gate some small piece of list maintenance code in your own VxD based on whether some other thread happens to be blocked on a page fetch, for example. Still, use of the critical section is widespread in Windows, and you might need to understand when it might be claimed behind your back. To this end, here is an incomplete list of common situations in which VxDs might claim the critical section:

■ During paging operations.

■ During calls to memory allocation functions, including *_HeapAllocate*, *_HeapFree*, *_PageAllocate*, and *_PageFree*, among others.

■ During calls to selector management functions such as *_Allocate_LDT_Selector* and others.

■ During calls to *VDMAD_Scatter_Lock*, because of its reliance on the *_LinPageLock* service.

■ During access to V86-mode services within the System VM. It's possible for a thread in the System VM to access V86 services while some other VM owns the critical section but *not* while some other thread in the System VM owns it. The VMM enforces this rule by maintaining a V86 mutex and a critical section mutex. Calling *Begin_V86_Serialization* takes the V86 mutex. Claiming the critical section in the System VM takes *both* mutexes.

BLOCK_SVC_IF_INTS_LOCKED

There's another critical section flag named *BLOCK_SVC_IF_INTS_LOCKED*. I'm sure you're all agog to know what it means, just like I was. Specifying this flag allows the VM to service interrupts only if the *VMSTAT_V86INTSLOCKED* flag is set. There, now you know.

I'll bet you're still not satisfied, are you? You probably want to know what the VM status flag means, too. This flag is left over from Windows 3.0, and Microsoft has been afraid to get rid of it even though *they* don't know of anyone actually using it anymore. The idea back then was that a paging driver would have to process events while waiting for disk I/O to complete. Setting the *VMSTAT_V86INTSLOCKED* flag is actually done by calling *SetResetV86Pageable*, which locks all pages containing global and instanced memory in addition to the local memory that's already locked by default. *SetResetV86Pageable* makes it possible to know that simulated hardware interrupts can't cause nested page faults, which therefore makes it safe for a pager to allow simulated hardware interrupts to occur. Hence, if you specified *BLOCK_SVC_IF_INTS_LOCKED*, you indicated that you could tolerate the servicing of interrupts if someone had used *SetResetV86Pageable* in this way.

■ At entry to DOS. DOS is still not reentrant, even in Windows 95. Therefore, the VMM components that need to call DOS services claim the critical section to guard against the forbidden reentrance.

■ When DOS programs issue INT 2Fh, function 1601h.

■ During calls to *System_Control*. In other words, whenever a VxD processes a system control message, it will be inside the critical section. Accordingly, it should not block. On the plus side, you needn't protect any of the code sections that execute *within* your system control message handlers. Preserving this behavior from Windows 3.1 was apparently a compatibility decision, because some non-Microsoft VxDs depend on it.

Because the critical section controls sensitive and time-critical operations, the VMM automatically boosts the execution priority of the section owner. The amount of the boost, *CRITICAL_SECTION_BOOST*, is numerically equal to 00100000h. This amount is smaller than the *TIME_CRITICAL_BOOST* (00400000h) applied to VMs that are handling hardware interrupts, but it's greater than the other priority boosts that are commonly applied. Thus, the owner of the critical section is pretty certain to execute, deferring only to hardware interrupts.

Critical Sections and Event Callbacks

I remarked earlier that it's very dangerous for an event callback procedure to block. Since *Begin_Critical_Section* can block and thereby create a deadlock condition, you might suppose that no event callback dares to issue this function. There certainly was a problem in Windows 3.1. Programmers evolved a technique that Microsoft calls "chasing the critical section," whereby a callback routine would keep scheduling itself in new tasks until it finally ended up in a task in which it could enter the section:

```
BeginProc OnSomeEvent
VMMCall Get_Crit_Section_Status
VMMCall Test_Cur_VM_Handle
jz      @F
mov     esi, offset32 OnSomeEvent
VMMCall Schedule_VM_Event
ret
@@:
mov     ecx, Block_Svc_Ints
VMMCall Begin_Critical_Section
...
VMMCall End_Critical_Section
ret
EndProc OnSomeEvent
```

You could initially schedule this function as a global event or as a VM event; it doesn't really matter which. The relatively terse code in this function works as follows. The initial call to *Get_Crit_Section_Status* returns with register EBX holding either the handle of the current VM (if no one owns the critical section) or the handle of the VM that owns the critical section. This function can also cause a task switch because of an optimization in the VMM that defers releasing the section until after it processes events. *Test_Cur_VM_Handle* asks if register EBX points to the current VM's control block. If so, it will be safe to issue a *Begin_Critical_Section* call for one of two reasons: either no one owns the critical section now and it can safely be claimed for the first time, or the current VM already owns it and it's safe to increment the claim count. If register EBX points to some other VM, however, the call to *Schedule_VM_Event* will schedule a callback to this same event procedure in the context of that other VM. We're hoping that the other VM still owns the critical section when control next comes back to the callback procedure. If not, the process is repeated.

In Windows 95, you don't need to write this complicated code. Instead, you can just schedule a restricted global event with the *PEF_Wait_Crit* flag:

```
mov     eax, PriorityBoost  ; 0 or something else
xor     ebx, ebx            ; indicate global event
mov     ecx, PEF_Wait_Crit  ; we need to enter critical section
mov     edx, ReferenceData  ; pass-through data to callback
mov     esi, offset32 OnSomeEvent ; callback function
mov     edi, TimeOut        ; in milliseconds
VMMCall Call_Restricted_Event
...
```

An event callback scheduled in this way occurs only when either no one owns the critical section or when the current VM owns it. Just as in the more complicated Windows 3.1 example, either of these situations means that the callback function can safely enter the critical section.

Synchronization Objects

In this section, I'll discuss the three classes of synchronization objects available to a VxD writer: semaphores, mutual exclusion (mutex) objects, and blocking identifiers. Before proceeding with the discussion, however, I want to mention some coding tricks that give you a high-performance way of synchronizing execution even in a highly volatile multitasking environment.

Implementing a Private Critical Section

The first coding trick isn't so much a trick as an observation that, on a uniprocessor system (the only kind currently supported by Windows 95), non–floating-point instructions cannot be interrupted. Even on a multiprocessor system, using the LOCK prefix (in front of an instruction that allows the prefix) guarantees that no other CPU can access shared memory until the current instruction completes. Thus, programmers commonly use XCHG and INC or DEC instructions to accomplish atomic operations because they realize that preemption can't affect the outcome.

So suppose you want to implement a private critical section to guard a resource that you share with other threads running an identical piece of code. Set aside a memory location to contain a claim counter. The counter's initial value is -1, meaning that no one has entered the critical section. A value of 0 denotes that one thread has entered the section, and a value greater than 0 specifies the number of threads that are blocked waiting to enter the section. Your code can claim the section in the normal case, when there's no competition, very quickly:

```
inc claimcount
jz  claimed    ; jump if claim counter == 0
```

At this point in the code, if the critical section has already been claimed, you will have incremented the counter past 0 and will need to explicitly wait on a semaphore. You should initialize this semaphore with a token count of 0 so that the first caller blocks.

Releasing the critical section is similarly painless if there's no competition:

```
dec claimcount
jl  released   ; jump if claim counter < 0 now
```

If the DEC instruction leaves the claim counter at 0 or above, it means that some thread somewhere has blocked while waiting to enter the critical section. In this case, signal the semaphore to release one of the waiting threads.

Don't, by the way, rely on the C-language ++ and -- operators. The compiler might not generate the INC and DEC instructions, which means that you can't be sure of getting the atomic behavior of a single instruction.

Using CMPXCHG

If you know that your code will be running on an Intel i486 or later processor, you can use the compare-and-exchange instruction to advantage. For example, suppose that multiple threads are maintaining a shared counter variable for use in assigning identifiers that must be unique across the system. You'd like to assign an identifier the value of the counter, then increment it, making sure that no other process increments the counter between these two steps.

A safe way to increment the counter with the CMPXCHG instruction is as follows:

```
    mov   eax, idcounter
@@: lea   ecx, [eax + 1]
    cmpxchg idcounter, ecx
    jnz   @B
```

When this code completes, the ECX register holds a unique identifier. The CMPXCHG instruction contains the magic to make this code thread-safe. At each iteration of the loop, register EAX contains our supposition about the current contents of *idcounter*. CMPXCHG compares register EAX with the *idcounter* variable. If they are equal, it means that our assumption was correct, and register ECX now holds the next value. In that case, CMPXCHG stores the contents of register ECX into *idcounter* and leaves the zero flag set to terminate the loop. If they're unequal, however, CMPXCHG reloads register EAX from *idcounter* and clears the zero flag, whereupon the loop will repeat. Since CMPXCHG does all of these things in one atomic operation, the loop can be preempted at any point without allowing two different threads to acquire the same identifier. The code will also work on a multiprocessor system if you add a LOCK prefix to the CMPXCHG instruction.

Here's another trick using CMPXCHG. Suppose you have a linked list shared by other processes. Each element in the list has a chaining field that occupies the first DWORD, and the chaining field in the last element is NULL. To safely add a new element whose address is in register ESI to the head of such a list, you could use the following:

```
    mov   eax, listhead    ; EAX -> head of list
@@: mov   [esi], eax       ; ESI's chain -> head
    cmpxchg listhead, esi  ; make [ESI] head if EAX still head
    jnz   @B               ; repeat with new head in EAX
```

But isn't it wasteful to execute this potentially infinite loop in ring-zero code? No, because it's very unlikely that the system would repeatedly preempt the loop without letting the thread execute at least a couple of instructions to get out of the loop. In fact, it's very unlikely that the loop will ever repeat even once, because it's so unlikely (as a general proposition, that is) that another thread would happen to be executing the same stretch of code at the time of a context switch. Still, we know that shared variables *do* sometimes need protection, and it's nice to have a low-cost way of achieving the protection in the overwhelmingly common case when no contention is actually occurring.

Semaphore Objects

Windows 3.1 introduced ring-zero semaphores as a way to synchronize VMs, and Windows 95 carries the semaphore concept forward to its thread-based multitasking model. Table 9-11 lists the VMM services you use for manipulating semaphores. A semaphore is essentially a counter with some associated semantics that the semaphore services implement. When you call *Create_Semaphore*, you specify an initial value for the token count:

```
VMM_SEMAPHORE sem = Create_Semaphore(initcount);
```

Service	Description
Create_Semaphore	Creates a new semaphore object
Destroy_Semaphore	Destroys a semaphore object
Signal_Semaphore	Signals a semaphore to release a waiting thread
Signal_Semaphore_No_Switch	Signals a semaphore without performing an immediate task switch
Wait_Semaphore	Waits for a semaphore to be signaled

Table 9-11. *Semaphore services.*

The initial count is usually 0, which creates a semaphore that will block the first time someone tries to wait on it. Someone who needs to wait for the resource controlled by the semaphore calls *Wait_Semaphore*:

```
Wait_Semaphore(sem, flags);
```

The *flags* argument specifies options concerning how interrupts can be serviced in the calling thread if the semaphore happens to block; these flags are the same as the ones I described earlier for *Begin_Critical_Section* (see page 229). This function decrements and then tests the token count for the semaphore. If the updated counter is less than 0, the *Wait_Semaphore* service blocks until someone signals the semaphore. Otherwise, it returns immediately.

To release a waiting thread, another thread must call *Signal_Semaphore*:

```
Signal_Semaphore(sem);
```

Signal_Semaphore increments the token count and then checks to see whether anyone is waiting on the semaphore. If so, it releases the highest priority blocked thread and might cause an immediate task switch. When *Signal_Semaphore* eventually returns (which might be right away, of course, if no task switch occurred), interrupts will be enabled.

If you don't want a thread switch to occur right away, or if interrupts are disabled and you want them to stay that way, call *Signal_Semaphore_No_Switch* instead of *Signal_Semaphore*. Any required context switch will occur when the VMM next processes events.

> **NOTE** Windows 95 implements *Signal_Semaphore* and *Signal_Sema-phore_No_Switch* with exactly the same code, meaning that calling *Signal_Semaphore* won't change the interrupt flag and won't cause a context switch. This congruence may change in the future, however, so you should write your code on the assumption that *Signal_Semaphore* might someday have the documented side effects.

Mutex Objects

The word *mutex* stands for *mutual exclusion*. You use a mutex to prevent two threads from executing certain sections of code at the same time. Table 9-12 lists the VMM services you use with a mutex. You initially create the mutex by calling *_CreateMutex*:

```
PVMMMUTEX mutex = _CreateMutex(boost, flags);
```

Here, *boost* is a priority boost that will automatically be applied to whichever thread owns the mutex. The *flags* parameter includes the bits I described earlier in connection with *Begin_Critical_Section* (see page 229). The *flags* parameter can also include *MUTEX_MUST_COMPLETE* to indicate that whoever owns the mutex from time to time has a charmed *must complete* status that precludes suspending or destroying the owner.

Service	Description
_CreateMutex	Creates a new mutex
_DestroyMutex	Destroys a mutex
_EnterMutex	Enters a mutual exclusion section
_GetMutexOwner	Determines which thread owns a mutex
_LeaveMutex	Leaves a mutual exclusion section

Table 9-12. *Mutex services.*

In normal processing, you bracket nonreentrant sections of code with *_EnterMutex* and *_LeaveMutex*:

```
_EnterMutex(mutex);
[sensitive code that only one thread can run at a time]
_LeaveMutex(mutex);
```

Blocking Identifiers

Ring-three Win32 programs can use *event objects* to synchronize threads. The purpose of an event object is to allow a thread to wait until some event occurs—that is, until some other thread finishes an operation. (The word *event* means something different here than it usually does for VxD programmers.) The VMM doesn't provide an object that exactly serves the purpose of a Win32 event object. The VMM does offer, however, a curious pair of synchronization services named *_BlockOnID* and *_SignalID* that you can use to implement an event object at relatively low cost.

Using *_BlockOnID* is simplicity itself. Just pick a random 32-bit number that you hope no one else is using for a blocking ID, and call the service:

```
VMMCall _BlockOnId, <random-32-bit-number, 0>
```

(The second argument to the *_BlockOnID* service contains the same flags you use with *Begin_Critical_Section* to control interrupt handling in the VM while it's blocked.) Now your thread is blocked until some other thread calls *_SignalID* with the same blocking identifier:

```
VMMCall _SignalID, <same-random-32-bit-number>
```

Did I say it was simple to use these services? Well, perhaps too simple. First of all, *_SignalID* acts sort of like a Win32 *PulseEvent* in that it releases only those threads that happen to be waiting at the exact moment you call it. Therefore, you must guard against the possibility of signaling the ID before someone else waits on it. Secondly, *_SignalID* wakes up every thread that's blocked on the same identifier. So if you and some other VxD happen to pick the same ID, you'll wake up to each other's signals. You must therefore have some additional means of knowing when a particular *_SignalID* is meant for you. Ordinarily, VxDs use the flat address of some function or data block they control as the blocking ID, thereby minimizing the chance of collision with some other VxD and simplifying the job of validating a wakeup call.

If you need a somewhat more robust event object than one that you can obtain by simple use of *_BlockOnID* and *_SignalID*, you can create one with a bit of programming. There are three steps you should follow to implement an event object using blocking identifier services:

1. Initialize two bits in memory to 0. One bit, which I'll call the *wait* bit, indicates that someone is waiting for the event. The other bit, which I'll call the *post* bit, indicates that the event has already occurred. (These terms were the ones that OS/360 used to describe the operations it provided for similar objects. Most readers of this book were not born long enough ago to know what OS/360 was. *Hint:* IBM produced it in the days when IBM was the dominant software company on the planet.) After this initialization, it's safe to begin the operation whose conclusion will eventually be awaited by some thread.

2. When a thread needs the results of the operation (whatever it happens to be) it performs a wait operation, as follows: If the post bit is set, the operation is complete and the program can proceed. Otherwise, it sets

the wait bit and calls _BlockOnID_ to suspend itself. When _BlockOnID_ returns, it goes back and tests the post bit again to guard against a coincidental duplication of blocking identifiers. Testing the post bit, setting the wait bit, and calling _BlockOnID_ must be done in such a way that it's impossible for another thread to call _SignalID_ in between. Otherwise, the _SignalID_ call might precede the _BlockOnID_ call, whereupon the thread will block forever. Disabling interrupts is sufficient protection if the code in question is page-locked.

3. When the program that's actually performing the operation completes, it performs a post operation, as follows: it sets the post bit; if the wait bit is also set, it calls _SignalID_ to wake up the thread that's currently blocked on the event. (Actually, it's safe to call _SignalID_ in any case. It's just faster to call it only when necessary.)

This explanation is rather a lot to digest. Happily, the code to implement the algorithm is pretty simple:

```
ecb       db    0
wait_bit equ    1
post_bit equ    2
...
        mov   ecb, 0        ; initialize event control block
...
wait_for_event:
        pushfd              ; save interrupt flag
@@:     cli                 ; disable interrupts
        test  ecb, post_bit ; event already posted?
        jnz   @F            ; if yes, proceed
        or    ecb, wait_bit ; indicate we're waiting
        VMMCall _BlockOnId, <<offset32 ecb>, 0>
        jmp   @B            ; guard against spurious wakeup
@@:     popfd               ; restore interrupt flag
...
post_event:
        or    ecb, post_bit ; indicate event is complete
        test  ecb, wait_bit ; anyone waiting?
        jz    @F            ; if not, no signal needed
        VMMCall _SignalID, <<offset32 ecb>>
@@:
```

Ring-Three vs. Ring-Zero Synchronization Objects

So far, we've been discussing synchronization primitives for VxDs running in ring zero. I have one more synchronization object to discuss before wrapping up this chapter. You can share a ring-three event object with a Win32 program by using some of the services provided by VWIN32 (see Table 9-13). Reinforcing the idea that the VxD and a Win32 application will be working together, the ring-three application must create the event object in the first place by calling *CreateEvent*, and it must then create a ring-zero handle for the event object by calling *OpenVxD-Handle*. The application then passes the ring-zero handle to the VxD using any convenient means. The VxD rather than the application has to eventually release this handle by calling *_VWIN32_CloseVxDHandle*.

Service	Description
_VWIN32_CloseVxDHandle	Closes the ring-zero handle to a ring-three event
_VWIN32_PulseWin32Event	Pulses a ring-three event
_VWIN32_ResetWin32Event	Resets a ring-three event to the unsignaled state
_VWIN32_SetWin32Event	Sets a ring-three event to the signaled state
_VWIN32_WaitMultipleObjects	Waits for one or more ring-three events to be signaled
_VWIN32_WaitSingleObject	Waits for a ring-three event to be signaled

Table 9-13. *Ring-three event services.*

NOTE It's important for you to know that these VWIN32 services are really register-oriented despite having a leading underscore in their names. Apparently, they were once C-convention services and got changed without anyone also changing the names.

In some earlier versions of the Windows 95 SDK, *OpenVxDHandle* was a symbol in the import library for KERNEL32.DLL. Since KERNEL32.LIB is supposed to be portable between Windows 95 and Windows NT, *OpenVxDHandle* is no longer available (as of Visual C++ 4.0, that is). You must link to it explicitly with code like the following:

```
typedef DWORD(*OPENVXDHANDLE)(HANDLE);
OPENVXDHANDLE OpenVxDHandle = (OPENVXDHANDLE)
    GetProcAddress(GetModuleHandle ("KERNEL32"),
    "OpenVxDHandle");
DWORD hr0Event = OpenVxDHandle(hEvent);
```

The VxD uses the ring-zero event handle in calls to the other VWIN32 services listed in Table 9-13. These act just as if a Win32 application had made the corresponding Win32 call.

Chapter 10

Helping Windows 95 Manage Virtual Machines

Most of the complication of VxD writing in previous versions of Windows derived from the need to support MS-DOS virtual machines in ways that made Windows seem to disappear. Even though graphically oriented Windows applications are clearly in the ascendancy vis-à-vis character-oriented MS-DOS applications, the MS-DOS applications are still very much with us and continue to require this kind of support. Furthermore, Windows applications execute in the confines of a VM too. Consequently, systems programmers still need to know many details about VMs.

VMs have a definite life cycle, governed by a set of system control messages that the SHELL virtual device sends to all VxDs as VMs come and go. Since it would be wasteful—not to mention logically incorrect—to have completely separate copies of the real-mode addressable first megabyte of memory in each virtual machine, the VMM goes to great trouble in its management of the V86 region of address space. In previous versions of Windows, MS-DOS was the "real" operating system behind the Windows operating environment. With real-mode device drivers and TSRs therefore forming the backbone of the system, the VMM provided elaborate support for the software interrupts that applications used to obtain system services. That support persists in Windows 95 for compatibility and to provide an alternative for vendors unable to move to a VxD-based solution.

Quite apart from satisfying the demands posed by virtualization, the VMM provides mechanisms that allow applications to communicate directly with VxDs and vice versa. Sixteen-bit applications use API addresses that they obtain by means of a software INT 2Fh interface, whereas 32-bit applications use a variation of the regular Win32 API. VxDs can post Windows messages to gain the attention of applications, and they can directly call 16-bit code at moments that carry the name "application time" or, more whimsically, "AppyTime." With more difficulty, and with greater cooperation on the part of the application, VxDs can also call 32-bit functions via the Windows 95 asynchronous procedure call facility.

THE LIFE CYCLE OF A VM

Virtualizing a device means presenting a fictitious piece of hardware to each VM. Doing so usually requires keeping track of VMs as they come and go. The VMM sends several system control messages over the lifetime of a VM to help you virtualize your device. I summarized these messages earlier in Chapter 4 (Table 4-2). I'll explain them now in more detail.

A user triggers the creation of a new VM by opening an MS-DOS prompt or executing an MS-DOS application from the Windows shell. Windows applications can also create new VMs by using the *WinExec* API function. Integrated development environments like Microsoft Developer Studio use undocumented methods to create hidden VMs, too. Whatever their genesis, VMs come into existence through the mediation of the SHELL virtual device, which performs a number of tasks that result in calls to the *System_Control* service. A VxD therefore participates in the creation of a new VM by responding to a series of system control messages:

1. The SHELL device generates a Create_VM message. In response, the VMM creates the control blocks necessary to describe the new VM and sends the Create_VM message to all devices. If you have reserved space in the VM control block (VMCB) using *_Allocate_Device_CB_Area*, now would be the time to initialize that memory. The Virtual Display Device (VDD), for example, initializes its per-VM information and also initializes any necessary memory or port traps (the subject of Chapter 13) so that it can virtualize I/O operations to the video hardware.

2. The VMM initially creates the VM in the suspended state and schedules events to finish initializing the new VM in its own context. The next step is therefore to call *Resume_VM* in order to make the VM (and, more importantly, the event routine that will finish creating it) eligible to run.

3. The SHELL device next sends a VM_Critical_Init message. You're not allowed to run ring-three code in the VM just yet. Any setup needed before ring-three code gets its first chance to do port I/O, issue software interrupts, and touch mapped memory locations must be finished before the VM_Init message unleashes the ring-three banshees. So you must do that setup either here or while handling the Create_VM message. The difference between this message and Create_VM is subtle, though. The VMM *System_Control* service claims the critical section around the calls it makes to VxD device control procedures. The Create_VM message happens in the context of some machine other than the one being created (usually the System VM, in fact). So the code that handles the VM_Critical_Init message is the place to do initialization steps that might need to claim the critical section on behalf of the new VM. For example, the VDD maps the physical video BIOS pages into a new VM in order to allow real-mode programs to actually use the video system—obviously a good idea. Since the mapping operation requires the critical section and might block, the VDD performs it at this stage. If you have less pathological initialization to do, you might not need to handle this message.

4. The SHELL device sends a VM_Init message. The VM is fully operational at this point. Now is the time to communicate with real-mode code whose assistance is needed to prepare the VM for executing its real-mode program. The VDD, for example, issues a number of INT 10h calls to initialize the real-mode video subsystem.

5. Finally, the SHELL sends a series of Set_Device_Focus messages to direct the drivers responsible for shared devices such as the display, mouse, and keyboard to assign ownership to the new VM. Switching device focus is more a part of assigning the execution focus to the new VM than part of creating it, of course.

NOTE You may have read in the DDK that interrupts are disabled during VM_Critical_Init and that the handler must not enable interrupts. This statement wasn't true in Windows 3.1, and it isn't true in Windows 95. I don't know why the DDK says what it does.

Having initialized the new VM, the VMM now allows it to enter into the normal fray of preemptive multitasking with all the other VMs. The application that created the VM in the first place will have established the program to be executed by calling *_DOSMGR_Set_Exec_VM_Data*. That program will execute. When it returns, the VMM regains control to destroy the VM in an orderly way. This orderly process proceeds with the system control messages VM_Terminate, VM_Terminate2,

VM_Suspend, VM_Suspend2, VM_Not_Executeable, VM_Not_Executeable2, Set_Device_Focus, Destroy_VM, and Destroy_VM2. (Recall that VxDs receive the "2" messages in reverse of the normal initialization order.)

NOTE If you monitor the system control messages that accompany the creation and destruction of an MS-DOS prompt, you'll also notice a thread being created and destroyed. WINOLDAP, the GUI interface for MS-DOS prompts, runs in this thread. There is also a second thread associated with the VM. The VMM uses this associated thread to schedule processor time for the VM, but it never sends the usual system control messages with respect to it.

There is also a not-so-orderly shutdown process that comes into play when something goes badly wrong in the VM, such as a general protection fault that no one handles. A VxD can call *Crash_Cur_VM* or the politically incorrect *Nuke_VM* service to abruptly terminate a VM. When that happens, the VMM bypasses the VM_Terminate message altogether. In this case, a VxD's first indication that a VM is shutting down is a VM_Not_Executeable message. For this reason, most drivers don't bother handling VM_Terminate because there's no certainty of ever receiving it.

Protected-Mode Applications

Pressing memory constraints once spawned an entire subindustry devoted to products generically named *DOS extenders*. A DOS extender is a system-level program that uses protected mode and extended memory to allow very large programs to run under MS-DOS. At the time Windows 3.0 appeared on the market, most major end-user applications used a DOS extender because the 640 KB real-mode region was just too small. Microsoft built DOS extender technology into Windows in the form of the DOS Protected Mode Interface (DPMI). Various VxDs augment the DPMI by providing protected-to-real-mode translation of the many interrupt-oriented APIs used by MS-DOS and 16-bit Windows programs.

The world of DOS extenders impinges on a VxD in several ways. I'll talk later in this chapter about how a VxD can supplement the DOS extender functionality already present in Windows 95. Right now I want to describe the two system control messages that pertain to DPMI. On a machine running MS-DOS without Windows, a DOS extender simply uses privileged instructions, including LGDT and MOV into register CR0, to switch the processor into protected mode. If Windows is running, it must instead use INT 2Fh, function 1687h, to obtain the address of a mode-switch routine. Calling this routine switches the VM from V86 mode to protected mode. Eventually, the application calls INT 21h, function 4Ch, to simultaneously terminate the program and return the VM to V86 mode.

When the real-mode program first calls the DPMI mode-switch routine, the VMM sends all drivers a Begin_PM_App system control message. When the protected-mode program terminates, the VMM sends an End_PM_App message. Drivers that are part of the VxD subsystem collectively known as DPMI respond to these messages. Exiting protected mode without releasing memory blocks allocated using DPMI function 0501h, for example, triggers automatic freeing of the memory.

After an application switches into protected mode, the VM control block's *VMSTAT_PM_APP* status flag will be set. If the application indicated that it was a 32-bit application in the initial mode-switch call, the *VMSTAT_PM_USE32* flag will be set as well. While the VM is in protected mode, the *VMSTAT_PM_EXEC* flag will also be set; this flag is cleared during intervals when the VM is running in V86 mode.

The System VM

I cast the preceding discussion in terms of MS-DOS VMs created *after* Windows is up and running. There is always at least one VM running when Windows is running, however: the System VM in which Windows programs run. The VMM creates the System VM automatically as part of the normal startup process. VxDs therefore never see the usual set of VM startup and shutdown messages for the System VM. Instead:

■ Any initialization a device would do while handling the Create_VM or VM_Critical_Init messages for the System VM should be done during one of the three device initialization stages.

■ A device can handle the Sys_VM_Init message, which is analogous to the VM_Init message. It's more usual, however, to simply call one's own VM_Init handler from within the Device_Init handler. Because driver initialization occurs in the context of the System VM, this time is as good as any to trigger the necessary functions.

■ A device can handle the Sys_VM_Terminate (and Sys_VM_Terminate2) message in addition to the VM_Terminate message. It's probably more usual to ignore this message and deal instead with the System_Exit message: you'll receive the System_Exit message even in situations in which the VMM bypasses generation of the Sys_VM_Terminate message.

THE V86 REGION

The *V86 region* of memory consists of all the linear addresses that a V86-mode program can address by using a segment:offset address. It amounts to almost 1.1 MB of memory beginning at 0000:0000 and extending through the last byte of the high memory area (HMA) at FFFF:FFFF. Figure 10-1 on the following page illustrates

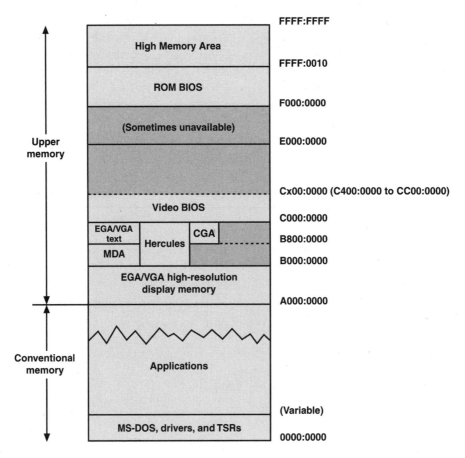

Figure 10-1. *Map of real-mode memory under MS-DOS.*

the familiar layout of real-mode memory when a PC is running MS-DOS. MS-DOS, the device drivers it loads during system startup, and any TSR utilities the user loads occupy the lowest addresses in memory. From the end of these resident programs and their data areas to the start of the *adapter memory area* at location A000:0000 is a large area in which MS-DOS applications execute. The contents of the adapter memory area vary depending on what hardware exists, but certain address assignments are predictable. For example, the video card's on-board memory occupies the region from A000:0000 to Cx00:0000, and the ROM BIOS occupies F000:0000 to F000:FFFF. As much as 128 KB of address space below the BIOS might not map to any physical memory at all.

The VMM's job insofar as the V86 region is concerned is to mimic this layout in a way that allows V86 programs to run normally in multiple VMs. Table 10-1 lists the VxD services that serve this purpose.

Service	Description
_AddInstanceItem	Designates a region of V86 memory as containing instance data that differs between VMs
_Allocate_Global_V86_Data_Area	Allocates memory (usually in small amounts) that a VxD can use to communicate with its real-mode counterparts
_Assign_Device_V86_Pages	Marks V86 region pages as being assigned, either globally or for a specific VM
_DeAssign_Device_V86_Pages	Marks an assigned V86 page as not being assigned anymore
_GetFirstV86Page	Retrieves the number of the first local page in a specified VM
_Get_Device_V86_Pages_Array	Retrieves a copy of the bit map describing assigned V86 pages
_GetLastV86Page	Retrieves the number of the last local page in a specified VM
GetSet_HMA_Info	Retrieves or alters information related to the high memory area
Hook_V86_Page	Establishes a handler for a page fault on specified V86 addresses
_LinMapIntoV86	Maps memory whose linear address you know into the V86 page table
_MapIntoV86	Maps memory whose block handle you know into the V86 page table
_PhysIntoV86	Maps memory whose physical address you know into the V86 page table
_TestGlobalV86Mem	Reports global, local, or instanced status of a range of addresses

Table 10-1. *V86 area management services.*

By default, the VMM classifies all memory that is in use when Windows starts as *global*. The global classification means that every VM will contain the same data at the same linear addresses. The program code within MS-DOS and the BIOS is global, which means that the System VM and every MS-DOS prompt will end up sharing a single physical copy of this code. Real-mode device drivers and TSRs are in the same category.

In contrast, *local* memory has different physical memory behind identical linear addresses in each VM. When you start Windows, most of the conventional memory area is free and becomes local memory. Then, each time you open a new MS-DOS prompt, you have the same large amount of conventional memory available for MS-DOS applications. Making this memory local to each VM is what makes the MS-DOS sessions in each VM separate from one another.

The local memory area is bounded by pages that you can find by calling _GetFirstV86Page and _GetLastV86Page. For example, one of the things the SHELL device does while creating a new VM is call *V86MMGR_Allocate_V86_Pages* to set up the base V86 memory. That service in turn uses _GetFirstV86Page and _Get-LastV86Page to determine the boundaries around the local memory region.

It's possible during device initialization for a VxD to allocate memory that will end up being globally available. _Allocate_Global_V86_Data_Area reserves a block of memory for use both by the VxD and by real-mode code with which the VxD communicates. Since a real-mode driver or TSR can't address memory outside the V86 region, this service allows a real-mode program to share memory with a VxD. You use this service if your architecture requires permanent V86 memory or if the real-mode program initiates calls to the VxD after filling a real-mode buffer with some data. If, however, the VxD initiates the call to real mode and needs to supply a pointer to a temporary data area, there are V86MMGR services designed for DOS extension purposes that are better suited to the task.

Instance Memory

Instance memory is global memory that must have different contents for each VM. A good example is the command recall buffer belonging to a program such as DOSKEY. It won't do for the keystrokes you type in one MS-DOS prompt to show up in another MS-DOS prompt, but DOSKEY itself is a TSR that would normally occupy global memory shared by all VMs. Instancing DOSKEY's recall buffer provides a physically separate copy of data that all VMs access at the same virtual address.

I know of five different ways to instance a block of memory. During the protected-mode initialization of a VxD (that is, before and during the Init_Complete message), you can call _AddInstanceItem:

```
#pragma VxD_IDATA_SEG
static InstDataStruc ids = {0, 0, 0, 0, ALWAYS_FIELD};
ids.InstLinAddr = linaddr;
ids.InstSize = size;
_AddInstanceItem(&ids, 0);
```

This call defines the memory area beginning at *linaddr* and extending for *size* bytes as containing instance data that will have a private value in each different VM. Note that the *InstDataStruc* passed to _AddInstanceItem must persist through Init_Complete. The easiest way to ensure the proper persistence without having the structure present for the entire Windows session is to declare it as a static variable in the initialization data segment.

You can also define memory for instancing during real-mode initialization. I described this interface in Chapter 8.

If the memory you want to instance happens to be an entire real-mode device driver, you can just call *DOSMGR_Instance_Device* during handling of the Init_Complete message. For example, to locate and instance a device named MS$MOUSE, you would use this statement:

```
DOSMGR_Instance_Device("MS$MOUSE");
```

Windows-aware drivers and TSRs should save you the trouble of having to instance memory from within a VxD by responding to the INT 2Fh, function 1605h, startup broadcast. On return from this interrupt, the ES:BX register pair points to a linked list of *startup info structures* that name VxDs to be statically loaded and that describe instance memory regions. For example, a Windows-aware driver should include code similar to the following:

```
sis         db    3, 0              ; SIS_Version
            dd    0                 ; SIS_Next_Dev_Ptr
            dd    0                 ; SIS_Virt_Dev_File_Ptr
            dd    0                 ; SIS_Reference_Data
            dd    ids               ; SIS_Instance_Data_Ptr
ids         dd    inststart         ; FAR* to start of region
            dw    instlength        ; length of instance region
            dd    0                 ; fence to end instance list
...
inststart equ $                     ; start of instance area
... [This area of memory is instanced in each VM]
instlength equ $-inststart          ; length of instance area
...
            assume ds:nothing, cs:@curseg
            align 4
org2f       dd    ?
int2f:      cmp   ax, 1605h         ; Windows startup?
            je    @F                ; if yes, skip ahead
chain2f:    jmp   [org2f]           ; chain to next handler
@@:         test  bx, 1             ; standard mode startup?
            jnz   chain2f           ; if yes, ignore
            pushf                   ; call next handler
            call  [org2f]           ;   ..
            mov   word ptr sis+2, bx ; build SIS chain
            mov   word ptr sis+4, es ;   ..
            mov   bx, cs            ; set ES:BX -> SIS chain
            mov   es, bx            ;   ..
            mov   bx, offset sis    ;   ..
            iret                    ; return to VMM32 startup
```

The Windows 3.1 Virtual Mouse Driver (VMD) illustrates several of these methods. I'm using this out-of-date VMD as an example because it's a fairly comprehensive sample for which Microsoft Development Platform subscribers have the source code (in the Windows 3.1 DDK). Bear in mind that the Windows 95 VMOUSE driver is completely different, except that it performs some of the same functions in order to provide compatible support for Windows 3.1 mouse drivers.

During handling of the Init_Complete message, the VMD issues an INT 2Fh, function 1607h, device call out (in real mode) to see whether the real-mode mouse driver is Windows-aware. If so, the real-mode driver will already have instanced itself appropriately by handling INT 2Fh, function 1605h, as described above. If not, the VMD checks to see whether the real-mode INT 33h (mouse services) handler is a TSR; if so, it calls _AddInstanceItem to instance the memory block that contains the INT 33h handler. If neither of these checks works, the VMD calls DOSMGR_Instance_Device as a last resort to instance a real-mode driver named MS$MOUSE. From this description, you can see that a mouse vendor can inadvertently defeat the VMD's instancing attempt by failing to hook INT 2Fh and by installing the driver as an MS-DOS device named something other than MS$MOUSE.

The fifth and final way to create instance memory is by means of a flag argument to _Allocate_Global_V86_Data_Area:

```
DWORD linaddr = _Allocate_Global_V86_Data_Area(nbytes,
    GVDAInstance);
```

Because the main reason you allocate a global V86 data area is to communicate with real-mode resident code, you'll convert this linear address to a segment:offset address somewhere down the line. This conversion is a simple arithmetic transformation of the linear address:

```
WORD segment = (WORD) (linaddr >> 4);
WORD offset = (WORD) linaddr & 0xF;
```

To create a protected-mode address that can be used by a 16-bit Windows application, be sure that your driver is running in the context of the System VM's protected-mode program and use Map_Lin_To_VM_Addr:

```
WORD selector;
DWORD offset;
PVMMCB hVM = Get_Cur_VM_Handle();
ASSERT(Test_Sys_VM_Handle(hVM)
    && (hVM->CB_VM_Status & VMSTAT_PM_EXEC));
Map_Lin_To_VM_Addr(linaddr, nbytes-1, &selector, &offset);
```

NOTE Microsoft officially discourages using *Map_Lin_To_VM_Addr* because it permanently consumes a selector. Windows itself uses this service to establish permanent mappings to addresses like 400h, A0000h, B0000h, B8000h, and so on. Usually you would allocate a global V86 data area because you wanted to share memory between a real-mode driver and a VxD. If you wanted to include a Win16 DLL driver in this sharing, it would be perfectly appropriate to create a permanent pointer to the shared memory.

You might be wondering how the VMM implements memory instancing. If a V86 page contains instance data, the VMM marks its page table entry as *not present* each time it performs a task switch to a new VM. If anyone tries to touch the page, the page-fault handler copies the instance values appropriate to the current VM into the physical page first. Thus, anyone who looks at or alters the instance data always sees the correct private copy. There's a small penalty to pay for accesses to noninstance data that happens to share a page with instance data, of course, but the penalty is much less onerous than copying all instance data on every task switch.

Device Memory

Each page within the V86 region can belong to a particular VxD. For example, the local memory area belongs to the V86MMGR device, and the various RAM areas associated with the video display belong to the Virtual Display Driver. The VMM maintains bit maps to describe page ownership, and it provides a simple reservation scheme that allows VxDs to manage those bit maps.

To take over ownership of a page, first call *_Get_Device_V86_Pages_Array* to obtain a local copy of the reservation map. Then test the appropriate bit to see whether some other VxD has reserved the same page. Finally, call *_Assign_Device_V86_Pages* to actually make the assignment. For example, the following code fragment globally assigns the page beginning at linear address 000B8000h (the start of the standard VGA text buffer):

```
DWORD devpages[9];    // room for all 110h bits needed
if (_Get_Device_V86_Pages_Array(NULL, devpages, 0)
    && !(devpages[0xB8 / 0x20] & (1 << (0xB8 % 0x20))))
    _Assign_Device_V86_Pages(0xB8, 1, NULL, 0);
```

There is a local assignment map for each VM and a separate global assignment map. A global assignment applies to all subsequently created VMs. A VxD normally makes global assignments during initialization—that is, during handling of the Sys_Critical_Init, Device_Init, or Init_Complete messages. A local assignment applies only to a specific VM and would normally occur during Create_VM processing.

The owner of a V86 page is responsible for supplying some physical memory to back up the virtual address. That's what the three xxx*IntoV86* services are for. For example, the V86 memory manager device exports a service named *V86MMGR_Allocate_V86_Pages* that the SHELL device uses to set up the base memory for a new VM. The major thing this service accomplishes is to define the contents of the local memory region of the VM. To do so, the V86MMGR allocates a block of linear address space by calling *_PageAllocate*, and it maps this memory block into the V86 region by calling *_MapIntoV86*. In this case, the V86MMGR makes a local assignment of the pages it maps.

As another example, consider the VGA text buffer beginning at 000B8000h. The Virtual Display Device globally assigns this region of memory in order to virtualize the display. It uses *Hook_V86_Page* to establish a page-fault handler that will receive control when the VM tries to touch this memory. If the VM is running in a window, the display device uses *_MapIntoV86* to map a private region of memory into the video RAM addresses. This mapping allows several VMs to run simultaneously, each one thinking that it is writing directly to hardware when it stores characters and attributes into the video RAM. If, however, the VM is running full screen, the display device uses *_PhysIntoV86* to map the real video RAM into the VM, thereby affording direct access to the hardware.

Upper Memory

Developers of MS-DOS applications have traditionally been willing to do just about anything to break the constraints of the 640-KB conventional memory region. One of the enduring solutions to "RAM cram" is essentially a kludge based on the observation that running an Intel 80386 or compatible processor in V86 mode also lets you enable paging for real-mode programs. By mapping otherwise inaccessible extended memory into V86 linear addresses, it's possible for MS-DOS, the BIOS, and other real-mode programs to actually use some of the megabytes of extended memory that might be installed on a particular machine. There's no getting around the fundamental 1.1 MB of real-mode addressability, however. Expanded memory manager products like EMM386, QEMM, and 386Max therefore locate holes in the physical memory between 0A0000h and 100000h. They create a page table that maps the actual physical memory on a physical-equals-virtual basis and that maps extended memory into the holes. These products can also create *upper memory blocks* (UMBs) that allow MS-DOS to allocate this virtual memory for its own use and for the use of MS-DOS applications.

You might think that expanded memory managers would now be of purely historical interest. They remain very much a part of the Windows 95 landscape, however, mostly because of the difficulty network vendors have had moving their drivers to protected mode. The third-party network I'm using at the moment needs almost 100 KB of real-mode drivers. I don't know why this network vendor hasn't supplied a protected-mode version of its software for Windows 95, but it hasn't. Installing EMM386 gains me about 80 KB of conventional memory, which can make the difference between being able to run some real-mode programs (mostly games) or not.

Handing off control of the paging hardware and of UMBs from the expanded memory manager to Windows requires some delicacy. The first step in the handoff is for the memory manager to use yet one more feature of the INT 2Fh, function 1605h, startup broadcast. Before returning, the memory manager can either switch the processor back to real mode or set the DS:SI register pair to point to a mode-switch routine that Windows can call to perform the switch at a more auspicious moment. Windows uses an additional, undocumented interface to determine the current state of memory. Basically, the V86MMGR issues an *IOCTL* call to the memory manager to retrieve a data structure that it can use to mimic the memory layout established by the memory manager.[1]

The timing of the memory management mimicry can assume importance for some VxDs. Until the V86MMGR sets up the machinery for addressing UMBs while processing the Sys_Critical_Init message, it's not safe to follow the MS-DOS memory chain from conventional memory into upper memory. Because real-mode drivers and TSRs, and even MS-DOS itself, may occupy UMBs, it's not even safe to examine the memory that contains a real-mode interrupt handler. The V86MMGR has a very high initialization ordinal (A0000000h). If you happen to need access to the first megabyte of memory while handling the Sys_Critical_Init message, you should use the special initialization order constant *UNDEF_INIT_TOUCH_MEM_INIT_ORDER* (A8000000h). If this initialization ordinal won't work for you, wait to access that memory until you receive the Device_Init message.

Accessing V86 Memory

Each VM owns a 4-MB region of the linear address space that maps one-for-one to the first megabyte of linear addresses. While the VM is active, the VMM duplicates the page table entries for this 4-MB region at address 0. That is, while the VM is running, its V86 region is simultaneously addressable beginning at linear address 0 and at the unique *high-linear address*. Windows accomplishes the dual mapping by simply installing a single 32-bit pointer in the page directory, since each page directory entry controls 1024 page table entries—equivalent to 1024 × 4096 bytes of virtual memory. The *CB_High_Linear* field of a VMCB contains the high-linear base address.

---

1 For full details, see "The Windows Global EMM Import Interface" by Taku Okazaki, in *Dr. Dobb's Journal*, September 1994.

A VxD should always access V86 memory using the high-linear version of the address. For example, the following code shows the approved way to access the COM1 port address held in the BIOS data area at 40:0h:

```
PVMMCB hVM = Get_Cur_VM_Handle();
WORD address = *(WORD *) (0x400 + hVM->CB_High_Linear);
```

The reason for restricting access to low memory is that the debug version of the VMM doesn't normally map the first megabyte of memory for VxD access. Not mapping this memory helps you catch NULL pointer references or references to structure fields located within a small offset from a NULL pointer. If you truly need to use the V86 address for some reason, bracket the reference with calls to *Enable_Touch_1st_Meg* and *Disable_Touch_1st_Meg*. Instead of calling the services directly, it's customary to use two macros from DEBUG.H for this purpose, as shown here:

```
#include <debug.h>
...
WORD address;
Begin_Touch_1st_Meg(); // enables first MB in debug build
address = *(WORD*) 0x400;
End_Touch_1st_Meg(); // disables first MB in debug build
```

The advantage of the macros is that they generate no code in a retail build, where there's no restriction on first-megabyte access anyway.

SOFTWARE INTERRUPTS

In the world of MS-DOS, programs communicate by issuing software interrupts and by sharing well-known data structures. Reflecting its real-mode roots, Windows continued to use MS-DOS and BIOS interrupts through version 3.1. As a matter of fact, 16-bit Windows programs *still* use software interrupts as their primary operating system API. In Chapters 5 and 6 I described how an interrupt issued in protected mode vectors through the processor's interrupt descriptor table to a protected-mode handler, and I also alluded to the VxD services that allow people such as you and I to install our own interrupt handlers. In this section, I'll complete the discussion of software interrupt handling.

Nothing I'm about to say has anything to do with Win32 programs. Thirty-two–bit Windows programs use the Win32 API, which is entirely based on function calls. At the innermost core of KERNEL32, a diligent reverse engineer can find a call to the VWIN32 VxD, which in turn calls one of a small number of ring-zero service routines. Not only do Win32 programs not issue software interrupts, they *cannot*; the VMM believes that any interrupt coming from the System VM must be from a 16-bit program and therefore saves and restores only part of the processor state.

Consequently, this discussion concerns only 16-bit Windows programs, MS-DOS programs (which are necessarily 16-bit), and extended DOS programs (which can be either 16-bit or 32-bit). This subset of applications is no longer commercially interesting, but compatibility requires that Windows continue to support them for a long time to come.

To make things concrete, suppose you were responsible for a Virtual Mouse Driver. In MS-DOS, one uses software interrupt 33h to talk to the real-mode mouse driver. Therefore, one of your jobs as a VxD writer will be to handle INT 33h calls coming from protected-mode programs. In Windows 3.1, the Windows mouse driver (MOUSE.DRV) used INT 33h. In Windows 95, extended DOS programs can still use the INT 33h interface.

Hooking an Interrupt

Set_PM_Int_Vector is the correct VxD service to use for hooking a protected-mode software interrupt. This service installs a gate directly into the IDT. If you use this service before the Sys_VM_Init message is generated, you specify the default handler for every VM. Otherwise, you specify the handler only for whatever VM happens to be current. The real Virtual Mouse Driver installs its INT 33h handler while processing the Sys_Critical_Init message so as to become the handler of last resort if no one else hooks it (and usually no one does). You should also install a handler while processing the Sys_Critical_Init message if your interrupt uses any pointer parameters that require translation from protected mode to real mode and if some other VxD might use *Exec_VxD_Int* to invoke your translation code while it is handling the Device_Init message.

You should always install a ring-three handler address into the IDT with *Set_PM_Int_Vector*. You *could* install a ring-zero address, but your code would then have the responsibility of setting up the ring-zero execution environment in exactly the same way that the VMM's first-level handlers already do. To hook an interrupt in such a way that you can handle it in a VxD, you create an object called a *protected-mode callback* by calling *Allocate_PM_Call_Back*:

```
mov      edx, refdata                 ; arbitrary pass-through data
mov      esi, offset32 i33callback  ; address of callback routine
VMMCall  Allocate_PM_Call_Back       ; create callback
jc       error                       ; handle error
```

Then you point the IDT to the protected-mode callback address:

```
movzx    edx, ax                ; cx:edx = first level handler
mov      ecx, eax               ;   ..
shr      ecx, 16                ;   ..
mov      eax, 33h               ; eax = interrupt number
VMMCall  Set_PM_Int_Vector      ; install default INT 33h handler
```

The preceding code fragment decomposes the 32-bit value returned in register EAX by *Allocate_PM_Call_Back* into a selector:offset address in the CX:EDX register pair, which is where *Set_PM_Int_Vector* wants to find the address of your interrupt handler. After you have taken these two steps, whenever a ring-three protected-mode program executes an INT 33h instruction, the VMM will route control to your *i33callback* routine with the register contents shown in Table 10-2. The callback routine can modify any general register and use any VxD service. (Even though the callback routine is handling an interrupt, it's not a *hardware* interrupt for which the draconian asynchronous-only restrictions apply.)

Register	*Contents*
EBX	Address of current VMCB
EDX	Reference data from the call to *Allocate_PM_Call_Back*
EDI	Address of current thread control block
EBP	Address of client register structure containing register values for the VM at the time it called the callback routine

Table 10-2. *Contents of registers at entry to a protected-mode callback routine.*

As a practical matter, the callback routine must be written in assembly language to accommodate the register parameters. You could code a callback as a simple wrapper for a C program if you wanted to:

```
            extrn  _OnInt33@16:near
BeginProc i33callback, pageable
            push   ebp            ; client registers
            push   edi            ; current thread
            push   edx            ; reference data
            push   ebx            ; current VM
            call   _OnInt33@16    ; handle interrupt
            ret                   ; return to caller

void __stdcall OnInt33(PVMMCB hVM, DWORD refdata,
                PTCB tcb, PCRS pRegs)
      {
      ...
      }
```

As you'll see, this approach might not be the best one because the API functions you use for translating pointers for real mode are very difficult to use in a high-level language. I'll therefore present the rest of this example in assembly language.

To recapitulate, the code fragments just described are the equivalent of hooking an interrupt by calling MS-DOS using INT 21h, function 35h, or *_dos_setvect*. Figure 10-2 on the following page diagrams what happens when protected-mode code in a VM issues the interrupt that we've hooked. The interrupt initially vectors to the INT 30h instruction at the address we installed by calling *Set_PM_Int_Vector*. The

---

V86 AND PROTECTED-MODE CALLBACKS

A *protected-mode callback* is an object that allows a ring-three protected-mode program to reach ring zero. When you call *Allocate_PM_Call_Back*, you supply the address of one of your own functions and a "reference data" value. The VMM assigns to you one of a fixed pool of INT 30h instructions located in segment 3Bh. (That segment contains nothing but INT 30h instructions, in fact.) When a ring-three program executes an INT 30h call, the VMM routes control to your function, providing the "reference data" value as an argument.

You can do one of two basic things with the address of a protected-mode callback. The text illustrates hooking a ring-three interrupt using a callback address. You can also give an application the callback address as a function pointer. When the application dereferences the pointer, it executes the INT 30h call and thereby transfers control to you. A protected-mode callback therefore gives you the ability to provide what amounts to a ring-zero subroutine to an application. The VMM uses protected-mode callbacks for additional purposes internally. For example, the VMM uses a protected-mode callback address to regain control following nested execution of ring-three code. The VMM also creates a protected-mode callback when an application uses INT 2Fh, function 1684h, to find the address of a VxD's protected-mode API.

The VMM provides a completely analogous set of services to V86-mode programs by means of *V86 callbacks*. You use V86 callbacks to hook V86-mode interrupts and to let V86-mode programs call you. You create a V86 callback by calling *Allocate_V86_Call_Back*. The resulting segment:offset address identifies an ARPL (adjust requested privilege level) instruction. Executing the ARPL instruction in V86 mode causes an Invalid Operation exception (INT 06h). Based on the address of the exception, the VMM can identify the callback as belonging to you and route control to your ring-zero callback routine. In some cases, the ARPL instruction is actually in the middle of a text string in the BIOS that just coincidentally has the right bit pattern—it happens to be 63h, which is the letter *c*. If you ever wondered what the *Locate_Byte_In_ROM* service was for, it's to search the BIOS for a 63h bit pattern that can do double duty as an ARPL.

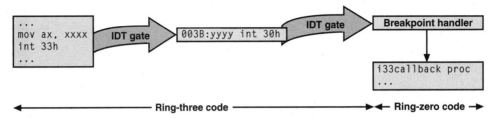

Figure 10-2. *Control flow during a protected-mode interrupt.*

VMM uses the address of the INT 30h instruction to locate our *i33callback* routine. When the handler returns, the VMM will redispatch the VM at its current CS:IP address. Without intervention from our callback routine, the same breakpoint INT 30h would execute over and over again. To prevent this infinite loop from happening, the callback must use *Simulate_Iret* to redirect the VM to the instruction following the original INT 33h:

```
BeginProc i33callback, pageable
VMMCall Simulate_Iret  ; arrange for VM to return
...
EndProc i33callback
```

Reflecting the Interrupt

You can find documentation for the INT 33h API in a variety of places. See, for example, Ralf Brown and Jim Kyle's *PC Interrupts* (Addison-Wesley, 1991). Let's consider an easy function first:

```
mov   ax, 2      ; function 2: hide mouse cursor
int   33h        ; issue mouse function call
```

As this fragment suggests, calls to the mouse driver use register AX to hold a function code, and function 02h hides the mouse cursor. In the absence of a real-mode mouse driver, ring-zero components would handle this call completely in protected mode. If the user has installed a real-mode driver, however, Windows defers control of the mouse to it. (The hardware mouse might, for example, require special software that hasn't yet been ported to Windows 95.) Sending the interrupt down to real mode is called *reflecting* the interrupt.

The mechanics of reflecting an interrupt involve the concept of *nested execution*. You create a nested execution block by calling *Begin_Nest_V86_Exec* (to execute real-mode code) or *Begin_Nest_Exec* (to execute protected-mode code). In the case we're considering, we would use *Begin_Nest_V86_Exec* because we want to execute the real-mode mouse driver to handle the Hide Cursor request. This service will install the current alternate set of client registers and set the virtual CS:IP to a V86 callback address. You use the *Exec_Int* service to execute the real-mode interrupt handler. *Exec_Int* pushes the client flags and instruction pointer onto the real-mode stack and changes the client CS:IP to point to the real-mode handler for a specific interrupt. Then it causes the VMM to dispatch the VM, thereby running the real-mode interrupt handler. The real-mode code performs an IRET to return to the V86 breakpoint belonging to the nested execution manager, whereupon you regain control at the instruction following your call to *Exec_Int*. Finally, you use *End_Nest_Exec* to restore the VM to its state before the nested execution block was executed. To perform these steps, your INT 33h handler might read as follows:

```
VxD_PAGEABLE_DATA_SEG
i33func  label  dword
         dd     offset32 i33_00
         dd     offset32 i33_01
         dd     offset32 i33_02
         ...
VxD_PAGEABLE_DATA_ENDS

BeginProc i33callback, pageable
         VMMCall Simulate_Iret  ; arrange for VM to return
         movzx  eax, [ebp + Client_AX] ; get function code
         jmp    [i33func + 4 * eax]    ; dispatch handler
         ...
i33_02:  call   reflect              ; hide cursor
         jmp    done
         ...
done:    ret
EndProc  i33callback

BeginProc reflect, pageable
         VMMCall Begin_Nest_V86_Exec
         mov    eax, 33h
         VMMCall Exec_Int
         VMMCall End_Nest_Exec
         ret
EndProc  reflect
```

You can think of *Exec_Int* as a function that executes in real mode because you don't regain control until after the VM returns. In reality, *Exec_Int* processes any waiting events and can trigger a task switch to some other VM. It might be a long time, in other words, before the VM actually executes the interrupt. If timing were critical, you could always use *Adjust_Exec_Priority* to boost the VM's priority to improve its chances of staying in control.

Although it is correct, this example glosses over some of the complications and generalities you need to know about when using nested execution blocks. The first thing to notice is that any changes made to general registers by the real-mode interrupt handler will be propagated back to the protected-mode client. Overwriting the original registers is intentional in the case of this interrupt handler, because the real-mode handler provides results in general registers. If you *don't* want the nested program to alter the general registers, you can save and restore them around the nested execution block:

```
...
Push_Client_State                ; save registers
VMMCall Begin_Nest_V86_Exec
...
VMMCall End_Nest_Exec
Pop_Client_State                 ; restore registers
```

Push_Client_State is a macro that decrements the stack pointer to make room for a data area, whose address it passes to the *Save_Client_State* service. Pop_Client_State is another macro, which calls *Restore_Client_State* and pops the stack back to its original position. You always use these two macros in a pair, as shown here.

Another thing you need to know is that there's a more general service than *Exec_Int* called *Resume_Exec*. *Resume_Exec* processes events and dispatches the VM, returning to your driver when the VM executes its breakpoint. To make *Resume_Exec* useful, you need to use some auxiliary services to manipulate the client registers and the stack beforehand (see Table 10-3). For example, you could implement *Exec_Int* by calling *Simulate_Int* followed by *Resume_Exec*. If it weren't for an important side effect of using *Simulate_Int* and *Exec_Int* (namely that they call hook procedures set up by *Hook_V86_Int_Chain*), you could use the following even more cumbersome and atomic code:

```
mov     eax, 33h                 ; eax = interrupt number
VMMCall Get_V86_Int_Vector       ; cx:edx = real-mode INT 33 vector
VMMCall Build_Int_Stack_Frame    ; build IRET frame using cx:edx
VMMCall Resume_Exec
```

or even the following ridiculous exercise in reinventing the wheel:

```
mov     ax, [ebp + Client_Flags]
VMMCall Simulate_Push
mov     ax, [ebp + Client_CS]
VMMCall Simulate_Push
mov     ax, [ebp + Client_IP]
VMMCall Simulate_Push
mov     eax, 33h
VMMCall Get_V86_Int_Vector
mov     [ebp + Client_CS], cx
mov     [ebp + Client_IP], dx
VMMCall Resume_Exec
```

Service	Description
Build_Int_Stack_Frame	Prepares the VM to execute an interrupt service routine
Simulate_Far_Call	Arranges CS:IP and the stack as if the VM had executed a far CALL instruction
Simulate_Far_Jmp	Arranges CS:IP as if the VM had executed a far JMP instruction
Simulate_Far_Ret	Arranges CS:IP and the stack as if the VM had executed a RETF instruction
Simulate_Far_Ret_N	Arranges CS:IP and the stack as if the VM had executed a RETF *n* instruction
Simulate_Int	Calls hook procedures, then arranges CS:IP and the stack as if the VM were interrupted
Simulate_Iret	Arranges CS:IP and the stack as if the VM had executed an IRET instruction
Simulate_Pop	Arranges the stack as if the VM had executed a POP instruction
Simulate_Push	Arranges the stack as if the VM had executed a PUSH instruction

Table 10-3. *Services for manipulating client registers.*

Incidentally, all of these register simulation services honor the application-bitness setting in the VMCB. Thus, if the VMM thinks a particular VM is running a 16-bit DPMI client (such as Windows), *Simulate_Push* pushes 2 bytes onto the SS:SP stack regardless of the actual bitness of the client stack and code segments. The correct behavior would be to push either 2 or 4 bytes (depending on whether the client CS is USE16 or USE32) onto either SS:SP or SS:ESP (depending on whether the client SS is USE16 or USE32). Since the VMM thinks that the System VM contains a 16-bit protected-mode program, you should use these client-register manipulation services only to interface with 16-bit programs.

Lastly, when you use *Begin_Nest_Exec* (as opposed to *Begin_Nest_V86_Exec*) to start a nested execution block for protected-mode code, you might also cause a stack switch in the VM. The VMM maintains a special 4-KB locked stack for each VM for use in nested execution. The locked stack's primary purpose is to allow virtual exception handlers and DPMI callbacks to ignore paging issues. So whenever you issue a *Begin_Nest_Exec* call, the VMM switches the VM to this locked stack if the VM wasn't already using it.

EXEC_VXD_INT AND EXEC_PM_INT

The VMM contains two additional services that execute software interrupt handlers within a VM. *Exec_VxD_Int* effectively lets you issue an inline call to a real-mode interrupt handler. You load the general registers appropriately for the interrupt, push the interrupt number onto the stack, and call this service. You don't change the segment registers, though. If the real-mode interrupt handler wants register pair ES:BX to hold some pointer, for example, simply load the flat version of the pointer into register EBX.

By means of some trickery, *Exec_VxD_Int* simulates the interrupt in such a way that VxD handlers get their chance to translate pointer arguments and reflect the interrupt to real mode. The net effect is the same as if a 32-bit protected-mode application in the current VM had issued the interrupt. Since this service is available during Device_Init, a great many VxD components use it to talk to their real-mode counterparts.

You may have read elsewhere that *Exec_VxD_Int* is not very useful due to a supposed bug in *Begin_Nest_Exec*. The bug (or limitation, or whatever it is) shows up if both of these constraints are true:

■ The current VM doesn't contain a protected-mode application. No MS-DOS prompt has a protected-mode application unless the user launched an application built on a DOS extender, and neither does the System VM until the Windows KERNEL uses the DPMI mode-switch call to enter protected mode.

■ The VxD handler for the interrupt you execute does a *Begin_-Nest_Exec* to execute protected-mode code. *Begin_Nest_Exec* isn't very usual in this context, because these interrupt handlers normally do a *Begin_Nest_V86_Exec* to reflect their interrupt to real mode. It's not exactly brain-dead to worry about the possibility, though, because something similar to *Begin_Nest_Exec* will happen if the interrupt handler decides to block on a semaphore.

This combination of circumstances shouldn't occur in Windows 95 (although it could arise in an Init_Complete message handler in Windows for Workgroups 3.11 if it has 32-bit file access enabled). Microsoft considers *Exec_VxD_Int* safe enough that its own system components use the service freely during Device_Init and later.

The other interrupt simulation service is *Exec_PM_Int. Exec_PM_Int* is like *Exec_VxD_Int* except that you use the current VM's client register structure instead of the real general registers for parameters. It's useful as a way to help a 32-bit ring-three program issue an interrupt and as a way to protect yourself from real-mode code that fails to preserve the high halves of extended registers.

Both of these services set the *VMSTAT_VXD_EXEC* status flag in the current VMCB for the duration of their *Exec_Int* calls. Although a protected-mode interrupt handler ought to be indifferent to the source of the interrupt it processes, it can inspect this flag if necessary to distinguish between an interrupt issued by the VM and one issued by a VxD.

The Windows 95 DDK documentation mandates that any handler you install for protected-mode interrupts be installed while processing the Sys_Critical_Init message. The reason for this mandate is that other VxDs that initialize before your VxD might start calling *Exec_VxD_Int* during Device_Init, by which time the pass-down handler must already be in place.

Translating Pointers for Real Mode

If all you're going to do is reflect your interrupt to real mode, there's no reason to write your own hook, because reflecting the interrupt is the default behavior. Many interrupt interfaces include far pointer parameters, however, and you will need to supply a translation service to deal with them. Translation is required because a protected-mode program uses selector:offset addressing for data anywhere in memory, whereas a real-mode program requires a segment:offset address of data in the first megabyte. The best general strategy is to copy whatever data the pointer points to into V86 memory and then generate a pointer to the copy. On return from real mode, you copy any changed data back to the original buffer.

The easiest way to handle pointer parameters is to use the V86MMGR services that were designed for the purpose (see Table 10-4 on the following page). The V86MMGR controls a *translation buffer* in low memory, and it copies data to and from this buffer in response to requests from other VxDs. You can either make explicit calls to translation services or you can build a translation script for *V86MMGR_Xlat_API* to execute. By means of *V86MMGR_Set_Mapping_Info*, you can also notify the translation service manager of your eventual requirements for translation buffer space. Although the DDK says that you can't use the V86 translation services until you receive the Init_Complete message, Microsoft's own drivers call them during Device_Init. So, I guess you and I can do it too.

Service	Description
V86MMGR_Allocate_Buffer	Reserves space in the translation buffer
V86MMGR_Free_Buffer	Releases space in the translation buffer
V86MMGR_Get_Xlat_Buff_State	Gets information about the translation buffer
V86MMGR_Load_Client_Ptr	Gets the address of the client buffer
V86MMGR_Set_Mapping_Info	Specifies translation service requirements
V86MMGR_Set_Xlat_Buffer_State	Switches to a new translation buffer
V86MMGR_Xlat_API	Interprets the translation script

Table 10-4. *V86MMGR pointer translation services.*

Your first step in using these services is to call *V86MMGR_Load_Client_Ptr* to set the FS:ESI register pair to the address of a protected-mode data area that you want to copy to real mode. Then you use *V86MMGR_Allocate_Buffer* to simultaneously reserve space in the translation buffer and copy the client data into it. After the real-mode program is finished, you use *V86MMGR_Free_Buffer* to copy the data back to the client buffer and to release the space in the translation buffer.

For example, consider mouse function 09h, which defines the bitmap for the graphical mouse cursor. This function uses ES:DX as a pointer to the new bitmap. You could handle this function with code such as the following:

```
BeginProc i33callback, pageable
        ...
i33_09: push    [ebp + Client_EDX]      ; save client's EDX (1)
        push    dword ptr [ebp + Client_Alt_ES]        ; (2)
        mov     ax, (Client_ES * 256) or Client_DX
        VxDCall V86MMGR_Load_Client_Ptr ; FS:ESI -> bitmap
        mov     ecx, 64                 ; bitmap is 64 bytes
        stc                             ; copy data to buffer
        VxDCall V86MMGR_Allocate_Buffer ; reserve space and copy
        mov     [ebp + Client_DX], di   ; EDI = pointer to copy
        shr     edi, 16                 ;  ..
        mov     [ebp + Client_Alt_ES], di ; ..
        call    reflect                 ; reflect to real mode
        clc                             ; don't copy back
        VxDCall V86MMGR_Free_Buffer     ; release ECX bytes
        pop     dword ptr [ebp + Client_Alt_ES]        ; (2)
        pop     [ebp + Client_EDX]      ; restore EDX (1)
        jmp     done                    ; done with function 09h
```

I'll go through this fragment step by step now. We start with the VM still in protected mode, which is a requirement for the V86MMGR services we're about to call. Since we will be temporarily changing the client DX register to point to a copy of the mouse cursor, we save it on our own ring-zero stack. It's not strictly necessary to save all 32 bits of register EDX, since the real-mode driver ought not to alter the high half of the register, but it's faster in general to always deal with 32-bit quantities in a VxD and it shouldn't do any harm. Furthermore, there's real-mode code out there that fails to preserve the high-order halves of extended registers. The *V86MMGR_Load_Client_Ptr* service uses registers AH and AL to index into the EBP client register structure and to compose an address in FS:ESI. Here we ask for the protected-mode equivalent of the address in the client ES:DX register pair.

The crucial call in this sequence is to *V86MMGR_Allocate_Buffer*. We set register ECX to the byte length of the data we want to pass to real mode. Setting the carry flag indicates that we want data copied from the buffer pointed to by FS:ESI into the translation buffer. The return value in register EDI is a far pointer to the real-mode copy of the data, which we want to store into the client ES:DX register pair. Since the VM is still in protected mode, the primary client ES register (*Client_ES*) is the protected-mode selector used by our immediate caller. We therefore change the *alternate* client ES register. *Begin_Nest_V86_Exec* will swap the primary and alternate values. There is, however, only one copy of general registers such as *Client_DX*.

V86MMGR_Allocate_Buffer can fail, and we will know that this has happened if the carry flag is set when it returns. It might also reserve less buffer space than we asked for, which we can detect by looking at the return value in register ECX. Robust coding would detect these failures and compensate for them if they occur.

Having set up the translation buffer, we call *reflect* to actually execute the interrupt in real mode. On return, register ECX still holds the byte length of the area we reserved in the translation buffer, and the VM is back in protected mode. We call *V86MMGR_Free_Buffer* to pop the number of bytes specified in register ECX off the translation buffer stack. Clearing the carry flag beforehand indicates that we don't wish to have the contents of the real-mode buffer copied back to protected mode.

Finally, we can restore the client registers that we altered and exit from the interrupt handler.

This example shows how to reserve translation buffer space and copy a data parameter from protected mode to real mode. There are other mouse services (such as function 16h, Save Driver State) that operate in the other direction. That is, they supply a pointer to a buffer area that the real-mode driver fills in. In this case, you would call *V86MMGR_Allocate_Buffer* with the carry flag clear and without necessarily setting up FS:ESI. When you call *V86MMGR_Free_Buffer*, you first set FS:ESI to the address of the protected-mode buffer and *set* the carry flag to indicate you want data copied back to protected mode.

An alternative to making your own explicit calls to the V86MMGR pointer translation services is to build a script for *V86MMGR_Xlat_API* to execute. This script contains operation codes that represent runtime calls to the more atomic services, but it encapsulates those calls in a more compact and easier-to-read form. Table 10-5 lists the V86MMGR.INC macros you use to build the script. The following code fragment illustrates how you could use them to handle the INT 33h, function 09h, example considered earlier:

```
VxD_PAGEABLE_DATA_SEG
xlat_09  label    byte
         Xlat_API_Fixed_Len es, dx, 64
         Xlat_API_Exec_Int 33h
VxD_PAGEABLE_DATA_ENDS

BeginProc i33callback, pageable
         ...
 i33_09: mov      edx, offset32 xlat_09
         VxDCall V86MMGR_Xlat_API
         jmp      done                    ; done with function 09h
         ...
EndProc  i33callback
```

Macro	Description
Xlat_API_ASCIIZ	Translates a null-terminated string (from protected mode to real mode only)
Xlat_API_ASCIIZ_InOut	Translates a null-terminated string (bidirectional)
Xlat_API_Calc_Len	Translates a buffer whose length is determined by calling a function you supply (bidirectional)
Xlat_API_Exec_Int	Performs an *Exec_Int* inside a nested V86 execution block
Xlat_API_Fixed_Len	Translates a fixed-length buffer (bidirectional)
Xlat_API_Jmp_To_Proc	Transfers control from the script processor to a function you supply to carry out special processing
Xlat_API_Return_Ptr	Creates a protected-mode version of a pointer returned by the real-mode program
Xlat_API_Return_Seg	Creates a selector mapping to a segment address returned by the real-mode program
Xlat_API_Var_Len	Translates a buffer whose length is in a register (bidirectional)

Table 10-5. *V86MMGR translation API macros.*

The translation API macros are appreciably easier to use for several reasons: They save and restore any client registers they use for translated addresses. They automatically issue the necessary *Begin_Nest_V86_Exec* and *End_Nest_Exec* calls around the *Exec_Int* call. And, not insignificantly, they hide the shenanigans surrounding the use of FS:ESI as a buffer pointer. These conveniences make it plausible to code many interrupt handlers in C. You would have to write your own C-language macros to generate the translation script, though.

Function Pointers

There are a few MS-DOS API functions that use function pointers. INT 21h, function 38h (Get Country-Specific Information), fills in a data structure with (among other things) the address of an uppercase translation routine. INT 33h, function 0Ch, supplies the address of a mouse event callback routine. Functions like these require additional work from a translation VxD because (obviously) a real-mode program can't directly call a protected-mode routine or vice versa.

To handle cases of the first kind (in which real-mode system code returns a function pointer), you must substitute a protected-mode address before returning to the protected-mode client. The most practical thing to do is to create a protected-mode callback. The callback routine, which the protected-mode client reaches when it calls through the function pointer, simulates a far call to the real-mode function within a nested execution block. Because there are a limited number of protected-mode callback objects and because there's no way of releasing one, you probably don't want to allocate a new one each time you handle the interrupt. You therefore need to remember the real-mode address of the function to call. In the particular case of INT 21h, function 38h, translating the case-conversion function has such marginal utility that Windows doesn't even bother—it just leaves the real-mode address in the returned structure, and woe betide anyone who tries to call it.

Handling cases of the second kind (in which a protected-mode program supplies a function pointer) is equally tricky. Here you substitute the address of a V86 callback in the call to real mode while saving the protected-mode address. When the callback occurs, you use *Begin_Nest_Exec* to force the VM into protected mode and simulate a far call to the protected-mode function whose address you've remembered.

V86 Interrupts

Software interrupts in V86 programs vector through the IDT to a VMM handler that normally turns around and reflects them back to V86 mode. As a VxD writer, you can affect events in two ways. You can use the *Set_V86_Int_Vector* service to change the 0:0 interrupt vector table. You *must* install a V86 far pointer with this service. If you're trying to handle the interrupt in a VxD, you need to create a V86 callback and install its address, which is a real-mode segment:offset address.

A somewhat more convenient way of dealing with V86 interrupts is to use the *Hook_V86_Int_Chain* service. Any number of VxDs can register hook functions for a V86 interrupt. A hook function can examine the parameters associated with the interrupt and decide to consume it (by returning with the carry flag clear) or to pass it along the chain to the next hook procedure (by returning with the carry flag set). If none of the hook procedures consumes the interrupt, the VMM reflects it to V86 mode at the address specified in the 0:0 interrupt vector. The hook procedure can also "hook the back end" of the interrupt by using *Call_When_VM_Returns* to establish a callback routine to gain control when the VM eventually performs an IRET instruction to return from the handler. In combination, these features allow a VxD to inspect, modify, or completely implement a V86 interrupt.

VxDs can use the *Simulate_Int* or *Exec_Int* services to generate V86 interrupts. Both of these services send the interrupt through the V86 hook chain before calling the virtual handler.

For example, the Windows 3.1 Virtual Mouse Driver needs to know what instructions real-mode code is giving to the real-mode mouse driver in order to correctly translate them into graphical mouse events. It therefore hooks into the V86 INT 33h chain. In most cases, the VMD's hook procedure just extracts a little bit of information from the interrupt parameters and passes the interrupt along to the real-mode driver. When dealing with a real-mode driver that isn't Windows aware, however, it filters out *Set Cursor* calls from background VMs to avoid having the mouse suddenly appear in a nonfocus window. (Windows-aware drivers know when they have the focus and act accordingly.)

Another function that's tangentially related to handling V86 interrupts is *Install_V86_Break_Point*. This service overstores the instruction at a designated address with an ARPL instruction that will cause control to pass to a callback function you provide. The purpose of the service is to trap real-mode code when an interrupt isn't in the picture. Consider, for example, a pre-Windows real-mode driver or TSR that uses extended memory. It should have used INT 2Fh, function 4310h, long ago to obtain the address of the XMS manager's API entry, and it will have saved that address in some internal location. Because the application will be making direct calls to the XMS manager without issuing any interrupts, the V86MMGR installs a V86 breakpoint within the XMS manager to trap the calls. Needless to say, this kind of tampering requires lots of assumption checking beforehand!

APPLICATION APIS

One of the main reasons to write a VxD is to extend the capabilities of the Windows operating system. To avoid the fruitless exercise of creating a program that never runs because no one knows how to call it, you'll obviously want to provide an API so that applications can reach your driver to request the unique services that it provides. You use two very different techniques for this purpose, depending on whether 16-bit or 32-bit applications will be calling your driver. In this section, I'll describe how a Win32 application uses *CreateFile* and *DeviceIoControl* to talk to a VxD. Then I'll talk about the Win16 interfaces originally created for Windows 3.0.

Calls from 32-bit Applications

A Win32 application that wants to call your VxD must use the *CreateFile*, *DeviceIo-Control*, and *CloseHandle* functions. In addition, your VxD must handle the W32_DeviceIoControl system control message. *CreateFile* is the Win32 API function that an application normally uses to open a file for input and output operations. By stretching the so-called Universal Naming Convention to its aesthetic limits, Microsoft provided a way for an application to obtain a special kind of *device handle*:

```
HANDLE hDevice = CreateFile("\\\\.\\name", ...);
```

Unlike the usual uses of *CreateFile*, a call with the strange \\.\ decoration preceding the filename doesn't actually open a file for I/O. Instead, it locates a device driver of the specified name and returns a handle by which the driver itself can later be accessed.

Much of the time, if a Win32 application needs to use a device driver, it makes sense to have the application actually load the driver dynamically. The complete call to *CreateFile* for opening and loading a device driver is as follows:

```
HANDLE hDevice = CreateFile("\\\\.\\pathname", 0, 0,
    NULL, 0, FILE_FLAG_DELETE_ON_CLOSE, NULL);
```

In this syntax, *pathname* specifies the executable file for the driver. The *FILE_FLAG_-DELETE_ON_CLOSE* flag indicates that you want to unload the driver when you later call *CloseHandle* to close the handle.

You use a device handle in calls to *DeviceIoControl*. The specification for this API function is so general as to be meaningless:

```
BOOL result = DeviceIoControl(
    HANDLE hDevice,       // handle of device driver
    DWORD code,           // I/O control code
    LPVOID inbuffer,      // input buffer
    DWORD cbinbuffer,     // size of input buffer
```

```
LPVOID outbuffer,      // output buffer
DWORD cboutbuffer,     // size of output buffer
LPDWORD pnumreturned,  // where to put the number of output bytes
LPOVERLAPPED povl);    // overlapped I/O structure
```

The fact is that the use of the parameters to this function is entirely up to the author of the driver that responds to it. In general, the *code* argument specifies an action for the driver to perform. The input buffer contains arguments to the driver, and the output buffer will hold any values returned by the driver. Even these uses for the arguments are conventional, though. You could decide to put the function code in place of the *cboutbuffer* argument if you wanted to, with the only drawback being that you might confuse other people who are trying to read your code. Well, this is not quite the only drawback. It turns out that your VxD must reply to control code 0 by returning 0 or the dynamic loading interface won't work right.

So let's assume that you're a slave to convention and will use the arguments to *DeviceIoControl* for their intended purpose. Internally, *DeviceIoControl* turns into a call to the VWIN32 driver through a secret and undocumented interface. Your VxD contains a handler for the W32_DeviceIoControl system control message, which is the quaint way in which VWIN32 tells you about a ring-three call to *DeviceIoControl*. You can handle this message most easily in C:

```
#include <vwin32.h>
DWORD __stdcall OnW32DeviceIoControl(PDIOCPARAMETERS p)
    {                          // OnW32DeviceIOControl
    switch (p->dwIoControlCode)
        {
    case DIOC_GETVERSION:    // i.e., control code 0
        return 0;
    ...
        }
    }                          // OnW32DeviceIOControl
```

The return value from this function is a Win32 error code, with 0 meaning "no error." The DIOCPARAMETERS structure whose address is passed to this function is essentially a copy of the arguments to the matching call to *DeviceIoControl* (the structure is defined as shown in Figure 10-3). Your driver must handle the DIOC_GETVERSION function as shown above in order to be dynamically loadable by calls to *CreateFile*. Other codes are, as I've said already, up to you. Suppose you wanted to implement a *GetVersion* service for use by your ring-three clients as function 1. Your VxD service routine could contain this fragment:

```
...
switch (p->dwIoControlCode)
    {
    ...
```

```
case 1:
    if (!p->lpvOutBuffer || p->cbOutBuffer < 2)
        return ERROR_INVALID_PARAMETER;
    *(WORD*)(p->lpvOutBuffer) = 0x0100; // major/minor
    if (p->lpcbBytesReturned)
        *(PDWORD)(p->lpcbBytesReturned) = 2;
    return 0;
    ...
    }
```

This program first executes a switch based on the value of the *dwIoControlCode* member of the DIOCPARAMETERS structure. This code is the same as the *code* argument to the *DeviceIoControl* call that got us here. The program verifies that the *DeviceIoControl* caller supplied an output buffer (that is, that *lpvOutBuffer* is not NULL) and that the buffer is at least 2 bytes long (*cbOutBuffer* >= 2). If one of these tests fails, it means that the caller coded the *DeviceIoControl* call incorrectly, so we return *ERROR_INVALID_PARAMETER*. This error code is one of the manifest constants in WINERROR.H (one of the Win32 SDK headers), and returning it or any other nonzero value will cause the original *DeviceIoControl* function to return FALSE. The application will then presumably call *GetLastError* and get back *ERROR_INVALID_PARAMETER*.

The *pnumreturned* parameter to *DeviceIoControl* is optional; if the caller supplied a NULL pointer for that parameter, the *lpcbBytesReturned* member of the DIOCPARAMETERS structure will be NULL as well. If that pointer is not NULL, however, you will want to use it to store the count of bytes actually copied into the output buffer.

```
typedef struct DIOCParams {
    DWORD Internal1;          // 00 pointer to client registers
    DWORD VMHandle;           // 04 VM handle
    DWORD Internal2;          // 08 pointer to DDB
    DWORD dwIoControlCode;    // 0C control code from DeviceIoControl call
    DWORD lpvInBuffer;        // 10 input buffer address from call
    DWORD cbInBuffer;         // 14 size of input buffer from call
    DWORD lpvOutBuffer;       // 18 output buffer address from call
    DWORD cbOutBuffer;        // 1C size of output buffer from call
    DWORD lpcbBytesReturned;  // 20 where to put output count (can be NULL)
    DWORD lpOverlapped;       // 24 overlapped I/O block from call
    DWORD hDevice;            // 28 ring-three device handle
    DWORD tagProcess;         // 2C process tag
} DIOCPARAMETERS;
```

Figure 10-3. *The DIOCParams structure used in W32_DeviceIoControl.*

The Win32 application that wants to know your driver's version number would contain the following code fragment:

```
WORD version;
HANDLE hDevice = CreateFile(...);
DeviceIoControl(hDevice, 1, NULL, 0, &version, sizeof(version),
    NULL, NULL);
```

Here the input buffer parameters are NULL because the function needs no input data. The output buffer is just the *version* variable. For purposes of this example, we'll scoff at errors and at the actual length of the returned data. Finally, by supplying a NULL overlapped I/O structure pointer, this code fragment requests that it not regain control until the control operation completes.

It's possible in Windows 95 to do asynchronous *DeviceIoControl* calls. To make asynchronous calls, you must specify the *FILE_FLAG_OVERLAPPED* flag when you open the device handle, and you must supply the address of an *OVERLAPPED* structure as the last argument to *DeviceIoControl*. The VxD returns immediately from its W32_DeviceIoControl handler. At some later time (presumably in an event callback routine), your VxD calls the *VWIN32_DIOCCompletionRoutine* service to signal the event associated with the overlapped I/O operation. This VWIN32 call allows you to synchronize with the ring-three application.

Calls from 16-bit Applications

In all releases of Windows since Windows 3.0, VxDs have been able to export application APIs simply by declaring them in the device description block (DDB). You can provide one API routine for use by V86-mode programs and a different API routine for use by protected-mode programs. You can specify the same routine for both, too. Two basic pieces underlie this process:

■ An application uses software interrupt 2Fh, function 1684h, to obtain a function address. When this function is called, your API routine will gain control.

■ Your API routine examines and alters the client registers belonging to the calling application.

On the application side, the programmer needs to know one of two things: either the 16-bit unique identifier of your VxD or the name that appears in the DDB. If the programmer knows the unique identifier (the *DriverId*), the application can execute code such as the following:

```
DWORD apiaddr;                          // address of VxD's API
_asm
    {                                   // get API address
    xor di, di
    mov es, di
    mov ax, 1684h
    mov bx, DriverId
    int 2fh
    mov word ptr apiaddr, di
    mov word ptr apiaddr+2, es
    }                                   // get API address
```

If the programmer doesn't know the *DriverId*, or if the ID is *Undefined_Device_ID*, the application sets register BX to 0 and points ES:DI to the 8-byte, blank-padded, case-sensitive name of the driver. For example:

```
char drivername[9] = "MYVXD    "; // three trailing blanks
DWORD apiaddr;                          // address of VxD's API
_asm
    {                                   // get API address
    xor bx, bx       ; or use mov bx, Undefined_Device_ID
    mov di, ss
    mov es, di
    lea di, drivername
    mov ax, 1684h
    int 2fh
    mov word ptr apiaddr, di
    mov word ptr apiaddr+2, es
    }                                   // get API address
```

If the interrupt returns with *apiaddr* nonzero, it means that the VxD that the application specified is loaded and exports an application API. Based on some agreed convention about what the registers contain, the application then makes calls through this pointer to talk to your driver. For example:

```
WORD version;
_asm
    {                       // call API
    mov ax, 0               ; function 0: get version
    call [apiaddr]
    mov version, ax
    }                       // call API
```

On the VxD side, first identify the API entry points when you initially define your device driver:

```
Declare_Virtual_Device MYVXD, ..., pmapi, v86api
```

The last two parameters to the macro identify your protected-mode and V86-mode API entry points, respectively. These are VxD functions that the VMM calls whenever the application calls your VxD through the INT 2Fh, function 1684h, *apiaddr* pointer. Then define the API procedure itself. The VMM will call your procedure with register EBX holding the current VM handle, register EDI holding the current thread handle, and register EBP pointing to the current thread's client register structure. An assembly-language API routine that implements a *GetVersion* function might appear as follows:

```
BeginProc pmapi, pageable
          movzx  eax, [ebp+Client_AX]
          test   eax, eax
          jnz    error
          mov    ax, word ptr MYVXD_DDB.DDB_Dev_Major_Version
          xchg   ah, al
          mov    [ebp+Client_AX], ax
          and    [ebp+Client_EFlags], not CF_Mask
          ret
error:    or     [ebp+Client_EFlags], CF_MASK
          ret
EndProc   pmapi
```

This sample extracts a function code from the client AX register. If the code is 0, it then composes the major and minor version numbers in the client AX register and clears the client's carry flag. If the function code is anything but 0, it sets the client's carry flag to indicate an error. After the API function returns to the VMM, the VMM will redispatch the VM with the altered flags and registers.

Those are the basics about application APIs. Here are two fine points: First of all, the application sample I showed you can be a DOS program running in V86 mode, a 16-bit Windows program (running in protected mode, of course), or an extended DOS program running under DPMI or some commercial DOS extender. The INT 2Fh, function 1684h, interface works equally well for all of them. The only difference between V86-mode callers and protected-mode callers is that you *may*—but you don't have to—use different API functions to service them. By using the *Map_Flat* service I talked about in Chapter 9 (on page 206), you can address data pointed to by client segment registers without needing to know your caller's mode of execution.

The second fine point about the API mechanism is that it works for 32-bit extended DOS programs *but not for 32-bit Windows programs*. A USE32 caller gets back a 16:32 far pointer to the application API entry instead of a 16:16 pointer. It should also use extended registers for its parameter passing, because that's what *Map_Flat* will be expecting. Other than that, the interface to the VxD can be identical to the 16-bit version. The reason that 32-bit Windows programs can't use this interface is that the VMM thinks that the System VM (in which such programs execute) is

---

CALLING VxDs FROM 32-BIT APPLICATIONS

You might be wondering what a bitness decision made during system initialization has to do with application APIs. The VMM doesn't always handle software interrupts correctly when they come from Win32 programs. Some software interrupts have 16-bit gates in the System VM's IDT. A 16-bit gate causes the processor to save only FLAGS (not EFLAGS), CS:IP (not CS:EIP), and SS:SP (not SS:ESP) registers. If a 32-bit program issues one of these interrupts, the VMM saves only a fraction of the program context on the stack and ends up performing an IRET instruction that returns to a random place with a random stack pointer. The INT 2Fh that's part of the API infrastructure doesn't have this particular problem: it uses a 32-bit gate that will preserve the full context. Unfortunately, code downstream from the first-level INT 2Fh handler uncritically assumes that it's dealing with a 16-bit caller and arranges to return incorrectly to the VM. Thus, the Win32 application can't even learn the address of an API entry point. There are ways around this problem if you're willing to hook INT 2Fh yourself and examine the caller's bitness. You'll eventually run up against an insoluble problem, however: the application must have a flat address to call, but the INT 30h handler will not honor a call into any segment but 3Bh. Also, the handler incorrectly returns as if the caller were 16-bit.

The moral of this particular story is that you shouldn't try to use methods appropriate for crotchety old 16-bit applications when you're dealing with spiffy new 32-bit applications. Microsoft wants Win32 to be *portable* across machine and operating system architectures. Portability precludes using software interrupts as a communication vehicle. Furthermore, Microsoft never intended you to be able to treat VxD code as integral to an application. That's why it's so hard to call back into VMs. If you absolutely need to do these things with 32-bit applications, you should use *DeviceIoControl* and *_VWIN32-_QueueUserApc*. These at least allow the application to remain as portable as possible.

running a 16-bit protected-mode DPMI client. The VMM stereotypes all applications based on how some real-mode program long ago (namely, during the initial startup of this Windows session) called the DPMI mode-switch function in order to enter protected mode. The Windows 95 KERNEL claims to be a 16-bit application, so the VMM assumes that all Windows 95 applications from then on are 16-bit applications too.

CALLING WINDOWS APPLICATIONS

Because VxDs are part of the operating system that underlies the Windows graphical operating environment, you might assume that it would be easy for a VxD to do the same things that applications do. Strangely, this assumption isn't true. In fact, until the release of Windows 95, it was unreasonably hard for a VxD to even make its presence known to ring-three code, never mind to interact with the user. In the previous section I showed how a VxD can export an API that will allow an application to request operating system services. In this section, I'll show the other half of the picture and explain how a VxD can talk back to an associated application.

To understand why this aspect of system programming is so hard, remember that the VMM's original job was to distribute interrupts among VMs. Working underneath and disassociated from the application code running in the VMs, the VMM had no particular need to work closely with that code. As a general rule, the VMM's only contribution to the internal life of a VM is to interrupt the orderly flow of ring-three execution and temporarily direct execution elsewhere. Complicating the situation is the fact that Windows itself is not reentrant. Thus, a program you reach by interrupting the System VM can't do very much. In previous versions of Windows, about all you could accomplish was to call *PostMessage*, which is one of the few Windows API routines that tolerates calls at interrupt time.

PostMessage in Windows 3.1

Because you might need to write a VxD that will be compatible with Windows 3.1, and because you might need to understand or maintain code written for Windows 3.1, you should understand how medieval VxD writers managed to do *PostMessage* calls. There are two pieces to this puzzle: a Windows application whose main job is to tell the VxD where *PostMessage* is, and a VxD that schedules interrupt-like calls to *PostMessage* when needed. The VxD exports a protected-mode API that the helper application can use to transmit the crucial *PostMessage* address.

The relevant portion of a helper Windows application locates the VxD's protected-mode API and passes it to the address of the Windows *PostMessage*

MORE ABOUT *POSTMESSAGE*

If you could call only one Windows API function from a VxD, *PostMessage* would be the one you'd choose. Its declaration is as follows:

```
BOOL WINAPI PostMessage(HWND hwnd, UINT msg,
    WPARAM wParam, LPARAM lParam);
```

The *hwnd* argument identifies one of the many window objects that currently exist, and the *msg* parameter identifies one of 65,536 possible Windows messages. The *wParam* and *lParam* parameters contain data whose meaning depends on which message you're posting. As the author of a Windows procedure, you can define your own messages, and you can decide that the *lParam* for some of them should be a pointer to something. And, given a pointer to play with, you can specify an arbitrarily complex set of function parameters with any type and amount of data.

PostMessage tries to place a Windows message in the message queue of the task that owns the window. It returns TRUE if it was able to do so. A FALSE return value might mean that the window doesn't exist or that the task's queue is full. (An application can use the *SetMessageQueue* API function to increase the size of its queue to head off *PostMessage* failures down the road.) There is a message loop somewhere in the code for the task that uses *GetMessage* or *PeekMessage* to extract messages from the queue and an API function such as *DispatchMessage* to send the message along to the appropriate Windows procedure. When the message loop takes its next turn on the CPU, it will poll for messages. Eventually, it will retrieve the one you posted, whereupon a ring-three Windows procedure will gain control to do your bidding.

routine. In general, the helper also needs to supply a window handle to which the VxD can post messages and, perhaps, a Windows message identifier. For example (this code is included on the companion disc in the \CHAP10\POSTMESSAGE-VTOOLSD directory):

The Windows Application

```
FARPROC aPostMessage = (FARPROC) PostMessage;
void (*apiaddr)();

_asm
    {                        // get API entry
```

(continued)

continued

```
        xor di, di
        mov es, di
        mov ax, 1684h
        mov bx, 4242h          ; use your own VxD ID here
        int 2fh
        mov word ptr apiaddr, di
        mov word ptr apiaddr+2, es
        }                      // get API entry

if (apiaddr)
    _asm
    {                          // register this application with the VxD
    mov ax, 1
    mov bx, hwnd
    mov cx, WM_USER+256
    mov di, word ptr aPostMessage
    mov si, word ptr aPostMessage+2
    call [apiaddr]
    }                          // register this application with the VxD
```

The first portion of this excerpt uses interrupt 2Fh, function 1684h, to obtain the API address of a VxD whose unique identifier is 4242h. (You would use your own assigned unique identifier in this spot. I used 4242h as an example because of the deep cultural significance of the number 42.) The second portion calls the API function 01h after loading parameters into several of the general registers.

The VxD responds to the function 01h (registration) call as follows:

The VxD (for Windows 3.1)

```
DWORD hwnd;
DWORD msg;
DWORD aPostMessage;

VOID PM_Api_Handler(VMHANDLE hVM, PCLIENT_STRUCT pRegs)
    {                          // PM_Api_Handler
    _clientEFlags &= ~CF_MASK;
    switch (_clientAX)
        {                      // select API function
        ...

    case 1:
        hwnd = _clientBX;
        msg = _clientCX;
```

(continued)

continued

```
        aPostMessage = ((DWORD) _clientSI << 16) |
                       ((DWORD) _clientDI & 0xFFFF);
        break;
        ...
        }                              // select API function
    }                                  // PM_Api_Handler
```

Basically, the handler for API function 01h simply copies parameters from (client) general registers into global variables belonging to the VxD. What the registration call from the application does, therefore, is give the VxD a window handle, a message identifier, and the ring-three address of the Windows *PostMessage* routine. It's surprising but true that a VxD has no other way to learn these facts in Windows 3.1.

To illustrate what you do with the information supplied by the helper application, let's suppose you wanted to write a VxD that would log the system control messages that occur when you create and destroy a new VM. You would add to each message handler a call to a common local routine (called *DoPostMessage* in this example) that would post a message to the helper application. (I wrote this sample using VTOOLSD to avoid bogging down in the mechanics of assembly-language callback routines.)

The VxD, Continued

```
BOOL OnCreateVm(VMHANDLE hVM)
    {
    DoPostMessage(CREATE_VM, hVM);
    return TRUE;
    }


...


typedef struct tagMSGSTUFF {
    DWORD hwnd;
    DWORD msg;
    DWORD wParam;
    DWORD lParam;
} MSGSTUFF, *PMSGSTUFF;

PriorityVMEvent_THUNK PostMessageThunk;
TIMEOUT_THUNK TimeoutThunk;
```

(continued)

continued

```
VOID DoPostMessage(DWORD event, VMHANDLE hVM)
    {
    PMSGSTUFF p;

    if (!aPostMessage) // a global variable
        return;

    p = (PMSGSTUFF) _HeapAllocate(sizeof(MSGSTUFF),
                            HEAPZEROINIT);
    Assert(p);
    p->hwnd = hwnd;    // hwnd is a global variable
    p->msg = msg;      // msg is a global variable
    p->wParam = event;
    p->lParam = (DWORD) hVM;

    Call_Priority_VM_Event(0, Get_Sys_VM_Handle(),
        PEF_WAIT_FOR_STI | PEF_WAIT_NOT_CRIT,
        p, PostMessageCallback, 0, &PostMessageThunk);
    }

VOID __stdcall PostMessageCallback(VMHANDLE hVM, PVOID refdata,
    PCLIENT_STRUCT pRegs, DWORD flags)
    {
    DoCallback((PMSGSTUFF) refdata, pRegs);
    }

VOID __stdcall TimeoutCallback(VMHANDLE hVM, PCLIENT_STRUCT
    pRegs, PVOID refdata, DWORD extra)
    {
    DoCallback((PMSGSTUFF) refdata, pRegs);
    }

BOOL DoCallback(PMSGSTUFF p, PCLIENT_STRUCT pRegs)
    {
    CLIENT_STRUCT saveregs;
    BOOL okay;

    Assert(aPostMessage); // aPostMessage is a global variable
    Save_Client_State(&saveregs);
    Begin_Nest_Exec();

    Simulate_Push(p->hwnd);
    Simulate_Push(p->msg);
    Simulate_Push(p->wParam);
```

(continued)

continued

```
    Simulate_Push(HIWORD(p->lParam));
    Simulate_Push(LOWORD(p->lParam));
    Simulate_Far_Call(HIWORD(aPostMessage),
        LOWORD(aPostMessage));
    Resume_Exec();

    okay = _clientAX;

    End_Nest_Exec();
    Restore_Client_State(&saveregs);

    if (okay)
        _HeapFree(p, 0);
    else
        Set_VM_Time_Out(100, Get_Sys_VM_Handle(), p,
                        TimeoutCallback, &TimeoutThunk);

    return okay;
    }
```

DoPostMessage in turn schedules a priority VM event callback in the System VM to actually perform the call. It uses a small piece of memory allocated from the system heap to hold the important parameters of the Windows message.

DoCallback is the function that actually calls *PostMessage*. Because the call to *PostMessage* will essentially interrupt whatever is currently running in the System VM, the first step is to preserve the current client register images by calling *Save_Client_State*. *Begin_Nest_Exec* initiates a nested execution block and forces the VM into protected mode (if it wasn't in that mode already). The *Simulate_Push* calls place the parameters to the Windows *PostMessage* function onto the virtual stack in the correct order for a __pascal-style call. *Simulate_Far_Call* pushes a return address onto the virtual stack and sets the virtual CS:IP register pair to the *PostMessage* address provided earlier by the test application. *Resume_Exec* allows the System VM to execute, whereupon *PostMessage* runs and enters a Windows message into the test application's queue. *End_Nest_Exec* and *Restore_Client_State* restore the System VM to its previous state. The results of running the test application included on the companion disk in the \CHAP10\POSTMESSAGE directory are shown in Figure 10-4 on the following page.

Notice that *DoPostMessage* actually schedules an event callback to *PostMessage-Callback*, which in turn calls *DoCallback*. The reason for this extra layer of subroutines is that the Windows *PostMessage* function can fail if, for example, the application's message queue is full. To handle this case, *DoCallback* captures *PostMessage*'s return value (the contents of the client AX register) before making the

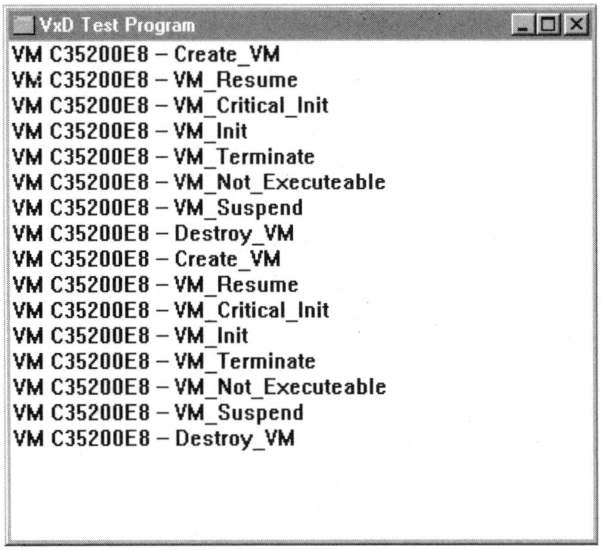

Figure 10-4. *Results of running the* PostMessage *test program.*

cleanup calls that will overwrite that value. If the value is TRUE, *DoCallback* releases the memory block used for parameters. If the value is FALSE, however, *DoCallback* schedules another event callback to occur when the System VM has executed for 100 milliseconds. The mechanics of VTOOLSD demand that this event use a different callback thunk and a different callback procedure, which is why I wrote *Timeout-Callback*, which does exactly the same thing as *PostMessageCallback*.

There are two potential problems with this code sample. First of all, *PostMessage* might fail for reasons other than the task queue being full. For example, the application might terminate and destroy its window. If the window handle passed to *PostMessage* is invalid, *PostMessage* will fail and this code will loop forever, retrying after every timeout. It's not possible for a VxD to determine whether a window handle is valid, nor is it possible to determine why *PostMessage* has failed. Thus, you might want to place some sort of limit on the number of times you try to deliver the message before giving up. It's not enough to rely on the application to deregister its window handle before it terminates because in the case of a crash, the application won't take the normal path out (unless the application developer has gone to the considerable trouble of creating a task termination callback using *ToolHelp*).

The second potential problem arises if you put this sample code into a dynamically loaded VxD. What happens if someone unloads the VxD while one or more of the events created by *DoPostMessage* is still outstanding? Unless you place the event-handling code into the static code segment, you run the risk of not having the callback there when the event happens. Handling this situation is a little complex because there can be more than one event outstanding at any given time. I didn't want to obscure the central point of the example by adding all this complication, but you'll need to consider these issues when you write a real VxD.

PostMessage in Windows 95

I'd like to report that calling *PostMessage* from a Windows 95 VxD is appreciably simpler, but I can't. It's only a little bit simpler. There is a new service in Windows 95 named *_SHELL_PostMessage* that handles the mechanics of finding and calling *PostMessage* with the normal four parameters. This service does not guarantee delivery, though, which means that you must still deal with the consequences of a *PostMessage* failure. Using this service allows you to recode the earlier VxD's *DoPostMessage* routine as follows (this code is included on the companion disc in the \CHAP10\SHELL_POSTMESSAGE-VTOOLSD directory):

The VxD (for Windows 95)

```
...
VOID DoPostMessage(DWORD event, VMHANDLE hVM)
    {
    PMSGSTUFF p;

    if (!hwnd)        // hwnd is a global variable
        return;

    p = (PMSGSTUFF) _HeapAllocate(sizeof(MSGSTUFF),
                            HEAPZEROINIT);
    Assert(p);
    p->hwnd = hwnd; // hwnd is a global variable
    p->msg = msg;   // msg is a global variable
    p->wParam = event;
    p->lParam = (DWORD) hVM;

    _SHELL_PostMessage((HANDLE) hwnd, msg, (WORD) event, (DWORD) hVM,
                    (PPostMessage_HANDLER) CheckPostMessage, p);
    }

VOID __cdecl CheckPostMessage(DWORD rc, PMSGSTUFF p)
    {
    if (rc)
        _HeapFree(p, 0);
    else
        Set_VM_Time_Out(100, Get_Sys_VM_Handle(), p,
                    TimeoutCallback, &TimeoutThunk);
    }
```

(continued)

continued

```
VOID __stdcall TimeoutCallback(VMHANDLE hVM,
    PCLIENT_STRUCT pRegs, PVOID refdata, DWORD extra)
    {
    PMSGSTUFF p = (PMSGSTUFF) refdata;
    _SHELL_PostMessage((HANDLE) p->hwnd, p->msg, (WORD) p->wParam,
    p->lParam, (PPostMessage_HANDLER)
    CheckPostMessage, p);
    }
```

_SHELL_PostMessage schedules an event and performs the operations necessary to call *PostMessage*. Then it calls the *CheckPostMessage* callback routine to report the return value from *PostMessage*. If *PostMessage* returned FALSE, *CheckPostMessage* schedules a timeout, after which the application repeats the call to *_SHELL_PostMessage*.

This example is (slightly) simpler than the one I showed earlier in two respects: the VxD needn't remember the address of *PostMessage*, and it needn't make all the service calls to set up the nested execution block, push parameters, and actually generate the call. It is, however, still necessary first to obtain a window handle and message identifier from an application and afterward to schedule a timeout to retry if *PostMessage* failed.

AppyTime Events

In contrast to earlier versions of Windows, Windows 95 provides a method by which a VxD can call regular 16-bit Windows functions in addition to *PostMessage*. The method revolves around the *AppyTime* (application time) event. First you schedule an event callback:

```
_SHELL_CallAtAppyTime(OnAppyTime, NULL, 0, 0);
```

At a later time, when Windows 95 is in a stable state in which API calls are permitted, the SHELL device calls your callback routine. You can then use some special SHELL application time services (listed in Table 10-6) to issue Windows API calls. For example, the following callback launches WinHelp to display help about the *_SHELL_CallDll* service that you use to actually make these API calls (this code is included on the companion disc in the \CHAP10\APPYTIME-DDK directory):

```
VOID __cdecl OnAppyTime(DWORD refdata)
    {                               // OnAppyTime
    #pragma pack(1)
    struct {
        DWORD dwData;
        WORD  fuCommand;
        DWORD lpszHelpFile;
```

```
        WORD hwnd;
} WinHelpArgs;
#pragma pack()

WinHelpArgs.hwnd = 0;
WinHelpArgs.lpszHelpFile = _SHELL_LocalAllocEx(LPTR +
    LMEM_STRING + LMEM_OEM2ANSI, 0,
    "D:\\DDK\\DOCS\\VMM.HLP");
WinHelpArgs.fuCommand = 0x101;        // HELP_KEY
WinHelpArgs.dwData = _SHELL_LocalAllocEx(LPTR +
    LMEM_STRING + LMEM_OEM2ANSI, 0,
    "_SHELL_CallDll");

_SHELL_CallDll("USER", "WinHelp", sizeof(WinHelpArgs),
    &WinHelpArgs);

_SHELL_LocalFree(WinHelpArgs.lpszHelpFile);
_SHELL_LocalFree(WinHelpArgs.dwData);
}                              // OnAppyTime
```

Service	Description
_SHELL_CallDll	Calls a function in a 16-bit DLL
_SHELL_FreeLibrary	Unloads a DLL
_SHELL_GetProcAddress	Locates an entry point in a DLL
_SHELL_LoadLibrary	Loads a DLL
_SHELL_LocalAllocEx	Allocates ring-three addressable memory
_SHELL_LocalFree	Releases ring-three addressable memory

Table 10-6. *Services for use at application time.*

_SHELL_CallDll is the basic service you use for making Windows API calls. You can use it as shown in this example, in which you specify the name of a DLL and the name of an entry point in that DLL. You can use an export ordinal instead. Or you can determine the 16:16 address of a function in some other way (by using *_SHELL_GetProcAddress*, for instance, or by having an application give it to you) and specify that address directly. With this service you also provide the address of a memory area in which you've already placed the function arguments in the order in which the 16-bit called function expects to find them on its stack.

To pass string arguments to a 16-bit routine, you need to come up with a 16:16 far pointer to the string. The *_SHELL_LocalAllocEx* function creates the requisite pointer for you by allocating memory within a local heap—a heap that belongs to a hidden message server application. You must explicitly release this memory when you no longer need it by calling *_SHELL_LocalFree*. If you're trying to pass a null-terminated string, you can use the *LMEM_STRING* flag to cause SHELL to count the string for you. Bear in mind, too, that VxDs use the OEM character set. If the API you're calling expects the ANSI character set (as do both of the APIs in the example), add the *LMEM_OEM2ANSI* flag.

Application time events are not especially convenient to use because the mechanics of calling ring-three functions are so cumbersome. There's one important restriction on the VMM services you can use within an application time callback: don't call *Begin_Nest_Exec* because it will probably crash Windows 95 if it is used at application time. Furthermore, you can only call *16-bit* programs in this way. You must use an asynchronous procedure call to call a 32-bit program. (And you needn't wait until application time to schedule such a call.)

Asynchronous Procedure Calls

So far, everything I've told you cleverly glosses over the problem of calling into Win32 code. As you saw earlier, you use *DeviceIoControl* and the W32_DeviceIo-Control message to call into a VxD from a Win32 application. In this subsection, I'll show you how a VxD can use a new mechanism called an *asynchronous procedure call* (or APC for short) to call into Win32 code. In brief, a Win32 application uses *DeviceIoControl* to send the address of a callback function to the VxD. The application then enters an alertable wait state. The VxD uses *_VWIN32_QueueUserApc* to schedule an asynchronous callback. The callback then occurs and the Win32 application wakes up from its wait.

The sample programs in this section that illustrate the APC mechanism provide a simple-minded monitor for V86 applications as they start and stop. (The code shown in this section is included on the companion disc in the \CHAP09\SERVICE-HOOK-ASM directory.) The Win32 application is responsible for printing messages about start and stop events. The VxD, as you can imagine, traps the start and stop events by hooking DOSMGR APIs, and queues APCs to alert the application.

On the Win32 side, the application dynamically loads the VxD and uses *DeviceIoControl* to supply the addresses of two callback routines:

```
HANDLE hDevice;
void (WINAPI *abegin)(DWORD) = beginapp;
void (WINAPI *aend)(DWORD) = endapp;

hDevice = CreateFile("\\\\.\\myvxd.vxd", 0, 0, NULL, 0,
    FILE_FLAG_DELETE_ON_CLOSE, NULL);
DeviceIoControl(hDevice, 1, &abegin, sizeof(abegin),
    NULL, 0, NULL, NULL);
DeviceIoControl(hDevice, 2, &aend, sizeof(aend),
    NULL, 0, NULL, NULL);
```

The VxD uses the *Hook_Device_Service* service described in the previous chapter to monitor *DOSMGR_Begin_V86_App* and *DOSMGR_End_V86_App* calls. When one of these calls occurs, the VxD queues an APC to one of the functions registered by these *DeviceIoControl* calls:

```
BeginProc BeginHook, service, hook_proc, next_begin, locked
        pushad
        mov    eax, beginfunc
        call   DoApc
        popad
        jmp    [next_begin]
EndProc BeginHook

BeginProc EndHook, service, hook_proc, next_end, locked
        pushad
        mov    eax, endfunc
        call   DoApc
        popad
        jmp    [next_end]
EndProc EndHook

BeginProc DoApc, locked
        test   eax, eax
        jz     doapc_done
        VxDCall _VWIN32_QueueUserApc, <eax, esi, appthread>

doapc_done:
        ret
EndProc  DoApc
```

In this fragment, *beginfunc* and *endfunc* are DWORD data variables in which the VxD has stored the addresses of the application's *beginapp* and *endapp* functions, and *appthread* holds the address of the application's thread control block. The operative part of the example is the call to *_VWIN32_QueueUserApc*. The first argument is the address of the Win32 function to call, the second argument is a single DWORD parameter to be passed to that function, and the third argument is the thread within whose context the call will occur. The "asynchronous" part of the term *asynchronous procedure call* manifests itself in the fact that this API returns immediately, without waiting for the call to actually take place in the VM.

Meanwhile, the application has placed itself into an alertable wait state by calling *SleepEx*, *WaitForSingleObjectEx*, or *WaitForMultipleObjectsEx*. I chose *SleepEx* for simplicity:

```
while (SleepEx(INFINITE, TRUE) == WAIT_IO_COMPLETION)
    ;                // i.e., wait forever or until error
```

The second argument to *SleepEx* indicates that we want the wait to be alertable. An *alertable* wait means that the VxD's APC will cause the thread to wake up and execute the designated callback routine, whereupon *SleepEx* will return with the *WAIT_IO_COMPLETION* return code. As coded, the application then repeats the wait forever. Pressing Ctrl-Break terminates the application and closes all of its handles. Closing the device driver handle also dynamically unloads the VxD because we used *FILE_FLAG_DELETE_ON_CLOSE*.

The application callback routines are declared as void __stdcall and receive a single DWORD argument, which is the same as the second argument to *_VWIN32_QueueUserApc*. For example:

```
void __stdcall beginapp(DWORD psp)
    {                                       // beginapp
    char name[9];
    printf("Starting V86 App %s\n", getname(psp, name));
    }                                       // beginapp

void __stdcall endapp(DWORD psp)
    {                                       // endapp
    char name[9];
    printf("Ending   V86 App %s\n", getname(psp, name));
    }                                       // endapp

char *getname(DWORD psp, char *name)
    {                                       // getname
    char *p  = (char *) (psp - 8);
    memcpy(name, p, 8);
    name[8] = 0;
    return name;
    }                                       // getname
```

Here the two DOSMGR services we're intercepting use ESI to point to the high-linear address of the V86 program's Program Segment Prefix (PSP). This pointer ends up being the argument to the *beginapp* and *endapp* functions. We're then relying on the feature of DOS 4.0 and later that specifies that the arena header just before the PSP contains the name of the program at offset 8. Thus, this tiny application prints out the names of each V86 application that starts or stops while it's active.

This example is probably too simple to be useful, primarily because the single DWORD parameter you use with an APC won't convey much information unless it's a pointer. So suppose the VxD allocates some memory, perhaps using *_HeapAllocate*, and passes the pointer to the Win32 application. The application can't release the memory, so it has to call back into the VxD (using yet another *DeviceIoControl* call) to perform the requisite *_HeapFree*. Not only is the bookkeeping associated with this logic a hassle, but the code is difficult to create and understand. For an example that goes this extra mile, look at the MONITOR sample for Chapter 15.

Part III

Input/Output Programming

Chapter 11

Introduction to Plug and Play

Do you know how many systems programmers it takes to change a light bulb? I don't know either—it sounds like a hardware problem.

The point of this incredibly lame joke is that personal computer hardware problems are cunning, baffling, and insidious. Most of us who claim some expertise in software still recoil in fear from the task of configuring a network card or a sound card. IRQ conflicts, DMA channel allocation, port addressing, memory assignment: without Plug and Play, you have to master all of these in order to do something as simple as upgrade a PC to play a multimedia game.

Add to the usual set of configuration puzzles the problems of dockable laptops and dynamically changeable PCMCIA cards. Add the fact that all of the devices attached to a PC need device drivers to work in Windows. Then you'll see why Microsoft desperately needed to invent a solution to device configuration that normal mortals could deal with. That's what the Plug and Play architecture of Windows 95 is all about.

Plug and Play encompasses a set of hardware standards and a software standard. The hardware standards govern how devices identify themselves and their resource requirements to an operating system. The software standard governs how systems programmers should write drivers that Windows 95 can find and load once it has identified particular hardware on the computer. I'll describe both aspects of Plug and Play in this chapter and the next. This being a book about systems programming, however, I'll concentrate on the software aspects. As you'll see, engineering the several components that dovetail with the Plug and Play software architecture causes considerable programmer annoyance but ensures end-user convenience.

How the Hardware Works

The various hardware standards I'm about to describe have two goals. The first goal is to allow an operating system to perform an automatic survey of the computer hardware. The second goal is to allow the operating system to automatically reconfigure the hardware to accommodate competing resource demands. For historical reasons, these standards evolved along with hardware bus standards that include specifications for clock rates, pin assignments, and other electronic details. I'll therefore organize the discussion by bus type, beginning with the crotchety old ISA bus.

The ISA Bus

The oldest, most prevalent, and cheapest of the bus standards is also the stupidest. The *Industry Standard Architecture* (ISA) bus predates the recognition of how hard it is to configure a modern system. Supporting Plug and Play for ISA bus machines requires the operating system to use a new scheme for self-identifying hardware cards. So-called "legacy" cards, which don't understand the Plug and Play conventions I'm about to describe, operate as they always have. That is, users continue to swear at documentation of varying quality as they set DIP switches or jumpers in their attempt to achieve conflict-free installation.

In brief, system software starts its hardware survey by first outputting a specific 32-byte data stream to a reserved I/O port. All Plug and Play devices attached to the ISA bus are simultaneously and continuously looking for this *initiation key* and respond by entering *configuration mode*. Software then isolates each Plug and Play card in turn to assign a unique handle (a *Card Select Number*, or CSN) to each card. Thereafter, software can read resource requirements and other information from the card, determine how best to allocate the computer's resources, and configure each of the cards. Finally, software activates all of the Plug and Play cards.

I won't go into all of the details about how Plug and Play cards identify their resource requirements and accept configuration instructions. Refer to the *Plug and Play ISA Specification 1.0A* (Microsoft Corporation; available on MSDN) for full information. I will, however, describe the initiation and isolation scheme in more detail.

To place all Plug and Play cards into configuration mode, software sends two 0 bytes plus the following 32-byte data stream to I/O port 279h:

```
6A B5 DA ED F6 FB 7D BE DF 6F 37 1B 0D 86 C3 61
B0 58 2C 16 8B 45 A2 D1 E8 74 3A 9D CE E7 73 39
```

Departing from the grand tradition of PC software, this sequence isn't anybody's name, or even the name of a restaurant in the developers' neighborhood. It represents instead successive values of a binary polynomial whose likelihood of random occurrence is vanishingly small. Port 279h is usually the LPT1 status port, which is normally read-only. Thus, this much of the Plug and Play protocol is pretty safe from inadvertent activation of the new functionality.

When all the Plug and Play cards are in the configuration state, software proceeds to isolate them one at a time to assign handles. The isolation algorithm depends on each card having a 64-bit identifier that's unique on the system. The identifier includes 32 bits of vendor identification and 32 bits of card identification. These 64 bits are sufficient to allow every person on earth to manufacture a card every second for the next millennium or so, thereby consuming all of the silicon, oxygen, and gold in the known universe and causing gravitational collapse of the Milky Way galaxy. Each card contains an 8-bit checksum as well, just to make sure there's no confusion of identifiers. (There is no truth to the rumor that science fiction author Douglas Adams has reserved manufacturer ID 0000002Ah.)

Card isolation is a high-tech game of odd man out. To isolate one card, software reads 144 bytes (2 bytes for each bit of the 64-bit card identifier and the 8-bit checksum) from the Plug and Play READ_DATA port. This port can be anywhere in the range 203h through 3FFh, depending on what the I/O configuration of the computer allows. The Plug and Play specification describes how the operating system can successively try different port addresses to find the one actually implemented by the computer manufacturer.

Each card begins an isolation round in the "sleep" state. Software sends a *WAKE(0)* command to place all cards that haven't yet been isolated—that is, whose CSN is still 0—into the isolation state. (See Figure 11-1 on the following page for an abbreviated state diagram.) As the read operations progress, each card consults successive bits of its unique identifier (low order to high order) to see how it will respond:

- **1-bit** The card sends 55h in response to the next even-byte read and AAh in response to the next odd-byte read.

- **0-bit** Rather than placing data on the bus, the card monitors the low-order two bits of the data bus to see what the other cards are doing. If the card notices that another card responds with 01 and 10 (the low-order two bits of 55h and AAh), it drops out of this round of the isolation game by switching back to the "sleep" state.

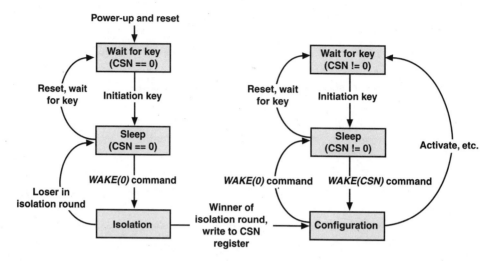

Figure 11-1. *State diagram for ISA Plug and Play cards.*

Because cards generate data on the bus only for 1-bits in their identifiers, this algorithm isolates the first card to have a 1-bit where all other cards have a 0-bit. The software driving the process can reconstruct the winning card's identifier if it wants to by treating the input sequence 55h AAh as denoting a 1-bit and any other 2-byte sequence as denoting a 0-bit. It's generally sufficient, however, to know that just one card will remain in the isolation state when the algorithm terminates.

Consider a simplified example in which cards have a 4-bit identifier with no checksum. Suppose we have three cards—A, B, and C—with identifiers 1010h, 1011h, and 0111h, respectively. Figure 11-2 diagrams the process by which software progressively isolates card C, then card B, and finally card A. An additional isolation round would yield an ID of 0000, indicating that no more Plug and Play devices exist.

Having isolated a card, software then assigns an 8-bit CSN for use as a handle in subsequent operations. By using the *WAKE* command with this CSN, the operating system can place this card into the configuration state later on. Once in the configuration state, the card will deliver its resource requirements (IRQ, DMA, memory, and port) on request and will accept configuration instructions. Since each card contains its own resource requirements in electronic form, there is no particular need for the manufacturer to supply a configuration file.

The EISA Bus

In an *Extended ISA* (EISA) system, each expansion slot in the PC has its own unique range of I/O port addresses, and each EISA card contains electronics for configuring

Round 1 (A, B, and C)			Round 2 (A and B)		Round 3 (A)
A	**B**	**C**	**A**	**B**	**A**
0 —	1 55h	1 55h	0 —	1 55h	0 —
—	AAh	AAh	—	AAh	—
(drops out)			(drops out)		
	1 55h	1 55h		1 55h	1 55h
	AAh	AAh		AAh	AAh
	0 —	1 55h		0 —	0 —
	—	AAh		—	—
	(drops out)				
		0 —		1 55h	1 55h
		—		AAh	AAh
Winner is C (0111)			**Winner is B (1011)**		**Winner is A (1010)**

Figure 11-2. *ISA card isolation algorithm (simplified).*

the other resources that might be needed by the card. The manufacturer of an EISA card supplies a disk containing a configuration file detailing the resource requirements of the card. A standalone configuration utility examines the configuration file and figures out how to harmonize all of the cards. The utility then records the configuration in nonvolatile memory such as battery-powered CMOS memory. During the power-on self test, the system BIOS reads the configuration information, verifies that the correct cards are in their expected slots, and dynamically configures the cards.

Software can identify an EISA card in slot x by reading a byte from each of the ports xC80h through xC83h. The returned data represents five compressed bytes—a 3-letter ASCII manufacturer code and a 4-digit hexadecimal (2-byte) device and revision number—as shown in Figure 11-3 on the following page. (The layout looks so peculiar because it's really big-endian in memory.)

Windows 95 continues to rely on the BIOS to identify EISA expansion cards. That is, the Configuration Manager notices only those devices that are recorded in the nonvolatile memory when it starts. To add a new EISA card, the end user needs to run the standalone configuration utility and reboot the computer.

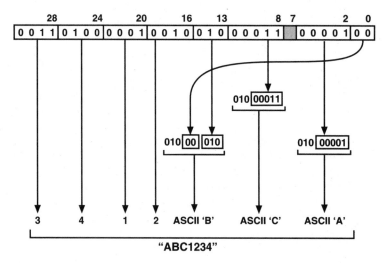

Figure 11-3. *Compressed EISA card identifier.*

The MCA Bus

The *Micro Channel Architecture* (MCA) bus in IBM PS/2 computers has a fairly limited scheme for adapter identification. Every MCA adapter card has eight *programmable option select* (POS) registers that software can address at ports 100h through 107h. Software selects a particular card's POS registers by writing to the adapter activation register at I/O port 096h (see Figure 11-4). Software can then read 16 bits of card identification data from ports 100h and 101h. IBM maintains the registry of card identifiers.

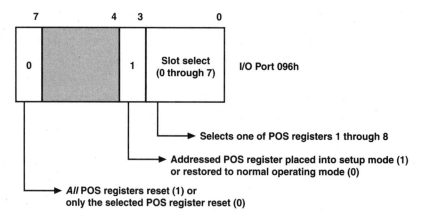

Figure 11-4. *MCA adapter activation register.*

MCA cards themselves contain no indication of what they are or what resources they need other than this 16-bit identifier. A disk accompanies each card, and the disk contains a set of setup files that describe in detail how to configure the card. A setup utility interprets these files and records the necessary configuration information in CMOS RAM for later use. As the machine boots, the system BIOS copies the configuration from CMOS to the POS registers on the cards. The BIOS is essentially an uncritical conduit for configuration data that it doesn't examine, except that it does verify that the expected card is still in the slot it's configuring.

You can get more information about the MCA bus and adapter cards at relatively high cost from the Micro Channel Developers Association, at (916) 222-2262. You will need several manuals, each costing $50 to $100, to make complete sense of the bus, the POS registers, and the setup utility. A better (and much more cost-effective) once-over-lightly treatment is Hans-Peter Messmer's *Indispensable PC Hardware Book: Your Hardware Questions Answered* (Addison-Wesley, 1994), pages 265–281.

The PCI Bus

The *Peripheral Component Interconnect* (PCI) local bus defines a hardware standard for self-identifying devices. Devices attached to the PCI bus have a *configuration space* (see Figure 11-5 on the following page) that contains 256 bytes of information, including the following:

- A 16-bit vendor identifier

- A 16-bit device identifier and an 8-bit version identifier

- A 24-bit device class code

- Up to six I/O or memory base addresses

- An option ROM address

- An IRQ number

Software can interrogate a particular configuration register in one of two ways. The preferred method is to first write a 32-bit device and register address (see Figure 11-6 on the following page) to the CONFIG_ADDRESS register (a 32-bit port at I/O address CF8h) and to then read the contents of the register from the CONFIG_DATA port at I/O address CFCh. Reading 64 registers with addresses 0, 4, and so on, allows you to accumulate all 256 bytes of a particular device's configuration space. To enumerate all the devices attached to the bus, you can loop over device numbers 0 through 31.

```
typedef struct tagCONFIG {      // PCI configuration space
    WORD vendorid;              // 00h vendor ID
    WORD deviceid;              // 02h device ID
    WORD command;               // 04h command register
    WORD status;                // 06h status register
    BYTE revision;              // 08h revision ID
    BYTE class[3];              // 09h class code
    BYTE cachesize;             // 0Ch cache line size
    BYTE latency;               // 0Dh latency timer
    BYTE hdrtype;               // 0Eh header type
    BYTE bist;                  // 0Fh built-in self-test control
    DWORD baseaddr[6]           // 10h base address registers
    DWORD cis;                  // 28h CardBus CIS pointer
    WORD subvendor;             // 2Ch subsystem vendor ID
    WORD subsystem;             // 2Eh subsystem
    DWORD romaddr;              // 30h expansion ROM base address
    DWORD reserved[2]           // 34h reserved
    BYTE irq;                   // 3Ch interrupt line
    BYTE ipin;                  // 3Dh interrupt pin
    BYTE min_gnt;               // 3Eh minimum burst on 33 MHz bus (1/4-
                                //     microsecond units)

    BYTE max_lat;               // 3Fh maximum latency on 33 MHz bus (1/4-
                                //     microsecond units)

    BYTE device[196];           // 40h device-specific information
} CONFIG, *PCONFIG;             // [100h] PCI configuration space
```

Figure 11-5. *Configuration space for a PCI device.*

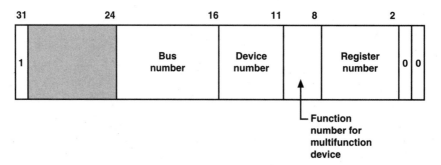

Figure 11-6. *Bit assignment within the PCI configuration address register.*

Another method of getting configuration information is defined only for backward compatibility. You first enable the configuration space by writing a 16-bit key to port CF8h. Then you read the configuration registers of up to 16 devices per bus at I/O ports C000h through CFFFh. While the configuration space is disabled, these ports function normally as I/O ports. Note that you get different behavior from the bus depending on whether you write 4 bytes or 2 bytes to CF8h!

You can obtain a copy of the PCI bus standard from the PCI Special Interest Group at (800) 433-5177 (from within the United States) or (503) 797-4207 (outside the United States). The cost is about $25. You might also want copies of the separate PCI BIOS and PCI-to-PCI Bridge specifications.

THE CONFIGURATION MANAGER

A new Windows 95 component called the *Configuration Manager* (CONFIGMG) controls the dynamic loading of device drivers and the configuration of hardware. The new hardware and software standards come into play even before Windows 95 starts, however. The computer needs a few devices—a display, a keyboard, and a disk drive, to name three—to boot in the first place. Even if these devices are capable of dynamic reconfiguration, they must power-up with a reasonable set of default assignments. The Plug and Play hardware specification allows the manufacturer to use jumpers or DIP switches for this limited purpose.

If your computer happens to have a new breed of BIOS that's built for Plug and Play compatibility, the BIOS automatically configures portions of your system when you boot the computer. To retain maximum flexibility, the BIOS should disable devices that aren't needed at this stage of system operation. Then, when Windows 95 eventually takes over in protected mode, the Configuration Manager can apply considerable knowledge to the problem of configuring the whole system.

The System Registry

The registry plays a key role in guiding the Configuration Manager through its tasks. The Windows 95 registry is a hierarchical database. Each node in the hierarchy is a *named key* that can have *named values* and *subkeys*. Named values are pairs of names and binary or ASCII values, and subkeys are named objects that themselves contain further named values and subkeys. Each node can also have a single unnamed value, but Windows 95 system software doesn't take advantage of this possibility. The Windows 95 Setup program creates the registry to begin with and populates it with information it discovers about the hardware and software environment. Various system components maintain the registry thereafter. The end user can manually inspect and modify the registry by using the REGEDIT application. Figure 11-7 on the following page shows the very important HKEY_LOCAL_MACHINE (HKLM for short) branch of the registry as displayed by REGEDIT.

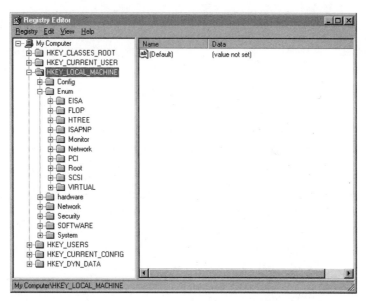

Figure 11-7. *The HKEY_LOCAL_MACHINE branch of the registry.*

Because of the registry's importance to the management of a Windows 95 system, it's worth exploring the various branches of this database:

HKEY_CLASSES_ROOT	OLE class information (an alias for HKLM\Software\Classes).
HKEY_CURRENT_USER	Customization information pertaining to the logon ID of the human being currently using the computer (an alias for some branch of HKEY_USERS).
HKEY_LOCAL_MACHINE	Hardware information.
Config	Details about hardware profiles.
0001	Details about hardware profile 1.
Enum	Information about all hardware ever installed on this computer.
enumerator	Information about devices found by the named bus enumerator—such as ISAPNP, PCI, and so on.
device-id	Information about devices of a particular type.
instance	Information about a particular device of the parent type. This key is also called the *hardware* key for the device. The named value Driver is especially important here.
ROOT	Information about legacy devices.
*device-id	Information about devices of a particular type. For example, *PNP0500 concerns serial ports.

`0000`	Information about the first device of a particular type. This key is also called the *hardware* key for the device. The named value Driver is especially important here.
`LogConfig`	Information about logical configurations of the device.
`Software`	Information about applications. This information supersedes that in INI files.
`Classes`	OLE class information.
`Manufacturer`	Information about a particular manufacturer's software on this system.
`ProductName`	Information about a particular product.
`CurrentVersion`	Information about the current version of the product.
`version`	Information about some other version of the product.
`System`	Detailed information about available devices.
`CurrentControlSet`	Detailed information about available devices.
`Control`	Detailed information about available devices.
`IDConfigDB`	Information about hardware profiles. The named values FriendlyName*nnnn* are especially important here.
`Services`	Information about device drivers.
`Arbitrators`	Control parameters for resource arbitrators.
`Class`	Information about each class of device.
`classname`	Information about devices of a particular class.
`0000`	Information about the first device of that class. This key is also called the *software* key for the device. Named values such as DevLoader, Enumerator, EnumPropPages, PortDriver, and so on, are crucial to the Configuration Manager.
`VxD`	Information about static device drivers.
`name`	Information about a particular driver, including settings formerly in the SYSTEM.INI file. The named value StaticVxD specifies the name of a driver file to load statically.
`HKEY_USERS`	Information about all users of this computer.
`HKEY_CURRENT_CONFIG`	Information about the current hardware profile (an alias for some branch of HKLM\Config).
`HKEY_DYN_DATA`	Dynamic data accessible through function calls wrapped by the registry API (in other words, not persistent).

Config Manager	Data maintained by the Configuration Manager.
Enum	The hardware tree.
xxxxxxxx	The DEVNODE at the specified linear address.
PerfStats	Performance counters.

The Mechanics of Plug and Play Drivers

There are some special requirements for building drivers intended to be part of the Configuration Manager system, and many of them aren't apparent without explanation. The Microsoft DDK works well for Plug and Play drivers written in high-level languages, so I'll present an example written in C using the DDK.

A Plug and Play device driver is a dynamic VxD. Therefore, you need to provide handlers for the Sys_Dynamic_Device_Init and Sys_Dynamic_Device_Exit system control messages. These handlers should simply return TRUE to indicate success:

```
BOOL OnSysDynamicDeviceInit()
    {                            // OnSysDynamicDeviceInit
    return TRUE;
    }                            // OnSysDynamicDeviceInit

BOOL OnSysDynamicDeviceExit()
    {                            // OnSysDynamicDeviceExit
    return TRUE;
    }                            // OnSysDynamicDeviceExit
```

There are some additional standard header files that are useful to include in a Plug and Play driver:

```
#define WANTVXDWRAPS
#include <basedef.h>
#include <vmm.h>
#include <debug.h>
#include <vmmreg.h>
#include <vxdwraps.h>
#include <configmg.h>
#include <regstr.h>
```

VMMREG.H declares services for examining and modifying the registry, and REGSTR.H defines manifest constants for many of the perplexingly ad hoc registry pathnames. CONFIGMG.H declares the interface to the Configuration Manager. REGSTR.H and CONFIGMG.H are exceptions to the rule I stated in Chapter 7 that all VxD include files should precede VXDWRAPS.H

The DDK defines Configuration Manager services whose names begin with _*CONFIGMG_*. This prefix is what you'd expect for C-callable VxD services in a VxD named CONFIGMG. You don't use the documented names when you write a driver, however. Instead, you replace the _CONFIGMG_ prefix with *CM_*. Thus, to call the _CONFIGMG_Register_Enumerator service, you actually code a call to *CM_Register_Enumerator*. (Note that the documentation for all these services confuses things even more by using a name prefix of *CONFIGMG_*, without the leading underscore.)

The Configuration Manager communicates with Plug and Play drivers by calling one or more special callback functions. The Configuration Manager needs a way to learn the addresses of these callbacks. Windows, however, can access a VxD only through the device control procedure mentioned in the VxD's Declare_Virtual_Device macro. Therefore, you write code in your device control procedure to handle the PNP_New_Devnode system control message. The Configuration Manager calls *VXDLDR_LoadDevice* to dynamically load your driver. The VxD loader returns the address of your driver's DDB, and the Configuration Manager then calls *Directed_Sys_Control* to send you the PNP_New_Devnode message. Thereupon, you use one or more registration API functions to inform the Configuration Manager about your callback routines.

There are two parameters for the PNP_New_Devnode message. One parameter is the address of a device node, or DEVNODE for short. The other parameter is a load type code (see Table 11-1) that indicates what the Configuration Manager expects your driver to do. A C program to handle the message would look like the following example, in which the return code *CR_DEFAULT* indicates that you want default handling for a load type code you didn't handle:

```
CONFIGRET OnPnpNewDevnode(DEVNODE devnode, DWORD loadtype)
    {                              // OnPnpNewDevnode
    ...
    return CR_DEFAULT;
    }                              // OnPnpNewDevnode
```

PNP_New_Devnode Load Type Codes	Description
DLVXD_LOAD_ENUMERATOR	Your driver is loaded as an enumerator
DLVXD_LOAD_DEVLOADER	Your driver is loaded as a device loader
DLVXD_LOAD_DRIVER	Your driver is loaded as a device driver

Table 11-1. *Reasons for PNP_New_Devnode messages.*

The actions the Configuration Manager expects you to take in each of the three PNP_New_Devnode roles are as follows:

- **Enumerator** Call *CM_Register_Enumerator* to register an enumeration function.

- **Device Loader** Dynamically load the device driver for the specified DEVNODE by calling *CM_Load_DLVxDs*. A side effect of this call will be to send the newly loaded driver(s) their own PNP_New_Devnode messages with the *DLVXD_LOAD_DRIVER* code. Returning *CR_SUCCESS* isn't enough to convince the Configuration Manager that you've succeeded as a device loader: something must also register as a device driver for the DEVNODE. One of the drivers you dynamically load will normally do so.

- **Device Driver** Call *CM_Register_Device_Driver* to register a configuration function. You can register a NULL configuration function, which means that the Configuration Manager will perform default handling for all configuration events.

The final advice I have to offer is that your driver will fit into the overall system architecture better if you include a version resource. For example, I created the following two files as part of the sample I'm about to show you (these files are included on the companion disc in the \CHAP11\SCHOOLBUS directory):

SCHOOL.RC

```
; SCHOOL.RC

#include <winver.h>
#include <version.h>

VS_VERSION_INFO VERSIONINFO
FILEVERSION     VERMAJOR, VERMINOR, 0, BUILD
PRODUCTVERSION  VERMAJOR, VERMINOR, 0, BUILD
FILEFLAGSMASK   VS_FFI_FILEFLAGSMASK
FILEFLAGS       VS_FF_DEBUG | VS_FF_PRERELEASE
FILEOS          VOS_DOS_WINDOWS32
FILETYPE        VFT_VXD
FILESUBTYPE     0
BEGIN
    BLOCK "StringFileInfo"
    BEGIN
        BLOCK "040904E4"
        BEGIN
            VALUE "CompanyName", "Walter Oney Software\0"
            VALUE "FileDescription", "School Bus Driver\0"
            VALUE "FileVersion", PRODVER
            VALUE "InternalName", "SCHOOL\0"
```

(continued)

continued

```
                VALUE "LegalCopyright", \
                    "Copyright (C) 1996 by Walter Oney Software\0"
                VALUE "OriginalFilename", "SCHOOL.VXD\0"
                VALUE "ProductName", "School Bus Sample Program\0"
                VALUE "ProductVersion", PRODVER
            END
        END
        BLOCK "VarFileInfo"
        BEGIN
            VALUE "Translation", 0x409, 1252
        END
    END
```

VERSION.H

```
// VERSION.H

#define VERMAJOR  1
#define VERMINOR  0
#define BUILD     003

#define PRODVER   "1.0.003\0"
```

The end user sees some of this information when he or she launches the System applet in the Windows 95 Control Panel and asks for the properties of the School Bus device (see Figure 11-8 on the following page). To add the version resource to your executable file, you must use the *16-bit* resource compiler and the DDK tool named ADRC2VXD. Your NMAKE script might contain the following:

```
all: school.vxd
...
.rc.res:
    c:\msvc\bin\rc -r $*.rc    # must use RC16 for this

school.vxd : s_ctl.obj $*.obj $*.def $*.res
    link @<<
-machine:i386 -def:$*.def -out:$@
-debug -debugtype:map
-map:$*.map -vxd vxdwraps.clb -nodefaultlib
s_ctl.obj $*.obj
<<
    adrc2vxd $*.vxd $*.res
```

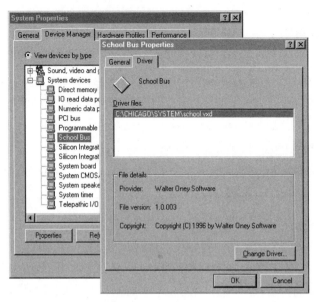

Figure 11-8. *Control Panel display of the version resource.*

Loading the Right Device Drivers

Mirroring the physical hardware, the Configuration Manager models the computer as containing one or more hardware *buses,* to which *devices* are attached. The Configuration Manager creates a hierarchical data structure called the *hardware tree* to describe the buses and their devices. Nodes in the tree are called DEVNODEs. The tree can be several nodes deep because some devices can in turn attach to other devices. For example, a SCSI controller attaches to a bus but in turn controls other devices.

The Configuration Manager relies heavily on the registry to build the hardware tree. The *root enumerator* (a component internal to the Configuration Manager) starts the process by adding the devices listed in HKLM\ENUM\ROOT to the hardware tree. One such device will be the primary bus on the computer. For example, the system I'm using right this minute has a PCI local bus as its primary bus. HKLM\ROOT\ENUM also lists so-called "legacy" devices. Legacy devices include standard components like the Direct Memory Access (DMA) controller and the Programmable Interrupt Controller (PIC). Because these components are classified as Plug and Play devices, the Configuration Manager needn't contain special code to set them up for each Windows 95 session. The category of legacy device also includes devices like the keyboard and standard serial ports that can't easily be detected automatically. The Windows 95 Setup program uses an elaborate—not to mention time-consuming and sometimes fragile—detection algorithm to locate legacy devices. Not only would it be silly for the Configuration Manager to rerun the detection algorithm anew each time you boot your computer, it would be wasteful and risky.

When the root enumerator finishes, the hardware tree contains DEVNODEs for all the legacy devices. Some of these DEVNODEs will have enumerators associated with them. The Configuration Manager calls these additional enumerators to further augment the hardware tree. The enumerators may find still more devices to which lower-level devices are attached. For example, my computer has an ISA bus connected via a bridge chip to the PCI local bus. The PCI bus enumerator therefore creates a DEVNODE for the ISA bus. The ISA bus enumerator then gets a chance to check for ISAPNP cards. The enumeration process continues in a recursive manner until the hardware tree mirrors the actual topology of the computer.

Device Identifiers

The Configuration Manager identifies devices with a three-part, backslash-delimited ASCII string that's unique within any given computer. The device ID is both the name of the DEVNODE and the name of the registry key that describes the device. The first portion of the string identifies the enumerator that detected the device—for example, ISAPNP or PCI. The second portion identifies the type of device, and the third portion identifies an instance of that type of device on the computer.

For example, the ID string of the IDE hard drive on my computer is PCI\VEN_1095&DEV_0640\BUS_00&DEV_0D&FUNC_00. Here, PCI identifies the bus, VEN_1095&DEV_0640 identifies the device type (PCI to IDE bridge from vendor number 1095), and BUS_00&DEV_0D&FUNC_00 identifies an instance of the device type. The instance identifier is merely a concatenation of the information contained in the PCI configuration space about this device: it's function 0 of device 0Dh on PCI bus number 0h. The registry key for this disk device is HKLM\Enum\PCI\ VEN_1095&DEV_0640\BUS_00&DEV_0D&FUNC_00.

Device identifiers often start with a * to indicate that they are EISA identifiers. An EISA identifier contains a 3-letter manufacturer prefix and a 4-digit hexadecimal number. A device manufacturer procures an EISA prefix from the central registry maintained by BCPR Services, Inc., in Spring, Texas. For devices that lack standard EISA IDs and for classes of devices for which an EISA ID is inappropriate, Microsoft reserved the prefix PNP and assigned pseudo-IDs to a large collection of devices. For example, a device ID that begins with *PNP0A00 is an ISA bus. Table 11-2 on the following page lists the possible device IDs for hardware buses. The complete list of IDs for all device classes appears in the Appendix. You can obtain an up-to-date list by downloading DEVIDS.TXT from the CompuServe PLUGPLAY forum.

Device ID	Description
PNP0A00	Industry Standard Architecture (ISA) bus
PNP0A01	Extended Industry Standard Architecture (EISA) bus
PNP0A02	Micro Channel Architecture (MCA) bus
PNP0A03	Peripheral Component Interconnect (PCI) bus
PNP0A04	Video Electronics Standards Association Local (VL) bus

Table 11-2. *Hardware bus device identifiers.*

Bus Enumerators

To illustrate how the Configuration Manager deals with buses, I'm going to present a simple example. Since the example is for instructional purposes, I'll describe how you could support a new hardware bus named the School Bus, for which we'll assume we've registered the fictitious device ID PNP0A05. Because of entries in a device information file that I'll describe later in this chapter, the Windows 95 Setup program will have copied the bus driver (SCHOOL.VXD) to the SYSTEM directory and will have created the registry entries shown in Figure 11-9.

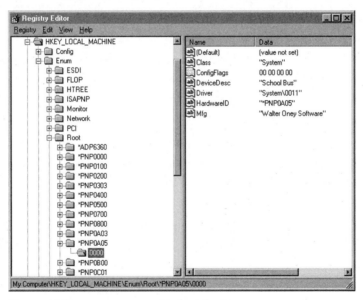

Figure 11-9. *Registry entries for the School Bus.*

When the root enumerator reaches the *PNP0A05 key in its enumeration of HKLM\Enum\Root, it reads the named value Driver to locate the bus enumerator. In Figure 11-9, this value is *System\0011* because the School Bus was the twelfth device of class System ever added to my computer. The root enumerator therefore opens the key HKLM\System\CurrentControlSet\Services\Class\System\0011 (see Figure 11-10). That key in turn indicates that the device loader (DevLoader) for the enumerator is SCHOOL.VXD.

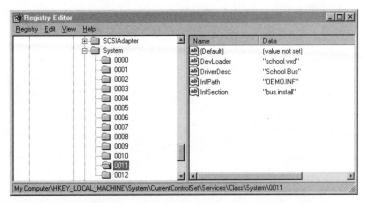

Figure 11-10. *Registry entries for the School Bus device driver.*

About Those Pseudo-EISA Identifiers If you install the School Bus driver from the companion CD included with this book, it won't end up in HKLM\Enum\Root*PNP0A05 as described in the text. It will end up in HKLM\Enum\SCHOOL instead. Only entries created by the automatic detection process end up in the root branch under those cryptic pseudo-EISA identifier names. Entries for devices you add manually end up in branches with more readable names. I manually renamed the automatically generated registry key to generate the screen shot in Figure 11-9.

The root enumerator now creates a DEVNODE to describe the bus and dynamically loads the specified device loader, namely SCHOOL.VXD. This VxD is really the bus enumerator, but the logic of the root enumeration process demands that it play the role of a device loader at this stage. SCHOOL.VXD then receives a Sys_Dynamic_Device_Init system control message, to which it typically responds simply by returning TRUE:

```
BOOL OnSysDynamicDeviceInit()
    {                               // OnSysDynamicDeviceInit
    return TRUE;
    }                               // OnSysDynamicDeviceInit
```

So far I've described nothing more than an especially elaborate scheme for dynamically loading a device driver. The Plug and Play architecture manifests itself in what happens next: the Configuration Manager sends SCHOOL.VXD a PNP_New_Devnode message directing it to load the driver for the DEVNODE representing the bus. The driver has actually already been loaded (SCHOOL.VXD is this very driver), but the Configuration Manager doesn't know it yet. Furthermore, SCHOOL.VXD uses the occasion of this message to do what it *really* wants to do, which is to register itself as a bus enumerator:

```
CONFIGRET OnPnpNewDevnode(DEVNODE devnode, DWORD loadtype)
    {                               // OnPnpNewDevnode
CONFIGRET code;
switch (loadtype)
        {                           // select function to perform

 case DLVXD_LOAD_DEVLOADER:
        code = CM_Register_Enumerator(devnode, OnEnumerate,
            CM_REGISTER_ENUMERATOR_HARDWARE);
        if (code != CR_SUCCESS)
            return code;
        return CM_Register_Device_Driver(devnode, NULL, 0,
            CM_REGISTER_DEVICE_DRIVER_REMOVABLE);
        }                           // select function to perform
return CR_DEFAULT;
    }                               // OnPnpNewDevnode
```

At this point, SCHOOL.VXD has registered itself as both the enumerator and the device driver for the DEVNODE representing the School Bus. We'll complete the enumeration function later in this chapter. A basic version of *OnEnumerate* looks like this:

```
CONFIGRET _cdecl OnEnumerate(CONFIGFUNC cf, SUBCONFIGFUNC scf,
    DEVNODE tonode, DEVNODE aboutnode, ULONG flags)
    {                               // OnEnumerate
return CR_DEFAULT;
    }                               // OnEnumerate
```

Notice that the School Bus enumerator doesn't seem to follow the rules I described earlier for responding to the PNP_New_Devnode message. It's an enumerator, but it responds only to a message with a *DLVXD_LOAD_DEVLOADER* load type. And instead of dynamically loading a driver as it's supposed to (according to the rules, that is), it performs the actions the other two types of drivers are supposed to do! These peculiarities result from trying to cram all the functionality for the bus driver into a single VxD. Microsoft's own PCI.VXD works exactly the same way, so the behavior I've shown you isn't idiosyncratic.

Table 11-3 lists the configuration messages an enumerator can receive. You don't pretend success for enumeration messages your driver doesn't handle; you return *CR_DEFAULT* to request that the default action occur. In fact, the debug version of the Configuration Manager sends the enumeration function a bogus message of 0x12345678 during the *CM_Register_Enumerator* call to see if it responds correctly.

Message	Description
CONFIG_APM	Notifies enumerator that a power management event is occurring
CONFIG_CALLBACK	Notifies enumerator that *CM_CallBack_Enumerator* has been called
CONFIG_ENUMERATE	Instructs enumerator to enumerate immediate children
CONFIG_FILTER	Instructs enumerator to filter (restrict) logical configurations for one of its devices
CONFIG_PREREMOVE	Notifies enumerator that one of its devices is about to be removed (sent from the bottom of the tree up)
CONFIG_PREREMOVE2	Notifies enumerator that one of its devices is about to be removed (sent from the top of the tree down)
CONFIG_PRESHUTDOWN	Notifies enumerator that the system is about to shut down
CONFIG_READY	Notifies enumerator that one of its devices has been set up
CONFIG_REMOVE	Notifies enumerator that one of its devices is being removed from the system
CONFIG_SETUP	Notifies enumerator that one of its devices has been set up for the very first time
CONFIG_SHUTDOWN	Notifies enumerator that the system is shutting down
CONFIG_TEST	Asks whether enumerator can stop using configuration or whether one of its devices can be removed
CONFIG_TEST_FAILED	Notifies enumerator that the previous CONFIG_TEST failed
CONFIG_TEST_SUCCEEDED	Notifies enumerator that the previous CONFIG_TEST succeeded

Table 11-3. *Configuration messages for enumerators.*

The Configuration Manager sends many function requests to a device's configuration function (discussed in the next chapter) as well as to the enumerator that owns the device. The duplication permits you to divide the responsibility for handling certain events in the most appropriate way. For example, a device driver might think it was perfectly okay to let itself be removed, but the enumerator might want to veto that decision.

An enumeration function receives two DEVNODEs as arguments. The *tonode* is the DEVNODE that represents the bus or other parent device. The *aboutnode* is usually the DEVNODE for a child device. There are some functions for which only one DEVNODE is relevant, and the *tonode* and *aboutnode* arguments will be the same.

The following pages describe the configuration functions for enumerators in greater detail.

The CONFIG_APM Function The Configuration Manager sends CONFIG_APM messages as part of the *Advanced Power Management* protocol. The subfunction argument (see Table 11-4) indicates the reason for the event. When you choose the *Suspend* command from the Start menu, for example, the Configuration Manager sends a series of messages to drivers and their enumerators, as follows:

■ CONFIG_APM_TEST_SUSPEND to the enumerator to see whether it's okay to suspend each attached device

■ CONFIG_APM_TEST_SUSPEND to each device

■ CONFIG_APM_TEST_SUSPEND to the enumerator to see whether it's okay to suspend the bus itself

Then, assuming that the suspend messages result in *CR_SUCCESS* return codes, the Configuration Manager sends this series of messages:

■ CONFIG_APM_TEST_SUSPEND_SUCCEEDED to each device

■ CONFIG_APM_TEST_SUSPEND_SUCCEEDED to the enumerator about each device

■ CONFIG_APM_TEST_SUSPEND_SUCCEEDED to the enumerator about the bus itself

Subfunction	Description
CONFIG_APM_TEST_STANDBY	Asks whether it is okay to change to standby (low-power) operation
CONFIG_APM_TEST_SUSPEND	Asks whether it is okay to change to suspended (*no-power*) operation
CONFIG_APM_TEST_STANDBY_FAILED	Indicates that the last standby request failed
CONFIG_APM_TEST_SUSPEND_FAILED	Indicates that the last suspend request failed
CONFIG_APM_TEST_STANDBY_SUCCEEDED	Indicates that the last standby request succeeded
CONFIG_APM_RESUME_STANDBY	Indicates the end of standby operation
CONFIG_APM_RESUME_SUSPEND	Indicates the end of suspended operation
CONFIG_APM_RESUME_CRITICAL	Indicates that critical operations are resuming

Table 11-4. *CONFIG_APM subfunctions.*

The enumerator returns *CR_SUCCESS* to approve TEST requests; it returns *CR_FAILURE* to disapprove them.

The CONFIG_CALLBACK Function There is an obscure Configuration Manager service for calling back to an enumerator:

```
CM_CallBack_Enumerator(OnEnumerate);
```

Calling this function causes the Configuration Manager to call the specified enumeration function with the CONFIG_CALLBACK message once for every DEVNODE *for which the function is the enumerator.* In other words, if you have a School Bus with ten attached devices, calling *CM_CallBack_Enumerator* with the School Bus bus enumerator function specified causes a single CONFIG_CALLBACK message, in which the *tonode* and *aboutnode* arguments both point to the bus's DEVNODE. No one gets called back about the attached devices.

As I understand it, no one actually uses *CM_CallBack_Enumerator* anymore, so you can probably not worry about this configuration function.

The CONFIG_ENUMERATE Function The CONFIG_ENUMERATE message is the most important message that gets sent to an enumerator. This message asks the enumerator to make the hardware tree agree with the devices actually attached to the bus. Assume that the School Bus can have one or more telepathic I/O channels. These are fictional devices that read the user's mind, and they have the equally fictional device ID WCO1234. In real life, the bus would have some way of knowing how many of these devices are attached. It might, for example, use a protocol like the ones described earlier for the ISA or EISA buses to dynamically figure out what devices really exist. Or it might do what the root enumerator does and read entries in the registry that were left around by a detection program at some point in the past.

However it learns of devices, an enumerator should manufacture a unique device ID for each device, and it should create DEVNODEs. It should then assign *logical configurations* that describe the devices' resource requirements. I'll talk about the configuration process in the next chapter. The DEVNODE creation part of an enumerator's job might look something like this:

```
case CONFIG_ENUMERATE:
    {
    DEVNODE device;
    CONFIGRET code = CM_Create_DevNode(&device,
        "SCHOOL\\WCO1234\\0000", tonode, 0);
    if (code == CR_SUCCESS)
        {                    // devnode added okay
        [add configurations to new devnode]
        }                    // devnode added okay
    else if (code == CR_ALREADY_SUCH_DEVNODE)
        code = CR_SUCCESS; // not an error
    return code;
    }
```

In this example, *CM_Create_DevNode* creates a new device node for the telepathic device as a child of the bus. The use of WCO1234 as the middle component of the three-part device identifier is essentially coincidental, since the Configuration Manager gleans no intelligence from the name itself. All that matters is that the device identifier be unique in the system and be reproducible from one session to the next.

This code fragment treats the *CR_ALREADY_SUCH_DEVNODE* error returned from *CM_Create_DevNode* as a normal condition. It's normal because the Configuration Manager can call the enumerator many times during one Windows 95 session to detect newly installed hardware. Each time it is called, the enumerator must make sure that the hardware tree agrees with the population of installed hardware. Some enumerators, like the one for PCMCIA cards, know when hardware gets removed and call *CM_Remove_SubTree* to remove obsolete DEVNODEs from the tree on a real-time basis.

Most enumerators don't know, however, when the user removes hardware for which they are responsible. But they do have an automatic way to verify the continued presence of their devices. To prune the hardware tree during an enumeration phase, these enumerators rely on a so-called *mark* attached to each DEVNODE, as follows:

```
case CONFIG_ENUMERATE:
    CM_Reset_Children_Marks(tonode, 0);
    [enumerate the bus]
    CM_Remove_Unmarked_Children(tonode, 0);
    return CR_SUCCESS;
```

CM_Reset_Children_Marks clears the mark on each DEVNODE that is a child of the *tonode* DEVNODE, which represents the bus. Each call to *CM_Create_DevNode* during the process of enumerating the bus sets the mark, even if the DEVNODE already exists. After the bus enumeration is complete, therefore, the only unmarked DEVNODEs will be the ones that were never visited during the enumeration. *CM_Remove_Unmarked_Children* deletes only those DEVNODEs, thereby pruning the tree to match the actual hardware.

The root enumerator doesn't fit either of the preceding two descriptions: it neither knows when hardware goes away nor has it any way to determine whether hardware is still present during a re-enumeration. The root enumerator is in the dark because it simply reads the registry to find out what devices might be present. It therefore sends *CONFIG_VERIFY_DEVICE* functions to the device drivers for its child nodes. The child drivers respond either *CR_SUCCESS* to indicate that the hardware is still present or *CR_DEVICE_NOT_THERE* to indicate that the hardware is no longer present.

The CONFIG_FILTER Function The Configuration Manager allows an enumerator to *filter* the configurations for its child device nodes—successive *aboutnodes*—after the device nodes themselves have had a chance to do so. The purpose of configuration filtering is to restrict overly optimistic claims about which resources devices can really support. For example, a PCMCIA card may ask for a memory resource anywhere in the 32-bit addressable range. The PCMCIA enumerator may need to restrict the allowable range to the first 16 MB instead.

The CONFIG_PREREMOVE and CONFIG_PREREMOVE2 Functions These functions indicate that the *aboutnode* DEVNODE is about to be removed. The Configuration Manager sends CONFIG_PREREMOVE starting with the DEVNODE and proceeding upward in the hardware tree; it sends CONFIG_PREREMOVE2 starting at the top of the hardware tree and proceeding downward. An enumerator can do appropriate cleanup while handling these two events.

The CONFIG_PRESHUTDOWN Function The Configuration Manager sends this message to an enumerator to prepare for system shutdown. The *tonode* and *aboutnode* arguments both point to the enumerator's own DEVNODE. This message is sent before CONFIG_REMOVE and CONFIG_SHUTDOWN messages about the enumerator and its devices.

The CONFIG_READY Function An enumerator receives this function when the DEVNODE pointed to by the *aboutnode* argument has been completely set up for the very first time, but not yet configured. That is, this message is sent following CONFIG_SETUP and before CONFIG_FILTER. The enumerator can make sure that logical configuration information is accurate at this time.

The CONFIG_REMOVE Function First device drivers, and then their enumerators, receive this message when the DEVNODE pointed to by the *aboutnode* argument is about to be removed from the system. The Configuration Manager will sometimes have already sent CONFIG_TEST and CONFIG_TEST_SUCCEEDED messages. The subfunction CONFIG_REMOVE_DYNAMIC indicates that Device Manager triggered the device removal dynamically. The subfunction CONFIG_REMOVE_SHUTDOWN indicates that the system is about to shut down. In either case, the device receives the CONFIG_REMOVE message first, and then its enumerator receives it.

The CONFIG_SETUP Function An enumerator receives this message when a DEVNODE it owns has been created for the very first time. The enumerator should load any additional drivers that the device will need. These might come, for example, from the device ROM. The enumerator should also construct identifier and description strings for the new device; the end user will see these strings in the Add New Hardware dialog box. After the enumerator handles this message but before the Configuration Manager starts configuring the device, the enumerator will receive a CONFIG_READY message.

For example, I implemented a CONFIG_SETUP function for the School Bus driver to make sure that the Windows 95 Add New Hardware wizard knew what kind of device was attached to the bus:

```
case CONFIG_SETUP:
    {                               // CONFIG_SETUP
    ULONG length;                   // length of class name
    char class[64];                 // device class
    length = sizeof(class);

    code = CM_Read_Registry_Value(aboutnode, NULL, "Class",
        REG_SZ, class, &length, CM_REGISTRY_HARDWARE);
    if (code == CR_NO_SUCH_VALUE)
            {                       // new device
        CM_Write_Registry_Value(aboutnode, NULL, "Class",
            REG_SZ, "System", 6, CM_REGISTRY_HARDWARE);
        CM_Write_Registry_Value(aboutnode, NULL,
            "HardwareID",
            REG_SZ, "WC01234", 6, CM_REGISTRY_HARDWARE);
            }                       // new device
    return CR_SUCCESS;
    }                               // CONFIG_SETUP
```

The call to *CM_Read_Registry_Value* reads the setting for the named value Class from the hardware key for the device. This key always exists unless the device is being added to the system, in which case the return code would be *CR_NO_SUCH_VALUE*. To cover that possibility, we use *CM_Write_Registry_Value* to record settings for named values Class and HardwareID. The Add New Hardware wizard will see these values and thereby know which .INF file to use to install the telepathic device attached to this bus.

The CONFIG_SHUTDOWN Function An enumerator receives this message after one of its devices does. The function indicates that the system is shutting down. Devices that were part of the boot configuration (that is, those that were visible in real mode before Windows 95 started) receive CONFIG_SHUTDOWN messages instead of CONFIG_REMOVE messages.

The CONFIG_START Function An enumerator receives this message about a particular DEVNODE (pointed to by the *aboutnode* argument) as an indication that the device has been configured and should now begin using its assigned configuration. The enumerator receives this message first, and then the device receives it. The subfunction code (either CONFIG_START_FIRST_START or CON-FIG_START_DYNAMIC_START) allows you to distinguish, if necessary, between the initial start of a device following the creation of its DEVNODE and later starts.

The CONFIG_STOP Function An enumerator receives this message about a particular DEVNODE (pointed to by the *aboutnode* argument) as an indication that the device should stop using its assigned configuration. The enumerator receives this message first, and then the device receives it.

The CONFIG_TEST Function The Configuration Manager uses the CONFIG_TEST message to inquire whether the enumerator can tolerate device removal (for which it uses subfunction CONFIG_TEST_CAN_REMOVE) or shutdown (for which it uses subfunction CONFIG_TEST_CAN_STOP). In either case, the *aboutnode* argument points to the DEVNODE for the device in question. A device receives this message after the enumerator returns *CR_SUCCESS*. An enumerator can also receive this message on behalf of its own DEVNODE. The enumerator returns *CR_SUCCESS* to approve the request or *CR_FAILURE* to disapprove.

The CONFIG_TEST_FAILED Function This message is sent after some driver or enumerator fails a CONFIG_TEST request.

The CONFIG_TEST_SUCCEEDED Function This message is sent after every driver and enumerator that needs to has approved a CONFIG_TEST request.

More About Device Loaders

The preceding example of a Plug and Play driver is slightly atypical in that it uses a device driver that's also its own device loader. Bus drivers and standalone device drivers have to be organized this way. For example, the named value Device in my Enum\Root*PNP0A03 (PCI bus) key points to a registry key with the named value DevLoader set to "*PCI.VXD*", which is both the bus driver and the enumerator. Similarly, the named value Device for my serial mouse (Enum\Root*PNP0F0C) is set to "Mouse\0000", which has its named value DevLoader set to "*vmouse". The "*vmouse" designator refers to the VMOUSE.VXD driver that is built into VMM32.VXD—it's primarily a driver rather than a loader.

Many of the device drivers that you'll write fit snugly into one of the new Windows 95 layered device architectures. For these drivers, you normally specify a Microsoft system component such as VCOMM or the IOS as your device loader. That component in turn expects to find the name of your driver in the named value PortDriver. For example, my COM1 key (Enum\Root*PNP0500\0000) contains a named value Driver set to "ports\0000". Figure 11-11 shows the registry entry for the driver. Note that the named value DevLoader is set to "*vcomm", meaning the VCOMM.VXD driver that is built into VMM32.VXD, and that the named value PortDriver is set to "serial.vxd".

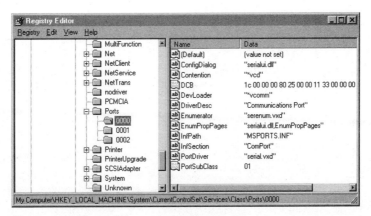

Figure 11-11. *The software key for COM1.*

The pieces that form the COM1 puzzle fit together in the following way: The root enumerator encounters the *PNP0500\0000 key in its enumeration of legacy devices and creates a DEVNODE for COM1. The Configuration Manager follows the Driver pointer to the "ports\0000" subkey of HKLM\System\CurrentControl-Set\Services\Class. There it learns that "*vcomm" is the device loader for this DEVNODE, so it sends VCOMM a PNP_New_Devnode message with the *DLVXD_LOAD_DEVLOADER* code. (The control flow isn't quite so straightforward, but what I've described is the net effect.) VCOMM calls *CM_Read_Registry_Value* to get the PortDriver value, namely "serial.vxd", from the software key. When COM1 is used for the first time, VCOMM calls *VXDLDR_LoadDevice* directly to load the SERIAL.VXD driver. In response to the Sys_Dynamic_Device_Init message, SE-RIAL.VXD calls *_VCOMM_Register_Port_Driver* to register its driver control procedure with VCOMM. Subsequent calls to the port driver are up to VCOMM. So far as the Configuration Manager is concerned, VCOMM is the device driver for the port, which relieves the port driver from the obligation to deal with configuration events.

In still other cases, you may wish to employ a separate device loader that actually loads device drivers. In response to a PNP_New_Devnode system control message, you would call the Configuration Manager's dynamic loading function:

```
code = CM_Load_DLVxDs(devnode, filenames, type, 0);
```

This call returns a CONFIGRET error code, as do all the other Configuration Manager functions we've been discussing. The *devnode* argument specifies the DEVNODE for which you're loading a driver, *filenames* specifies a space-delimited or comma-delimited list of filenames (including extensions), and *type* is one of the *DLVXD_LOAD*_xxxx codes you're used to from handling PNP_New_Devnode messages (see Table 11-1 on page 303). Of course, you don't *have* to specify more than one file; a single null-terminated string will do.

An odd situation can occur with static VxDs that are also Plug and Play device loaders. VMOUSE.VXD is an example. VMOUSE.VXD is statically loaded because it needs to hook and virtualize INT 33h while handling the Sys_Critical_Init message. It won't know all the facts it needs for configuring the mouse until it receives the Device_Init message. The Configuration Manager initializes before VMOUSE.VXD, however. Therefore, VMOUSE.VXD will receive a PNP_New_Devnode message before it's ready to act as a device loader. To handle this situation, VMOUSE.VXD initially returns *CR_DEVLOADER_NOT_READY*. This return code causes the Configuration Manager to defer handling the mouse. When VMOUSE.VXD receives the Device_Init message, it calls *CM_Register_DevLoader* to indicate that it's ready to act as a device loader. At the next opportunity, the Configuration Manager reissues the PNP_New_Devnode message to load the mouse driver.

DEVICE INFORMATION FILES

If you've ever built an installation program for a Windows application, you'll be overjoyed to know that you don't have to build your own installer for your device driver. Microsoft has done all the work for you in the Windows 95 Add New Hardware wizard. All you need to do is provide a *device information file* (an .INF file) that describes your device and its accompanying software.

The DDK contains comprehensive information about how to build an .INF file using the INFEDIT utility that comes with the DDK. I'll summarize the basics about .INF files here.

Even though you'll probably be using INFEDIT to create and maintain your .INF files, you'll benefit from an understanding of the underlying structure and syntax of the raw files themselves. Physically, an .INF file looks a lot like a traditional Windows .INI file. It contains a number of sections with bracketed names, each of which contains a number of named values. (An example appears at the end of this chapter.) The .INF syntax is designed to make it easy to localize the strings that may be visible to the end user (in messages and dialog boxes). So wherever you see a percent-delimited keyword like *%String0%*, look in the [Strings] section of the file to find the corresponding substitution text. Thus, to figure out who created the WCO.INF file shown at the end of this chapter, you look in the [Version] section for the Provider value. The Provider value takes you to the String0 value in the [Strings] section, where you learn that Walter Oney Software (yours truly) provided the file. Here's the relevant portion of our example:

```
[Version]
Signature=$CHICAGO$
Class=System
Provider=%String0%

...

[Strings]
String0="Walter Oney Software"
String1="Walter Oney Software"
String2="School Bus"
```

An .INF file really represents a hierarchical data structure laced together with pointers. The central structure is the [Manufacturer] section (see Figure 11-12). This section lists the manufacturers whose software appears on a set of installation disks. (The .INF file itself appears on the first or only disk of the set.) This list of manufacturer names is also the source of the first screen an end user sees after specifying a class of devices or clicking on the Have Disk button and specifying a disk drive in the Add New Hardware wizard (see Figure 11-13 on the following page).

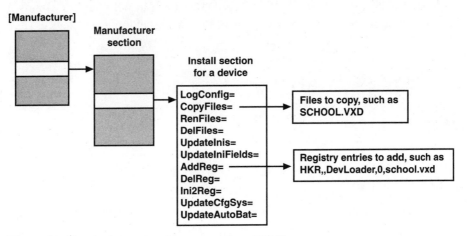

Figure 11-12. *The hierarchical structure of an .INF file.*

Values in the [Manufacturer] section are of the form *company-name=section-name*. For example, the line *Walter Oney Software=SECTION_0* indicates that you can find information about Walter Oney Software's devices in [SECTION_0]. Each of the individual manufacturer sections lists the devices provided by that manufacturer in a *device line* together with the name of the install section for each device and the device's hardware ID. In the WCO.INF file at the end of this chapter, you see that Walter Oney Software provides a School Bus, which has an install section named

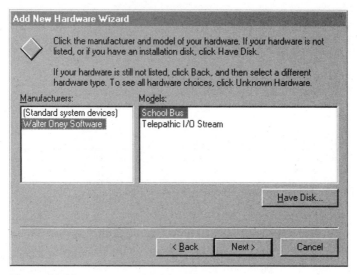

Figure 11-13. *A sample manufacturer list.*

"bus.install" and a hardware ID of *PNP0A05. Each install section contains further pointers to sections that specify in detail how to install the given device. Here's the relevant portion of our example:

```
...
[Manufacturer]
%String1%=SECTION_0

[SECTION_0]
%String2%=bus.install,*PNP0A05
...
```

Install Sections

A device's install section gives you considerable flexibility in installing or updating software and specifying configuration information. Each entry in an install section is a pointer to yet another section that contains the actual installation instructions. You're almost certain to need AddReg and CopyFiles entries. The other possible entries have more esoteric purposes. Syntactically, an install section looks like the following, where *install-name* is the name you used in a device line within some manufacturer section:

```
[install-name]
AddReg=AddReg-name
CopyFiles=CopyFiles-name
...
```

The subsection pointers you can specify are as follows:

AddReg The AddReg section indicates how to update the registry when installing this device. Entries in this section have the form

root-key, subkey, name, flag, value

The *root-key* and *subkey* parameters together specify the registry key you want to add or modify. The most usual choices for these parameters are HKR and an empty string, respectively, which indicate that you want to add or modify an entry in the device's software key (the one below \HKLM\System\CurrentControl-Set\Services\Class). The *name* and *value* parameters specify a named value below the subkey. The *flag* argument indicates the data type and replacement option for the subkey: bit 0 is 0 if the value is an ANSI string or 1 if it's hexadecimal, and bit 1 is 0 if you want to replace an existing registry key or 1 if you don't want to replace it. (Don't worry about keeping these bits straight. The INFEDIT utility I'll describe later keeps them straight for you.)

In the example, installing a School Bus causes the installer to process the [bus.registry] section, which contains this one line:

```
HKR,,DevLoader,0,school.vxd
```

This line inserts a "DevLoader school.vxd" entry into the software key for the bus. As described earlier (on pages 308-309), this registry entry is the one that eventually causes the Configuration Manager to load the School Bus enumerator.

CopyFiles The CopyFiles section specifies the files you want the installer to copy from the installation disks to the hard disk. Each line in this section has the form

destination-file, source-file, temporary-file, flag

Each of the parameters except *destination-file* is optional. The *destination-file* parameter holds the filename and extension of a file as it will appear on the hard disk. The *source-file* parameter names the file as it appears on the installation disk; omit the destination name if the source and destination names are the same. Use the *temporary-file* name if the file is likely to be open during installation. Windows 95 installs the file under this name and renames it during the next system startup. Finally, you can specify an optional *flag* value of 2 if successful installation of this file is critical to the overall installation process.

In the WCO.INF example on pages 334-335, the School Bus's CopyFiles section is named [bus.files] and specifies copying SCHOOL.VXD from the installation disk to the hard disk.

You're probably wondering about two things right now: how does the Add New Hardware wizard locate files on the installation disks, and how does it know what directory to put files into on the hard disk? There's a set of .INF sections that describes the installation disks, and it's completely independent of the [Manufacturer] branch we've been discussing. The [SourceDiskNames] section enumerates the disks that form the installation package; this section includes the electronic labels of the disks as well as the names printed on the disks so that the installer can verify correct insertion. The [SourceDiskFiles] section lists *all* of the files in your installation package and the disks on which they can be found. In the WCO.INF example on pages 334-335, SCHOOL.VXD lives on DISK1, which carries the external label *School Bus Installation Disk*.

To choose a destination directory for a file, the Add New Hardware wizard refers to the [DestinationDirs] section. The DefaultDestDir entry specifies a default to use if there's no other information. In the WCO.INF example on pages 334-335, this entry has the value 11, which is the mnemonic for the SYSTEM directory. Well, okay, it's not very mnemonic. Table 11-5 lists the possible values for this parameter. You don't need to refer to this list if you use INFEDIT, because INFEDIT presents a pick list of directories from which you can choose.

Destination Code	Description
1	Source drive and pathname
2	Temporary setup directory (valid only during setup)
3	Uninstall directory (such as \UNINSTAL.000)
4	Backup directory
10	Windows directory (such as \WINDOWS)
11	System directory (such as \WINDOWS\SYSTEM)
12	I/O subsystem directory (such as \WINDOWS\SYSTEM\IOSUBSYS)
13	Command directory (such as \WINDOWS\COMMAND)
14	Control Panel directory
15	Printer directory
16	Workgroup directory
17	.INF directory (such as \WINDOWS\INF)
18	Help directory (such as \WINDOWS\HELP)
19	Administration directory (such as \WINDOWS)
20	Fonts directory (such as \WINDOWS\FONTS)
21	Viewers directory (such as \WINDOWS\SYSTEM\VIEWERS)
22	VMM32 directory (such as \WINDOWS\SYSTEM\VMM32)
23	Color directory (such as \WINDOWS\SYSTEM\COLOR)

Table 11-5. *Destination directory codes.* *(continued)*

continued

Destination Code	Description
25	Shared directory (such as \WINDOWS)
26	Windows boot directory (such as \WINDOWS)
27	Machine specific
28	Host boot directory (such as \WINDOWS)
30	Root directory of the boot drive
31	Root directory for the host drive of a virtual boot drive
32	Old boot directory
33	Old Windows directory
34	Old DOS directory

You can also specify entries of this form:

section-name=code [,subdir]

In this entry, *section-name* is the name of a CopyFiles section, *code* is one of the destination codes from Table 11-5, and *subdir* is an optional subdirectory below the directory identified by *code*. The section name can also be the name of a RenFiles or DelFiles section.

Note that all the files in a particular CopyFiles section end up in the same directory on the hard disk. If you need to send files to different directories, you need to add multiple CopyFiles entries to the install section.

DelFiles You can delete one or more pre-existing hard disk files in a DelFiles section. Each entry is of the form

filename[,,,flag]

where *filename* is the name and extension of the target file and *flag* is an optional flag that, when set, will cause Windows 95 to queue the file deletion of an in-use file until the next system restart. The directory portion of the filename comes from the [DestinationDirs] section. The installer deletes the files you specify in a DelFiles section *during installation*. Windows 95 has no way to automatically delete files when the user removes your device. (Windows 95 *does* clean up the files associated with network protocols, but a different system component is responsible.)

DelReg You can delete one or more values or entire keys from the registry in a DelReg section. Each entry is of the form

root-key[,subkey][,name]

where the parameters have the same meaning as in an AddReg section. As with DelFile entries, the entries in a DelReg section pertain to *installation* of the device rather than removal.

Ini2Reg The Ini2Reg section allows you to convert sections of old-style .INI files to parallel registry entries. An entry in an Ini2Reg section has the form

%*dest*%*filename,ini-section,[ini-key],root-key,[subkey][,flags]*

where *dest* is a destination directory code (see Table 11-5), *filename* is the name of an .INI file (with file extension), *ini-section* is the name of a bracketed section in the .INI file, *ini-key* optionally specifies a keyword on the left side of an equals sign in the .INI file, *root-key* is a registry root key, *subkey* optionally specifies a registry subkey, and *flags* specifies optional flags. Bit 0 of *flags* is 0 if you don't want to delete the .INI entry (or section) or 1 if you do want to delete the entry (or section). Bit 1 is 0 if you don't want to replace an existing registry subkey or 1 if you do want to replace it. INFEDIT takes care of setting these flags correctly for you.

LogConfig A LogConfig section specifies the contents of one logical configuration. You need to specify this information if neither the device driver nor its enumerator has any other way to learn the resource requirements of the device. Only Plug and Play ISA cards can provide resource information, and you might well mistrust the degree to which card manufacturers will adhere to the complete standard. Thus, you might find that you always must supply logical configurations in the .INF file.

This section can contain one ConfigPriority item and one or more items specifying resource requirements. You can repeat the resource keywords if the device needs more than one instance of a resource. The possible items are:

ConfigPriority={HARDWIRED | DESIRED | NORMAL | SUBOPTIMAL |
    DISABLED | RESTART | REBOOT | POWEROFF | HARDRECONFIG}
DMAConfig=[{D | W}:]*channel-number*[,*channel-number*] ...
IOConfig=*io-range*[,...]
IRQConfig=[S:]*irq-number*[,*irq-number*] ...
MemConfig=*mem-range*[,...]

The *D* and *W* modifiers in DMAConfig refer to DWORD (32-bit) or WORD (16-bit) width; the default is 8 bits if you specify neither. The *S* in IRQConfig indicates that the IRQ is shared with other devices, meaning that the driver will virtualize it as a shared IRQ and disambiguate the source of each interrupt.

An *io-range* uses one of these two forms:

start-end[([*decode-mask*]:[*alias-offset*]:)]
size@*min-max*[%*align-mask*] [([*decode-mask*]:[*alias-offset*]:)]

Here the hyphens separating *start* and *end* and *min* and *max* are syntax elements.

The following example indicates that the device requires 8 consecutive ports starting at either 1F8h, 2F8h, or 3F8h:

```
IOConfig=1F8-1FF(3FF::), 2F8-2FF(3FF::), 3F8-3FF(3FF::)
```

The next example indicates that the device requires 8 consecutive ports on an 8-byte boundary beginning at 300, 308, 310, 318, 320, or 328:

```
IOConfig=8@300-328%FF8(3FF::)
```

Memory ranges (*mem-range* parameters) are similarly expressed, except that you need to use a full 32 bits to specify the alignment mask:

```
[size@]min-max[%align-mask]
```

The following example indicates that the device uses memory from C000:0000h to C000:7FFFh:

```
MemConfig=C0000-C7FFF
```

The next example describes a more flexible device that needs any 8000-byte aligned block beginning at C000:0000h, C800:0000h, D000:0000h, or D800:0000h:

```
MemConfig=8000@C0000-D8000%FFFF8000
```

If you use LogConfig sections in the .INF file to create logical configurations, they show up as LogConfig entries in the hardware registry key. The root enumerator reads these registry entries to get the *BASIC_LOG_CONF* value. If there were an MCA enumerator, it would do so as well.

RenFiles The RenFiles section lets you rename files as part of the installation process, using the following syntax:

```
new-name,old-name
```

You specify the directory that contains the files to be renamed in the [DestinationDirs] section.

UpdateAutoBat The UpdateAutoBat section lets you add or modify entries in the AUTOEXEC.BAT file. You shouldn't usually need to modify AUTOEXEC.BAT, because everything you do should be possible within Windows 95 itself. But, just in case you do, you can use items like these:

```
CmdAdd=command-name[,"parameters"]
CmdDelete=command-name[,flag]
PrefixPath=destination-code[,...]
RemOldPath=destination-code[,...]
TmpDir=destination-code[,subdirectory]
UnSet=environment-variable-name
```

Deleting a command means deleting any line that includes the specified command; adding the optional flag value *1* causes the line to be commented out instead of deleted. Since you wouldn't usually want to delete all SET commands, you use *UnSet* to selectively delete environment settings.

RemOldPath indicates path directories that should be removed, whereas *PrefixPath* designates path directories that the Add New Hardware wizard should place at the head of the path. For example, SETUPC.INF (the .INF file that helps drive the Windows 95 Setup program) contains the following two path maintenance directives:

```
PrefixPath=26,25,10,13
RemOldPath=33,32
```

In other words, these directives remove the old Windows and boot directories and add the new Windows boot, Windows shared, Windows, and Command directories. Since some of these directories are the same, the net effect on one of my systems was to change this path:

```
path C:\DOS;C:\TOOLS;C:\WINDOWS
```

to this one:

```
path C:\WINDOWS;C:\WINDOWS\COMMAND;C:\TOOLS
```

UpdateCfgSys The UpdateCfgSys section lets you add or modify entries in the CONFIG.SYS file. As with AUTOEXEC.BAT, you shouldn't normally need to change CONFIG.SYS in Windows 95. But if you do, you can use the following items:

Buffers=*number*
DelKey=*key*
DevAddDev=*driver-name,*{device | install}[,*flag*][,"*parameters*"]
DevDelete=*driver-name*
DevRename=*old-name,new-name*
Files=*number*
PrefixPath=*destination-code*[,*destination-code*]
RemKey=*key*
Stacks=*number*

UpdateIniFields The UpdateIniFields section allows you to selectively modify fields in .INI file settings that pertain to more than one component. An entry has the following form:

%*dest*%*filename,ini-section,key,*[*old-field*],[*new-field*][,*flags*]

Bit 0 of *flags* is 0 if you want to treat * literally or 1 if you want * to be a wildcard character. Bit 1 is 0 if you want to use a blank as the separator when adding a new field or 1 if you want to use a comma.

For example, WINPAD.INF has the following UpdateIniFields section:

```
[WinPadFields]
system.ini,boot,drivers,hhsystem.dll
```

This entry means that, in the drivers= setting of the [boot] section of SYSTEM.INI, the field reading "hhsystem.dll" should be replaced with nothing (in other words, it should be removed).

As another example, take a look at the following item, which would add an entry to the load= setting in the [Windows] section of the WIN.INI file in case you're too lazy to update the StartUp program group:

```
win.ini,Windows,load,,myapp.exe,2
```

UpdateInis You use an UpdateInis section to add or modify complete entries in .INI files. In general, you should be using the registry to store parameter values in Windows 95. But in case you need to use an old-style .INI file, here's what you'd code:

$$%dest%\filename,ini-section,[old-entry],[new-entry][,flags]$$

The *flags* parameter gives you great flexibility in handling existing .INI file entries. Refer to the Windows 95 DDK section titled "Update INI File Sections" for details about this parameter. The default value of 0 is adequate for most needs. It directs the Add New Hardware wizard to replace the *old-entry* value with the *new-entry* value. If you omit the *old-entry* parameter, you end up adding the *new-entry* value. Furthermore, only the keyword part of the *old-entry* value is considered. Thus, the line

```
win.ini,Desktop,Wallpaper=0,Wallpaper=1
```

changes the Wallpaper= setting in the [Desktop] section of the WIN.INI file from 0 to 1.

Using INFEDIT

Keeping track of the syntax of all of the .INF entries, the linkages between sections, and the alternatives at each stage would be very difficult. Luckily, Microsoft provides an .INF file editor, INFEDIT, with the DDK. INFEDIT provides a graphical environment within which you can create and edit .INF files that will automatically be syntactically correct.

I'm going to lead you through the process of creating a simple .INF file using INFEDIT. In brief, the steps will be as follows:

1. Complete the [Version] section with file header information.

2. Complete the [Manufacturer] section by adding a new manufacturer and a new device.

3. Create a CopyFiles section that describes which files will be copied to the user's hard disk.

4. Update the Disk Names section to reflect how all the installation files will be placed on installation disks.

5. Create an Add Registry section.

6. Complete the Install section for the device.

To get started with INFEDIT, run INFEDIT.EXE from the \BIN directory of the Windows 95 DDK. Choose the File/New command and then select the top-level folder, which has the name <NEWINF.INF> (see Figure 11-14).

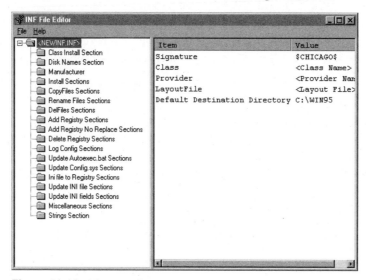

Figure 11-14. *The initial INFEDIT screen.*

You will need to fill in the Class setting to be the name of the device class your .INF file designates (*System* in this example) and the Provider setting to be your own company name (since you're creating this .INF file). If you have a complicated set of installation disks, you might also want to specify a disk layout file here too. For the purposes of this example, we won't have a layout file, so you will change the LayoutFile item to be blank.

To change a value, double-click on the item name (in the Item column) in the right-hand pane of the INFEDIT window. INFEDIT displays a dialog box in which to specify the new value (see Figure 11-15).

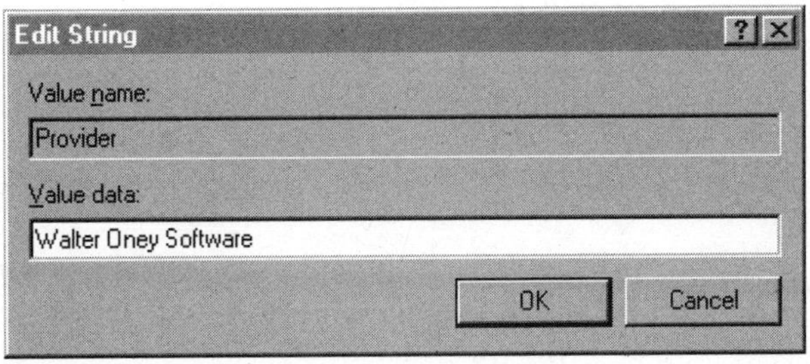

Figure 11-15. *A value editing dialog box.*

You specify all item values in INFEDIT in similar dialog boxes, but some items give you more complicated dialog boxes with multiple fields to complete and pick lists to help you. See Figure 11-16 for an example.

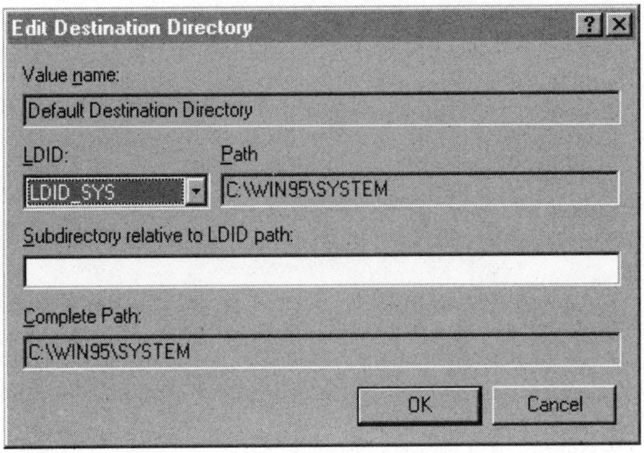

Figure 11-16. *Editing the default destination directory.*

Now right-click on the Manufacturer folder in the left-hand pane to get a small shortcut menu, and select the New Manufacturer choice. Then move down a level in the tree (select the New Manufacturer folder) and change the Company Name item to your own company's name. The result is shown in Figure 11-17 on the following page. Right-clicking on a folder in the left-hand pane is the way you create new sections and delete old ones in INFEDIT. Since INFEDIT knows what the possible choices are, the shortcut menus limit your options appropriately at each step.

Now right-click on the company name folder you just created and select the New Device choice. Select the <Device description> folder and modify the items. In my example, I'm creating entries for the School Bus, which will use an install section named bus.install, which has a hardware ID of *PNP0A05, and which is not compatible with any other device. When you specify the name bus.install in the right-hand pane, INFEDIT automatically creates an empty install section by that name (see Figure 11-18 on the following page).

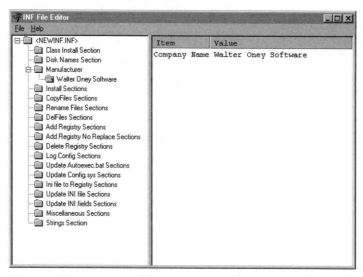

Figure 11-17. *The new manufacturer section.*

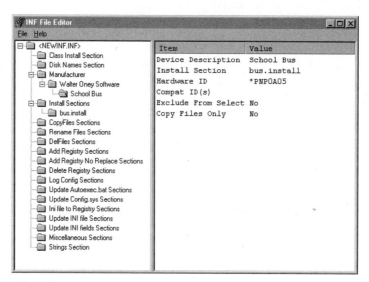

Figure 11-18. *Results of completing new-device information.*

Before trying to fill out the bus.install section, it's more convenient to specify information about the installation disks and their contents first. Therefore, right-click on the CopyFiles Sections folder and add a new section. Move down to that folder and change the Section Name item to bus.files. Then right-click on the bus.files folder you just created and select the Add File Name choice. Change the File Name item to use a Destination Name of SCHOOL.VXD. Now move to the

Disk Names section (near the top of the left-hand pane) and add a new disk. The printed label (the Disk Description item) on this disk will be School Bus Installation Disk, and the disk will be labeled electronically (the Disk Label item) as DISK1. The Disk serial number should be made blank instead of 0000-0000 (see Figure 11-19).

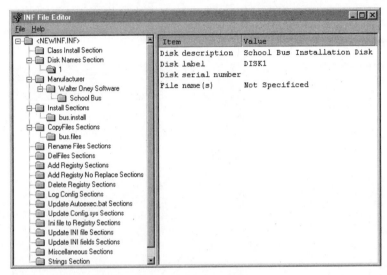

Figure 11-19. *Adding a new installation disk.*

This is the point at which you actually partition files onto their respective installation disks. When you change the File Name(s) item in a Disk Names section, INFEDIT gives you a pick list of all the files that it currently knows about from the CopyFiles sections (see Figure 11-20). You do the CopyFiles sections first so you

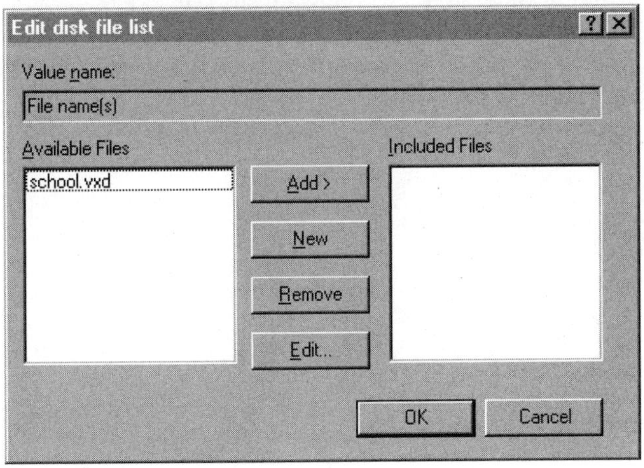

Figure 11-20. *File pick list.*

can get a pick list at this point in the process. In the Edit Disk File List dialog box, add SCHOOL.VXD to the Included Files list and click on the OK button.

Before you can go back to the install section, you need to create a new Add Registry section. Change the Section Name item to bus.registry, then create a new Section Value. You'll need to have a DevLoader item in the software branch. Although INFEDIT doesn't make it clear, HKR is the right root key to use here. Set up the Section Value items as shown in Figure 11-21.

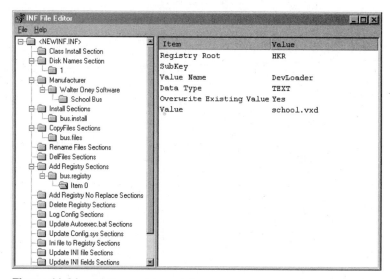

Figure 11-21. *Adding registry entries.*

Return now to the bus.install section and fill in the CopyFiles Sections item (add bus.files) and the AddReg item (add bus.registry). INFEDIT provides pick lists for these items, which is why we created the subsidiary sections first.

At this point, you can save the new .INF file. I've saved my example under the name WCO.INF. The completed .INF file looks like this:

```
[Version]
Signature=$CHICAGO$
Class=System
Provider=%String0%

[DestinationDirs]
DefaultDestDir=11

[Manufacturer]
%String1%=SECTION_0

[SECTION_0]
%String2%=bus.install,PNP0A05
```

```
[bus.install]
CopyFiles=bus.files
AddReg=bus.registry

[bus.files]
school.vxd

[bus.registry]
HKR,,DevLoader,0,school.vxd

[ControlFlags]

[SourceDisksNames]
1=School Bus Installation Disk,DISK1,

[SourceDisksFiles]
school.vxd=1

[Strings]
String0="Walter Oney Software"
String1="Walter Oney Software"
String2="School Bus"
```

Chapter 12

Configuring Devices

In the previous chapter, I showed how the Configuration Manager determines what hardware is physically present on the computer and how it loads the drivers to support that hardware. In this chapter, I'll go into detail about the configuration process. When you configure the devices attached to a system you first determine their resource requirements and then allocate the available resources among all the devices that need them. In brief, the steps of this process are as follows:

1. Create *logical configurations* for each device that describe that device's resource requirements and allowable alternatives for satisfying them.

2. *Filter* the logical configurations to further restrict the allowable alternatives for resource assignment.

3. Assign resources to devices in such a way that conflicts are eliminated and the highest performance is ensured.

4. Configure the hardware itself.

LOGICAL CONFIGURATIONS

Each device that needs resources ends up having one or more logical configurations attached to its DEVNODE. A logical configuration represents a possible set of resource assignments. Each DEVNODE can have as many as five different kinds of logical configurations:

- The *boot* configuration describes the resources assigned to a device at boot time by the system BIOS.

- The end user can create a *forced* configuration in the Control Panel by specifying resource assignments.

- An enumerator can create a linked list of *basic* configurations to describe possible resource assignments.

- Enumerators and device drivers can copy and modify the basic configuration list to produce another linked list of *filtered* configurations.

- The Configuration Manager and its resource arbitrators eventually create a single *allocated* configuration to describe the resources actually assigned to the device.

Since there can be more than one logical configuration in the basic and filtered configuration lists, the Configuration Manager needs some way to order configurations. Each logical configuration therefore carries a *priority* that indicates how relatively good or bad that configuration might be (see Table 12-1). The *LCPRI_FORCECONFIG* and *LCPRI_BOOTCONFIG* values are used only with forced and boot configurations respectively, and their only purpose is to allow an experienced programmer to spot the source of a configuration while debugging. The other priority values represent real gradations of preference among configurations, however.

Priority	*Description*
LCPRI_FORCECONFIG	This configuration was forced by the user through the Control Panel.
LCPRI_BOOTCONFIG	This configuration was established at boot time by the BIOS or the card.
LCPRI_DESIRED	This configuration is the preferred configuration and gives the best performance.
LCPRI_NORMAL	This configuration gives an acceptable performance.

Table 12-1. *Logical configuration priorities.*   *(continued)*

continued

Priority	Description
LCPRI_SUBOPTIMAL	This is a workable configuration but gives poor performance.
LCPRI_RESTART	This configuration will require restarting Windows.
LCPRI_REBOOT	This configuration will require a soft reboot of the computer.
LCPRI_POWEROFF	This configuration will require a hard reboot of the computer.
LCPRI_HARDRECONFIG	This configuration will require the user to change a jumper.
LCPRI_HARDWIRED	This is the only possible configuration.

At first blush, the ability to have multiple logical configurations with different levels of preference seems like needless generality given the modest needs of current hardware. Now that the operating system is able to handle more sophisticated hardware, however, this flexibility will probably become more important. Just imagine, for example, a frame capture card that works best when it can directly address a large amount of memory but that can still work, albeit more slowly, by doing DMA transfers instead. Such a device would have an *LCPRI_DESIRED* configuration that demands memory and an *LCPRI_NORMAL* or *LCPRI_SUBOPTIMAL* configuration that demands a DMA channel.

Discovering the resource requirements of a device and creating logical configurations is generally the responsibility of the enumerator that creates the corresponding DEVNODE. Many devices can provide requirement information automatically, and the enumerator normally retrieves these requirements in order to build logical configurations. The enumerator uses *CM_Add_Empty_Log_Conf* to create each logical configuration and *CM_Add_Res_Des* to add each set of resource requirements (in the form of a *resource descriptor*).

To make things concrete once again, let's suppose that the School Bus introduced in Chapter 11 supports a telepathic I/O stream device that reads the user's mind. The School Bus's *OnEnumerate* function might contain the following enumeration code:

```
case CONFIG_ENUMERATE:          // cf == 5
    {                           // CONFIG_ENUMERATE
    DEVNODE device;             // DEVNODE for device
    LOG_CONF logconf;           // logical configuration
    RES_DES resource;           // resource descriptor handle
```

```
static IRQ_DES irq = {{0, 0, 0xFFFF, 0}};

CM_Create_DevNode(&device, "SCHOOL\\WC01234\\0000",
    tonode, 0);
CM_Add_Empty_Log_Conf(&logconf, device,
    LCPRI_NORMAL,
    BASIC_LOG_CONF | PRIORITY_EQUAL_LAST);
CM_Add_Res_Des(&resource, logconf, ResType_IRQ,
    &irq, sizeof(irq), 0);
return CR_SUCCESS;
}                          // CONFIG_ENUMERATE
```

The call to *CM_Add_Empty_Log_Conf* creates an empty logical configuration. If we did nothing more than create an empty configuration, the device would claim no resources. The call to *CM_Add_Res_Des* adds a resource requirement to the logical configuration. In this case, the third field in the *irq* structure indicates that the device needs an IRQ in the range 0 through 15. (The *IRQ_DES* structure is explained in the next section, "Resource Descriptors".)

The registry records the logical configurations for legacy devices in the LogConfig subkey of the device's registry entry. See Figure 12-1 for an example. The root enumerator uses *CM_Read_Registry_Log_Confs* to automatically create the in-memory logical configurations from the registry entries.

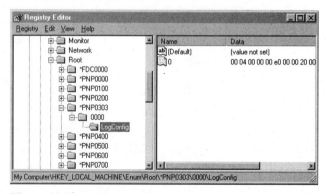

Figure 12-1. *Example of a logical configuration in the registry.*

A single logical configuration can allow several choices for each of the standard resource classes (IRQ, memory, I/O address, and DMA). In fact, Microsoft's *Hardware Design Guide for Microsoft Windows 95* (Microsoft Press, 1994) mandates that Plug and Play expansion cards and motherboard components support as many different configurations as possible to ensure maximum flexibility. The suggested requirements for "PC 95" certification include:

- At least eight IRQ alternatives, one of which can be disabled.

- At least eight memory base addresses, one of which can be disabled, for direct memory access and for option ROM.

- At least eight I/O base addresses, one of which can be disabled.

- At least three DMA channel alternatives plus a disabled configuration.

An ideal device would have a single logical configuration that allows for any possible assignment in each category. Making devices this flexible makes them more expensive, though, which is why the certification requirements are less stringent.

Resource Descriptors

The Configuration Manager represents each resource requirement and assignment in a resource descriptor structure. A logical configuration can have any number of resources of each type, and each resource will have its own descriptor. The descriptors are bidirectional in a sense. In one direction, you inform the Configuration Manager of the requirements for your device by completing a resource descriptor and adding it to a logical configuration. The Configuration Manager makes an internal copy of your structure, preceded in memory by a standard header. In the other direction, you can later retrieve and work with the Configuration Manager's copies of your descriptors.

Resource descriptors have different formats depending on the type of resource being described. The four types of resource descriptors are explained in the following sections.

Interrupt Request Lines (IRQs)

An *IRQ_DES* structure describes a single IRQ:

```
typedef struct IRQ_DES_s
    {
    WORD   IRQD_Flags;       // 00 shared/unshared flags
    WORD   IRQD_Alloc_Num;   // 02 IRQ actually allocated
    WORD   IRQD_Req_Mask;    // 04 mask of acceptable IRQs
    WORD   IRQD_Reserved;    // 06 (reserved)
    } IRQ_DES;               // 08
```

IRQD_Flags can be *fIRQD_Share* to indicate that the device shares an IRQ, or 0 to indicate that the device needs an exclusive IRQ. *IRQ_Req_Mask* is a bit mask in which bit *n* is 1 if the device supports use of IRQ *n*. A device that can handle any IRQ would use *FFFFh* for this parameter; a device that needs either IRQ 3 or IRQ 4 would use *0018h*. In the *IRQ_DES* structure that the Configuration Manager eventually creates for the allocated logical configuration, *IRQ_Alloc_Num* will hold the IRQ actually assigned to the device.

Memory

A memory resource descriptor employs a *MEM_DES* structure immediately followed in memory by one or more *MEM_RANGE* structures:

```
typedef struct Mem_Des_s
    {
    WORD   MD_Count;      // 00 number of MEM_RANGEs that follow
    WORD   MD_Type;       // 02 always equal to MTypeRange
    ULONG  MD_Alloc_Base; // 04 base of allocated memory
    ULONG  MD_Alloc_End;  // 08 end of allocated memory
    WORD   MD_Flags;      // 0C flags
    WORD   MD_Reserved;   // 0E (reserved)
    } MEM_DES;            // 10

typedef struct Mem_Range_s
    {
    ULONG  MR_Align;      // 00 mask for base alignment
    ULONG  MR_nBytes;     // 04 byte count
    ULONG  MR_Min;        // 08 minimum address
    ULONG  MR_Max;        // 0C maximum address
    WORD   MR_Flags;      // 10 flags
    WORD   MR_Reserved;   // 12 (reserved)
    } MEM_RANGE;          // 14
```

MD_Count is the number of *MEM_RANGE* structures that follow the *MEM_DES* structure in memory. *MD_Type* may have had more general pretensions at one point in its evolution, but it now holds the value *MTypeRange*, which is simply the size of a *MEM_RANGE* structure. Within each *MEM_RANGE* structure, *MR_Align* specifies how the allocated memory must be aligned. For example, *FFFFF000h* denotes page (4096-byte–boundary) alignment. *MR_nBytes* contains the byte length of the required memory area. *MR_Min* and *MR_Max* indicate the bounds on the base address. To insist that a page-aligned memory block be in the adapter region of memory, for example, specify *000A0000h* and *000FFFFFh* for these values. The *MR_Max* value (*000FFFFFh* in the example) is the largest possible *ending address* for the memory block. *MR_Flags* can include either *fMD_ROM* or *fMD_RAM* plus either *fMD_24* or *fMD_32*. *MR_Reserved* should be 0.

In the *MEM_DES* structure that the Configuration Manager eventually creates for the allocated logical configuration, *MD_Alloc_Base* and *MD_Alloc_End* will hold the starting and ending addresses of the assigned block. *MD_Flags* will hold the flags from the *MEM_RANGE* entry that the arbitrator ended up using to satisfy the requirement.

I/O Port Addresses

I/O port address descriptors, like memory resource descriptors, use a header structure followed by an array of range structures:

```
typedef struct IO_Des_s
    {
    WORD IOD_Count;        // 00 number of IO_RANGEs that follow
    WORD IOD_Type;         // 02 always IOType_Range
    WORD IOD_Alloc_Base;   // 04 allocated base address
    WORD IOD_Alloc_End;    // 06 allocated end of range
    WORD IOD_DesFlags;     // 08 flags
    BYTE IOD_Alloc_Alias;  // 0A allocated alias offset
    BYTE IOD_Alloc_Decode; // 0B allocated alias decode mask
    } IO_DES;              // 0C

typedef struct IO_Range_s
    {
    WORD IOR_Align;        // 00 mask for base alignment
    WORD IOR_nPorts;       // 02 number of ports needed
    WORD IOR_Min;          // 04 lowest allowable address
    WORD IOR_Max;          // 06 highest allowable address
    WORD IOR_RangeFlags;   // 08 flags
    BYTE IOR_Alias;        // 0A alias offset
    BYTE IOR_Decode;       // 0B alias decode mask
    } IO_RANGE;            // 0C
```

The meaning of most of these fields is analogous to the similar fields in memory resource descriptors. For example, an ISA card needing 16 ports starting on a 16-byte boundary would specify:

```
IOR_Align = 0xFFF0;
IOR_nPorts = 0x10;
IOR_Min = 0x0100;
IOR_Max = 0x03FF;
```

The *IOR_Min* and *IOR_Max* values shown in this example follow from the fact that the standard ISA bus provides for only 10 bits of I/O port addressing and reserves addresses 00h through FFh. *IOR_Max* is the largest allowable *end address* for the allocated ports. That is, since the largest 16-byte–aligned base address is 3F0h, the last of the 16 requested ports would be at 3FFh.

In the *IO_DES* structure that the Configuration Manager eventually creates for the allocated logical configuration, *IOD_Alloc_Base*, *IOD_Alloc_End*, *IOD_DesFlags*, *IOD_Alloc_Alias*, and *IOD_Alloc_Decode* will describe the port(s) actually assigned to the device.

The DDK presents a confusing description of how to use the *IOR_Alias* and *IOR_Decode* fields to do a couple of different things. One use for these fields is to describe how many bits of I/O port address the card decodes. A standard ISA card, for example, decodes only the low-order 10 bits, meaning that addresses 3F8h, 7F8h, BF8h, and so on, are all equivalent ways of addressing the same physical hardware port. Another use for *IOR_Alias* and *IOR_Decode* is to describe cards that use multiple addresses that happen to differ by 400h, 800h, or some other value larger than 1024 (2^{10}). This scheme is so complex that Microsoft is planning to change it for the sequel to Windows 95. The only settings for these fields should be the ones shown in Table 12-2.

IOR_Alias	IOR_Decode	Meaning
0	0	Card decodes all 16 bits of I/O address
4	3	Card decodes 10 bits of I/O address
16	15	Card decodes 12 bits of I/O address
255	0	Card is a PCI card that can use ports that would otherwise be reserved as 10-bit synonyms for ISA card ports

Table 12-2. *Possible* IOR_Alias/IOR_Decode *settings for an I/O resource.*

The setting *IOR_Alias* = 255 and *IOR_Decode* = 0 requires special explanation. Normally, the I/O arbitrator—which allocates I/O port addresses among competing devices—automatically reserves all the 10-bit synonyms of any port address in recognition of the way ISA cards decode addresses. That is, if a card receives ports 3F8h through 3FFh, the arbitrator will normally not give any other card addresses like 7F8h through 7FFh or BF8h through BFFh, whose low-order 10 bits can't be distinguished. In a system with both a PCI bus and an ISA bus, the primary bus is the PCI bus, and the ISA bus is attached via a bridge. The ISA bus never sees I/O addresses bigger than 3FFh, which means that PCI cards can use the 10-bit synonym addresses with impunity. The special *IOR_Alias/IOR_Decode* setting of *255/0* tells the I/O arbitrator to assign port addresses without worrying about 10-bit synonyms, in order to take advantage of this feature of the PCI bus.

One final note: EISA cards use I/O port addresses that are determined by the slot they occupy. Such cards need not specify an I/O resource at all because the EISA enumerator deduces it automatically.

Direct Memory Access (DMA) Channels

You describe a DMA resource with a *DMA_RES* structure:

```
typedef struct DMA_Des_s
    {
    BYTE DD_Flags;          // 00 flags
    BYTE DD_Alloc_Chan;     // 01 allocated channel
    BYTE DD_Req_Mask;       // 02 mask for supported channels
    BYTE DD_Reserved;       // 03 (reserved)
    } DMA_RES;              // 04
```

DD_Flags indicates the width of the required channel: *fDD_BYTE*, *fDD_WORD*, or *fDD_DWORD*. *DD_Req_Mask* indicates which channels can be used. For example,

60h indicates that the device can use channel 5 or 6. The number of the actual channel assignment will appear in *DD_Alloc_Chan* in the *DMA_RES* structure that the Configuration Manager eventually creates for the allocated logical configuration.

DEVICE DRIVERS

A Plug and Play device driver is a dynamic VxD that provides a *configuration function* in addition to low-level hardware support code and virtualization functions. The configuration function replaces traditional ways of learning about the hardware resources dedicated to a device.

Prior to Windows 95, VxDs interrogated profile settings in the SYSTEM.INI file or elsewhere to determine which resources to use, or else they made ad hoc assumptions. The Windows 3.1 Virtual Mouse Device (VMD), for example, relied on its real-mode initializer to discover whether it was managing a bus or serial mouse and to learn which IRQ (if any) it was managing. The VMD's real-mode initializer, in turn, relied on the real-mode mouse driver for these facts. The information gathered in this way by the VMD and other drivers ultimately depended on the end user to enter the correct settings in CONFIG.SYS, SYSTEM.INI, and perhaps other files.

Since end users often have great difficulty configuring devices correctly and communicating the desired settings to software drivers, the Configuration Manager tries to automate the process. That's where a device driver's configuration function comes into play.

The driver responds to the PNP_New_Devnode system control message by registering itself as a device driver and supplying the address of its configuration function. For example:

```
CONFIGRET OnPnpNewDevnode(DEVNODE devnode, DWORD loadtype)
    {                               // OnPnpNewDevnode
    switch (loadtype)
        {                           // select function to perform

    case DLVXD_LOAD_DEVLOADER:  // loadtype == 2
        return CM_Register_Device_Driver(devnode, OnConfigure,
            0, (CM_REGISTER_DEVICE_DRIVER_REMOVABLE
            | CM_REGISTER_DEVICE_DRIVER_DISABLEABLE));
        }                           // select function to perform

    return CR_DEFAULT;
    }                               // OnPnpNewDevnode
```

This function (part of TELEPATH.C in the \CHAP11\SCHOOLBUS directory on the companion disc) examines the *loadtype* parameter to see why the Configuration Manager has called it. The code *DLVXD_LOAD_DEVLOADER* means that the

Configuration Manager wants the function to locate and load the correct device driver. Device drivers frequently disobey this instruction. Here, the function calls *CM_Register_Device_Driver* to register the configuration function for the given DEVNODE. The call, by setting flag bits in the final argument, indicates that this particular device driver supports dynamic removal and reconfiguration.

The Configuration Function

The configuration function responds to configuration events initiated by the Configuration Manager. The message codes are from the same series of *CONFIG_* manifest constants that the enumeration function discussed in the previous chapter uses. Table 12-3 lists the messages that are relevant to the configuration function for a device driver. In skeletal form, a configuration function reads like this:

```
CONFIGRET OnConfigure(CONFIGFUNC cf, SUBCONFIGFUNC scf,
    DEVNODE devnode, DWORD refdata, ULONG flags)
    {                              // OnConfigure
    switch (cf)
        {                          // select on message
        ...
    default:
        return CR_DEFAULT;
        }                          // select on message
    }                              // OnConfigure
```

Message	Description
CONFIG_APM	Notifies the driver that a power management event is occurring
CONFIG_CALLBACK	Notifies the driver that *CM_CallBack_Device_Driver* has been called
CONFIG_FILTER	Instructs the driver to filter (restrict) logical configurations
CONFIG_PREREMOVE	Notifies the driver that the device is about to be removed (sent from the bottom of the tree up)
CONFIG_PREREMOVE2	Notifies the driver that the device is about to be removed (sent from the top of the tree down)
CONFIG_PRESHUTDOWN	Notifies the driver that the system is about to shut down

Table 12-3. *Configuration function messages for device drivers.*   *(continued)*

continued

Message	Description
CONFIG_REMOVE	Notifies the driver that the device is being removed from the system
CONFIG_SHUTDOWN	Notifies the driver that the system is shutting down
CONFIG_START	Instructs the driver to start using the allocated configuration
CONFIG_STOP	Instructs the driver to stop using the current configuration
CONFIG_TEST	Tests whether the driver can stop using the configuration or whether the device can be removed
CONFIG_TEST_FAILED	Notifies the driver that the previous CONFIG_TEST failed
CONFIG_TEST_SUCCEEDED	Notifies the driver that the previous CONFIG_TEST succeeded
CONFIG_VERIFY_DEVICE	Tests whether a legacy device is present

As with enumeration functions, configuration functions receive a bogus 0x12345678 configuration message in a debug build to see whether they correctly return CR_DEFAULT. You should return CR_SUCCESS only if you actually succeed in handling a particular request. The following sections elaborate on how a configuration function should respond to some of theses messages.

The CONFIG_START Function The device obtains its configuration and extracts information about the assigned resources in response to a CONFIG_START message. In fact, an average Plug and Play VxD does most of its initialization during processing of the CONFIG_START message. If the device uses only the standard resource types, the easiest way to get the resource assignments is to call *CM_Get_Alloc_Log_Conf*:

```
int irq;
...
CMCONFIG config;
CM_Get_Alloc_Log_Conf(&config, devnode,
    CM_GET_ALLOC_LOG_CONF_ALLOC);
irq = config.bIRQRegisters[0];
return CR_SUCCESS;
```

CM_Get_Alloc_Log_Conf fills in a *CMCONFIG* structure (see Figure 12-2 on the following page) with information about the assigned resources. The structure records up to 7 IRQ assignments, up to 9 memory blocks, up to 20 I/O base addresses, and up to 7 DMA channels.

```
typedef struct Config_Buff_s {
    WORD   wNumMemWindows;                        // 00 Number of memory windows
    DWORD  dMemBase[MAX_MEM_REGISTERS];           // 02 Memory window base [9]
    DWORD  dMemLength[MAX_MEM_REGISTERS];         // 26 Memory window length [9]
    WORD   wMemAttrib[MAX_MEM_REGISTERS];         // 4A Memory window Attrib [9]
    WORD   wNumIOPorts;                           // 5C Number of I/O ports
    WORD   wIOPortBase[MAX_IO_PORTS];             // 5E I/O port base [20]
    WORD   wIOPortLength[MAX_IO_PORTS];           // 86 I/O port length [20]
    WORD   wNumIRQs;                              // AE Number of IRQ info
    BYTE   bIRQRegisters[MAX_IRQS];               // B0 IRQ list [7]
    BYTE   bIRQAttrib[MAX_IRQS];                  // B7 IRQ Attrib list [7]
    WORD   wNumDMAs;                              // BE Number of DMA channels
    BYTE   bDMALst[MAX_DMA_CHANNELS];             // C0 DMA list [7]
    WORD   wDMAAttrib[MAX_DMA_CHANNELS];          // C7 DMA Attrib list [7]
    BYTE   bReserved1[3];                         // D5 Reserved
} CMCONFIG;                                       // D8
```

Figure 12-2. *The* CMCONFIG *structure.*

The *wNumIRQs* field in a *CMCONFIG* structure indicates how many IRQs have been assigned to the device, and entries in the array *bIRQRegisters* indicate which ones. The *bIRQAttrib* array records attributes for each IRQ; the only current attribute is the *fIRQD_Share* flag, which indicates that the IRQ is shared with other devices. You'll normally want to call *VPICD_Virtualize_IRQ* to virtualize each of the IRQs you own.

The *wNumMemWindows* member indicates how many memory blocks were assigned, and entries in *dMemBase* record their base addresses. The *dMemLength* array entries give the lengths of the memory blocks, and *wMemAttrib* array elements specify block attributes. The base addresses are physical addresses and can, in general, occupy any location in the 32-bit address space. Most often, devices use memory in the adapter region of the first megabyte—that is, addresses in the range 000A0000h through 000FFFFFh. An entry in the *wMemAttrib* array indicates the location of the assigned memory and can contain either *fMD_ROM* or *fMD_RAM* and either *fMD_24* or *fMD_32*.

To access a memory block from a VxD, you need to convert the physical address in a *dMemBase* array element to a virtual address. In Windows 3.1, you would have called *_MapPhysToLinear* to assign an address that would always refer to the same physical location for the duration of the Windows session. You can call *_MapPhysToLinear* in Windows 95, but there's a major disadvantage: if your device is reconfigured to use a different memory address, the region of linear address space you were using is effectively lost for the rest of the session. What you should do instead of calling *_MapPhysToLinear* is to use some of the new page mapping services in Windows 95:

```
ULONG npages = (physsize + 4095) >> 12;
ULONG firstpage = physaddr >> 12;
DWORD linaddr = _PageReserve(firstpage, npages, PR_FIXED);
_PageCommitPhys(linaddr >> 12, npages, firstpage,
    PC_INCR | PC_WRITEABLE);
_LinPageLock(linaddr >> 12, npages, 0);
```

This sequence begins with *physsize* holding the byte length of a block of physical memory (for example, *config.dMemLength[something]*) and *physaddr* holding its physical address (for example, *config.dMemBase[something]*). This code assumes that the physical address is aligned on a page (4096-byte) boundary. It uses *_PageReserve* to allocate a sufficient number of virtual address pages to span the device memory; the *PR_FIXED* flag indicates that the physical addresses associated with the memory block are not allowed to change. The call to *_PageCommitPhys* builds the page tables by which the memory can be accessed. The *PC_INCR* flag instructs *_PageCommitPhys* to step the linear and physical addresses in parallel as it builds page tables; the *PC_WRITEABLE* flag indicates that the memory can be written as well as read. If ring-three programs require access to the memory, you can also specify the *PC_USER* flag.

The *wNumIOPorts* field in a *CMCONFIG* structure indicates how many blocks of port addresses have been assigned to the device. Each assignment includes a base address (a *wIOPortBase* array element) and a port count (a *wIOPortLength* array element).

Finally, the *wNumDMAs* field indicates how many DMA channels have been assigned to the device, and the *bDMALst* array contains their numbers. The *wDMAAttrib* array indicates the width of the assigned channels as *fDD_BYTE*, *fDD_WORD*, or *fDD_DWORD*.

As an alternative to calling *CM_Get_Alloc_Log_Conf*, you can use a more cumbersome approach based on enumerating all of the resource descriptors for the allocated configuration:

```
LOG_CONF logconf;
RES_DES hres;
RESOURCEID restype;

CM_Get_First_Log_Conf(&logconf, devnode, ALLOC_LOG_CONF);
hres = (RES_DES) logconf;
while (CM_Get_Next_Res_Des(&hres, hres,
    ResType_All, &restype, 0) == CR_SUCCESS)
    {                           // for each resource
    switch (restype)
        {                       // select on resource code
    case ResType_IRQ:
        {                       // IRQ resource
        IRQ_DES* pirq = (IRQ_DES*) hres;
```

```
            [do something with pirq->IRQD_Alloc_Num]
            break;
            }                          // IRQ resource
    case ResType_Mem:
        ...
    case ResType_IO:
        ...
    case ResType_DMA:
        ...
            }                          // select on resource code
        }                              // for each resource
```

The call to *CM_Get_First_Log_Conf* retrieves the first logical configuration of the type specified by the last argument. We are interested in the "allocated" configuration, which contains the resources we've been assigned. Each call to *CM_Get_Next_Res_Des* retrieves a new resource descriptor. You start a loop over the resource descriptors by setting *hres* equal to the logical configuration handle. During each iteration of the loop, you supply the handle of the previous resource descriptor (or of the logical configuration) as the second argument and the type of resource you're interested in as the third argument. *ResType_All* means you're interested in all resource types. The first argument points to a location where the next resource handle will be stored, and the fourth argument points to a location where the type of the resource will be stored. You can supply NULL for either or both of these pointers if you're not interested in that particular item of information. The last argument contains flags that must currently be 0.

Each time *CM_Get_Next_Res_Des* returns a resource descriptor, the preceding example uses a switch statement to decode the *restype* return value. The returned *hres* resource handle is just the flat address of the Configuration Manager's internal copy of a resource descriptor that has the format implied by *restype*. For example, if *CM_Get_Next_Res_Des* retrieves a *ResType_IRQ* resource, *hres* will point to an *IRQ_DES* structure.

The second method of retrieving configuration information (looping over resource descriptors) looks so much harder than the first method (calling *CM_Get_Alloc_Log_Conf*) that you might wonder why you'd ever do it. The only real reason I can think of is that you might be using a private resource (that is, one for which you've supplied you own arbitrator). The loop-over-configurations method is the only way to extract information about a private resource, since the *CMCONFIG* structure doesn't provide for this situation.

The CONFIG_FILTER Function Before it assigns resources, the Configuration Manager gives devices and their enumerators a chance to *filter* their logical configurations by sending the CONFIG_FILTER message. The problem solved by filtering is the possibility that the configurations may initially be unrealistically optimistic about how flexibly the device or its driver can really be configured. To handle the request, you would loop over all logical configurations and then over all resources, modifying the resource descriptors that you didn't like:

```
LOG_CONF logconf;
code = CM_Get_First_Log_Conf(&logconf, devnode,
    FILTER_LOG_CONF);
while (code == CR_SUCCESS)
    {                             // for each configuration
    RESOURCEID restype;
    RES_DES hres = (RES_DES) longconf;
    while (CM_Get_Next_Res_Des(&hres, hres, ResType_All,
        &restype, 0) == CR_SUCCESS)
        {                         // for each resource
        switch (restype)
            {                     // process this resource
            [filter resource requirements]
            }                     // process this resource
        }                         // for each resource
    code = CM_Get_Next_Log_Conf(&logconf, logconf, 0);
    }                             // for each configuration
```

This example employs an outer loop over all logical configurations. You call *CM_Get_First_Log_Conf* to obtain the first logical configuration of a given type. Here, we want the first "filtered" configuration. To iterate the outer loop, you call *CM_Get_Next_Log_Conf*. An inner loop calls *CM_Get_Next_Res_Des* to obtain successive resource descriptors. The logic of this loop is the same as the one discussed earlier for the CONFIG_START message. Within the inner loop, you treat the *hres* variable as a pointer to a resource descriptor of the *restype* type, and you make any required changes directly to that descriptor.

PCMCIA cards provide an example of why configurations might need to be filtered. A card that needs a memory resource can ask for the memory anywhere in the 32-bit linear address space and can indicate any random alignment requirement and size. On an ISA bus machine, however, DMA is possible only within the first 16 megabytes of memory. Furthermore, for the sake of efficiency, it's helpful to have the assigned memory be page-aligned and be a multiple of the page size in length. The PCCARD device must therefore modify all the memory resource descriptors to restrict the allowable memory ranges. In the context of the preceding example, the modification might be accomplished by using the following case of the switch statement in the innermost loop. (The adjustments made by PCCARD are much more complicated, but this example conveys the general idea.)

```
case ResType_Mem:
    {                             // filter memory resource
    MEM_DES* mem = (MEM_DES*) hres;
    int i;
    MEM_RANGE* range = (MEM_RANGE*) (mem+1);
```

```
        ULONG maxmax;

        for (i = 0; i < mem->MD_Count; ++i)
            {                           // for each memory range
            range->MR_Align &= ~4095; // require page alignment
            range->MR_nBytes = (range->MR_nBytes + 4095) & ~4095;
            maxmax = 0x00FFFFFF - range->MR_nBytes;
            if (range->MR_Max > maxmax)
                range->MR_Max = maxmax;
            ASSERT(range->MR_Min <= range->MR_Max);
            range = (MEM_RANGE*) ((DWORD) range + mem->MD_Type);
            }                           // for each memory range
        }                               // filter memory resource
```

The CONFIG_REMOVE, CONFIG_SHUTDOWN, and CONFIG_STOP Functions
The Configuration Manager sends one of three requests when it wants to remove
the device (CONFIG_REMOVE), shut the system down (CONFIG_SHUTDOWN), or
change resource allocations to accommodate a new device (CONFIG_STOP). The
driver should stop using its current configuration. If your driver is currently
virtualizing an IRQ, for example, it would stop doing so. Your driver can receive
CONFIG_STOP messages in the middle of a Windows session when the Configuration Manager wants to reconfigure your driver in order to steal a resource. Your
driver can receive CONFIG_REMOVE messages in the middle of a Windows session
as well, when they indicate that the end user is removing your device. (In reality,
Windows 95 uses CONFIG_REMOVE instead of CONFIG_STOP, but later versions
of Windows will be using CONFIG_STOP.) As the system shuts down, your driver
will receive either CONFIG_SHUTDOWN (if it was part of the boot configuration)
or CONFIG_REMOVE (if it was not part of the boot configuration).

The CONFIG_TEST Function The CONFIG_TEST message is a request for permission either to invalidate the current configuration (requested with the *CON-
FIG_TEST_CAN_STOP* subfunction) or to remove the device (requested with the
CONFIG_TEST_CAN_REMOVE subfunction). Your driver should return *CR_SUCCESS*
to grant permission or *CR_FAILURE* to withhold permission.

The CONFIG_VERIFY_DEVICE Function The root enumerator initiates the CON-
FIG_VERIFY_DEVICE message when it receives a *CR_DEVNODE_ALREADY_THERE*
return value while it is enumerating legacy devices. The function's purpose is
to allow the root enumerator to find out whether the device is still present. Your
driver should return *CR_SUCCESS* if the device is physically present or *CR_DE-
VICE_NOT_THERE* if it isn't.

RESOURCE ARBITRATORS

Each class of resource (IRQ, memory address, I/O address, and DMA) has a *resource arbitrator* that is responsible for allocating that resource among all competing devices. Microsoft believes that very few developers will need to write arbitrators; accordingly, the directions for doing so are remarkably sparse. In order to illustrate how the arbitration process works, I'm going to present an arbitrator for a fictitious telepathic channel resource, one of which is needed by every telepathic I/O stream device attached to the School Bus. To identify this resource, I'll use an identifying convention documented in CONFIGMG.H whereby Microsoft assigns a 10-bit OEM ID that I combine with a 5-bit resource code. I'll pretend that I'm OEM number 10h (0 through F being reserved by Microsoft) and that this resource is the sixth I've ever defined:

```
#define ResType_Telepath ((0x10 << 5) | 5)
```

Note that this resource identification scheme accounts for only 15 bits out of 32. The 00008000h-bit is defined in CONFIGMG.H as ResType_Ignored_Bit; setting this bit in a resource ID means that the resource has no arbitrator. The remaining 16 bits aren't used simply because Microsoft wants to make it easy for 16-bit code to work with the Configuration Manager.

You register a resource arbitrator by calling *CM_Register_Enumerator*:

```
REGISTERID arbid;
CONFIGRET OnArbitrateTelepath(ARBFUNC af, ULONG refdata,
    DEVNODE devnode, NODELIST_HEADER h);
...
CM_Register_Arbitrator(&arbid, ResType_Telepath,
    OnArbitrateTelepath, 0, NULL, ARB_GLOBAL);
```

In this example, I'm registering an arbitrator for a new global resource, so I use the *ARB_GLOBAL* flag in a call to *CM_Register_Arbitrator* and supply *NULL* for the next-to-last parameter. You may have a resource that belongs to a specific DEVNODE. In such a case, use *ARB_LOCAL* and pass the DEVNODE address as the next-to-last parameter. You define the arbitration function like this:

```
CONFIGRET OnArbitrateTelepath(ARBFUNC af, ULONG refdata,
    DEVNODE devnode, NODELIST_HEADER h)
    {                           // OnArbitrateTelepath
    switch (af)
        {                       // select on function
        ...
        }                       // select on function
    }                           // OnArbitrateTelepath
```

Here the *af* parameter is one of the messages listed in Table 12-4, *refdata* is whatever reference data was supplied as the fourth argument to *CM_Register_Arbitrator* (I used 0 in the example), *devnode* is whatever DEVNODE was the fifth argument to *CM_Register_Arbitrator*, and *h* is a pointer to a *nodelistheader* structure that in turn points to the head and tail of a list describing the DEVNODEs that need configuration (see Figure 12-3). Each node in the list points to a DEVNODE (*nl_ItsDevNode*) and to a logical configuration (*nl_Test_Req*). Each node also has a field (*nl_ulSortDWord*) for the arbitrator to use as a sorting ordinal. The logical configuration associated with each node contains resource descriptors, some of which may be for the resource we're arbitrating.

Message	Description
ARB_TEST_ALLOC	Directs the arbitrator to perform trial allocation of the resource
ARB_RETEST_ALLOC	Directs the arbitrator to verify the previous trial allocation
ARB_FORCE_ALLOC	Directs the arbitrator to retest but doesn't fail the previous trial allocation
ARG_SET_ALLOC	Directs the arbitrator to commit the previous trial allocation
ARB_RELEASE_ALLOC	Directs the arbitrator to discard the previous trial allocation
ARB_QUERY_FREE	Requests information about free resources
ARB_REMOVE	Directs the arbitrator to prepare for removal of the arbitrator

Table 12-4. *Arbitrator function messages.*

The arbitration function should return *CR_SUCCESS* for all of the standard function codes unless there's really an error but should return *CR_DEFAULT* for any unknown function code. The Configuration Manager can use the *CR_DEFAULT* return value to test version compatibility in future releases of Windows.

The Configuration Manager's basic resource assignment algorithm is to call all resource arbitrators with the ARB_TEST_ALLOC message to perform a trial allocation. Once the arbitrators generate a working set of assignments, the Configuration Manager commits the trial allocations by issuing ARB_SET_ALLOC messages. In order to perform these and the other arbitrator functions, the sample arbitrator maintains an allocation map, called *free_map*, consisting of a short bit string. Bit *n* in the map is 1 if telepathic channel number *n* is free and 0 if channel number *n* has been

```
struct nodelistheader_s
    {                                   // node list header
    struct nodelist_s* nlh_Head;        // 00 head of list
    struct nodelist_s* nlh_Tail;        // 04 tail of list
    };                                  // 08 node list header

struct nodelist_s
    {                                   // node list element
    struct nodelist_s* nl_Next;         // 00 chain to next element
    struct nodelist_s* nl_Prev;         // 04 chain to previous element
    struct devnode_s* nl_ItsDevNode;    // 08 a device node that needs
                                        //    resources
    struct Log_Conf* nl_Test_Req;       // 0C a configuration for that DEVNODE
    ULONG  nl_ulSortDWord;              // 10 sort order for CM_Sort_NodeList
    };                                  // 14 node list element
```

Figure 12-3. *Arbitrator node structures.*

assigned to a device. The following sections describe in detail how a resource arbitrator should respond to each arbitrator message.

The ARB_TEST_ALLOC Function ARB_TEST_ALLOC is simultaneously the most basic and the most complicated of the arbitration messages to handle. Its job (in our example) is to try to assign a telepathic channel to each device that needs one. The following code (part of SCHOOL.C in the \CHAP11\SCHOOLBUS directory on the companion disc) implements a typical algorithm (the variables and helper functions will be explained in the rest of this section):

```
case ARB_TEST_ALLOC:          // af == 0
    {                         // ARB_TEST_ALLOC
    sortnodes((NODELISTHEADER) h);
    free_copy = free_map;
    release((NODELISTHEADER) h, &free_copy);

    ALLOCPLACE place = {((NODELISTHEADER)h)->nlh_Head,
        NULL};
    if (allocate(place, &free_copy))
        return CR_SUCCESS;
    else
        return CR_FAILURE;
    }                         // ARB_TEST_ALLOC
```

The first step in the assignment algorithm is to sort the devices so that the fussiest ones are first in the list. We can assign each device a fussiness index according to how many different channels will satisfy its requirements. Fussier devices support fewer alternatives than less fussy devices. Here's what a telepathic resource descriptor looks like:

```
#define ResType_Telepath ((0x10 << 5) | 5)

typedef struct
    {
    int allocated;   // index of allocated channel (-1 --> none)
    ULONG requested; // mask for requested channels
    } TELEPATH_RESOURCE;
```

I wrote some helper functions to perform the sort. The *bitcount* function simply counts the number of bits that are turned on in a mask. The *sortnodes* function sorts the nodes based on their bit count.

```
typedef struct nodelistheader_s *NODELISTHEADER;
typedef struct nodelist_s *PNODE;

int bitcount(ULONG mask)
    {                           // bitcount
    int nbits = 0;
    while (mask)
        {                       // count bits
        if (mask & 1)
            ++nbits;
        mask >>= 1;
        }                       // count bits
    return nbits;
    }                           // bitcount

void sortnodes(NODELISTHEADER h)
    {                               // sortnodes
    PNODE node = h->nlh_Head;
    while (node)
        {                           // for each node
        RES_DES hres = (RES_DES) node->nl_Test_Req;
        #define pres ((TELEPATH_RESOURCE *) hres)

        node->nl_ulSortDWord = 0;
        while (CM_Get_Next_Res_Des(&hres, hres,
            ResType_Telepath, NULL, 0) == CR_SUCCESS)
            node->nl_ulSortDWord += bitcount(pres->requested);
        node = node->nl_Next;

        #undef pres
        }                           // for each node
    CM_Sort_NodeList((NODELIST_HEADER) h, 0);
    }                               // sortnodes
```

The sorting function performs a loop over the node list in order to calculate sorting ordinals (based on the telepathic resource descriptor's *requested* field), and then it calls *CM_Sort_NodeList* to actually perform the sort. Within the loop, it performs a *CM_Get_Next_Res_Des* loop over telepathic resources and accumulates a count of channel alternatives. The *bitcount* helper function counts the 1 bits in the TELEPATH_RESOURCE *requested* field, which is a bit mask that indicates which channels the device supports.

We now make a copy of the real allocation map. We'll use the copy to record the trial allocation we end up with. Assuming that a computer can accommodate 8 or fewer channels, the "real" map and the copy can both just be static DWORD variables. A simple assignment statement therefore suffices to create the working copy:

```
static DWORD free_map = 0x000000FF;
static DWORD free_copy;
...
free_copy = free_map;
```

The initial value of *free_map* indicates that channels 0 through 7 are initially free.

The third step in the trial allocation is to update the trial allocation map so that any resources used by any of the contending devices appear free. After all, we will be assigning new channels to these devices. I wrote another helper function to perform this step:

```
void release(NODELISTHEADER h, PULONG pmap)
    {                                   // release
    PNODE node = h->nlh_Head;
    while (node)
        {                               // for each node
        LOG_CONF logconf;

        if (CM_Get_First_Log_Conf(&logconf,
            (DEVNODE) node->nl_ItsDevNode, ALLOC_LOG_CONF)
            == CR_SUCCESS)
            {                           // release channel(s)
            RES_DES hres = (RES_DES) logconf;
            #define pres ((TELEPATH_RESOURCE *) hres)
            while (CM_Get_Next_Res_Des(&hres, hres,
                ResType_Telepath, NULL, 0) == CR_SUCCESS)
                if (pres->allocated >= 0)
                    *pmap |= 1 << pres->allocated;
            #undef pres
            }                           // release channel(s)
        node = node->nl_Next;
        }                               // for each node
    }                                   // release
```

For each node in the list, we call *CM_Get_First_Log_Conf* to find the one and only "allocated" logical configuration for the associated device. (The allocated channel is stored in the *allocated* field of the telepathic resource descriptor.) If there is one, we loop over all of the telepathic channel resources to clear the bit representing the currently assigned channel in the *pmap* bit map.

The fourth and final step in the trial allocation is to attempt to locate free channels for the devices that need them. One device can theoretically need more than one channel, but this fact will appear only when we traverse multiple telepathic channel resource descriptors in the logical configuration associated with the device's entry in the node list. The entity to which we assign channels is therefore really a resource descriptor instead of a configuration or a device, and the resource descriptors are located in an interrupted list, as shown in Figure 12-4.

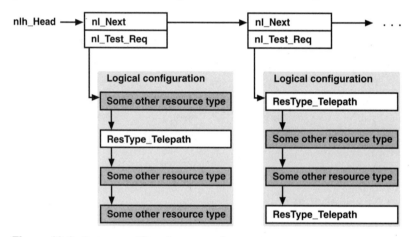

Figure 12-4. *Interrupted list of resource descriptors.*

To make it as easy as possible to traverse the interrupted list, I defined a helper structure to represent a position within the list:

```
typedef struct
    {                                   // allocation placeholder
    PNODE node;                         // current node
    TELEPATH_RESOURCE* pres;            // current resource descriptor
    } ALLOCPLACE, *PALLOCPLACE;         // allocation placeholder
```

Here, *node* is the address of a node list element and *pres* is the address of one of the resource descriptors belonging to the *nl_Test_Req* logical configuration for that node. The following helper function steps from one position in the list to the next:

```
BOOL nextres(PALLOCPLACE p)
    {                                   // nextres
    ASSERT(p->node && p->node->nl_Test_Req);
```

```
    if (!p->pres)
        p->pres = (TELEPATH_RESOURCE *) p->node->nl_Test_Req;
    while (CM_Get_Next_Res_Des((RES_DES*) &p->pres,
        (RES_DES) p->pres, ResType_Telepath, NULL, 0)
        != CR_SUCCESS)
        {                               // no more of our resource
        if (!(p->node = p->node->nl_Next))
            return FALSE;          // no more nodes in the list
        p->pres = (TELEPATH_RESOURCE *) p->node->nl_Test_Req;
        }                               // no more of our resource
    return TRUE;
    }                               // nextres
```

The function that actually performs the trial allocation, finally, and which is called by our ARB_TEST_ALLOC message-handling code on page 355, is as follows:

```
BOOL allocate(ALLOCPLACE place, PULONG map)
    {                               // allocate
    if (!nextres(&place))           // no resource descriptors...
        return TRUE;                // ...nothing to do
    (place.pres->allocated = -1;
    for (int channel = 0; channel < 8; ++channel)
        {                               // try to allocate a channel
        ULONG mask = 1 << channel;
        ULONG tempmap = *pmap;
        if ((tempmap & mask) && (place.pres->requested & mask))
            {                           // do trial allocation
            tempmap &= ~mask;
            if (allocate(place, &tempmap))
                {                       // successful allocation
                *pmap = tempmap;
                place.pres->allocated = channel;
                return TRUE;
                }                       // successful allocation
            }                           // do trial allocation
        }                               // try to allocate a channel
    return FALSE;                       // all channels in use
    }                               // allocate
```

This function recursively descends through the interrupted list of resource descriptors to assign channels to each one. Each instance of the function corresponds to one demand for a telepathic channel. The function loops over all possible channels to see whether the channel corresponding to the loop index can be used to satisfy the demand. The first test (*tempmap & mask*) determines whether the channel is free within the allocation map supplied by the previous level of recursion. (Recall that a set bit indicates that the channel is free.) The outermost level of recursion received the *free_copy* map belonging to the arbitrator, whereas inner levels receive another copy belonging to their parents. If that test passes, the next test (*place.pres->requested & mask*) determines whether the channel meets the device's requirements (as specified by its telepathic resource descriptor). If that test also passes, we mark the channel as used in our own temporary map (*tempmap &= ~mask*) and attempt to satisfy all the remaining demands by calling *allocate* recursively. If the recursive call succeeds, we copy our temporary map back to our caller's map and record the current channel in the resource descriptor. If the recursive attempt fails, however, we repeat the whole attempt with the next channel.

Each recursive call to *allocate* receives a copy (the *place* variable) of its caller's *ALLOCPLACE* structure. The reason we make a copy is so that the initial call to *nextres* will always locate the same resource descriptor each time the call to *allocate* is repeated for a particular level in the recursive descent.

If the outermost allocation attempt succeeds (see page 355), the arbitrator will return *CR_SUCCESS* while saving the results of the successful trial allocation in the *free_copy* map. Otherwise, the arbitrator returns *CR_FAILURE* to indicate inability to satisfy all the demands expressed in the node list.

The ARB_RETEST_ALLOC and ARB_FORCE_ALLOC Functions The Configuration Manager uses the ARB_RETEST_ALLOC message to see whether the resource assignment recorded in a particular set of logical configurations is still workable. ARB_FORCE_ALLOC is similar but must not fail. It will be easier for you to understand why the Configuration Manager uses these two messages after you know how to implement handlers for them. Here's an example:

```
case ARB_RETEST_ALLOC:      // af == 1
case ARB_FORCE_ALLOC:       // af == 6
    free_copy = free_map;
    release((NODELISTHEADER) h, &free_copy);

    if (reallocate((NODELISTHEADER) h, &free_copy,
        af == ARB_FORCE_ALLOC))
        return CR_SUCCESS;
    else
        return CR_FAILURE;
```

This fragment uses the *release* helper function to release resources in the temporary allocation map and then calls *reallocate*, shown on the following page, to allocate the resources described by the *ul_Test_Req* configurations in the node list:

```
BOOL reallocate(NODELISTHEADER h, PULONG pmap, BOOL forced)
    {                           // reallocate
    PNODE node = h->nlh_Head;

    while (node)
        {                           // for each node
        RES_DES hres = (RES_DES) node->nl_Test_Req;
        #define pres ((TELEPATH_RESOURCE *) hres)

        while (CM_Get_Next_Res_Des(&hres, hres,
            ResType_Telepath, NULL, 0) == CR_SUCCESS)
            {                       // requires our resource
            ULONG mask;

            ASSERT(pres->allocated >= 0);
            mask = 1 << pres->allocated;
            if ((*pmap & mask) && !forced)
                return FALSE;// one or more still in use
            *pmap &= ~mask;
            }                       // requires our resource
        node = node->nl_Next;

        #undef pres
        }                           // for each node
    return TRUE;
    }                               // reallocate
```

The *reallocate* function performs a loop over nodes and, within that loop, another loop over telepathic channel resources. Each of the resource descriptors should contain a channel assignment (*pres->allocated*). If that channel is free, we mark it as allocated. If that channel isn't free, however, the action we take depends on whether the message we received was ARB_RETEST_ALLOC or ARB_FORCE_ALLOC. In the "retest" case, we fail the call. In the "force" case, we allow the duplicate assignment to persist anyway.

A conceivable purpose for the ARB_RETEST_ALLOC message is to return to a workable but suboptimal configuration that the Configuration Manager considered at an earlier time. There are two other reasons why the Configuration Manager sends this message to an arbitrator, however. The first reason is to initialize the allocation map with any resource assignments left over from boot time. To perform this initialization, the Configuration Manager sends each arbitrator an ARB_RETEST_ALLOC request with a node list pointing to the boot logical configurations. The DEVNODEs involved in the calls might not have "allocated" logical configurations at all, in which case the *release* step would do nothing.

The second case in which the Configuration Manager uses ARB_RETEST_AL-LOC is during the removal of a DEVNODE. In this case, the Configuration Manager sends the request with a single node list entry describing the device that is being removed. The *ul_Test_Req* logical configuration doesn't have any resources, so the *reallocate* step does nothing. Indeed, the message is sent by the Configuration Manager only to release the resources claimed in the DEVNODE's "allocated" configuration.

The purpose of the ARB_FORCE_ALLOC message is to implement a configuration forced by the user through the Control Panel. Duplicate assignments are permitted in such a case because the end user must be presumed to know best.

The ARB_SET_ALLOC Function After a successful ARB_TEST_ALLOC, ARB_RE-TEST_ALLOC, or ARB_FORCE_ALLOC call, the Configuration Manager calls the arbitrator to commit the trial allocation by performing an ARB_SET_ALLOC call:

```
case ARB_SET_ALLOC:            // af == 2
    ASSERT(free_copy != 0xDEADBEEF);
    free_map = free_copy;
    free_copy = 0xDEADBEEF;
    return CR_SUCCESS;
```

This function copies the current trial allocation map (*free_copy*) on top of the "real" map (*free_map*). In this sample, I also reinitialized the copy to a recognizable bit pattern to make it obvious when someone tries to work with an uninitialized version of the trial map. The constant *DEADBEEFh* appears many places in the Configuration Manager as a way to indicate uninitialized data.

The ARB_RELEASE_ALLOC Function In the imperfect real world, it won't always be possible to satisfy every device. We might, for example, have two devices that can use only channel number 0. In such a case, *allocate* will return *FALSE* and the arbitrator will fail the test allocation by returning *CR_FAILURE*. The Configuration Manager will issue an ARB_RELEASE_ALLOC message to allow the arbitrator to discard the now useless trial allocation, and it will then attempt trial allocations using any alternative logical configurations that may exist. If no allocation is possible, the Configuration Manager will disable one of the devices. The Device Manager will report the conflict so that the user will understand why the disabled device can't be used.

In general, you may have memory or other program resources tied up in the trial map. Now is the time to release them. In the sample arbitrator we're considering, this function is almost trivial:

```
case ARB_RELEASE_ALLOC:     // af == 3
    free_copy = 0xDEADBEEF;
    return CR_SUCCESS;
```

The ARB_QUERY_FREE Function The Configuration Manager sends an ARB_-QUERY_FREE message when a VxD or an application calls either *CM_Query_Arbitrator_Free_Size* or *CM_Query_Arbitrator_Free_Data*. These functions retrieve either the size of the internal data used by the arbitrator to control allocation or the actual data itself. For this function, the Configuration Manager overloads the *NODELIST_HEADER* argument by passing instead the address of an *arbitfree_s* structure:

```
struct arbitfree_s {
    PVOID *af_PointerToInfo;  // the arbitrator's info
    ULONG af_SizeOfInfo;      // length of the info
};
```

The arbitrator fills in this structure with the address and size of its internal data. For example:

```
case ARB_QUERY_FREE:         // af == 4
    {                        // ARB_QUERY_FREE
    struct arbitfree_s *p = (struct arbitfree_s *) h;
    p->af_SizeOfInfo = sizeof(ULONG);
    p->af_PointerToInfo = (PVOID*) &free_map;
    return CR_SUCCESS;
    }                        // ARB_QUERY_FREE
```

For the returned information to be of any use, the ultimate caller must be privy to the internal data structures used by the arbitrator. Except in the case of the DMA arbitrator (for which source code is provided with the DDK), Microsoft hasn't published the formats used by the standard arbitrators. Therefore, this function will be useful mostly for private resources.

The ARB_REMOVE Function The Configuration Manager issues the ARB_REMOVE message when it deregisters the arbitrator. For a local arbitrator connected to a particular DEVNODE, deregistration is automatic when the DEVNODE disappears. For a global arbitrator, deregistration occurs only (if at all) when a VxD (probably the one that registered the arbitrator in the first place) calls *CM_Deregister_Arbitrator*. In any case, the arbitrator's job is to release any memory or other program resources it's been using. In the case of the telepathic channel arbitrator, there's nothing to do:

```
case ARB_REMOVE:             // af == 5
    return CR_SUCCESS;
```

HARDWARE PROFILES

Windows 95 supports the ability to define multiple configurations for a single computer. Multiple configurations are probably most useful for laptop computers equipped with docking hardware, because they allow the system to automatically configure itself appropriately for whatever docking station the computer happens to be attached to. The user of a desktop system might also find reasons to employ the concept.

The Windows 95 Setup program initially creates a single *hardware profile* with the friendly name "Original Configuration." Windows 95 will notice if you dock your laptop in a new station, and it will automatically launch a full hardware detection scan to discover the characteristics of the new environment. You can also manually create a new hardware profile by first making a copy of the original profile and then altering the assignment of devices to the new profile. Suppose, for example, you wanted to make the telepathic I/O stream device available only in a configuration called "Intellectual Configuration." You'd first use the Hardware Profiles tab of the System icon in the Control Panel to create the new profile and then use the Device Manager tab of the System icon to display the device's property sheet, in which you would remove the device from "Original Configuration" (see Figure 12-5).

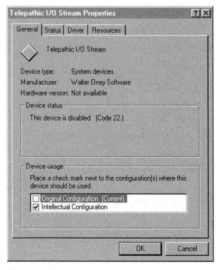

Figure 12-5. *Removing a device from a hardware profile.*

The existence of the new hardware profile will cause some changes to occur in the way you boot the computer. As indicated above, the usual reason for defining a new profile is to support a new docking mode. If your computer has a Plug and Play BIOS, it will compute a *docking ID* by interrogating the hardware. MS-DOS will search the Windows 95 registry database to select a hardware profile that includes that docking ID (see Figure 12-6). If it finds more than one matching profile in the registry, it will prepare a menu of the possibilities for you to choose from. A similar process occurs even without a Plug and Play BIOS, except that you *always* get the configuration menu because MS-DOS always discovers the same default docking ID:

```
Windows cannot determine what configuration your computer is in.
Select one of the following:

1. Original Configuration
2. Intellectual Configuration
3. None of the above
```

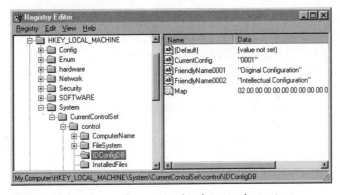

Figure 12-6. *The configuration database in the registry.*

After you select a configuration, MS-DOS extracts the friendly name of the hardware profile from the registry. In the example, the name would be either "Original Configuration" or "Intellectual Configuration." MS-DOS now searches your CONFIG.SYS file for a [menu] section having a menuitem entry with the same friendly name. If there is one, MS-DOS automatically chooses that branch of CONFIG.SYS. If you have a configuration [menu] section but no matching menuitem entry, MS-DOS gives you the standard CONFIG menu to make you choose; the menu is just MS-DOS version 6 or later at work. However it determines the appropriate configuration, MS-DOS executes the CONFIG.SYS commands located in the selected branch and also sets the CONFIG environment variable to the short name of the configuration.

For example, your CONFIG.SYS file might contain the following:

```
[menu]
menuitem=original,Original Configuration
menuitem=smart,Intellectual Configuration

[original]
...(normal configuration commands)

[smart]
include=original
...(special configuration commands)
```

Your AUTOEXEC.BAT file might then make further decisions based on finding the CONFIG environment variable equal to *ORIGINAL* or *SMART*.

As Windows 95 starts, the real-mode initializer for CONFIGMG.VXD sends an IOCTL request to the real-mode CONFIG$ device to learn which hardware profile is in effect. It passes this information along to the protected-mode initialization routines in the Configuration Manager as reference data. The Configuration Manager can then automatically disable any devices that aren't present in the current profile.

If all the pieces dovetail properly, the end user never notices the process. The BIOS identifies the docking station, MS-DOS finds a single hardware profile that matches the docking ID and selects the right block in the CONFIG.SYS file, and AUTOEXEC.BAT executes all the right commands. The Configuration Manager never enables the devices that aren't present, and the Device Manager shows the actual configuration of the computer. The only thing that's awkward about this mechanism is the unintelligible explanation displayed in the Device Status area of the General tab of the properties sheet for the device: "This device is disabled. (Code 22.)" You'd have to be a knowledgeable user indeed to realize that it's disabled because it's absent from the current hardware profile.

INTERACTING WITH THE USER

Windows 95 includes a device installer (the Add New Hardware wizard) and the Device Manager, both of which are reachable through the Windows 95 Control Panel. These components present a unified interface to the end user, who (presumably) will be less bewildered about his or her hardware as a result. The existence of these user interface components requires writers of device drivers to be aware of some application-level concepts that used to be part of applications only. I'll discuss two of these factors in this section, beginning with how to customize the display of device properties.

Property Page Providers

The Windows 95 Device Manager is one of the programs behind the System icon in the Control Panel. You use the Device Manager to examine the configuration of your system. The Device Manager provides two ways for you to customize the information presented to the user by replacing or adding pages in the properties sheet the user sees when he or she chooses the Properties button from the Device Manager tab of the System icon in the Control Panel. The first method is to provide a custom property sheet provider for the device. The second method, used as a fallback if there's no custom provider, is to call entry points in the class installer (if any) for the device class to which your device belongs. I'll talk about the first, and simplest, method here.

A property sheet provider for the Device Manager is a *16-bit* dynamic link library. In its simplest form, the provider exports a single function named *Enum-PropPages*. It also contains a resource that defines a property page and the dialog function needed to manage that page. Before displaying the properties sheet, the Device Manager calls your *EnumPropPages* function to allow you to add your own pages to the sheet or to replace the standard ones if you're brave enough. Thereafter, the Windows 95 property sheet manager calls your dialog procedure(s) in a completely normal way. Here's an example of an *EnumPropPages* function for the telepathic I/O stream device we've been working with in this chapter (it is part of SCHOOLUI.C in the \CHAP11\SCHOOLBUS directory on the companion disc):

```
#include <windows.h>
#include <commctrl.h>
#include <setupx.h>

#include "resource.h"

BOOL WINAPI EXPORT StatusDlgProc(HWND, UINT, WPARAM, LPARAM);

BOOL WINAPI EXPORT EnumPropPages(LPDEVICE_INFO pdi,
    LPFNADDPROPSHEETPAGE AddPage, LPARAM lParam)
    {                               // EnumPropPages
    PROPSHEETPAGE status;           // status property page
    HPROPSHEETPAGE hstatus;

    status.dwSize = sizeof(PROPSHEETPAGE);
    status.dwFlags = PSP_USETITLE;
    _asm mov status.hInstance, ds
    status.pszTemplate = MAKEINTRESOURCE(IDD_STATUS);
    status.hIcon = NULL;
    status.pszTitle = "Status";
    status.pfnDlgProc = StatusDlgProc;
    status.lParam = (LPARAM) pdi->dnDevnode;
```

```
status.pfnCallback = NULL;
hstatus = CreatePropertySheetPage(&status);
if (!hstatus)
    return TRUE;                 // display sheet even if we fail

if (!AddPage(hstatus, lParam))
    DestroyPropertySheetPage(hstatus);
return TRUE;
}                                 // EnumPropPages
```

The WINDOWS.H, COMMCTRL.H, and SETUPX.H header files are part of the DDK; you'll find them in the INC16 subdirectory. SETUPX.H also includes PRSHT.H, which defines the property sheet interface, and it defines the *DEVICE_INFO* structure.

This function is completely boring to experienced Windows programmers except for two minor points. First of all, when the user first views our custom page, Windows 95 will send our dialog function a WM_INITDIALOG message whose *lParam* will be the address of a copy of the property page structure. The *dnDevnode* member of the *DEVICE_INFO* structure is the (flat) address of the DEVNODE about which we're reporting. Setting the *status.lParam* field to the DEVNODE address from the *DEVICE_INFO* block therefore makes it possible for the dialog procedure to know the DEVNODE address. The second notable point is that the *AddPage* argument to *EnumPropPages* is a pointer to a function that will add our custom page to the sheet. When we call it, we must pass it the *lParam* argument we received unchanged. The function will return *TRUE* if it successfully added the page.

Your provider can call the the Configuration Manager through its protected-mode API. CONFIGMG.H is set up in such a way that you can include it in a 16-bit program and can simply call the same entries you're now used to calling from a VxD. To do so, you need to include CONFIGMG.H in a peculiar way:

```
#define Not_VxD
#include <vmm.h>
#define MIDL_PASS
#include <configmg.h>
```

Defining *Not_VxD* suppresses all the declarations in VMM.H and CONFIGMG.H that are interesting only to VxD writers. Defining *MIDL_PASS* avoids a warning from the 16-bit compiler about a #pragma pack(push) statement.

As an example of getting information from the Configuration Manager, here's the dialog procedure for a simple custom page (see Figure 12-7 on page 370):

```
BOOL WINAPI EXPORT StatusDlgProc(HWND hdlg, UINT msg,
    WPARAM wParam, LPARAM lParam)
    {                                 // StatusDlgProc
    switch (msg)
        {                             // process message
```

```
    case WM_INITDIALOG:
        {                               // WM_INITDIALOG

        #define ResType_Telepath ((0x10 << 5) | 5)

        typedef struct
            {
            ULONG allocated;
            ULONG requested;
            } TELEPATH_RESOURCE;

        LOG_CONF logconf;
        RES_DES hres;
        DEVNODE devnode = (DEVNODE)
            ((LPPROPSHEETPAGE) lParam)->lParam;

        if (CM_Get_First_Log_Conf(&logconf, devnode,
                ALLOC_LOG_CONF) == CR_SUCCESS
            && CM_Get_Next_Res_Des(&hres, (RES_DES) logconf,
                ResType_Telepath, NULL, 0) == CR_SUCCESS)
            {                           // has telepath channel
            TELEPATH_RESOURCE res;
            int channel;
            DWORD mask;

            CM_Get_Res_Des_Data(hres, &res, sizeof(res), 0);
            if (res.allocated >= 0)
                SetDlgItemInt(hdlg, IDC_CHANNEL, res.allocated,
                    FALSE);
            }                           // has telepath channel
        break;
        }                               // WM_INITDIALOG

        }                               // process message
    return FALSE;
    }                                   // StatusDlgProc
```

This dialog procedure handles only WM_INITDIALOG. It retrieves the address of the telepathic device's DEVNODE as previously described and then uses familiar Configuration Manager calls to locate the allocated logical configuration and the telepathic channel resource descriptor within it. Although we're able to use the ring-zero flat address of the DEVNODE as an argument to a function such as *CM_Get_First_Log_Conf*, we have no use for the ring-zero flat address of the telepathic resource descriptor we get back from *CM_Get_Next_Res_Des*. That's where *CM_Get_Res_Des_Data* comes into play. This function is for use only by ring-three

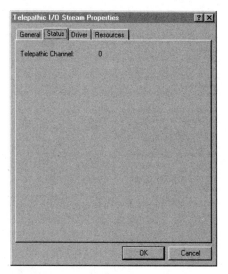

Figure 12-7. *A simple custom property page.*

programs like this one that want to get a copy of one of the Configuration Manager's resource descriptors. Once we have our own copy, we can use the *allocated* field of the telepathic resource descriptor to set the text of the appropriate item of the property page.

Handling Private Resources

The sample property page I just described is less than ideal from an end user's perspective. Since I defined a private telepathic channel resource, I could best serve end-user convenience by listing the channel along with all the other resources on the Resources page of the property sheet. You can do so by first adding a property page that will contain all the resource information and then setting the *DI_RESOURCEPAGE_ADDED* flag in the *DEVICE_INFO* structure:

```
pdi->Flags |= DI_RESOURCEPAGE_ADDED;
```

(You can replace the General page by setting the *DI_GENERALPAGE_ADDED* flag.)

If you replace the Resources page, however, you must unfortunately also duplicate all of the functionality that's in that page. Duplication will be a major pain in the neck because it involves dealing with the configuration profile list, reporting resource conflicts, initiating reconfiguration requests, and so on. Also, the list box that displays resource information is an owner-draw list box.

The WM_DEVICECHANGE Message

In addition to giving you the ability to customize device-related portions of the user interface, Windows 95 also offers application builders the WM_DEVICECHANGE message. This message is like WM_WININICHANGE or WM_SYSCOLORCHANGE, which Windows broadcasts to all top-level windows when a systemwide change occurs that many applications may be interested in. And, like other broadcast messages, most applications pass this message along to a default procedure that ignores it. After I describe how to react to this message in an application, we'll be ready to leave the subject of Plug and Play.

The *wParam* value of a WM_DEVICECHANGE message indicates the reason for sending the message, and the *lParam* value contains data (often a pointer) that depends on the value of *wParam* (see Table 12-5). The symbols in the table appear in DBT.H, which also defines some other structures and constants that will be useful in handling this message.

wParam Value	*Description*
DBT_CONFIGCHANGED	Indicates that the current configuration has changed
DBT_DEVNODESCHANGED	Indicates that the hardware tree has changed
DBT_DEVICEARRIVAL	Indicates that a new device has been installed or new media has been inserted
DBT_DEVICEQUERYREMOVE	Queries whether it is okay to remove a device
DBT_DEVICEQUERYREMOVEFAILED	Indicates that the previous QUERYREMOVE failed
DBT_DEVICEREMOVEPENDING	Indicates that the device is being removed
DBT_DEVICEREMOVECOMPLETE	Indicates that the device has been removed
DBT_DEVICETYPESPECIFIC	Indicates that a device-specific event has occurred

Table 12-5. *WM_DEVICECHANGE parameters.*

For all of the DBT_DEVICE messages, *lParam* points to one of several possible self-identifying structures. The first 12 bytes of each possible structure are the same, however, so you can always cast *lParam* to be a pointer to a *_DEV_BROAD-CAST_HEADER* structure (see Figure 12-8). The *dbcd_devicetype* field of the structure indicates which additional data follows the fixed header. The following section describes the possible values for this field.

```
struct _DEV_BROADCAST_HEADER
    {
    DWORD dbcd_size;           // 00 size of entire structure
    DWORD dbcd_devicetype;     // 04 type of structure this really is
    DWORD dbcd_reserved;       // 08 reserved for future use
    };                         // 0C
```

Figure 12-8. *Header of a DBT_DEVICE message structure.*

DBT_DEVTYP_OEM If the value is *DBT_DEVTYP_OEM*, *lParam* points to a *DEV_BROADCAST_OEM* structure:

```
typedef struct _DEV_BROADCAST_OEM
    {
    DWORD        dbco_size;
    DWORD        dbco_devicetype;
    DWORD        dbco_reserved;
    DWORD        dbco_identifier;
    DWORD        dbco_suppfunc;
    } DEV_BROADCAST_OEM, DBTFAR* PDEV_BROADCAST_OEM;
```

The values of the *dbco_identifier* and *dbco_suppfunc* members depend on who is sending the message and why.

DBT_DEVTYP_DEVNODE If the value is *DBT_DEVTYP_DEVNODE*, *lParam* points to a *DEV_BROADCAST_ DEVNODE* structure:

```
typedef struct _DEV_BROADCAST_DEVNODE
    {
    DWORD        dbcd_size;
    DWORD        dbcd_devicetype;
    DWORD        dbcd_reserved;
    DWORD        dbcd_devnode;
    } DEV_BROADCAST_DEVNODE, DBTFAR *PDEV_BROADCAST_DEVNODE;
```

The *devnode* member is the ring-zero linear address of the device node about which the message was sent. For example, a DBT_DEVICEARRIVAL message denotes the creation of a new DEVNODE.

As you know, the Configuration Manager will give you all sorts of information about a DEVNODE. To call the Configuration Manager from a 16-bit application, you use the techniques shown earlier in this chapter in connection with custom property page providers. That is, you #define the symbol *Not_VxD* and include both VMM.H and CONFIGMG.H. Then you can code calls to functions like *CM_Get_Al-loc_Log_Conf* just as you would in a VxD.

Strangely, you can't reach the Configuration Manager directly from a Win32 application in Windows 95, although you'll be able to in future releases. To legally learn more about what a particular DEVNODE pointer represents, you can interrogate a so-called *dynamic key* in the registry:

```
#define tp ((struct _DEV_BROADCAST_DEVNODE*) lParam)
DWORD devnode = tp->dbcd_devnode;
HKEY devkey;
char keyname[256];
DWORD lkeyname;

_snprintf(keyname, sizeof(keyname),
    "Config Manager\\Enum\\%8.8lX", devnode);
RegOpenKeyEx(HKEY_DYN_DATA, keyname, 0, KEY_READ, &devkey);
lkeyname = sizeof(keyname);
RegQueryValueEx(devkey, "HardwareKey", NULL, NULL, keyname,
    &lkeyname);
...
if (devkey)
    RegCloseKey(devkey);
#undef tp
```

This code relies on the barely documented fact that the HKEY_DYN_DATA branch of the registry contains a Config Manager\Enum branch with entries for each DEVNODE in the hardware tree. The named value HardwareKey for a particular DEVNODE gives the registry path from HKLM\Enum to the hardware key for the device, from which you can find other information. Learning about the current resource assignments for the device is not possible, however, without relying on undocumented knowledge about control block contents. For this reason, Microsoft discourages applications from handling messages that have *dbcd_devicetype* set to *DBT_DEVTYP_DEVNODE*; they don't occur in Windows NT anyway, which is another reason not to rely on them.

DBT_DEVTYP_VOLUME If the value of the *dbcd_devicetype* field is *DBT_-DEVTYP_VOLUME*, *lParam* points to a *DEV_BROADCAST_VOLUME* structure:

```
typedef struct _DEV_BROADCAST_VOLUME
    {
    DWORD       dbcv_size;
    DWORD       dbcv_devicetype;
    DWORD       dbcv_reserved;
    DWORD       dbcv_unitmask;
    WORD        dbcv_flags;
    } DEV_BROADCAST_VOLUME, DBTFAR *PDEV_BROADCAST_VOLUME;
```

The *dbcv_unitmask* member is a bit mask that indicates which disk device this message concerns, with bit 0 meaning drive A, and so on. The *dbcv_flags* member can include the bit DBTF_MEDIA (indicating that the change affects the media in the drive rather than the drive itself) and the bit DBTF_NET (indicating that the drive is a network drive).

For example, inserting a new CD-ROM disc in my drive D generates a DBT_DEVICEARRIVAL message with this subtype, a flag of DBTF_MEDIA, and a unit mask of 00000008h.

I was disappointed to note that pressing the eject button on my CD-ROM drive doesn't generate any query messages about whether it is okay to remove the disc. Instead, I just get a *DBT_DEVICEREMOVECOMPLETE* message to tell me that the disc is gone. With a floppy drive, you don't even get these two messages, as the hardware doesn't lend itself to noticing diskette changes, which are detected only by laborious polling. In other words, the WM_DEVICECHANGE message won't help you deal in a smarter way with a user who wants to remove the disc that contains the very file you're working with. The best you can do is detect that you're dealing with a file on a CD-ROM and prevent the user from removing the disc using the 21/440D media locking function described in the *Programmer's Guide to Microsoft Windows 95* (Microsoft Press, 1995); this interface is, of course, only for 16-bit callers.

DBT_DEVTYP_PORT If the value of the *dbcd_devicetype* field is *DBT_DEVTYP_-PORT*, *lParam* points to a *DEV_BROADCAST_PORT* structure:

```
typedef struct _DEV_BROADCAST_PORT
    {
    DWORD       dbcp_size;
    DWORD       dbcp_devicetype;
    DWORD       dbcp_reserved;
    DWORD       dbcp_name[1];
    } DEV_BROADCAST_PORT, DBTFAR *PDEV_BROADCAST_PORT;
```

The *dbcp_name* member is a null-terminated string containing the friendly name—such as *Communications Port (COM3)*—of the communications port the message is about. By way of example, if you use the Control Panel to add a completely bogus communications port, you'll get *two* DBT_DEVICEARRIVAL messages: one with *DBT_DEVTYP_PORT* and the other with *DBT_DEVTYP_DEVNODE*.

I found it instructive—and a little surprising—to monitor the WM_DEVICE-CHANGE messages that occurred when I added and then deleted the School Bus and its associated telepathic device. (An application to monitor these messages is included on the companion disc in the \CHAP12\WM_DEVICECHANGE directory.) Figure 12-9 shows the messages that occurred while I was adding the bus, and Figure 12-10 shows the ones that occurred while I was deleting the bus. If you look carefully at Figure 12-9, you'll see several DEVNODEs that don't seem to have anything to do with the School Bus being created and destroyed. In order to verify that the resources needed by a new device are free, Windows 95 creates a temporary DEVNODE. Additionally, when it comes time to reprocess the DEVNODE, Windows 95 performs a re-enumeration of the entire system. The ISAPNP driver always recreates the read-data port DEVNODE, and the Virtual Display Device always removes and recreates the MONITOR DEVNODE.

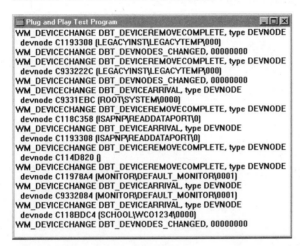

Figure 12-9. *WM_DEVICECHANGE messages that appear while a device is being added.*

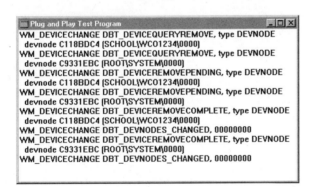

Figure 12-10. *WM_DEVICECHANGE messages that appear while a device is being deleted.*

Chapter 13

Input/Output Programming

The previous two chapters on Plug and Play explained how the Windows 95 Configuration Manager parcels out I/O resources to the devices and drivers that need them. This chapter explains how to actually use those resources in a Windows 95 driver. You will learn how to use memory mapped directly to a device, how to control access to a device's I/O ports, how to handle hardware interrupts, and how to use DMA transfers to and from a device.

Originally, the Windows VMM served the primary purpose of virtualizing hardware for the benefit of multiple VMs. Real-mode drivers were paramount in the early (Windows 3.0) days of enhanced-mode Windows. The VMM therefore aimed to give real-mode drivers precedence in I/O programming, intervening only as necessary for virtualization. Real-mode drivers have become increasingly less important with successive versions of Windows and will eventually disappear altogether. But to understand how to write a modern VxD, you also have to understand something about the underlying IBM PC/AT I/O architecture and about how real-mode drivers did their work.

After discussing the hardware features that underlie most I/O programming, I'll explain how to write a VxD that virtualizes these features so that multiple VMs can pretend they have exclusive access to the hardware. If you want to move forward with Microsoft, however, you should plan on writing VxDs that completely handle your hardware in ring zero instead of virtualizing it for ring-three drivers. Writing ring-zero drivers is therefore the last topic in this chapter.

HARDWARE UNDERPINNINGS

I/O device programming on PC/AT-compatible computers involves mapped memory access, I/O port operations, hardware interrupt requests (IRQs), and so-called direct memory access (DMA). The Intel processor chip and a variety of standardized helper chips mediate these operations. In this section, we'll explore the standard way drivers use the helper chips and processor features.

Mapped Memory

Although DMA stands for "direct memory access," some devices use a memory access strategy that's even more direct: they *map* memory directly into the processor's address space. Software accesses the hardware by reading and writing the mapped memory just as it would read and write ordinary data. The most familiar example of this strategy is a standard Video Graphics Array (VGA) display operating in text mode. Memory locations starting at physical address B8000h control the characters that appear on the display. Thus, the simple DEBUG script

```
C:\>debug
-e b800:0 41 20
-
```

places a black letter *A* at the top-left corner of the display, with a cyan background. (Be sure to clear the screen before you run DEBUG when you try this, or the results of your test may scroll out of sight before you see them!)

I/O Ports

The processor implements an I/O address space in addition to a regular memory address space. Locations in the I/O address space are called *ports*. The IN and OUT instructions, and their several variants, access I/O ports instead of memory. Just as with regular memory, however, port access can occur in units of 1 byte, 2 bytes, or 4 bytes. Furthermore, software can use the INS and OUTS instructions, with or without a REP prefix, to automatically adjust an address register and a count register after a port transfer.

I/O port addresses are 16 bits in width. A number of standard design features conspire to prevent you from attaching 65,536 separately addressable devices to a real PC/AT-compatible computer, though. The standard architecture reserves port addresses 00h through FFh for certain standard devices (see Table 13-1). The Industry Standard Architecture (ISA) bus decodes only the low-order 10 bits of an I/O address, reducing the number of distinct port addresses to 768 (2^{10} minus the 256 reserved addresses). Other hardware buses decode the full 16-bit I/O addresses, however. In addition, a system that contains a PCI bus usually has a *bridge chip* connecting the PCI bus to an ISA bus. The bridge lets the ISA bus see only the I/O addresses in the 0FFh through 3FFh range. Devices attached directly to the PCI bus can therefore use 16-bit port addresses whose low-order 10 bits might otherwise conflict with an ISA device.

Port Address (Hexadecimal)	Description
00	DMA channel 0, address register
01	DMA channel 0, count register
02	DMA channel 1, address register
03	DMA channel 1, count register
04	DMA channel 2, address register
05	DMA channel 2, count register
06	DMA channel 3, address register
07	DMA channel 3, count register
08	DMA status register for channels 0 through 3
0A	DMA mask register for channels 0 through 3
0B	DMA mode register for channels 0 through 3
0C	DMA clear-byte pointer
0D	DMA master clear byte
0E	DMA clear-mask register for channels 0 through 3
0F	DMA write-mask register for channels 0 through 3
18	DMA extended function register
1A	DMA extended function execute register
20	In-service register for master PIC
21	Master PIC command and mask register
40	Interval timer counter 0
42	Interval timer counter 2
43	Control register for interval timer counters 0 and 2
44	Interval timer counter 3
47	Control register for interval timer counter 3
60	Keyboard controller
61	System control port B (PS/2)
64	PS/2 peripheral controller command and status register
70	CMOS address register
71	CMOS data register

Table 13-1. *Reserved I/O port assignments.* *(continued)*

continued

Port Address (Hexadecimal)	Description
74-75	Extended CMOS address register
76	Extended CMOS data register
80	DMA address register
81	DMA page register for channel 2
82	DMA page register for channel 3
83	DMA page register for channel 1
87	DMA page register for channel 0
89	DMA page register for channel 6
8A	DMA page register for channel 7
8B	DMA page register for channel 5
8F	DMA page register for channel 4
90	DMA arbitration register
91	DMA feedback register
92	System control port A (PS/2)
94	System board setup enable register (PS/2)
96	Programmable option select register (PS/2)
A0	In-service register for slave PIC
A1	Slave PIC command and mask register
C0	DMA address register for channel 4
C2	DMA count register for channel 4
C4	DMA address register for channel 5
C6	DMA count register for channel 5
C8	DMA address register for channel 6
CA	DMA count register for channel 6
CC	DMA address register for channel 7
CE	DMA count register for channel 7
D0	DMA status register for channels 4 through 7
D4	DMA mask register for channels 4 through 7
D6	DMA mode register for channels 4 through 7
D8	DMA clear-word pointer
DA	DMA master clear word
DC	DMA clear-mask register for channels 4 through 7
DE	DMA write-mask register for channels 4 through 7
F0-FF	Math coprocessor register

Hardware Interrupts

Most devices use an interrupt to notify the operating system that they have completed an operation. Using an interrupt in this way allows the CPU to do other things while I/O is occurring, thereby improving the overall throughput of the system. The computer contains a *Programmable Interrupt Controller* (also known as a PIC) to manage the interrupt system. Figure 13-1 shows a simplified block diagram of the PIC. You'll notice that the illustration shows eight interrupt request lines coming into the PIC, whereas you probably already know that IRQs can have numbers as high as fifteen. As I'll explain presently, there are really *two* PICs in the computer, each of which handles eight input lines. For more information about the PIC, see Intel's *Peripheral Components* (Intel Corporation, 1993) and Hans-Peter Messmer's *Indispensible PC Hardware Book; Your Hardware Questions Answered* (Addison-Wesley, 1994).

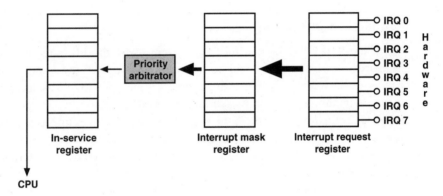

Figure 13-1. *Programmable Interrupt Controller architecture.*

Each hardware device that can generate an interrupt has a logical connection to one of the PIC's interrupt request (IRQ) lines. Some of the assignments of devices to IRQs are standardized among all PC/AT-compatible computers (see Table 13-2 on the following page). When a device needs to interrupt the CPU, it signals the PIC on its dedicated IRQ line, thereby setting a bit in the PIC's *interrupt request register* (IRR). The IRR has a set bit for each IRQ that's currently trying to interrupt and a clear bit for each IRQ that isn't currently trying to interrupt. The PIC consults its *interrupt mask register* (IMR) to decide whether to allow the interrupt or not. A set bit in the IMR means that the corresponding interrupt is disabled, or "masked;" a clear bit means that the interrupt is enabled, or "unmasked."

IRQ	Standard Assignment
0	Interval timer
1	Keyboard
2	Summarizes IRQs 8 through 15 from the slave PIC (see text)
3	COM2
4	COM1
5	LPT2 (if installed), often available for use
6	Floppy disk controller
7	LPT1
8	Real-time clock
13	Math coprocessor error signal
14	Hard disk controller

Table 13-2. *Standard IRQ assignments.*

If the IMR indicates that the IRQ is unmasked, the PIC attempts to interrupt the processor. The interrupt will be allowed if and only if the interrupt flag in the processor's flags register is set. If the interrupt is allowed, the PIC selects the highest priority IRQ among all the unmasked interrupts that are currently requesting service and sets the corresponding bit in the *in-service register* while simultaneously clearing the bit in the interrupt request register. It also causes the CPU to interrupt on an interrupt number computed by adding the IRQ number to an internal interrupt base address.

As I mentioned, there are two interrupt controllers in a computer. The first PIC, known as the *master PIC,* services interrupt requests 0 through 7 and vectors them to interrupts 08h through 0Fh in a standard real-mode system. The second PIC, known as the *slave PIC,* services interrupt requests 8 through 15 and vectors them to interrupts 70h through 77h. But, because the processor has only a single interrupt line, the slave PIC connects to the master PIC's IRQ 2 line instead of to the CPU. As a result, interrupts on IRQs 8 through 15 occur because the master PIC recognizes IRQ 2.

The standard real-mode BIOS programs the PICs to operate in what's called "fully nested mode." In this mode, each IRQ has a strict priority that blocks higher-numbered IRQs on the same PIC. Because the slave PIC connects to the master PIC's IRQ 2 line, the priority order of interrupt requests, from highest to lowest, is 0 through 1, 8 through 15, 3 through 7. For example, while a keyboard interrupt (IRQ 1) is being serviced, only timer interrupts (IRQ 0) can occur. And no hardware can interrupt the timer interrupt service routine.

The interrupt service routines (ISRs) for hardware interrupts generally need to do pretty much the same things:

1. The ISR should enable interrupts as soon as possible by executing an STI instruction. In a real-mode operating system, the ISR begins execution with interrupts disabled because that's just the way the Intel processor works. In a protected-mode environment, an ISR will also begin with interrupts disabled if the IDT contains an *interrupt gate* for the interrupt. (It's possible for the operating system to install a *trap gate,* which would cause the ISR to gain control with interrupts enabled. Systems don't usually use trap gates for hardware interrupts because hardware ISRs usually have some code that must be executed without possibility of interruption.)

2. The ISR should also send the PIC an *end-of-interrupt* (EOI) *command* to dismiss the interrupt as soon as possible. Because the BIOS programs the PIC to nest interrupts strictly according to interrupt priority, most real-mode software uses a *nonspecific EOI command* to dismiss an interrupt in the knowledge that no other interrupt can be pending when the EOI command is executed. An ISR for a master-PIC interrupt sends an EOI command by using the OUT instruction to write the byte 20h to I/O port 20h. An ISR for a slave-PIC interrupt sends an EOI command by writing 20h to *both* ports 20h and A0h. (It should send an EOI command to the slave PIC first and then to the master PIC.) Windows uses a *specific EOI command* to dismiss a specific interrupt to be extra sure that the correct interrupt gets dismissed. Whichever kind of EOI command is used, the EOI command releases the PIC so that lower-priority interrupts can occur and so that interrupts from the same source can once more occur.

3. When it is finished handling the interrupt, the ISR executes an IRET instruction to return to the program that was originally interrupted.

Handling IRQ 9   The IBM PC/XT architecture included just one PIC. To preserve software compatibility when the PC/AT architecture added a second PIC, the BIOS was made to do an apparently strange thing: handle INT 71h by sending an EOI command to the slave PIC and then issuing an INT 0Ah. INT 71h is from IRQ 9, whereas INT 0Ah is from IRQ 2. Since IRQ 2 is used for cascading the master and slave PICs, it's no longer available for use by other hardware. Hardware that used to use IRQ 2 on the XT was simply redirected to IRQ 9. If no one hooks INT 71h, the BIOS provides a default handler. The default handler arranges to pass control to the original IRQ 2 ISR after first ensuring that it will be okay for the ISR to just send an EOI command to the master PIC. If you hook INT 71h to handle IRQ 9, you'll become responsible for sending both EOI commands. If you hook INT 0Ah to handle IRQ 2, your code will work fine even though the hardware will actually be signalling IRQ 9.

Direct Memory Access

DMA transfers allow an I/O device to move data to and from main memory without needing software to execute each time a unit of data is transferred. By alternately locking and unlocking memory, the DMA controller creates the appearance that data transfer occurs simultaneously with program execution. In brief, software uses port I/O operations to store the starting address, length, and direction (that is, whether the transfer is to or from memory) in DMA controller registers. Software then *unmasks* the channel to initiate the transfer. A subsequent hardware interrupt alerts software that the transfer is complete. The ultimate source of information about the DMA controller chip is Intel's *Peripheral Components*. You can find other useful discussions in Messmer's *Indispensible PC Hardware Book; Your Hardware Questions Answered* and in Frank Van Gilluwe's *The Undocumented PC* (Addison-Wesley, 1994). Be aware that the code samples in both of these books have errors, however.

Figure 13-2 is a simplified block diagram of the standard DMA hardware in a PC. There are eight DMA channels, four for each of two DMA controller chips. Channels 0 through 3 provide for 8-bit transfers, while channels 5 through 7 provide for 16-bit transfers. Channel 4 is used to cascade two physical DMA controller chips and is therefore unavailable for programmatic use. Conventionally, channel 0 is reserved for use in driving the memory refresh cycles required by DRAM memory chips, and channel 2 is reserved for floppy disk operations. Other than these reserved

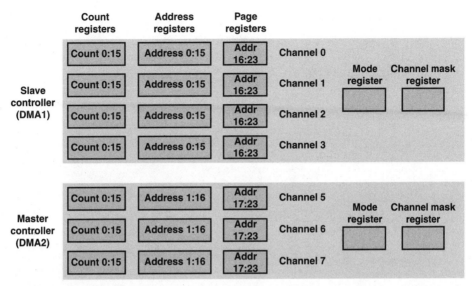

Figure 13-2. *Architecture of the DMA hardware. (Channel 4 cascades the master control-ler to the slave controller.)*

channels, two 8-bit channels (1 and 3) and three 16-bit channels (5, 6, and 7) are available for expansion cards.

Each DMA channel has a 16-bit *address* register, an 8-bit *page* register, and a 16-bit *count* register. The page and address registers together provide access to the first 16 MB of physical memory. Each DMA controller has a *mode* register and a *channel mask* register. Each controller also has additional registers designed for use by the BIOS during the system boot process; I won't discuss those registers here.

To transfer data, system software must establish the base address, data count, and transfer mode for a DMA channel that the hardware device in question is already prepared to work with. For example, the following code fragment initializes DMA channel 2 to transfer a 512-byte sector from a floppy disk to memory. (The numbers shown in bold correspond to the discussion on pages 387–388.)

1.

```
                       ; DMA channel mask register
mov   al, 06h          ; xxxxx 1 10 => mask channel 2
out   0Ah, al          ;   ..
iodelay                ;   ..
```

(continued)

continued

2.

```
                        ; DMA mode register:
mov    al, 46h          ; 01 0 0 01 10
out    0Bh, al          ; |  | | |  |
iodelay                 ; |  | | |  +-> channel 2
                        ; |  | | +-> write transfer mode
                        ; |  | +-> autoinitialize inactive
                        ; |  +-> increment address
                        ; +-> single transfer mode
```

3.

```
movzx eax, word ptr buffer+2 ; segment portion of buffer address
movzx ecx, word ptr buffer   ; offset portion
shl    eax, 4            ; compute physical address
add    eax, ecx         ;  ..

out    0Ch, al          ; output anything at all to 0C
iodelay                 ;    to reset the even/odd flip-flop
out    04h, al          ; low byte of address
iodelay                 ;  ..
shr    eax, 8           ; high byte of address
out    04h, al          ;  ..
iodelay                 ;  ..
shr    eax, 8           ; page address
out    81h, al          ;  ..
iodelay                 ;  ..
```

4.

```
mov    al, 0FFh         ; set count register to 511
out    05h, al          ;  ..
iodelay                 ;  ..
mov    al, 1            ;  ..
out    05h, al          ;  ..
iodelay                 ;  ..
```

5.

```
mov    al, 02h          ; xxxxx 0 10 => unmask channel 2
out    0Ah, al          ;  ..
```

In this fragment, iodelay is a macro that generates two short jumps to unload the processor's instruction pipeline in order to permit an OUT instruction to finish before the next one starts. The *buffer* variable is a real-mode far pointer to a data buffer. The logic of the fragment is as follows:

1. Port 0Ah is the channel mask register for DMA controller 1, which governs channels 0 through 3 (see Figure 13-3). Writing 06h to this port "masks" channel 2 so that we can safely program it: the low-order two bits (10b) designate channel 2, and bit 2 (1b) indicates that we want to mask the channel.

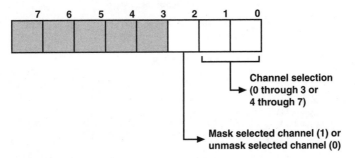

Figure 13-3. *DMA channel mask register.*

2. Port 0Bh is the mode register for DMA controller 1 (see Figure 13-4 on the following page). Writing 46h to this port signifies the following: the low-order two bits (10b) indicate that we're setting the mode for channel 2. Bits 2 and 3 (01b) indicate that this is a write operation; that is, we're reading from the I/O device and writing to memory. Bit 4 indicates that we do not wish the DMA channel to reinitialize itself for an additional transfer once this one completes. (I'll explain later why you don't normally use the "autoinitialization" mode indicated by a set bit in this position under Windows 95.) Bit 5 (0b) indicates that we want the controller to increment the address register after each transfer; the alternative is to decrement the register instead. Finally, bits 6 and 7 (01b) select the single transfer mode expected by a floppy disk controller. Alternatives for the transfer mode in bits 6 and 7 are 00b (demand mode) and 10b (block mode); the value 11b means "cascade" and is used only for channel 4.

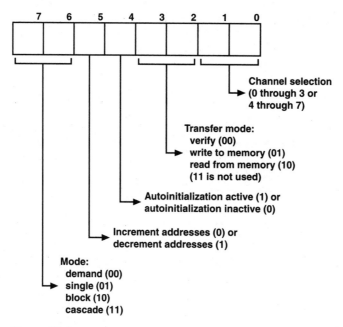

Figure 13-4. *DMA mode register.*

3. Port 04h is the address register for channel 2, and port 81h is the page register. We write the low-order 16 bits of the physical buffer address to port 04h one byte at a time, and then we write the high-order byte to the page register. To save circuitry, the chip has an internal flip-flop to tell it whether it's receiving the low-order or high-order byte of the 16-bit address and count registers. To place this flip-flop into a known state denoting that the low-order byte is expected next, we write any value at all to port 0Ch.

4. Port 05h is the count register for channel 2. We write to this register—also one byte at a time—the quantity one less than the data count we want to transfer. (The same flip-flop mentioned in the preceding paragraph controls whether a byte is interpreted as low-order or high-order. The second of the writes to port 04h in step 3 leaves the flip-flop in the correct state for this step.)

5. Finally, writing 02h to port 0Ah unmasks channel 2 so that the controller can begin transferring data as soon as the device is ready.

If you really wanted to read a sector from a floppy disk, you would now program the floppy disk controller to turn on its motor and perform a sector read using DMA. As soon as the controller receives the last byte of the sector-read command sequence, it will move the read/write head to the designated track, search for the start of the designated sector, and begin transferring data bytes to the memory bus. Each time the floppy disk controller reads a new data byte, it will signal the DMA controller. The DMA controller in turn shuts out the CPU (and other users of memory) from access to memory and gates the data byte into the next buffer location. While the floppy disk controller is moving the head and searching for the right sector, and in between actual transfer of data bytes, the CPU will be able to access memory normally. When the transfer finally finishes, either because the DMA controller exhausts its count or because the floppy disk controller finishes the disk operation, the floppy disk controller signals the PIC on a reserved IRQ line (usually IRQ 6, corresponding to interrupt 0Eh in a real-mode system). System software fields the interrupt by sending an EOI command to the interrupt controller and reading status bytes from the floppy disk controller.

The historical evolution of PC design really shows through when you examine the DMA architecture. The DMA chips use *physical* instead of virtual addresses. An operating system like Windows 95 that uses paging must therefore do a great deal of translation and page-locking work to prepare for a DMA transfer. Figure 13-5 illustrates what a device driver that wants to transfer 512 bytes of data might have to do to prepare for the transfer. The device driver starts with a virtual buffer address. Since the DMA controller understands only physical addresses, the driver must first

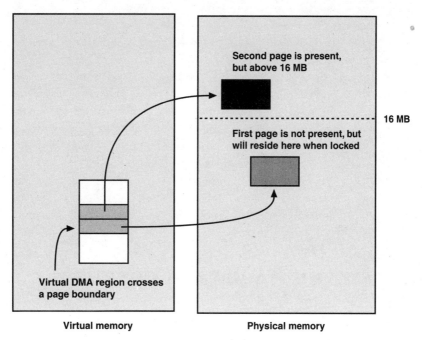

Figure 13-5. *DMA transfer from a buffer in virtual memory.*

translate its virtual buffer address to a physical address by referring to a set of page tables. The driver must also *lock* the buffer in memory to prevent the paging subsystem from using the same physical memory for some other purpose while the transfer occurs. In addition, it might happen that the buffer crosses the boundary between two virtual pages (as shown in the figure). In that case, the driver needs to address the likelihood that the buffer won't occupy adjacent physical pages. Depending on hardware, the driver may need to program two transfers or arrange for a discontiguous transfer using a hardware *scatter/gather* mechanism.

The difficulties posed by virtual memory aren't over yet, though. Recall that the DMA controller has a 24-bit address, which is sufficient to address only 16 MB of physical memory. Suppose the pages containing the buffer happen to lie beyond the 16-MB line? The Windows 95 VDMAD VxD handles transfers to and from memory beyond the line by copying data to or from a preallocated DMA buffer that's locked into physical memory below the line.

There's an additional wrinkle to consider for the 16-bit DMA channels. The DMA controller insists that you transfer data beginning on a word (16-bit) boundary in memory. In effect, the controller essentially shifts the 24-bit quantity held in the page and address registers left by one bit (losing the high-order bit) to generate memory addresses, and it interprets the count register as a *word* count instead of a byte count. Thus, you can transfer up to 128 KB in word units using one of the 16-bit DMA channels.

If the address register happens to overflow or underflow during a transfer, the DMA controller doesn't automatically increment or decrement the page register. So, suppose you programmed a 512-byte transfer beginning at physical address 4FFFh:0000h (4FFF0h). You would set the page register to 4 and the address register to FFF0h. After transferring 16 bytes, the DMA controller would increment the address register past its 16-bit maximum, and the next memory location would be 40000h instead of 50000h. In other words, you must be sure not to cross 64-KB (128-KB in the case of 16-bit DMA) boundaries during DMA transfers.

With an EISA bus in the computer, DMA is a bit simpler. EISA supports 32-bit transfers in addition to 8-bit and 16-bit transfers. Also, EISA supports 32-bit buffer addressing. Therefore, the EISA bus allows DMA transfers to any area of memory, whether above or below 16 MB.

VIRTUALIZING HARDWARE RESOURCES

Prior to Windows 95, the purpose of a VxD was to virtualize real hardware on behalf of ring-three drivers running in VMs. The idea behind this virtualization was to let existing real-mode drivers continue to handle the hardware so that hardware vendors wouldn't immediately have to build VxDs. Although the "immediately" I'm talking about was six years ago when Windows 3.0 first appeared, plenty of hardware vendors haven't caught up yet. Windows 95 therefore continues to support the virtualization techniques I'm about to describe.

Virtualizing Mapped Memory

The problem with memory-mapped devices is that the hardware responds to a particular range of *physical* addresses and that software using the hardware needs to use *virtual* addresses that are all numerically identical with the physical addresses. I'll use the term *hardware address* to describe the address to which the hardware responds; for example, the hardware address for the VGA text-mode display is B8000h. (The DDK refers to this as the *physical address*.) The basic strategy for virtualizing mapped memory involves two steps. First, you provide physically separate areas of memory for each VM that will share the device. Second, if it's possible for a single owner of the device to emulate the hardware for more than one simultaneous VM (as is true for the display screen, which you already know from having seen windowed MS-DOS sessions on the desktop), you arrange for each VM's page tables to map the virtual hardware address to the per-VM memory area. If only one VM at a time can own the device, you instead arrange to completely swap the contents of the mapped memory each time ownership of the device changes.

Swapping the State of a Memory-Mapped Device

The Windows 95 Virtual Display Device (VDD) VxD combines both the approaches mentioned in the previous paragraph. To handle a windowed MS-DOS VM, the VDD allows the VM to access its own private (virtual) display memory at the usual addresses. The VDD works closely with two other components—the video "grabber" and the WINOLDAP Windows application—to update the VM's window in a more-or-less timely fashion. WINOLDAP owns the screen window within which the VM's display appears. It calls the grabber to perform screen update and selection operations within the window, and the grabber in turn calls the VDD's API function. (Chapter 3 of the *Device Driver Adaptation Guide* [part of the Windows 3.1 DDK; Microsoft Corporation, 1992] provides more information about video grabbers.)

The user, by way of the Windows 95 taskbar or some similar user interface component, selects a VM to have the focus. The focus VM moves to foreground status. The SHELL VxD uses the Set_Device_Focus system control message to shift ownership of hardware to the new focus VM as well. If the new focus VM happens to be running in a desktop window, SHELL will shift ownership of many devices, including the display, to the System VM. If the new focus VM is running full-screen, SHELL assigns the display to that VM instead. The VDD responds to the Set_Device_Focus message by saving the state of the previous owner of the display and installing the state of the new owner.

In general, saving and restoring state information for a modern super VGA display system is very complicated, especially if the display is in a graphical mode in one or both of the VMs. To simplify the discussion, suppose that both VMs were using video mode 3 (the standard 25-line text mode of the display). The only thing that would actually be different between the two states would then be the content of the video RAM beginning at virtual address B8000h.

While a full-screen VM is in the foreground, the VDD maps the VM's virtual B8h page, B9h page, and so on directly to those same physical memory locations. (Since a page is 1000h bytes long, page B8h corresponds to linear address B8000h.) Therefore, whenever a foreground program stores a character or attribute in the video RAM, the physical display changes immediately. While a full-screen VM is in the background, however, the VDD maps its video RAM pages to extended memory pages. Therefore, whenever a background program stores a character or attribute in the video RAM, the change is invisible. To switch from one foreground VM to another, then, the VDD merely needs to copy the physical video RAM to an extended memory buffer belonging to the outgoing VM and copy the extended memory buffer belonging to the incoming VM into the physical video RAM. After the switchover, any changes made to the incoming VM's video RAM while that VM was in the background become apparent to the user.

A sketch of how you would implement the memory-swapping strategy is as follows. This isn't *nearly* complete enough for a real driver; it's just an illustration of how you might handle a device that's too simple to be useful in a real computer. In fact, all I'll promise you is that this example (included on the companion disk in the \CHAP13\MEMORYVIRTUALIZATION directory) compiles correctly.

```
PVMMCB hOwner;
PBYTE GetPrivateVideoBuffer(PVMMCB);
PBYTE GetRealVideoBuffer(void);
void MapPrivateVideoPages(PVMMCB);
void MapRealVideoPages(PVMMCB);
#define BUFSIZE (8*4096) // Eight pages of data

BOOL OnSetDeviceFocus(PVMMCB hVM, DWORD devid, DWORD flags,
    PVMMCB hProblemVM)
    {                      // OnSetDeviceFocus
    if (devid && devid != MYVXD_DEVICE_ID)
        return TRUE;   // ignore request for another device
    memcpy(GetPrivateVideoBuffer(hOwner), GetRealVideoBuffer(),
        BUFSIZE);
    memcpy(GetRealVideoBuffer(), GetPrivateVideoBuffer(hVM),
        BUFSIZE);
    MapPrivateVideoPages(hOwner);
```

```
MapRealVideoPages(hVM);
hOwner = hVM;
return TRUE;
}                       // OnSetDeviceFocus
```

This code fragment requires a good deal of explanation and elaboration. The Set_Device_Focus system control message includes a VxD ID as a parameter, the idea being that the identified VxD should switch the focus of the devices it manages. Each VxD receives Set_Device_Focus messages for all devices, though, not just the ones it's managing. By convention, a Set_Device_Focus message with a device ID of 0 sets the focus of every device for which focus is a meaningful concept. The first statement in the subroutine detects these cases so as to ignore requests specific to other drivers.

I used a helper function named *GetRealVideoBuffer*, whose purpose is to return the linear address of the real video buffer located at physical address B8000h. It would not be correct for this routine to just return the value B8000h, however. The pointer that is returned will be interpreted as a virtual address according to whatever page tables are currently in place. Depending on which VM is current, locations in the first megabyte (that is, in the V86 region of the address space) may be mapped to identical physical locations, or they may be mapped instead to unique pages in extended memory. Since we don't have any way of knowing a priori which VM will be current when we receive a Set_Device_Focus message, we shouldn't assume that virtual address B8000h will map to physical address B8000h. The correct way to implement *GetRealVideoBuffer* is therefore to use the *_MapPhysToLinear* VxD service:

```
PBYTE GetRealVideoBuffer(void)
    {                       // GetRealVideoBuffer
    return _MapPhysToLinear(0xB8000, BUFSIZE, 0);
    }                       // GetRealVideoBuffer
```

The linear address obtained in this way stays the same for the duration of a Windows 95 session. In fact, we would probably make the *_MapPhysToLinear* call once during device initialization and save the returned value in a global variable. Doing the call during initialization saves repeating the overhead within *_MapPhysToLinear* that would be required to check whether the mapping had already been done.

The fact that *_MapPhysToLinear* creates a permanent mapping of a linear address to physical memory creates a problem in Windows 95 because it's possible for the physical device address to change during a Windows 95 session. (The address of the video display won't change because the configuration of the video driver is fixed at boot time and can't change until the machine is rebooted. But, in general, the Configuration Manager can reassign memory addresses along with all other I/O resources.) To avoid chewing up linear address space that can't ever be recovered, you would want to use a different technique in a Plug and Play driver. Within the CONFIG_START handler in your configuration function, use _PageReserve, _PageCommitPhys, and _LinPageLock to map the assigned memory. Within the CONFIG_STOP and CONFIG_REMOVE handlers, undo those functions. The following code shows how this is done:

```
case CONFIG_START:
    [determine physical memory address "physaddr" and length "npages"]
    ULONG linaddr = _PageReserve(PR_SYSTEM, npages,
        PR_FIXED);
    _PageCommitPhys(linaddr >> 12, npages, physaddr >> 12,
        PC_INCR | PC_WRITEABLE);
    _LinPageLock(linaddr >> 12, npages, 0);
    ...
case CONFIG_STOP:
case CONFIG_REMOVE:
    _LinPageUnlock(linaddr >> 12, npages, 0);
    _PageFree(linaddr, 0);
    ...
```

In the CONFIG_START case, the call to _PageReserve allocates a range of virtual addresses by which we can address the device's memory. _PageCommitPhys instructs the paging manager to create page table entries that map the physical memory to those virtual addresses. _LinPageLock then ensures that the virtual-to-physical mapping can never change. By the way, DDK documentation to the effect that you can't lock memory that you've mapped with _PageCommitPhys is incorrect: you can lock it as shown in this sample. In the CONFIG_STOP and CONFIG_REMOVE cases, the calls to _LinPageUnlock and _PageFree undo the work done during CONFIG_START.

I used another helper routine named GetPrivateVideoBuffer to access an 8-page private memory block containing a copy of a given VM's video RAM. You could allocate this buffer by calling _PageAllocate in response to a Create_VM control message and save its address in the VM control block. Reserving space in the VM control block is something you most often do during device initialization. Therefore, in order to implement the GetPrivateVideoBuffer function, you end up with more code than you probably expected:

```
typedef struct tagMYSTUFF
    {
    PVOID pVidBuff;        // linear address of video buffer
    } MYSTUFF, *PMYSTUFF;
DWORD cboffset;            // offset of MYSTUFF in VMCB
#define GetStuff(hvm) ((PMYSTUFF) ((DWORD) hvm + cboffset))
```

```
BOOL OnDeviceInit(PVMMCB hVM, DWORD refdata)
    {                   // OnDeviceInit
    if (!_Assign_Device_V86_Pages(0xB8, 8, NULL, 0))
        return FALSE;   // can't globally assign pages
    cboffset = _Allocate_Device_CB_Area(sizeof(MYSTUFF), 0);
    if (!cboffset)
        return FALSE;
    return OnCreateVM(hVM); // initialize system VM data now
    }                   // OnDeviceInit

BOOL OnCreateVM(PVMMCB hVM)
    {                   // OnCreateVM
    PVOID pVidBuff;
    pVidBuff = _PageAllocate(8, PG_VM, (HVM) hVM, 0, 0, 0, 0,
        PAGEZEROINIT);
    if (!pVidBuff)
        return FALSE;
    GetStuff(hVM)->pVidBuff = pVidBuff;
    return TRUE;
    }                   // OnCreateVM

BOOL OnDestroyVM(PVMMCB hVM)
    {                   // OnDestroyVM
    _PageFree(GetStuff(hVM)->pVidBuff, 0);
    return TRUE;
    }                   // OnDestroyVM

PBYTE GetPrivateVideoBuffer(PVMMCB hVM)
    {                   // GetPrivateVideoBuffer
    return GetStuff(hVM)->pVidBuff;
    }                   // GetPrivateVideoBuffer
```

The *OnDeviceInit* function first uses *_Assign_Device_V86_Pages* to mark the video RAM pages in the V86 region as belonging to our VxD. *_Assign_Device_V86_Pages* checks a bit map that records whether or not each V86 page is owned by some VxD or another; the bit map doesn't actually indicate *who* owns a page, merely whether a page is owned or not. If the eight pages we're going to virtualize aren't owned by any other VxD, *_Assign_Device_V86_Pages* marks them as owned and returns TRUE; otherwise, it returns FALSE. In a real situation, it would be very unusual for the assignment call to fail, because there should only be one VxD interested in each block of V86 pages.

After reserving the video RAM pages, the *OnDeviceInit* function uses *_Allocate_Device_CB_Area* to reserve device-specific space within each VM control block. We will use this space to remember the address of the private video buffer we'll allocate. Finally, *OnDeviceInit* calls *OnCreateVM* to initialize the System VM; recall that no Create_VM message ever occurs for the System VM, so VxDs usually do any per-VM initialization needed for the System VM during Device_Init.

The _PageAllocate Function The _PageAllocate function is the most basic of all the memory allocation API functions a VxD can use. This function reserves a contiguous range of linear address space and commits memory to back up those addresses. *Committing* a memory block means making sure that there is sufficient physical memory to hold the contents of the block plus all the other currently committed memory. The needed physical memory can come either from RAM or from space in the swap file. The reason Windows 95 commits memory is to be sure that a page fault can never fail due to an inability to write a page to the swap file. If you wish, you can perform the two steps of reserving address space and committing pages separately by calling _PageReserve and _PageCommit separately, instead of simply calling _PageAllocate.

The prototype for _PageAllocate (defined in VXDWRAPS.H) is

```
PVOID _PageAllocate(DWORD nPages, DWORD pType, HVM hvm,
    DWORD AlignMask, DWORD minPhys, DWORD maxPhys,
    PVOID *PhysAddr, DWORD flags);
```

The *nPages* argument is the number of pages you want to allocate. The *pType* argument is one of the manifest constants *PG_SYS* or *PG_VM*. *PG_SYS* pages are allocated in the shared system region of the address space (from C0000000h up), while *PG_VM* pages are allocated in the shared application region (from 80000000h to C0000000h). There is an additional manifest constant named *PG_HOOKED* that, for Windows 95, means the same thing as *PG_VM*. The third argument is a VM handle (that is, a pointer to a VM control block); note that the DDK defines a typedef symbol named *HVM* as a simple DWORD, but an *HVM* is really the same entity as a *PVMMCB*. If you allocate pages with the *PG_VM* or *PG_HOOKED* type, the handle identifies the VM that owns the pages. If you allocate *PG_SYS* pages, the argument should be NULL because no VM owns the pages.

The *flags* argument allows you to tailor the allocation for special purposes. You compose the argument by ORing zero or more manifest constants describing your special requirements. The *PAGEZEROINIT* flag means what you think it does. *PAGEFIXED* and *PAGELOCKED* both lock the allocated pages; that is, they cause the page manager to immediately reserve physical memory pages that can't be stolen for other pages. The difference between these two flag bits is that *PAGEFIXED* indicates that the pages will never be unlocked, whereas *PAGELOCKED* indicates that you plan to call _PageUnLock later on to unlock the pages.

The *PAGELOCKEDIFDP* flag also locks the pages like *PAGELOCKED* does, but only if Windows 95 is using MS-DOS or BIOS functions to perform paging I/O (which is not the usual case). You would use this flag if you needed to access the memory block during an event callback where you don't know in advance that paging will be okay. The VMM doesn't know until the Init_Complete message is sent whether MS-DOS or ring-zero VxD code will be responsible for paging. A static driver can wait until Init_Complete to allocate a block that needs this conditional locking behavior. A dynamic driver can achieve the same result with code like the following:

```
BOOL OnSysDynamicDeviceInit()
    {                           // OnSysDynamicDeviceInit
    if (VMM_GetSystemInitState() >= SYSSTATE_VXDINITCOMPLETED)
        return OnInitComplete(Get_Sys_VM_Handle(), 0);
    else
        return TRUE;
    }                           // OnSysDynamicDeviceInit


BOOL OnInitComplete(PVMMCB hVM, DWORD refdata)
    {                           // OnInitComplete
    _PageAllocate(..., PAGELOCKEDIFDP);
    ...
    }                           // OnInitComplete
```

In this code fragment, we use *VMM_GetSystemInitState* to determine whether Init_Complete has already occurred. If not, we simply wait for that message to arrive. If so, we call the function that would have handled Init_Complete had the driver been loaded at the time.

The *PAGEUSEALIGN* flag for *_PageAllocate* allows you to control where *PAGELOCKED* pages will be placed in physical memory. If you specify both *PAGEUSEALIGN* and *PAGELOCKED*, the four arguments I haven't described yet come into play. *AlignMask* can be one of the values 0h, 01h, 03h, 07h, 0Fh, or 1Fh to specify alignment on a particular page boundary. Specifying an *AlignMask* of 0Fh, for example, indicates that the physical address must be a multiple of 16 pages, which means 64-KB alignment. The *minPhys* and *maxPhys* arguments specify minimum and maximum physical addresses for the memory block. The *PhysAddr* argument, if nonzero, is the address of a location where *_PageAllocate* will store the physical address it assigns. Finally, if you have specified *PAGEUSEALIGN* and *PAGELOCKED*, you can also specify *PAGECONTIG* to be sure that the allocated physical memory will be contiguous.

One purpose of the extra arguments is to make it possible for the VDMAD to use *_PageAllocate* to allocate a DMA buffer. The VDMAD would typically ask for 128-KB alignment (*AlignMask* equal to 1Fh) with a maximum physical address of 16 MB. The VDMAD would also insist on contiguous physical memory (using the *PAGECONTIG* flag), and it would want to know the resulting physical address (*PhysAddr* not NULL).

The return value from *_PageAllocate* is the linear address of the allocated memory block, which also serves as a handle when calling other page allocation services. In previous versions of Windows, *_PageAllocate* returned a separate handle in addition to a linear address. If you need to write a VxD that will be compatible with Windows 3.x, you will need to write your own C-language wrapper with an additional pointer argument so you can return both the handle and the linear address.

Mapping Pages into the VM The two remaining helper functions are *MapPrivateVideoPages* and *MapRealVideoPages*, which install the page table entries for the private and real video RAM areas, respectively:

```
void MapPrivateVideoPages(PVMMCB hVM)
    {                               // MapPrivateVideoPages
    _MapIntoV86(GetStuff(hVM)->pVidBuff, (HVM) hVM, 0xB8, 8,
        0, 0);
    }                               // MapPrivateVideoPages


void MapRealVideoPages(PVMMCB hVM)
    {                               // MapRealVideoPages
    _PhysIntoV86(0xB8, (HVM) hVM, 0xB8, 8, 0);
    }                               // MapRealVideoPages
```

The *_MapIntoV86* function maps some or all of the pages in a memory block into a VM at a specified virtual address, while *_PhysIntoV86* maps physical pages into a VM. The term *mapping* means setting up page table entries to point to specific physical pages. *MapPrivateVideoPages* installs page table entries for virtual addresses B8000h through BF000h that point to the pages in the private video RAM buffer. *MapRealVideoPages* installs page table entries for virtual addresses B8000h through BF000h that point to physical addresses B8000h through BF000h.

Dynamically Allocating Memory

The sample code I've just explained has one major problem in real life: it wastes virtual memory. Take a look at that call to *_PageAllocate* in *OnCreateVM*, and you'll realize that far more than eight pages will be needed to record the complete state of a large display that has graphics and text modes. Suppose we allocate all those many megabytes of memory each time we create a new VM. Since allocating the memory requires Windows 95 to commit space in the swap file, the swap file will grow without apparent bound. So will the amount of virtual address space dedicated to private display memory buffers. Wouldn't it be silly to do this if all the user plans to do is type one little *ver* command in a 25-line text window? (Answer: Yes; besides, you don't get any useful information from *ver* anyway.)

At least in the case of memory mapped into the V86 region of the virtual address space, it's possible to arrange to have the VM announce its need for various portions of the device's mapped memory by means of page faults. The standard way to prepare for demand allocation of V86 memory is to call *Hook_V86_Page* in order to establish a page-fault callback for the device address range. Unfortunately, the technique I'm about to describe doesn't work for devices whose mapped memory is outside the V86 region of memory, because there are no VxD services to let you manage the page tables that map these addresses. If you're virtualizing such a device, you'll just have to preallocate the buffer in which you plan to save the device state.

Continuing the previous example, your Device_Init handler might hook the VGA text buffer like this:

```
BOOL OnDeviceInit(PVMMCB hVM, DWORD refdata)
    {                               // OnDeviceInit
    DWORD page;

    if (!_Assign_Device_V86_Pages(0xB8, 8, NULL, 0))
        return FALSE;               // can't globally assign pages

    cboffset = _Allocate_Device_CB_Area(sizeof(MYSTUFF), 0);
    if (!cboffset)
        return FALSE;

    for (page = 0xB8; page < 0xC0; ++page)
        if (!Hook_V86_Page(page, OnPageFault))
            {                           // couldn't hook page
            while (--page >= 0xB8)
                Unhook_V86_Page(page, OnPageFault);
            return FALSE;               // couldn't hook page
            }

    return OnVMCriticalInit();
    }                               // OnDeviceInit
```

You no longer need to allocate a buffer during Create_VM, but you need to handle the VM_Critical_Init message to prepare the mapped pages to actually generate page faults:

```
BOOL OnVMCriticalInit(PVMMCB hVM)
    {                               // OnVMCriticalInit
    return _ModifyPageBits((HVM) hVM, 0xB8, 8, ~P_PRES, 0,
        PG_HOOKED, 0);
    }                               // OnVMCriticalInit
```

The _ModifyPageBits function has the following prototype:

```
BOOL _ModifyPageBits(HVM hVM, DWORD VMLinPgNum,
    int nPages, const int bitAND,
    const int bitOR, DWORD pType, DWORD flags);
```

The function modifies the *nPages* page table entries for the *hVM* virtual machine beginning at page number *VMLinPgNum* by first ANDing the *bitAnd* mask and then ORing the *bitOr* mask. We're using the function here to reset the "present" bit in the video RAM pages so that the next reference to any virtual address in the range B8000h through BFFFFh will cause a page fault. We already established our *OnPageFault* function as a page-fault callback routine when we "hooked" the B8h through BFh pages.

There is a reason why I placed the call to *_ModifyPageBits* within the handler for the VM_Critical_Init system control message. Recall that creating a new VM causes three system control messages to be sent to each VxD: Create_VM, VM_Critical_Init, and VM_Init. The Create_VM message occurs in the context of whichever VM happens to be current at the time the new VM is created; usually, it's the System VM that's current because the signal to create a new VM usually comes from a function like *WinExec*. VM_Init occurs in the context of the new VM, and any VxD is free to use *Resume_Exec* to run V86-mode code in the VM. In general, we want our device set up in the context of the new VM but before any V86-mode code has a chance to try to reference our device. That's what the VM_Critical_Init message is for: it occurs in the context of the new VM, but no VxD can execute V86-mode code until after all VxDs have processed it.

Eventually, some V86 program running in the new VM will try to use our device by touching the memory at B8000h through BFFFFh. Because we marked all the pages in this range "not present," a page fault will occur. Control will come to the page-fault callback routine we established via *Hook_V86_Page*:

```
void __declspec(naked) OnPageFault()
    {                                // OnPageFault
    _asm
        {                            // handle page fault
        push    ebx             ; current VM handle
        push    eax             ; page number that caused the fault
        call    HandlePageFault ; call real handler
        add     esp, 8          ; lose args
        ret                     ; return to caller
        }                            // handle page fault
    }                                // OnPageFault

void HandlePageFault(DWORD page, PVMMCB hVM)
    {                                // HandlePageFault
    PBYTE pVidBuff = (PBYTE) _PageAllocate(8, PG_HOOKED,
        (HVM) hVM, 0, 0, 0, 0, PAGEZEROINIT);
    if (pVidBuff)
        {                            // map private buffer
        GetStuff(hVM)->pVidBuff = pVidBuff;
        _MapIntoV86(pVidBuff, (HVM) hVM, 0xB8, 8, 0, 0);
        }                            // map private buffer
    else
        Nuke_VM(hVM);
    }                                // HandlePageFault
```

The page fault handler needs to be written in assembly language because its arguments arrive in registers from which they can't reliably be extracted in the body of a standard C function. I used the *__declspec(naked)* directive to force the compiler to leave out all prolog and epilog code so I could just write a small inline assembler wrapper for the *HandlePageFault* C function. The latter routine does all the work. It first tries to allocate an 8-page buffer. If the allocation succeeds, it calls *_MapIntoV86* to install the allocated buffer into the VM's page tables. The allocation might fail, of course. In real life, we would then present a blue-screen message explaining why it was necessary to crash the VM before calling *Nuke_VM* to terminate the VM.

The dynamic allocation example I just described needs some additional logic to make it useful for a real video display device. I'll explain what's required and leave the details as an exercise for the reader. Notice that I waited for a page fault and then installed a private buffer address into the VM's page table entries for B8000h, and so on. This is correct for a display driver only if the VM happens to be running in a window. If the VM were running full-screen, the driver would need to work a little differently. You would still trap page faults. But instead of allocating a private buffer and plugging the buffer pages into the VM page table at the time of the page fault, you'd set a flag indicating that the VM accessed the text-mode memory. Then you'd call *_PhysIntoV86* to turn the VM loose on the real hardware. If the VM loses focus later on, your Set_Device_Focus handler would see that the flag was set and allocate the buffer in order to save the VM's state. Conversely, when switching focus to a VM that's never had a buffer allocated for it, you'd notice that the flag *wasn't* set. The absence of the flag would indicate that there's no saved state to be restored, so you'd initialize the video hardware directly instead.

Virtualizing I/O Ports

Virtualizing I/O ports relies on the *I/O permission mask* feature of Intel processors. The one and only task state segment (TSS) used by Windows 95 contains a variable-length permission mask in which each bit corresponds to an 8-bit I/O port. Two adjacent bits control a 16-bit port, and four adjacent bits control a 32-bit port. Before allowing V86 or protected-mode programs running in ring three to access a port, the processor inspects the bit(s) corresponding to the port. If all the bits are 0, the processor allows the operation to proceed. If any bit is 1, the processor generates a general protection fault to allow the VMM to intervene. Ring-zero programs have unfettered access to all I/O ports, however.

More About the I/O Permission Mask The Intel processor always checks the I/O permission mask before allowing access to an I/O port if the processor is running in V86 mode. If the processor is in protected mode, however, the access control mechanism is more complicated. The Flags register contains two bits called the *I/O privilege level* (IOPL). Recall that the current code selector determines the *current privilege level* (CPL), which is the privilege ring of the current program. If the CPL is less than or equal to the IOPL, I/O is allowed to proceed unchecked. Conversely, if the CPL is greater than the IOPL, the processor investigates the permission mask. You already know that the VMM and other VxDs run in protected mode at ring zero (CPL == 0), so these rules imply that any VxD can access any port. You also already know that Windows applications also run in protected mode, but at ring three (CPL == 3). You need to know that the VMM forces the IOPL to 0 while running protected-mode applications. Therefore, application access to ports is subject to the permission mask. (The IOPL is usually 3 while running V86 programs, for reasons explained in Chapter 5, but the IOPL doesn't have anything to do with I/O in V86 mode in the first place.)

The VMM initializes the I/O permission mask to 0. By default, therefore, any given I/O port is available for use by any program at all. I guess that means that I can start serial communication programs in two different MS-DOS boxes and have them both access the COM1 ports at 3F8h through 3FFh, thereby intermixing data and totally confusing the universal asynchronous receiver-transmitter (UART) about communication settings, eh? (Answer: Yes, except that the I/O permission mask doesn't get left in its default state, so someone will trap these accesses.)

Trapping I/O Ports

To prevent unfortunate collisions between VMs that both want to access the same unshareable ports, you must *trap* your ports by calling *Install_IO_Handler* to register an I/O callback routine with the VMM. The VMM will call your routine whenever ring-three code tries to access a port. The callback routine will then do any of several things:

- Perform the I/O operation on behalf of the program. This means issuing IN or OUT instructions directly to the hardware. Since the callback routine is part of a ring-zero VxD, these instructions aren't subject to permission mask checking.

■ Simulate the I/O operation. One situation for which you'd simulate an operation is when you have a device that can't tolerate a high *latency period* between when it interrupts and when the driver reacts. Reacting to an interrupt entirely in ring zero is much faster than switching to ring three first. Another reason to simulate an operation is to create a fictitious piece of hardware. Still a third reason is to allow a program to run while some other program owns and interacts with the real hardware; virtualizing the video display, for example, allows you to have an MS-DOS session running within a graphical window.

■ Discover that two different VMs are trying to access the same hardware. In this case, your VxD will probably alert the user to the contention and terminate one or the other of the contending VMs.

■ Disable the port trap whenever the same VM is running. Disabling the trap for one VM effectively gives that VM ownership of the port and improves performance by avoiding subsequent calls to your callback routine.

As I'll explain, it's much easier to write I/O callback routines in assembly language than in C, so the examples in this section will be in assembler. A VxD establishes a port trap during initialization and cancels it during termination. A Plug and Play driver would perform these operations in its configuration function in response to CONFIG_START and CONFIG_STOP (and/or CONFIG_REMOVE) requests, respectively. A dynamically loaded VxD that isn't part of Plug and Play would perform them during Sys_Dynamic_Device_Init and Sys_Dynamic_Device_Exit. A static VxD would probably establish port traps during Device_Init and simply not cancel the traps. In fact, Windows 3.x (which supported only static VxDs) didn't provide any way to remove an I/O trap and required traps to be installed no later than Init_Complete.

You establish a port trap by calling *Install_IO_Handler*:

```
mov      esi, offset32 IoCallback  ; I/O callback routine
mov      edx, port                 ; port number
VMMCall  Install_IO_Handler
jc       error
```

IoCallback is the name of your I/O callback routine, and *port* is the number of the port you want to trap. As usual, a return with the carry flag set indicates an error (which usually means that some other VxD is already trapping the port), while a return with the carry flag clear indicates success. Since you often need to trap more than one port, there's also an *Install_Mult_IO_Handlers* service that installs multiple traps. For example:

```
mov      edi, offset32 iotable      ; I/O table address
VMMCall  Install_Mult_IO_Handlers
jc       error
...
Begin_VxD_IO_Table iotable
         3F8h, TrapXmitHoldingReg
         3F9h, TrapInterruptEnableReg
         [etc.]
End_VxD_IO_Table iotable
```

If this function fails, the EDX register will hold the address of the port on which the failure occurred; cleanup requires you to remove traps for ports earlier in the table than the one in EDX.

Cancelling the traps later uses analogous *Remove_* services:

```
mov      edx, port           ; port address
VMMCall  Remove_IO_Handler
```

or

```
mov      edi, offset32 iotable    ; same one we installed with
VMMCall  Remove_Mult_IO_Handlers
```

The I/O Callback Routine

When a V86 or ring-three program tries to access a trapped port, either for reading or for writing, the VMM passes control to the I/O callback routine you designated for the port. The purpose of your callback is to perform or simulate the instruction that caused the trap. Table 13-3 lists the register parameters to the callback routine. If you're performing a single input-type operation to read 8, 16, or 32 bytes, you'll return the input data in register EAX; in other cases, the return value doesn't matter. If you're performing a single output type operation to write 8, 16, or 32 bytes, the data you're supposed to output comes to you in the EAX register. Part of the reason you want to program in assembly language is that so many parameters come to you in registers, but there's a more important reason I'll get to in a moment.

Register	Contents
EAX	Output data for output operations, undefined for input operations
EBX	Current VM handle (VMCB address)
ECX	Flags denoting type of I/O operation; one of the following:

Flag	Description
BYTE_INPUT	Single-byte input operation
BYTE_OUTPUT	Single-byte output operation
DWORD_INPUT	Double-word input operation
DWORD_OUTPUT	Double-word output operation
WORD_INPUT	Word input operation
WORD_OUTPUT	Word output operation

plus zero or more of the following:

Flag	Description
ADDR_32_IO	INS or OUTS operation is using 32-bit addressing
REP_IO	INS or OUTS operation has a repeat prefix
REVERSE_IO	INS or OUTS operation has the direction flag set (that is, decrement address)
STRING_IO	Operation is an INS or OUTS operation (and HIWORD(ECX) will hold the selector of the data buffer)

Register	Contents
EDX	I/O port address
EBP	Client registers for current VM

Table 13-3. *Register parameters to an I/O callback routine.*

The flag bits in the ECX register tell you what kind of I/O operation the ring-three program is trying to perform. There are 54 different possibilities in all. The program may have used an INS or OUTS instruction to perform a string I/O operation, in which case there are eight different combinations of the *ADDR_32_IO*, *REP_IO*, and *REVERSE_IO* flags. (These three flag bits make sense only if *STRING_IO* is set.) A ninth possibility (which is actually the most likely one) is that the program is trying to do a single IN or OUT operation. Multiply these nine possibilities by three sizes (8, 16, or 32 bytes) and two directions (input or output) to obtain 54.

The prospect of coding a 54-way switch to handle all the possibilities in an I/O callback routine is pretty daunting. Luckily, the VMM provides some additional service API functions that make the job easier. First of all, there's a service named *Simulate_IO* that you can call to handle all the cases more complicated than single-byte IN or OUT operations. *Simulate_IO* expects exactly the same register contents as an I/O callback. It decodes the ECX flag bits and calls your I/O callback recursively to do a series of *BYTE_INPUT* or *BYTE_OUTPUT* operations in order to emulate the more complicated operations. You don't usually *call Simulate_IO*, by the way: you usually use the VMMJmp macro to jump to it instead; that way, it returns directly to your caller. In addition, there's a macro named Dispatch_Byte_IO that checks the ECX register to see if you're facing one of the complicated cases. If so, the macro jumps to *Simulate_IO*. If you're confronted with *BYTE_INPUT* or *BYTE_OUTPUT* operations, however, the macro jumps to a label in your own program to let you carry out the operation.

Using the Dispatch_Byte_IO macro simplifies the coding job to something like the following skeleton:

```
BeginProc IOCallback, locked
        Dispatch_Byte_IO Fall_Through, byteout
        in      al, dx
        ret
byteout: out    dx, al
        ret
EndProc  IOCallback
```

I used a shortcut here by coding *Fall_Through* in place of the byte input routine label. Using this keyword in place of either or both of the labels suppresses explicit JMP instructions, which improves performance. I also wrote simple routines for handling the two cases that Dispatch_Byte_IO doesn't hand off to *Simulate_IO*. Notice that the VMM already set up the DX register with the port address (what a coincidence, given that IN and OUT require DX to contain the address!), so you can just issue an IN or OUT instruction and return. The efficiency of this code is another reason why it's better to write I/O callbacks in assembler.

The most important reason to write an I/O callback in assembler instead of C has to do with the jump to *Simulate_IO*. As I mentioned, *Simulate_IO* wants the same register parameters as an I/O callback routine, and this includes the EBP register. All C compilers I know about use the EBP register to point to the stack frame for the current procedure, and they access arguments and automatic variables via EBP. Accurate coding is therefore required to reach *Simulate_IO* from a C-language callback routine. If you're determined to code in C, the following fragment (taken from a driver I built with VTOOLSD) may be helpful:

```
DWORD __stdcall IOCallback(VMHANDLE hVM, DWORD IOType,
    DWORD Port, PCLIENT_STRUCT pRegs, DWORD Data)
    {                                   // IOCallback
    if (IOType == BYTE_INPUT)
        {                               // read character
        char ch;
        [read input somehow into "ch"]
        return ch;
        }                               // read character
    else if (IOType == BYTE_OUTPUT)
        {                               // write character
        [output LOBYTE(Data) somehow]
        return 0;
        }                               // write character

    _asm mov eax, Data
    _asm mov ebx, hVM
    _asm mov ecx, IOType
    _asm mov edx, Port
    _asm push ebp
    _asm mov ebp, pRegs

    VxDCall(Simulate_IO);

    _asm pop ebp
    }                                   // IOCallback
```

Notice that you reload the EBP register just before calling *Simulate_IO* because you won't have access to arguments after reloading it. In addition, you *call* *Simulate_IO* instead of jumping to it because its eventual RET instruction would cause havoc if executed on the same stack you received. Finally, you take care to save and restore the EBP register so that your function epilog will work correctly (the epilog will include a LEAVE or a MOV ESP, EBP instruction).

Simulating a Device

Occasionally you want to simulate a device in your I/O callback routine instead of simply executing IN and OUT instructions on behalf of the application. The usual reason for simulating a device is performance. There are devices that can easily generate interrupts much faster than Windows 95 can tolerate without data loss if it has to switch back to ring three to service the interrupt. The standard serial port is an example of such a device. When it is receiving data at a modest (by today's standards, anyway) rate of 9600 baud, the port will generate an interrupt every 950 microseconds or so. Software must read data from the chip before the next interrupt or else risk losing data, but Windows 95 can't handle the interrupt and return to ring three to do the input operation without either falling behind or neglecting other tasks.

The Windows 95 virtual communications device (VCD) driver solves the latency problem for serial ports by handling interrupts entirely within ring zero and by simulating serial port I/O done by applications. (The VCD subsumes the job done in earlier versions of Windows by two VxDs named VCD and COMBUFF.) When a data byte arrives, the VCD immediately reads the byte into its own buffer, thereby releasing the serial chip for the next byte. Ring-three code asks in its own good time for the next byte by executing an IN instruction. The VCD traps the instruction and returns the next byte from its internal buffer. The VCD buffers output data in a similar way.

Another reason to simulate an I/O port is to create fictitious hardware. Vendors of new kinds of communications boards might, for example, use a VxD to translate I/O directed to a standard 8250-class serial chip into requests to their own hardware. In effect, simulation amounts in this case to treating the serial port interface as an API that you implement in a nontraditional way.

Here's an example of a VxD that simulates a hardware device by trapping a port. (The expanded version of this code, presented in the next section, is included on the companion disk in the \CHAP13\PORTVIRTUALIZATION directory.) The simulated device has one read-only port at address 1234h. Reading this port delivers successive characters of the string "Hello, world!":

```
        name   myvxd
        .386p
        include vmm.inc
        include debug.inc

Declare_Virtual_Device MYVXD, 1, 0, MYVXD_control, \
        Undefined_Device_ID, Undefined_Init_Order

Begin_Control_Dispatch MYVXD
Control_Dispatch Sys_Dynamic_Device_Init, \
    OnSysDynamicDeviceInit
Control_Dispatch Sys_Dynamic_Device_Exit, \
    OnSysDynamicDeviceExit
End_Control_Dispatch   MYVXD

VxD_LOCKED_DATA_SEG
data       db     'Hello, world!', 0
pdata      dd     offset32 data
VxD_LOCKED_DATA_ENDS
```

```
BeginProc OnSysDynamicDeviceInit, locked
        mov    esi, offset32 IOCallback
        mov    edx, 1234h
        VMMCall Install_IO_Handler
        ret
EndProc OnSysDynamicDeviceInit

BeginProc OnSysDynamicDeviceExit, locked
        mov    edx, 1234h
        VMMCall Remove_IO_Handler
        ret
EndProc OnSysDynamicDeviceExit

BeginProc IOCallback, locked
        Dispatch_Byte_IO Fall_Through, byteout
bytein:
        mov    esi, pdata
        xor    eax, eax
        lodsb
        test   al, al
        jnz    @F
        mov    esi, offset32 data
@@:
        mov    pdata, esi
byteout:
        ret
EndProc  IOCallback

        end
```

Here's a short test program that you can use to verify that this sample VxD does what it's supposed to:

```
D:\CHAP13\PortVirtualization>debug testport.com
File not found

-a 100
30CD:0100 mov di,200
30CD:0103 mov dx,1234
30CD:0106 in al,dx
30CD:0107 test al,al
30CD:0109 jz 10e
30CD:010B stosb
30CD:010C jmp 106
30CD:010E mov byte ptr [di], 0d
30CD:0111 mov byte ptr [di+1], 0a
30CD:0115 mov byte ptr [di+2], 24
30CD:0119 mov dx,0200
```

```
30CD:011C mov ah,9
30CD:011E int 21
30CD:0120 mov ax,4c00
30CD:0123 int 21
30CD:0125
-g
Hello, world!
```

The test program executes the IN instruction at location 106h until it reads a null byte. Then the program uses INT 21h, function 09h, to output the string to the console and terminates.

Now let's trace through the way TESTPORT works with the VxD in place trapping port 1234h. Each time TESTPORT tries to execute the IN instruction at location 106h, the processor consults the I/O privilege mask and determines that port 1234h is trapped. A general protection fault therefore ensues that causes control to pass eventually to MYVXD's *IOCallback* routine. The flag bits in the ECX register will equal *BYTE_INPUT* because the trapped instruction is just a simple IN to the AL register. The EDX register will equal 1234h. The other registers don't matter. The Dispatch_Byte_IO macro will check register ECX and end up falling through to the simulation code for byte input. (None of the other cases that Dispatch_Byte_IO is prepared for will ever happen with the TESTPORT test program.) To simulate the operation, the callback routine loads a static pointer (*pdata*) to the next input byte into the ESI register. Then it uses the LODSB instruction to simultaneously load the next byte and advance the pointer. If the input byte is 0, we've reached the end of the string and want to reset the data pointer back to the start. That way, the next time we call TESTPORT, it will retrieve the complete string all over again. Finally, the callback routine returns with the new input byte in the AL register. The VMM will take care of putting this data byte into the client AL register before returning to the VM.

Handling Contention

Ordinarily, only one virtual machine at a time should be accessing a given I/O port. Providing *contention resolution* is another function of the I/O callback routine for a trapped port. Resolving contention requires you to keep track of the virtual machine that currently "owns" the device. You must allow only the current owner to use the device. If some other VM tries to access the device, you have to tell the end user about the problem and allow him or her to decide what to do. The *SHELL_Resolve_Contention* service is tailor-made for interacting with the user. After asking the user to make a decision, you may need to do something draconian like terminate one of the VMs in order to halt an otherwise never-ending stream of requests for I/O service.

Here's an expanded version of the earlier I/O callback routine that deals with the contention issue:

```
BeginProc IOCallback, locked
        cmp    ebx, owner
        je     okayio
        cmp    owner, 0
        jne    contend
        mov    owner, ebx
        jmp    okayio

contend:
        push   eax
        mov    eax, owner
        mov    esi, offset32 MYVXD_DDB + DDB_Name
        VxDCall SHELL_Resolve_Contention
        pop    eax

        jc     cantresolve
        cmp    ebx, owner
        je     cantresolve
        mov    owner, ebx

okayio:
        Dispatch_Byte_IO Fall_Through, byteout

bytein:
        mov    esi, pdata
        xor    eax, eax
        lodsb
        test   al, al
        jnz    @F
        mov    esi, offset32 data
@@:
        mov    pdata, esi

byteout:
        ret

cantresolve:
        VMMCall Crash_Cur_VM
        ret
EndProc  IOCallback
```

Figure 13-6 on the following page illustrates the logic behind the contention resolution. The basic idea is to check whether the current VM (whose handle arrives as an argument to the I/O callback routine in the EBX register) is the owner or if there isn't an owner. In either case, it will be okay to proceed. If some other VM owns the device, we call *SHELL_Resolve_Contention* to let the user sort out the confusion. On return, the carry flag will indicate whether resolution was possible and, if it was possible, the EBX register will hold the handle of the VM that won the contention. If the original owner won, we have to do something to stop the current VM from continuing to try to access the port. For this example, I chose to just crash the VM. No message tells the user what happened, however, so you'd want to do something a little friendlier in a real driver. For example, you might call *SHELL_Message* to display an explanatory message.

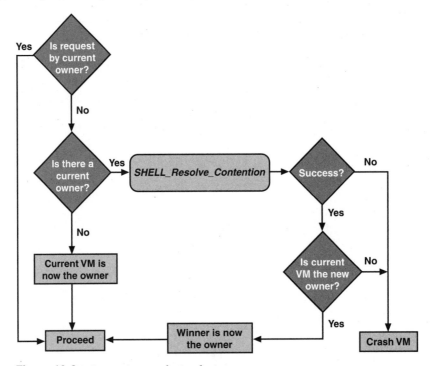

Figure 13-6. *Contention resolution logic.*

To test the contention resolution, you can run TESTPORT from two different MS-DOS prompts in succession. The test will work normally in the first MS-DOS box. Figure 13-7 shows the dialog box that *SHELL_Resolve_Contention* displays when you try the experiment in the second MS-DOS box. Can you tell which MS-DOS Prompt option you should pick to terminate one VM or the other? (Answer: The top one is the current owner.) The reason the message is so uninformative is that SHELL is just using the virtual machine title string associated with the VM. It would be better if SHELL would also include the application title string so that the message would at

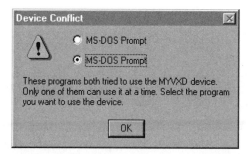

Figure 13-7. *Contention resolution dialog box.*

least match the title bar of the window. Windows 95 provides an INT 2Fh interface for MS-DOS applications to use to change the VM title (see Article 27 in the *Programmer's Guide to Microsoft Windows 95* [Microsoft Corporation, 1995]), but my experience leads me to believe that the interface isn't very reliable. Consequently, *SHELL_Resolve_Contention* is useful only if the contending VMs have different titles resulting from different PIF file settings—er, Object Properties.

Enabling and Disabling Trapping

One more refinement to I/O port virtualization concerns the *trap state*. A trap state is either on or off. The VMM maintains a *trap state* for each port and VM. You can alter the trap state for a given port in a single VM by calling *Enable_Local_Trapping* or *Disable_Local_Trapping*. You can alter the trap state in *every* VM by calling *Enable_Global_Trapping* or *Disable_Global_Trapping*. The state you establish by calling one of the global trapping calls is also the initial state for every VM that subsequently gets created.

You might wonder why you would want to control the trap state at all. The answer is that a ring-three driver will run much faster if its IN and OUT instructions go directly to the hardware instead of being trapped by a VxD. In many cases, therefore, a driver will disable local trapping for its own ports in the VM it considers to be the owner of the device. By leaving local trapping enabled in other VMs, the driver ensures that it will recognize contention for the device.

Virtualizing Hardware Interrupts

The Virtual Programmable Interrupt Controller Device (VPICD) handles all hardware interrupts in Windows 95. Instead of directly hooking an interrupt vector to take over a device interrupt, a VxD instead "virtualizes the IRQ" by calling a VPICD service. Table 13-4 on the following page lists all of the VPICD services that are involved in hardware interrupt handling. But before delving into those services in detail, you need to first understand the process the VPICD normally follows when it receives a hardware interrupt. You also need to keep in mind the VM-centric view of the world that the VPICD has even in Windows 95. That is, the VPICD's main job is to route hardware interrupts to device drivers located in VMs and allow *them* to work pretty much as they would have without Windows being in the picture. The VPICD also virtualizes the interrupt controller on behalf of virtual machine drivers, allowing drivers to virtually mask and unmask interrupt requests, interrogate a virtual in-service register, and so on.

Service	*Description*
VPICD_Auto_Mask_At_Inst_Swap	Causes an IRQ to be masked during an instance data swap.
VPICD_Begin_Inst_Page_Swap	Notifies the VPICD that an instance data swap is commencing (internal use only).
VPICD_Call_When_Hw_Int	Installs a callback to be called on every hardware interrupt.
VPICD_Clear_Int_Request	Clears a virtual interrupt request for a VM.
VPICD_Convert_Handle_To_IRQ	Retrieves the IRQ number for a virtualized IRQ.
VPICD_Convert_Int_To_IRQ	Determines which IRQ corresponds to a given interrupt number in a given VM.
VPICD_Convert_IRQ_To_Int	Determines which interrupt number corresponds to a given IRQ in a given VM.
VPICD_End_Inst_Page_Swap	Notifies the VPICD that an instance data swap is finished (internal use only).
VPICD_Force_Default_Behavior	Unvirtualizes an IRQ.
VPICD_Force_Default_Owner	Sets global/local status, ownership, and certain default handling options for an IRQ identified by IRQ number.
VPICD_Get_Complete_Status	Retrieves the complete status of a virtualized IRQ.
VPICD_Get_IRQ_Complete_Status	Retrieves the complete status of an IRQ given its number.
VPICD_Get_Status	Retrieves the commonly used subset of the complete status for a virtualized IRQ.
VPICD_Get_Version	Retrieves the VPICD version number, PIC configuration, and maximum supported IRQ.

Table 13-4. *VPICD services.*   *(continued)*

continued

Service	Description
VPICD_Get_Virtualization_Count	Retrieves the number of times an IRQ identified by number has been virtualized.
VPICD_Phys_EOI	Indicates completion of processing for an interrupt (actually unmasks the IRQ instead of sending an EOI command).
VPICD_Physically_Mask	Masks a virtualized IRQ.
VPICD_Physically_Unmask	Unmasks a virtualized IRQ.
VPICD_Set_Auto_Masking	Enables automatic masking of a virtualized IRQ. When automatic masking is enabled, the physical IRQ is unmasked if and only if some VM has it unmasked.
VPICD_Set_Int_Request	Sets a virtual interrupt request (simulates an interrupt) for a virtualized IRQ in a specified VM.
VPICD_Test_Phys_Request	Tests the physical in-service register for a virtualized IRQ.
VPICD_Virtual_EOI	Performs a virtual EOI command for a virtualized IRQ in a specified VM.
VPICD_Virtualize_IRQ	Establishes nondefault handlers for an IRQ.
VPICD_VM_SlavePIC_Mask_Change	An internal service used when a VM masks or unmasks IRQ 2. Use *Hook_Device_Service* if you want to know when this happens.

Default IRQ Handling

Figure 13-8 on the following page diagrams the overall process of handling a hardware interrupt in the default case. Hardware interrupts vector through the IDT entries for interrupts 50h through 5Fh. These interrupt numbers differ from the standard real-mode vector assignments because the VPICD alters the master and slave PIC base vectors to 50h and 58h, respectively. Changing the base vectors makes it much easier and faster for the VPICD to tell the difference between a hardware interrupt and a software interrupt or processor exception that coincidentally uses the same real-mode vector number. For example, it would otherwise be hard to tell the difference between a page fault (exception 0Eh) and IRQ 6. INT 56h, on the other hand, is unambiguously devoted to IRQ 6.

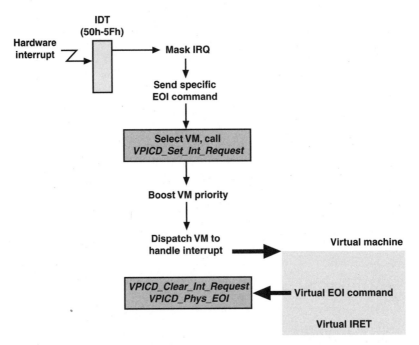

Figure 13-8. *Default process for handling a hardware interrupt.*

A Note on INT 50h Through 5Fh The Descriptor Privilege Level (DPL) in the IDT gate entries for interrupts 50h through 5Fh is 0. If a ring-three program issues an INT instruction for one of these interrupts, a general protection fault occurs instead. The VMM investigates and discovers that the program is trying to execute an INT instruction, and it routes control to the software interrupt handler for that interrupt. Since no ring-zero program should ever be using one of these interrupts in an INT instruction, the VPICD can simply assume that such a situation connotes a hardware interrupt. I used this fact in one of the sample programs for this chapter, in fact, by using an INT 5Ch in a VxD to simulate an IRQ 12 for testing a driver's virtualization of IRQ 12. You should never fake hardware interrupts in a released product, because future versions of Windows might not always handle hardware interrupts in exactly the same way as Windows 95 does.

The VPICD contains the second-level interrupt handler for each hardware interrupt. Each handler masks its IRQ off by writing to the PIC's IMR, and it then issues a specific EOI command to clear the interrupt. From the discussion earlier in the chapter, you know that these two steps allow lower priority or higher priority interrupts to occur but prevent a recursive interrupt on the same IRQ. By actual count, the VPICD's first-level and second-level interrupt handlers, together with common state-saving code in the core of the VMM, execute either 24 or 31 instructions before reaching the point of doing the EOI, depending on whether the interrupt came from V86 or protected mode, respectively. On an i486 processor, the instructions consume between 100 and 150 clock cycles.

The VPICD next selects some VM or other to handle the interrupt. The VM selected depends on whether the IRQ is considered *global* or *owned*. A global IRQ is one that was unmasked (that is, for which the IMR contained a 0-bit) when Windows 95 started up. The real-mode ISR for the IRQ in question was already in place when Windows 95 started and occupies global V86 memory. In other words, the ISR exists in every VM, and it therefore doesn't really matter which VM handles the interrupt. Accordingly, the VPICD normally selects the current VM to perform the office of servicing a global IRQ. If, however, some other VM happens to have claimed the critical section, the VPICD gives the interrupt to the critical section owner instead.

A local IRQ is one that first becomes unmasked after Windows 95 starts. Code running in some VM or other will have written to the IMR in either the master PIC or the slave PIC. The VPICD traps these writes so that it knows when VM code is trying to manipulate the PIC, and it makes the newly unmasked IRQ local to the VM that unmasked it. By default, the VPICD also sends interrupts on a local IRQ to the owning VM.

You can change the classification of an IRQ from global to local, or vice versa, by calling *VPICD_Force_Default_Owner*. A parameter to that service also allows you to direct the VPICD to choose the execution-focus VM instead of the current VM for handling a global IRQ if no VM owns the critical section. As an example, a client of mine needed to be sure that an interrupt always got serviced in the System VM because their code relied on a DPMI real-mode callback to get to a Windows application. Since the IRQ in question was unmasked when Windows 95 started, the VPICD's default handling was to treat the IRQ as global and route it to the current VM. A simple VxD that called *VPICD_Force_Default_Owner* with the System VM handle solved that particular problem. A converse problem can arise if the BIOS fails to unmask the floppy disk IRQ (as some do), so the Virtual Floppy Driver uses this service to force the floppy disk IRQ to be global.

Having chosen a VM to service the interrupt, the VPICD uses one of its own services—*VPICD_Set_Int_Request*—to mark the VM as having a pending interrupt on the IRQ. The interrupt will be simulated into the VM (using the normal real-mode vector numbers, by the way) either immediately or at some later point when all of the following conditions are true:

■   The VM must be enabled for interrupts. The VMM traps CLI and STI instructions coming from ring-three protected-mode programs and re-cords a virtual enable state that doesn't have any correlation with the state of the real machine's interrupt flag. Since V86 code normally runs with the IOPL equal to 3, a CLI instruction from V86 mode normally disables the real machine, but there are situations in which a V86 program might be only virtually disabled. In any case, it's the virtual interrupt state that's important for hardware interrupt simulation.

■   The VM must not have masked the IRQ by writing a 1-bit to its virtual IMR. The VPICD traps the PIC control ports and maintains virtual mask and in-service registers for each VM. While a particular IRQ is being serviced by the VPICD, it will be physically masked. It's the virtual mask state that determines whether the interrupt can be simulated in a VM, however.

■   No higher priority IRQ can be in service within the VM. This mimics the way the real machine works.

■   The VM must be ready to run, which means that it's not suspended and not blocked in such a way that interrupts are disallowed. Recall that synchronization primitives like Begin_Critical_Section, Wait_Semaphore, and the like, have a flag argument that allows a VM to field interrupts even while blocked.

■   The interrupt must not have been cancelled by some VxD calling *VPICD_Clear_Int_Request*.

The virtual machine ISR eventually gains control as a result of the call to *VPICD_Set_Int_Request*. Typically, the ISR will attempt to send an EOI command to the PIC at some point, and it will eventually execute an IRET instruction to return to the point of interrupt. The VPICD intervenes at the point of the EOI command by virtue of having trapped the PIC control ports. When the virtual EOI command occurs, the VPICD calls more of its own services: *VPICD_Clear_Int_Request* and the misleadingly named *VPICD_Phys_EOI*. *VPICD_Clear_Int_Request* clears the virtual interrupt request from the VM. Clearing the request is required because the VPICD simulates a *level-triggered* PIC, which will keep interrupting as long as the interrupt request remains asserted. Since the real physical EOI command occurred shortly after the interrupt, *VPICD_Phys_EOI* doesn't issue an EOI command at all. Instead, it unmasks the physical IRQ. (The *VPICD_Physically_Unmask* service also physically unmasks an IRQ. These two services differ in how they maintain internal data structures, so one is not a substitute for the other.)

The VPICD also intervenes at the point of the IRET from the ring-three ISR. Trapping the IRET allows the VPICD to undo the priority boost described in the next paragraph. Furthermore, the VPICD allows the same VM to handle any interrupt on the same IRQ that occurs before the IRET. (Doing otherwise might result in incorrect handling of cascading interrupts.) Trapping the IRET causes the VPICD to clear its memory of which VM is currently handling the interrupt so that the regular VM selection rules will apply to the next interrupt on the same IRQ.

It's usually a good idea to service hardware interrupts as quickly as possible, so the VPICD boosts the priority of the VM that will handle an interrupt by the very large amount TIME_CRITICAL_BOOST. This boost value is larger than any priority boost commonly used elsewhere in the system, so a VM whose priority has been boosted by this amount is pretty much guaranteed to run next (unless there are several VMs all handling different interrupts, in which case the scheduler will be called on to share the processor among them all). The boost lasts until the virtual ISR returns or until 500 milliseconds elapse, whichever comes first.

Virtualizing an IRQ

If you want to override the default handling of an IRQ, you use *VPICD_Virtualize_IRQ* to supply a table of pointers to functions that allow you to intervene at defined points. The calling sequence to this service is as follows:

```
include vpicd.inc
...
mov      edi, offset32, vid    ; virtual irq descriptor
VxDCall  VPICD_Virtualize_IRQ
jc       error                 ; jump if error
mov      hIrq, eax             ; handle of virtualized IRQ
```

Figure 13-9 on the following page shows the format of the *Virtual IRQ Descriptor* (VID) structure that describes the virtualization of the IRQ. The *VID_IRQ_Number* and *VID_Hw_Int_Proc* fields are required; the remaining fields are optional and should be set to 0 if not used. I'll discuss the meaning of the various flag bits in the VID structure later. The return value from *VPICD_Virtualize_IRQ* is an *IRQ handle* that you should save in a global variable for later use. The handle is a parameter to many VPICD services, most notably *VPICD_Force_Default_Behavior*, which is the service you use to "unvirtualize" an IRQ as part of your driver's cleanup.

The VPICD will call your virtualization functions at the points indicated in Figure 13-10 on page 421. If you don't override one or more of the *Virt_Int_Proc*, *EOI_Proc*, and *IRET_Proc* procedures by supplying a nonzero pointer, the VPICD doesn't do anything when the corresponding events occur. When you're virtualizing an IRQ to allow it to be serviced in a VM, you would therefore usually supply both a *Hw_Int_Proc* procedure and an *EOI_Proc* procedure. (As we'll see in the last section of the chapter, when you're virtualizing an IRQ to provide ring-zero handling of an interrupt, you would only need the *Hw_Int_Proc* procedure because you won't be reflecting the interrupt to a VM.)

```
VPICD_IRQ_Descriptor STRUC
    VID_IRQ_Number         dw   ?     ; 00 number of IRQ (0-15) (required)
    VID_Options            dw   0     ; 02 option flags (listed below)
    VID_Hw_Int_Proc        dd   ?     ; 04 address of hardware interrupt
                                      ; procedure (required)
    VID_Virt_Int_Proc      dd   0     ; 08 virtual interrupt procedure
                                      ; (optional)
    VID_EOI_Proc           dd   0     ; 0C EOI procedure (optional)
    VID_Mask_Change_Proc   dd   0     ; 10 mask-change procedure (optional)
    VID_IRET_Proc          dd   0     ; 14 IRET procedure (optional)
    VID_IRET_Time_Out      dd   500   ; 18 maximum time to leave VM's priority
                                      ; boosted
    VID_Hw_Int_Ref         dd   ?     ; 1C reference data for hardware
                                      ; interrupt procedure
VPICD_IRQ_Descriptor ENDS


; Flags in VID_Options:

VPICD_OPT_READ_HW_IRR        EQU 0001h  ; Read physical IRR to see if the
                                        ; interrupt is in service
VPICD_OPT_CAN_SHARE          EQU 0002h  ; Virtual IRQ can be shared
VPICD_OPT_REF_DATA           EQU 0004h  ; Pass reference data to hardware
                                        ; interrupt procedure
VPICD_OPT_VIRT_INT_REJECT    EQU 0010h  ; Don't allow interrupt to be
                                        ; reflected to ring three
VPICD_OPT_SHARE_PMODE_ONLY   EQU 0020h  ; Interrupt can be shared only if
                                        ; handled entirely in ring zero
```

Figure 13-9. *Virtual IRQ Descriptor (VID) structure passed to* VPICD_Virtualize_IRQ.

In the remainder of this subsection, I'll describe the callback routines you can supply when you virtualize an IRQ.

The Hardware Interrupt Procedure (*Hw_Int_Proc*) A hardware interrupt procedure receives control shortly after the hardware interrupt occurs. The VPICD has masked the associated IRQ and issued a specific EOI command to the PIC. Interrupts are disabled for the real machine. The EAX register contains the virtual IRQ handle previously returned by *VPICD_Virtualize_IRQ*, and the EDX register contains the reference data (if any) you specified in the VID structure. The EBX register fortuitously points to the current VM control block, the EDI register points to the current thread control block, and the EBP register points to the current VM's client registers. There's almost no reason why you should need to reference the EBX, EDI, and EBP registers, however, because the identity and context of the VM that got interrupted is practically irrelevant to handling a hardware interrupt.

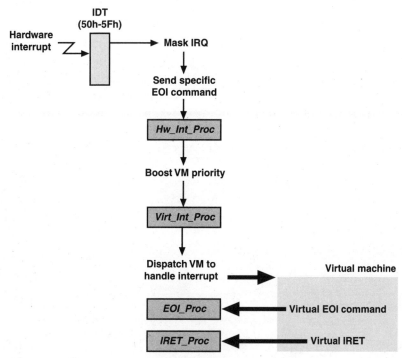

Figure 13-10. *Handling a virtualized IRQ.*

Your hardware interrupt procedure should return with the carry flag clear if it processed the interrupt. If you indicated in your VID structure that the IRQ was shareable (by setting the *VID_OPT_CAN_SHARE* flag), you can return with the carry flag set to indicate that your procedure didn't handle the interrupt. In such a case, the VPICD will call the next handler in the list of handlers for this shared IRQ.

The *VPICD_OPT_SHARE_PMODE_ONLY* Flag You can set this flag in the Virtual IRQ Descriptor you use in the call to *VPICD_Virtualize_IRQ* to indicate that the IRQ can be shared only if the handlers run in ring zero (which is probably the only way IRQ sharing can be made to work in the first place). This flag doesn't do anything in the retail build of Windows 95. In the debug version, however, it generates a debug warning if someone calls *VPICD_Set_Int_Request* to service the IRQ in ring three. You want to make sure that doesn't happen because of the fact that the hardware interrupt routine won't know whether to return with the carry flag set or clear; it won't know whether to set the carry flag because it *can't* know whether the ring-three handler will actually handle the interrupt or not.

Although your hardware interrupt procedure can enable interrupts, it must use only page-locked code and data, and it can call only those VxD services designated as "asynchronous." Since the VPICD has sent a physical EOI command to the PIC, interrupts of both higher *and* lower priority can occur if your procedure enables interrupts. No interrupt on your IRQ can occur because the VPICD has masked it off. Although your procedure may be interrupted by other hardware, you can be sure of regaining control as soon as the inner interrupt's hardware interrupt procedure returns. In particular, the VMM doesn't process events until the outermost of a nested set of hardware interrupt procedures has returned.

A common reason to virtualize an IRQ that you will end up reflecting into a VM is to override the VPICD's selection of a VM to handle the interrupt. For example, suppose your device has an "owner." (Typically, you assign ownership based on Set_Device_Focus messages or on the outcome of a contention algorithm.) You would probably want the device's interrupts serviced in the VM that owns the device. A hardware interrupt procedure that accomplishes that result is as follows:

```
BeginProc Hw_Int_Proc, locked
        cmp    owner, 0          ; anyone own the device?
        je     @F                ; if not, reflect to current VM
        mov    ebx, owner        ; point to device owner
@@:     VxDJmp VPICD_Set_Int_Request ; set request for owner
EndProc  Hw_Int_Proc
```

The effect of this procedure is to send the interrupt into the owner VM if there is one. If no VM owns the device, this procedure sends the interrupt into the current VM. If you wanted to mimic the VPICD's default handling instead of just sending the interrupt to the current VM, you would need much more elaborate code that we won't go into here.

The Virtual Interrupt Procedure (*Virt_Int_Proc*) The VPICD calls your virtual interrupt procedure when it's about to reflect a hardware interrupt into a particular VM. The EAX register holds the IRQ handle, and the EBX register holds the handle of the VM that's about to receive the interrupt. The usual reason for providing a virtual interrupt procedure is so that you can surround the virtual handler with a critical section, as shown in this example:

```
BeginProc Virt_Int_Proc, locked
        xor    ecx, ecx
        VMMCall Begin_Critical_Section
        ret
EndProc  Virt_Int_Proc
```

If you claim the critical section in the virtual interrupt procedure, you should also provide an IRET procedure to release the section.

Another reason to provide a *Virt_Int_Proc* procedure is to selectively prevent interrupts from being reflected to a VM. The *VPICD_OPT_VIRT_INT_REJECT* flag prevents *any* interrupt from being reflected. To prevent only selected interrupts from being reflected, leave that flag 0 and return from your *Virt_Int_Proc* procedure with the carry flag set to prevent reflection or clear to permit reflection.

The End-of-Interrupt Procedure (*EOI_Proc*) A virtual interrupt service routine usually sends an EOI command to the interrupt controller when it's ready to tolerate another interrupt from the same device. For a device that uses IRQ 0 through 7 (an interrupt request on the master PIC), a ring-three interrupt handler would issue an EOI command like this:

```
out   20h, 20h    ; EOI for our IRQ on the master PIC
```

For a device that uses IRQ 8 through 15 (an interrupt request on the slave PIC), a ring-three interrupt handler would issue an EOI command like this:

```
out   0A0h, 20h  ; EOI for our IRQ on the slave PIC
out   20h, 20h   ; EOI for IRQ 2 to the master PIC
```

I want to emphasize that I'm showing you what a ring-three interrupt handler does. A VxD (other than the VPICD, that is) shouldn't be sending EOI commands directly to the PIC. It should instead use the *VPICD_Phys_EOI* service to signify completion of an interrupt.

The VPICD traps these references to the interrupt controller ports and calls your *EOI_Proc* procedure with the EAX register holding the IRQ handle and the EBX register holding the handle of the current VM. You would normally clear the virtual interrupt request and notify the VPICD that the interrupt has been completely processed:

```
BeginProc EOI_Proc, locked
          VxDCall VPICD_Clear_Int_Request
          VxDJmp VPICD_Phys_EOI
EndProc   EOI_Proc
```

If you forget to clear the virtual interrupt, the VPICD will try to reflect the interrupt into the VM again and again. This is because the VPICD simulates a *level-triggered* interrupt controller, which requests an interrupt as long as the hardware request line remains asserted.

Recall that *VPICD_Phys_EOI* doesn't, despite its name, actually do a physical EOI. It unmasks the physical interrupt instead. The physical EOI happened long before, shortly after the interrupt occurred.

The Mask-Change Procedure (*Mask_Change_Proc*) Whenever a virtual machine tries to change the masking of the IRQ you've virtualized, the VPICD calls your

Mask_Change_Proc procedure. The EAX register holds the handle of the IRQ, the EBX register holds the handle of the current VM, and the ECX register holds a flag indicating whether the IRQ has been masked (ECX is nonzero) or unmasked (ECX is 0). You might provide a *Mask_Change_Proc* procedure to manage contention for your device. We already discussed device contention in connection with port trapping, so there's no need to discuss the subject again.

Note that there is no way for your *Mask_Change_Proc* procedure to restore the virtual IMR to what it was prior to the trapped instruction that caused your handler to be called.

The IRET Procedure (*IRET_Proc*) There's one more callback procedure you can specify when you virtualize an IRQ: the IRET procedure. The virtual interrupt service routine eventually issues an IRET instruction to terminate its processing of the interrupt. The VPICD then calls your IRET procedure, if you've provided one. You would usually have an *IRET_Proc* procedure only if you also have a *Virt_Int_Proc* procedure, and its purpose would be to undo whatever *Virt_Int_Proc* did. If your *Virt_Int_Proc* procedure claimed the critical section, for example, your *IRET_Proc* procedure would release it by calling *End_Critical_Section*.

Virtualizing DMA

If you were daunted by the earlier discussion of how to set up and perform a DMA transfer, you're probably quite worried at this point that your VxD will have to do a lot of work to support DMA transfers by ring-three programs. Luckily, the VDMAD does all the work. A V86-mode driver running in a virtual machine can simply program the transfer in the normal way by writing to the DMA page, address, and count registers, and it can initiate the transfer by unmasking the DMA channel and programming the device. The VDMAD traps all the DMA controller ports in order to virtualize the transfer. The VDMAD fetches and locks the pages that are involved in the transfer, and it translates virtual addresses to physical addresses. If necessary, the VDMAD supplies its own buffer below the 16-MB physical memory line and copies data to or from the virtual machine buffer as necessary.

The VDMAD can pretty much handle any standard DMA programming that a real-mode driver throws its way. An exception to the rule occurs in *autoinitialization* mode. Programming a DMA channel in autoinitialization mode indicates that you want the address and count to be automatically restored each time the channel exhausts the count. In normal circumstances, this mode is used only to cause channel 0 to continuously refresh memory. If you program an autoinitialize transfer from a buffer that is discontiguous or that lies beyond the 16-MB limit, the VDMAD declines to perform the transfer because the bookkeeping is too complicated to really be worth it, given the low utility of this transfer mode.

Protected-mode ring-three programs can't, however, use DMA in the usual way. The VDMAD supports the *Virtual DMA Standard* (VDS) for protected-mode DMA. The VDS specification is available on the MSDN discs; I won't discuss it in this book.

The only respect in which you need to worry about DMA for your device concerns the size and location of the DMA buffer the VDMAD will use. The VDMAD allocates this buffer during the processing of the Init_Complete message. At any time prior to the VDMAD's processing of this message, you can call *VDMAD_Reserve_Buffer_Space* to indicate the size and maximum physical address of the buffer required by your device. For example, suppose you knew that the V86-mode driver for your device would do DMA transfers for 8192 bytes. In your Device_Init handler, you would tell the VDMAD about this requirement:

```
            include vdmad.inc

BeginProc Device_Init, init
          mov     eax, 2     ; 8192 bytes = 2 pages
          xor     ecx, ecx   ; we don't care about buffer addr
          VxDCall VDMAD_Reserve_Buffer_Space
          ...
EndProc   Device_Init
```

Very few VxDs should be interested in the physical location of the DMA buffer, by the way. The location of the buffer depends primarily on which hardware bus is in the computer, and the VDMAD already factors that into its algorithm.

Advanced Virtualization Techniques

Two additional virtualization techniques are available for special situations. It's possible to write interrupt handlers that run in ordinary 16-bit DLLs in ring zero. It's also possible to write *bimodal* interrupt handlers that execute in whatever mode the processor happens to be in at the time of the interrupt. The purpose of both of these techniques is to minimize the number of ring transitions required, in order to improve the performance of high-speed devices. Neither technique is well documented in the DDK, but Karen Hazzah's *Writing Windows VxDs and Device Drivers* (R&D Press, 1995) contains an excellent discussion along with code samples.

In my opinion, both of these advanced interrupt handling techniques are basically hacks aimed at letting you conserve code that you really ought to just rewrite as a VxD. That's why I'm not going to discuss either of them further in this book.

WRITING RING-ZERO DRIVERS

Now that you've read the preceding lengthy discussion of how a VxD goes about virtualizing I/O resources, I have a secret to share: the knowledge you just gained ought to be obsolete. In the best of all possible worlds, there wouldn't be any ring-three device drivers and there wouldn't be any need to worry about them doing port I/O, handling interrupts, or programming DMA transfers. If it weren't for concerns about compatibility, you'd never have to think about virtualizing a device.

Microsoft is moving toward an architecture in which all device drivers run in 32-bit protected mode and in which there are no more real-mode drivers. Whether the architecture will ultimately include VxDs in their traditional form is unclear as of the time I'm writing, but there will surely be a transition phase in which VxDs implement most device driver functions. In this section, I'll discuss how to write a purely ring-zero device driver.

A modern ring-zero driver would have the following components:

■ Machinery to connect with the Configuration Manager for the purpose of cooperating in the management of I/O resources. Your configuration function's CONFIG_START handler would extract resource assignments and initialize the device. Your CONFIG_STOP and CONFIG_REMOVE handlers would take steps to stop using the resources.

■ A VPICD hardware interrupt procedure to handle hardware interrupts on any assigned IRQs. The interrupt procedure would completely handle the interrupt without ever reflecting it to a VM.

■ An API to allow application programs to interact with the device via function calls. The API takes the place both of I/O port trapping and of elaborate ways to emulate the behavior of memory-mapped devices. (You might very well allow applications to directly access mapped memory, but you would make them explicitly serialize their access by making API calls.)

■ Ring-zero code to use the VDMAD services for any required DMA transfers.

NOTE Code for the example presented in this section is included on the companion disk in the \CHAP13\RING0DMA directory. Use caution if you build and execute this sample—it would be quite easy to overwrite critical data on your hard disk if you get the I/O commands or the transfer direction wrong by accident.

We've already discussed all these pieces except the last one. To illustrate DMA in ring zero, I'll show an example that reads the boot sector from a floppy disk. The Plug and Play connection consists of the following subroutines:

```
DMAHANDLE dmahandle;        // virtualized DMA channel handle
HIRQ irqhandle;             // virtualized IRQ handle
DWORD baseport;             // I/O base address (i.e., 3F2)

CONFIGRET OnPnpNewDevnode(DEVNODE devnode, DWORD loadtype)
    {                           // OnPnpNewDevnode
    return CM_Register_Device_Driver(devnode, OnConfigure,
        0, CM_REGISTER_DEVICE_DRIVER_REMOVABLE
        | CM_REGISTER_DEVICE_DRIVER_DISABLEABLE);
    }                           // OnPnpNewDevnode

CONFIGRET CM_HANDLER OnConfigure(CONFIGFUNC cf, SUBCONFIGFUNC
    scf, DEVNODE devnode, DWORD refdata, ULONG flags)
    {                           // OnConfigure
    switch (cf)
        {                       // handle configuration function

    case CONFIG_START:
        {                       // CONFIG_START
        CMCONFIG config;
        DWORD channel;
        DWORD irq;
        VID vid = {0, 0, (DWORD) Hw_Int_Proc_Thunk};

        CM_Get_Alloc_Log_Conf(&config, devnode,
            CM_GET_ALLOC_LOG_CONF_ALLOC);
        baseport = config.wIOPortBase[0]; // 3F2h
        channel = config.bDMALst[0];      // 2
        irq = config.bIRQRegisters[0];    // 6
        dmahandle = VDMAD_Virtualize_Channel(channel, NULL);
        vid.VID_IRQ_Number = (USHORT) irq;
        irqhandle = VPICD_Virtualize_IRQ(&vid);

        return CR_SUCCESS;
        }                       // CONFIG_START

    case CONFIG_STOP:
    case CONFIG_REMOVE:
        if (dmahandle)
            {                       // unvirtualize DMA channel
            VDMAD_Unvirtualize_Channel(dmahandle);
            dmahandle = NULL;
            }                       // unvirtualize DMA channel
```

```
              if (irqhandle)
                  {                           // unvirtualize IRQ
                  VPICD_Force_Default_Behavior(irqhandle);
                  irqhandle = NULL;
                  }                           // unvirtualize IRQ
              return CR_SUCCESS;

          default:
              return CR_DEFAULT;
              }                       // handle configuration function
          }                           // OnConfigure
```

In conjunction with an .INF file having a hardwired configuration that requires ports 3F2h through 3F5h, DMA channel 2, and IRQ 6, the configuration function will take over the I/O resources associated with a standard floppy disk controller.

Our virtualization of IRQ 6 in this example has only a *Hw_Int_Proc* procedure, which contains the following code to fetch status bytes from the controller and to dismiss the interrupt:

```
void __declspec(naked) Hw_Int_Proc_Thunk()
    {                               // Hw_Int_Proc_Thunk
    _asm
        {                           // call Hw_Int_Proc
        push edx                    ; reference data (if any)
        push eax                    ; IRQ handle
        call Hw_Int_Proc            ; call C program
        add  esp, 8                 ; lose arguments
        cmp  eax, 1                 ; turn TRUE return into CLC
        ret                         ; return to VPICD
        }                           // call Hw_Int_Proc
    }                               // Hw_Int_Proc_Thunk

VMM_SEMAPHORE waitsem;              // semaphore to wait on

BOOL Hw_Int_Proc(HIRQ hirq, DWORD refdata)
    {                               // Hw_Int_Proc
    int i;
    BYTE status[7];                 // 7 status bytes

    for (i = 0; i < 7; ++i)
        {                           // read status from controller
        BYTE c;
        FdcWait(baseport);
        _asm
            {                       // read next status byte
            mov edx, baseport       ; DX = port to read from
            add dx, 3               ;  ..
            in  al, dx              ; read status byte
```

```
            mov c, al           ;  ..
            }                   // read next status byte
        status[i] = c;
        }                       // read status from controller

    VPICD_Phys_EOI(hirq);
    Schedule_Global_Event(FdcWakeup, waitsem);
    return TRUE;
    }                           // Hw_Int_Proc

void __declspec(naked) FdcWakeup()
    {                           // FdcWakeup
    _asm mov eax, edx       ; EDX (ref data) = semaphore handle
    VMMCall(Signal_Semaphore_No_Switch) // wakeup thread
    _asm ret
    }                           // FdcWakeup

void FdcWait(DWORD baseport)
    {                           // FdcWait
    _asm
        {                       // wait for floppy disk controller
        mov edx, baseport       ; base port address
        add dx, 2               ; point to status port
    waitloop:
        in  al, dx              ; read status byte
        test al, 80h            ; wait for ready bit to be 1
        jz  waitloop            ;  ..
        }                       // wait for floppy disk controller
    }                           // FdcWait
```

In this sample, *FdcWait* is a helper routine that waits for the floppy disk controller to be ready to accept or deliver another status or command byte. The call to *Schedule_Global_Event* illustrates how a hardware interrupt procedure might notify a waiting thread that an I/O operation is complete. *FdcWakeup*, the event callback routine, signals a semaphore whose handle is passed in as reference data. Since *Signal_Semaphore* is not an asynchronous service, it's not possible for the hardware interrupt procedure to call it directly. As discussed earlier in the book, if an interrupt procedure needs to perform nonasynchronous services, it schedules an event callback. The event callback routine is free to issue any service call subject to the constraints previously discussed with respect to causing page faults when MS-DOS is being used for paging I/O.

I built a simple API function for this sample VxD that initializes the floppy disk controller and programs a DMA transfer over channel 2. I'll discuss the DMA transfer aspect of this in the next section. A test application uses the API interface by loading the DS:BX register pair with the address of a 512-byte buffer and calling the INT 2Fh, function 1684h, API entry point. On return, the application's

buffer will contain the contents of the boot sector of the disk in drive A. The API
function looks like this:

```
void ApiEntry(HVM hVM, PTCB tcb, PCRS pRegs)
    {                               // ApiEntry
    static BYTE cmd[] = {3, 0xAF, 2, 0xE6, 0, 0, 0, 1, 2,
        0x12, 0x1B, 255};
    DWORD buffer;
    DWORD code;

    _asm
        {                           // initialize floppy disk controller
        mov edx, baseport           ; DX = base port (3F2)
        mov al, 1Ch                 ; turn on drive A motor
        out dx, al                  ;   ..
        jmp delay1
delay1:
        jmp delay2
delay2:
        add dx, 5                   ; DX = 3F7
        xor al, al
        out dx, al
        }                           // initialize floppy disk controller

    // INITIALIZE FOR DMA TRANSFER

    FdcWrite(baseport, cmd, sizeof(cmd));

    Wait_Semaphore(waitsem, BLOCK_SVC_INTS);

    _asm
        {                           // turn motor off
        mov edx, baseport
        mov al, 0Ch
        out dx, al
        }                           // turn motor off
    }                               // ApiEntry

void FdcWrite(DWORD baseport, BYTE* data, int length)
    {                               // FdcWrite
    while (length-- > 0)
        {                           // for each byte
        BYTE c = *data++;           // next byte to write
        FdcWait(baseport);          // wait until okay to write
        _asm
            {                       // write data byte
            mov edx, baseport       ; compute port address
            add dx, 3               ;   ..
```

```
                mov al, c        ; AL = next data byte
                out dx, al       ; output data byte
            }                    // write data byte
        }                        // for each byte
    }                            // FdcWrite
```

The *ApiEntry* function programs the floppy disk controller to read sector 0 from drive A. The floppy disk controller will start the operation as soon it receives the last command byte, so it behooves us to have prepared the DMA controller ahead of time. Once the operation commences, the *ApiEntry* function waits on a semaphore. Specifying *BLOCK_SVC_INTS* as a flag argument to *Wait_Semaphore* makes it possible for our own thread to handle events if necessary. The semaphore will be signalled by the global event callback scheduled by the IRQ 6 hardware interrupt handler. In other words, the *ApiEntry* function will wake up when the read operation completes. Thereupon, it turns the motor off and returns to the application.

Using VDMAD Services

Although the VDMAD virtualizes DMA transfers initiated by VMs, it requires you to use its exported services if you want to use DMA from a VxD driver. I'll therefore describe the VDMAD in more detail. When you're done reading about the VDMAD, you'll know all you need to know to write a typical hardware device driver for Windows 95.

Table 13-5 lists the services provided by the VDMAD.

Service	*Description*
VDMAD_Copy_From_Buffer	Copies data from the VDMAD buffer to the associated DMA region
VDMAD_Copy_To_Buffer	Copies data from a DMA region to the associated VDMAD buffer
VDMAD_Default_Handler	Performs a transfer using values specified by a VM and default algorithms
VDMAD_Disable_Translation	Disables automatic translation of a standard DMA channel
VDMAD_Enable_Translation	Undoes the effect of a previous *VDMAD_-Disable_Translation* service
VDMAD_Get_EISA_Adr_Mode	Determines the addressing and transfer mode for a channel
VDMAD_Get_Region_Info	Retrieves information about the region currently assigned to a DMA channel

Table 13-5. *VDMAD services.*   *(continued)*

continued

Service	Description
VDMAD_Get_Version	Determines which version of the VDMAD is running
VDMAD_Get_Virt_State	Retrieves the virtual state of a DMA channel
VDMAD_Lock_DMA_Region	If possible, locks the pages of a region to be used for a DMA transfer
VDMAD_Mask_Channel	Masks a DMA channel
VDMAD_Phys_Mask_Channel	Masks a DMA channel without checking its terminal count
VDMAD_Phys_Unmask_Channel	Unmasks a DMA channel without checking its terminal count
VDMAD_Release_Buffer	Releases a VDMAD buffer previously assigned by *VDMAD_Request_Buffer*
VDMAD_Request_Buffer	Reserves the VDMAD buffer to transfer a given region
VDMAD_Reserve_Buffer_Space	During initialization, notifies the VDMAD of requirements for buffer space
VDMAD_Scatter_Lock	Locks all pages mapped to a DMA region and provides a scatter translation map
VDMAD_Scatter_Unlock	Unlocks pages previously locked by *VDMAD_Scatter_Lock*
VDMAD_Set_EISA_Adr_Mode	Sets the EISA extended addressing mode
VDMAD_Set_EISA_Phys_State	Sets the transfer mode for a DMA channel (EISA only)
VDMAD_Set_IO_Address	Changes the port associated with a DMA channel (PS/2 machines only)
VDMAD_Set_Phys_State	Sets the transfer mode for a DMA channel
VDMAD_Set_PS2_Phys_State	Sets the transfer mode for a DMA channel (PS/2 machines only)
VDMAD_Set_Region_Info	Sets information about the region currently associated with a DMA channel
VDMAD_Set_Virt_State	Modifies the virtual state of a DMA channel
VDMAD_Unlock_DMA_Region	Unlocks the DMA region associated with a channel

(continued)

continued

Service	Description
VDMAD_Unlock_DMA_Region_No_Dirty	Unlocks the DMA region, but doesn't mark the pages as dirty
VDMAD_UnMask_Channel	Physically unmasks a DMA channel
VDMAD_Unvirtualize_Channel	Releases the virtualization of a DMA channel
VDMAD_Virtualize_Channel	Takes ownership of a DMA channel

The first step to perform if you're going to be programming DMA transfers in your driver is to obtain a handle to a virtualized DMA channel:

```
DMAHANDLE dmahandle = VDMAD_Virtualize_Channel(channel, NULL);
```

The first argument to *VDMAD_Virtualize_Channel* is simply the channel number (0 through 7). The second argument is the address of a callback procedure that the VDMAD will call whenever a VM changes the virtual state of the same channel. For our present purposes, we're not going to allow VMs to program our channel, so we can supply a NULL address. Virtualizing the channel has the side effect of reserving the DMA channel within the DMA arbitrator too. You shouldn't depend on the side effect, of course: you should allow the Configuration Manager to assign a DMA channel first and *then* virtualize it.

The call to *VDMAD_Virtualize_Channel* occurs when you initialize the driver, most likely in the CONFIG_START handler of your configuration function. You match this call with a subsequent call to *VDMAD_Unvirtualize_Channel* from your termination routine, most likely in the CONFIG_STOP and CONFIG_REMOVE handlers of your configuration function.

A VDMAD Shortcut

In general, programming a DMA transfer in ring zero can be very complex. I'll show you a shortcut based on the fact that the sample program we're working with operates in the context of a particular VM. Then I'll explain how you would use lower-level VDMAD services to accomplish the same result. The overall strategy of the shortcut is to use *VDMAD_Set_Virt_State* to set the virtual state of the DMA channel *as if* code running in the VM had programmed the same transfer we're going to perform. We then call *VDMAD_Default_Handler* to handle the physical transfer. We will want to work with the virtual address of the application's buffer, so we use *Client_Ptr_Flat* to determine that address based on the client registers:

```
buffer = Client_Ptr_Flat(DS, BX);
```

Client_Ptr_Flat is a macro wrapper around *Map_Flat*. In assembly language, there's already such a macro. I defined the macro for purposes of this sample because it's so much more convenient to use than a direct call to *Map_Flat*:

```
#define Client_Ptr_Flat(seg, off) Map_Flat(\
    FIELDOFFSET(struct Client_Reg_Struc, Client_##seg), \
    FIELDOFFSET(struct Client_Word_Reg_Struc, Client_##off))
```

We also want to be absolutely sure that *VDMAD_Set_Virt_State* will be expecting a virtual address instead of a physical address when we call it. The VDMAD maintains a *translation disable counter* for each channel in each VM. *VDMAD_Disable_Translation* increments this counter, and *VDMAD_Enable_Translation* decrements it. While the counter is nonzero, the VDMAD expects that any buffer address you send to it via *VDMAD_Set_Virt_State* is a physical address. To make sure that translation is enabled, we need to call *VDMAD_Enable_Translation* over and over again until it returns with the carry flag set, which means that translation was already enabled before the call. Since I had to write a VDMAD.H file (there being none in the DDK), I defined the wrapper for this function as follows:

```
#define ET_WASENABLED   0x0100 // translation already enabled
#define ET_NOTENABLED   0x0001 // not yet enabled

VXDINLINE DWORD VDMAD_Enable_Translation(DMAHANDLE hdma,
    HVM hVM)
    {
    _asm mov eax, hdma
    _asm mov ebx, hVM
    VMMCall(VDMAD_Enable_Translation)
    _asm mov eax, 0
    _asm setz al
    _asm setc ah
    }
```

Thus, the code within *ApiEntry* that is preparing the DMA transfer reads as follows:

```
do  {
    code = VDMAD_Enable_Translation(dmahandle, hVM);
    }
while ((code & ET_WASENABLED) != ET_WASENABLED);
```

Finally, the program can make the following two calls to program and initiate the DMA transfer:

```
VDMAD_Set_Virt_State(dmahandle, hVM, buffer,
    512, DMA_type_write | DMA_single_mode);
VDMAD_Default_Handler(dmahandle, hVM);
```

Notice that I didn't supply the *DMA_masked* flag in the call to *VDMAD_-Set_Virt_State*. Consequently, that call unmasks the virtual channel. *VDMAD_Default_Handler* notices that the channel is virtually unmasked and proceeds to lock the buffer, to program the physical DMA registers, and to unmask the physical channel.

Low-Level VDMAD Programming

It's probably obvious that *VDMAD_Default_Handler* employs elaborate machinery to set up and perform a physical DMA transfer. Unfortunately, that function operates *only* in the context of a particular VM whose DMA controllers have a virtualized state. If your driver needs to operate outside the context of a VM, you will need to duplicate much of what *VDMAD_Default_Handler* does. Luckily, the source code for the VDMAD is part of the DDK, so people like you and I have a chance of figuring out how to do the required steps.

Your driver will need to proceed as follows to duplicate what *VDMAD_Default_Handler* does:

1. Locate a physical buffer that's acceptable to the DMA controller. If possible, you should do this by page-locking your own buffer. The VDMAD refers to your buffer as the *DMA region*. If the region lies beyond the address range available to the controller (that is, beyond the first 16 MB on an ISA system), or if it occupies discontiguous memory, or if it crosses a DMA page boundary (64 KB for byte transfers, 128 KB for word transfers), you will need to borrow the VDMAD's buffer. You may also have to break up the transfer into pieces acceptable to the controller.

2. Program the physical DMA controller registers with the address, count, and mode appropriate for your transfer.

3. Unmask the physical channel. As you know, this allows the transfer to proceed as soon as the device starts delivering or requesting data bytes and notifying the DMA controller.

4. Arrange to get control when the transfer completes, whereupon you immediately mask the DMA channel. If you needed to program multiple transfers, you would start the next one now. If you borrowed the VDMAD's buffer, you would give it back. If you locked any pages, you would unlock them.

5. After unmasking the channel, you should also arrange a timeout in case some device problem prevents the transfer from happening. If the timeout expires, you could abort the DMA transfer. Most importantly, you could return the VDMAD buffer if you borrowed it.

Locking the DMA Region

The first of these five steps is the most complex. You first determine the address, size, and alignment requirement of the DMA region and attempt to lock the region using code such as the following:

```
DWORD code;              // return code
DWORD address;           // linear address of DMA region
DWORD size;              // byte size of DMA region
DWORD result;            // result of lock attempt
BYTE align;              // 1 for 64 KB, 2 for 128 KB
code = VDMAD_Lock_DMA_Region(address, size, align, &result);
```

If the lock attempt succeeds, *code* will be 0 and *result* will be the physical address of the locked region. If the lock attempt fails, *code* will be either *DMA_Not_Contiguous*, *DMA_Not_Aligned*, or *DMA_Lock_Failed*; and *result* will be the number of bytes that could have been locked at the beginning of the region. You could decide to break up the transfer into multiple pieces if you get a failure code from *VDMAD_Lock_DMA_Region*. Even if the function returns success, you're not out of the woods yet, because you must still verify that the physical address is usable by the DMA controller. The VDMAD provides an undocumented service for determining the maximum physical page number for DMA:

```
DWORD maxpage = VDMAD_Get_Max_Phys_Page();
if (code == 0 && result >= (maxpage << 12))
    {                      // beyond maximum
    VDMAD_Unlock_DMA_Region(address, size);
    code = DMA_Invalid_Region;
    }                      // beyond maximum
```

Determining the maximum physical DMA address on your own is complex, because it depends on what hardware bus you have (an EISA bus allows any 32-bit address; ISA and MCA buses allow only 16 MB), what processor chip you have (a PC/XT accelerator only allows 1 MB; others don't impose a limit), and what the user specified in various SYSTEM.INI settings. But be aware that *VDMAD_Get-_Max_Phys_Page* is new to Windows 95, so you can't use it if your driver must be compatible with Windows 3.1.

If you got through the locking and maximum address tests okay, you could proceed to program the DMA transfer as follows:

```
VDMAD_Set_Region_Info(dmahandle, 0, TRUE, address, size, result);
VDMAD_Set_Phys_State(dmahandle, mode);
VDMAD_UnMask_Channel(dmahandle, Get_Sys_VM_Handle());
```

The second argument to my wrapper for *VDMAD_Set_Region_Info* is a buffer identifier; 0 means that we're not using the VDMAD's buffer. The third argument indicates whether or not we have already locked the pages that will be involved in the transfer. The *address* argument specifies the virtual address of the DMA region, which has no actual utility to the VDMAD when we're programming the transfer at this low level. The *size* and *result* arguments specify the physical size and address of the actual DMA buffer; they are the values that will eventually be programmed into the physical DMA controller.

The *mode* argument to *VDMAD_Set_Phys_State* contains mode and extended mode settings (see Table 13-6); these are basically the same settings you use when programming a real DMA controller, except that you leave out the channel number in the low-order two bits. Finally, the second argument to *VDMAD_UnMask_Channel* is a VM handle. You must supply a valid VM handle even though the transfer isn't on behalf of any particular VM. The VM handle ends up being ignored for most purposes, but NULL (which you might have wanted to use instead of the System VM handle shown in the example) has a special meaning for certain kinds of error correction.

Mode Flag	Description
DMA_type_verify	Verifies the operation
DMA_type_write	Writes to memory
DMA_type_read	Reads from memory
DMA_AutoInit	Specifies autoinitialization mode
DMA_AdrDec	Specifies address decrement mode
DMA_demand_mode	Specifies demand mode
DMA_single_mode	Specifies single transfer mode
DMA_block_mode	Specifies block transfer mode
DMA_cascade	Cascades from master DMA controller
Programmed_IO	(Extended mode)
PS2_AutoInit	(Extended mode)
Transfer_Data	(Extended mode)
Write_Mem	(Extended mode)
_16_bit_xfer	(Extended mode)

Table 13-6. *Mode flags for* VDMAD_Set_Phys_State.

Borrowing the VDMAD's Buffer

If you *didn't* get through the locking and maximum address test phases unscathed, you'll need to borrow a buffer to perform the transfer. The VDMAD allocates a page-locked buffer that has the right alignment and location characteristics during its processing of the Init_Complete message. You can set a minimum size for the buffer by calling *VDMAD_Reserve_Buffer_Space* at any time prior to the VDMAD's Init_Complete processing. The purpose of the buffer is to provide a memory area with which to perform DMA transfers when the DMA region is unusable for some reason. The DMA region is unusable if it's discontiguous, crosses a DMA page boundary, lies above the maximum address, or is simply unlockable for some other reason.

To borrow the DMA buffer, you call *VDMAD_Request_Buffer*:

```
BYTE id;                     // buffer ID for VDMAD_Set_Region_Info
code = VDMAD_Request_Buffer(address, size, &result, &id);
```

If successful, *VDMAD_Request_Buffer* returns 0 and sets *result* equal to the physical address of the assigned buffer area and *id* equal to the buffer identifier. You pass the buffer identifier and physical address to *VDMAD_Set_Region_Info* later on. If *VDMAD_Request_Buffer* fails, the return code will be either *DMA_Buffer_Too_Small* or *DMA_Buffer_In_Use*. In the first case, you need to break up the transfer into smaller pieces. In the second case, you need to wait for the buffer to become free. The VDMAD's default handler simply calls *Time_Slice_Sleep* to wait 100 milliseconds, and then it tries again.

Once you have claimed a portion of the VDMAD's DMA buffer, you proceed to set up the transfer much as you would when you merely locked your own buffer. The only differences are that you supply a buffer identifier to *VDMAD_Set_Region_Info* and that you must arrange to have data copied to the buffer if necessary, as shown here:

```
VDMAD_Set_Region_Info(dmahandle, id, TRUE, address, size, result);
if (mode & DMA_type_read)
    VDMAD_Copy_To_Buffer(id, address, 0, size);
VDMAD_Set_Phys_State(dmahandle, mode);
VDMAD_UnMask_Channel(dmahandle, Get_Sys_VM_Handle());
```

VDMAD_Copy_To_Buffer copies data from the DMA region located at linear address *address* for *size* bytes to the *id* buffer, beginning at an offset specified by the third argument. You should copy data to the buffer before unmasking the channel if you're doing a *DMA_type_read* operation (that is, if you're reading memory and writing to the device).

Handling Transfer Completion

When the DMA transfer is complete, your device generates a hardware interrupt. You should mask the DMA channel you were using to prevent spurious transfers. If you've borrowed a buffer from the VDMAD, you should copy data from that buffer to the DMA region; in addition, you should release the buffer you were using, as shown here:

```
VDMAD_Mask_Channel(dmahandle);
if (id)
    {                        // finish buffered transfer
```

```
        if (mode & DMA_type_write)
            VDMAD_Copy_From_Buffer(id, address, 0, size);
        VDMAD_Release_Buffer(id);
        }                      // finish buffered transfer
    else
        if (mode & DMA_type_write)
            VDMAD_Unlock_DMA_Region(address, size);
        else
            VDMAD_Unlock_DMA_Region_No_Dirty(address, size);
```

The cleanup calls expose the last piece of dirty laundry we have to consider about I/O programming with VxDs. If the transfer was a *DMA_write_type* operation (from a device to memory), we've modified some pages. Ordinarily, when you write to memory, the paging logic in the processor automatically marks a page as dirty in the page table entry. The dirty flag tells the paging system to write the contents of the memory page to the swap file if it steals the same page frame for another page. The paging system will never know about our modifications to the DMA region, though, because the DMA controller bypasses all of the page translation logic in the processor. Therefore, *VDMAD_Unlock_DMA_Region* sets the dirty flag for each page involved in the transfer. If we did a *DMA_type_read* operation (from memory to a device), however, we didn't dirty the pages. Therefore, we call a different service (*VDMAD_Unlock_DMA_Region_No_Dirty*) that doesn't set the dirty flags.

Avoiding Complexity

I want to end this lengthy chapter with some simplifying advice. Evidently, you have a complex chore if you want to do DMA transfers to an arbitrary buffer. You can avoid the need to lock a region, borrow a buffer from the VDMAD, and so on, if you reserve your own buffer of appropriate size and location during your own device initialization. You would use the *PAGEUSEALIGN*, *PAGEFIXED*, and *PAGECONTIG* options to *_PageAllocate* to allocate the buffer, and you would specify either 64-KB or 128-KB alignment, depending on whether you were going to be doing 8-bit or 16-bit transfers, respectively. Furthermore, you could specify a maximum address of 16 MB (page number 01000h) and be sure of ISA, MCA, and EISA compatibility. The only disadvantage to this approach (and it may be a big one) is that you will tie up physical memory for your DMA buffer as long as your driver is loaded. For a highly active device, devoting resources permanently to the device would be entirely appropriate, of course. Mind you, in Windows 95 you can use the *PAGEUSEALIGN* and related options at any time (Windows 3.1 restricted these options to device initialization), but you run the risk of having *_PageAllocate* fail at an inopportune time.

Chapter 14

Communications Drivers

The computer's serial port is the user's window on the world. Through it flows an ever-increasing amount of information in a bewildering variety of formats. Armed with a serial port and a modem, the user can send and receive mail and fax transmissions, manage investments, debate the issues of our time, view images from space, conduct a courtship, embezzle money, and plot the overthrow of governments. It's fair to say that communications hardware lets a person use a PC as just another tool in the business of life, for good or for evil according to inclination. The immense popularity of the Internet and the World Wide Web and the deployment of high-speed digital communications technologies such as the Integrated Services Digital Network (ISDN) promise to make external communications even more important to PC users than it already is.

The parallel port provides another kind of window for the personal computer user. From its original purpose as a connector to an output-only printer, the parallel port has grown to serve additional needs. Clever programming allows Traveling Software's LapLink to connect two PCs for file transfer using the parallel port. External SCSI adapters can connect to the parallel port. Xircom markets a network interface that plugs into the parallel port; it's a godsend for laptop owners, who face a shortage of ways to augment already ultraminiaturized hardware. Several companies sell "dongles" that plug into the parallel port and act as security keys for expensive software. And printers have finally become smart enough to talk back to the operating system and explain their needs and capabilities.

Hardware needs software to make it work, of course. Underneath glitzy Web browsers are the drivers and APIs that are the province of systems programmers. A static VxD named VCOMM is the focal point for I/O involving serial and parallel ports in Windows 95. VCOMM works with *port driver* and *port virtualization* VxDs to coordinate the use of physical ports and to provide a degree of device independence to applications.

ARCHITECTURAL OVERVIEW

As with other areas of Windows, it's easier to understand where we are if we understand where we've been. I'll therefore briefly discuss the operation of the standard serial chip and the architecture of serial communications drivers in earlier versions of Windows. Then I'll describe the architecture of VCOMM and its satellites in Windows 95.

A Historical Perspective

Users of early PCs sometimes added option cards that contained serial and parallel ports to their computers. Early serial ports were based on the Intel 8250 universal asynchronous receiver-transmitter (UART) chip. The standard system BIOS provides cumbersome access to the serial port via INT 14h. MS-DOS supports serial communications through the AUX device or through devices named COM1, COM2, and so on. Both the BIOS and MS-DOS interfaces have always been too slow. Those interfaces also rely on continuous polling of input data, which makes them unsuitable either for full duplex communications or for multitasking systems.

To overcome the limitations of the BIOS and MS-DOS serial APIs, programmers learned early on how to directly program the 8250 chip. The major benefit you get from directly programming the chip is that you can make the chip generate a hardware interrupt when a new input character arrives or when the chip is ready to send another output character, rather than being forced to continuously poll the port. Another benefit is that you can program the baud-rate generator to achieve higher rates than the BIOS maximum of 9600.

Windows has always included a DLL driver (COMM.DRV) to interface between USER.EXE and the 8250 chip. Applications communicate with USER.EXE using low-level API calls such as *OpenComm*, *ReadComm*, and the like. USER.EXE calls COMM.DRV at entry points with names such as *inicom* and *reccom*. In Windows

3.x, COMM.DRV wrote directly to the 8250 ports and fielded the ensuing hardware interrupts. Enhanced-mode Windows 3.0 included a VxD named the VCD (Virtual Communications Device) to handle contention between different VMs for the hardware ports. It proved difficult for Windows 3.0 to sustain communications faster than 4800 baud, so Windows 3.1 added another VxD named COMBUFF. COMBUFF's job was to buffer all the input and output to and from the UART. COMBUFF also virtualized the serial ports and IRQs so as to supply prebuffered input to virtual machine programs (including COMM.DRV) and to buffer output to the UART. Figure 14-1 illustrates the architecture for serial communications in Windows 3.1.

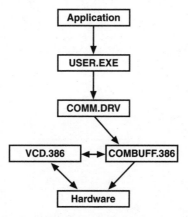

Figure 14-1. *Serial communications architecture in Windows 3.1.*

With COMBUFF in the picture, higher-speed communications became possible, but Windows applications still suffered performance penalties because of the baroque path through USER.EXE and COMM.DRV. Vendors routinely supplied their own versions of COMM.DRV, VCD.386, and COMBUFF.386. Relative chaos ensued, since independent vendors naturally didn't agree about how best to solve all the problems and didn't necessarily craft compatible replacements for Microsoft's components.

Programming the 8250 Chip

Since so much of the serial communications software architecture grew from the need to support one particular chip (the 8250 UART), it's important to understand the basic operation of that chip. Figure 14-2 on the following page is a simplified block diagram of the 8250 (actually, the figure shows its higher-performance descendant, the 16550) that emphasizes the features accessible to programmers. The chip requires eight 8-bit I/O ports. In a standard configuration, COM1 uses ports 3F8h through 3FFh, and COM2 uses ports 2F8h through 2FFh. The chip also requires an IRQ, which is usually IRQ 4 for COM1 and IRQ 3 for COM2.

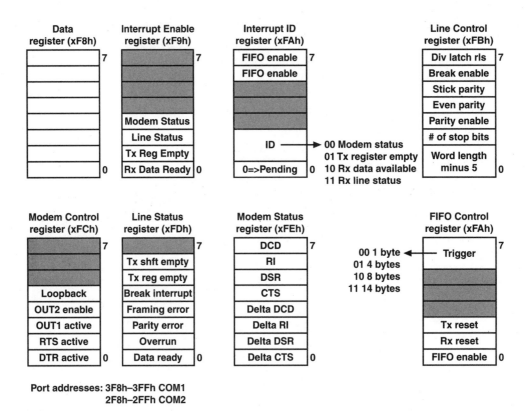

Figure 14-2. *Programming architecture of the 16550 UART.*

To prepare the chip for operation, you write configuration information to the Line Control, FIFO Control, and Interrupt Enable registers. Programming the baud rate requires you to output a 16-bit clock divisor to the divisor register pair. The divisor register pair is normally hidden from view. If you set bit 7 of the Line Control register, the divisor register pair becomes visible at the chip's base address and base address plus one. To determine the baud rate, divide 115,200 (the maximum data rate) by the value of the divisor. Thus, to set the chip for 9600 baud, you set the divisor register pair to 12.

The UART will generate interrupts upon the occurrence of those events that you indicated you wanted to handle by setting a bit in the Interrupt Enable register. Modem Status and Line Status interrupts occur when there's a change in the Modem Status or Line Status register, respectively. A Modem Status interrupt indicates a change in the RS-232 control signal lines connected to the UART, and a Line Status interrupt generally indicates an error. A Transmit Register Empty interrupt occurs when the chip finishes sending an output character; the interrupt indicates that it would be possible to send another character. A Receive Data Ready interrupt occurs when the chip receives an input character. Software must read the input byte before the next byte arrives to clear the interrupt and avoid an overrun error.

The Modem Control and Modem Status registers govern the RS-232 protocol that the UART uses to talk to the world outside the PC. Most often, the UART connects to a modem, which is why these registers have the word *modem* in their names. The six bits in these registers labeled DTR (Data Terminal Ready), RTS (Request To Send), DCD (Data Carrier Detect), RI (Ring Indicate), DSR (Data Set Ready), and CTS (Clear To Send) correspond to the six standard control lines specified by the RS-232 standard.

Because modems and communications protocols differ so widely, most communications programs bring low-level concepts like line control settings and RS-232 signals forward into the user interface. End users and applications require detailed control over how the UART operates, so device drivers for communications must provide a low-latency pathway for the transfer of information between the application and the hardware. To give one example of many, the end user can elect to use so-called "hardware flow control." Flow control refers to a mechanism for gating data transmission according to whether the receiver is ready to receive data or not. Hardware flow control relies on the RTS and CTS control lines. For a cooperatively multitasked application to be able to effectively perform flow control this way, it needs almost immediate access to an image of the Modem Status register (where the CTS signal appears). Thus, the Windows communications drivers have always provided a way for an application to get a pointer to the location at which the hardware interrupt handler stores the Modem Status register after an interrupt.

VCOMM Architecture

The Virtual Communications Driver (VCOMM) is the centerpiece of the Windows 95 architecture for serial and parallel communications. Figure 14-3 on the following page diagrams the interrelationships between VCOMM and other components in a Windows 95 system.

To perform serial communications, 16-bit Windows applications use standard Windows 3.x API calls implemented by the 16-bit USER.EXE module. USER.EXE translates the API calls into calls to the COMM.DRV driver. Whereas in earlier versions of Windows COMM.DRV fielded serial port interrupts and issued port I/O operations, the Windows 95 version of COMM.DRV simply calls VCOMM through a standard INT 2Fh, function 1684h, API call (see Table 14-1 on the following page).

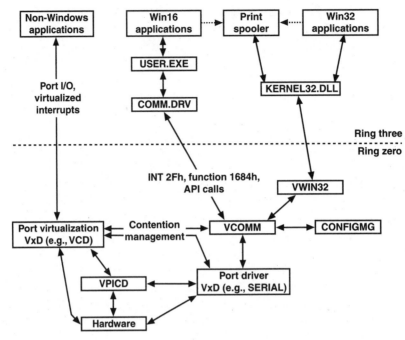

Figure 14-3. *Serial communications with VCOMM.*

Function Number	Mnemonic	Description
0	VCOMM_PM_API_OpenCom	Opens a communications device
1	VCOMM_PM_API_SetCom	Sets the port state from a DCB structure (like the Win16 *SetCommState* function)
2	VCOMM_PM_API_Setup	Sets input and output queue sizes
3	VCOMM_PM_API_ctx	Sends a high-priority character
4	VCOMM_PM_API_TrmCom	Closes a port
5	VCOMM_PM_API_StaCom	Determines port status
6	VCOMM_PM_API_cextfcn	Performs an extended control function (like the Win16 *EscapeCommFunction* function)
7	VCOMM_PM_API_cFlush	Flushes the input or output queue
8	VCOMM_PM_API_cevt	Registers an event word and an event mask (like the Win16 *SetCommEventMask* function)

Table 14-1. *VCOMM API functions for Windows applications.*   *(continued)*

continued

Function Number	Mnemonic	Description
9	VCOMM_PM_API_cevtget	Obtains the current event word and clears selected events (like the Win16 *GetCommEventMask* function)
10	VCOMM_PM_API_SetMSRShadow	Registers a byte to receive an up-to-date copy of the Modem Status register each time the register changes
11	VCOMM_PM_API_WriteString	Sends output data to the port
12	VCOMM_PM_API_ReadString	Reads input data from the port
13	VCOMM_PM_API_EnableNotify	Registers a notification function and receives and transmits queue size notification thresholds

Thirty-two–bit Windows programs use the regular *CreateFile* API function to open a file handle for a communications port, and they perform serial I/O operations using other Win32 API calls (see Table 14-2 on the following page). Internally, KERNEL32.DLL uses an undocumented interface with the VWIN32 VxD to reach VCOMM services. (VCOMM's VxD services are shown in Table 14-3 on page 449.) The print spooler is a Win32 program that interfaces between the GDI and VCOMM using the same undocumented VWIN32 pathway.

VCOMM services serial I/O requests from Windows programs and VxD callers of its service entry points by calling a *port driver* VxD. Table 14-4 on page 450 lists the functions each port driver exports for use by VCOMM.

Software running in an MS-DOS virtual machine hooks the standard serial port hardware interrupts and issues reads and writes to the standard I/O ports. A *port virtualization* VxD virtualizes the interrupts and the I/O ports. The standard port virtualization VxD is named VCD, just as it was in earlier versions of Windows. In addition to virtualizing the serial ports on behalf of virtual machine programs, however, a port virtualization VxD also provides *contention management* facilities for VCOMM.

Win32 API Function	Description
BuildCommDCB	Builds a control structure for a communications port
BuildCommDCBAndTimeouts	Builds a DCB and a COMMTIMEOUTS structure
ClearCommBreak	Clears a break condition
ClearCommError	Obtains and resets communication errors
CloseHandle	Closes a communications port
CommConfigDialog	Obtains configuration parameters from the user
CreateFile	Opens a communications port
EscapeCommFunction	Performs an extended control function
GetCommConfig	Determines communication configuration
GetCommMask	Gets the event mask
GetCommModemStatus	Gets the current modem status
GetCommProperties	Obtains the communications device properties
GetCommState	Gets the current device state
GetCommTimeouts	Determines the timeout settings
GetDefaultCommConfig	Gets the default configuration
PurgeComm	Purges the input and/or output queues
ReadFile	Reads data from a file
SetCommBreak	Sends a break signal
SetCommConfig	Sets the port configuration
SetCommMask	Sets the event mask
SetCommState	Sets the port state
SetCommTimeouts	Sets the port timeout values
SetDefaultCommConfig	Sets the default configuration
SetupComm	Establishes the input and output queue sizes
TransmitCommChar	Sends a priority character
WaitCommEvent	Waits for an overlapped (asynchronous) port operation to complete
WriteFile	Writes data to a file

Table 14-2. *Win32 API functions used for serial communications.*

Service	*Description*
_VCOMM_Acquire_Port	Acquires exclusive control of a port
_VCOMM_Add_Port	Adds a new port
_VCOMM_ClearCommError	Obtains and clears communication errors
_VCOMM_CloseComm	Closes a port
_VCOMM_EnableCommNotification	Registers an event notification callback
_VCOMM_EscapeCommFunction	Performs an extended control function
_VCOMM_GetCommEventMask	Gets current events and clears selected events
_VCOMM_GetCommProperties	Gets the properties of a port
_VCOMM_GetCommQueueStatus	Gets the status and queue sizes of a port
_VCOMM_GetCommState	Gets the current state of a port
_VCOMM_GetLastError	Gets the most recent error code
_VCOMM_GetModemStatus	Gets the current modem status
_VCOMM_GetSetCommTimeouts	Gets or sets timeouts for a port
_VCOMM_OpenComm	Opens a port
_VCOMM_PurgeComm	Purges the input or output queue
_VCOMM_ReadComm	Reads input data
_VCOMM_Register_Enumerator	Registers an enumerator for Plug and Play devices
_VCOMM_Register_Port_Driver	Registers a port driver
_VCOMM_Release_Port	Releases control of a port
_VCOMM_SetCommEventMask	Registers an event word and sets the event mask
_VCOMM_SetCommState	Sets the port state
_VCOMM_SetReadCallback	Registers a callback and sets the input queue size threshold
_VCOMM_SetupComm	Sets queue sizes and addresses
_VCOMM_SetWriteCallback	Registers a callback and sets the output queue size threshold
_VCOMM_TransmitCommChar	Sends a priority output character
_VCOMM_WriteComm	Sends output data

Table 14-3. *VCOMM API services for VxD callers.*

Port Driver Function	Description
ClearError	Gets and clears errors
Close	Closes the port
EnableNotification	Registers the event notification procedure
EscapeFunction	Performs an extended control function
GetCommConfig	Gets the port configuration
GetCommState	Gets the port state
GetError	Gets the last error
GetEventMask	Gets current events and clears selected events
GetModemStatus	Gets the current modem status
GetProperties	Gets the port properties
GetQueueStatus	Gets the port status and queue counts
Open	Opens a port
Purge	Purges the input or output queue
Read	Reads input data
SetCommConfig	Sets the port configuration
SetCommState	Sets the port state
SetEventMask	Registers an event word and sets the event mask
SetModemStatusShadow	Registers a byte to receive an up-to-date copy of the Modem Status register each time the register changes
SetReadCallback	Registers the callback and sets the input queue threshold
Setup	Sets the queue sizes and addresses
SetWriteCallback	Registers the callback and sets the output queue threshold
TransmitChar	Sends a priority character
Write	Sends output data

Table 14-4. *Port driver functions.*

SERIAL PORT DRIVERS

In this section, we'll discuss the details of a serial port driver. Refer once again to Figure 14-3 on page 446 and notice that VCOMM uses port driver VxDs as the device drivers for physical ports. VCOMM itself serves both as the intermediary between port drivers and Windows applications and as the point of contact between the Windows 95 Configuration Manager and the port drivers.

Microsoft supplies a port driver named SERIAL.VXD as one of the standard Windows 95 components. The source code for SERIAL.VXD, which Microsoft coded in assembly language, is part of the Windows 95 DDK. To explore in detail how port drivers work, you usually have to decipher the assembly-language version of SERIAL.VXD. In this book, however, I'll illustrate the inner workings of port drivers by showing you a C++ version of SERIAL.VXD instead.

About the Sample Version of SERIAL.VXD In contrast to most of the sample programs on which the examples in this book are based, the SERIAL.VXD sample is a complete, working serial port driver. I chose to write it in C++ because the architecture of port drivers seems to cry out for class inheritance and virtual functions. I also chose to use the standard DDK header files rather than a toolkit like VTOOLSD because I wanted to avoid the considerable complication of dealing with someone else's complete class library. The code presented in this chapter is included on the companion disc in the \CHAP14\PORTDRIVER directory.

Although the discussion in this section explicitly concerns a port driver for a serial port, much of it also pertains to parallel port drivers. The similarity between the two kinds of drivers arises from the fact that both kinds of ports move data bytes at relatively slow speed into and out of the computer. Furthermore, printer technology includes both serial and parallel varieties, so it would be silly to provide widely disparate driver interfaces for ring-three programs to deal with.

Loading Port Drivers

The overall process by which port drivers end up loaded in memory and able to control a physical serial port is somewhat complicated. Let's consider as an example a computer that has the standard two serial ports (COM1 and COM2). The Windows 95 Setup program would have detected these two ports as legacy devices and would have added subkeys to the HKLM\Enum\Root branch of the registry (see Figure 14-4 on the following page). The named value Driver in these *hardware* subkeys points to so-called *software* subkeys of HKLM\System\CurrentControlSet\Services\Class (see Figure 14-5 on the following page). Named values in each software key designate VCOMM as the device loader and SERIAL.VXD as the port driver.

As indicated in the preceding chapters on Plug and Play, the root enumerator will create a DEVNODE for each serial port, whereupon the Configuration Manager

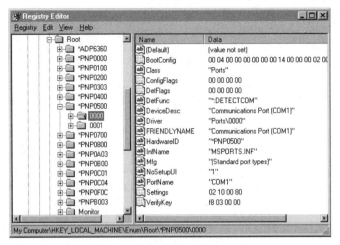

Figure 14-4. *The hardware key for COM1.*

will send VCOMM a PNP_New_Devnode system control message that includes the *DLVXD_LOAD_DEVLOADER* argument. This argument indicates that VCOMM is supposed to act as the device loader for the DEVNODE. VCOMM instead registers itself as the device driver for the DEVNODE and supplies the address of a configuration function. When the Configuration Manager configures a serial port, it calls VCOMM's configuration function, whereupon VCOMM determines which I/O ports and which IRQ belong to the serial port. Normally, COM1 owns I/O ports 3F8h through 3FFh and IRQ 4, and COM2 owns I/O ports 2F8h through 2FFh and IRQ 3. VCOMM also reads the named value PortDriver from each DEVNODE's software key and thereby determines that SERIAL.VXD is the port driver for both standard serial ports.

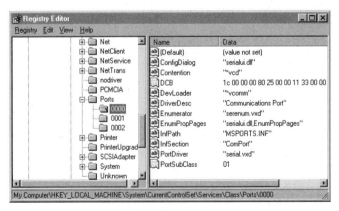

Figure 14-5. *The software key for COM1.*

Eventually, some client of VCOMM will attempt to open a port. As we'll see, the port open request eventually turns into a *_VCOMM_OpenComm VxD* service call. The client might be a 16-bit Windows application, which will use the Win16 API *OpenComm* function. *OpenComm*, an entry point to USER.EXE, will call the *inicom* entry in COMM.DRV (a 16-bit DLL), which will thereupon call VCOMM's protected-mode API entry to perform the *VCOMM_PM_API_OpenCom* function. Internally, this API entry point issues a VxD-level service call to *_VCOMM_OpenComm*.

The VCOMM client attempting to open the port might instead be a Win32 application. It will call the regular Win32 API *CreateFile* function, designating COM1 or COM2 as the name of the file to open. The KERNEL32.DLL implementation of *CreateFile* uses an undocumented interface to call the VWIN32 VxD. VWIN32 in turn calls VCOMM at another undocumented entry point, which ends up issuing the same *_VCOMM_OpenComm* service call to open the port.

Finally, the VCOMM client in question might just be another VxD, which would issue a *_VCOMM_OpenComm* call directly. The only standard VxD I know of that acts as a VCOMM client is the UNIMODEM driver for AT-command-compatible modems. You might need to write your own VCOMM client VxD to support an application, too.

However it originates, the *_VCOMM_OpenComm* call includes a string argument that designates the port to be opened. At this point, VCOMM consults its internal data structures to determine that SERIAL.VXD is the port driver for the port. VCOMM dynamically loads SERIAL.VXD. As part of the process of dynamically loading SERIAL.VXD, the VMM will send SERIAL.VXD a Sys_Dynamic_Device_Init system control message. SERIAL.VXD then calls VCOMM to register as a port driver:

```
SYSCTL BOOL OnSysDynamicDeviceInit()
    {                               // OnSysDynamicDeviceInit
    return VCOMM_Register_Port_Driver((PFN) DriverControl);
    }                               // OnSysDynamicDeviceInit
```

There are three mundane things to explain about this short code fragment. In my sample program, the symbol *SYSCTL* is simply #defined as *extern "C"* to make it easier to reference system control message handlers from the assembly-language device control procedure. The standard VXDWRAPS.H header uses PFN as a generic function pointer type, but PFN rarely matches the actual arguments to any of the function pointers it purports to describe. Hence, it's usually necessary to cast function arguments to VxD service calls as shown in this fragment. Finally, VXDWRAPS.H defines function wrappers for VCOMM entries without any leading underscore, in defiance of the usual convention. For instance, VCOMM exports a C-convention service named _VCOMM_Register_Port_Driver, but VXDWRAPS.H declares the wrapper for this service without the leading underscore.

The purpose of *VCOMM_Register_Port_Driver* is to register a so-called driver control function with VCOMM. The prototype for the driver control function is as follows:

```
BOOL DriverControl(DWORD cf, DEVNODE devnode,
    DWORD refdata, ...)
```

The *cf* argument denotes a control function code, *devnode* is a pointer to a device node, and *refdata* is a piece of so-called "reference data" to be passed through to downstream VCOMM functions. The remaining variable arguments depend, supposedly, on which *cf* is being requested.

Despite the grandiose description I just gave of the driver control function, only one control function is currently defined, namely *DC_Initialize*. The variable arguments for the *DC_Initialize* function are the base I/O port address (a DWORD), the IRQ (also a DWORD), and the name of the device (a pointer to a string). In response to *DC_Initialize*, the port driver should call *VCOMM_Add_Port* to erect the machinery for managing the port. In my sample driver, I accomplished this step in the following way:

```
#include <stdarg.h>
...
BOOL DriverControl(DWORD cf, DEVNODE devnode,
    DWORD refdata, ...)
    {                             // DriverControl
    va_list ap;
    va_start(ap, refdata);

    DWORD iobase = va_arg(ap, DWORD);
    DWORD irq    = va_arg(ap, DWORD);
    char *name   = va_arg(ap, char *);

    va_end(ap);

    CSerialPort* port = new CSerialPort(name,
        iobase, irq, devnode);
    if (!port->AddPort(refdata))
        {                         // unable to add port
        delete port;
        return FALSE;
        }                         // unable to add port

    return TRUE;
    }                             // DriverControl
```

```
...
BOOL CPort::AddPort(DWORD refdata)
    {                               // CPort::AddPort
    if (!VCOMM_Add_Port(refdata, (PFN) CPort::PreOpen, m_name))
        return FALSE;
    if ((m_contend = (PCONTENTIONPROC)
        VCOMM_Get_Contention_Handler(m_name)))
        m_resource = VCOMM_Map_Name_To_Resource(m_name);
    return TRUE;
    }                               // CPort::AddPort
```

The first argument to *VCOMM_Add_Port* is whatever reference data was supplied to the driver control procedure. The second argument is the address of a function that VCOMM can call to open the port; in this case, it's the *PreOpen* member function of the *CPort* class. The third argument is the name of the port (for example, "COM2"); this value is the same one supplied as the third of the variable arguments to the driver control procedure. I'll discuss the purpose of the call to *VCOMM_Get_Contention_Handler* later on.

To make complete sense of this code fragment, you have to see the following excerpt from the complete declarations of the *CSerialPort* and *CPort* classes. (The complete *CPort* declaration appears later in this chapter; the *CSerialPort* declaration is available in machine-readable form on the companion disc.) Here's the excerpt:

```
class CPort
{
public:
    CPort(char *name, DWORD iobase, DWORD irq, DWORD devnode);
    char            m_name[8];
    DWORD           m_iobase;
    DWORD           m_irq;
    DEVNODE         m_devnode;
    PCONTENTIONPROC m_contend;
    DWORD           m_resource;
};

class CSerialPort : public CPort
{
public:
    CSerialPort(char *name, DWORD iobase, DWORD irq,
        DWORD devnode);
};
```

This snippet illustrates the fact that I defined two C++ classes to implement the driver sample. *CPort* encapsulates all the device-independent functionality of a VCOMM port driver. *CSerialPort*, which is derived from *CPort*, implements an 8250-compatible serial port driver. As you might imagine, the constructor for *CPort* initializes member variables and performs other housekeeping chores that don't involve calling VxD services (other than _HeapAllocate, which gets called implicitly by *operator new*).

A Note on Documentation   The documentation for VCOMM's service entries and its protected-mode API, as well as for the data structures and functions in a port driver, is found in VCOMM.DOC on the Windows 95 DDK disc. This particular document has many mistakes. VCOMM.DOC says the driver control function doesn't return a value. It really does, though, and that return value becomes the return value from *VCOMM_Register_Port_Driver*. (If the driver control function were truly a void procedure, there would be no way to abort the loading of the port driver VxD if the call to *VCOMM_Add_Port* failed or if something else went wrong.) VCOMM.DOC also misspells the one and only function code as *DC_InitializePort*, whereas it's really spelled *DC_Initialize*. Finally, VCOMM.DOC mixes up the order of the variable arguments, saying that the port name is first when it's really last. I've done my best to report things correctly in this book, since there's no other way to make a real driver work. The WinHelp annotation file that appears on the companion disc also notes the corrections I discovered.

Opening the Port

After you call *VCOMM_Add_Port*, VCOMM finally has the address of one of your functions that it can call to actually open the port. In my sample driver, I wrote the port open routine as a static member function of the generic *CPort* class, as follows:

```
PortData* CPort::PreOpen(char *name, HVM hVM, int* pError)
    {                               // CPort::PreOpen
    CPort* port;

    for (port = CPortAnchor; port; port = port->m_next)
        if (strcmp(name, port->m_name) == 0)
            {                       // try to open port
            if (port->m_open)
                {                   // already open
                *pError = IE_OPEN;
                return NULL;
                }                   // already open
            if (port->Open(hVM, pError))
                {                   // opened okay
                port->m_open = TRUE;
                return &port->m_pd;
                }                   // opened okay
```

```
        port->Release();
        return NULL;
        }                         // try to open port

    *pError = IE_HARDWARE;
    return NULL;
    }                             // CPort::PreOpen
```

The first argument to the *PreOpen* function is the name of the port VCOMM is trying to open. This name originates in an application as an argument to *OpenComm* or *CreateFile*, or in a client VxD as an argument to *VCOMM_OpenComm*. The name should match the name of one of the ports our driver registered with VCOMM by calling *VCOMM_Add_Port*. To satisfy VCOMM's call to the open routine, a port driver needs some way to locate its own private data structures starting from the name. In my own driver, I used a linked list anchored in a static member variable (*CPortAnchor*) and chained with member variables (*m_next* and *m_prev*). The *CPort* constructor and destructor are responsible for maintaining the links.

The second argument to the open function is a VM handle, which we'll use as part of the contention management protocol described in the section titled "Managing Contention" on page 463. The third and last argument is the address of a DWORD in which to record the reason for any failure in the open routine. Possible settings for this variable are *IE_OPEN* (the port is already open) and *IE_HARDWARE* (the port doesn't exist or has some other hardware problem that prevents it from being opened).

The purpose of the open routine is to finish initializing data structures, reserve the device through an elaborate contention management protocol, and return to VCOMM the address of a *PortData* structure that you have completely initialized. VCOMM and the port driver share the *PortData* structure as a way to manage the device while it's open. In fact, VCOMM uses the address of your *PortData* structure as a handle argument to all of the port driver functions you supply besides the open routine.

The *PortData* Structure

Understanding the *PortData* structure is key to learning how VCOMM and a port driver cooperate to manage an open port. Figure 14-6 on the following page illustrates the layout of this important structure. Since VCOMM.DOC documents the *PortData* structure so incompletely, we'll go through the structure field by field now.

PDLength holds the length of your structure so that VCOMM can verify that you've used the correct declaration of the *PortData* structure in building your driver. You simply set this value to *sizeof(PortData)*. *PDVersion* is a version number used for a similar purpose; we are using version 1.10 of the structure, so we initialize this field to 0x010A.

```
typedef struct _PortData {
  WORD PDLength;                  // 00 size of this structure
  WORD PDVersion;                 // 02 version of structure
  PortFunctions *PDfunctions;     // 04 table of port driver functions
  DWORD PDNumFunctions;           // 08 number of functions in PDfunctions table
  DWORD dwLastError;              // 0C 0 or error resulting from last port
                                  //    driver function
  DWORD dwClientEventMask;        // 10 reserved for use by VCOMM
  DWORD lpClientEventNotify;      // 14 client's event notification procedure
  DWORD lpClientReadNotify;       // 18 client's receive notification procedure
  DWORD lpClientWriteNotify;      // 1C client's transmit notification procedure
  DWORD dwClientRefData;          // 20 reference data for lpClientEventNotify
  DWORD dwWin31Req;               // 24 reserved for use by VCOMM
  DWORD dwClientEvent;            // 28 reserved for use by VCOMM
  DWORD dwCallerVMId;             // 2C reserved for use by VCOMM
  DWORD dwDetectedEvents;         // 30 default location to store currently
                                  //    detected events
  DWORD dwCommError;              // 34 current communication error flags
  BYTE bMSRShadow;                // 38 default shadow of Modem Status register
  WORD wFlags;                    // 39 reserved for use by VCOMM
  BYTE LossByte;                  // 3B contention management flag
  DWORD QInAddr;                  // 3C input queue address
  DWORD QInSize;                  // 40 input queue size
  DWORD QOutAddr;                 // 44 output queue address
  DWORD QOutSize;                 // 48 output queue size
  DWORD QInCount;                 // 4C number of bytes now in input queue
  DWORD QInGet;                   // 50 input queue offset to get next byte from
  DWORD QInPut;                   // 54 input queue offset to put next byte into
  DWORD QOutCount;                // 58 number of bytes now in output queue
  DWORD QOutGet;                  // 5C output queue offset to get next byte
                                  //    from
  DWORD QOutPut;                  // 60 output queue offset to put next byte
                                  //    into
  DWORD ValidPortData;            // 64 reserved for use by VCOMM
  DWORD lpLoadHandle;             // 68 reserved for use by VCOMM
  COMMTIMEOUTS cmto;              // 6C reserved for use by VCOMM
  DWORD lpReadRequestQueue;       // 80 reserved for use by VCOMM
  DWORD lpWriteRequestQueue;      // 84 reserved for use by VCOMM
  DWORD dwLastReceiveTime;        // 88 default location to store time of last
                                  //    receive
  DWORD dwReserved1;              // 8C reserved for use by VCOMM
  DWORD dwReserved2;              // 90 reserved for use by VCOMM
} PortData;                       // [94]
```

Figure 14-6. *The layout of the* PortData *structure.*

PDfunctions is the address of a function pointer table, and *PDNumFunctions* is the number of pointers in that table. (Even though *PDfunctions* is defined as a pointer to a *PortFunctions* structure, it really points to an array of function pointers than can be shorter than the *PortFunctions* declaration seems to require.) The function pointer table serves a purpose similar to that of a virtual function table in a C++ class object, because it directs VCOMM to your port driver's service functions; I'll have more to say about this table in the section titled "Port Driver Functions" on page 469.

The *dwLastError* member holds 0 or the error code with which the most recent port driver function ended. Table 14-5 lists the possible values for this variable. As we will see, all the port driver functions (except *Open*) are Boolean functions that return TRUE if they succeed and FALSE if they don't. Even though there is a port driver function named *GetError* that's presumably supposed to return the *dwLastError* value, the implementation of *GetError* in Microsoft's SERIAL.VXD doesn't do anything. VCOMM actually uses the *dwLastError* value to diagnose errors for its own callers without bothering to call the port driver.

Error Code	Description
IE_BADID	Indicates that the device is an invalid or unsupported device
IE_OPEN	Indicates that the port is already open
IE_NOPEN	Indicates that the port isn't open
IE_MEMORY	Indicates that there is insufficient memory
IE_DEFAULT	Indicates that there is an error in the default parameters
IE_INVALIDSERVICE	Indicates that the port driver doesn't support this function
IE_HARDWARE	Indicates that the hardware is not present
IE_BYTESIZE	Indicates that there is an invalid byte size in the DCB
IE_BAUDRATE	Indicates that there is an invalid baud rate in the DCB
IE_EXTINVALID	Indicates use of an invalid escape function
IE_INVALIDPARAM	Indicates the passage of an invalid parameter
IE_TRANSMITCHARFAILED	Indicates that there is a priority character already waiting to be sent

Table 14-5. *Error codes in the* dwLastError *member of* PortData.

VCOMM maintains the three fields named *lpClientEventNotify*, *lpClientRead-Notify*, and *lpClientWriteNotify*. Each field contains the address of a client callback function, which can be located in ring three. The port driver should maintain *separate* function pointers for event, receive, and transmit notifications; VCOMM calls your *EnableNotification*, *SetReadCallback*, and *SetWriteCallback* functions to register these function pointers. The pointers refer to functions within VCOMM that wrap the client callbacks. Each callback also has a (different) DWORD of associated reference data supplied to you in the registration call. You need to reserve three DWORDs somewhere to hold the reference data values for the callbacks.

The event notification callback function registered by *EnableNotification* handles communication events detected by the port driver. Table 14-6 lists the flags for the events that might occur. Whenever the port driver detects an event, it sets the appropriate event flag in the current *event word*. The driver clears events when instructed to do so by a call to the *GetEventMask* function. The *dwDetectedEvents* member of the *PortData* structure is not, as you might suppose, the place to record events. The port driver should instead maintain a separate LPDWORD variable that points to the current event word, which can be changed by calls to *SetEventMask*. The initial value of this pointer variable might as well be the address of the *dwDetectedEvents* member, since that member won't be used for any other purpose.

Event Flag	Description
EV_RXCHAR	Indicates that a character (any character at all) was received
EV_RXFLAG	Indicates that the special "event character" specified in the DCB was received
EV_TXEMPTY	Indicates that the transmit queue is empty
EV_CTS	Indicates that the CTS bit has changed state
EV_DSR	Indicates that the DSR bit has changed state
EV_RLSD	Indicates that the carrier detect line state has changed
EV_BREAK	Indicates that a break signal was received
EV_ERR	Indicates that a Line Status interrupt (indicating an error) has occurred
EV_RING	Indicates that the RI (Ring Indicate) line became active
EV_PERR	Indicates that a printer error has occurred
EV_CTSS	Indicates that the CTS is active
EV_DSRS	Indicates that the DSR is active
EV_RLSDS	Indicates that the carrier detect line is active

Table 14-6. *Communication event flags.*   *(continued)*

continued

Event Flag	Description
EV_RingTe	Indicates that the ring trailing-edge was detected
EV_TXCHAR	Indicates that a character was transmitted
EV_DRIVER	Indicates that a driver-specific event occurred
EV_UNAVAIL	Indicates that the port was stolen
EV_AVAIL	Indicates that a previously stolen port has become available again

The port driver uses *dwCommError* to record communication errors. Table 14-7 lists the flag bits that denote various errors. Errors accumulate until they are cleared by a call to the *ClearError* port driver function. The existence of any error also aborts any Read operation unless someone has issued the *IGNOREERRORONREADS* escape function.

Error Flag	Description
CE_RXOVER	Indicates that the input queue is full
CE_OVERRUN	Indicates that there was a receive overrun error
CE_RXPARITY	Indicates that there was a parity error
CE_FRAME	Indicates that there was a framing error
CE_BREAK	Indicates that there was a break detected
CE_CTSTO	Indicates that there was a CTS timeout
CE_DSRTO	Indicates that there was a DSR timeout
CE_RLSDTO	Indicates that there was a carrier detect timeout
CE_TXFULL	Indicates that the output queue is full
CE_PTO	Indicates that there was a printer timeout
CE_IOE	Indicates that there was a printer I/O error
CE_DNS	Indicates that there was a printer device-not-selected error
CE_OOP	Indicates that the printer is out of paper
CE_MODE	Indicates that the requested mode is not supported

Table 14-7. *Error flags in* dwCommError.

A standard UART alerts the processor to a change in the Modem Status register by generating an interrupt. The port driver should maintain a PBYTE variable that points to a location in which its interrupt routine will save the then-current value of the Modem Status register. The *bMSRShadow* field of the *PortData* structure is the initial location of this "shadow" copy of the register; the location can be changed by calling the *SetModemStatusShadow* port driver function.

According to the official documentation, *LossByte* is reserved for use by VCOMM. This isn't accurate, however, in that a port driver for one of the standard COM ports needs to inspect and modify the low-order bit in this byte to correctly handle the contention protocol implemented by the VCD. I'll talk more about the contention protocol in the next section.

The port driver manages input and output queues as ring buffers using fields reserved in the *PortData* structure. Figure 14-7 illustrates the relationship between the buffering parameters. The port driver's *Setup* function records each queue's buffer address *(QInAddr* and *QOutAddr)* and size *(QInSize* and *QOutSize)*; the buffers can belong to an external caller, or the port driver itself can allocate storage for them. Each queue has a count *(QInCount* and *QOutCount)*, which indicates how many bytes of data are currently in the buffer. A program that adds data to the buffer does so at the offset held in a "put" pointer *(QInPut* or *QOutPut)*, which it then increments. A program that removes data from the buffer does so from the offset held in a "get" pointer *(QInGet* or *QOutGet)*, which it also increments. Each kind of program also adjusts the associated count value to indicate whether it just added or removed data. The difference between the "get" and the "put" pointers, when expressed modulo the buffer size, should always be equal to the count of data bytes in the buffer. Because the buffer is used as a ring buffer, the "get" pointer may be greater than the "put" pointer, which means that the portion of the buffer occupied by data wraps around the end of the buffer back to the beginning.

To provide for timing out an idle port, the port driver must record the system time at which the most recent data byte was received. Since there is an escape function *(SETUPDATETIMEADDR)* to specify the location of a DWORD to receive

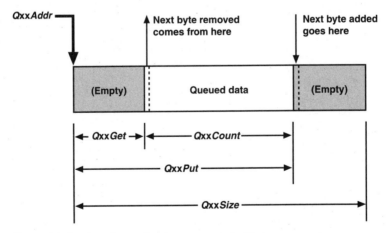

Figure 14-7. *The relationship between port buffering parameters.*

this time stamp, the driver needs to provide its own PDWORD variable to point to the current time stamp location. The driver should initialize the variable so that it points to the *dwLastReceiveTime* field of the *PortData* structure.

VCOMM reserves the *PortData* structure members not specifically mentioned above for its own use. In addition to fields whose names obviously indicate that they are reserved, these fields include *dwClientEventMask, dwWin31Req, dwClientEvent, dwCallerVMId, wFlags, ValidPortData, lpLoadHandle, cmto, lpReadRequestQueue,* and *lpWriteRequestQueue*.

Managing Contention

Windows can't allow two applications to simultaneously share a given serial port. This probably seems obvious, since the two applications are likely to require different communications settings and probably won't be able to multiplex their input and output traffic through a shared serial port. *Contention management* is the generic term that describes how Windows makes sure that only one application at a time has access to each port.

The software registry key for a port contains the named value Contention that designates a VxD to manage contention among VCOMM port drivers for that port. The VCD provides contention management for serial ports, and the Virtual Printer Device (VPD) does the same for parallel ports. The contention VxD for a port normally also virtualizes the port for virtual machine software that wants to use the port directly. Virtualizing the port means trapping port I/O operations and hooking the associated hardware interrupt using techniques described in the previous chapter. It makes sense to combine virtualization and contention management into a single VxD because the only way a VxD can discover that MS-DOS or other virtual machine software is trying to use the port is by trapping an I/O operation. Furthermore, as we saw in the previous chapter, part of the job of virtualizing a hardware resource is handling contention between different virtual machines.

A contention VxD contains a *contention function*. VCOMM learns the address of this function by sending the VxD a GET_CONTENTION_HANDLER system control message. The VxD responds by returning the address of the contention function in the EAX register and by clearing the carry flag. A port driver learns the address of the contention function for its port by calling VCOMM. In the *CPort::AddPort* function of my example, I used the following call

```
m_contend = (PCONTENTIONPROC)
    VCOMM_Get_Contention_Handler(m_name);
```

where *m_contend* is a member variable that is used to hold the address of the contention function while the port remains open.

The contention function is actually six different functions multiplexed via a subfunction code supplied as the first argument (see Table 14-8). The details of these functions are discussed in the following pages.

Subfunction Code	Description
MAP_DEVICE_TO_RESOURCE	Obtains the contention resource handle for a named port
ACQUIRE_RESOURCE	Acquires ownership of a port
STEAL_RESOURCE	Steals a port from its current owner
RELEASE_RESOURCE	Releases a previously acquired port
ADD_RESOURCE	Adds a port to the list managed by the called contention function
REMOVE_RESOURCE	Removes a port from the list managed by the called contention function

Table 14-8. *Subfunction codes for contention functions.*

The *MAP_DEVICE_TO_RESOURCE* Subfunction The calling sequence for the contention function using the *MAP_DEVICE_TO_RESOURCE* subfunction is:

```
DWORD hResource = Contend(MAP_DEVICE_TO_RESOURCE, PCHAR name,
    DEVNODE devnode, DWORD IOBase);
```

The return value is 0 if the contention function doesn't know about the *name* port. Otherwise, the return value is a resource handle that has meaning to the contention function.

A port driver doesn't need to call the contention function directly to perform the resource mapping because VCOMM provides a service to hide this particular interface. In my sample driver, the *CPort::AddPort* function contains this call:

```
m_resource = VCOMM_Map_Name_To_Resource(m_name);
```

Here, *m_resource* is a member variable that holds the resource handle while the port remains open. Note that the subfunction code here doesn't exactly match the VCOMM service name.

The *ACQUIRE_RESOURCE* Subfunction The calling sequence for the contention function using the *ACQUIRE_RESOURCE* subfunction is:

```
DWORD hContend = Contend(ACQUIRE_RESOURCE, DWORD hResource,
    PFN NotifyProc, DWORD NotifyData, BOOL bSteal);
```

The *ACQUIRE_RESOURCE* subfunction asks the contention function to assign ownership of the port represented by *hResource* to the caller. The *hResource* handle is the one returned by a previous call to *MAP_DEVICE_TO_RESOURCE*. If the *bSteal* argument is TRUE, the contention function will attempt to steal the port from its current owner if it is currently owned. If the flag is FALSE, the contention function won't try to reassign the port if it is currently owned. *NotifyProc* is the address of a notification function that will be called during the process of assigning ownership, and *NotifyData* is an arbitrary quantity to be passed to the notification function as reference data.

If the contention function was able to assign the resource, it returns a DWORD handle to the port; otherwise, the function returns NULL. In practice, the handle returned from a successful call is the same as the resource handle used as the *hResource* argument. In the case of the VCD's contention function, in fact, both handles are the address of the VCD's internal *VCD_COM_Struc* structure for the port. Therefore, you could treat *ACQUIRE_RESOURCE* as a Boolean function and just test the return value for 0.

In my sample driver, I wrote a *CPort::Acquire* member function to obtain ownership of a port that's in the process of being opened:

```
BOOL CPort::Acquire(HVM hVM)
    {                               // CPort::Acquire
    if (m_contend)
        {                           // have a contention procedure
        if (!m_resource)
            return FALSE;           // but no resource handle
        m_hContend = (*m_contend)(ACQUIRE_RESOURCE, m_resource,
            pPortStolen, this, TRUE); // try to steal if owned
        if (m_hContend)
            {                       // we've got it
            m_owner = hVM;
            return TRUE;
            }                       // we've got it
        return FALSE;
        }                           // have a contention procedure
    m_owner = hVM;
    return TRUE;
    }                               // CPort::Acquire
```

(The *pPortStolen* variable is a static pointer to the *CPort::OnPortStolen* function I'll show you in a moment. I needed a pointer to overcome a limitation in the C++ compiler having to do with passing a pointer to a member function as one of the variable arguments to the contention function.)

The notification function receives two arguments: the first argument is the *NotifyData* reference data and the second is a Boolean value that indicates whether the port has been acquired by the driver (TRUE) or lost to another driver (FALSE). The contention VxD will call this function during the *ACQUIRE_RESOURCE* call and at other times when ownership of the port changes. In the sample driver, I use a static member function to handle ownership change notifications (it needs to be static because the VCD calls it directly as a C-language function):

```
BOOL CPort::OnPortStolen(CPort* port, BOOL owned)
    {                                  // OnPortStolen
    if (owned)                         // we own the port
        port->m_pd.LossByte &= ~1;     // set low bit to 0
    else                               // we lost the port
        port->m_pd.LossByte |= 1;      // set low bit to 1
    return TRUE;                       // answer !owned with "OK"
    }                                  // OnPortStolen
```

(The *m_pd* member of *CPort* is the *PortData* structure for this port.) The return value matters only when the *owned* argument is 0, meaning that the contention VxD wants to steal the port. You return TRUE to allow the port to be stolen and FALSE to prevent it from being stolen.

My *OnPortStolen* function mimics what the official SERIAL.VXD code does when VCOMM notifies it of ownership changes. The low-order bit of *LossByte* is 0 when the port driver owns the port and 1 otherwise. Various functions in the port driver, such as the interrupt routine and other functions that want to do I/O operations to the UART, need to check this bit first. If the bit is 1, meaning that the contention VxD has stolen the port, the port driver can try to steal it back by issuing a *STEAL_RESOURCE* call.

The *STEAL_RESOURCE* Subfunction The calling sequence for the contention function using the *STEAL_RESOURCE* subfunction is:

```
BOOL bStolen = Contend(STEAL_RESOURCE, DWORD hResource,
    PFN NotifyProc);
```

The *hResource* argument is the resource handle from *MAP_DEVICE_TO_RE-SOURCE*, and *NotifyProc* is the address of the same notification procedure used in an earlier *ACQUIRE_RESOURCE* call. The notification procedure uses the *NotifyProc* address both to identify the caller as a previous owner of the resource *and* to notify it when it has regained ownership, so it's important for the caller to always use the same procedure address for *ACQUIRE_RESOURCE* and *STEAL_RESOURCE* calls.

STEAL_RESOURCE returns TRUE if the contention VxD was able to reassign control over the port and FALSE otherwise. Before returning, it calls the previous

WHY NOT USE *VCOMM_ACQUIRE_PORT*?

According to the official documentation in VCOMM.DOC, a port driver is supposed to call *VCOMM_Acquire_Port* to gain ownership of a port and *VCOMM_Release_Port* to release ownership later. Don't you believe it! First of all, VCOMM.DOC misdocuments *VCOMM_Acquire_Port*. The correct calling sequence to this function is

```
DWORD hContend = VCOMM_Acquire_Port((HANDLE) hPort,
    DWORD lPortNum, HVM hVM, DWORD lFlags, char *vxdname);
```

where *hPort* is the VCOMM port handle (the *PortData* structure address) for the port; *lPortNum* is either the 1-based port number (1 means COM1) or the base I/O address for the port, depending on the setting of bit 2 of the *lFlags* argument; *hVM* is the handle of the VM that will own the port or -1 if your VxD will take over the port; *lFlags* is composed by ORing together 01h (meaning "steal the port even if it's already owned") and 02h (meaning "*lPortNum* is the I/O base address instead of the port number"); and *vxdname* is the null-terminated name of your VxD in case you supplied -1 for the *hVM* argument. The *vxdname* argument isn't used if you give a real VM handle for *hVM*. You probably wouldn't want to take over the port by using -1 for the *hVM* argument because you would then have complete responsibility for virtualizing the port as well. If you're this brave, first carefully read the source code for the VCD (on the Windows 95 DDK disk in the \COMM\SAMPLES\VCD directory).

If we were going to call this function in our sample port driver, the call would look like the following:

```
m_hContend = VCOMM_Acquire_Port((HANDLE) &m_pd, m_iobase, hVM,
    3, NULL);
```

VCOMM will call *VCD_Acquire_Port_Windows_Style* to claim ownership of the port. The VCD will also know to clear the low-order byte of your *PortData* structure's *LossByte* field so you can know when the port has been stolen away from you. Unfortunately, you end up with no method to steal the port back. If you call the contention function directly, as I'm recommending here, your callback routine (the *CPort::OnPortStolen* function, for example) will alert you to the fact that your port has been stolen. You can later do a *STEAL_RESOURCE* call to regain control, as SERIAL.VXD does.

owner's notification procedure to indicate loss of the port (the *owned* argument is set to FALSE), and it calls the new owner's notification procedure to indicate restoration of control (the *owned* argument is set to TRUE). Because *STEAL_RE-SOURCE* calls notification procedures, it's not strictly necessary for a port driver to test the return value. In my sample driver, however, I mimicked what the official SERIAL.VXD code does to steal the port:

```
BOOL CPort::StealPort()
    {                               // CPort::StealPort
    if (!(m_pd.LossByte & 1))
        return TRUE;                // we never lost it
    if ((*m_contend)(STEAL_RESOURCE, m_hContend, pPortStolen))
        {                           // stole it back
        m_pd.LossByte &= ~1;
        return TRUE;
        }                           // stole it back
    return FALSE;
    }                               // CPort::StealPort
```

The *RELEASE_RESOURCE* Subfunction The calling sequence for the contention function using the *RELEASE_RESOURCE* subfunction is:

```
Contend(RELEASE_RESOURCE, DWORD hResource, PFN NotifyProc);
```

The *hResource* argument is the resource handle from *MAP_DEVICE_TO_RE-SOURCE*, and *NotifyProc* is the address of the same notification procedure used in an earlier *ACQUIRE_RESOURCE* call. Before returning, *RELEASE_RESOURCE* calls the notification function to indicate loss of the resource (the *owned* argument is set to FALSE).

In the sample driver, I wrote a member function to relinquish control during the process of closing the port:

```
void CPort::Release()
    {                               // CPort::Release
    m_owner = NULL;
    if (m_hContend)
        {                           // release port
        (*m_contend)(RELEASE_RESOURCE, m_hContend,
            pPortStolen);
        m_hContend = NULL;
        }                           // release port
    }                               // CPort::Release
```

The *ADD_RESOURCE* Subfunction The calling sequence for the contention function using the *ADD_RESOURCE* subfunction is:

```
BOOL bAdded = Contend(ADD_RESOURCE, DWORD iobase, DWORD irq,
    DEVNODE devnode);
```

In this sequence, *iobase* is the base I/O address for the port, *irq* is the allocated IRQ number, and *devnode* is the address of a Configuration Manager device node. VCOMM uses *ADD_RESOURCE* to notify a contention VxD that the Configuration Manager has detected a new port. The return value simply indicates whether the contention VxD was able to update its internal data structures to reflect the existence of the new port (TRUE) or not (FALSE).

The *REMOVE_RESOURCE* Subfunction The calling sequence for the contention function using the *REMOVE_RESOURCE* subfunction is

```
void Contend(REMOVE_RESOURCE, DWORD iobase);
```

where *iobase* is the base I/O address for the port. VCOMM calls *REMOVE_RESOURCE* when the Configuration Manager removes the underlying DEVNODE.

Port Driver Functions

Once VCOMM has opened a port by successfully calling the port driver's open function, it communicates with the port driver by calling the functions whose pointers appear in the function pointer table pointed to by the *PDfunctions* field of the *PortData* structure. There are 22 such functions, as shown earlier in Table 14-4 on page 450. (*Open*, the 23rd function, is not reached via a pointer in this table.) I'll describe each of them in this section in order to clarify the official documentation in VCOMM.DOC. I'll illustrate the device-independent parts of their operation by examples drawn from the *CPort* class in my sample driver, and I'll briefly describe the device-dependent functionality provided by the *CSerialPort* class I derived from *CPort*.

Interfacing to Virtual Functions

As I mentioned in an earlier note, the architecture of a VCOMM port driver seems to cry out for a derived class implementation with virtual functions in C++. Translating VCOMM's C-language calls into calls to C++ member functions, however, posed a small challenge. All of the port driver functions expect a *port handle* (which is really a pointer to a *PortData* structure) as the first argument, and they all return a Boolean value indicating success or failure. The 22 port driver functions differ in the type and number of other arguments that they require, however. To create the necessary function pointer table, I first created a macro to turn a port handle into a *this* pointer for member function calls:

```
#define CPORT(hp) ((CPort *) ((DWORD) hp - \
    FIELDOFFSET(CPort, CPort::m_pd)))
```

FIELDOFFSET is a more-or-less standard macro for delivering the offset of a member of a structure:

```
#define FIELDOFFSET(type, field) ((DWORD)(&((type *)0)->field))
```

The *CPORT* macro takes advantage of the fact that a successful *CPort::PreOpen* function call returns to VCOMM the address of the *PortData* structure built into the *CPort* object as *m_pd*. VCOMM uses this same address as the port handle in all calls to port driver functions. (To provide a little bit of paranoia in the debugging version of the driver, I also implemented an *m_signature* field containing an eye-catching string and an *ASSERT_VALID_CPORT* macro to test this in each member function.)

Since I'm a lazy typist, I wrote a series of macros like these to help me declare C-language functions to interface between VCOMM and my C++ member functions:

```
#define PF0(f) BOOL f(PortData* hp) {return CPORT(hp)->f();}
#define PF1(f, alt) BOOL f(PortData* hp, alt a1)\
    {return CPORT(hp)->f(a1);}
[etc.]
```

PF0 is for a member function that has no arguments, *PF1* is for a member function that has one argument, and so on. Then I coded the actual function definitions using these macros:

```
PF2(ClearError, _COMSTAT*, int*)
PF0(Close)
[etc.]
```

These statements generate the following interface routines:

```
BOOL ClearError(PortData* hp, _COMSTAT* a1, int* a2)
    {
    return CPORT(hp)->ClearError(a1, a2);
    }

BOOL Close(PortData* hp)
    {
    return CPORT(hp)->Close();
    }
```

[etc.]

To declare the function pointer table itself, I wrote yet another macro so I wouldn't have to type the same cast over and over again:

```
#define PF (BOOL (*)())
```

Finally, the function pointer table to which the *PortData* structure's *PDfunctions* member ends up pointing is simply:

```
PortFunctions functions =
{PF SetCommState, PF GetCommState, PF Setup, PF TransmitChar,
PF Close, PF GetQueueStatus, PF ClearError,
PF SetModemStatusShadow,
PF GetProperties, PF EscapeFunction, PF Purge, PF SetEventMask,
```

```
PF GetEventMask, PF Write, PF Read, PF EnableNotification,
PF SetReadCallback, PF SetWriteCallback, PF GetModemStatus,
PF GetCommConfig, PF SetCommConfig, PF GetError, NULL};
```

Let's trace an example call to a port driver function to see how this apparently complex linkage works out in practice. VCOMM opens the port by calling our *CPort::PreOpen* routine, whose address it initially obtained from our call to *VCOMM_Add_Port*. The *PreOpen* routine calls the *CPort::Open* function, which sets the *m_pd.PDfunctions* member of the *CPort* class object to point to the *functions* table shown just above. The fifth entry in the table (corresponding to the *pPortClose* member of a *PortFunctions* structure) points to the simple *Close* function shown above. When VCOMM wants to close the port, it calls through the *pPortClose* function pointer to *Close*, passing the address of the *m_pd* member of our *CPort* structure as the only argument (*hp*). *Close* uses the *CPORT* macro to back up from that address to the start of the *CPort* instance and calls that instance's *CPort::Close* member function.

I declared all of the port driver member functions as *virtual* to allow for overrides in a derived class:

```
class CPort
{
...
virtual BOOL    ClearError(_COMSTAT* pComstat, int* pError);
virtual BOOL    Close();
...
};
```

Thus, the C-language wrappers that VCOMM talks to directly may end up calling either base-class or derived-class functions, depending on how they've been implemented for a particular port driver.

By the way, you can use a NULL pointer in the *PortFunctions* array for any port driver function you don't implement *except* (if yours is a serial port driver) the *SetModemStatusShadow* function. VCOMM doesn't try to call a port driver function for which you use a NULL pointer. (Unfortunately, VCOMM doesn't perform any default processing in this case either.) The reason for the exception is that the UNIMODEM modem driver calls your *SetModemStatusShadow* function directly through the function pointer table without first checking to see whether it's NULL. If you use any telephony applications such as HyperTerminal, you will end up taking a path into UNIMODEM.VXD that makes this naïve call.

The NULL pointer in the last entry of my *PortFunctions* table is a placeholder for a port driver *IOCTL* function. Microsoft hasn't documented the calling sequence to this function.

The *CPort* Class

I declared the *CPort* class interface in a C++ header file named VPORT.H. The complete header is on the CD that accompanies this book. You need to have a large portion of this header file in front of you to make sense of the function descriptions that I'm about to present:

VPORT.H

```
// vport.h -- Interface to CPort class
// Copyright (C) 1996 by Walter Oney
// All rights reserved

#ifndef VPORT_H
#define VPORT_H

typedef void (*PCOMMNOTIFYPROC)(PortData* hPort, DWORD refdata,
    DWORD lEvent, DWORD lSubEvent);
typedef DWORD (*PCONTENTIONPROC)(int, ...);

///////////////////////////////////////////////////////////////
// Base class for serial ports

class CPort
{
public:
    static CPort*   CPortAnchor;    // anchor of CPort list


// Nonstandard flags in m_NfyFlags (#define so we can use
// inline assembler with them)

#define CN_IDLE         0x80        // host has gone idle
#define CN_NOTIFY       0x40        // notifications enabled

// Flags in m_MiscFlags

enum MISCFLAGS
    {MF_TXQSET          = 0x0001    // transmit queue set up
    ,MF_RXQINTERNAL     = 0x0002    // we allocated Rx queue
    ,MF_TXQINTERNAL     = 0x0004    // we allocated Tx queue
    ,MF_CLRTIMER        = 0x0008    // timer logic disabled
    ,MF_IGNORECOMMERROR = 0x0010    // ignore read errors
    ,MF_DISCARD         = 0x0020    // discard input characters
    ,MF_STATESETONCE    = 0x0040    // SetCommState done once
    };
```

(continued)

continued

```
// Attributes

public:
    CPort*            m_next;          // chain to next port
    CPort*            m_prev;          // chain to previous port

    PortData          m_pd;            // VCOMM PortData structure
    _DCB              m_dcb;           // ring-zero DCB
    DWORD             m_signature;     // signature "PORT"
    char              m_name[8];       // name of port (COMx)
    DWORD             m_iobase;        // base I/O address
    DWORD             m_irq;           // IRQ number
    DEVNODE           m_devnode;       // our device node
    PCONTENTIONPROC   m_contend;       // contention function
    DWORD             m_resource;      // resource handle
    DWORD             m_hContend;      // contention handle
    BOOL              m_open;          // true when port is open
    HVM               m_owner;         // handle of VM owner
    PDWORD            m_pRxTime;       // last receive time
    PDWORD            m_pEvent;        // address of event word
    DWORD             m_eventmask;     // mask for notify events
    PBYTE             m_pMsrShadow;    // address of MSR shadow byte
    DWORD             m_TxTrigger;     // transmit trigger
    DWORD             m_RxTrigger;     // receive trigger

    DWORD             m_EvData;        // reference data for EvNotify
    DWORD             m_RxData;        // reference data for RxNotify
    DWORD             m_TxData;        // reference data for TxNotify
    PCOMMNOTIFYPROC   m_EvNotify;      // ring-zero notification
                                       // procedure
    PCOMMNOTIFYPROC   m_RxNotify;      // ring-zero read notify
                                       // procedure
    PCOMMNOTIFYPROC   m_TxNotify;      // ring-zero write notify
                                       // procedure
    WORD              m_MiscFlags;     // miscellaneous flags

    BYTE              m_NfyFlags;      // flags for notifications

// Methods

public:
    CPort(char *name, DWORD iobase, DWORD irq, DWORD devnode);
    virtual ~CPort();
```

(continued)

continued

```
       static void DeleteAll();
       static PortData* PreOpen(char *name, HVM hVM, int* pError);
       static void OnPortStolen(CPort* port, BOOL stolen);
       static void ManageTimer();
       static void OnTimeout(DWORD extra, DWORD refdata);


       BOOL            AddPort(DWORD refdata);

// Overridable functions

       virtual BOOL    Acquire(HVM hVM);
       virtual void    CallNotifyProc(int code);
       virtual BOOL    ClearError(_COMSTAT* pComstat, int* pError);
       virtual BOOL    Close();
       virtual BOOL    EnableNotification(PCOMMNOTIFYPROC
                       pCallback, DWORD refdata);
       virtual BOOL    EscapeFunction(DWORD lFunc, DWORD InData,
                       PVOID pOutData);
       virtual BOOL    GetCommConfig(PCOMMCONFIG lpCC, PDWORD lpSize);
       virtual BOOL    GetCommState(_DCB* pDCB);
       virtual BOOL    GetEventMask(DWORD mask, PDWORD pEvents);
       virtual BOOL    GetProperties(_COMMPROP* pCommProp);
       virtual BOOL    GetQueueStatus(_COMSTAT* pComstat);
       virtual BOOL    GetError(int* pError);
       virtual BOOL    GetModemStatus(PDWORD pModemStatus);
       virtual BOOL    Open(HVM hVM, int* pError);
       virtual BOOL    Purge(DWORD qType);
       virtual BOOL    Read(PCHAR buf, DWORD cbRequest, PDWORD pRxCount);
       virtual void    Release();
       virtual BOOL    SetCommConfig(PCOMMCONFIG lpCC, DWORD dwSize);
       virtual BOOL    SetCommState(_DCB* pDCB, DWORD ActionMask);
       virtual BOOL    SetEventMask(DWORD mask, PDWORD pEvents);
       virtual BOOL    SetModemStatusShadow(PBYTE pShadow);
       virtual BOOL    SetReadCallback(DWORD RxTrigger,
                       PCOMMNOTIFYPROC pCallback, DWORD refdata);
       virtual BOOL    Setup(PCHAR RxQueue, DWORD cbRxQueue,
                       PCHAR TxQueue, DWORD cbTxQueue);
       virtual BOOL    SetWriteCallback(DWORD TxTrigger,
                       PCOMMNOTIFYPROC pCallback, DWORD refdata);
       virtual BOOL    StealPort();
       virtual BOOL    TransmitChar(CHAR ch);
       virtual BOOL    Write(PCHAR buf, DWORD cbRequest, PDWORD pTxCount);
```

(continued)

continued

```
// Mini-driver callouts

    virtual BOOL    cextfcn(DWORD lFunc, DWORD InData,
                        PVOID pOutData);
    virtual BOOL    inicom(int* pError); // part of Open
    virtual BOOL    trmcom(); // part of Close

    virtual void    BeginSetState();
    virtual void    EndSetState(DWORD ChangedMask);
    virtual void    Flush(DWORD qType); // part of Purge
    virtual BOOL    CheckState(_DCB* pDCB, DWORD ActionMask);
    virtual DWORD   GetProviderSubType();
    virtual void    KickTx();
};


#define ASSERT_VALID_CPORT(p) \
    ASSERT(((CPort *) p)->m_signature == 'TROP')


#endif // VPORT_H
```

The Port Driver Functions

This subsection presents a detailed description of each of the 22 port driver functions. In the code samples, I've left out debugging code in the interest of clarity, and I've felt free to collapse detail that doesn't serve the primary expository purpose. Once again, refer to the CD accompanying the book if you want all the gory details.

ClearError *ClearError* returns the current collection of communication errors and resets all error indicators to 0:

```
BOOL CPort::ClearError(_COMSTAT* pComstat, int* pError)
    {                               // CPort::ClearError
    if (pComstat)
        GetQueueStatus(pComstat);
    *pError = (int) m_pd.dwCommError;
    m_pd.dwCommError = 0;
    m_pd.dwLastError = 0;
    return TRUE;
    }                               // CPort::ClearError
```

An application generates *ClearError* calls by calling *GetCommError* (Win16) or *ClearCommError* (Win32). The *Read* function normally aborts immediately if any error indicators are set. The application can override the error-checking feature of *Read* by using the *IGNOREERRORONREADS* escape function.

pComstat is optional. If it's not NULL, the driver should fill it in just like *GetQueueStatus* would. I'll discuss *_COMSTAT* in connection with *GetQueueStatus*.

Note that setting *dwLastError* to 0 means *ClearError* itself succeeded. All port driver functions must clear *dwLastError* if they succeed. I won't mention this again.

There's normally no need for a derived class to override *ClearError*, since all of the functionality is device-independent.

Close *Close* closes the port. An application triggers a call to *Close* by calling *CloseComm* (if it is a Win16 application) or *CloseHandle* (if it is a Win32 application). My sample driver implements *Close* as follows:

```
BOOL CPort::Close()
    {                               // CPort::Close
    m_pd.dwLastError = 0;           // assume no problems
    if (!m_open)
        return TRUE;                // not open in the first place

    if (!trmcom())
        return FALSE;               // mini-driver couldn't close
    Release();                      // release from contention manager
    m_open = FALSE;

    if (m_MiscFlags & MF_RXQINTERNAL)
        _HeapFree((PVOID) m_pd.QInAddr, 0);

    if (m_MiscFlags & MF_TXQINTERNAL)
        _HeapFree((PVOID) m_pd.QOutAddr, 0);

    m_MiscFlags |= MF_CLRTIMER;
    ManageTimer();
    return TRUE;
    }                               // CPort::Close
```

This base-class function calls a virtual function named *trmcom* to perform device-dependent operations needed to close the port. My *CSerialPort::trmcom* function, for example, waits for the output queue to drain, instructs the UART to prevent further interrupts, and unvirtualizes the associated IRQ.

The device-independent part of closing a port is shown above. Since we acquired the port from the contention VxD, it's necessary to release it now. I showed the *CPort::Release* function earlier in connection with the contention management discussion. Our *CPort::Setup* routine may have allocated receive and/or transmit buffers, so *CPort::Close* needs to release them. Finally, we may have created a timer to handle one or more timeout events associated with one of the ports managed by our driver; *ManageTimer* will cancel the timeout event if there are no other ports that depend on it. Since the base-class *Close* function calls the virtual *trmcom* function at an appropriate point in processing, there should be no need for a derived class to override *Close*.

EnableNotification *EnableNotification* allows VCOMM to register a notification procedure for any of the events that were listed in Table 14-6 on pages 460-461. Here's how I implemented it for the *CPort* class:

```
BOOL CPort::EnableNotification(PCOMMNOTIFYPROC pCallback,
    DWORD refdata)
    {                                   // CPort::EnableNotification
    ClrNfyFlag(CN_NOTIFY);
    m_EvNotify = pCallback;
    m_EvData = refdata;
    if (pCallback)
        {                               // wants notifications
        _asm pushfd
        _asm cli
        m_NfyFlags |= CN_NOTIFY;
        DWORD pending = m_eventmask & *m_pEvent;
        _asm popfd
        if (pending)
            CallNotifyProc(CN_EVENT);
        }                               // wants notifications
    m_pd.dwLastError = 0;
    return TRUE;
    }                                   // CPort::EnableNotification
```

The *m_eventmask* member variable contains a bit mask indicating the events for which the client program wants to receive notifications. The *m_pEvent* variable points to a DWORD provided by the client in which the port driver records pending events. *SetEventMask* sets both of these variables.

A Win16 application tells USER.EXE to send it WM_COMMNOTIFY messages by calling *EnableCommNotification*. USER.EXE calls an entry in COMM.DRV that relays a *VCOMM_PM_API_EnableNotify* request to VCOMM. VCOMM calls the port driver after substituting a suitable ring-zero callback routine that uses nested execution to awaken the application. Win32 applications can't establish an event notification routine, although they can use *WaitCommEvent* to wait for events to occur.

Functions within the port driver that discover events should check to see whether a notification callback is currently registered and, if so, call it. For example, the hardware interrupt handler for *CSerialPort* contains the following event recognition logic:

```
BOOL CSerialPort::HwIntProc()
    {                                   // CSerialPort::HwIntProc
    DWORD oldevents = *m_pEvent;    // current event word

    do {                            // handle pending interrupts
        [interrupt handling code that may set *m_pEvent bits]
```

```
        }                               // handle pending interrupts
    while ([expression indicating pending interrupts]);

    VPICD_Phys_EOI(m_irqhandle);

    // Notify client of any new events

    *m_pEvent &= m_eventmask;    // clear uninteresting events
    if ((m_NfyFlags & CN_NOTIFY) && (*m_pEvent & ~oldevents))
        CallNotifyProc(CN_EVENT);
    return TRUE;                       // i.e., we've handled it
    }                                  // CSerialPort::HwIntProc
```

CPort::CallNotifyProc is a general routine for calling client notification procedures:

```
    void CPort::CallNotifyProc(int code)
        {                               // CPort::CallNotifyProc

    _asm mov ebx, this
    _asm mov al, byte ptr code
    _asm or [ebx]CPort.m_NfyFlags, al
    DWORD events = *m_pEvent;
    switch (code)
        {                               // select notify proc to call

    case CN_EVENT:
        (*m_EvNotify)(&m_pd, m_EvData, code, events);
        break;

    case CN_RECEIVE:
        (*m_RxNotify)(&m_pd, m_RxData, code, events);
        break;

    case CN_TRANSMIT:
        (*m_TxNotify)(&m_pd, m_TxData, code, events);
        break;
        }                               // select notify proc to call
    }                                  // CPort::CallNotifyProc
```

Since event notification can occur while a hardware interrupt is being handled, the notification procedure must be reentrant and page-locked, and it can use only asynchronous VxD services. Note that I took care in *EnableNotification* and *CallNotifyProc* to avoid several possible races between these functions and an interrupt routine that might also want to alter *m_NfyFlags*. *ClrNfyFlag* is a macro that uses inline assembler to alter *m_NfyFlags* in one atomic operation. *EnableNotification* also illustrates the correct way to clear and later restore the interrupt flag when you don't know a priori what the original state of the flag might be: you save the current flags on the stack with PUSHFD, execute CLI to clear interrupts, and later restore the interrupt flag by executing POPFD.

Note also that the client can supply a NULL notification function address, which has the effect of disabling event notification.

There's a special reason why I used the EBX register in the first three lines of this function. Even though the notification callback routines (*m_EvNotify*, *m_RxNotify*, and *m_TxNotify*) are supposed to be C-callable, they might fail to restore the EBX register as they're supposed to. Using the EBX register, as shown, causes the compiler to save and restore EBX during the prolog and epilog of *CPort::CallNotifyProc*, thereby averting problems in the calling functions.

Since *EnableNotification* is device-independent, there should be no reason for a derived class to override it. Derived classes still have to worry about maintaining the event word and triggering notification calls, however.

EscapeFunction *EscapeFunction* performs an extended control function on the port. Table 14-9 lists each possible escape function along with a code that indicates whether each function is device-dependent or device-independent. An application reaches *EscapeFunction* by calling *EscapeCommFunction* (in Win16 or Win32).

Escape Function	Device-Dependent (D) or Device-Independent (I)	Description
SETXOFF	D (COM)	Acts as though an X-Off (DC3) character had been received from the host
SETXON	D (COM)	Acts as though an X-On (DC1) character had been received from the host
SETRTS	D (COM)	Sets the RTS line
CLRRTS	D (COM)	Clears the RTS line
SETDTR	D (COM)	Sets the DTR line
CLRDTR	D (COM)	Clears the DTR line
RESETDEV	D (LPT)	Resets the device
GETCOMBASEIRQ	D	Determines the I/O base address and IRQ
SETBREAK	D (COM)	Asserts a break signal on the RS-232 line
CLEARBREAK	D (COM)	Removes the break signal

Table 14-9. *Device escape functions.*

(continued)

continued

Escape Function	Device-Dependent (D) or Device-Independent (I)	Description
CLRTIMERLOGIC	I	Disables timeout logic
GETDEVICEID	D (LPT)	Gets the device identifier
SETECPADDRESS	D (LPT)	Sets the ECP channel address
ENABLETIMERLOGIC	I	Enables timeout logic
IGNOREERRORONREAD	I	Allows read operations even if errors are pending
SETUPDATETIMEADDR	I	Saves a new address for recording the last-receive time value
PEEKCHAR	I	Examines the next character (if any) in the input queue

In my sample driver, I implemented the device-independent escape functions in the following way:

```
BOOL CPort::EscapeFunction(DWORD lFunc, DWORD InData,
    PVOID pOutData)
    {                               // CPort::EscapeFunction
    m_pd.dwLastError = 0;

    switch (lFunc)
        {                           // process escape function

    case PEEKCHAR:                  // lFunc == 200
        if (!m_pd.QInCount)
            return FALSE;           // no pending input character
        *(PBYTE) pOutData = ((char *) m_pd.QInAddr)[m_pd.QInGet];
        break;

    case ENABLETIMERLOGIC:          // lFunc == 21
        m_MiscFlags &= ~MF_CLRTIMER;
        break;

    case IGNOREERRORONREADS:        // lFunc == 20
        m_MiscFlags |= MF_IGNORECOMMERROR;
        break;

    case CLRTIMERLOGIC:             // lFunc == 16
        m_MiscFlags |= MF_CLRTIMER;
        break;
```

```
    case SETUPDATETIMEADDR:      // lFunc == 19
        m_pRxTime = (PDWORD) InData;
        break;

    default:
        if (cextfcn(lFunc, InData, pOutData))
            break;               // mini-driver handled it
        m_pd.dwLastError = (DWORD) IE_EXTINVALID;
        return FALSE;            // unknown escape
        }                       // process escape function
    return TRUE;
    }                           // CPort::EscapeFunction
```

The *cextfcn* virtual function handles device-dependent escapes. Since the base-class function calls *cextfcn* at an appropriate point in processing, there's no particular reason for a derived class to override *EscapeFunction*.

Here's what the device-independent escape functions mean:

- **PEEKCHAR** The *PEEKCHAR* escape function allows the caller to examine the next character (if any) in the input queue. The *QInCount* member of the port's *PortData* structure will be nonzero if any characters are currently queued, in which case the next character can be found at offset *QInGet* from the start of the input buffer at *QInAddr*.

- **ENABLETIMERLOGIC** The *ENABLETIMERLOGIC* escape function enables a timer that acts as a backstop for client programs that depend on the input queue filling up. The way the timer works is as follows: Every 100 milliseconds, the driver wakes up and examines all the ports it manages. If a port has requested input queue notifications by calling *SetReadCallback*, and if there is data in the port's input queue but the most recent data arrived before the previous timeout, the port driver calls the client's input callback routine even if the queue hasn't reached the specified threshold. The idea is to keep the application busy reading input data even when the host isn't transmitting very quickly.

- **IGNOREERRORONREADS** The *IGNOREERRORONREADS* escape function tells the port driver to perform read operations even if there are uncleared error conditions. Normally, calls to *Read* fail immediately if any errors have been detected and recorded in *dwCommError,* and the client must call *ClearError* to clear the error flags and allow reads to proceed once more.

- **CLRTIMERLOGIC** The *CLRTIMERLOGIC* escape function tells the port driver to stop sending the client input notifications every 100 milliseconds.

■ **SETUPDATETIMEADDR** The *SETUPDATETIMEADDR* escape function specifies a new address for the DWORD in which the port driver's interrupt routine will record the time at which each input byte arrives. The time stamp is the one delivered by *Get_Last_Updated_System_Time*, which may be inaccurate by up to 50 milliseconds but has the virtue of requiring almost no time to compute.

GetCommConfig *GetCommConfig* completes a *COMMCONFIG* structure to describe the current configuration of the port. *GetCommConfig* services a call to the Win32 API of the same name; Win16 applications don't use this port driver function. I implemented it as follows:

```
BOOL CPort::GetCommConfig(PCOMMCONFIG lpCC, PDWORD lpSize)
    {                               // CPort::GetCommConfig
    DWORD size = *lpSize;
    *lpSize = sizeof(COMMCONFIG);

    if (size < sizeof(COMMCONFIG) || !lpCC)
        return TRUE;

    lpCC->dwProviderOffset = 0;
    lpCC->dwProviderSize = 0;
    lpCC->dwSize = sizeof(COMMCONFIG);
    lpCC->wVersion = 0x0100;
    lpCC->dwProviderSubType = GetProviderSubType();
    VCOMM_Map_Ring0DCB_To_Win32(&m_dcb, &lpCC->dcb);

    return TRUE;
    }                               // CPort::GetCommConfig
```

The *lpSize* argument points to a DWORD that initially contains the size of the *COMMCONFIG* structure pointed to by *lpCC*. *GetCommConfig* updates that DWORD to hold the actual size of the structure. If the original size is too small, *GetCommConfig* returns TRUE without doing anything except setting the size value. If the size is adequate, however, *GetCommConfig* fills in the structure.

The *COMMCONFIG* structure (see Figure 14-8) is documented in the online Win32 Programmer's Reference section of the Win32 SDK. Initializing the *dwProviderOffset* and *dwProviderSize* members to 0 indicates that there is no provider-specific data in the *wcProviderData* area of the structure. The *dwProviderSubType* value is device-dependent, so I provided a virtual function named *GetProviderSubType* to determine it. *CSerialPort::GetProviderSubType* returns the value *PST_RS232* to indicate that *CSerialPort* implements a serial port driver.

The most interesting configuration information is in the *dcb* member of the *COMMCONFIG* structure. This member is a Win32-format device control block

```
typedef struct _COMM_CONFIG {
   DWORD     dwSize;              // 00 size of the structure
   WORD      wVersion;            // 04 version of the structure (0x0100 = 1.00)
   WORD      wAlignDCB;           // 06 padding to DWORD boundary
   WIN32DCB dcb;                  // 08 Win32-format device control block
   DWORD     dwProviderSubType;   // 24 provider subtype (PST_xxx)
   DWORD     dwProviderOffset;    // 28 offset of provider data from start
                                  //    of structure
   DWORD     dwProviderSize;      // 2C length of provider data that follows
                                  //    structure
} COMMCONFIG, *PCOMMCONFIG;       // [30]
```

Figure 14-8. *The* COMMCONFIG *structure.*

(DCB). Since the format of the ring-zero DCB with which VCOMM and port drivers work is different from the Win32 format, VCOMM provides conversion services to translate one format to the other. In this case, we want to translate the ring-zero DCB in the *CPort* object to the Win32-format DCB contained in the *COMMCONFIG* structure, so we call *VCOMM_Map_Ring0DCB_To_Win32*.

Since the provider subtype is the only piece of information that varies between devices, there's no particular reason for a derived class to override *GetCommConfig*. It should suffice to provide an appropriate *GetProviderSubType* function.

GetCommState *GetCommState* returns the current state of a communications port by filling in a device control block provided by the caller. Win16 and Win32 applications use their respective *GetCommState* APIs to reach this port driver function. Here's my implementation:

```
BOOL CPort::GetCommState(_DCB* pDCB)
   {                                 // CPort::GetCommState
   *pDCB = m_dcb;
   m_pd.dwLastError = 0;
   return TRUE;
   }                                 // CPort::GetCommState
```

Agreeably simple, isn't it? There's also probably no reason to override *GetCommState*.

GetError It's anybody's guess what *GetError* is supposed to do. The SERIAL.VXD program's function does nothing, while the LPT.VXD program's function examines the *PortData dwCommError* field to turn printer-specific error flags into regular WINERROR.H (that is, Win32 *GetLastError*) codes. VCOMM.DOC doesn't document the port function, but it does claim that the *_VCOMM_GetLastError* service returns one of the IE series of communication port errors. In fact, *_VCOMM_GetLastError* returns whatever the port driver has left in the *dwLastError* field of the *PortData* structure (which therefore ought to be an IE-series error code). What a mess! I ended up implementing the function as follows.

```
BOOL CPort::GetError(int* pError)
    {                           // CPort::GetError
    *pError = m_pd.dwLastError;
    return TRUE;
    }                           // CPort::GetError
```

There's no reason for a derived class to override *GetError*.

GetEventMask *GetEventMask* performs two functions. First of all, it copies the current event word (which records events in which the client expressed interest by calling *SetEventMask*) to a location supplied by the caller. Second, it masks off selected events in the event word. Sixteen-bit applications use *GetCommEventMask* to trigger a call to this function; Win32 applications don't use it at all. Here's the sample implementation of *GetEventMask*:

```
BOOL CPort::GetEventMask(DWORD mask, PDWORD pEvents)
    {                           // CPort::GetEventMask
    _asm pushfd
    _asm cli
    *pEvents = *m_pEvent;       // return all current events
    *m_pEvent &= ~mask;         // clear selected events
    _asm popfd
    m_pd.dwLastError = 0;
    return TRUE;
    }                           // CPort::GetEventMask
```

Another Documentation Mixup The VCOMM documentation says that the *pEvents* argument to *GetEventMask* can be NULL. Well, it can't! (Okay, the LPT.VXD version of this routine checks the pointer, but SERIAL.VXD doesn't.) The documentation also seems to imply that a non-NULL *pEvents* argument will become the new address of the event word. Well, it won't! The only way to change the location of the event word is to call *SetEventMask*. Adding to the confusion, Microsoft's documentation for this function and for *SetEventMask* also uses the term *mask* inconsistently. For the sake of precision, I've used the term *event word* to describe the place where the port driver records enabled events by setting bits, and I've used the word *mask* to describe an array of bits that indicates which events are currently enabled. When Microsoft named *GetEventMask* (and the corresponding Win16 API function), they used *event mask* to mean *event word* instead. The Win32 API has functions named *SetCommMask* and *GetCommMask* that truly work with the "mask," not the event word. Mind you, it's not very useful to get back just the mask without knowing which events have occurred, but at least the API is consistent!

Since the functionality of *GetEventMask* is device-independent, there's no reason for a derived class to override the base-class function.

GetModemStatus *GetModemStatus* returns the current modem status. This function services the Win32 *GetCommModemStatus* API function. A derived class could override this function in order to retrieve the current status from hardware. For example:

```
BOOL CSerialPort::GetModemStatus(PDWORD pModemStatus)
    {                               // CSerialPort::GetModemStatus
    *pModemStatus = in(m_iobase + MSR) & MS_Modem_Status;
    return TRUE;
    }                               // CSerialPort::GetModemStatus
```

GetProperties *GetProperties* fills in a *_COMMPROP* structure (see Figure 14-9 on the following page) with information about the port. This function exists to service the Win32 API function *GetCommProperties*. My sample completes the device-independent portion of the properties structure as follows:

```
BOOL CPort::GetProperties(_COMMPROP* pCommProp)
    {                               // CPort::GetProperties
    memset(pCommProp, 0, sizeof(_COMMPROP));
    pCommProp->wPacketLength = sizeof(_COMMPROP);
    pCommProp->wPacketVersion = 2;
    pCommProp->dwServiceMask = SP_SERIALCOMM;
    pCommProp->dwCurrentRxQueue = m_pd.QInSize;
    pCommProp->dwCurrentTxQueue = m_pd.QOutSize;

    m_pd.dwLastError = 0;
    return TRUE;
    }                               // CPort::GetProperties
```

SP_SERIALCOMM is the only value defined for *dwServiceMask*. It doesn't make sense for someone to call *GetProperties* to get information about a parallel port. LPT.VXD valiantly tries to deal with the call anyway, but it only sets the *dwCurrentxxQueue* values.

A derived class should override the function, calling the base-class function and then filling in the device-dependent portions of the structure. For example:

```
BOOL CSerialPort::GetProperties(_COMMPROP* pCommProp)
    {                               // CSerialPort::GetProperties
    if (!CPort::GetProperties(pCommProp))
        return FALSE;

    pCommProp->dwMaxBaud = BAUD_USER;
    pCommProp->dwProvSubType = PST_RS232;
    ...
    return TRUE;
    }                               // CSerialPort::GetProperties
```

```
typedef struct _COMMPROP {    // cmmp
  WORD  wPacketLength;         // 00 length of this structure
  WORD  wPacketVersion;        // 02 version of this structure
  DWORD dwServiceMask;         // 04 bit mask indicating services provided
  DWORD dwReserved1;           // 08 reserved
  DWORD dwMaxTxQueue;          // 0C maximum transmit queue size
  DWORD dwMaxRxQueue;          // 10 maximum receive queue size
  DWORD dwMaxBaud;             // 14 maximum baud supported
  DWORD dwProvSubType;         // 18 specific COMM provider type
  DWORD dwProvCapabilities;    // 1C flow control capabilities
  DWORD dwSettableParams;      // 20 bit mask indicating parameters that can
                               //    be set
  DWORD dwSettableBaud;        // 24 bit mask indicating baud rates that
                               //    can be set
  WORD  wSettableData;         // 28 bit mask indicating number of data bits
                               //    that can be set
  WORD  wSettableStopParity;   // 2A bit mask indicating allowed stop bits
                               //    and parity checking
  DWORD dwCurrentTxQueue;      // 2C current size of transmit queue
  DWORD dwCurrentRxQueue;      // 30 current size of receive queue
  DWORD dwProvSpec1;           // 34 used if clients have intimate
                               //    knowledge of format
  DWORD dwProvSpec2;           // 38 used if clients have intimate
                               //    knowledge of format
  WCHAR wcProvChar[1];         // 3C used if clients have intimate
                               //    knowledge of format
  WORD    filler;              // 3E to make it multiple of 4
} COMMPROP;                    // [40]
```

Figure 14-9. *The* _COMMPROP *structure.*

GetQueueStatus The inaptly named *GetQueueStatus* function returns a status flag and information about the current amount of queued data in a *_COMSTAT* structure (see Figure 14-10). Applications usually reach this function indirectly, by calling *GetCommError* (Win16) or *ClearCommError* (Win32) and supplying a non-NULL _COMSTAT pointer. The device-independent portion of this function is:

```
BOOL CPort::GetQueueStatus(_COMSTAT* pComstat)
{                                  // CPort::GetQueueStatus
  m_pd.dwLastError = 0;
  pComstat->cbInque = m_pd.QInCount;
  pComstat->cbOutque = m_pd.QOutCount;
  return TRUE;
}                                  // CPort::GetQueueStatus
```

A derived class should override this function, filling in the *BitMask* field and calling the base-class function.

```
typedef struct _COMSTAT {
  DWORD BitMask;            // 00 flags
  DWORD cbInQue;            // 04 number of bytes in input queue
  DWORD cbOutQue;          // 08 number of bytes in output queue
} _COMSTAT;                // 0C
```

Figure 14-10. *The _COMSTAT structure.*

Purge *Purge* discards the current contents of the input or output buffer. *Purge* services the Win32 API function *PurgeComm*. This function is mostly independent of device:

```
BOOL CPort::Purge(DWORD qType)
    {                           // CPort::Purge
    switch (qType)
        {                       // purge requested queue

    case 0:                     // Tx queue
        {                       // flush Tx queue
        DWORD count = m_pd.QOutCount;
        _asm pushfd
        _asm cli
        m_pd.QOutCount = 0;
        m_pd.QOutGet = 0;
        m_pd.QOutPut = 0;
        _asm popfd

        if (count && m_TxTrigger)
            CallNotifyProc(CN_TRANSMIT);

        Flush(qType);
        break;
        }                       // flush Tx queue

    case 1:                     // Rx queue
        _asm pushfd
        _asm cli
        m_pd.QInCount = 0;
        m_pd.QInGet = 0;
        m_pd.QInPut = 0;
        _asm popfd

        Flush(qType);
        ClrNfyFlag(CN_RECEIVE);

        break;
```

```
default:
    break;
    }                               // purge requested queue
m_pd.dwLastError = 0;
return TRUE;
    }                               // CPort::Purge
```

A derived class can override the *Flush* member function to provide additional processing. My *CSerialPort::Flush* routine, for example, checks to see if filling the input queue previously caused the driver to use a flow control mechanism (such as sending an X-Off character) to halt host transmission. If so, purging the read queue means that the host should be notified to resume transmission.

Read *Read* retrieves data from the input queue. Applications trigger calls to the port driver *Read* function by calling *ReadComm* (Win16) or *ReadFile* (Win32). Most of the work in performing a read operation is managing the ring buffer. My sample driver implements *Read* this way:

```
BOOL CPort::Read(PCHAR buf, DWORD cbRequest, PDWORD pRxCount)
    {                               // CPort::Read
    if (!(m_MiscFlags & MF_IGNORECOMMERROR) &&
        m_pd.dwCommError)
        {                           // pending errors
        m_pd.dwLastError = m_pd.dwCommError;
        return FALSE;
        }                           // pending errors

    m_pd.dwLastError = 0;
    DWORD numread = m_pd.QInCount;
    if (!numread)
        {                           // quick out if queue empty
        *pRxCount = 0;
        return TRUE;
        }                           // quick out if queue empty

    if (numread > cbRequest)
        numread = cbRequest;
    DWORD get = m_pd.QInGet;
    DWORD ncopy = m_pd.QInSize - get;
    if (ncopy > numread)
        ncopy = numread;
    memcpy(buf, (PCHAR) m_pd.QInAddr + get, ncopy);

    if (ncopy == numread)
        get += ncopy;
    else
        {                           // wraparound to start
        buf += ncopy;
```

```
        ncopy = numread - ncopy;
        memcpy(buf, (PCHAR) m_pd.QInAddr, ncopy);
        get = ncopy;
        }                             // wraparound to start
    m_pd.QInGet = get;

    _asm pushfd
    _asm cli
    m_pd.QInCount -= numread;
    m_NfyFlags &= ~CN_RECEIVE;
    _asm popfd

    *pRxCount = numread;
    return TRUE;
    }                                 // CPort::Read
```

The *MF_IGNORECOMMERROR* flag will be set if someone has issued an *IGNOREERRORONREADS* escape function; this option indicates that read operations should proceed even if there are communication errors that haven't yet been cleared by a call to *ClearError*. I copied the code from SERIAL.VXD that sets *dwLastError* equal to *dwCommError*. The CE-series communication error bits in *dwCommError* don't equal the IE-series error codes that belong in *dwLastError,* so this code is flat wrong, of course. I already remarked in the *GetError* discussion that confusion surrounds the error codes that port drivers are supposed to store in *dwLastError,* so this additional evidence of confusion shouldn't be too surprising.

The buffer management and copy logic in *Read* are pretty straightforward. Refer back to Figure 14-7 on page 462 for a picture of how the buffering parameters relate to each other. Updating the buffer count and the notify callback flag must be done without interference from an interrupt routine, so I protected those steps by clearing the interrupt flag around them.

A derived class should override *Read*, calling the base-class function and then checking whether removing data from the input buffer makes it possible to notify the host to resume transmission.

SetCommConfig *SetCommConfig* is the reverse of *GetCommConfig*. It sets the state of a port based on a Win32-format device control block:

```
BOOL CPort::SetCommConfig(PCOMMCONFIG lpCC, DWORD dwSize)
    {                                 // CPort::SetCommConfig
    if (dwSize < sizeof(COMMCONFIG))
        {                             // too small
        m_pd.dwLastError = (DWORD) IE_INVALIDPARAM;
        return FALSE;
        }                             // too small
    _DCB r0dcb;
    VCOMM_Map_Win32DCB_To_Ring0(&lpCC->dcb, &r0dcb);
```

```
      return SetCommState(&r0dcb, 0xFFFFFFFF);
}                               // CPort::SetCommConfig
```

This function services the Win32 API function *SetCommConfig*; there is no Win16 counterpart. There's no reason for a derived class to override this function, since the base-class *SetCommState* includes logic for handling device-dependent functions.

SetCommState *SetCommState* is the basic API function for setting communications parameters. This function uses a device control block (*_DCB*) structure (see Figure 14-11) to describe the communications protocol. Win16 and Win32 applications reach this port driver function by calling their respective *SetCommState* API functions.

```
typedef struct _DCB {
   DWORD DCBLength;            // 00 size of (DCB)
   DWORD BaudRate ;            // 04 baud rate at which running
   DWORD BitMask;             // 08 flag DWORD
   DWORD XonLim;              // 0C transmit X-On threshold
   DWORD XoffLim;             // 10 transmit X-Off threshold
   WORD  wReserved;           // 14 reserved
   BYTE  ByteSize;            // 16 number of bits/byte, 4-8
   BYTE  Parity;              // 17 0-4 = none, odd, even, mark, space
   BYTE  StopBits;            // 18 0,1,2 = 1, 1.5, 2
   char  XonChar;             // 19 Tx and Rx X-On character
   char  XoffChar;            // 1A Tx and Rx X-Off character
   char  ErrorChar;           // 1B parity error replacement character
   char  EofChar;             // 1C end of input character
   char  EvtChar1;            // 1D special event character
   char  EvtChar2;            // 1E another special event character
   BYTE  bReserved;           // 1F reserved
   DWORD RlsTimeout;          // 20 timeout for RLSD to be set
   DWORD CtsTimeout;          // 24 timeout for CTS to be set
   DWORD DsrTimeout;          // 28 timeout for DSR to be set
   DWORD TxDelay;             // 2C amount of time between characters
} _DCB;                        // [30]
```

Figure 14-11. *Format of a device control block (DCB).*

The arguments to *SetCommState* include the address of a *_DCB* structure and a bit mask that indicates which fields are to be altered. To maximize the amount of common code, I wrote the following base-class function:

```
BOOL CPort::SetCommState(_DCB* pDCB, DWORD ActionMask)
   {                               // CPort::SetCommState
   if ((m_pd.LossByte & 1) && !StealPort())
      {                            // port stolen
      m_pd.dwLastError = (DWORD) IE_DEFAULT;
```

```
            return FALSE;
        }                              // port stolen
    if (!CheckState(pDCB, ActionMask))
        return FALSE;                  // error in miniport-specific parts
    BeginSetState();                   // prepare to change state of port

    DWORD ChangedMask = 0;             // assume nothing changed yet

    #define ss(m) if (ActionMask & f##m) { \
                    if (m_dcb.m != pDCB->m) ChangedMask |= f##m; \
                    m_dcb.m = pDCB->m;}

ss(BaudRate)
    ss(BitMask)
    ss(XonLim)
    ss(XoffLim)
    ss(ByteSize)
    ss(Parity)
    ss(StopBits)
    ss(XonChar)
    ss(XoffChar)
    ss(ErrorChar)
    ss(EofChar)
    ss(EvtChar1)
    ss(EvtChar2)
    ss(RlsTimeout)
    ss(CtsTimeout)
    ss(DsrTimeout)
    ss(TxDelay)

    EndSetState(ChangedMask);    // install new parameters
    m_MiscFlags |= MF_STATESETONCE;
    m_pd.dwLastError = 0;
    return TRUE;
    }                              // CPort::SetCommState
```

The *ss* macro, designed to save typing, generates code such as the following for each field in the *_DCB* structure:

```
if (ActionMask & fBaudRate)
    {
    if (m_dcb.BaudRate != pDCB->BaudRate)
        ChangedMask |= fBaudRate;
    m_dcb.BaudRate = pDCB->BaudRate;
    }
```

Thus, at the end of all the calls to *ss*, the port's *_DCB* structure has been updated and *ChangedMask* indicates which fields actually changed.

There are three device-dependent steps to processing *SetCommState*: verifying the correctness and consistency of the parameters in the *_DCB* structure (performed by *CheckState*), preparing the device to permit changes to the *_DCB* structure (performed by *BeginSetState*), and reprogramming the device once all the changes have been made (performed by *EndSetState*). A derived class should override all three of these functions.

SetEventMask *SetEventMask* works in conjunction with *EnableNotification* to provide for client notification of communications events. Applications trigger calls to this port driver function by calling *SetCommEventMask* (Win16) or *SetCommMask* (Win32). This function sets an *event mask* that governs which events will be recorded. It also gives you the option of setting the address of the *event word* that holds the masked event flags:

```
BOOL CPort::SetEventMask(DWORD mask, PDWORD pEvents)
    {                           // CPort::SetEventMask
    m_eventmask = mask;
    if (pEvents)
        m_pEvent = pEvents;
    m_pd.dwLastError = 0;
    return TRUE;
    }                           // CPort::SetEventMask
```

Calling *SetEventMask* with a NULL *pEvents* argument is not an error: this is how a client can change just the mask without affecting where events are stored. Also, the port driver must maintain a PDWORD (such as *m_pEvent* in my sample) that points to the current event word. The driver should initialize the pointer with the address of the *dwDetectedEvents* member of the *PortData* structure.

I believe that this implementation of *SetEventMask* correctly interprets the purpose of the application-level API functions. If an application tries to set the event mask for a *parallel* port, however, a surprise will occur: the LPT.VXD implementation of *SetEventMask* ORs the *mask* argument into the event word instead of saving it as a true mask. LPT.VXD also uses *dwDetectedEvents* as a pointer to the event word instead of as the initial event word itself.

There's no reason for a derived class to override *SetEventMask*.

SetModemStatusShadow *SetModemStatusShadow* sets the address of a BYTE in which the port driver's interrupt routine will save the Modem Status register each time it changes:

```
BOOL CPort::SetModemStatusShadow(PBYTE pShadow)
    {                                 // CPort::SetModemStatusShadow
    m_pMsrShadow = pShadow;
    m_pd.dwLastError = 0;
    return TRUE;
    }                                 // CPort::SetModemStatusShadow
```

There's no reason for a derived class to override this function. There's also no direct way for an application to reach this routine.

SetReadCallback *SetReadCallback* establishes a threshold queue size (a *trigger*) for the input queue and registers a callback routine to be called when the queue grows larger than the threshold:

```
BOOL CPort::SetReadCallback(DWORD RxTrigger,
    PCOMMNOTIFYPROC pCallback, DWORD refdata)
    {                              // CPort::SetReadCallback
    if (RxTrigger != 0xFFFFFFFF && RxTrigger > m_pd.QInSize)
        RxTrigger = m_pd.QInSize;   // make it sensible
    if (!pCallback)
        RxTrigger = 0xFFFFFFFF; // reset if no callback function

    _asm pushfd
    _asm cli
    m_RxNotify = pCallback;
    m_RxData = refdata;
    m_RxTrigger = RxTrigger;
    _asm popfd

    if (!m_pd.QInCount)
        *m_pRxTime = 0;
    ManageTimer();
    return TRUE;
    }                              // CPort::SetReadCallback
```

The meaning of the threshold value is as follows: each time the input queue grows to contain the specified number of data bytes (or more), the port driver will call the specified callback routine. Calling the callback routine disarms the trigger until the input queue falls below the threshold. Additionally, if timer logic is enabled for the port, a callback will occur every 100 milliseconds (provided the callback is armed), even if the input queue never reaches the threshold. (Timer logic is enabled by default and can be controlled by the *ENABLETIMERLOGIC* and *CLRTIMERLOGIC* escape functions.) Calling the client every 100 milliseconds helps keep data moving out of the input buffer during periods while the host is failing to deliver data rapidly.

Specifying a trigger value of -1 or a NULL callback address disables the callback mechanism. The default input trigger is -1, which means that input callbacks are initially disabled when someone opens the port.

There's no reason for a derived class to override *SetReadCallback*. Win16 applications reach this function indirectly by calling *EnableCommNotification*. Win32 applications don't use this function.

Setup *Setup* initializes the sizes and locations of the input and output queues. Win32 applications can control queue sizes by calling *SetupComm*; Win16 applications specify the queue sizes as optional parameters to *OpenComm*. My implementation of *Setup* is as follows:

```
BOOL CPort::Setup(PCHAR RxQueue, DWORD RxLength,
    PCHAR TxQueue, DWORD TxLength)
    {                                   // CPort::Setup
    m_pd.dwLastError = 0;       // no error
    m_pd.QInCount = 0;
    m_pd.QInGet = 0;
    m_pd.QInPut = 0;
    m_pd.QOutCount = 0;
    m_pd.QOutGet = 0;
    m_pd.QOutPut = 0;

    if (!RxQueue)
        {                               // need internal buffer
        if (m_MiscFlags & MF_RXQINTERNAL)
            {                           // reallocate existing buffer
            RxQueue = (PCHAR) _HeapReAllocate((PVOID)
                m_pd.QInAddr, RxLength, 0);
            if (!RxQueue)
                return FALSE;
            }                           // reallocate existing buffer
        else
            {                           // allocate buffer the first time
                RxQueue = (PCHAR) _HeapAllocate(RxLength, 0);
            if (!RxQueue)
                return FALSE;   // means no change made
            m_MiscFlags |= MF_RXQINTERNAL;
            }                           // allocate buffer the first time
        }                               // need internal buffer
    m_pd.QInAddr = (DWORD) RxQueue;
    m_pd.QInSize = RxLength;

    if (!TxQueue)
        if (TxLength)
            {                           // need internal buffer
            if (m_MiscFlags & MF_TXQINTERNAL)
                {                       // reallocate existing buffer
                TxQueue = (PCHAR) _HeapReAllocate((PVOID)
                    m_pd.QOutAddr, TxLength, 0);
                if (!TxQueue)
                    return FALSE;
                }                       // reallocate existing buffer
            else
                {                       // allocate buffer the first time
```

```
                        TxQueue = (PCHAR) _HeapAllocate(TxLength, 0);
                        if (!TxQueue)
                            {               // can't allocate
                            if (m_MiscFlags & MF_RXQINTERNAL)
                                {           // release internal buffer
                                _HeapFree((PVOID) m_pd.QInAddr, 0);
                                m_MiscFlags &= ~MF_RXQINTERNAL;
                                }           // release internal buffer
                            return FALSE;
                            }               // can't allocate
                        m_MiscFlags |= MF_TXQINTERNAL;
                        }                   // allocate buffer the first time
                    }                       // need internal buffer

    m_pd.QOutAddr = (DWORD) TxQueue;
    m_pd.QOutSize = TxLength;
    if (TxQueue)
        m_MiscFlags |= MF_TXQSET;

    return TRUE;
    }                                       // CPort::Setup
```

This function looks more complex than it really is. If the client specifies the address of a buffer, the port driver will use that buffer. If the client specifies a buffer size and a NULL buffer address, the driver will allocate its own buffer of the given size. If the client specifies neither a buffer size nor an address, *Setup* doesn't change the corresponding queue address or size.

I essentially copied the logic of the equivalent function from Microsoft's SERIAL.VXD. As it stands, the implementation can potentially lead to a memory leak. The leak occurs if *Setup* allocates an internal buffer during one call and then receives a subsequent call that specifies a client-owned buffer. In that case, *Setup* won't release the original buffer.

There's no reason for a derived class to override *Setup*.

SetWriteCallback *SetWriteCallback* establishes a threshold queue size (a *trigger*) for the output queue and registers a callback routine to be called when the queue falls below the threshold:

```
BOOL CPort::SetWriteCallback(DWORD TxTrigger,
    PCOMMNOTIFYPROC pCallback, DWORD refdata)
    {                                   // CPort::SetWriteCallback
    if (TxTrigger == 0xFFFFFFFF)
        TxTrigger = 0;          // -1 => no callback
    if ((m_MiscFlags & MF_TXQSET)
        && TxTrigger > m_pd.QOutSize)
        TxTrigger = m_pd.QOutSize;
```

```
if (!pCallback)
    TxTrigger = 0;

_asm pushfd
_asm cli
m_TxNotify = pCallback;
m_TxData = refdata;
m_TxTrigger = TxTrigger;
if (m_pd.QOutCount < TxTrigger)
    m_NfyFlags |= CN_TRANSMIT;
_asm popfd

return TRUE;
}                              // CPort::SetWriteCallback
```

The meaning of the threshold value is as follows: each time the output queue falls below the specified number of data bytes, the port driver will call the specified callback routine. Calling the callback routine disarms the trigger until the output queue reaches the threshold again. The purpose of the callback is to allow the client program to refill the output buffer to keep up a steady flow of data to the host.

I preserved a curious piece of logic from Microsoft's SERIAL.VXD that allows a *TxTrigger* value of -1 to mean "no trigger." A 0 value is the correct "no trigger" value to store, since it's impossible for the queue size to fall below 0. In fact, 0 is the initial value assigned to *m_TxTrigger*, so transmit notifications are initially disabled.

There's no reason for a derived class to override *SetWriteCallback*. Win16 applications reach this function indirectly by calling *EnableCommNotification*. Win32 applications don't use this function.

TransmitChar *TransmitChar* queues a high-priority output character. Applications call *TransmitCommChar* (Win16 or Win32) to reach *TransmitChar*. This function is inherently device-specific. Strictly speaking, there is supposed to be only one high-priority character outstanding at a time, and the port driver ought to diagnose an error (specifically, *IE_TRANSMITCHARFAILED*) if a second one arrives. Microsoft's SERIAL.VXD doesn't check for this error case, however, so neither did I in my driver:

```
BOOL CSerialPort::TransmitChar(CHAR ch)
    {                          // CSerialPort::TransmitChar
    m_ImmedChar = ch;  // save char to transmit BEFORE setting flag
    SetFlag(fTxImmed); // remember we have a character to transmit
    KickTx();
    return TRUE;
    }                          // CSerialPort::TransmitChar
```

KickTx is a device-dependent routine that attempts to restart pending output.

Write *Write* transmits data to the host. Applications reach *Write* by calling *Write-Comm* (Win16) or *WriteFile* (Win32). Just as is true with *Read*, most of the work of *Write* revolves around managing the ring buffer:

```
BOOL CPort::Write(PCHAR buf, DWORD cbRequest, PDWORD pTxCount)
    {                               // CPort::Write
    DWORD nwritten;
    m_pd.dwLastError = 0;

    if (m_MiscFlags & MF_TXQSET)
        {                           // using an output buffer
        nwritten = m_pd.QOutSize - m_pd.QOutCount;
        if (nwritten > cbRequest)
            nwritten = cbRequest;

        DWORD put = m_pd.QOutPut; // where we can start copying
        DWORD ncopy = m_pd.QOutSize - put; // most we can copy
        if (ncopy > nwritten)
            ncopy = nwritten;
        memcpy((PCHAR) m_pd.QOutAddr + put, buf, ncopy);

        if (ncopy == nwritten)
            put += ncopy;           // only need one copy
        else
            {                       // wraparound
            buf += ncopy;
            ncopy = nwritten - ncopy; // amount left to do
            memcpy((PCHAR) m_pd.QOutAddr, buf, ncopy);
            put = ncopy;
            }                       // wraparound

        m_pd.QOutPut = put;

        _asm pushfd
        _asm cli
        if ((m_pd.QOutCount += nwritten) >= m_TxTrigger)
            m_NfyFlags &= ~CN_TRANSMIT;
        _asm popfd
        }                           // using an output buffer
    else
        {                           // no output buffer set up
        _asm pushfd
        _asm cli
        m_pd.QOutAddr = (DWORD) buf;
        m_pd.QOutSize = cbRequest;
```

```
        m_pd.QOutCount = cbRequest;
        m_pd.QOutPut = 0;
        m_pd.QOutGet = 0;
        if (cbRequest >= m_TxTrigger)
            m_NfyFlags &= ~CN_TRANSMIT;
        _asm popfd

        nwritten = cbRequest;    // pretend all of it written
        }                        // no output buffer set up

    KickTx();                    // try to restart output
    if (nwritten < cbRequest)
        m_pd.dwCommError |= CE_TXFULL; // buffer became full
    *pTxCount = nwritten;
    return TRUE;
    }                            // CPort::Write
```

The *else* branch of the first *if* statement handles the case in which the client never set up an output queue by tricking the rest of the driver into treating the caller's output buffer as the missing queue.

A derived class should override *Write*, calling the base-class function after verifying that the host hasn't forbidden transmission via the current flow control mechanism.

OTHER VxDs IN VCOMM'S ORBIT

As I indicated earlier, VCOMM works in conjunction with several kinds of VxDs to handle the communications workload. We've discussed serial port driver VxDs already. The remaining categories of VxDs that work with VCOMM are parallel port drivers, port virtualization drivers, and modem drivers.

Parallel Port Drivers

The preceding section of this chapter dealt in great detail with an example that can serve as a replacement for the official SERIAL.VXD port driver for standard serial ports. VCOMM also uses port drivers for parallel ports, however. The standard LPT.VXD driver operates in much the same way as the serial port driver we just studied, but it's a great deal simpler because parallel port programming is appreciably easier than serial port programming.

I wondered how Microsoft shoehorned a driver for parallel ports into an architectural mode designed for more complicated serial ports. I wondered, for example, how LPT.VXD would deal with data structures like the _DCB_ and _COMMCONFIG_ structures that are heavily oriented toward serial communications.

Unfortunately, Microsoft didn't supply the source code for LPT.VXD on the Windows 95 DDK disc. I had to fall back on well-proven techniques of reverse engineering to learn the details about LPT.VXD, whereupon I found the answer that I should have expected all along: LPT.VXD just ignores the structures and fields that don't pertain to it. For example, _GetCommState_, _SetCommState_, _GetCommConfig_, and _SetCommConfig_ are basically no-operation functions in LPT.VXD: if you should happen to call them, they set a last-error of 0 and return TRUE. And _GetQueueStatus_ fills in the queue count fields of its _COMSTAT_ structure but just sets the _BitMask_ member to 0.

LPT.VXD also takes advantage of the fact that VCOMM won't call port driver functions whose entries in the _PortFunctions_ array are NULL. LPT.VXD doesn't have _SetModemStatusShadow_ or _GetModemStatus_ functions, and it uses NULL pointers in the corresponding _PortFunctions_ slots. (Leaving the _SetModemStatusShadow_ pointer NULL isn't dangerous because UNIMODEM will have no business loading a parallel port driver.)

Port Virtualization Drivers

Windows 95 includes two port virtualization VxDs: the VCD for serial ports and the VPD for printer ports. Virtualization in Windows 95 is primarily a way to preserve compatibility for legacy applications. In a better world, all applications would use the new VCOMM interfaces to deal with serial and parallel ports; there wouldn't be any code left that directly accessed I/O ports or depended on hooking hardware interrupts. Since we haven't yet attained this utopian state, however, we need to understand in more detail how the VCD and VPD do their jobs so that we can predict the behavior of the system. Since the source code for both of these VxDs is on the Windows 95 DDK disc, it's easy to explore.

Printer Port Trapping

Both the VCD and the VPD use _Install_IO_Handler_ to trap their respective I/O ports. The two VxDs differ markedly in their strategies for handling contention, however. The VPD normally leaves trapping globally disabled for printer ports. While trapping is disabled, ring-three code in any VM can freely talk to the printer. The resulting free-for-all can produce odd and unexpected results. Figure 14-12 on the following page illustrates the outcome of a planned experiment involving printing from two different MS-DOS boxes simultaneously.

When someone uses the VCOMM contention mechanism to reserve the port—that is, when some VxD calls the VPD's contention function with the

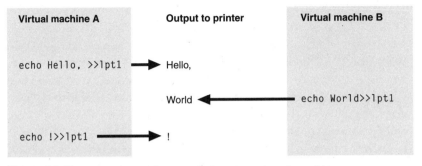

Figure 14-12. *Printing simultaneously from two virtual machines.*

ACQUIRE_RESOURCE function code—the VPD calls *Enable_Global_Trapping* to trap the printer I/O ports in all virtual machines. The Windows 95 spooler uses VCOMM services and, therefore, explicitly reserves the printer. So when the spooler is printing a document, the VPD won't permit interference from an MS-DOS program. If an MS-DOS program tries to write to the printer, the VPD presents a contention dialog box to allow the user to choose between the MS-DOS program and the Windows 95 spooler. The converse isn't true: the VPD will allow the Windows 95 spooler to preempt an MS-DOS printing program. The preemption occurs because the VPD doesn't initially know that there is a ring-three user of the printer (because trapping has been disabled until this point) and therefore assigns ownership to the system VM without demur. The next I/O operation from the MS-DOS program *will* be trapped, though, and the VPD will simulate a busy status that results in an MS-DOS critical error.

There are two anomalies about the VPD's contention management strategy worth noting. First of all, you could have a pathological situation in which some Windows-based program tried to directly access the printer while the Windows 95 spooler (the "official" print program in the system VM) was printing. This situation would slip through the cracks because printer ownership is a per-VM concept. That is, the VPD would trap the out-of-band I/O from the unofficial program, see that it was coming from the VM that owns the printer, and allow it to proceed. Second, the VPD assigns ownership to the System VM whenever *any* VM uses the VCOMM contention mechanism. There's not much else the VPD can do, of course, because the contention architecture doesn't provide for passing a VM handle to the *ACQUIRE_RESOURCE* function.

Serial Port Trapping

In contrast to the VPD, the VCD usually leaves the I/O ports for a serial device trapped except when a VCOMM port driver is in control. A VM becomes the owner simply by attempting an I/O operation. The Windows 95 version of the VCD also subsumes the functionality of the Windows 3.1 COMBUFF driver by buffering physical I/O and simulating port I/O requests from VMs. These actions ensure that the operating system responds as quickly as possible to serial interrupts while still allowing virtual interrupt handlers (which are subject to the scheduling vagaries inherent in multitasking) to believe that they are servicing real hardware. If another VM subsequently tries to access the hardware, the VCD fails the attempt without providing any notification to the end user. The user can alter the contention behavior by altering the *COMxAutoAssign* option setting in the SYSTEM.INI file.

SERIAL PORT VIRTUALIZATION AND VCOMM

It's important to realize that the VCD is *not* a VCOMM client. In other words, any I/O operations it virtualizes go directly to the hardware rather than through VCOMM to a port driver VxD. If you're attempting to provide modem redirection across a network, or if you want to trap serial operations for standard ports coming from an MS-DOS program, you will have to take over the standard ports from the VCD and you will have to craft your own mechanism for contention.

VCD_Virtualize_Port allows you to assume responsibility for virtualizing a port so that you can redirect I/O operations through VCOMM. You can find documentation for this service in the Windows 3.1 DDK or in the VCD source code on the Windows 95 DDK disc. Contrary to what the documentation says, you must call this service after CONFIGMG's Device_Init but before the VCD's Device_Init. The peculiar timing requirement arises because the VCD builds its intermediate data structures in response to *ADD_RESOURCE* calls to its contention procedure and then creates its final data structures during its own Device_Init. *VCD_Virtualize_Port* operates only on the intermediate data structures and is therefore useless except within the interval between these two events. Practically speaking, this requirement means that you should specify an initialization order slightly before the VCD and place your *VCD_Virtualize_Port* call in your Device_Init handler.

Contention handling is an issue because the VCD's *ACQUIRE_RESOURCE* procedure will give ownership of the port to the System VM. If you want to intercept serial I/O operations from an MS-DOS VM, you'll want to give ownership to that VM instead. To do so, you'll need to call *VCD_Acquire_Port_Windows_Style* on behalf of the MS-DOS VM and with the other arguments that the VCD's contention function uses.

The *COMxAutoAssign* Option   For each COM port, the user can set the *COMxAutoAssign* option in the SYSTEM.INI file (*COM1AutoAssign*, *COM2AutoAssign*, and so on) to a timeout value in seconds. For example, *COM2AutoAssign=2* means that the VCD should judge that a previous owner of COM2 is done using the port if 2 seconds have elapsed since the last I/O operation. An option value of 0 means that the VCD should always reassign ownership without any timeout, while -1 means that the VCD should always present a contention dialog box. The undocumented value of -2, which is the default setting, means that the VCD should always fail contending access attempts without comment.

The virtualization picture changes slightly when a VCOMM port driver uses the VCD's contention function to acquire ownership of a port. The contention function uses the *VCD_Acquire_Port_Windows_Style* service to give the System VM ownership of the port. In handling this service call, the VCD disables local trapping within the new owner VM while leaving trapping enabled for all other VMs. Disabling trapping has the theoretical effect of allowing the System VM to directly access the hardware, but applications that use the Windows 95 version of COMM.DRV won't take advantage of this freedom: they'll be calling VCOMM, and all the port I/O will happen within the ring-zero port driver anyway.

Finally, it's worth noting that the Windows 95 version of the VCD continues to compatibly support communication drivers from Windows versions 3.0 and 3.1. The support includes such archeological curiosities as 16-bit ring-zero DLLs. Explaining how the support works is beyond the scope of this book (and, indeed, my span of attention).

Modem Drivers

Nobody should need to write a special VxD to handle a modem in Windows 95. Nearly all modems on the market understand the AT command set invented by Hayes, and Microsoft has provided a generic set of ring-three and ring-zero drivers for AT-command-compatible modems. All that most modem manufacturers need to do in order to gain Windows 95 compatibility is to create an .INF file that defines the commands and responses that their particular modem understands.

The VxD that supports AT-command-compatible modems for telephony applications (that is, applications that use TAPI, the Telephony API) is UNIMODEM.VXD. Microsoft hasn't published the source code for UNIMODEM.VXD, but there's probably no need for them to do so given how unlikely it is that anyone will need to duplicate it. UNIMODEM.VXD is a peculiar animal: it's both a VCOMM port driver *and* a client of VCOMM. I'll explain what I mean in the next few paragraphs, after which we'll be done discussing communications in Windows 95.

To determine how UNIMODEM.VXD fits into the system architecture, I used the Add New Hardware wizard to install a generic 28,800 bps modem. I ended up with registry entries that, among other things, designated VCOMM as the device loader for the device (see Figure 14-13). Notice in the figure that the modem's software key has subkeys with names like Answer, Hangup, and so on. These subkeys contain command strings and responses for the modem. For example, Hangup has a single named value (1), which is set to ATH<cr>; you'll probably recognize this as the standard Hayes modem command for hanging up the phone.

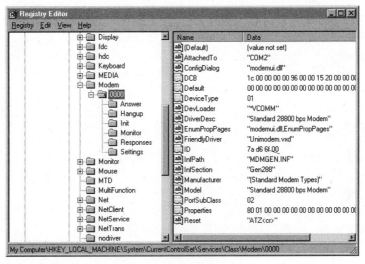

Figure 14-13. *Software key for a modem.*

In contrast to the software key for other Plug and Play devices we've studied in this book, the modem's software key doesn't have a named value PortDriver. The important named values for our purposes are FriendlyDriver (which is set to UNIMODEM.VXD) and AttachedTo (which is set to COM*x*). Together, these values tell VCOMM that UNIMODEM.VXD is the port driver for a device opened under the particular friendly name for this modem and that the modem is attached to the COM*x* port.

When a telephony application opens a line using the friendly name given to this modem, VCOMM ends up loading UNIMODEM.VXD as the port driver. UNIMODEM.VXD goes through all the same work we discussed earlier to register a driver control procedure, call *_VCOMM_Add_Port*, and so on. When asked to open its port, however, UNIMODEM.VXD turns around and calls *_VCOMM_OpenComm* to open the AttachedTo port. This nested open call causes VCOMM to load SERIAL.VXD; you know what happens then with respect to COM*x*.

Many of UNIMODEM.VXD's port driver function entries are straight pass-throughs to the underlying serial port driver. In fact, UNIMODEM.VXD breaks the published rules by calling directly through the *PortFunctions* table belonging to the serial driver. In all cases but one, it first checks the function pointer for 0. (The exception is an early call to the serial driver's *SetModemStatusShadow* function, in which it doesn't check for 0 first. This call is the reason a serial port driver must supply this port driver function even though all others are optional.) UNI-MODEM.VXD obtains the address of the *PortFunctions* table by looking inside the *PortData* structure, whose address it obtains by calling *_VCOMM_OpenComm*. Even though the official documentation says that the handle returned by *_VCOMM_Open-Comm* isn't necessarily the same one as that returned by a port driver open routine, you can see that it really is the same. I would imagine that one incarnation of UNIMODEM.VXD used the published VCOMM service API to get to the port driver but that performance concerns prompted a switch to the kludgier, faster method now used.

Those of UNIMODEM.VXD's port driver functions that aren't simple pass-throughs to the serial port driver involve very little additional processing. For example, UNIMODEM.VXD makes its own copy of the MSR shadow byte before calling the serial driver to handle *SetModemStatusShadow*. Its *Read* and *Write* routines update statistical counters, but otherwise defer to the serial port driver. In fact, UNIMODEM.VXD acts much like a C++ class derived from a serial port class similar to the *CSerialPort* class discussed in this chapter.

Chapter 15

Block Device Drivers

The more you know about the insides of Windows 95, the more you think someone highly placed at Microsoft must have once wondered aloud about MS-DOS, "Will no one rid me of this real-mode operating system?" In previous versions of Windows, two of the major impediments to dispensing altogether with MS-DOS were the FAT file system and the disk I/O subsystem underneath it. I'll talk in the next chapter about the Windows 95 Installable File System Manager that has finally supplanted MS-DOS's file system. In this chapter, I'll discuss the new 32-bit protected-mode subsystem for disk I/O.

It's hard to overstate the importance of the technology that allows Windows 95 to do disk I/O without leaving 32-bit protected mode. The constant need to switch to V86 mode in order to run MS-DOS disk drivers for page swapping operations put previous versions of Windows in a straightjacket. MS-DOS wasn't (and still isn't) reentrant, so you couldn't allow recursive page faults to occur. Indeed, you couldn't allow any page faults whatsoever to occur while MS-DOS was active. Programs that violated the rule could leave the system in a state in which it would need to recursively enter MS-DOS to fetch a page. One implication was that no ring-zero code could be pageable; if it were, you might have event callbacks that inadvertently faulted while they innocently called presumably legal nonasynchronous VxD services. And you couldn't forbid event service during paging I/O because the system wouldn't be able to handle the interrupts that signal I/O completion. Another implication of real-mode paging was that the page manager would end up owning the one-and-only ring-zero critical section for long periods of time in order to protect paging I/O from the forbidden reentrance. So Windows 95's ability to do paging I/O in ring zero frees the entire system and relaxes many of the rules that used to be needed to prevent deadlock.

Despite the many benefits that accrue from having a 32-bit protected-mode disk subsystem, programmers of Windows 95 VxDs still have to worry about the old rules because of two compatibility features. First, real-mode drivers are still with us, and it's possible that Windows 95 will end up using real-mode code for page swapping just because third-party vendors haven't yet gotten with the program by converting to VxDs. And second, the end user can foil the most capable ring-zero implementation by demanding that Windows 95 use real-mode drivers anyway.

Notwithstanding the inconvenient persistence of real mode as a compatibility escape, the file systems and other components that rely on the Input/Output Supervisor (IOS) for disk access use 32-bit interfaces to reach the IOS. Real mode, if it intrudes at all, does so sometime during the IOS's handling of requests. We'll study the IOS in detail here, and I'll show you how to build a port driver (which operates at nearly the lowest level of a layered hierarchy of drivers) and a "vendor-supplied" driver (which operates at an intermediate level).

THE ARCHITECTURE OF THE IOS

Windows 95 abstracts disks as *block devices,* that is, devices that move data in fixed-size blocks at relatively high speeds. A VxD known as the Input/Output Supervisor (IOS) implements a layered device driver model that accommodates current and foreseeable disk technologies. The IOS works with many other VxD components—some supplied by Microsoft and some supplied by hardware and software manufacturers—to coordinate block I/O operations for clients such as the page swapper and the file system manager. The IOS even handles I/O requests generated by MS-DOS programs running in V86 mode. The official documentation of the IOS is Microsoft's *Layered Block Device Drivers* (in the "Design and Imple-mentation Guide" section of the Windows 95 DDK), but you'll probably find the rest of this chapter to be a useful supplement.

The IOS provides a small number of services to the rest of the Windows 95 system (see Table 15-1). The primary clients of the IOS are file system drivers, which translate application requests for access to files into appropriate I/O operations to be performed on a volume mounted on a block device. *IOS_SendCommand* is the primary service by which file systems and other IOS clients launch I/O requests and monitor their status. The IOS uses other VxD components—collectively known as *layer drivers*—to perform the requests that clients submit to it. Most of the story in this chapter relates to these layer drivers.

Service	Description
IOS_BD_Command_Complete	Indicates completion of an I/O request using the BlockDev interface.
IOS_BD_Register_Device	Registers a BlockDev-compatible VxD.
IOS_Exclusive_Access	Locks a drive for exclusive access by a single virtual machine.
IOS_Find_Int13_Drive	Finds the BlockDev device descriptor for a device that was visible in real mode prior to Windows 95 startup.
IOS_Get_Device_List	Retrieves the head of the list of BlockDev device descriptors.
IOS_Get_Version	Gets the IOS version number.
IOS_Register	Registers a layer driver with the IOS.
IOS_Requestor_Service	Performs a function on behalf of an originator of I/O requests.
IOS_Send_Next_Command	Sends the next command to a device.
IOS_SendCommand	Sends an I/O request to a device. (This is the method used to do I/O with block devices.)
IOS_Set_Async_Timeout	Creates an asynchronous timeout (same as the VMM service *Set_Async_Timeout* service).
IOS_Signal_Semaphore_No_Switch	Same as the VMM service *Signal_Semaphore_No_Switch* service.
IOSIdleStatus	Determines whether the IOS is idle.
IOSMapIORSToI21	Maps an IOS error code to its INT 21h equivalent.
IOSMapIORSToI24	Maps an IOS error code to its INT 24h equivalent.

Table 15-1. *IOS services.*

IOS Clients

Although this chapter is really about how to write VxDs that fit into the IOS's internal architecture, it's helpful to know a little about how external client VxDs call into the IOS. Clients deal with *logical disk drives* and *volumes*. A volume is the abstract container of a large number of fixed-size data blocks "mounted" on an equally abstract unit that the client can address separately. That is, the logical disk drive is a software stand-in for a physical disk drive, and a volume is the software stand-in for a physical disk spinning on a drive spindle. For most purposes, you can think of a logical drive and the volume it contains as being the same entity.

In the physical world, logical disk drives correspond to the partitions on physical disks. The end user participates in the creation of logical drives by using the FDISK utility on a new hard disk. Small computer system interface (SCSI) hard disks and CD-ROMs routinely have control and other information physically present but hidden from casual view behind the logical volume facade.

It's difficult to describe how an IOS client uses IOS services before talking about the IOS's central data structures: the device control block (DCB), the volume request parameters block (VRP), and the I/O request descriptor (IOR). It's also hard to describe these structures without first talking about how they're used. I decided, therefore, to briefly explain in a name-dropping manner the process an IOS client goes through to perform I/O operations. That is, I'll refer to various data structures as if they were old friends. Then, in the remainder of this section on architecture, I'll discuss the data structures in detail. In the last section of this chapter, I'll return to how programmers use the data structures with various IOS services to accomplish useful results.

Windows 95 IOS Clients

An IOS client needs some extrinsic way of knowing what devices are present on the system. The Installable File System (IFS) Manager provides this knowledge for file system drivers (FSDs) by means of a volume mounting protocol. We'll talk later in the book about IFS. For now, all you need to know is that FSDs use a DCB to describe a logical disk drive and a VRP to describe the volume mounted on a logical drive. The IFS Manager uses subfunctions of *IOS_Requestor_Service* to create and manage VRPs in the first instance. Starting with a DCB and a VRP, a client goes through the following steps to perform an I/O operation such as reading a sector:

1. Create an IOR and fill it in with information about the operation to be performed. The client uses an IOS service routine to allocate the memory for the IOR.

2. Invoke the so-called "criteria" routine to massage the I/O request to conform to the requirements of the drivers that will handle it. The criteria routine does such things as convert the transfer count from sectors to bytes and convert virtual addresses to physical address scatter/gather descriptors.

3. Pass the IOR address to *IOS_SendCommand*. Despite documentation that suggests that you also pass the DCB address, the IOS actually locates the DCB on its own. A flag bit in the IOR indicates whether the operation should be handled synchronously or not. For a synchronous operation, the IOS waits for the operation to complete before returning. For an

asynchronous operation, the IOS returns after queueing the operation; when the operation later completes, the IOS will call a completion routine whose address appears in the IOR.

4. Analyze the completion status of the operation and take appropriate action.

5. Release the memory occupied by the IOR by calling an IOS service.

A short sample program (IOSCaller) on the companion disc illustrates the process. It can be found in the \CHAP15\IOSCALLER directory.

Windows 3.1 Block Device Clients

VxDs that aren't Windows 95 file system drivers can use *IOS_Find_Int13_Drive* to find a specific physical drive or *IOS_Get_Device_List* to enumerate physical drives. These two IOS services exist only for compatibility purposes to support VxDs that used the Windows 3.1 block device driver. VxDs that use the old block device interface to INT 13h drives use a BlockDev device descriptor (BDD) to describe a physical drive (there being no purely logical INT 13h drives). They don't use the VRP structure at all because Windows 3.1 didn't have a corresponding concept.

The IOS maintains the BDD structures as parts of its own DCBs. The BDD begins at offset C3h in the DCB, in fact. Because nearly all control blocks used by Windows 95 begin on a 4-byte boundary, you can easily spot BDDs during debugging by their (literally) odd addresses.

VxDs that use the block device interface from Windows 3.1 perform the following steps to do I/O operations:

1. Create a *BlockDev_Command_Block* (BCB) structure describing the operation. Clients use their own storage for these structures.

2. Pass the BCB and BDD addresses to *IOS_SendCommand*. The IOS differentiates between this kind of call (with BCB and BDD pointers) and a Windows 95-style call (with IOR and DCB pointers) by means of a flag bit. The *IOR_flags* member of the IOR structure is at offset 08h; its 400h bit is called *IORF_VERSION_002*. The *BD_CB_Flags* member of the BCB structure is also at offset 08h and didn't assign the 400h bit in Windows 3.1. Hence, if *IOS_SendCommand* sees the 400h bit set at offset 08h from the start of the request structure, it concludes that it has a Windows 95–style request. Otherwise, it concludes that it has a block device request.

3. Wait until the IOS calls the callback procedure specified in the BCB to investigate the completion status of the request. (All operations using the block device interface are asynchronous.)

IOS Layer Drivers

The IOS defines 32 levels of driver functionality (see Figure 15-1). The purpose of the layered architecture is to segregate functionality according to one possible abstract model of how block devices operate and fit into the overall system. The IOS represents each physical device with a DCB. A DCB contains an ordered *calldown list* of functions that participate in handling I/O requests for the associated physical device. Each function in the calldown list occupies one of the 32 possible layers and receives I/O request packets from the level above it. The function can

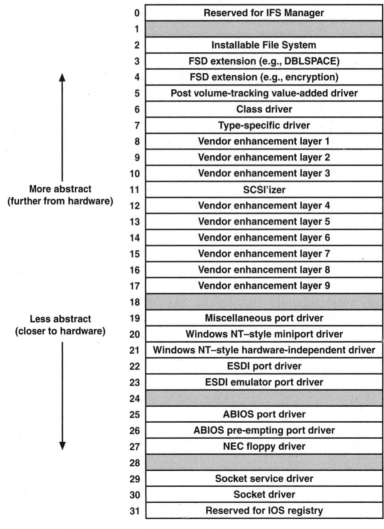

0	Reserved for IFS Manager
1	
2	Installable File System
3	FSD extension (e.g., DBLSPACE)
4	FSD extension (e.g., encryption)
5	Post volume-tracking value-added driver
6	Class driver
7	Type-specific driver
8	Vendor enhancement layer 1
9	Vendor enhancement layer 2
10	Vendor enhancement layer 3
11	SCSI'izer
12	Vendor enhancement layer 4
13	Vendor enhancement layer 5
14	Vendor enhancement layer 6
15	Vendor enhancement layer 7
16	Vendor enhancement layer 8
17	Vendor enhancement layer 9
18	
19	Miscellaneous port driver
20	Windows NT–style miniport driver
21	Windows NT–style hardware-independent driver
22	ESDI port driver
23	ESDI emulator port driver
24	
25	ABIOS port driver
26	ABIOS pre-empting port driver
27	NEC floppy driver
28	
29	Socket service driver
30	Socket driver
31	Reserved for IOS registry

More abstract (further from hardware) ↑

Less abstract (closer to hardware) ↓

Figure 15-1. *Layers of driver functionality.*

process the packet completely, it can modify the packet and pass it along to the next lower level in the calldown list, or it can execute completely new requests that cumulatively implement the original request.

Although there are 32 layers in the complete IOS driver model, only a few of those layers are actually occupied by drivers for any given piece of hardware. Figure 15-2 illustrates the actual layering of drivers for three disk drives on my own system. My floppy disk drive includes five layers of drivers: a volume tracker (level 5), a type-specific driver (level 7), a secret IOS internal component (level 18), a floppy driver (level 27), and a handler of last resort (level 31). Not only can layers

	Floppy disk drive	Hard disk drive	CD-ROM
0			
1			
2			
3			
4			
5	VOLTRK		VOLTRK
6			CDTSD
7	Disk TSD	Disk TSD	
8			
9			
10			
11			
12			
13			CDVSD
14			
15			SCSI1HELP
16			
17			
18	Secret IOS thingy		
19		Miscellaneous port driver	
20			SCSIPORT
21			
22		ESDI_506 port driver	
23			
24			
25			
26			
27	HSFLOP port driver		
28			
29			
30			
31	IOS handler of last resort	IOS handler of last resort	IOS handler of last resort

Figure 15-2. *Layering of disk drivers on my system.*

be vacant, but different devices can have some layers containing the same or different drivers. All devices share the IOS last-resort handler at level 31, for example. My CD-ROM drive shares the volume tracker (level 5) with my floppy drive because both drives have removable media. An Integrated Device Electronics (IDE) hard disk drive on my system has nothing at level 5 (its media can never change), but it has a "miscellaneous" port driver at level 19 and an Enhanced Small Device Interface (ESDI) port driver at level 22.

Functions of Layer Drivers

Drivers in each layer have definite responsibilities. Except in the case of drivers at the lowest levels, which you can lump together under the rubric "port drivers," Microsoft hasn't provided a detailed specification of these responsibilities. No detailed specification is probably needed, though, because Microsoft itself provides most of the drivers at high and intermediate levels, and because the large class of vendor-supplied drivers has a deliberately vague and broad charter.

File System Drivers

File system drivers (FSDs) manage high-level I/O requests from applications. I'll have a lot more to say about file system drivers in Chapter 16 when I talk about the IFS Manager.

Volume Trackers

As its name suggests, a volume tracker (such as VOLTRACK.VXD) keeps track of which volume is currently inserted into a device that has removable media. The volume tracker monitors the device for media changes and interacts with the end user to be sure that the expected media is actually present. One of the implicit parameters of an I/O request is a structure (a VRP) designating the media that the IOS client believes it wants to talk to. The data structures describing physical devices likewise include VRPs. So a volume tracker would verify that the device has the volume that the client wants to work with and would take steps to correct any mismatch.

Type-Specific Drivers

A type-specific driver (TSD) has overall responsibility for devices of a certain class. A typical system contains a Disk TSD (DISKTSD.VXD) and a CD-ROM TSD (CDTSD.VXD). Among the things a TSD does are the following:

■   Examine BIOS and MS-DOS data about disk devices that were visible in real mode prior to Windows 95 startup in order to provide for protected-mode driver access to the same devices.

- Read the partition table from a hard disk's master boot record and build the data structures that describe the logical devices that share the physical media.

- Convert requests from logical to physical sector basing.

Vendor-Supplied Drivers

Vendor-supplied drivers (VSDs) defy easy categorization. One purpose of a VSD is to allow a hardware or software vendor to implement nonstandard or proprietary functionality. Some VSDs are standard parts of the system, however. Note that the VSD layer numbers (8 through 10 and 12 through 17) bracket the layer (11) at which a SCSI'izer operates. Thus, a VSD can insert itself into the calldown stack either above or below the SCSI'izer, as appropriate.

Most VSDs pertain to SCSI devices. Non-SCSI devices are implemented primarily in the port driver, and there's no real need for additional layers of drivers. The standard CDVSD, DISKVSD, and SCSI1HLP drivers are examples of SCSI-related VSDs. CDVSD generates SCSI commands for SCSI-2 CD-ROM and audio devices, while DISKVSD does so for SCSI-2 disk drives. SCSI1HLP converts SCSI-2 packets to whatever nonstandard format a SCSI-1 device happens to need.

We'll talk in this chapter about how to build a VSD for the almost trivial purpose of monitoring the flow of I/O requests in order to educate systems programmers. You could write a VSD to perform compression or encryption, or for any other purpose you can dream up. Unfortunately, the fact that the IOS uncritically loads any VxD it finds in the IOSUBSYS directory and treats it as a VSD provides a relatively easy pathway for a virus, too.

SCSI'izers

A SCSI'izer (such as APIX.VXD) builds SCSI command descriptor blocks for a specific class of device, and it performs device-level error recovery and logging.

Port Drivers

Windows 95 uses Windows NT–style miniport drivers for SCSI devices. SCSI miniport drivers have .MPD as their file extension. Miniport drivers for Windows 95 are slightly improved versions of Windows NT miniport drivers. They use the portable executable (PE) file format and are therefore directly usable in binary form under Windows NT, in fact. A miniport driver handles adapter-specific tasks on behalf of the device-independent SCSI port driver supplied by Microsoft. Such tasks include tracking state transitions, introducing necessary delays at specific points in an operation, translating status codes to standard values, and so on. To learn more about SCSI miniport drivers, refer to the Windows NT 3.51 DDK, in the section titled "Kernel-Mode Drivers," subsection "Reference," in the set of documents grouped under the heading "Part 3 SCSI Drivers." (Search for "Part 3 SCSI Drivers" to find this section in the DDK.) I won't discuss them further in this book.

For non-SCSI devices, the IOS uses port drivers with the .PDR extension. A port driver generates I/O commands for a physical device, programs DMA transfers, interprets status information, and handles hardware interrupts. Microsoft supplies port drivers for certain generic kinds of devices. ESDI_506.PDR, for example, is the port driver for ESDI and IDE disk drives, and HSFLOP.PDR is the port driver for NEC floppy drives. Hardware manufacturers may need to supply individualized port drivers too.

We'll talk in this chapter about how to build a port driver for a RAM disk, which doesn't (thankfully) require sophisticated port programming or interrupt handling.

Real-Mode Mappers

Some devices will continue to require real-mode device drivers. There might not be an acceptable protected-mode driver for the device, or the real-mode driver that Windows 95 found when it started up might provide functionality that no protected-mode driver emulates. (Adding the missing functionality would be a good reason to create a VSD.) In such cases, Windows 95 has to pass I/O requests along to the pre-existing MS-DOS drivers using the same interrupt pass-down mechanisms we discussed in Chapter 10. The real-mode mapper is responsible for the pass-down operation.

Loading Layer Drivers

The IOS uses a flexible scheme for loading all of the device drivers needed to make a particular configuration work. The Configuration Manager drives the process by identifying all the adapters and controllers on the system. The software key for a block device controller designates *IOS as the device loader and names a particular port driver as the port driver. See Figure 15-3 for an example. All IOS port driver VxDs have the file extension .PDR and are located in the IOSUBSYS subdirectory of the Windows system directory. (SCSI miniport drivers are in the same directory, with a file extension of .MPD. They aren't VxDs, however.) As the IOS initializes each port driver, the port driver verifies that its controller hardware is actually present. The IOS then creates a DCB for each physical device attached to the controller.

The IOS also loads all *value-added* drivers (files that have the .VXD extension) that it finds in the IOSUBSYS directory. These files are the VxDs that populate the higher levels of the IOS driver hierarchy. The IOS gives each of these value-added

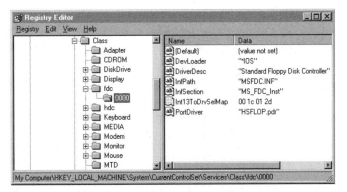

Figure 15-3. *Sample port driver software registry key.*

drivers the opportunity to insert itself into the calldown list of each DCB. VxDs that end up not attaching to any existing device simply unload, thereby freeing memory for more useful purposes.

THE MECHANICS OF WORKING WITH THE IOS

If you've been progressing in a straight line through this book, you now have a firm grounding in the mechanical aspects of building VxDs in the source language of your choice. There are a few additional rules to learn about when working with the IOS. First of all, you'd better be prepared to do a lot of typing: there are about two dozen header files to include, and they define structures whose member names are very long. Not only that, most of the pointer values in the structures are defined as *ULONG* or *PVOID*, which requires you to constantly supply casts to the correct pointer type. Instead of using regular VxD service calls to request services from the IOS, you use a function-based mechanism that relies on a table of function pointers provided by the IOS. The service calls use parameter "packets" instead of arguments on the stack, which makes their use a little different from that of normal subroutines.

The IOS Header Files

In contrast to other components of Windows 95, the IOS tends to use a separate header file for each major data structure. Table 15-2 on the following page lists the header files you may need in a full-blown project. Some of these header files (the ones marked with an asterisk in the table) can be found in the \DDK\BLOCK\INC directory on the DDK disc; the DDK Setup program doesn't copy these to the standard \DDK\INC32 directory on your hard disk.

Header File (.H or .INC)	Contents
AEP[†]	Asynchronous event codes and structures.
BLOCKDEV	Compatibility declarations for Windows 3.x block devices.
CONFIG (*)	Manifest constants for IOS design limits.
DCB (*)	Device control block (major structure for a physical or logical device).
DDB (*)	Device data block (major structure for a controller).
DEFS (*)	Random type definitions plus a few 8250-related constants.
DRP	Driver registration packet.
DVT (*)	Driver vector table (major structure for a VxD that works with the IOS).
ERROR (*)	Standard runtime library header defining MS-DOS error codes.
IDA (*)	IOS internal data structure.
ILB	IOS linkage block (defines function pointers for calling the IOS).
IODEBUG (*)	Debugging declarations for IOS VxDs.
IOP (*)	I/O request packet (IOP) structure (major structure for each I/O request).
IOR	I/O request descriptor (part of an IOP, but nevertheless a separate structure and header file).
IOS	IOS service declarations. Only the .INC file is of any use.
IRS	*IOS_Requestor_Service* function codes and structures.
ISP	IOS service request function codes and structures (major interface between VxDs and the IOS).
IVT (*)	Internal IOS vector table structure.
MINIPORT (*)	Declarations for SCSI miniport drivers.
SCSI (*)	SCSI port and class driver declarations.
SCSIDEFS (*)	SCSI request declarations.
SCSIPORT (*)	A few more declarations concerning the SCSI port driver.
SGD	Scatter/gather descriptor.
SRB (*)	SCSI request block.

† AEP.H on the Windows 95 DDK contains a syntax error in the definition for the *AEP_rpm_change* structure. I've included a correct version of this file on the companion disc in subdirectories of \CHAP15 and \CHAP16. You should copy the corrected version to your \DDK\INC32 directory.

Table 15-2. *IOS header files.*

I'd hoped to find a blanket header file named IOS.INC or IOS.H that would include all the necessary components. Since there isn't any such blanket header, you can either create one yourself, or else include all of the necessary files individually. If you want to write in C or C++, you'll also have to provide your own service table declaration and function wrappers, because the DDK doesn't have any. In fact, the IOS.H file in the DDK is practically all comments (and not very useful comments at that). For purposes of the examples I'll be presenting in this chapter, I built my own IOSDCLS.H file (included in all of the subdirectories under \CHAP15 on the companion disc), which looks like this:

```
#ifndef IOSDCLS_H
#define IOSDCLS_H

#ifdef __cplusplus
extern "C" {
#endif

#define WANTVXDWRAPS
#include <basedef.h>
#include <vmm.h>

#include <aep.h>
#include <blockdev.h>
#include <config.h>
#include <dcb.h>
#include <ddb.h>
#include <drp.h>
#include <dvt.h>
#include <ida.h>
#include <ilb.h>
#include <ior.h>
#include <iop.h>
#include <irs.h>
#include <isp.h>
#include <ivt.h>
#include <sgd.h>
#include <vrp.h>

#undef _IRS_H            // suppress extra IOS_Requestor_Service
#include <vxdwraps.h>

// Some annoying inconsistencies in typedef spelling:

typedef pIOP PIOP;
typedef pDDB PDDB;


...


[MANY additional declarations]
```

```
    ...

    #ifdef __cplusplus
    }
    #endif

    #endif // IOSDCLS_H
```

Driver Initialization

A VxD that works with the IOS initializes in a very different way than a normal VxD does. The VxD is dynamically loadable and must be installed in the IOSUBSYS directory with a file extension of .PDR or .VXD. You put a pointer to a special data structure (the driver registration packet, or DRP) in your driver's Declare_Virtual_Device macro. The only system control message you handle is Sys_Dynamic_Device_Init. Within your handler for that message, you call the *IOS_Register* service. You inspect the result of *IOS_Register* to decide whether your driver should stay loaded or not, and the return value from your Sys_Dynamic_Device_Init handler will reflect that decision.

The Driver Registration Packet

Figure 15-4 shows the format of the DRP structure. The DRP is a temporary structure that you use only for the purpose of calling *IOS_Register*. You might as well put the structure into your initialization data segment. The *DRP_eyecatch_str* field contains 'XXXXXXXX', which may help you spot the structure while debugging.

```
typedef struct DRP {
  CHAR   DRP_eyecatch_str[8];  // 00 EyeCatcher 'XXXXXXXX'
  ULONG  DRP_LGN;              // 08 flags for levels at which driver
                              //    operates
  PVOID  DRP_aer;              // 0C asynchronous event procedure
  PVOID  DRP_ilb;              // 10 address of permanent IOS linkage block
  CHAR   DRP_ascii_name[16];   // 14 name of driver
  BYTE   DRP_revision;         // 24 revision level
  ULONG  DRP_feature_code;     // 25 options for how asynchronous events are
                              //    sent to driver
  USHORT DRP_if_requirements;  // 29 compatible system bus types
  UCHAR  DRP_bus_type;         // 2B controller bus type (port drivers only)
  USHORT DRP_reg_result;       // 2C return code from IOS_Register
  ULONG  DRP_reference_data;   // 2E reference data for AEP_INITIALIZE
  UCHAR  DRP_reserved1[2];     // 32 alignment
  ULONG  DRP_reserved2[1];     // 34 reserved
} DRP, *PDRP;                  // 38
```

Figure 15-4. *Layout of the Driver Registration Packet.*

DRP_LGN is a bit mask in which you specify one of the 32 possible driver levels (shown in Figure 15-1) at which you will operate. It's possible (but unusual) to set more than one bit in this mask. Table 15-3 lists the manifest constants you use for bits in this mask.

Level	Load Group Masks	Description
0	DRP_IFS	IFS Manager
2	DRP_FSD	Installable File System
3 and 4	DRP_FSD_EXT_1, DRP_FSD_EXT_2	FSD extensions
5	DRP_VOLTRK	Volume tracker
6	DRP_CLASS_DRV	Class driver
7	DRP_TSD	Type-specific driver
8 through 10	DRP_VSD_1 through DRP_VSD_3	Vendor-specific driver
11	DRP_SCSI_LAYER	SCSI'izer
12 through 17	DRP_VSD_4 through DRP_VSD_9	Vendor-specific driver
19	DRP_MISC_PD	Miscellaneous port driver
20	DRP_NT_MPD	Windows NT–style miniport driver
21	DRP_NT_PD	Windows NT–style hardware-independent port driver
22	DRP_ESDI_PD	ESDI port driver
23	DRP_ESDIEMUL_PD	ESDI emulator port driver
25	DRP_ABIOS_PD	ABIOS port driver
26	DRP_ABIOS_PREMPT_PD	ABIOS pre-empting port driver
27	DRP_NEC_FLOPPY	NEC floppy driver
29	DRP_SOC_SER_DRV	Socket service driver
30	DRP_SOC_DRV	Socket driver
31	DRP_IOS_REG	IOS registry

Table 15-3. *Mask values for load group numbers.*

DRP_aer points to a function in locked code that the IOS will call to handle asynchronous events. *DRP_ilb* points to an IOS linkage block (ILB) structure you must allocate in locked memory and that the IOS will fill in; the ILB plays a central role in how you invoke the IOS's service functions later on. *DRP_ascii_name* and *DRP_revision* are optional fields that the IOS disregards.

DRP_feature_code is a bit mask that specifies options about how you want asynchronous events sent to your driver. I'll discuss the bits in this mask when I talk about asynchronous events. *DRP_if_requirements* stands for "interface requirements" but isn't used anymore. *DRP_bus_type* indicates what kind of I/O bus your driver deals with (see Table 15-4). The way you set this field tells the IOS how to send you asynchronous *AEP_DEVICE_INQUIRY* events (which are discussed later). The IOS sets *DRP_reg_result* as the return code from *IOS_Register*; the value of this field eventually tells you whether to stay loaded or not. *DRP_reference_data* is 32 bits of arbitrary data that the IOS will pass to your aysnchronous *AEP_INITIALIZE* event handler.

Bus Type Code	Description
DRP_BT_ESDI	ESDI bus or an ESDI emulator (including IDE)
DRP_BT_SCSI	SCSI bus or SCSI emulator
DRP_BT_FLOPPY	NEC floppy bus or floppy emulator
DRP_BT_SMART	Smart device bus
DRP_BT_ABIOS	ABIOS bus or ABIOS emulator

Table 15-4. *Values for the* DRP_bus_type *field.*

A port driver written in C using the DDK normally includes one small assembly-language program to declare the VxD and to define its control procedure. You might place the DRP into this file. For example:

DEVDCL.ASM

```
; DEVDCL.ASM:
        .386p
        include vmm.inc
        include drp.inc
        include ilb.inc

        extrn _OnAsyncRequest:near

VxD_IDATA_SEG
        public _theDRP

;    Declare this driver as a level 19 port driver:

_theDRP  DRP    <EyeCatcher, DRP_MISC_PD, \
    offset32 _OnAsyncRequest, \
    offset32 _theILB, 'Sample Port Dvr', 0, 0, 0>
```

(continued)

continued

```
VxD_IDATA_ENDS

VxD_LOCKED_DATA_SEG
        public _theILB
_theILB  ILB  <>                    ; I/O subsystem linkage block
VxD_LOCKED_DATA_ENDS

Declare_Virtual_Device RAMDISK, 1, 0, RAMDISK_control,\
    Undefined_Device_ID, Undefined_Init_Order,,,_theDRP

Begin_Control_Dispatch RAMDISK
Control_Dispatch Sys_Dynamic_Device_Init, \
    _OnSysDynamicDeviceInit, cCall
End_Control_Dispatch    RAMDISK


        end
```

The crucial feature of this file (included on the companion disc in the
\CHAP15\PORTDRIVER directory) is the last argument to the Declare_Virtual_Device macro. This last argument ends up in the *DDB_Reference_Data* field of the
VxD's device description block. Its purpose is to give the IOS a quick way to find
the DRP as soon as the IOS dynamically loads the driver.

Registering the Driver

The handler for Sys_Dynamic_Device_Init is deceptively simple:

```
extern DRP theDRP;                   // device registration packet

BOOL OnSysDynamicDeviceInit()
    {                                // OnSysDynamicDeviceInit
    IOS_Register(&theDRP);
    return theDRP.DRP_reg_result == DRP_REMAIN_RESIDENT;
    }                                // OnSysDynamicDeviceInit
```

Taking this function at face value, you call *IOS_Register*, passing the address
of your DRP as an argument. Then you inspect whatever return code comes back
in *DRP_reg_result* and set your own return value accordingly. *DRP_REMAIN_RESIDENT* means your driver is supposed to stay loaded.

NOTE If you look at the DRP.H header, you'll find a result code named
DRP_MINIMIZE, which the DDK sample programs use as a synonym
for *DRP_REMAIN_RESIDENT*. The IOS no longer uses this return code,
however.

You can't quite take the OnSysDynamicDeviceInit routine at face value, though. While you're away in *IOS_Register*, the IOS will call your asynchronous event procedure (the function at the end of the *DRP_aer* pointer) to handle an *AEP_INITIALIZE* event. You'll do your *real* initialization while handling that event.

Calling IOS Service Functions

As you'd expect, the IOS exports a number of services for use by port and value-added drivers. In contrast to the way other system components work, however, the IOS doesn't make these services visible as normal VxD services. Instead, the IOS gives you a number of pointers to its internal functions and defines a packet-based way to call those functions through the pointers. The function pointers themselves end up in the ILB to which your DRP points. Table 15-5 lists the service routines pointed to by the ILB. You have to know a lot about IOS programming before most of these functions make any sense. But you have to know about the *ILB_service_rtn* service right away.

Service	Description
ILB_service_rtn	Main IOS service entry.
ILB_dprintf_rtn	Debugging output routine for use with debugging version of the IOS.
ILB_Wait_10th_Sec	Delays 100 milliseconds.
ILB_internal_request	Performs an I/O request.
ILB_io_criteria_rtn	Converts scatter/gather descriptors in an IOR from linear to physical addresses. Used by external IOS clients.
ILB_int_io_criteria_rtn	Same as *ILB_io_criteria_rtn*, only starting with an IOP instead of an IOR. Used by layer drivers to prepare internal requests.
ILB_enqueue_iop	Enqueues an IOP.
ILB_dequeue_iop	Dequeues an IOP.

Table 15-5. *IOS service functions in the ILB.*

The main IOS service routine is the one pointed to by *ILB_service_rtn*. To request a service, you first complete an IOS service packet (ISP) structure of the type appropriate to the service. Then you call the service routine. The results come back in various fields of the ISP. You'll observe that this process is especially cumbersome in a C program. To allocate a device data block (DDB), for example, you might code something like the following:

```
PDDB ddb;
{
ISP_ddb_create isp;
isp.ISP_ddb_hdr.ISP_func = ISP_CREATE_DDB;
isp.ISP_ddb_size = sizeof(DDB);
isp.ISP_ddb_flags = 0;
// Call the service:
(* (void (*)(ISP_ddb_create*)) theILB.ILB_service_rtn)(&isp);
if (isp.ISP_ddb_hdr.ISP_result == 0)
    ddb = (PDDB) isp.ISP_ddb_ptr;
else
    ddb = NULL;
}
```

NOTE Don't confuse the IOS DDB structure with a VxD's device description block, which is also often abbreviated as "DDB".

Creating a DDB is one of the things you'd normally do while handling *AEP_INITIALIZE*, by the way. There are more than 20 different ISP-series services (see Table 15-6), each of which has its own packet structure in the ISP family.

Service	Description
ISP_ALLOC_MEM	Allocates memory. Used only for small amounts of memory associated with I/O requests.
ISP_ASSOCIATE_DCB	Associates a logical DCB with a physical device.
ISP_BROADCAST_AEP	Broadcasts an asynchronous event.
ISP_CREATE_DCB	Creates a new DCB.
ISP_CREATE_DDB	Creates a new DDB.
ISP_CREATE_IOP	Creates a new IOP.
ISP_DEALLOC_DDB	Deallocates a DDB.
ISP_DEALLOC_MEM	Releases memory allocated by *ISP_ALLOC_MEM*.
ISP_DELETE_LDM_ENTRY	Destroys a logical device map entry.
ISP_DESTROY_DCB	Destroys a DCB.
ISP_DEVICE_ARRIVED	Announces the arrival of a device.
ISP_DEVICE_REMOVED	Announces the removal of a device.
ISP_DISASSOCIATE_DCB	Disconnects a logical DCB from a device.

Table 15-6. *IOS service request function codes.*   *(continued)*

continued

Service	Description
ISP_DRIVE_LETTER_PICK	Picks a drive letter for a DCB.
ISP_FIND_LDM_ENTRY	Finds a logical device map entry.
ISP_GET_DCB	Finds the DCB for a physical drive.
ISP_GET_FIRST_NEXT_DCB	Finds the first or next DCB in a loop over all DCBs.
ISP_INSERT_CALLDOWN	Adds an entry to a DCB's calldown list.
ISP_QUERY_MATCHING_DCBS	Finds logical DCBs that match a physical DCB.
ISP_QUERY_REMOVE_DCB	Queries whether it is okay to remove a DCB.
ISP_REGISTRY_READ	Reads a named value from the registry.

There's no predictable rule for guessing the name of the packet structure given the name of the service function code, and there's no predictable rule for guessing the name prefixes for members of those packet structures. I'd estimate that I would generate at least one bug or compilation error each time I coded a sequence like the one I just showed you. Rather than present an unreadable sample, I built a bunch of inline function definitions in my IOSDCLS.H file to create the appearance of a rational, function-oriented interface to the service routine. For example, my header includes the following two definitions:

```
VXDINLINE DWORD NAKED IlbService(PVOID isp)
{
    _asm jmp [theILB.ILB_service_rtn]
}
...
VXDINLINE PDDB IspCreateDdb(USHORT size, UCHAR flags)
{
    ISP_ddb_create isp = {{ISP_CREATE_DDB, 0}, size, 0, flags};
    IlbService(&isp);
    if (isp.ISP_ddb_hdr.ISP_result == 0)
        return (PDDB) isp.ISP_ddb_ptr;
    return NULL;
}
```

Consequently, the code to create a DDB can be a good deal more readable:

```
PDDB ddb = IspCreateDdb(sizeof(DDB), 0);
```

Because I think the official service interface is so hard to use from C, I'm not going to explain any more of the details of how to use it directly. I'll refer instead to the wrapping functions in my IOSDCLS.H file. If you want to see the gory details in order to write assembly-language code (or out of simple perversity), please consult the machine-readable copy of IOSDCLS.H on the companion disc.

Important Data Structures

Although the IOS uses a large number of data structures, three of them—the DCB, the IOP, and the VRP—have pervasive importance. It's much easier to understand how the IOS and layer drivers work if you understand these three structures first.

The Device Control Block

Figure 15-5 (starting on the following page) shows the format of the device control block (DCB). (Note that each of the substructures shown in the figure is actually defined as a separate structure in DCB.H. I put them together for purposes of illustration.) DCB structures can have one of four different sizes in memory, depending on what kind of device they represent:

■ A *logical* device has only a *DCB_COMMON* structure. The TSD creates a logical DCB for each partition on a physical drive. Logical DCBs are therefore the structures most closely associated with drive letters. You can tell you're dealing with a logical DCB by the fact that the *DCB_DEV_LOGICAL* flag is set in *DCB_device_flags*.

■ A *physical* device has a *DCB_COMMON* structure plus the fields I labeled as "extension for physical DCBs" in the figure. Port drivers indirectly create physical DCBs by the way they respond to *AEP_DE-VICE_INQUIRY* events. A physical DCB has the *DCB_DEV_PHYSICAL* flag set in *DCB_device_flags*.

■ A physical device has a *_DCB_BLOCKDEV* extension as well. The *_DCB_BLOCKDEV* structure offers compatibility for Windows 3.1 drivers.

■ A *CD-ROM* device has the three DCB portions discussed above plus a special CD-ROM extension (a *DCB_cdrom* structure) not shown in the figure.

The DCB structure has a bewildering amount of detail, most of which needn't concern the average author of port drivers and VSDs. Knowing which fields you need to care about is much of the battle of learning how to write VxDs to work with

Common header for all kinds of DCBs. This is the only portion present for logical DCBs.

```
typedef struct _DCB {
  struct _DCB_COMMON {
    ULONG    DCB_physical_dcb;        // 00 DCB for physical device
    ULONG    DCB_expansion_length;    // 04 total length of IOP extensions
    PVOID    DCB_ptr_cd;              // 08 pointer to calldown list
    ULONG    DCB_next_dcb;            // 0C link to next DCB
    ULONG    DCB_next_logical_dcb;    // 10 pointer to next logical DCB
    BYTE     DCB_drive_lttr_equiv;    // 14 logical drive number
                                      //    (A = 0, etc.)
    BYTE     DCB_unit_number;         // 15 physical drive number
    USHORT   DCB_TSD_Flags;           // 16 flags for TSD
    ULONG    DCB_vrp_ptr;             // 18 pointer to VRP for this DCB
    ULONG    DCB_dmd_flags;           // 1C demand bits of the topmost layer
    ULONG    DCB_device_flags;        // 20 device flags
    ULONG    DCB_device_flags2;       // 24 more device flags
    ULONG    DCB_Partition_Start;     // 28 sector where partition starts
    ULONG    DCB_track_table_ptr;     // 2C (internal) track table pointer
    ULONG    DCB_bds_ptr;             // 30 DOS BDS corresponding to this DCB
    ULONG    DCB_Reserved1;           // 34
    ULONG    DCB_Reserved2;           // 38
    BYTE     DCB_apparent_blk_shift;  // 3C log of apparent_blk_size
    BYTE     DCB_partition_type;      // 3D partition type
    USHORT   DCB_sig;                 // 3E padding and signature
    BYTE     DCB_device_type;         // 40 device type
    ULONG    DCB_Exclusive_VM;        // 41 handle for exclusive access to
                                      //    this device
    UCHAR    DCB_disk_bpb_flags;      // 45 BPB flags
    UCHAR    DCB_cAssoc;              // 46 count of logical drives
    UCHAR    DCB_Sstor_Host;          // 47 Super Store volume
    USHORT   DCB_user_drvlet;         // 48 user drive letter settings
    USHORT   DCB_Reserved3;           // 4A
    ULONG    DCB_Reserved4;           // 4C
  } DCB_cmn;
```

Extension for physical DCBs

```
    ULONG    DCB_max_xfer_len;        // 50 maximum transfer length
    ULONG    DCB_actual_sector_cnt[2]; // 54 number of sectors as seen below
                                      //    TSD
    ULONG    DCB_actual_blk_size;     // 5C actual block size of the device
    ULONG    DCB_actual_head_cnt;     // 60 number of heads as seen below TSD
    ULONG    DCB_actual_cyl_cnt;      // 64 number of cylinders as seen below
                                      //    TSD
```

Figure 15-5. *Format of a device control block.*

(continued)

continued

```
    ULONG    DCB_actual_spt;         // 68 number of sectors per track as
                                     //    seen below TSD
    PVOID    DCB_next_ddb_dcb;       // 6C link to next DCB on DDB chain
    PVOID    DCB_dev_node;           // 70 pointer to DEVNODE
    BYTE     DCB_bus_type;           // 74 type of I/O BUS (ESDI, SCSI, etc.)
    BYTE     DCB_bus_number;         // 75 channel (cable) within adapter
    UCHAR    DCB_queue_freeze;       // 76 queue freeze depth counter
    UCHAR    DCB_max_sg_elements;    // 77 maximum number of scatter/gather
                                     //    elements
    UCHAR    DCB_io_pend_count;      // 78 number of requests pending
    UCHAR    DCB_lock_count;         // 79 number of media locks minus unlocks
    USHORT   DCB_SCSI_VSD_FLAGS;     // 7A flags for SCSI'izer
    BYTE     DCB_scsi_target_id;     // 7C SCSI target ID
    BYTE     DCB_scsi_lun;           // 7D SCSI logical unit number
    BYTE     DCB_scsi_hba;           // 7E SCSI host bus adapter number
    BYTE     DCB_max_sense_data_len; // 7F maximum sense data length
    USHORT   DCB_srb_ext_size;       // 80 miniport SRB extension length
    BYTE     DCB_inquiry_flags[8];   // 82 device inquiry flags
    BYTE     DCB_vendor_id[8];       // 8A vendor ID string
    BYTE     DCB_product_id[16];     // 92 product ID string
    BYTE     DCB_rev_level[4];       // A2 product revision level
    BYTE     DCB_port_name[8];       // A6
    UCHAR    DCB_current_unit;       // AE used to emulate multiple logical
                                     //    devices
    ULONG    DCB_blocked_iop;        // AF pointer to requests for an
                                     //    inactive volume
    ULONG    DCB_vol_unlock_timer;   // B3 unlock timer handle
    UCHAR    DCB_access_timer;       // B7 used to measure time between
                                     //    accesses
    UCHAR    DCB_Vol_Flags;          // B8 flags for volume tracking
    BYTE     DCB_q_algo;             // B9 queuing algorithm (FIFO, sorted)
    BYTE     DCB_unit_on_ctl;        // BA relative device number on
                                     //    controller
    ULONG    DCB_Port_Specific;      // BB bytes for port driver use
    ULONG    DCB_spindown_timer;     // BF timer for drive spin-down
```

Extension for INT 13h drives

```
struct _DCB_BLOCKDEV {
    ULONG    DCB_BDD_Next;              // C3 chain to next BDD (also
                                       //    embedded in a DCB)
    BYTE     DCB_BDD_BD_Major_Version; // C7 major version of driver
    BYTE     DCB_BDD_BD_Minor_Version; // C8 minor version of driver
    BYTE     DCB_BDD_Device_SubType;   // C9 BlockDev device type (usually
                                       //    0, in fact)
```

(continued)

continued

```
       BYTE    DCB_BDD_Int_13h_Number;        //  CA INT 13h unit number
       ULONG   DCB_BDD_flags;                 //  CB BDF series flags from
                                              //     BLOCKDEV.H
       ULONG   DCB_BDD_Name_Ptr;              //  D3 name of device
       ULONG   DCB_apparent_sector_cnt[2];    //  D7 number of sectors as seen
                                              //     by TSD and above
       ULONG   DCB_apparent_blk_size;         //  DF block size of device as
                                              //     seen by TSD and above
       ULONG   DCB_apparent_head_cnt;         //  E3 number of heads as seen
                                              //     by TSD and above
       ULONG   DCB_apparent_cyl_cnt;          //  E7 number of cylinders as seen
                                              //     by TSD and above
       ULONG   DCB_apparent_spt;              //  EB number of sectors per track
                                              //     as seen by TSD and above
       ULONG   DCB_BDD_Sync_Cmd_Proc;         //  EF command handling procedure
       ULONG   DCB_BDD_Command_Proc;          //  F3 command handling procedure
       ULONG   DCB_BDD_Hw_Int_Proc;           //  F7 interrupt procedure
       ULONG   DCB_BDP_Cmd_Queue_Ascending;   //  FB head of ascending cylinder
                                              //     queue
       ULONG   DCB_BDP_Cmd_Queue_Descending;  //  FF head of descending cylinder
                                              //     queue
       ULONG   DCB_BDP_Current_Flags;         // 103 flags
       ULONG   DCB_BDP_Int13_Param_Ptr;       // 107
       ULONG   DCB_BDP_Current_Command;       // 10B
       ULONG   DCB_BDP_Current_Position[2];   // 10F
       ULONG   DCB_BDP_Reserved[5];           // 117
       ULONG   DCB_fastdisk_bdd;              // 12B
    } DCB_bdd;
 } DCB, *PDCB;                                // 12F
```

the IOS. The following list provides information about the important fields in the DCB. Any field that I don't mention in the ensuing discussion is one that the IOS or some other Microsoft component uses exclusively for its own purposes. Since I'm not trying to provide an exposé of the undocumented features of Windows 95, I didn't even try to figure out what most of those fields were for once I determined that you and I could get our jobs done while remaining ignorant about them. (I made some exceptions for fields that will help you debug your drivers.) In addition, unless I say otherwise, you and I can ignore 95 percent of what's in a DCB except while debugging.

DCB_cmn.DCB_physical_dcb This field points to the DCB for the physical device associated with this DCB. If this DCB has the *DCB_DEV_PHYSICAL* flag set, the pointer will point to this DCB. The TSD (which creates logical DCBs and associates them with physical DCBs) is responsible for filling in this field.

DCB_cmn.DCB_expansion_length This field contains the total length of the IOP expansion area. The expansion area is memory that the IOS reserves when it allocates IOP structures. The IOS calculates this value after all the layer drivers that want to insert themselves into the calldown stack have done so.

DCB_cmn.DCB_ptr_cd This field points to the list of *DCB_cd_entry* structures that describe the calldown stack for this device. The IOS maintains this value and uses it when it initializes IOP packets. Layer drivers look at the current calldown pointer in an IOP rather than at this field of the DCB.

DCB_cmn.DCB_next_logical_dcb In a physical DCB, this field points to the first logical DCB associated with this device. In a logical DCB, it points to the next logical DCB associated with the same physical DCB as this one. If this DCB is both logical and physical, this field will be NULL.

DCB_cmn.DCB_drive_lttr_equiv This field contains the zero-based index of the drive letter for a logical DCB. That is, 0 means drive A, and so forth.

DCB_cmn.DCB_TSD_Flags This field contains flags used internally by the TSD. Port drivers should nonetheless set the *DCB_TSD_ACTUAL_PRE_SET* and/or *DCB_-TSD_APPARENT_PRE_SET* flags if they complete the actual or apparent geometry fields of the DCB during *AEP_CONFIG_DCB*. If these flags are set, the TSD won't try (possibly incorrectly) to figure out the geometry on its own.

DCB_cmn.DCB_dmd_flags This field contains the same *demand flags* as the topmost calldown stack entry. When a driver hooks into the calldown stack during *AEP_CONFIG_DCB*, it passes a demand mask in which it has cleared bits for lower-level demands that it will implement itself and in which it has set bits for additional demands it places on higher-level drivers. The IOS contains a so-called *criteria* routine that assumes responsibility for implementing the demands that appear at the DCB level.

The IOS maintains the *DCB_dmd_flags* field as the calldown stack grows during initialization. A layer driver's *AEP_CONFIG_DCB* handler uses the then-current value as a starting point for the demand flags it passes to *ISP_INSERT_CALL-DOWN* but doesn't directly change this field in the DCB. Table 15-7 on the following page lists the demand flags that have meaning for port drivers and VSDs.

DCB_cmn.DCB_device_flags This field contains flags about this device. All 32 bits in this DWORD field are defined, but you and I are only concerned with the ones listed in Table 15-8 on page 531.

Demand Flag	Description
DCB_dmd_srb_cdb	This flag indicates that I/O packets require a SCSI request block (SRB) and a command description block (CDB). A SCSI'izer hooks into the calldown stack to implement this demand, which should therefore not be expressed at the top level.
DCB_dmd_physical	This flag indicates that a driver requires physical rather than logical DCBs. The TSD services this demand, which should therefore not be expressed at the top level. In fact, the TSD puts a physical DCB address into IOP structures even without this flag being set, so there's no real reason to assert it in the first place.
DCB_dmd_small_memory	This flag indicates that data buffers must be in the first 16 MB of physical memory. This constraint originates in a port driver on a large-memory machine with an ISA bus, because the DMA controller understands only those addresses in the first 16 MB. BIGMEM.DRV (a Microsoft-supplied VxD) implements this demand.
DCB_dmd_word_align DCB_dmd_dword_align	This flag indicates that data buffers must have the specified alignment. These requirements are also DMA-related, and BIGMEM.DRV also satisfies them.
DCB_dmd_phys_sgd	This flag indicates that the port driver depends on having the *IOR_sgd_lin_phys* array of scatter/gather descriptor (SGD) structures completed.
DCB_dmd_do_a_b_toggling	This flag is set by the TSD to tell the volume tracker to keep track of whether a floppy drive on a single-floppy drive system is currently being treated as drive A or drive B.
DCB_dmd_lock_unlock_media	This flag is set by the port driver to indicate that the hardware supports software control over whether the user can remove media. This is more of an announcement than a "demand."

Table 15-7. *Demand flags.* (continued)

continued

Demand Flag	Description
DCB_dmd_load_eject_media	This flag is set by the port driver to indicate that software can load or eject media. This too is more of an announcement than a demand.
DCB_dmd_serialize	This flag indicates that a driver requires that requests be serialized before they reach it. An internal IOS component handles this demand by automatically queueing requests, so the demand ought not be expressed at the top level.

Device Flag	Description
DCB_DEV_SPINDOWN_SUPPORTED	This flag is set by an IDE port driver for a hard disk that supports spin-down.
DCB_DEV_SPUN_DOWN	This flag is set by an IDE port driver when the disk appears to be spun down.
DCB_DEV_IO_ACTIVE	This flag is set by a port driver to indicate that it's busy. Whichever component is responsible for queueing requests checks this flag before passing a request along to the port driver.
DCB_DEV_ASYNC_MED_CHG_SUPPORT	This flag is set by a port driver if the physical device can asynchronously report (via an interrupt) that the media has been removed.
DCB_DEV_SYNC_MED_CHG_SUPPORT	This flag is set by a port driver if the device can synchronously report media changes by means of an error code on the next access.
DCB_DEV_PHYSICAL	This flag indicates that this is a "physical" DCB. (DCB_DEV_LOGICAL can also be set.)

Table 15-8. *Important flags in* DCB_device_flags. *(continued)*

continued

Device Flag	Description
DCB_DEV_LOGICAL	This flag indicates that this is a "logical" DCB. (DCB_DEV_PHYSICAL can also be set.)
DCB_DEV_REMOVABLE	This flag is set by the port driver if the device has removable media. This flag signals that a volume tracker should hook into the calldown stack.
DCB_DEV_WRITEABLE	This flag indicates that the device is writeable. It is normally set by the TSD after the TSD checks the hardware.
DCB_DEV_INT13_DRIVE	This flag indicates that this device was visible in real mode before Windows 95 started. It is set by the TSD.

DCB_cmn.DCB_Partition_Start This field records the physical sector at which this logical device's partition begins. It is maintained and used only by the TSD.

DCB_cmn.DCB_partition_type This field indicates the type of this partition. It is copied by the TSD from the type indicator in the partition record in the master boot record. The most common values are probably 4 (16-bit FAT partition) and 6 (MS-DOS Large File System partition).

DCB_cmn.DCB_sig This field contains 0x4342, which shows up as the characters *BC* in a memory dump. This signature helps you identify DCBs when you're debugging. For assembly-language programmers, there is a set of IOS debugging macros with names like Assert_DCB that check signature fields such as this to help validate pointers.

DCB_cmn.DCB_device_type This field contains the device type (see Table 15-9). The IOS determines the device type automatically for SCSI devices by reading the SCSI inquiry data. Port drivers for non-SCSI devices should set this field while processing *AEP_CONFIG_DCB*. VSDs commonly inspect the device type when they later receive *AEP_CONFIG_DCB* to decide whether or not to hook into the calldown stack.

DCB_max_xfer_len This field contains the maximum data transfer length. Only a port driver can determine this value. Common choices are 0xFFFFFFFF and 0x00FFFFFF. This value represents the largest single transfer that the port driver is prepared to handle. The IOS will break larger requests into pieces to honor this setting.

Device Type	Value	Description
DCB_type_disk	0h	Generic nonremovable direct-access device (i.e., a fixed disk)
DCB_type_tape	01h	Generic sequential access device
DCB_type_printer	02h	Printer device
DCB_type_processor	03h	Processor-type device
DCB_type_worm	04h	Write-once, read-many optical drive
DCB_type_cdrom	05h	CD-ROM device
DCB_type_scanner	06h	Scanner device
DCB_type_optical_memory	07h	An optical disc other than a CD-ROM device
DCB_type_changer	08h	Disk changer device
DCB_type_comm	09h	Communication device
DCB_type_floppy	0Ah	Floppy disk device
DCB_type_optical_nec	84h	NEC 5.25-inch optical disc device

Table 15-9. *DCB device types.*

DCB_actual_xxx The "actual" fields (*DCB_actual_sector_cnt*, *DCB_actual_blk_size*, *DCB_actual_head_cnt*, *DCB_actual_cyl_cnt*, and *DCB_actual_spt*) describe the actual geometry of a device. The port driver can set these fields during processing of *AEP_CONFIG_DCB* or in response to an *IOR_COMPUTE_GEOM* request. The disk TSD will set these fields from BIOS tables during initialization unless the port driver does it first and sets the *DCB_TSD_ACTUAL_PRE_SET* flag.

DCB_next_ddb_dcb This field contains the address of the next physical DCB belonging to the same controller. A port driver creates a DDB during the processing of *AEP_INITIALIZE*. The DDB describes an adapter that has one or more attached devices, each of which has a physical DCB. The *DDB_dcb_ptr* field in the DDB points to the first DCB, and this field is used to link DCBs after the first.

DCB_dev_node This field contains the address of the Configuration Manager DEVNODE for this device. (You could also reach the DEVNODE from the DDB, but it may be more convenient to use this field instead.)

DCB_max_sg_elements This field is set by the port driver, during the processing of *AEP_CONFIG_DCB*, to the largest number of scatter/gather elements it can handle. (There won't be more than 17 in any case.) Any higher-level driver can make the number smaller while processing *AEP_CONFIG_DCB*.

DCB_srb_ext_size This field contains the size of the miniport extension in SCSI request blocks generated for this device. The SCSI port driver determines this value by querying the miniport driver, so no one else should need to worry about this field.

The Input/Output Packet

Figure 15-6 shows the format of an I/O request packet (IOP). IOS clients (both internal and external) allocate and release the memory that holds an IOP, but they do so in a ritualized way. For example, a layer driver with access to a physical DCB would do it this way:

```
USHORT offset = (USHORT) (dcb->DCB_cmn.DCB_expansion_length
    + FIELDOFFSET(IOP, IOP_ior));
USHORT size = offset + sizeof(IOR)
    + dcb->DCB_max_sg_elements * sizeof(SGD);
PIOP iop = IspCreateIop(size, offset, ISP_M_FL_MUST_SUCCEED);
PIOR ior = &iop->IOP_ior;

[do something that needs an IOP, such as IlbInternalRequest]

IspDeallocMem((PBYTE) iop - dcb->DCB_cmn.DCB_expansion_length);
```

An external IOS client starts with the current VRP for a desired volume. From there, the process is similar to what an internal client does, except that the external client works solely with the IOR embedded within the IOP:

```
USHORT size = vrp->VRP_max_req_size
    + vrp->VRP_max_sgd * sizeof(SGD);
USHORT offset = (USHORT) vrp->VRP_delta_to_ior;
PIOR ior = IspCreateIor(size, offset, ISP_M_FL_MUST_SUCCEED);

[do something that needs an IOR, such as IOS_SendCommand]

IspDeallocMem((PBYTE) ior - offset);
```

In both cases, the requestor uses the *ISP_CREATE_IOP* subfunction of the *ILB_service_rtn* service. That subfunction returns the address of a memory block that has essentially not been initialized in any way. If you call the service directly, you need to add the size of the expansion area to the returned pointer to get to the IOP. My wrapper functions (*IspCreateIop* and *IspCreateIor*, defined in IOSDCLS.H) perform these additions before returning, which is why you didn't see that particular complication in these code fragments. Figure 15-7 on page 536 shows the overall layout of the memory block that contains an I/O request.

```
typedef struct _IOP {
  ULONG    IOP_physical;              // 00 physical address of IOP
  ULONG    IOP_physical_dcb;          // 04 pointer to physical DCB
  ULONG    IOP_original_dcb;          // 08 pointer to DCB designated by IOR
  USHORT   IOP_timer;                 // 0C current timeout value
  USHORT   IOP_timer_orig;            // 0E original timeout value
  ULONG    IOP_calldown_ptr;          // 10 pointer to next calldown routine
  ULONG    IOP_callback_ptr;          // 14 pointer to current callback
                                      //    address
  ULONG    IOP_voltrk_private;        // 18 private to volume tracker
  ULONG    IOP_Thread_Handle;         // 1C owning thread
  ULONG    IOP_srb;                   // 20 SRB address
  ULONG    IOP_reserved[2];           // 24
  IOP_callback_entry IOP_callback_table[IOP_CALLBACK_TABLE_DEPTH];
                                      // 2C the callback stack
  BYTE     IOP_format_head;           // 5C for use in low-level formatting
  BYTE     IOP_format_xfer_rate;      // 5D
  USHORT   IOP_format_track;          // 5E
  ULONG    IOP_format_num_sectors;    // 60
  struct _IOR {
    ULONG    IOR_next;                // 64/00 chaining pointer
    USHORT   IOR_func;                // 68/04 function to perform
    USHORT   IOR_status;              // 6A/06 status of request
    ULONG    IOR_flags;               // 6C/08 flags
    CMDCPLT  IOR_callback;            // 70/0C client callback function
    ULONG    IOR_start_addr[2];       // 74/10 starting sector
    ULONG    IOR_xfer_count;          // 7C/18 bytes or sectors to transfer
    ULONG    IOR_buffer_ptr;          // 80/1C buffer or BlockDev scatter/
                                      //       gather pointer
    ULONG    IOR_private_client;      // 84/20 reserved for use by client
    ULONG    IOR_private_IOS;         // 88/24 reserved for use by IOS
    ULONG    IOR_private_port;        // 8C/28 reserved for use by port
                                      //       driver
    union    urequestor_usage _ureq;  // 90/2C IOCTL parameters
    ULONG    IOR_req_req_handle;      // A4/40 reference data for callback
                                      //       routine
    ULONG    IOR_req_vol_handle;      // A8/44 media handle supplied by
                                      //       requestor
    ULONG    IOR_sgd_lin_phys;        // AC/48 address of SGD array
    UCHAR    IOR_num_sgds;            // B0/4C number of SGDs in array
    UCHAR    IOR_vol_designtr;        // B1/4D drive letter (0 = A, etc.)
    USHORT   IOR_ios_private_1;       // B2/4E padding
    ULONG    IOR_reserved_2[2];       // B4/50
  } IOP_ior;                          //   /58
} IOP, *pIOP;                         // BC
```

Figure 15-6. *Format of an input/output request packet.*

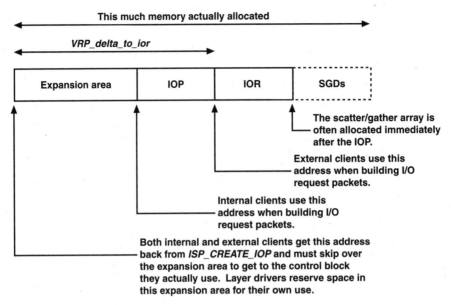

The scatter/gather array is often allocated immediately after the IOP.

External clients use this address when building I/O request packets.

Internal clients use this address when building I/O request packets.

Both internal and external clients get this address back from *ISP_CREATE_IOP* and must skip over the expansion area to get to the control block they actually use. Layer drivers reserve space in this expansion area for their own use.

Figure 15-7. *How the memory for an IOP is used.*

The IOP expansion area is memory that physically precedes the IOP structure within the memory block allocated for the IOP. Layer drivers tell the IOS how much expansion data they require when they call *ISP_INSERT_CALLDOWN* to insert themselves into the calldown stack. The IOS totals the requirements and saves the total in *DCB_expansion_length*. IOS clients end up reserving memory for the expansion area when they allocate new IOPs. The request routines of layer drivers use their respective calldown list entries to locate the (negative) offset of their own expansion areas from the start of the IOP.

The list that follows provides information about the important fields in the IOP and the IOR.

IOP_physical This field contains the physical address of the IOP. There's no known use for this.

IOP_physical_dcb This field contains the address of the physical DCB to which the request relates. Layer drivers below the TSD will find this field completed all the time whether or not they assert the *DCB_dmd_physical* demand. Layer drivers that originate internal requests and use the internal criteria routine must complete this and the next fields of the IOP before calling the criteria routine, which will otherwise crash.

IOP_original_dcb This field contains the address of the DCB passed in by the IOS client, which is the logical DCB for the volume against which the request is generated. Layer drivers that originate internal requests and use the internal criteria routine must complete this and the previous fields of the IOP before calling the criteria routine, which will otherwise crash.

IOP_timer This field contains the number of half-second units that remain until expiration of the 7.5-second interval the IOS allows before it decides that this request may be in trouble. The IOS simply counts this field down each half-second or so. Layer drivers might modify this field to restart a request or as part of handling an *AEP_IOP_TIMEOUT* event.

IOP_timer_orig This field contains the original value the IOS put into *IOP_timer*. This would be the value to restore into *IOP_timer* if you wanted to give a timed-out request a second chance.

IOP_calldown_ptr This field contains the pointer to the current calldown stack entry, which is a *DCB_cd_entry* structure, as shown here:

```
typedef struct _DCB_cd_entry {
    PVOID   DCB_cd_io_address;      // 00 address of request routine
    ULONG   DCB_cd_flags;          // 04 demand bits for this layer
    ULONG   DCB_cd_ddb;            // 08 driver's DDB pointer
    ULONG   DCB_cd_next;           // 0C pointer to next cd entry
    USHORT  DCB_cd_expan_off;      // 10 offset of expansion area
    UCHAR   DCB_cd_layer_flags;    // 12 flags for layer's use
    UCHAR   DCB_cd_lgn;            // 13 load group number
} DCB_cd_entry, *pDCB_cd_entry;    // 14
```

A layer driver uses and updates the calldown pointer to call down to the next layer. For example:

```
void __declspec(naked) DoCallDown(PIOP iop)
    {                               // DoCallDown
    _asm
        {                           // call down to next layer
        mov ecx, [esp+4]
        mov eax, [ecx]IOP.IOP_calldown_ptr
        mov eax, [eax]DCB_cd_entry.DCB_cd_next
        mov [ecx]IOP.IOP_calldown_ptr, eax
        jmp [eax]DCB_cd_entry.DCB_cd_io_address
        }                           // call down to next layer
    }                               // DoCallDown
```

> **NOTE** There is code in the Layered Block Device Drivers section on the Windows 95 DDK that shows a different method of calling down, involving adding a constant to the current calldown pointer to reach the next entry. That code is incorrect; you must chain from one calldown entry to the next as shown in the preceding code fragment.

IOP_callback_ptr This field contains the pointer to the current callback stack entry. Each entry looks like this:

```
typedef struct IOP_callback_entry {
  ULONG  IOP_CB_address;        // 00 callback address
  ULONG  IOP_CB_ref_data;       // 04 reference data for callback
} IOP_callback_entry;
```

The IOP itself contains an array (*IOP_callback_table*) of these structures, and this pointer ought to point to an element of that array.

When a layer driver finishes handling an I/O request, it doesn't just return to its caller. After all, the request may have been queued for a while, and the immediate caller may be a VMM event function or some other agent that has no interest in the results of the I/O operation. Instead, the driver "calls the request back" (in the words used by official IOS documentation) by popping the callback stack and calling the function at the new top of the stack. Even though there is "reference data" in the callback entry, the callback function has only one argument (an IOP pointer) and returns no value. Sample code to execute a callback is as follows:

```
void __declspec(naked) DoCallBack(PIOP iop)
    {                                 // DoCallBack
    _asm
        {                             // call back to previous layer
        mov ecx, [esp+4]
        sub [ecx]IOP.IOP_callback_ptr, size IOP_callback_entry
        mov eax, [ecx]IOP.IOP_callback_ptr
        jmp [eax]IOP_callback_entry.IOP_CB_address
        }                             // call back to previous layer
    }                                 // DoCallBack
```

There's always at least one callback routine on the stack; it is provided by the IOS so that a layer driver can't accidentally jump off into never-never land. If you want *your* driver to be called back when the layer below it finishes the request, you push an entry onto the callback stack:

```
void InsertCallBack(PIOP iop, VOID (*callback)(PIOP),
    ULONG refdata)
    {                                 // InsertCallBack
    IOP_callback_entry* cbp = (IOP_callback_entry*)
        iop->IOP_callback_ptr;
```

```
ASSERT(cbp >= iop->IOP_callback_table
    && cbp < iop->IOP_callback_table
    + arraysize(iop->IOP_callback_table));
cbp->IOP_CB_address = (ULONG) callback;
cbp->IOP_CB_ref_data = refdata;
iop->IOP_callback_ptr += sizeof(IOP_callback_entry);
}                              // InsertCallBack
```

If you want access to the reference data you saved along with the callback function pointer, you must fetch the value out of the callback structure yourself.

IOR_next This is a linking field used by anyone who wants to put the IOR onto a queue. The client should initialize this field to 0. If I were you, I wouldn't assume that this field ever got initialized.

IOR_func This field contains the I/O operation to perform (see Table 15-10). The client program fills this in. Layer drivers inspect it within their request functions to see whether they want to handle particular requests.

I/O Function Code	*Description*
IOR_READ	Reads data from the device.
IOR_WRITE	Writes data to the device.
IOR_VERIFY	Verifies data written to the device.
IOR_WRITEV	Writes data to the device with verification.
IOR_MEDIA_CHECK_RESET	Checks to see whether media has changed.
IOR_LOAD_MEDIA	Loads removable media.
IOR_EJECT_MEDIA	Ejects removable media.
IOR_LOCK_MEDIA	Locks removable media in the drive (increments a counter shared with UNLOCK_MEDIA).
IOR_UNLOCK_MEDIA	Unlocks removable media (decrements a counter shared with LOCK_MEDIA).
IOR_REQUEST_SENSE	Reads sense data from the device (SCSI only).
IOR_COMPUTE_GEOM	Recomputes volume and device characteristics.
IOR_GEN_IOCTL	Performs a generic I/O control operation.
IOR_FORMAT	Issues a low-level format packet.
IOR_SCSI_PASS_THROUGH	Passes a SCSI command through unchanged to a SCSI port driver.
IOR_CLEAR_QUEUE	Drains the queue (that is, waits for it to empty naturally).
IOR_DOS_RESET	Resets the device after an INT 13h reset request (used only by HSFLOP right now).

Table 15-10. *IOR function codes.* (continued)

continued

I/O Function Code	Description
IOR_SCSI_REQUEST	Sends an SRB to a SCSI device (originated by layer drivers).
IOR_SET_WRITE_STATUS	Sets the *DCB_DEV_WRITEABLE* flag according to actual media (used only by HSFLOP right now).
IOR_RESTART_QUEUE	Used in an IOR whose purpose is to mark a place in the request queue. Should be used only by IOS internal components.
IOR_ABORT_QUEUE	Flushes the request queue.
IOR_SPIN_DOWN	Spins down the drive.
IOR_SPIN_UP	Spins up the drive.
IOR_FLUSH_DRIVE	Forces out queued data.
IOR_FLUSH_DRIVE_AND_DISCARD	Flushes and then discards queued data.
IOR_FSD_EXT	Sends a private command to an FSD. Lower levels should never receive one of these.

IOR_status This field contains the status code with which an operation completes. Values below *IORS_ERROR_DESIGNTR* (equal to 16) denote successful completion, while values greater than or equal to *IORS_ERROR_DESIGNTR* denote errors. The successful completion codes include three cases: *IORS_SUCCESS* (0), *IORS_SUC-CESS_WITH_RETRY* (1), and *IORS_SUCCESS_WITH_ECC* (2). (Values 3 through 15 are not used.)

IOR_flags Only a handful of the flag bits within an I/O request matter to clients or to VSDs and port drivers. *IORF_CHAR_COMMAND* indicates to a port driver that the data counts in the request are in bytes; otherwise, they are in units of whatever the device's block size happens to be (usually 512). Clients can set *IORF_DATA_IN* and *IORF_DATA_OUT* if they want to; these flags actually matter only if the BIGMEM.DRV driver can't tell which direction data will move for a given operation, and they allow BIGMEM.DRV to peform only the necessary copy operations.

Clients set *IORF_DOUBLE_BUFFER* to ask the IOS to copy the client data back and forth to IOS internal buffers and to perform the operation using those internal buffers. Clients can also set *IORF_HIGH_PRIORITY* to move a request to the head of any internal queues, although it's more usual for layer drivers to ask for priority handling of internal requests. The IOS's own queue manager honors the flag, so layer drivers don't need to examine it.

As it happens, most IOS clients provide a physical sector address by adding a logical sector address to the partition bias (that is, the physical sector number where a partition starts) for the volume they're addressing. If you want to supply a logical address instead, you must set the *IORF_LOGICAL_START_SECTOR* flag. The TSD will add in the appropriate partition bias once, setting the *IORF_PARTI-TION_BIAS_ADDED* flag to prevent it from doing so again should the request be retried.

A client can set *IORF_QUIET_VOLTRK* to prevent the volume tracker from alerting the user about incorrect media. File systems use this flag when they are reading ahead to fill their caches, since it would be incorrect to bother the user if the read-ahead data isn't actually required.

A client sets *IORF_SCATTER_GATHER* if *IOR_buffer_ptr* points to an array of scatter/gather descriptors. Otherwise, *IOR_buffer_ptr* points to a data buffer.

IORF_SYNC_COMMAND indicates a synchronous command. The IOS waits until a synchronous command completes before returning to the requesting client. If this flag is clear, the IOS returns after queueing the request, and it calls the *IOR_callback* routine when the command later completes. Most IOS clients generate only asynchronous requests and contain their own code to await completion. Therefore, this flag is used sparingly outside the IOS itself.

Clients set *IORF_VERSION_002* to indicate that they are providing an IOR structure. The corresponding bit (namely 400h) at the corresponding offset (namely 8) of a *BlockDev_Command_Block* structure (BCB) is 0. If *IOS_SendCommand* finds this flag set, it actually ignores the parameter passed in the EDI register (which is supposed to hold the address of a DCB); in this case, the IOS uses *IOR_vol_designtr* to locate the correct DCB.

IOR_callback This field points to the completion routine the IOS should call when an asynchronous command finishes. The prototype for this function is as follows:

```
void __cdecl callback(DWORD refdata);
```

The "reference data" the IOS supplies to the callback function is whatever the client places into the *IOR_req_req_handle* field of the IOR.

Layer drivers don't use this callback pointer. They "call a request back" by using the callback stack pointed to by *IOP_callback_ptr*. *IOR_callback*, in contrast, is for *IOS_SendCommand* or some other top-level IOS function to use.

IOR_start_addr This field contains the starting sector address for the request. This is a 64-bit integer occupying two DWORDS. The first DWORD holds the low-order part of the address, and the second DWORD holds the high-order part. If *IORF_LOGI-CAL_START_SECTOR* is set, the address will be relative to the start of the partition. Otherwise, it will be relative to the start of the physical surface.

IOR_xfer_count This field contains the transfer count in units of bytes (if *IORF_CHAR_COMMAND* is set) or sectors (if *IORF_CHAR_COMMAND* is clear). If *IORF_SCATTER_GATHER* is set, this field is actually redundant because you can infer the count by summing the counts for each scatter/gather descriptor. This field must nonetheless be filled in by the client because some programs use it.

IOR_buffer_ptr If *IORF_SCATTER_GATHER* is set, *IOR_buffer_ptr* is the linear address of an array of BlockDev scatter/gather descriptors. Each element of the array has this format:

```
typedef struct BlockDev_Scatter_Gather {
  ULONG BD_SG_Count;       // 0 number of bytes or sectors
  ULONG BD_SG_Buffer_Ptr;  // 4 address of buffer
} _BlockDev_Scatter_Gather;
```

Note that the members of this structure are in the opposite order of the SGD structure used internally by the IOS. The buffer pointers in the scatter/gather descriptors will always be linear addresses.

If *IORF_SCATTER_GATHER* is clear, however, *IOR_buffer_ptr* is the linear address of a data buffer.

IOR_private_xxx The *IOR_private_client*, *IOR_private_IOS*, and *IOR_private_-port* fields contain data private to the originating client, to the IOS, and to the port driver, respectively.

Microsoft's drivers frequently use the *IOR_private_client* field as a convenient place to save the offset of the IOR from the memory block that embeds it. They use the field when releasing the memory used by an IOR. For example:

```
ior->IOR_private_client = vrp->VRP_delta_to_ior;
...
IspDeallocMem((PVOID) ((DWORD) ior - ior->IOR_private_client));
```

_ureq This field contains the parameters for an IOCTL request.

IOR_req_req_handle This field contains 32 bits of arbitrary data to be passed as the one-and-only argument to the *IOR_callback* routine when an asynchronous request completes.

IOR_req_vol_handle This field is set by the client to the address of the desired VRP and is used by the volume tracker to verify that the correct media is present.

IOR_sgd_lin_phys This field contains a linear address of an array of SGDs. Each SGD has this format:

```
typedef struct _SGD {
ULONG SG_buff_ptr;    // 0 physical address of buffer
ULONG SG_buff_size;   // 4 size of the buffer in bytes
} SGD, *PSGD;
```

The pointers inside the SGD structures are always physical addresses, despite the implication inherent in the *lin_phys* part of this field name. The so-called "criteria" routine will build the SGD array and convert transfer counts from sectors to bytes if the port driver asserted the *DCB_dmd_phys_sgd* demand.

There is a demand flag named *DCB_dmd_phys_sgd_ptr* that supposedly causes the *IOR_sgd_lin_phys* address to be a physical address instead of a linear address. A physical address would be very useful to a hardware DMA controller that could directly support scatter/gather operations. I'm told, however, that the demand is not actually used or supported at the present time.

Don't do as I initially did and confuse the SGD structures pointed to by this member with the *_BlockDev_Scatter_Gather* structures pointed to by *IOR_buffer_ptr*. Not only do the two structures have fields in the opposite order, but this structure uses physical addresses whereas the BlockDev structure uses linear addresses.

IOR_num_sgds This field is set by the criteria routine to equal the number of elements in the *IOR_sgd_lin_phys* array of SGDs.

IOR_vol_designtr This field is set by the client to be the logical drive index (0 means A, and so forth) for the target volume.

The Volume Request Parameters Block

The IOS uses a structure called a volume request parameters block (VRP) to describe the volume mounted on a particular device (see Figure 15-8).

```
typedef struct _VRP {
  ULONG    VRP_demand_flags;         // 00 demand flags
  ULONG    VRP_event_flags;          // 04 event flags
  USHORT   VRP_max_sgd;              // 08 maximum number of SGDs supported by
                                     //    port driver
  USHORT   VRP_max_req_size;         // 0A size of I/O request packets
  ULONG    VRP_delta_to_ior;         // 0C offset of IOR from start of packet
                                     //    memory
  ULONG    VRP_block_size;           // 10 sector size on this device
  ULONG    VRP_fsd_hvol;             // 14 FSD's handle for this volume
  ULONG    VRP_fsd_entry;            // 18 FSD's IFS request handler
  ULONG    VRP_device_handle;        // 1C BDD address
  ULONG    VRP_partition_offset;     // 20 physical sector where partition starts
  ULONG    VRP_next_vrp;             // 24 internal VRP chaining field
  ULONG    VRP_logical_handle;       // 28 DCB for logical device
  ULONG    VRP_reserved;             // 2C (reserved)
} VRP, *PVRP;                        // 30
```

Figure 15-8. *Format of a volume request parameters block.*

The IOS creates a VRP in response to an *IOR_Requestor_Service* call from the IFS Manager, and IFS and the various file system drivers pass it around as a handle to the media on which they wish to operate. The structure also holds values that govern how external clients build I/O requests. The fields in a VRP are discussed below:

VRP_demand_flags This field contains flags that indicate the demands the client must satisfy by calling the (external) criteria routine. The bits in this field have the same meaning as the bits in *DCB_demand_flags*, but the demands in the VRP aren't necessarily identical to the ones in the corresponding DCB. On my system, for example, my CD-ROM's DCB expresses the *DCB_dmd_load_eject_media* demand (among others), while the VRP expresses *DMD_dmd_query_remov* (among others) instead.

VRP_event_flags This field contains flags to alert the client to facts that the volume tracker has recently discovered about the volume (see Table 15-11). Of these, only the *VRP_ef_media_changed* and *VRP_ef_media_uncertain* flags are useful to a client.

Flag	*Description*
VRP_ef_media_changed	The media on the device that used to (and maybe still does) contain this volume has changed since the most recent I/O operation
VRP_ef_media_uncertain	The media *might* have changed
VRP_ef_prompting	The volume tracker is currently prompting the user to (re)insert the media containing this volume
VRP_ef_input_share	The input stream of a character device is shareable
VRP_ef_output_share	The output stream of a character device is shareable
VRP_ef_user_canceled	The user canceled the volume tracker's request to (re)insert the volume
VRP_ef_write_protected	This volume is write-protected
VRP_ef_real_mode_mapped	This volume is currently being accessed by a real-mode driver instead of a 32-bit driver
VRP_ef_ios_locked	The device containing this volume is locked

Table 15-11. VRP_event_flags *flags*.

VRP_max_sgd This field holds the maximum number of scatter/gather descriptors needed for an I/O request packet. A client uses either this number or 17 (whichever is smaller) when determining the size required for a new I/O packet:

```
USHORT numsgd = min(vrp->VRP_max_sgd, 17);
USHORT size = vrp->VRP_max_req_size + numsgd * sizeof(SGD);
```

Scatter/gather descriptors don't *have* to be part of the same memory block as an I/O packet, but they do have to occupy a locked page that meets DMA controller requirements. Therefore, it's much easier for everyone if you simply tack the space for these descriptors onto the end of the IOP.

VRP_max_req_size This field contains the number of bytes required for each I/O request packet directed to the device that contains this volume. There's only one size for each device, which is determined after the calldown stack is complete. So I don't see where the "max" part of this field's name comes into play. The size includes the IOP expansion area, the IOP, and the embedded IOR. It does *not* include space for scatter/gather descriptors.

VRP_delta_to_ior This field contains the offset of an IOR from the start of the memory block that contains an I/O packet for the device containing this volume. Refer to Figure 15-7 on page 536 for a picture showing what one of these memory blocks looks like. The "delta" value gets you past the expansion area and the IOP to the start of the IOR. External clients depend on this field to locate the IOR portion of a request packet without necessarily knowing how big the expansion area and IOP portions are.

VRP_block_size This field holds the size in bytes of each sector on the volume. This is usually 512. It *must* be a power of two because code (such as the criteria routine) that converts transfer counts to bytes uses the *DCB_apparent_blk_shift* value as a shift count. I would be reluctant to bet that all components of Windows 95 robustly handle nonstandard block sizes.

VRP_fsd_bvol This field holds the handle by which the client VxD knows the volume. The format of the structure to which this points is entirely up to the individual client.

VRP_fsd_entry This field holds the address of the *FS_MountVolume* routine within the client file system driver. IOS components such as the volume tracker call that function directly, as discussed in the next chapter.

VRP_device_handle This field holds the address of the BDD that describes the device that contains this volume. This address will point C3h bytes into the physical DCB for the device.

VRP_partition_offset This field holds the sector number of logical sector 0 on the physical volume. Although it's possible for a client to pass a logical sector number to the IOS as a starting address, most clients actually perform the translation from logical to physical sectors themselves by adding the partition offset. The reason for this apparently odd behavior is that many clients actually call *IOS_SendCommand* with the address of the BDD instead of the logical DCB. Since the BDD describes a physical device, the IOS can't easily work backwards to find the partition starting address.

VRP_next_vrp This field holds the address of the next VRP. The IOS uses this field to maintain a list of VRPs for all the volumes mounted on any device.

VRP_logical_handle This field holds the address of the DCB that describes the logical device that contains this volume.

Handling Asynchronous Events

The IOS uses asynchronous events to initialize and terminate layer drivers and to alert them to events that occur while the system is running. Your VxD will have an asynchronous event handling procedure. The procedure can be called at interrupt time, so it must be in the locked code segment. It is a *void* function that requires a single argument, namely a pointer to an asynchronous event packet (AEP):

```
void OnAsyncRequest(PAEP aep)
    {
    // do something based on aep->AEP_func
    // store result of doing it in aep->AEP_result
    }
```

In common with other "packet" structures used by the IOS, the AEP structure is actually the parent of a family of structures that share a common header:

```
typedef struct AEPHDR {
  USHORT  AEP_func;       // 00 function code
  USHORT  AEP_result;     // 02 result
  ULONG   AEP_ddb;        // 04 pointer to DDB
  UCHAR   AEP_lgn;        // 08 current load-group number
  UCHAR   AEP_align[3];   // 09 alignment
} AEP, *PAEP;             // 0C
```

Because there are 24 possible function codes in the AEP structure, there are (naturally) 24 child structures, all of which have *different* names for the common header and *different* interior name qualifiers, like the *AEP_bi_i* prefix in the *AEP_INITIALIZE* structure. The proliferation of structures and the lexicographic length of member names inside them are two reasons why I said earlier that you must be prepared to do a lot of typing when you write a VxD to work with the IOS.

Although some of the asynchronous event procedures need to be in locked code, most don't. It therefore made sense to me to code my *OnAsyncRequest* routine in the following way:

```
VOID OnAsyncRequest(PAEP aep)
    {                               // OnAsyncRequest
    typedef USHORT (*PEF)(PAEP);
    static PEF evproc[AEP_MAX_FUNC+1] =
        {(PEF) OnInitialize     //  0 AEP_INITIALIZE
        ,NULL                   //  1 AEP_SYSTEM_CRIT_SHUTDOWN
        ,(PEF) OnBootComplete   //  2 AEP_BOOT_COMPLETE
        ...
        ,NULL                   // 23 AEP_CHANGE_RPM
        };
    PEF proc;

    ASSERT(aep->AEP_func < arraysize(evproc));
    if (aep->AEP_func < arraysize(evproc)
        && (proc = evproc[aep->AEP_func]))
        aep->AEP_result = proc(aep);
    else
        aep->AEP_result = (USHORT) AEP_FAILURE;
    }                               // OnAsyncRequest
```

That is, I wrote a separate procedure for each of the asynchronous events I wanted to handle and dispatched each one from this one function. I made the individual event functions return a result so I could dispense with the following sort of rococo nonsense:

```
void OnInitialize(PAEP_bi_init aep)
    {
    ...
    aep->AEP_bi_i_hdr.AEP_result = AEP_SUCCESS;
    }
```

and could instead code something more evocative like this:

```
USHORT OnInitialize(PAEP_bi_init aep)
    {
    ...
    return AEP_SUCCESS;
    }
```

Of course, there's still a bit of residual nonsense because the *AEP_FAILURE* error code (which is destined for a USHORT field, mind you) is defined as -1, practically guaranteeing a complaint from the compiler.

The IOS distinguishes between three kinds of drivers when it decides how and when to send asynchronous event notifications. "Noncompliant" drivers include the

IFS, the FSD, and Windows NT port drivers (layers 0, 2, and 21); they are not considered to be "registered" and never receive asynchronous events. "Port" drivers include all layer drivers in layers 19 through 30 (except layer 21). "Generic" drivers include everything else. In general, as you can see, port drivers are responsible for specific pieces of hardware, whereas generic drivers are busybodies that might concern themselves with any and all devices.

The following sections describe the AEP events:

AEP_1_SEC The IOS sends an *AEP_1_SEC* event to notify you that 1 second has elapsed since the last *AEP_1_SEC* event. You request these notifications by setting the *DRP_FC_1_SEC* flag in the *DRP_feature_code* field before calling *IOS_Register*. At least, that's how it's supposed to work. Even if you ask for 1-second notifications, you will also get them every half second because DRP.H defines the *DRP_FC_1_SEC* flag to be the same numeric value as the *DRP_FC_HALF_SEC* flag. You can judge the importance of this bug by the fact that it's been in the IOS basically from the beginning.

AEP_2_SECS The IOS sends an *AEP_2_SECS* event to notify you that 2 seconds have elapsed since the last *AEP_2_SECS* event. You request these notifications by setting the *DRP_FC_2_SECS* flag in the *DRP_feature_code* field before calling *IOS_Register*.

AEP_4_SECS The IOS sends an *AEP_4_SECS* event to notify you that 4 seconds have elapsed since the last *AEP_4_SECS* event. You request these notifications by setting the *DRP_FC_4_SECS* flag in the *DRP_feature_code* field before calling *IOS_Register*.

AEP_ASSOCIATE_DCB A TSD initiates this event to discover any additional volumes that belong to a particular physical device that it couldn't deduce on its own. The event procedure receives an *AEP_assoc_dcb* packet:

```
typedef struct AEP_assoc_dcb {
  struct AEPHDR AEP_a_d_hdr;     // 00 standard header
  PVOID         AEP_a_d_pdcb;    // 0C physical DCB address
  ULONG         AEP_a_d_drives;  // 10 bit map of associated drives
} AEP_assoc_dcb, *PAEP_assoc_dcb;
```

A layer driver that has the additional information being sought by the TSD should modify the *AEP_a_d_drives* bit map. Suppose your driver is an FSD responsible for compression on the physical drive represented by the *AEP_a_d_pdcb* DCB and that you know that the Q drive is one of yours. You would set bit 16 of the bit mask (bit 0 corresponding to drive A and Q being the 17th letter of the alphabet).

AEP_BOOT_COMPLETE The IOS sends an *AEP_BOOT_COMPLETE* event when it finishes a series of operations that may have added or removed DCBs from the system. The event routine receives an *AEP_boot_done* packet, which contains only the standard AEP structure header. The driver should determine whether it remains responsible for any devices. If so, it should return *AEP_SUCCESS*; if not, it should return *AEP_FAILURE*.

A layer driver should maintain a static variable that records the number of DCBs for which the driver is responsible. The *AEP_CONFIG_DCB* handler increments the variable, and the *AEP_UNCONFIG_DCB* handler decrements the variable for DCBs that truly represent the driver's own devices. The *AEP_BOOT_COMPLETE* handler is then very simple:

```
static int ndevices = 0;
...
USHORT OnBootComplete(PAEP_boot_done aep)
    {                           // OnBootComplete
    return ndevices ? AEP_SUCCESS : AEP_FAILURE;
    }                           // OnBootComplete
```

AEP_CONFIG_DCB The IOS sends a layer driver an *AEP_CONFIG_DCB* event to set up a DCB. Port drivers receive this event only for DCBs that represent physical devices for which they are directly responsible. Generic drivers receive the event for every DCB in the system. The event routine receives an *AEP_dcb_config* packet:

```
typedef struct AEP_dcb_config {
  struct AEPHDR AEP_d_c_hdr;     // 00 standard header
  ULONG         AEP_d_c_dcb;     // 04 DCB address
} AEP_dcb_config, *PAEP_dcb_config;
```

Here, *AEP_d_c_dcb* is the address of a DCB that's in the process of being configured.

A port driver should fill in geometry and other device-specific information about the device. For example, in my RAM-disk driver (code for which is included on the companion disc in the \CHAP15\PORTDRIVER directory), I decided to create a 2-MB drive that appears to have one cylinder, one track, and 4096 sectors of 512 bytes each:

```
dcb->DCB_cmn.DCB_device_type = DCB_type_disk;
dcb->DCB_cmn.DCB_device_flags |= DCB_DEV_WRITEABLE;

dcb->DCB_max_xfer_len = 0xFFFFFFFF;
dcb->DCB_actual_sector_cnt[0] = 4096;
dcb->DCB_actual_sector_cnt[1] = 0;
dcb->DCB_actual_blk_size = 512;
dcb->DCB_actual_head_cnt = 1;
dcb->DCB_actual_cyl_cnt = 1;
dcb->DCB_actual_spt = 4096;
dcb->DCB_cmn.DCB_TSD_Flags |= DCB_TSD_ACTUAL_PRE_SET;
```

A port driver might also want to set other device flags such as *DCB_DEV_SPIN-DOWN_SUPPORTED, DCB_DEV_SPUN_DOWN, DCB_DEV_ASYNC_MED_CHG_SUP-PORT, DCB_DEV_SYNC_MED_CHG_SUPPORT,* and *DCB_DEV_REMOVABLE.* You can also set *DCB_max_sg_elements* if your limits are smaller than the default 17.

A Caution About Removable Media Drives   In their zeal to be sure that they never write to the wrong volume, Microsoft's file system drivers do something I consider very questionable with removable media. Each time they detect a new read/write volume in a drive, they rewrite the 8-byte vendor identifier in the boot sector of the disk. The revised identifier, which is supposed to be statistically unique, begins with the characters *CHI* and contains five additional bytes computed by randomizing the time of day and other factors. The purpose of writing a unique identifier is to allow Windows 95 to distinguish mass-produced floppy disks that don't have unique serial numbers. If you're responsible for virus detection software, you'll need to allow boot sector rewrites that change only the vendor ID. But if you have software that bases decisions on seeing strings like "MSDOS5.0" in the vendor ID field of a floppy disk boot sector, that software is now broken. There is commercially important software that *does* depend on the vendor ID. Stacker, for example, identifies its compressed volumes this way. The file system drivers therefore avoid rewriting boot sectors that match specifications held in the HKLM\System\CurrentControlSet\Control\FileSystem\ NoVolTrack branch of the registry.

A layer driver uses the *AEP_CONFIG_DCB* event as the occasion to insert itself into the calldown stack for a DCB in which it's interested by calling the following routine:

```
BOOL IspInsertCalldown(PDCB dcb, VOID (*calldown)(PIOP),
    PDDB ddb, USHORT expand, DWORD demand, UCHAR loadgroup);
```

In this prototype, *dcb* is the DCB (physical, logical, or both) into whose calldown stack you want to insert an entry. The *calldown* argument is the address of your I/O request handling procedure; I'll discuss this very important procedure in more detail in the next major section of this chapter when I describe how to build a port driver.

The *ddb* argument is the address of the DDB for this driver; I mention the fact because "generic" layer drivers have a DDB (whose address is supposed to be used in this argument slot) that differs from the DDB for the VxD that created the DCB. Furthermore, this argument points to an IOS *DDB* structure rather than to a VxD's device description block, which sometimes also carries the name *DDB*.

The *expand* argument gives the number of bytes this driver requires for its expansion area in all IOP packets created for this device. The IOS will compute a *negative* offset value for the expansion area and place it in the *DCB_cd_expan_off* member of the *DCB_cd_entry* structure it creates for your calldown stack entry. Your calldown routine can add this offset to the address of the IOP to find an area for its own use as big as the number of bytes specified by the *expand* argument.

In the *demand* argument you express your demands for I/O packet conversion services. You construct the argument by starting with whatever bits are already in *DCB_dmd_flags*. If there are particular demands that your driver satisfies, you turn off the corresponding bits. If your driver were the SCSI'izer, for example, you would clear the *DCB_dmd_srb_cdb* demand in the argument value you're building. If there are particular demands that you want higher layers to satisfy, you turn on the corresponding bits.

The last argument, *loadgroup,* is the number of the layer at which you want to insert your calldown entry. Most layer drivers use the number that comes into the event function as *AEP_lgn*, which usually corresponds to the one-and-only load group bit set in the *DRP_LGN* field. Theoretically, you could specify any load group index here. More than one driver can hook in at the same level. The order in which the IOS calls drivers that share a level isn't defined, however.

A successful *ISP_INSERT_CALLDOWN* call adds a *DCB_cd_entry* structure to the calldown list for the DCB (anchored on *DCB_ptr_cd*) and updates the *DCB_expansion_length* and *DCB_dmd_flags* members of the DCB. When all layer drivers have had their chance to hook into the calldown stack, what's left in the DCB is the address of the topmost calldown entry, the total of all layer driver expansion-area sizes, and the demand flags still not satisified by any of the layer drivers.

In my RAM-disk driver, I used the following call to hook my port driver into the calldown stack:

```
if (!(IspInsertCalldown(dcb, OnRequest,
    (PDDB) aep->AEP_d_c_hdr.AEP_ddb, 0,
    dcb->DCB_cmn.DCB_dmd_flags | DCB_dmd_serialize,
    aep->AEP_d_c_hdr.AEP_lgn)))
    return (USHORT) AEP_FAILURE;

++ndevices;
return AEP_SUCCESS;
```

To avoid having to worry about queueing requests, I asserted the *DCB_dmd_serialize* demand. The *ndevices* variable is the global static integer mentioned on page 549 that keeps track of how many DCBs we've decided to hook into. The purpose of this counter is to tell the *AEP_BOOT_COMPLETE* handler how to respond.

AEP_CREATE_VRP The IFS Manager initiates this event after creating a VRP for a newly mounted parent volume. The event handler receives an *AEP_vrp_create_destroy* packet:

```
typedef struct AEP_vrp_create_destroy {
  struct AEPHDR AEP_v_cd_hdr;   // 00 standard header
  PVOID         AEP_v_cd_pvrp;  // 0C address of the VRP
  ULONG         AEP_v_cd_drive; // 10 drive number
} AEP_vrp_create_destroy, *P AEP_vrp_create_destroy;
```

Drivers that you and I are likely to write can ignore this event, which is purely informational.

AEP_DCB_LOCK The IOS sends this event while servicing an *IRS_QUERY_VOL-UME_LOCK* requestor service call to indicate that it's servicing an exclusive volume lock request. The event handler receives an *AEP_lock_dcb* packet:

```
typedef struct AEP_lock_dcb {
  struct AEPHDR AEP_d_l_hdr;       // 00 standard header
  PVOID         AEP_d_l_pdcb;      // 0C logical DCB being locked
  ULONG         AEP_d_l_drives;    // 10 bit map of logical drives
  UCHAR         AEP_d_l_designtr;  // 14 volume index (0 = A)
  UCHAR         AEP_d_l_align[3];  // 15
} AEP_lock_dcb, *PAEP_lock_dcb;
```

A driver (such as a disk compression driver) that knows the facts should update the *AEP_d_l_drives* bit map to indicate which other logical drives need to be locked too. If, for example, the *AEP_d_l_pdcb* DCB happened to be the host volume for the compressed Q drive, the compression driver would set bit 16 of the bit map (because *Q* is the 17th letter of the alphabet).

Additionally, any driver responsible for the DCB being locked should take note of the lock and stop doing things (such as caching) that shouldn't be done on a locked volume.

The *AEP_d_l_designtr* value in the packet, by the way, is the same "designator" supplied in the *IRS_QUERY_VOLUME_LOCK* call. Since the IOS has already used this value to find the appropriate DCB, layer drivers probably needn't use it for anything.

AEP_DESTROY_VRP The IFS Manager initiates this event after determining that the volume represented by a particular VRP has been dismounted. The event handler receives an *AEP_vrp_create_destroy* packet:

```
typedef struct AEP_vrp_create_destroy {
  struct AEPHDR AEP_v_cd_hdr;   // 00 standard header
  PVOID         AEP_v_cd_pvrp;  // 0C address of the VRP
  ULONG         AEP_v_cd_drive; // 10 drive number
} AEP_vrp_create_destroy, *PAEP_vrp_create_destroy;
```

Drivers that you and I are likely to write can ignore this event, which is purely informational.

AEP_DEVICE_INQUIRY The IOS determines how many disk drive units are attached to your controller by sending your port driver a series of *AEP_DEVICE_IN-QUIRY* events. The event handler receives a pointer to an *AEP_inquiry_device* structure:

```
typedef struct AEP_inquiry_device {
  struct AEPHDR AEP_I_d_hdr;      // 00 standard header
  ULONG         AEP_I_d_dcb;      // 0C address of DCB
} AEP_inquiry_device, *PAEP_inquiry_device; // 10
```

The *DCB_unit_on_ctl* field of the DCB pointed to by the packet is the zero-based index of the unit about which the IOS is inquiring. That is, that field will be 0 for the first inquiry call, 1 for the second, and so on. A non-SCSI port driver should check this unit index against the actual population of the controller to see if the unit exists. If not, the driver should return the *AEP_NO_INQ_DATA* status. The driver can also return *AEP_NO_MORE_DEVICES* to signal the IOS that there are no more units, in which case the IOS will stop sending inquiry events. The IOS will stop after 128 inquiries anyway. If the unit does exist, the driver should complete several fields of the DCB to describe the device; the vendor and product ID will end up appearing in the Device Manager's list of devices, among other places. For example:

```
USHORT OnDeviceInquiry(PAEP_inquiry_device aep)
    {                              // OnDeviceInquiry
    PDCB dcb = (PDCB) aep->AEP_i_d_dcb;
    ASSERT(dcb);
    if (dcb->DCB_unit_on_ctl > 0)
        return AEP_NO_MORE_DEVICES;

    memcpy(dcb->DCB_vendor_id, "WALTONEY", 8);
    memcpy(dcb->DCB_product_id, "RAM Disk        ", 16);
    memcpy(dcb->DCB_rev_level, "0001", 4);

    return AEP_SUCCESS;
    }                              // OnDeviceInquiry
```

A SCSI port driver operates a little differently. Before returning from *AEP_IN-ITIALIZE*, the port driver sets the *AEP_bi_i_max_target* and *AEP_bi_i_max_lun* fields to specify the number of units serviced by the port. The port driver can also set the optional *AEP_BI_FL_SCSI_SCAN_DOWN* flag in *AEP_bi_flags*. The IOS then sends only the specified number of inquiry events. If the *AEP_BI_FL_SCSI_SCAN_DOWN* flag was set, the IOS sends the events from largest to smallest unit number; otherwise, it sends them from smallest to largest. Scanning in reverse might be necessary in some future operating system to mimic the way some BIOSs assign drive letters. In Windows 95, however, the IOS also computes drive letters in such a way that the scan order doesn't matter. Therefore, there's probably no reason to ever set the *AEP_BI_FL_SCSI_SCAN_DOWN* flag.

The IOS also accommodates—by means of a hack—SCSI miniport drivers taken directly from Windows NT. If the *AEP_INITIALIZE* handler sets the *AEP_BI_-FL_SEND_CONFIG_AGAIN* flag, the IOS will start the inquiry process over again by sending *AEP_INITIALIZE* followed by a complete set of *AEP_DEVICE_INQUIRY* events. This sequence allows a miniport driver to make the equivalent of a return that says, "I found one of my adapters, but there might be more." Miniport drivers that have been properly revised for Windows 95 don't need to implement this special behavior.

Finally, a SCSI port driver should return *AEP_NO_INQ_DATA* to halt the enumeration of devices (instead of *AEP_NO_MORE_DEVICES*), and it should be sure to fill in the *DCB_inquiry_flags* field with the SCSI-2 inquiry data from the device.

AEP_HALF_SEC The IOS sends an *AEP_HALF_SEC* event to notify you that 0.5 second has elapsed since the last *AEP_HALF_SEC* event. You request these notifications by setting the *DRP_FC_HALF_SEC* flag in the *DRP_feature_code* field before calling *IOS_Register*. You will also get *AEP_1_SEC* notifications (half as frequently) if you ask for the half-second notifications.

AEP_INITIALIZE *AEP_INITIALIZE* is the first asynchronous event the IOS sends to a port driver, and it occurs even before the driver's own *IOS_Register* call returns. The event handler receives a pointer to an *AEP_bi_init* structure, which contains the following:

```
typedef struct AEP_bi_init {
    struct AEPHDR   AEP_bi_i_hdr;          // 00 standard header
    ULONG           AEP_bi_reference_data; // 0C reference data from DRP
    UCHAR           AEP_bi_flags;          // 10 flags
    CHAR            AEP_bi_i_max_target;   // 11 maximum SCSI ID
    CHAR            AEP_bi_i_max_lun;      // 12 maximum SCSI LUN
    ULONG           AEP_bi_i_dcb;          // 13 initial DCB
    PVOID           AEP_bi_i_hdevnode;     // 17 DEVNODE address
    PVOID           AEP_bi_i_regkey;       // 1B registry key
    UCHAR           AEP_bi_i_align[1];     // 1F DWORD alignment
} AEP_bi_init, *PAEP_bi_init;              // 20
```

The *AEP_bi_reference_data* field contains whatever value was in *DRP_reference_data* when the driver called *IOS_Register*. The *AEP_bi_i_hdevnode* value is the handle of the Configuration Manager DEVNODE for the controller device. The *AEP_bi_flags, AEP_bi_i_max_target,* and *AEP_bi_i_max_lun* fields are output fields for use by SCSI device drivers; I described their purpose in connection with the

AEP_DEVICE_INQUIRY event. The *AEP_bi_i_dcb* and *AEP_bi_i_regkey* values in this structure are meaningless.

The port driver should create a DDB to describe the physical controller. The IOS defines a basic DDB structure in the format shown in Figure 15-9. The only standard DDB field you'll probably ever have any use for is *DDB_devnode_ptr*, which points to the same DEVNODE as the *AEP_bi_i_hdevnode* parameter to the *AEP_INITIALIZE* event. You'll often want to define your own larger structure with room for additional fields specific to your device. For example, you might want to remember the IRQ and base I/O address that the Configuration Manager gave you, using a structure like the following:

```
typedef struct tagRAMDISKDDB
    {                              // RAMDISKDDB
    struct DDB;                    // 00 basic DDB
    DWORD   irq;                   // 20 assigned IRQ
    DWORD   iobase;                // 24 base port address
    HIRQ    irqhandle;             // 28 virtualized IRQ handle
    BOOL    busy;                  // 2C busy with a request?
    } RAMDISKDDB, *PRAMDISKDDB;    // 30
```

Of course, the RAM-disk driver I'm using as an example doesn't need an IRQ or a base I/O port. I'm showing you how to deal with those resources here to keep this example from being completely sterile. Note, by the way, the use of an unnamed structure member in the preceding declaration. The ability to embed an unnamed structure inside another structure or union is a felicitous Microsoft language extension that allows you to reference fields inside the substructure without adding a level of name qualification. This feature requires less typing, which means that I approve of it.

```
typedef struct DDB {
    ULONG    DDB_phys_addr;       // 00 physical address of this structure
    ULONG    DDB_Next_DDB;        // 04 next DDB for this device (internal use)
    ULONG    DDB_Next_DDB_init;   // 08 next DDB on init chain (internal use)
    ULONG    DDB_dcb_ptr;         // 0C first DCB for this device
    UCHAR    DDB_number_buses;    // 10 number of buses supported by device
    UCHAR    DDB_ios_flags;       // 11 flags for internal use
    USHORT   DDB_sig;             // 12 signature 0x4442 ('BD')
    PVOID    DDB_dvt;             // 14 address of DVT for owning driver
    PVOID    DDB_devnode_ptr;     // 18 DEVNODE for this device
    PVOID    DDB_reserved;        // 1C (reserved)
} DDB , *pDDB;                    // 20
```

Figure 15-9. *Format of an IOS device data block.*

Here's an example of how to allocate a DDB within the context of the *AEP_INITIALIZE* handler:

```
USHORT OnInitialize(PAEP_bi_init aep)
    {                               // OnInitialize
    PRAMDISKDDB ddb;                // pointer to new DDB
    CMCONFIG config;                // allocated configuration info
    CONFIGRET code;                 // configmg return code

    ddb = (PRAMDISKDDB) IspCreateDdb(sizeof(RAMDISKDDB), 0);
    if (!ddb)
        return (USHORT) AEP_FAILURE;    // couldn't create DDB
    return AEP_SUCCESS;             // pointer to new DDB is stored in ISP
    }                               // OnInitialize
```

For a real device, you would also want to determine which I/O resources the Configuration Manager had assigned to you and do something with them. For example:

```
    ...
    CMCONFIG config;
    CONFIGRET code;

    ddb->irqhandle = NULL;
    code = CM_Get_Alloc_Log_Conf(&config,
        (DEVNODE) aep->AEP_bi_i_hdevnode,
        CM_GET_ALLOC_LOG_CONF_ALLOC);
    if (code != CR_SUCCESS)
        {                           // no configuration
    error:
        IspDeallocDdb((PDDB) ddb);
        return (USHORT) AEP_FAILURE;
        }                           // no configuration

    if (config.wNumIRQs)
        {                           // have an IRQ
        VID vid;                    // IRQ descriptor

        ASSERT(config.wNumIRQs == 1); // should only be 1

        ddb->irq = vid.VID_IRQ_Number = config.bIRQRegisters[0];
        vid.VID_Options = VPICD_OPT_REF_DATA;
        if (config.bIRQAttrib[0] & fIRQD_Share)
            vid.VID_Options |= VPICD_OPT_CAN_SHARE;
        vid.VID_Hw_Int_Proc = (ULONG) HwIntProc;
        vid.VID_EOI_Proc = 0;
        vid.VID_Mask_Change_Proc = 0;
        vid.VID_IRET_Proc = 0;
```

```
        vid.VID_IRET_Time_Out = 500;
        vid.VID_Hw_Int_Ref = (ULONG) ddb;

        if (!(ddb->irqhandle = VPICD_Virtualize_IRQ(&vid)))
            goto error;
        }                           // have an IRQ
    if (config.wNumIOPorts)
        {                           // have an I/O port
        ASSERT(config.wNumIOPorts == 1); // should only be 1
        ddb->iobase = config.wIOPortBase[0];
        }                           // have an I/O port
    ...
```

In this code fragment, we use *CM_Get_Alloc_Log_Conf* to fill the *config* structure with information about the allocated logical configuration for our DEVNODE. If an IRQ was assigned to our device, we build a VID structure and call *VPICD_Virtualize_IRQ* to virtualize it. We also save the resulting IRQ handle in the DDB so we can unvirtualize the IRQ during *AEP_UNINITIALIZE*. If a base I/O port was assigned, we remember that in the DDB as well. Presumably, we would do IN and OUT operations to this port in order to handle I/O requests.

It's important to realize that *AEP_INITIALIZE* and the DDB structure apply to a single addressable device, such as a typical disk controller. If the same VxD will handle more than one controller, it will receive separate *AEP_INITIALIZE* events for each one, and it will create a separate DDB for each one as well.

AEP_IOP_TIMEOUT The IOS sends an *AEP_IOP_TIMEOUT* event to every driver in the system when an I/O request (for *any* device) fails to complete (with or without an error) within a timeout period that defaults to 7.5 seconds. The event routine receives an *AEP_iop_timeout_occurred* structure:

```
typedef struct AEP_iop_timeout_occurred {
  struct AEPHDR AEP_i_t_o_hdr;        // 00 standard header
  ULONG         AEP_i_t_o_iop;        // 0C IOP that timed out
} AEP_iop_timeout_occurred, *PAEP_iop_timeout_occurred;
```

This event is mostly intended to be handled by port drivers. Its goal is to protect the system from the lockup that occurs when the port driver launches an I/O request into the void but the adapter doesn't respond. When handling this event, if it's possible to reset the adapter, the port driver should do so and then retry the request after resetting the *IOP_timer* value equal to *IOP_timer_orig*. Other possible actions would be:

■ Store a completion code in *IOR_status* and call the request back.

■ Reset *IOP_timer* and do nothing else. This would be the right thing to do if the request has simply timed out while sitting in a queue but will eventually get serviced.

But before taking any of these actions, a layer driver receiving this event should first determine whether it has even seen the IOP in question or not. If it has not, it should return *AEP_FAILURE* (or any other nonzero value). If it has seen the IOP, it should take whatever corrective action it can and return *AEP_SUCCESS*. You'd expect the IOS to stop sending *AEP_IOP_TIMEOUT* events to drivers as soon as someone returns *AEP_SUCCESS*. At the present time, however, the IOS keeps on sending *AEP_IOP_TIMOUT* events to the remaining list of drivers anyway. You should nevertheless return the right code because this compulsive behavior might change someday.

AEP_MOUNT_NOTIFY The IFS Manager initiates an *AEP_MOUNT_NOTIFY* event when it has successfully mounted a new volume. The event routine receives an *AEP_mnt_notify* packet:

```
typedef struct AEP_mnt_notify {
    struct AEPHDR AEP_m_n_hdr;                      // 00 standard header
    PVOID         AEP_m_n_pvrp;                     // 0C VRP of new volume
    ULONG         AEP_m_n_drivemap;                 // 10 child volume map
    ULONG         AEP_m_n_drive;                    // 14 drive just mounted
    ULONG         AEP_m_n_effective_drive;          // 18 effective drive number
    ULONG         AEP_m_n_atual_drive;              // 1C actual drive number
} AEP_mnt_notify, *PAEP_mnt_notify;
```

The main purpose of this event is to notify compression managers such as DRVSPACE that a new volume has arrived. The manager would look on the new volume for the special files in which it stores compressed information and arrange to have them appear as drive letters. Explaining how this is implemented is beyond the scope of this book.

AEP_PEND_UNCONFIG_DCB The IOS sends an *AEP_PEND_UNCONFIG_DCB* event when a DCB is about to be removed. The event routine receives an *AEP_dcb_unconfig_pend* packet:

```
typedef struct AEP_dcb_unconfig_pend {
    struct AEPHDR AEP_d_u_hdr;     // 00 standard header
    ULONG         AEP_d_u_dcb;     // 0C address of DCB
} AEP_dcb_unconfig_pend, *PAEP_dcb_unconfig_pend;
```

Since the DCB will be going away soon, any interested driver should stop using it and prevent any further I/O with the device. For example, if an operation is in process, the port driver should halt it. If any operations are queued, whoever is responsible for queueing should flush the queue.

If your driver is virtualizing an IRQ, this is *not* the right time to stop handling interrupts because the controller (the entity that actually generates interrupts) is still present. Wait until the *AEP_UNINITIALIZE* event, which signifies that the DDB with which the IRQ is most clearly associated is going away.

AEP_REAL_MODE_HANDOFF The IOS sends an *AEP_REAL_MODE_HANDOFF* event when the IFS Manager is about to take over INT 21h handling from the initialization-only code that passed MS-DOS file system calls down to real mode. The handoff is *from* real mode *to* protected mode. The event routine receives an *AEP_rm_handoff* packet that contains just the standard header. Probably no driver you or I ever write will care about this event.

AEP_REFRESH_DRIVE The IOS sends an *AEP_REFRESH_DRIVE* event when whoever was locking a volume releases the lock. The event routine receives an *AEP_drive_refresh* packet:

```
typedef struct AEP_drive_refresh {
  struct AEPHDR AEP_d_r_hdr;    // 00 standard header
  ULONG         AEP_d_r_drive;  // 0C drive number
} AEP_drive_refresh, *PAEP_drive_refresh;
```

If you recorded the absolute location of data on a drive, you would now want to refresh your records because that data might have moved while the volume was locked. This event is the opposite of *AEP_DCB_LOCK*, so you can now clear whatever flag you set to note that the volume was locked.

AEP_SYSTEM_CRIT_SHUTDOWN The IOS sends the *AEP_SYSTEM_CRIT_SHUT-DOWN* event to all registered drivers during the processing of the Sys_Critical_Shutdown system control message. The event routine receives an *AEP_sys_crit_shutdown* packet, which contains only the standard header. The contents of the packet don't matter anyway, because the event is notifying you of a systemwide event. Just be careful not to enable interrupts or to try to execute any V86-mode code, because the system is in no state to tolerate things like that. You could, of course, just handle the Sys_Critical_Init control message on your own. The only reason to use the IOS asynchronous notification is that you might need to do something at the IOS's spot in the shutdown order rather than at your own spot in the shutdown order.

AEP_SYSTEM_SHUTDOWN The IOS sends an *AEP_SYSTEM_SHUTDOWN* event to all registered drivers during the processing of the System_Exit system control message. The event routine receives an *AEP_sys_shutdown* packet, which contains only the standard header. The contents of the packet don't matter, because the event is notifying you of a systemwide event.

AEP_UNCONFIG_DCB The IOS sends all drivers an *AEP_UNCONFIG_DCB* event when the device represented by a DCB is disappearing. The driver receives an *AEP_dcb_unconfig* packet:

```
typedef struct AEP_dcb_unconfig {
    struct AEPHDR AEP_d_u_hdr;      // 00 standard header
    ULONG         AEP_d_u_dcb;      // 0C DCB being deleted
}   AEP_dcb_unconfig, *PAEP_dcb_unconfig;
```

The main purpose of this event is to notify vendor-supplied drivers (VSDs) that a DCB is disappearing. The VSD would handle the event by checking to see if it had put itself into the DCB's calldown stack. If so, if would decrement the counter that the *AEP_BOOT_COMPLETE* handler inspects:

```
USHORT OnUnconfigDcb(PAEP_dcb_unconfig aep)
    {                          // OnUnconfigDcb
    PDCB dcb = (PDCB) aep-AEP_d_u_dcb;
    if (<expression that's TRUE if we hooked this dcb>)
        --ndevices;
    return AEP_SUCCESS;
    }                          // OnUnconfigDcb
```

The IOS later sends an *AEP_BOOT_COMPLETE* event, and the VSD can once again decide whether to stay loaded or not.

AEP_UNINITIALIZE When an adapter is going away, the IOS sends the associated port driver an *AEP_UNINITIALIZE* event for each DDB that belongs to the driver. The event routine receives an *AEP_bi_uninit* packet, which contains only the standard header. Even though you allocated memory for the DDB during the *AEP_INITIALIZE* event, you need not explicitly release the DDB because the IOS will do so automatically. But you should clean up all other interfaces and data structures that were created during the *AEP_INITIALIZE* event. If the driver has been handling a hardware interrupt, for example, you should restore the IRQ to its original behavior.

In handling *AEP_UNINITIALIZE*, you need to be somewhat careful to undo only actions that *AEP_INITIALIZE* actually completed. The reason for this caution is that the IOS will send an *AEP_UNINITIALIZE* event if the initialization handler calls the *ISP_DEALLOC_DDB* service (which it would do if it was unable to successfully complete initializing). Suppose your driver virtualizes an IRQ. You would normally save the virtual IRQ handle in the DDB so you could undo the virtualization later. By initializing the IRQ handle field of the DDB before there's any possibility of calling *ISP_DEALLOC_DDB*, your *AEP_UNINITIALIZE* handler can easily avoid making a mistake by checking whether the IRQ handle has been changed from its initial state:

```
USHORT OnInitialize(PAEP_bi_init aep)
    {                              // OnInitialize
```

```
        PRAMDISKDDB ddb;

        if (!(ddb = (PRAMDISKDDB) IspCreateDdb(sizeof(RAMDISKDDB),
            0)))
            return (USHORT) AEP_FAILURE;
        ddb->irqhandle = NULL;     // initialize IRQ handle field
        ...
        ddb->irqhandle = VPICD_Virtualize_IRQ(&vid);
        ...
error:
    IspDeallocDdb((PDDB) ddb);
    return (USHORT) AEP_FAILURE;
    }                             // OnInitialize

USHORT OnUninitialize(PAEP_bi_uninit aep)
    {                             // OnUninitialize
    PRAMDISKDDB ddb = (PRAMDISKDDB) aep->AEP_bi_u_hdr.AEP_ddb;

    if (!ddb)
        return AEP_SUCCESS;

    if (ddb->irqhandle)
        {                             // unvirtualize IRQ
        VPICD_Force_Default_Behavior(ddb->irqhandle);
        ddb->irqhandle = NULL;
        }                             // unvirtualize IRQ

    return AEP_SUCCESS;
    }                             // OnUninitialize
```

When the code is organized this way, *OnUninitialize* will always do the right thing with respect to unvirtualizing the IRQ, no matter how *OnUninitialize* happens to be reached, because the *irqhandle* member of the DDB can only be 0 or the handle of a virtualized IRQ; it can never be a bogus, uninitialized value.

BUILDING DRIVERS

In this section, I'll discuss two small programming projects that use the information so laboriously presented in the previous sections of this chapter. Most programmers will never need to write a VxD that works with the IOS in the first place. Those who do will probably need to write either a port driver for a particular piece of hardware or a vendor-supplied driver to supplement or correct the behavior of an existing stack of drivers. Therefore, the examples I'll present here illustrate only those two options.

Building a Port Driver

The lowest real level of the IOS driver hierarchy contains a port driver that controls a hardware disk controller and its collection of disk drives. An IOS port driver includes an asynchronous event handler, an I/O request handler that's part of the calldown stack for one or more DCBs, and (often) a VPICD hardware interrupt handler.

To create a meaningful example of a port driver without getting bogged down in the details of control signals and interrupt timing, I decided to write a RAM-disk driver. A RAM disk, for those of you born recently, is a virtual disk drive that uses memory to hold data but that responds to the system as if it were a disk drive. RAM disks were popular in the early days of personal computing because they provided a worthwhile performance boost (memory being much faster than rotating media) while also providing an excuse to add some extended memory to your computer. On a modern virtual memory system with robust disk caching, a RAM disk is fundamentally silly because it consumes virtual memory that the system might be able to use more efficiently. But for our purposes it makes a good example, and if you're ever brave enough to build your own file system, a RAM disk would be the place to test it until it's healthy enough to point at actual hardware.

Housekeeping

We've already been through code samples that illustrate the housekeeping aspects of building a RAM-disk port driver. Specifically, the port driver included in the \CHAP15\PORTDRIVER directory on the companion disc does the following things that you now know all about:

■   It handles the Sys_Dynamic_Device_Init message by calling *IOS_Register* with a DRP that indicates that our driver is a DRP_MISC_PD (level 19) layer driver.

■   It handles *AEP_INITIALIZE* by creating a DDB.

■   It handles *AEP_CONFIG_DCB* by filling in geometry parameters that indicate one cylinder, one track per cylinder, and 4096 sectors (of 512 bytes each) per track. That is, the disk contains 2 MB of storage. The *AEP_CONFIG_DCB* handler also inserts the driver into the calldown stack at level 19 and updates a global counter of affected DCBs. It does one more thing (allocating memory to simulate disk space) that I'll describe in the next section.

■   It handles *AEP_UNCONFIG_DCB* by decrementing the counter of affected DCBs. It does one more thing that I'll briefly allude to later.

■ It handles *AEP_BOOT_COMPLETE* by examining the counter of affected DCBs and asking to stay loaded if the counter is nonzero.

I also built a standard .INF file to install the driver (RAMDISK.PDR) in the IOSUBSYS directory as a class *hdc* (hard disk controller) device. You'll find the .INF file on the companion disc if you want to experiment.

Simulating a Disk

The steps I left out of earlier discussions about this driver have to do with actually simulating a disk drive. During the *AEP_CONFIG_DCB* event, the driver allocates a 2-MB block of virtual memory to serve as the simulated media:

```
USHORT OnConfigDcb(PAEP_dcb_config aep)
    {
    ...
    if (!(dcb->DCB_Port_Specific = (ULONG) _PageAllocate(2048,
        PG_SYS, NULL, 0, 0, 0, NULL,
        PAGEZEROINIT | PAGELOCKEDIFDP)))
        return (USHORT) AEP_FAILURE;
    ...
    }
```

The call to *_PageAllocate* allocates and commits 2048 pages (2 MB) of memory. If MS-DOS is being used for paging (which it never is on my system), the memory will also be page locked. The *AEP_CONFIG_DCB* handler saves the resulting linear address in the *DCB_Port_Specific* field of the DCB for later use. It also initializes a master boot record at the beginning of the allocated memory area and a dummy file allocation table 512 bytes later, but the code to do this initialization is too boring to be repeated here. It turns out to be crucial, by the way, to incorporate a valid partition table and an AA55h signature at the end of the boot record; otherwise, the disk TSD refuses to mount a logical volume for the disk. Since I did all the steps right (eventually, that is), I was rewarded by having a disk appear both at a Windows 95 MS-DOS prompt and in the Windows 95 shell each time I used the Add New Hardware wizard to install it.

The memory allocation step gets undone during the *AEP_UNCONFIG_DCB* event:

```
USHORT OnUnconfigDcb(PAEP_dcb_unconfig aep)
    {                               // OnUnconfigDcb
    PDCB dcb = (PDCB) aep->AEP_d_u_dcb;
    ASSERT(dcb);

    if (!(dcb->DCB_cmn.DCB_device_flags & DCB_DEV_PHYSICAL)
        || memcmp(dcb->DCB_vendor_id, "WALTONEY", 8) != 0)
        return AEP_SUCCESS;
```

```
if (dcb->DCB_Port_Specific)
    {                             // release memory
    _PageFree((PVOID) dcb->DCB_Port_Specific, 0);
    dcb->DCB_Port_Specific = 0;
    }                             // release memory
--ndevices;
ASSERT(ndevices >= 0);
return AEP_SUCCESS;
}                             // OnUnconfigDcb
```

Handling I/O Requests

The whole purpose of the layered architecture we've been discussing is to get I/O
requests routed into device-specific code that you've written. The request handler
for the RAM-disk driver needs to handle only read and write requests, and the bulk
of the code is identical for both types of requests. Here is the function in its entirety:

```
#pragma VxD_LOCKED_CODE_SEG

VOID OnRequest(PIOP iop)
    {                             // OnRequest
#define ior iop->IOP_ior
DWORD funcode = ior.IOR_func;
PDCB dcb = (PDCB) iop->IOP_physical_dcb;

ior.IOR_status = IORS_SUCCESS; // assume it'll succeed
dcb->DCB_cmn.DCB_device_flags |= DCB_DEV_IO_ACTIVE;

switch (funcode)
    {                             // dispatch function processor

//////////////////////////////////////////////////////////////

case IOR_READ:              // IOR_func == 0
    {                       // IOR_READ
    DWORD sector = ior.IOR_start_addr[0];
    PBYTE diskdata = (PBYTE) (dcb->DCB_Port_Specific +
        sector * dcb->DCB_actual_blk_size);

    ASSERT(sector < dcb->DCB_actual_sector_cnt[0]);
    ASSERT(ior.IOR_start_addr[1] == 0);

    if (ior.IOR_flags & IORF_SCATTER_GATHER)
        {                       // have scatter/gather structures
        _BlockDev_Scatter_Gather* sgd =
            (_BlockDev_Scatter_Gather*) ior.IOR_buffer_ptr;
        PBYTE memdata;
        DWORD nbytes;
        while ((nbytes = sgd->BD_SG_Count))
```

```
            {               // for each s/g structure
        memdata = (PBYTE) sgd->BD_SG_Buffer_Ptr;
        if (!(ior.IOR_flags & IORF_CHAR_COMMAND))
            nbytes *= dcb->DCB_actual_blk_size;
        memcpy(memdata, diskdata, nbytes);
        diskdata += nbytes;
        ++sgd;
            }               // for each s/g structure
        }                   // have scatter/gather structures
    else
        {                   // have simple buffer address
        PBYTE memdata = (PBYTE) ior.IOR_buffer_ptr;
        DWORD nbytes = ior.IOR_xfer_count;
        if (!(ior.IOR_flags & IORF_CHAR_COMMAND))
            nbytes *= dcb->DCB_actual_blk_size;
        memcpy(memdata, diskdata, nbytes);
        }                   // have simple buffer address

    break;
    }                       // IOR_READ

/////////////////////////////////////////////////////////////

case IOR_WRITE:             // IOR_func == 1
    {                       // IOR_WRITE
    DWORD sector = ior.IOR_start_addr[0];
    PBYTE diskdata = (PBYTE) (dcb->DCB_Port_Specific +
        sector * dcb->DCB_actual_blk_size);

    ASSERT(sector);         // rewriting boot sector??
    ASSERT(sector < dcb->DCB_actual_sector_cnt[0]);
    ASSERT(ior.IOR_start_addr[1] == 0);

    if (ior.IOR_flags & IORF_SCATTER_GATHER)
        {                   // have scatter/gather structures
        _BlockDev_Scatter_Gather* sgd =
            (_BlockDev_Scatter_Gather*) ior.IOR_buffer_ptr;
        PBYTE memdata;
        DWORD nbytes;
        while ((nbytes = sgd->BD_SG_Count))
            {               // for each s/g structure
            memdata = (PBYTE) sgd->BD_SG_Buffer_Ptr;
            if (!(ior.IOR_flags & IORF_CHAR_COMMAND))
                nbytes *= dcb->DCB_actual_blk_size;
            memcpy(diskdata, memdata, nbytes);
            diskdata += nbytes;
            ++sgd;
            }               // for each s/g structure
```

```
        }                       // have scatter/gather structures
    else
        {                       // have simple buffer address
        PBYTE memdata = (PBYTE) ior.IOR_buffer_ptr;
        DWORD nbytes = ior.IOR_xfer_count;
        if (!(ior.IOR_flags & IORF_CHAR_COMMAND))
            nbytes *= dcb->DCB_actual_blk_size;
        memcpy(diskdata, memdata, nbytes);
        }                       // have simple buffer address

    break;
    }                           // IOR_WRITE


//////////////////////////////////////////////////////////////

default:
    dcb->DCB_cmn.DCB_device_flags &= ~DCB_DEV_IO_ACTIVE;
    DoCallDown(iop);
    return;
    }                           // dispatch function processor

dcb->DCB_cmn.DCB_device_flags &= ~DCB_DEV_IO_ACTIVE;
DoCallBack(iop);            // we're done with this request

#undef ior
}                               // OnRequest
```

We've already gone through the *DoCallDown* and *DoCallBack* functions that this routine uses. Here I'll discuss all the other details of *OnRequest*.

OnRequest is in the locked code segment. This isn't strictly necessary for this driver, since it won't hurt to take a page fault while handling a request against the RAM drive. We won't, after all, be putting the swap file on this dummy disk. In general, however, your driver will have request-handling code that gets called during the processing of your own hardware interrupt. You know that such code has to be in page-locked memory and can use only asynchronous VxD services.

The only argument to *OnRequest* is the address of an IOP. We're interested in the DCB and calldown stack to which the IOP points. Other than that, we're only interested in the IOR structure embedded within the IOP. I used a macro (*ior*) to shorten references to the embedded IOR because, as you know by now, I abhor long strings of meaningless, duplicative syntax.

In this driver, I asserted the *DCB_dmd_serialize* demand when I inserted *OnRequest* into the calldown stack. This demand causes code upstream from this driver to queue and dequeue requests. All I have to do in my driver is set and clear the *DCB_DEV_IO_ACTIVE* flag around request activity. In other cases, you might want to handle queueing yourself by calling *IlbEnqueueIop* and *IlbDequeueIop*. You would certainly want to have a hardware interrupt routine that, at a minimum, cleared *DCB_DEV_IO_ACTIVE* to release the queue.

The handling for read and write requests is practically identical, so I'll describe them both together. The disk location *(sector)* from which we'll read, or to which we'll write, is a physical sector number. It should be an integer between 0 and 4095, inclusive. The source or target data *(diskdata)* is located *sector* units of 512 bytes *(DCB_actual_blk_size)* into the memory area we allocated during *AEP_CONFIG_DCB*.

We never asked to have the *IOR_sgd_lin_phys* array constructed because we're working exclusively with linear addresses. In a more realistic driver, you would assert the *DCB_dmd_phys_sgd* demand in order to ask higher layers to create the SGD array, which would then hold the physical addresses of the data buffer(s). You would probably also use the VDMAD services we discussed in Chapter 13 to set up DMA transfers to and from your device.

In this simplified example, we are working directly with the buffer pointer set up by the original IOS client. Normally, only the criteria routine looks at this buffer pointer. The client provides a single buffer or an array of scatter/gather structures in the BlockDev format. The RAM-disk driver tells the difference by looking at the *IORF_SCATTER_GATHER* flag. If the flag is set, we step through the array of *_BlockDev_Scatter_Gather* structures until we reach a zero DWORD. For each scatter/gather structure, we read or write the specified amount of data *(BD_SG_Count)* into or out of the specified buffer *(BD_SG_Buffer_Ptr*, which is a linear address rather than a physical address). The transfer count in each scatter/gather descriptor is expressed in bytes if *IORF_CHAR_COMMAND* is set; otherwise, it's expressed in units of the device's block size (in our case, 512 bytes).

If *IORF_SCATTER_GATHER* is clear, we're faced with a single data buffer instead of a series of buffers. In this case, *IOR_xfer_count* is the number of bytes (or sectors) that we should transfer.

This driver always handles read and write requests completely and successfully, so *OnRequest* ends by calling the request back with a 0 completion code *(IORS_SUC-CESS)*. This driver doesn't handle anything else, so it simply calls down to the next layer (if any) to handle other requests. We will get requests, for example, to recompute geometry or to check media, but we can ignore them.

Building a Vendor-Supplied Driver

Vendor-supplied drivers (VSDs) serve diverse purposes in the scheme of the IOS. Writing a VSD lets you intervene in the handling of any I/O request for any device you choose. Since there are nine layers reserved for VSDs, you can select an insertion point in the calldown stack that best suits your needs. A VSD for a SCSI device can, for example, intervene either before or after the SCSI'izer builds a SCSI request block. There aren't any hard-and-fast rules for why you might write a VSD. The reasons are as diverse as hardware and imagination can provide.

Architecturally, the main difference between a VSD and a port driver lies in how many times the VSD receives an *AEP_CONFIG_DCB* event. A port driver sees this event only for devices it created. A VSD sees this event for every DCB in the system. This fact allows a VSD to hook into the calldown stack for any and all devices.

To provide an example of a VSD, I wrote a small VSD that monitors I/O requests by sending an information packet about every request to a Windows-based application. The VSD and the application are similar in purpose to the sample described in "Examining the Windows 95 Layered File System," by Mark Russinovich and Bryce Cogswell (*Dr. Dobb's Journal*, December 1995). Figure 15-10 shows a sample of the request log generated for a DIR A: command on my system.

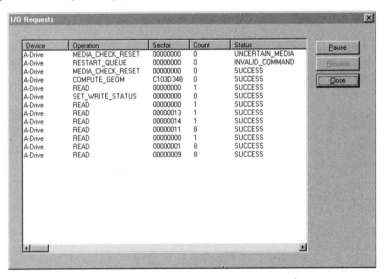

Figure 15-10. *Sample output from the MONITOR example.*

Housekeeping

Most of the work in this sample application (included on the companion disc in the \CHAP15\IOSMONITOR directory) is in the ring-three application that paints the screen. I won't go into that work here. The VSD itself is relatively simple. Mechanically, it does the following things that you already understand:

■   It handles Sys_Dynamic_Device_Init by calling *IOS_Register* with a DRP that indicates a DRP_VSD_9 (level 17) layer driver. In addition, this particular VSD uses the regular *List_Create* service to allocate a linked list of memory blocks that can be accessed during the I/O request routine later on:

```
extern DRP theDRP;                  // device registration packet

BOOL OnSysDynamicDeviceInit()
    {                               // OnSysDynamicDeviceInit
    list = List_Create(LF_ASYNC | LF_ALLOC_ERROR,
        sizeof(MONINFO));
    if (!list)
        return FALSE;
    IOS_Register(&theDRP);
    return TRUE;
    }                               // OnSysDynamicDeviceInit
```

The *MONINFO* structure referred to in this fragment is one I declared to hold all the interesting data about an I/O request that the Windows-based application will report. The *list* variable is a global pointer to the linked list object. This driver destroys the linked list during Sys_Dynamic_Device_Exit:

```
BOOL OnSysDynamicDeviceExit()
    {                               // OnSysDynamicDeviceExit
    if (list)
        List_Destroy(list);
    return TRUE;
    }                               // OnSysDynamicDeviceExit
```

■ It ignores the *AEP_INITIALIZE* and *AEP_UNINITIALIZE* events. That is, it returns *AEP_SUCCESS* for both events without actually doing anything.

■ It handles *AEP_CONFIG_DCB* by hooking into the calldown stack for every physical DCB:

```
USHORT OnConfigDcb(PAEP_dcb_config aep)
    {                               // OnConfigDcb
    PDCB dcb = (PDCB) aep->AEP_d_c_dcb;
    if (!(dcb->DCB_cmn.DCB_device_flags & DCB_DEV_PHYSICAL))
        return AEP_SUCCESS;
    if ((IspInsertCalldown(dcb, OnRequest,
        (PDDB) aep->AEP_d_c_hdr.AEP_ddb, 0,
        dcb->DCB_cmn.DCB_dmd_flags, aep->AEP_d_c_hdr.AEP_lgn)))
        ++ndevices;
    return AEP_SUCCESS;
    }                               // OnConfigDcb
```

■ It handles *AEP_UNCONFIG_DCB* by always decrementing the *ndevice* counter for physical DCBs:

```
USHORT OnUnconfigDcb(PAEP_dcb_unconfig aep)
    {                               // OnUnconfigDcb
    PDCB dcb = (PDCB) aep->AEP_d_u_dcb;
    if (!(dcb->DCB_cmn.DCB_device_flags & DCB_DEV_PHYSICAL))
        return AEP_SUCCESS;
    ASSERT(ndevices > 0);
    --ndevices;
    return AEP_SUCCESS;
    }                               // OnUnconfigDcb
```

■ It handles *AEP_BOOT_COMPLETE* by returning *AEP_SUCCESS* if it has hooked into any DCB's calldown stack:

```
USHORT OnBootComplete(PAEP_boot_done aep)
    {                               // OnBootComplete
    return ndevices ? AEP_SUCCESS : AEP_FAILURE;
    }                               // OnBootComplete
```

Monitoring Requests

The request handler for this VSD is also quite simple:

```
VOID OnRequest(PIOP iop)
    {                               // OnRequest
    if (userproc)                   // APC callback routine
        InsertCallBack(iop, OnRequestComplete, 0);
    DoCallDown(iop);
    }                               // OnRequest
```

This request routine simply adds an entry to the callback list for the request, as you can see. The VSD transacts its real business when a lower-level driver calls the request back to signify completion:

```
VOID OnRequestComplete(PIOP iop)
    {                               // OnRequestComplete
    #define ior iop->IOP_ior
    DWORD funcode = ior.IOR_func;
    PDCB dcb = (PDCB) iop->IOP_physical_dcb;
    PMONINFO mip = GetBlock();

    if (mip)
        {                           // notify ring-three app
        mip->dcb = dcb;
        mip->opcode = (BYTE) ior.IOR_func;
        mip->status = (BYTE) ior.IOR_status;
        mip->sector = ior.IOR_start_addr[0];
```

```
            mip->nbytes = 0;
            if (ior.IOR_func <= IOR_WRITEV)
                {                       // compute transfer length
                if (ior.IOR_flags & IORF_SCATTER_GATHER)
                    {           // request used scatter/gather records
                    _BlockDev_Scatter_Gather* sgp =
                        (_BlockDev_Scatter_Gather*)
                        ior.IOR_buffer_ptr;
                    while (sgp->BD_SG_Count)
                        mip->nbytes += sgp->BD_SG_Count, ++sgp;
                    }           // request used scatter/gather records
                else
                    mip->nbytes = ior.IOR_xfer_count;
                }               // compute transfer length

            if (!userproc || !_VWIN32_QueueUserApc(userproc,
                (DWORD) mip, thread))
                ReturnBlock(mip);
            }                       // notify ring-three app

    DoCallBack(iop);
    }                           // OnRequestComplete
```

GetBlock and *ReturnBlock* are helper functions that allocate and release memory from the asynchronous linked list that was set up during the processing of Sys_Dynamic_Device_Init:

```
    void ReturnBlock(PMONINFO mip)
        {                       // ReturnBlock
        _asm pushfd
        _asm cli
        List_Deallocate(list, (VMMLISTNODE) mip);
        _asm popfd
        }                       // ReturnBlock

    PMONINFO GetBlock()
        {                       // GetBlock
        PMONINFO mip;

        _asm pushfd
        _asm cli
        mip = List_Allocate(list);
        _asm popfd

        return mip;
        }                       // GetBlock
```

SOME DETAILS ABOUT THE **MONITOR** APPLICATION

The MONITOR application, which displays the request log, has some interesting details. It uses *CreateFile* to obtain a device handle for the VSD, and it then uses several *DeviceIoControl* calls to communicate with the VSD. Most VSDs don't, of course, have applications associated with them and so wouldn't support *DeviceIoControl*. One of the *DeviceIoControl* calls registers the APC callback routine *(userproc)* called by *OnRequest*. Another calls *ReturnBlock* to release a *MONINFO* block once the Windows application is done with it.

The MONITOR application itself spawns a thread whose sole purpose is to wait for APC calls from the VSD. The thread also looks for an event that means that the end user wants to pause or close the display of events:

```
DWORD __stdcall DoMonitor(CRequestLog* log)
    {                           // DoMonitor
    void (WINAPI *acallback)(PMONINFO) = callback;
    if (!DeviceIoControl(log->m_reqmon,
        REQMON_SETMONITORADDRESS,
        &acallback, sizeof(acallback), NULL, 0, NULL, NULL))
        {                       // can't establish callback
        PostMessage(log->m_hWnd, WM_COMMAND, IDB_PAUSE, 0);
        return 1;
        }                       // can't establish callback
    logptr = log;
    while (WaitForSingleObjectEx(log->m_evkill, INFINITE, TRUE)
        == WAIT_IO_COMPLETION)
        ;                       // until told to quit
    acallback = NULL;
    DeviceIoControl(log->m_reqmon, REQMON_SETMONITORADDRESS,
        &acallback, sizeof(acallback), NULL, 0, NULL, NULL);
    log->m_thread = NULL;   // we're out of here
    return 0;
    }                           // DoMonitor
```

We talked in Chapter 10 about using the "extended" form of API functions such as *WaitForSingleObjectEx* to perform an alertable wait to support APC calls from VxDs. The APC callback routine simply posts a message to the main application thread:

```
void WINAPI callback(PMONINFO mip)
    {                        // callback
    PostMessage(logptr->m_hWnd, WM_USER+256, 0, (LPARAM) mip);
    }                        // callback
```

The handler for the private *WM_USER+256* message adds a row to the list control in the application window and returns the *MONINFO* block back to the VSD by means of the second *DeviceIoControl* call referred to above.

The operation of *OnRequest* is as follows: It allocates a *MONINFO* block from the linked list. As prescribed for manipulating asynchronous lists, the *GetBlock* helper function disables interrupts around the call to *List_Allocate*. Using an asynchronous list allows this VSD to safely monitor requests even for the swapping device. *OnRequest* fills in most of the *MONINFO* fields by simply copying the corresponding data from the I/O request packet. Filling in the transfer count (misleadingly called *nbytes*) requires summation over the scatter/gather descriptors (if any). Once the *OnRequest* routine completes the *MONINFO* block, it uses *_VWIN32_QueueUserApc* to schedule an asynchronous procedure call (APC) back to the Windows-based application, which will format a description of the request for the end user to see.

The only important way in which this VSD differs from others you might write is that it doesn't construct any I/O requests on its own. One of the reasons you write a VSD is to supplement or correct the behavior of existing drivers, and one of the things you might need to do is formulate and execute your own requests. The way to execute requests is to create and submit an I/O request packet using *internal* mechanisms. I described the mechanics of doing this earlier in connection with the IOP data structure discussion. In the context of this VSD, you might have code like the following:

```
USHORT offset = (USHORT) (dcb->DCB_cmn.DCB_expansion_length
    + FIELDOFFSET(IOP, IOP_ior));
USHORT size = offset + sizeof(IOR)
    + dcb->DCB_max_sg_elements * sizeof(SGD);
PIOP iop = IspCreateIop(size, offset, ISP_M_FL_MUST_SUCCEED);
PIOR ior = &iop->IOP_ior;

iop->IOP_original_dcb = (ULONG) dcb;
iop->IOP_physical_dcb = (ULONG) dcb->DCB_cmn.DCB_physical_dcb;
```

```
ior->IOR_next = 0;
ior->IOR_start_addr[1] = 0;
ior->IOR_flags = IORF_VERSION_002;
ior->IOR_private_client = offset;
ior->IOR_req_vol_handle = dcb->DCB_cmn.DCB_vrp_ptr;
ior->IOR_sgd_lin_phys = (ULONG) (ior + 1);
ior->IOR_num_sgds = 0;
ior->IOR_vol_designtr = dcb->DCB_cmn.DCB_unit_number;

[fill in remaining IOR fields to describe request]

IlbIntIoCriteria(iop);
IlbInternalRequest(iop, dcb, OnRequest);
IspDeallocMem((PVOID) ((DWORD) ior - ior->IOR_private_client));
```

The third argument to *IlbInternalRequest* tells the IOS where in the calldown stack to start processing this request. It specifies the calldown routine for the level *above* the one you want to start with. (You extract this poiner from one of the calldown stack entries.) As shown here, we are asking to have the calldown entry after our own invoked first. If you supply a NULL pointer the request will start at the top of the calldown stack; be careful about the recursion through your own request routine that will then occur.

Part IV

Extending the
Operating System

Chapter 16

Installable
File Systems

Previous versions of Windows were tied to MS-DOS's apron strings because only MS-DOS knew how to manage files on disk. Real mode is a *terrible* place to have your one-and-only file system: multiple processes can't simultaneously do file operations without proceeding one at a time through the Windows critical section; network redirectors have to support an undocumented INT 2Fh protocol; CD-ROM drives have to piggyback onto the file system through the kludgery of MSCDEX, which mimics a network redirector in some ways. Windows 95 avoids these problems by means of the *Installable File System (IFS) Manager*.

Figure 16-1 on the following page diagrams the position the IFS Manager holds in the Windows 95 architecture. The IFS Manager exports a number of VxD-level services for use by other parts of the system. It calls on file system drivers (FSDs) to implement diverse file systems like FAT and CD-ROM file systems, and the FSDs in turn talk to disk drivers within the overall framework of the I/O Supervisor discussed in Chapter 15. FSDs also provide the necessary redirection of file operations to network connections. The subject of network redirectors is beyond the scope of this book.

Although Microsoft provides a pretty good document in the DDK that describes how a driver calls and is called by the IFS Manager, Microsoft hasn't given much guidance about how to write file system drivers. To develop the information I'm about to give you, I needed to write a very simple example of a file system (the Low

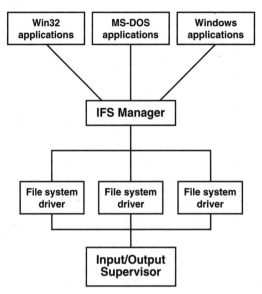

Figure 16-1. *Overall architecture of the Installable File System.*

Performance File System, or LPFS) and do a good deal of reverse engineering of components such as the IFS Manager and VFAT. LPFS is pretty wimpy as file systems go, but it still involves a lot of code.

USING IFS SERVICES

The IFS Manager provides many services that are primarily useful to FSDs, as well as a few services that are more generally useful. Many IFS services involve a ubiquitous control block called an *ioreq* that records information about a particular file system request. Among the services that are generally useful to VxD callers are *IFSMgr_Ring0_FileIO*, which allows a VxD to work directly with local or remote files, and *IFSMgr_InstallFileSystemApiHook*, which allows a VxD to intercept (and modify, if desired) a request before an FSD ever sees it. The IFS Manager also provides a set of pathname and time conversion services that are mostly useful to FSDs but that might be helpful in other situations.

The IFS I/O Request Structure

The IFS Manager and its satellite VxDs use the I/O request structure (*ioreq*) diagrammed in Figure 16-2. A key feature of the *ioreq* structure is that many of its fields can be overlaid by several different fields, depending on the purpose for which

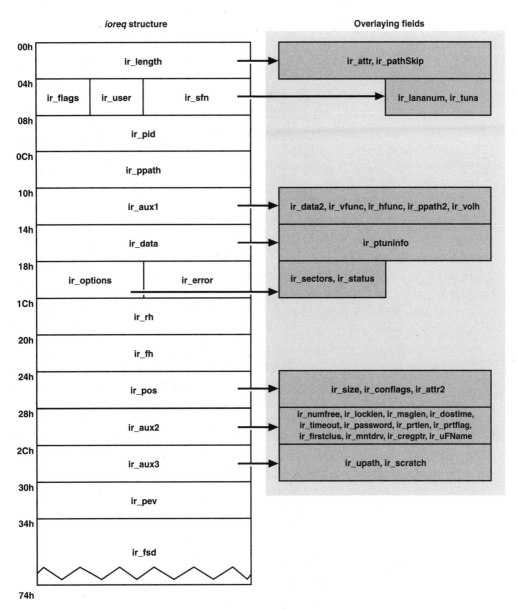

Figure 16-2. *The IFS I/O request structure.*

the structure is being used. The same portion of the structure is sometimes used both for input and for output by a single request, possibly under different names. In such cases, you must be careful not to store an output value before you use the input value that occupies the same space.

The various fields have the following uses:

ir_length The primary use for the 32-bit field at offset 0 is to hold the data length for read and write requests. This field is overlaid by *ir_attr* in calls (such as *FS_FindFirstFile*) that involve pathnames, in which case the field contains a file attribute mask. The *FS_ConnectNetResource* request uses this field as an output parameter under the name *ir_pathSkip* to indicate how many components of the input pathname were used to specify the remote resource.

ir_flags The 8-bit *ir_flags* field often contains a subfunction code. For example, in an *FS_FileAttributes* request, *ir_flags* differentiates between a "get attributes" and a "set attributes" subfunction. The field also contains flag values for some requests.

ir_user The 8-bit *ir_user* field contains the user ID for a file system request. A network redirector uses this field to differentiate between users. A local FSD has no use for this field. The overlaying field *ir_drivenum* defined in IFS.H is not used anywhere.

ir_sfn The 16-bit *ir_sfn* field contains a *system file number* used internally by the IFS Manager as a global file handle. FSDs aren't supposed to do anything with this value. Some network-oriented requests use this field under the name *ir_lananum* to designate a LAN adapter number. A volume mounting request uses this field under the name *ir_tuna* as an output parameter to indicate the FSD's support for *tunneling*. I'll explain what tunneling is all about when I discuss how to rename a file.

ir_pid The *ir_pid* field designates the process that generated the current request. An FSD should use this field only as a unique process identifier without making any assumptions about what it might mean.

ir_ppath The *ir_ppath* field points to a parsed pathname structure. I'll discuss parsed pathnames later in this chapter.

ir_aux1 The multipurpose *ir_aux1* field can be used for any of the following purposes:

■ Under the name *ir_data2* it's a pointer to the output buffer for an *FS_TransactNamedPipe* call.

■ A volume mounting request uses this field under the name *ir_volh* as an input parameter to specify the IOS volume request parameters structure and under the name *ir_vfunc* as an output parameter to supply the IFS Manager with the address of a table of functions for handling volume-oriented requests.

■ The *FS_OpenFile* and *FS_FindFirstFile* requests use it under the name *ir_hfunc* as the address of a table of handle-oriented request function pointers for the FSD to fill in.

■ The *FS_RenameFile* request uses this field under the name *ir_ppath2* to designate the parsed new name of the file.

ir_data The main use for the *ir_data* field is as a data buffer pointer. *FS_OpenFile* and *FS_RenameFile* requests use the field under the name *ir_ptuninfo* to point to tunneling information.

ir_options The 16-bit *ir_options* field often contains flag bits pertaining to a request. The *FS_GetDiskInfo* request uses it on output under the name *ir_sectors* to indicate how many sectors are in each cluster. Named pipe calls provide status feedback here using the name *ir_status*.

ir_error FSDs set the *ir_error* field on output, setting it to a standard MS-DOS error code, with 0 denoting normal completion. FSD functions also return the same numeric value, as an integer return value, in the EAX register. The IFS Manager sometimes uses the return value and sometimes uses the *ir_error* value to discern the result of a function call to an FSD, so you must be careful both to return a code *and* to set *ir_error*. Since there is a difference between the error codes used by the IFS Manager and the IOS, you sometimes need to use *IOSMapIORSToI21* or *IOSMapIORSToI24* to convert an IOS error code to one usable as an *ir_error* value.

ir_rh Most requests use the *ir_rh* field as an input parameter to point to whatever internal data structure the FSD uses to keep track of a logical volume. A volume mount request uses it on input to point to the MS-DOS disk parameter block (DPB) chain, however. The FSD sets *ir_rh* to the address of its internal control block as part of handling a successful volume mount.

ir_fh Handle-based requests (that is, requests that deal with an open file identified by a handle rather than by a path) use the *ir_fh* field as an input parameter to point to whatever internal data structure the FSD uses to keep track of a file contained by the logical volume. The FSD supplies this value on output from a successful *FS_OpenFile* or *FS_FindFirstFile* request.

ir_pos Read and write requests use the *ir_pos* field to specify a file position. *FS_ConnectNetResource* requests use it under the name *ir_conflags* for connection flags. *FS_RenameFile* requests use it under the name *ir_attr2* for a second set of file attributes; these attributes govern treatment of the destination name. This field is also used as an undocumented input parameter for the *IR_FSD_MAP_DRIVE* request to denote a new "original" drive letter for a mapped volume.

In the original IFS design, file open and truncate requests were to use this field under the name *ir_size* to specify the size of a file. This truncation feature was eventually dropped, however, so that you now truncate a file by seeking to the appropriate offset and writing zero bytes. Accordingly, this field is no longer used under the name *ir_size*.

ir_aux2 This multipurpose field can be used for any of the following purposes:

- As *ir_numfree* to hold the number of free clusters on output from an *FS_GetDiskInfo* request.

- As *ir_locklen* to hold the length of a record in a region locking request.

- As *ir_msglen* to hold the length of a message sent to a named pipe or mailslot.

- As *ir_dostime* to hold a date and time value in the MS-DOS format.

- As *ir_timeout* to contain a timeout value.

- As *ir_password* to point to the password for an *FS_ConnectNetResource* request.

- As *ir_prtlen* to hold the length of a printer setup string.

- As *ir_prtflag* to hold the various printer flags.

- As *ir_firstclus* to point to the first cluster of a file. This value is an optional output value from *FS_FindFirstFile* and *FS_SearchFile*, used only by VFAT.

- As *ir_mntdrv* to contain the drive letter for a newly mounted volume.

- As *ir_cregptr* to point to a client register structure containing IOCTL parameters.

- As *ir_uFName* to point to the case-preserved Unicode name associated with certain requests. In many situations an FSD uses this name for a new or renamed file.

ir_upath The *ir_upath* field points to the unparsed Unicode pathname associated with requests that have pathnames. (Although this field is part of a union named *ir_aux3*, there are no other uses for the field at this offset.)

ir_pev In a request that occurs during processing of an IFS event, the *ir_pev* field points to the event structure that describes the event. Elaboration of the IFS event scheduling mechanism is beyond the scope of this book.

ir_fsd The 64-byte *ir_fsd* field is available for use by the FSD for any purpose.

You must not try to allocate your own *ioreq* blocks, by the way. The IFS Manager maintains an internal pool of these structures, and they are longer than the structure declared for you and me to use. The IFS Manager uses the space past the declared end of the *ioreq* structure for its own purposes.

There is one situation in which you should explicitly release an *ioreq* block. You can use *IFSMgr_SchedEvent* and *IFSMgr_QueueEvent* to schedule timeout events. The IFS Manager passes an *ioreq* to your event callback routine so you can call back into the IFS Manager. When you're done processing the event, you should call *IFSMgr_FreeIoreq* to release this *ioreq*. You don't use *IFSMgr_FreeIoreq* for any other purpose.

Ring-Zero File Operations

A major advantage to having a ring-zero file system is that it allows VxDs to access disk files almost as easily as applications can. To appreciate the advantage, consider what VxDs needed to do in previous versions of Windows to access a disk file. Opening a file was simple: you could just call the VMM *OpenFile* service and hang on to the resulting MS-DOS file handle. From there on, you had two options. You could either perform INT 21h functions inside a nested V86 execution block, or you could rely on *Exec_VxD_Int* and built-in INT 21h translation services to handle the nested execution mechanics for you. Either way, you had to run parts of MS-DOS in V86 mode. Consequently, whenever you wanted to do file I/O, you needed to worry about whether you'd trigger an illegal recursion into MS-DOS.

The *IFSMgr_Ring0_FileIO* service implements analogs (see Table 16-1 on the following page) to the basic MS-DOS file system calls we've all come to know and love. This service is register-based. To use it, you load the EAX register with a subfunction code such as *R0_OPENCREATFILE*, and you load other general registers with parameters that depend on the subfunction you're invoking. Just like its various MS-DOS counterparts, the *IFSMgr_Ring0_FileIO* service indicates success or failure by clearing or setting the carry flag. If the call succeeds, it clears the carry flag and returns the results in the general registers. If an error occurs, it sets the carry flag and returns the error code in the AX register. This service often uses general registers for the same parameters and results as a 32-bit version of MS-DOS would, but there are exceptions.

Subfunction	Description
R0_CLOSEFILE	Closes a file.
R0_DELETEFILE	Deletes a file. This subfunction is equivalent to INT 21h, function 7141h, which is the long-name equivalent of INT 21h, function 41h. Like INT 21h, function 7141h, this function accepts a file-search attribute mask to restrict wildcard matching.
R0_FINDCLOSEFILE [sic]	Closes a find-file handle. This subfunction is equivalent to INT 21h, function 71A1h, which has no real-mode equivalent.
R0_FINDFIRSTFILE	Finds the first matching file. This subfunction is equivalent to INT 21h, function 714Eh, which is the long-name equivalent of INT 21h, function 4Eh.
R0_FINDNEXTFILE	Finds the next matching file. This subfunction is equivalent to INT 21h, function 714Fh, which is the long-name equivalent of INT 21h, function 4Fh.
R0_FILEATTRIBUTES	Gets or sets file attributes. This subfunction is equivalent to INT 21h, function 7143h, which is the long-name equivalent of INT 21h, function 43h.
R0_GETFILESIZE	Determines the size of a file. This subfunction is equivalent to INT 21h, function 4202h, except that it doesn't set a file position.
R0_GETDISKFREESPACE	Determines free space information about a logical volume. This subfunction is equivalent to INT 21h, function 36h.
R0_FILELOCKS	Locks or unlocks a file. This subfunction is equivalent to INT 21h, function 5Ch.
R0_OPENCREATFILE and R0_OPENCREAT_IN_CONTEXT	Open or create a file. These functions are equivalent to INT 21h, function 716Ch, which is the long-name equivalent of INT 21h, function 6Ch.
R0_READFILE and R0_READFILE_IN_CONTEXT	Read a file. These functions are equivalent to INT 21h, function 3Fh, except that you can supply a 32-bit count and a file position.
R0_READABSOLUTEDISK	Reads sectors from a logical volume. This subfunction is equivalent to INT 25h.

Table 16-1. *Subfunctions of* IFSMgr_Ring0_FileIO. *(continued)*

continued

Subfunction	Description
R0_RENAMEFILE	Renames a file. This subfunction is equivalent to INT 21h, function 7156h, which is the long-name equivalent of INT 21h, function 56h.
R0_WRITEABSOLUTEDISK	Writes sectors to a logical volume. This subfunction is equivalent to INT 26h.
R0_WRITEFILE and R0_WRITEFILE_IN_CONTEXT	Write a file. These functions are equivalent to INT 21h, function 40h, except that you can supply a 32-bit count and a file position.

Using *IFSMgr_Ring0_FileIO*

Suppose you had already opened a file for writing and wanted to write the string "Hello, world!". If you were writing in assembly language, you'd use code like this:

```
handle  dd      0               ; from R0_OPENCREATFILE call
string  db      'Hello, world!'
lstring equ     $-string
filepos dd      0               ; position in file
...
        mov     eax, R0_WRITEFILE
        mov     ebx, handle
        mov     ecx, lstring
        mov     edx, filepos
        mov     esi, offset string
        VxDCall IFSMgr_Ring0_FileIO
        jc      error           ; skip if error
        cmp     eax, ecx        ; or if less than all bytes
        jne     error           ;   got written
        add     filepos, ecx
```

Except for needing to keep track of the file position yourself, and except for using ESI instead of EDX as the data pointer, this code is very similar to what you would have used in a real-mode program that was talking to MS-DOS.

To provide a slightly more complete example in C, I needed to build a C-language header file to match the IFSMGR.INC file in the DDK. I elected to build a set of inline function declarations to simplify calling *IFSMgr_Ring0_FileIO*. (You can find my IFSMGR.H header on the companion disc in any of the subdirectories under \CHAP16.) The complete code to create a file containing the string "Hello, world!" using my IFSMGR.H header looks like this:

```
DWORD hfile;
int code;
DWORD action;
```

```
static unsigned char *data = "Hello, world!";
DWORD nwritten;

code = R0_OpenCreatFile(FALSE, ACCESS_READWRITE |
    SHARE_DENYREADWRITE, 0, ACTION_CREATEALWAYS, 0,
    "HelloWorld.txt", &hfile, &action);
if (code == 0)
    {                             // file opened okay
    R0_WriteFile(FALSE, hfile, strlen(data), 0, data,
        &nwritten);
    R0_CloseFile(hfile);
    }                             // file opened okay
```

This sample (included on the companion disc in the \CHAP16\FILEIO directory) opens a file named HELLOWORLD.TXT in the Windows directory because I didn't specify a full pathname. You can use a complete pathname if you want. The various flag arguments to *R0_OpenCreatFile* (*ACCESS_READWRITE* and so on) are manifest constants from IFS.H and translate directly to their MS-DOS equivalents. The first argument, which is *FALSE* in the example, indicates that we're opening the file in *global context;* I'll discuss the concept of file context in more detail on the following page.

My *R0_OpenCreatFile* function returns an MS-DOS error code as its result. A 0 return value denotes success. You can use the manifest constants in the Win32 header WINERROR.H to test other return values. *ERROR_PATH_NOT_FOUND*, for example, would mean that you had supplied the name of a nonexistent directory. Following a successful open call, *hfile* will hold a ring-zero file handle that you can use for subsequent operations. The *action* variable will tell you what action the function took with respect to creating or opening a file; its possible values are the same as those returned from an MS-DOS open call.

If the open call succeeds, the example goes on to call *R0_WriteFile* to write the data string at file offset 0 and then calls *R0_CloseFile* to close the file handle. Both operations use the file handle returned by *R0_OpenCreatFile*. If you happened to have a file handle that you'd obtained in some other way—from an application, or by calling MS-DOS directly—you could *not* use it for ring-zero file I/O operations; you can only use a file handle returned by *R0_OpenCreatFile*.

A more elegant way to proceed would be to implement the Win32 file API functions as ring-zero functions that issue *IFSMgr_Ring0_FileIO* calls. You could then call your versions of the Win32 file API functions directly from your VxD. If you were even more ambitious, you could use your Win32 substitutes as the bottom layer of a regular C runtime library, thereby allowing you to use regular *fopen* or *_open* function calls in your VxD.

You can perform ring-zero file operations only after the IFS Manager has finished its Device_Init phase of initialization. If your initialization order is later than the IFS Manager's (which would usually be true of an FSD), you should wait until you receive the Device_Init message. If your initialization order is earlier, you should wait until you receive the Init_Complete message. If your driver is a dynamic VxD, use *VMM_GetSystemInitState* to verify that the system has reached the Device_Init phase (if you know your driver is being loaded by a component that initializes after the IFS Manager) or the Init_Complete phase (if you know your driver is being loaded by a component that initializes before the IFS Manager or if you don't know the initialization order of the component that's loading your driver).

Global and Thread Contexts

The open, read, and write subfunctions of *IFSMgr_Ring0_FileIO* have two variants: a *global context* version and a *thread context* version. You indicate thread context by using the XXX_*IN_CONTEXT* version of the subfunction name in an assembly-language call or by passing a first argument value of *TRUE* to my C-language wrappers. You indicate global context by using the unadorned version of the sub-function name or by passing a first argument value of *FALSE*.

If you open a file in thread context, the current process owns the resulting file handle. The IFS Manager won't allow any other process to access the file using this handle. Furthermore, you should use the thread-context versions of *R0_READ_FILE* and *R0_WRITE_FILE* with that file. You should use the thread-context versions of these three API functions if you are acting on behalf of some application, particularly if you need to read or write data using addresses in the private memory area of the process.

If you open a file in global context, any process can use the resulting file handle. In this case, it's an error to use the XXX_*IN_CONTEXT* versions of *R0_READ_FILE* and *R0_WRITE_FILE*. A VxD that wants to access files for its own benefit (as opposed to the benefit of some application it's assisting) would normally use global context to avoid being limited to performing its operations only when a particular process is current.

Why Two Versions of *R0_READ_FILE* and *R0_WRITE_FILE*?

I wondered why the read and write operations had global and thread context versions, since the IFS Manager enforces a rule that you must use the same context in these operations as you did when you opened the file. After all, if the IFS Manager knows enough to complain, it knows enough to choose the right context. It turns out that the system performs ring-zero read and write operations on ring-three file handles to optimize performance. Distinguishing these reads and writes requires the different operation codes.

Character Conversions and Pathnames

The IFS Manager works internally with Unicode pathnames, even though Windows 95 itself at the application level does not. Thus, if you issue an MS-DOS command such as *TYPE F:\CHAP16\LPFS\FILESYSTEM.CPP*, the IFS Manager converts the pathname to Unicode before passing it to any file system drivers. The IFS Manager offers several conversion services to make it easy for VxD writers to convert strings back and forth between Unicode and the "base" character set (BCS) used by Windows applications (see Table 16-2).

Service	*Description*
UniToBCS	Converts a Unicode string (not a parsed pathname) to a BCS string
BCSToUni	Converts a BCS string to Unicode
BCSToBCS	Converts a BCS string to another BCS string using a different code page
UniCharToOEM	Converts a Unicode character to a BCS character in the OEM code page
UniToUpper	Converts a mixed-case Unicode string to its uppercase equivalent

Table 16-2. *IFS services for pathname conversion.*

The conversion functions don't form a complete set of all possible conversions. You can't convert, for example, Unicode or BCS strings to *lowercase*, or single Unicode characters directly to the ANSI code page. The particular set of functions listed in Table 16-2 happens to be what the IFS Manager needs to turn user and program input into Unicode strings for use by file system drivers. If I issue the MS-DOS *TYPE* command mentioned earlier, you can imagine the IFS Manager going through two steps: first, calling *BCSToUni* to convert the filename argument to Unicode, and then calling *UniToUpper* to convert it to uppercase. For example, the IFS Manager *might* do something like the following (I haven't disassembled it to see if it actually does, and I'm pretty sure I wouldn't find all of these steps in such close proximity):

```
USHORT uniname[MAX_PATH];
PBYTE *oemname = Client_Ptr_Flat(DS, DX);
UINT len = strlen(oemname);
UINT nbytes = BCSToUni(uniname, oemname, len, BCS_OEM);
UniToUpper(uniname, uniname, nbytes);
```

In this code fragment, we're taking a pointer coming from a virtual machine in the DS:DX register pair (which is where an MS-DOS INT 21h, function 716Ch, call would expect such a pointer) and treating it as a string that uses the OEM code page.

BCSToUni converts it to Unicode, and *UniToUpper* converts the resulting mixed-case Unicode string to uppercase.

A Note on Data Types   If you're used to Win32 applications programming, you might have expected to see Unicode strings declared using a type name such as WCHAR, wchar_t, or the like. The DDK always uses USHORT, however.

If you wanted to display the resulting Unicode string on the debugging terminal (which is probably using the OEM character set), you would use *UniToBCS* to convert it:

```
BYTE bcsname[MAX_PATH];
int len = UniToBCS(bcsname, uniname, nbytes,
    sizeof(bcsname)-1, BCS_OEM);
bcsname[len] = 0;
```

This service does not automatically add a null terminator to the string it returns, so you often need to add one yourself, as shown above.

Here's an example that shows how a VxD built using the Windows ANSI character set in the Microsoft Developer Studio would convert a string constant to the OEM character set:

```
BCSToBCS(bcsname, "Grüß Gott", BCS_OEM, BCS_WANSI,
    sizeof(bcsname));
```

(Freely translated, *Grüß Gott* is how a Bavarian says, "Hello, world!" Just call any random phone number in Munich to prove the point.)

Here are two final examples of character conversions:

```
UniCharToOEM(0x00FC);
UniCharToOEM(0x015C);
```

Assuming that code page 437 (MS-DOS Latin US) is the current OEM code page, the first example maps the Latin character *ü* (which is code point 00FCh in Unicode) to its code page 437 equivalent (81h). The second example attempts to map the Unicode character S-circumflex (Ŝ) to code page 437. Since the mapping is impossible (there's no such character in code page 437), the function returns 5Fh, which is the ASCII underscore character.

Pathname Parsing

Not only does the IFS Manager deal internally with Unicode strings, it also provides one additional felicitous service for file system drivers: it parses every pathname according to Windows 95 rules before calling down to file system drivers. If you've ever written application code that was littered with calls to *_splitpath* and other string

From *c:\Chap16\Lpfs\FileSystem.cpp*, we get:

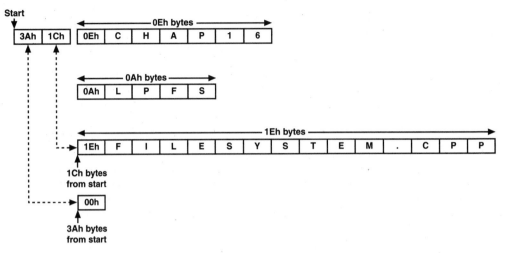

Figure 16-3. *Example of a parsed pathname.*

manipulation functions, you'll immediately appreciate what a boon pre-parsing is. Figure 16-3 shows the structure of an example parsed pathname.

The *ParsedPath* structure begins with a WORD (*pp_totalLength*) that gives the overall byte count of the parsed name, including the header. The second WORD (*pp_prefixLength*) gives the offset (again in bytes) of the last *PathElement* item in the structure; this element represents the last component of the pathname. After this header is a series of *PathElement* structures, one per directory level in the pathname. Each element begins with a WORD (*pe_length*) that gives the byte length of the element (including the WORD containing the length) and contains zero or more Unicode characters. A 00h WORD (not included in *pp_totalLength*) follows the whole structure in memory. Note that all the counts and offsets are in *bytes* rather than characters.

IFS.H contains some macros that are useful in manipulating pathnames:

- *IFSPathSize* returns the size of a *ParsedPath* structure, including the null terminator.

- *IFSPathLength* returns the total length of the *PathElement* components in a *ParsedPath* structure. That is, it subtracts the length of the *ParsedPath* header from the *pp_totalLength* value.

- *IFSLastElement* returns a pointer to the last *PathElement* component in a *ParsedPath* structure. The last element represents the filename portion of a pathname.

- *IFSNextElement* returns the address of the next *PathElement* component after a given *PathElement* component.

- *IFSIsRoot* returns *TRUE* if a *ParsedPath* structure represents the root directory. (It determines this by ascertaining that there are no *PathElement* components in the pathname, so the *pp_totalLength* field equals 4, which is the size of the *ParsedPath* header.)

You almost never need to parse a pathname yourself. From within a file system driver request-handling function, you can call *IFSMgr_FSDParsePath* if you've received a pathname (in the base character set) through some private API function rather than from the IFS Manager itself. That service requires a pointer to an *ioreq*, which you can't allocate for yourself. As an example of how you'd use the service, suppose you used *IFSMgr_SetReqHook* to hook a private INT 21h call that includes a pathname. The IFS Manager doesn't know anything about your private API function and can't realize that the pathname needs to be parsed. Since your hook function gets control with an *ioreq* block, it can call *IFSMgr_FSDParsePath* to parse the pathname. Except in this unusual kind of situation, you'll always get a pre-parsed pathname from the IFS Manager.

I already mentioned the *UniToBCS* service for converting a Unicode string to the base character set. There's an analogous service named *UniToBCSPath* for converting a parsed pathname to the base character set. Much of the time, you get a pointer to the parsed pathname in the *ir_ppath* member of an *ioreq* structure. You could convert it (for diagnostic printing or for some other purpose) as follows:

```
BYTE bcsname[MAX_PATH];
int len = UniToBCSPath(bcsname, pir->ir_ppath->pp_element,
    sizeof(bcsname)-1, BCS_OEM);
bcsname[len] = 0;
```

UniToBCSPath traverses the parsed pathname starting with a given element until it reaches the null terminator. For each element, it inserts a backslash followed by the base-character-set version of the element. Although the documentation for this function claims that it doesn't null-terminate the string it returns, it actually does add a null terminator unless it overflows your buffer (which you could detect because the returned length would equal the size of your buffer). Furthermore, the length you supply, *sizeof(bcsname) -1*, reserves room for you to add the null terminator that the function will actually add. Since the behavior I just described isn't documented, Microsoft can feel free to make the software correspond to the documentation. Therefore, you and I should use the function as documented—and as shown in the example above—even though doing so is less convenient.

It's obvious how to step from one element of a parsed pathname to the next. What isn't obvious is exactly what to do with each element. The IFS Manager contains some additional services beyond the character translation services we've already discussed that simplify common operations on path elements (see Table 16-3).

Service	Description
CreateBasis	Maps a Unicode path element to a basis name (an 8.3 name with no dot)
MatchBasisName	Compares a basis name with a file control block–format (FCB-format) name
AppendBasisTail	Appends a unique identifying integer to a basis name
FcbToShort	Translates an FCB-format name to the Unicode 8.3 format
ShortToFcb	Translates a Unicode 8.3-format name to the FCB format
ShortToLossyFcb	Translates a Unicode 8.3-format name to an FCB-format name using only OEM characters

Table 16-3. *IFS services for manipulating path elements.*

FCB and Basis Names

The so-called *FCB format* with which some of the services described in Table 16-3 work is 11 characters long: it has an 8-character primary name and a 3-character extension. Each component is padded with blanks, if necessary, to fill its allotted space. Thus, the FCB-format version of FUBAR.TXT is FUBAR   TXT (three blanks between the name and the extension). The characters are in Unicode format, so the name totals 22 bytes in length.

A *basis* name is a Unicode FCB-format name created from a path element according to a standard set of rules for turning long names into names with 8-byte primary names and 3-byte extensions.

An *8.3* name—also known as a *short* name—contains a name of as many as 8 characters, a dot, and an extension of as many as 3 characters. There aren't any padding spaces in a short name. For example:

```
USHORT uniname[MAX_PATH];
USHORT name_8_3[12];
USHORT fcbname[11];

BCSToUni(uniname, "FileSystem.cpp", 14, BCS_WANSI);
CreateBasis(fcbname, uniname, 28);
AppendBasisTail(fcbname, 1);
FcbToShort(name_8_3, fcbname, FALSE);
```

In this fragment of code,

■   *CreateBasis* applied to FileSystem.cpp creates FILESYSTCPP.

- *AppendBasisTail* applied to FILESYSTCPP with a numeric tail value of 1 creates FILESY~1CPP.

- *FcbToShort* applied to FILESY~1CPP creates FILESY~1.CPP.

You'll undoubtedly recognize these steps as parts of the process by which a VFAT-compatible file system would create an 8.3 alias for a long filename.

Date and Time Conversions

Careful management of date and time information has become a great deal more important since the days when all computing was done in batch mode on machines that could talk to each other across a room only with great difficulty. The advent of local- and wide-area networks and of routine international exchanges of digital information has created a demand for precise thinking about time. One example of why time is more important occurs every day in software development. Most software developers use desktop systems connected by a LAN, yet each system has its own clock and software for maintaining it. It wouldn't be unusual for a development project to span several time zones, either. So is your copy of a file stamped at 02:25 more—or less—recent than my copy stamped at 02:26? (Notice that I picked time values corresponding to the normal working times of many programmers.) Without someone explicitly keeping track of the vagaries of PC clock settings and time zones, it wouldn't be possible for a MAKE script or version control system to answer that question, which depends on whether we're in the same time zone, how accurate we've been in setting our clocks, and perhaps other factors.

IFS provides for three different styles of time data. The *MS-DOS format*, in use for well over a decade, records a timestamp in 32 bits, as shown in Figure 16-4. The time value is expressed in terms of 2 seconds and is always based on the local time zone of a particular computer. This format is only capable of expressing a moment between the years 1980 and 2107. The FAT file system uses this format to record the time a file was last modified.

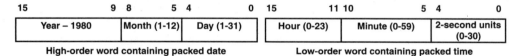

15	9	8	5	4	0	15	11	10	5	4	0
Year – 1980		Month (1-12)		Day (1-31)		Hour (0-23)		Minute (0-59)		2-second units (0-30)	

High-order word containing packed date   Low-order word containing packed time

Figure 16-4. *MS-DOS–format timestamp.*

Windows NT pioneered the use of *coordinated universal time* (UTC), which expresses in 64 bits the number of 100-nanosecond units since January 1, 1601, GMT. If you know a lot about the calendar, this particular choice of origin is the obvious one: it's the start of a 4-century period that ends in a leap year. If you know just a little about the calendar and history, you might think that the choice has something to do with an apple hitting Isaac Newton. Either way, you're likely to be bemused by the 100-nanosecond precision. Assuming that international priorities for space exploration remain at their present low level, we're unlikely to regret the grandiose description of this time standard as "universal" before the systems that use it become obsolete. I predict, however, that 100 nanoseconds will seem much too coarse-grained before long.

While FAT files use the MS-DOS format and Win32 APIs use the Windows NT format, networks use yet a different format called, appropriately enough, *network time*. A network time timestamp uses 32 bits to record the number of seconds since January 1, 1970, GMT. This time format is the same one used by UNIX systems and UNIX-derived functions such as *time* in the standard runtime library. People sometimes refer to this format of time as based on coordinated universal time (meaning GMT) too, perpetuating a confusion between the Win32 64-bit format and the time zone to which a network time value refers.

Converting a time value from one of these formats to another requires a lot of intricate code. The IFS Manager provides several services (see Table 16-4) to perform the conversions for you. For example, to convert the last-modification time recorded for a FAT file to the 64-bit Win32 format, you would call *IFSMgr_DosToWin32Time*. The only function missing from the otherwise complete set is one to obtain the current time in Win32 format. You wouldn't normally need to use the time zone bias returned by *IFSMgr_GetTimeZoneBias*, by the way, since the conversions to and from MS-DOS time (the only one expressed in local time) automatically apply the bias.

Service	Description
IFSMgr_Get_NetTime	Gets the current network time
IFSMgr_Get_DOSTime	Gets the current local time in MS-DOS format
IFSMgr_NetToDosTime	Converts a network time to MS-DOS format
IFSMgr_DosToNetTime	Converts an MS-DOS local time to network format
IFSMgr_DosToWin32Time	Converts an MS-DOS local time to Win32 format
IFSMgr_Win32ToDosTime	Converts a Win32 time to MS-DOS format
IFSMgr_NetToWin32Time	Converts a network time to Win32 time
IFSMgr_Win32ToNetTime	Converts a Win32 time to network time
IFSMgr_GetTimeZoneBias	Obtains the local time zone bias in minutes

Table 16-4. *IFS services for time conversions.*

As an example of using some of these date and time services, suppose your FSD had just created a file and you wanted to record the current time as the creation, modification, and access time in your own directory entry. You could call *IFSMgr_Get_DOSTime*, as follows:

```
e.created = e.modified = e.accessed = IFSMgr_GetDOSTime();
```

If your FSD later needed to fill in a *WIN32_FIND_DATA* structure as part of the implementation of the Win32 *FindFirstFile* API function, you could convert your MS-DOS–format timestamps like this:

```
_WIN32_FIND_DATA* fdp;
fdp->ftCreationTime   = IFSMgr_DosToWin32Time(e.created);
fdp->ftLastAccessTime = IFSMgr_DosToWin32Time(e.accessed);
fdp->ftLastWriteTime  = IFSMgr_DosToWin32Time(e.modified);
```

In this code fragment, note the leading underscore in the name *_WIN32_FIND_-DATA*. The official IFS.H file declares a copy of the Win32 structure using this name to make it easier for you to include IFS.H in a compilation that uses regular Win32 headers. (Unfortunately, the official IFS.H file also defines the Win32 structures *_FILETIME* and *_BY_HANDLE_INFORMATION*, so I needed to add some conditional compilation to the official file for use with some of the projects in this chapter.)

File System API Hooking

One of the most popular things to do with file system calls is hook them. I can't explain the impulse to intervene in other people's I/O operations, but I can't deny it either. The *IFSMgr_InstallFileSystemApiHook* service makes it easy for you to be a busybody if you're so inclined. You install and remove an API hook as follows:

```
ppIFSFileHookFunc prevhook;
...
BOOL OnSysDynamicDeviceInit()
    {
    prevhook = IFSMgr_InstallFileSystemApiHook(HookProc);
    return TRUE;
    }

BOOL OnSysDynamicDeviceExit()
    {
    IFSMgr_RemoveFileSystemApiHook(HookProc);
    return TRUE;
    }
```

That is, you install the hook when your VxD initializes, and you remove the hook when your VxD terminates. *IFSMgr_InstallFileSystemApiHook* takes the address of your hook procedure as an argument, and it returns the address of a DWORD containing a pointer to another hook procedure. You remove your hook by passing to *IFSMgr_RemoveFileSystemApiHook* the address of your hook procedure. Internally, the IFS Manager maintains its own list of API hooks so that you and other people can add and remove them in any order.

The hook procedure has the following prototype:

```
int HookProc(pIFSFunc fsdproc, int fcn, int drive, int flags,
    int cp, pioreq pir);
```

Here, *fsdproc* is the address of the function (located in some file system driver or other) that the IFS Manager would normally call to implement this particular I/O request. The *fcn* parameter is a code indicating one of 30 possible I/O request codes; the codes correspond to functions that file system drivers implement. The drive letter index (1 meaning drive A) for the logical volume to which the request is directed arrives as the *drive* parameter, and *flags* indicates what kind of device that drive happens to be. The *cp* value (*BCS_ANSI* or *BCS_OEM*) indicates whether the IFS Manager's caller passed it an ANSI or an OEM string. Finally, *pir* points to an IFS I/O request structure that contains all the parameters for the request.

If there weren't any hook procedure in place, the IFS Manager would simply have performed a function call equivalent to this one:

```
int status = (*fsdproc)(pir);
```

That is, the IFS Manager would have called the function pointed to by the *fsdproc* argument with the address of the I/O request structure and would have saved the return value as a status code. If you wanted to pass the request along from your hook function in a transparent way, you could write a hook function having the following form:

```
int HookProc(pIFSFunc fsdproc, int fcn, int drive, int flags,
    int cp, pioreq pir)
    {
    return (*fsdproc)(pir);        // don't do this
    }
```

Not only would there not be much point in coding so simple a hook function, it would also be wrong. If you can hook API functions, so can other VxDs. You must give the other potential hooks their chance to look at each request, too, so even the smallest hook function you could write should chain the call instead of just processing it:

```
int HookProc(pIFSFunc fsdproc, int fcn, int drive, int flags,
    int cp, pioreq pir)
    {
    return (**prevhook)(fsdproc, fcn, drive, flags, cp,
        pir);
    }
```

In this example, you use the *prevhook* value returned by your initial call to *IFSMgr_InstallFileSystemApiHook* to locate the next hook function in the chain, and you call it with the same parameters you received. If no other VxD has actually hooked file system API calls, you will end up reaching a default hook function within the IFS Manager that calls the *fsdproc* procedure with the *pir* request, thereby actually performing the I/O request.

The IFSMonitor sample on the companion disc shows how to use a file system API hook for the nearly trivial purpose of monitoring file system calls in your system. The VxD portion of this sample hooks API calls in the manner just described and uses an asynchronous list to record information about each call. It uses the asynchronous procedure call mechanism to send the list elements to a Windows-based application (really not much more than a standard Windows 95 list control with a frame around it) for display. In fact, the overall architecture of this monitor application is the same as the IOS request monitor I described in Chapter 15.

Figure 16-5 shows the request activity that resulted from starting the monitor and stopping it a few seconds later. What you see is a series of page read operations from different locations in a file into a particular page buffer. Nothing else was actually happening on my system at the time I recorded the log.

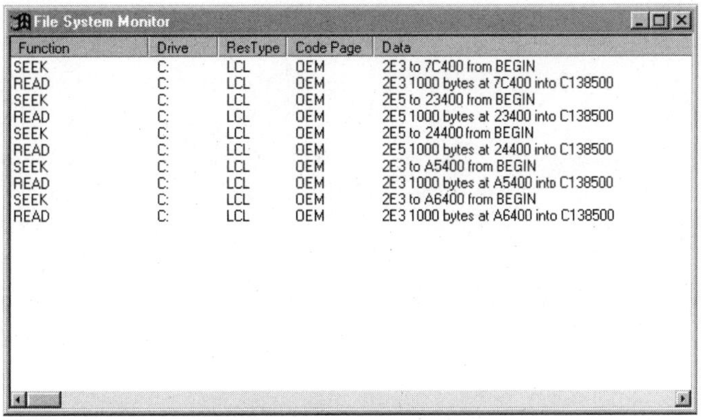

Figure 16-5. *Sample output from the IFSMonitor application.*

The ability to hook file system API calls is obviously pretty powerful. There are already commercial virus scanners that rely on API hooks to detect infection, even across the network. You could use an API hook to implement per-file compression or encryption, too. Now that it's possible to hook API calls (and, what's probably most important, to be *sure* you'll see all of them), many more applications will probably occur to the entrepeneurs among us.

Seeing All API Calls?   Just at press time, I learned that an API hook *might* not actually see all file system API calls after all. It was reported on the WINSDK forum that requests for a CD-ROM drive that uses a real-mode MSCDEX will bypass the hook.

LOCAL FILE SYSTEM DRIVERS

A *local file system driver* (local FSD) implements the Windows 95 file system model on a local device—that is, a device attached to the computer on which the driver is installed as opposed to a device attached to some other computer over a network. You certainly have the VFAT file system on your computer; VFAT is the 32-bit version of the venerable MS-DOS FAT (file allocation table) file system that offers long filename support and other nifty features. VFAT is implemented by VFAT.VXD, which is one of the standard VxDs packaged in VMM32. You also have the VDEF (default) file system; that's what allows you to access a blank disk in order to format it. You probably also have the CD file system (CDFS), which supports CD-ROM devices. The CD file system includes the VCDFSD component of VMM32 as well as an FSD component such as CDFS.VXD from the IOSUBSYS directory.

Introducing the Low Performance File System

Implementing a real file system as an *example* is far beyond the scope of reason and good sense. I wanted to present enough of a sample to be able to accurately describe the service functions that a file system needs to provide, however. I decided, therefore, to implement a very low performance file system for use with the RAM-disk drive developed in Chapter 15 (No way would I trust one of my hard disks to a file system under development!) I call the end result the Low Performance File System (LPFS). VTHIN (the opposite of VFAT, that is) would have been another good name, I suppose.

LPFS has a root directory that contains only one file. The file can have any name you like. You can't delete this file, but you can open it for reading or writing, and you can rename it. I put these limits on the functionality of LPFS so I wouldn't have to clutter the examples with the complications associated with directory structures, sector allocation, and the like.

It made sense to me to build LPFS in C++ using the class hierarchy shown in Figure 16-6. I defined a base class named *CFileSystem* that encapsulates the behavior of an IFS file system. From that class I derived *CLocalFileSystem* (a file system on a local device) and *CNetworkFileSystem* (a file system on a remote device—that is, a network redirector). The distinction between a local and a network file system is that the local file system uses IOS services to perform I/O operations against a local resource, whereas the network redirector transmits requests over a network. Both types of file systems respond to most of the same calls from the IFS Manager. Furthermore, the server that answers requests for remote file operations would itself contain a local file system to carry out the requests. LPFS is an example of a local file system, so I derived *CLpfs* from *CLocalFileSystem*, as shown in the figure.

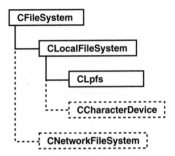

Figure 16-6. *Class hierarchy for the LPFS file system sample.*

Some IFS Mechanics

Like other local FSDs, LPFS is a static VxD with an initialization order of *FSD_Init_Order* that uses both IFS and IOS services. Most of the VxDs we've discussed in this book are dynamic, and they perform initialization and shutdown processing when the Sys_Dynamic_Device_Init and Sys_Dynamic_Device_Exit messages are processed. Furthermore, their initialization order doesn't matter. However, as a static VxD, LPFS needs to handle the Device_Init message and needs to have a specific initialization order to fit itself correctly into the overall Windows 95 scheme. I used *FSD_Init_Order + 100h* as the initialization order so that my VxD would initialize after the VFAT and other file system drivers. I'll explain later in the note titled "The Importance of Registration Order" (see page 603) why this particular initialization order is so important to the example.

LPFS.CPP is the main program for this VxD, and it also contains the implementation of the *CLpfs* class. The portion relevant to VxD initialization is as follows:

```
#define NULL 0

extern "C" {
#define WANTVXDWRAPS
#include <basedef.h>
#include <vmm.h>
#include <debug.h>
#include <vxdwraps.h>
#include <winerror.h>
#include "iosdcls.h"
#include "ifsmgr.h"
    } // extern "C"

#pragma hdrstop

#include "lpfs.h"
```

```
void OnAsyncEvent(PAEP aep);
CFileSystem* CreateInstance();

#pragma VxD_INIT_CODE_SEG
#pragma VxD_INIT_DATA_SEG

extern "C" extern DRP theDRP;

SYSCTL BOOL OnDeviceInit(HVM hVM, DWORD refdata)
    {                           // OnDeviceInit
    if (!IOS_Get_Version())
        return FALSE;           // IOS not loaded (?)
    theDRP.DRP_aer = (PVOID) OnAsyncEvent;
    IOS_Register(&theDRP);

    return CLpfs::Register(CLpfs::CreateNew);
    }                           // OnDeviceInit
```

You wouldn't expect to have to define NULL yourself, but BASEDEF.H defines it (incorrectly) as '\0'. C++ compilers are unwilling to accept this signed character as equivalent to a NULL pointer value. Luckily, BASEDEF.H's definition is surrounded by an *#ifndef*, making it possible to supply a definition that works. Bracketing the DDK headers with *extern "C" {...}* avoids the embarrassment of a program that demands VxD service wrappers with C++ decorated names. IFSMGR.H is the header I wrote as a stand-in for the one I expected to find (but didn't) in the DDK; it includes a slightly modified version of the DDK header called IFS.H; my modifications make it possible to include IFS.H and regular Win32 headers in the same compilation. IOSDCLS.H is the same header we used in Chapter 15 for accessing the Input/Output Supervisor.

The Device_Init system control message handler registers with the IOS and, indirectly, with the IFS Manager. Like other file system drivers, LPFS needs to call functions that can be reached only through the IOS linkage block (ILB). To obtain an ILB, you have to call *IOS_Register*. If you register with *IOS_Register*, you have to supply a driver registration packet and an asynchronous event handler procedure. I defined the DRP in the DEVDCL.ASM file as follows:

```
VxD_IDATA_SEG
        public _theDRP
_theDRP  DRP    <EyeCatcher, DRP_TSD, 0, offset32 _theILB, \
                'LowPerfFileSys ', 0, 0, 0>
VxD_IDATA_ENDS
```

The asynchronous event procedure can be empty, like this one:

```
#pragma VxD_LOCKED_CODE_SEG
#pragma VxD_LOCKED_DATA_SEG
```

```
void OnAsyncEvent(PAEP aep)
    {                                   // OnAsyncEvent
    aep->AEP_result = AEP_SUCCESS;
    }                                   // OnAsyncEvent
```

You need the excess baggage of an event procedure unless you register with the IOS as a so-called "noncompliant" layer driver. Since our driver is an FSD, you might have guessed that we'd register as an FSD, which is by definition a noncompliant driver that doesn't need an asynchronous event procedure. Strangely, all of Microsoft's FSDs tell the IOS that they are type-specific drivers (TSDs), which *do* need event procedures. Go figure!

The IFS registration call is buried in the *Register* member function, and I'll describe it later, in the section titled "Registering LPFS." The call to *Register* includes the address of a *CLpfs* static member function that creates a new instance of *CLpfs*:

```
CFileSystem* CLpfs::CreateNew()
    {                                   // CreateInstance
    return new CLpfs();
    }                                   // CreateInstance
```

I'll show later, in the note titled "Creating an LPFS Instance" (see page 605), how this function fits into the overall picture.

CFileSystem, the base class for all the file system classes, has the following interface:

```
class CFileSystem
    {                                   // CFileSystem
public:
    CFileSystem();
    ~CFileSystem();

    static CFileSystem* (*CreateNewFcn)();
    static int ProviderId;
    static BOOL Register(CFileSystem* (*createnew)());
    };                                  // CFileSystem
```

The *Register* function simply saves its function pointer argument in the *CreateNewFcn* variable:

```
BOOL CFileSystem::Register(CFileSystem* (*createnew)())
    {                                   // CFileSystem::Register
    CreateNewFcn = createnew;
    return TRUE;
    }                                   // CFileSystem::Register
```

More About LPFS   The complete source code for LPFS is on the companion disc. I'm not going to reproduce all of it here because all I want to show you is how to combine IFS and IOS services to accomplish the basic operations of a file system. Moreover, if you look at the machine-readable source code, you'll discover that I sometimes implemented the functions in different or more general ways than described here in the text. I'm not trying to show off my skills (or lack thereof) at designing a C++ class library for file system development. I'm only going to explain enough about the implementation to let you make sense of the code fragments in the text.

Volume Mounting

A local FSD registers with the IFS Manager by calling *IFSMgr_RegisterMount*,

```
int code = IFSMgr_RegisterMount(mountfunc, version, type);
```

where *mountfunc* identifies your volume mount function and *version* designates the lowest version of the IFS Manager that you can work with. The *type* argument indicates whether yours is the default FSD or not. You usually specify the constants *IFSMGRVERSION* and *NORMAL_FSD* for the last two parameters. Microsoft's VDEF.VXD (the only FSD for which source code appears in the DDK) uses *DEFAULT_FSD* for the last parameter instead; it's the only FSD that does so. I'll explain later the significance of being the default FSD. The return code is a *provider ID* that identifies the file system. (In Windows 95, the provider ID of a local file system provider indexes the IFS Manager's internal arrays. This simple correspondence to an array index will be changed in the next release of Windows, so you shouldn't rely on it now except to help you debug an FSD.)

Volume mounting requests originate in the Input/Output Supervisor when someone recognizes that a new disk drive has appeared or that the media in an existing drive has changed. The IFS Manager then polls all the FSDs that have registered a mount function in order to connect an FSD to the volume. The polling occurs in reverse of the order in which the FSDs registered, except that the one-and-only default FSD gets polled last no matter when it registered. To poll a file system, the IFS Manager calls the registered mount function, whose prototype is as follows:

```
int FS_MountVolume(pioreq pir);
```

In this call, *pir* points to an IFS I/O request in which *ir_flags* designates the *IR_FSD_MOUNT* subfunction, *ir_volh* points to the IOS VRP structure for the logical volume, *ir_rh* points to the head of the MS-DOS DPB chain, and *ir_mntdrv* designates the drive letter for the volume. Your mount function should determine whether it recognizes the file system on the volume. If not, it should simply set *ir_error* to an error code and return the same error code as its return value. If it does recognize the file system, it should erect whatever machinery your FSD needs to manage the volume, set several output values, and return 0. The output values you should set are as follows:

- Within the *ioreq*, you set the *ir_rh* field to point to your internal volume-oriented data structure. The IFS Manager won't look inside this structure, but it will pass the pointer back to you in the *ir_rh* field of all subsequent function calls related to this volume.

- Also within the *ioreq*, you set *ir_vfunc* to the address of a *volfunc* structure, which contains pointers to fifteen functions that the IFS Manager will call to handle volume-oriented requests such as *FS_OpenFile*.

- Within the VRP, you set *VRP_fsd_entry* to point to your *FS_MountVolume* function. Various IOS components will call your function directly on occasion. *VOLTRACK*, for example, calls it to perform an *IR_FSD_VERIFY* function when the port driver for the physical device decides that the media has changed.

- Also within the VRP, you set *VRP_fsd_hvol* to point to your internal volume-oriented data structure. IOS components will use this value to initialize *ir_rh* when they construct I/O requests for your *FS_MountVolume* function.

The Importance of Registration Order   I learned the following lesson the hard way: If you modify the *ioreq* block and then decide to reject the new volume, your modifications will be preserved in the mount calls the IFS Manager makes to lower-priority file systems (that is, file systems that registered with the IFS Manager before yours did). In particular, if you modify *ir_rh*, lower-priority file systems will probably crash if they interpret the value as a DPB pointer. Moral: don't change the *ioreq* or the VRP unless you mean it. Notwithstanding this advice, the VFAT *does* modify the *ir_rh* field even if it decides to reject the new volume. The CDFS and the VDEF, which are normally the only other two file systems present, don't care about *ir_rh* as an input field. If your file system's priority is below VFAT's and you *do* care, you're in trouble. My advice is to use an initialization order bigger than *FSD_Init_Order*. You'll then load and register later than VFAT, causing you to see mount requests before VFAT has a chance to corrupt *ir_rh*.

Registering LPFS

As shown earlier, LPFS's Device_Init handler calls the *Register* function to register the file system with the IFS Manager. That function contains the following code:

```
BOOL CLocalFileSystem::Register(CFileSystem* (*createnew)())
    {                         // CLocalFileSystem::Register
    if (!CFileSystem::Register(createnew))
        return FALSE;
    if (IFSMgr_Get_Version() < IFSMGRVERSION)
        return FALSE;         // back-level system
    if ((ProviderId = IFSMgr_RegisterMount(MountVolumeThunk,
        IFSMGRVERSION, NORMAL_FSD)) < 0)
        return FALSE;
    return TRUE;
    }                         // CLocalFileSystem::Register
```

The call to *CFileSystem::Register* simply records the *CLpfs::CreateNew* function address for later use. The call to *IFSMgr_Get_Version* serves two purposes. If the IFS Manager happens not to be loaded (it's unclear how that could ever actually happen), we don't want to load our driver either. In addition, if we find ourselves running on a back-level system (a system older than the one for which the driver was written), we may not want to stay loaded. *IFSMGRVERSION* will be the version of the IFS Manager whose interfaces our driver is compiled to use and whose functionality we (presumably) understand. Comparing the return value from *IFSMgr_Get_Version* to this constant therefore tells us whether there's a version of the IFS Manager present that we can work with. If not, we return *FALSE*, and the Device_Init handler will then return a failure code to the VMM that causes it to unload LPFS. The IFS Manager in turn decides whether it can work with *us* by inspecting the version number constant we pass into the registration API.

Mounting LPFS Volumes

CLocalFileSystem has a static member function named *MountVolumeThunk* that handles mount-related requests from the IFS Manager and from IOS layer drivers such as VOLTRACK. The mount protocol begins with an *IR_FSD_MOUNT* request, as follows:

```
int CLocalFileSystem::MountVolumeThunk(pioreq pir)
    {                         // CLocalFileSystem::MountVolumeThunk
    pir->ir_error = ERROR_ACCESS_DENIED; // assume error

    switch (pir->ir_flags)
        {                     // select volume mount function

    case IR_FSD_MOUNT:
        {                     // IR_FSD_MOUNT
        CLocalFileSystem* lfs = (CLocalFileSystem*)
```

```
            (*CreateNewFcn)();
        lfs->m_vrp = (PVRP) pir->ir_volh;
        lfs->m_drive = lfs->m_origdrive =
            (BYTE) pir->ir_mntdrv;
        lfs->m_dpb = pir->ir_rh;
        if ((pir->ir_error = lfs->MountVolume(pir)) == 0)
            {                       // successfully mounted
            pir->ir_rh = (rh_t) lfs;
            lfs->m_vrp->VRP_fsd_hvol = (ULONG) lfs;
            lfs->m_vrp->VRP_fsd_entry = (ULONG)
                MountVolumeThunk;
            }                       // successfully mounted
        else
            delete lfs;            // error trying to mount volume
        break;
        }                          // IR_FSD_MOUNT
    ...
    }                              // select volume mount function

    return pir->ir_error;
    }                              // CLocalFileSystem::MountVolumeThunk
```

We initially assume that the function will fail. *ERROR_ACCESS_DENIED* is a convenient error code we use to mean, "I don't recognize this volume." The IFS Manager handles some error codes as special cases when the mount function returns, but this particular code is not one of the special cases. Whatever is left in *ir_error* becomes the return code from the function.

Creating an LPFS Instance The mount function must be a static function because its purpose is to decide whether it makes sense to create an instance of a file system object. To make the decision, it first creates a file system object (which may be discarded later) simply to ease the mechanics of investigating the volume. Here is where the *CreateNew* function comes into play: we need to create an instance of some class derived from *CLocalFileSystem*, but we don't know when we compile LOCALFILESYS-TEM.CPP what class that will be. C++ doesn't readily support creating classes whose type is determined at runtime (hence the machinery of *CObject* and *CRuntimeClass* in MFC). *CreateNewFcn* is a pointer to a static function belonging to the derived class in question that creates an instance of its own class.

With the new file system object in hand, the mount function can copy the important parameters from *ioreq* into the object. These parameters include a VRP address (*ir_volh*), a drive letter index (*ir_mntdrv*), and an MS-DOS DPB address (*ir_rb*). We then call *MountVolume*, which is a virtual member function that can be overridden if necessary. I didn't need to override *MountVolume* in this example, so it's just a part of *CLocalFileSystem*:

```
int CLocalFileSystem::MountVolume(pioreq pir)
    {                               // CLocalFileSystem::MountVolume
    if (!OurVolume(pir))
        return ERROR_ACCESS_DENIED;
    for (CLocalFileSystem* fs = First; fs; fs = fs->m_next)
        if (fs != this && SameVolume(fs))
            return ERROR_IFSVOL_EXISTS;
    pir->ir_vfunc = &volfuncs;
    return 0;
    }                               // CLocalFileSystem::MountVolume
```

In this example, *volfuncs* is a static variable of type *volfunc* that specifies a table of pointers to virtual functions that implement volume-oriented functions such as *FS_OpenFile*.

OurVolume is a virtual function that you should override, since it decides whether the current volume contains an instance of the file system we're trying to implement. When you build a file system, you would have a function that occupies this architectural niche and investigates the contents of the disk volume to see whether you recognize it. In this simplified example, I just check the vendor ID in the master boot record to see whether I'm dealing with one of the RAM disks we looked at in Chapter 15:

```
BOOL CLpfs::OurVolume(pioreq pir)
    {                               // CLpfs::OurVolume
    PBYTE bootsec = ReadBootSector();
    if (!bootsec)
        {                           // can't read boot sector
        pir->ir_error = m_error;
        return FALSE;
        }           (               // can't read boot sector
    BOOL ours = (memcmp(bootsec + 3, "WALTONEY", 8) == 0);
    _HeapFree(bootsec, 0);
    return ours;
    }                               // CLpfs::OurVolume
```

You would also have a function like the one called *SameVolume*, which checks for a duplicate mount request. I'll describe *SameVolume* later on in connection with the *IR_FSD_VERIFY* request, which also uses it.

Reading the Boot Sector

ReadBootSector is a part of *CLocalFileSystem*. It uses a number of helper routines to create and execute a read operation to fetch sector 0 from the logical volume. There is one new feature of this operation beyond what we discussed in Chapter 15, so I'll present some of the code. *ReadBootSector* itself looks like this:

```
PBYTE CLocalFileSystem::ReadBootSector()
    {                         // CLocalFileSystem::ReadBootSector
    PBYTE buffer = (PBYTE) _HeapAllocate(m_vrp->VRP_block_size,0);
    if (!buffer)
        return NULL;
    if (m_error = ReadSectorNow(0, buffer))
        {                            // request had error
        _HeapFree(buffer, 0);
        return NULL;
        }                            // request had error
    return buffer;
    }                         // CLocalFileSystem::ReadBootSector
```

This function allocates a block of memory large enough to hold one disk sector. It extracts the length of a sector from the IOS VRP. The function then calls a helper function named *ReadSectorNow* to read sector 0 into the allocated memory. *ReadSectorNow* looks like this:

```
int CLocalFileSystem::ReadSectorNow(ULONG sector, PBYTE buffer)
    {                         // CLocalFileSystem::ReadSectorNow
    PIOR ior = CreateIOR(IOR_READ,
        IORF_BYPASS_VOLTRK | IORF_HIGH_PRIORITY);
    ior->IOR_start_addr[0] = sector;
    ior->IOR_buffer_ptr = (ULONG) buffer;
    ior->IOR_xfer_count = 1;
    SatisfyCriteria(ior);
    SendCommandAndWait(ior);
    int status = (int) ior->IOR_status;
    DestroyIOR(ior);

    if (status >= IORS_ERROR_DESIGNTR)
        return IOSMapIORSToI21(status);
    else
        return 0;
    }                         // CLocalFileSystem::ReadSectorNow
```

ReadSectorNow uses *CreateIOR* to create a new I/O request descriptor using IOS services we discussed in Chapter 15. *SatisfyCriteria* calls the IOS criteria routine to prepare the request for actual transmittal to the top level of the IOS layer drivers. *SendCommandAndWait*, which I'll discuss in detail shortly, executes the I/O request and waits for it to finish. *DestroyIOR* returns the IOR to the IOS. If you omit the *DestroyIOR* step, Windows 95 will hang when the user eventually exits, because the IOS thinks there's still an outstanding request for which it should wait. Finally, this function uses *IOSMapIORSToI21* to map any error return value from the IOS set of error codes to the IFS set.

A Note on Error Checking The *ReadBootSector* and *ReadSector-Now* functions illustrate a basic way of detecting and reporting disk errors. In most of the examples that follow, I won't actually do anything with these particular return values. In a production file system, you should *always* test for errors. Error checking makes programs hard to read, however, so I left it out in the interest of clarity. (I'm not trying to teach you how to program, but rather how to work with IFS.) Testing for unusual or alternative conditions is a different matter, though, so I *didn't* leave out such tests.

SendCommandAndWait illustrates the way file system drivers generally perform synchronous I/O operations:

```
#define IOR_event _ureq._IOR_requestor_usage[0]

void CLocalFileSystem::SendCommandAndWait(PIOR ior)
    {                      // CLocalFileSystem::SendCommandAndWait
    ior->IOR_event = 0;
    ior->IOR_callback = (CMDCPLT) OnCommandComplete;
    ior->IOR_req_req_handle = (ULONG) ior;
    SendCommand(ior);

    while (TRUE)
        {                      // wait for command to finish
        _asm pushfd
        _asm cli
        if (ior->IOR_event)
            break;             // it's done
        IFSMgr_Block((ULONG) &ior->IOR_event);
        _asm popfd
        }                      // wait for command to finish
    _asm popfd
    }                          // CLocalFileSystem::SendCommandAndWait

void CLocalFileSystem::OnCommandComplete(PIOR ior)
    {                      // CLocalFileSystem::OnCommandComplete
    ior->IOR_event = 1;
    IFSMgr_Wakeup((ULONG) &ior->IOR_event);
    }                      // CLocalFileSystem::OnCommandComplete
```

As I mentioned in Chapter 15, most IOS clients avoid using the *IORF_SYNC_COMMAND* flag when they have a synchronous command to perform. Instead, they have some other way of waiting for requests to complete. The method shown in this code fragment is very similar to what VFAT does.

The IOS I/O request descriptor (IOR) contains a field named _ureq that is used either for IOCTL parameters or for any purpose the IOS client dreams up. Here we use one of the DWORDs in the _ureq union as a completion flag. Before sending the I/O request to the IOS, we set the flag to 0. Our I/O completion routine (*OnCommandComplete*) will set the flag to 1 when the operation eventually finishes. To wait for the operation, we call *IFSMgr_Block*, passing it the address of the flag word. *IFSMgr_Block* is a thin wrapper for calling the _BlockOnID service with the BLOCK_SVC_INTS and BLOCK_SVC_ENABLE_INTS flags. As you know, _BlockOnID blocks the current thread until someone calls _SignalID with the same 32-bit blocking ID as its argument. *IFSMgr_Wakeup*, used in *OnCommandComplete*, performs that very function. Thus, the call to *IFSMgr_Block* will return after the function we're waiting for finishes.

As you also know, _BlockOnID and _SignalID treat their arguments as arbitrary 32-bit values. It's possible (albeit very unlikely) for two different VxDs to pick the same blocking ID by accident. Therefore, whenever you use these two functions to synchronize an operation, you need to have an extrinsic way to verify that the wakeup call you're getting is the one you're expecting. The *while* loop inside *SendCommandAndWait* accomplishes this verification by checking to see whether the flag word has become nonzero. If not, someone has fortuitously used the address of the flag word in a call to _SignalID intended for someone else, and you need to repeat the loop. (You don't *have* to use the address of the extrinsic flag as the blocking ID, but you usually do.)

This code sample illustrates one more nuance of _BlockOnID and _SignalID. It's very important not to block if the signal has already occurred, because you'll never wake up. (_SignalID acts much like the Win32 *PulseEvent* API function in that it only releases a thread that happens to already be waiting.) Therefore, you must check the event flag before blocking. And, to prevent a race between your check and the asynchronous completion routine, you must be sure that you can't be interrupted. Disabling interrupts is part of the insurance, but you must also take care not to cause a page fault. The wait loop must therefore be in the locked code segment.

Operations on Volumes

After the IFS Manager has made a successful *IR_FSD_MOUNT* call to your *MountVolume* function, it makes your volume available to other components of the system. You can now receive additional calls to your *MountVolume* function with subfunction codes other than *IR_FSD_MOUNT*, and you can receive calls to the functions you specify in the *ir_vfunc* table you returned to the IFS Manager.

Additional *MountVolume* Subfunctions
IFS and IOS layer drivers can call your *MountVolume* function to handle the following additional subfunctions.

IR_FSD_MAP_DRIVE The IFS Manager issues an *IR_FSD_MAP_DRIVE* request to support some drive compression schemes (such as Microsoft's DRVSPACE) that require the exchange of drive letters. That is, the compression driver might initially create a compressed drive Q from a file located on drive C, but it requires the compressed drive to be accessed with the letter *C* and the base drive with the letter *Q*. To support this feature, the FSD needs to keep track of two drive letters: a *current* drive letter and an *original* drive letter. The FSD uses the current drive letter when calling I/O requests down to the IOS and holds the original letter in reserve to handle a subsequent *IR_FSD_UNMAP_DRIVE* request. For example:

```
class CLocalFileSystem : public CFileSystem
{
...
BYTE m_drive;     // current drive number (A = 0)
BYTE m_origdrive; // original drive number (A = 0)
...
};

int CLocalFileSystem::MapDrive(pioreq pir)
    {                           // CLocalFileSystem::MapDrive
    m_drive = (BYTE) pir->ir_options;
    m_origdrive = (BYTE) pir->ir_pos; // undocumented!
    return 0;
    }                           // CLocalFileSystem::MapDrive
```

The fact that *ir_pos* contains a new (therefore *more* original) value for the "original" drive letter is undocumented, by the way. The initial value for both drive letters is the *ir_mntdrv* parameter in the original *IR_FSD_MOUNT* request.

IR_FSD_MOUNT_CHILD The IFS Manager uses the *IR_FSD_MOUNT_CHILD* request to mount a volume that's physically a child of another volume. For example, a compressed drive is a child of the volume on which its file lives. You might be able to use the very same code for child and parent volume mounts. The VFAT has slightly different routines for these two requests (*IR_FSD_MOUNT* and *IR_FSD_MOUNT_CHILD*) because it does two things for parent volumes (boot sector smashing for removable media and DPB lookup) that aren't relevant (or even correct) for a child volume.

For reasons I don't understand, parent and child volumes must use the same file system. Thus, it's not possible (for example) for CDFS to provide a compressed logical volume that contains data managed by VFAT.

IR_FSD_UNLOAD An IOS layer driver can send the FSD an *IR_FSD_UNLOAD* request to force the FSD to dismount a volume. You should flush any cache and clean up any other resources you're holding on behalf of the volume. You can still receive other requests for the volume, however, so you don't want to release the memory containing your internal data structures. (Wait until you receive an *FS_DisconnectResource* call to release the memory.)

IR_FSD_UNMAP_DRIVE An IOS layer driver responsible for compression sends an FSD the *IR_FSD_UNMAP_DRIVE* request to undo the effect of an earlier *IR_FSD_MAP_DRIVE* request. The undocumented but entirely expected entry condition is that *ir_rh* points to the FSD's internal control block for the volume. The FSD should resume using the "original" drive letter. For example:

```
int CLocalFileSystem::UnmapDrive(pioreq pir)
    {                              // CLocalFileSystem::UnmapDrive
    m_drive = m_origdrive;
    return 0;
    }                              // CLocalFileSystem::UnmapDrive
```

IR_FSD_VERIFY VOLTRACK (the volume tracking layer driver that handles removable-media devices) calls your *MountVolume* function directly with this subfunction code whenever the port driver indicates that the media has changed. Your FSD's job is to see whether the volume now mounted on the physical device is the same as the volume that was mounted prior to the media change. (The signal from the port driver may have been spurious, or the user may have ejected and immediately reinserted a volume.)

The calling sequence for this function isn't documented, but it was easy enough for me to figure out by judicious disassembly of VFAT.VXD and VOLTRACK.VXD. On input, *ir_drvh* points to your handle for the volume that used to be mounted on the drive and *ir_data* points to a 256-byte area where you can place the label from any new volume. You should return 0 (and set *ir_error* to 0) if the drive still contains the old volume. You should return -1 (and set *ir_error* to -1) if the drive contains a new volume, in which case you should also fill in the *ir_data* area and set *ir_aux2* to the 32-bit volume serial number. As it happens, VOLTRACK doesn't do anything with the output data, but that might change someday.

Here's how LPFS handles the *IR_FSD_VERIFY* subfunction:

```
int CLocalFileSystem::MountVolumeThunk(pioreq pir)
    {                          // CLocalFileSystem::MountVolumeThunk
    pir->ir_error = ERROR_ACCESS_DENIED; // assume error

    switch (pir->ir_flags)
        {                          // select volume mount function
        ...
    case IR_FSD_VERIFY:
        {                              // IR_FSD_VERIFY
        CLocalFileSystem* lfs = (CLocalFileSystem*) CreateNew();
        CLocalFileSystem* old = (CLocalFileSystem*) pir->ir_drvh;
        lfs->m_drive = lfs->m_origdrive = old->m_drive;
        lfs->m_vrp = old->m_vrp;
```

```
                  pir->ir_error = lfs->VerifyVolume(pir);
                  delete lfs;              // used only for verification
                  break;
                  }                        // IR_FSD_VERIFY
                  ...
                  }                        // select volume mount function

            return pir->ir_error;
            }                          // CLocalFileSystem::MountVolumeThunk

      int CLocalFileSystem::VerifyVolume(pioreq pir)
            {                          // CLocalFileSystem::VerifyVolume
            if (SameVolume((CLocalFileSystem*) pir->ir_drvh))
                return 0;
            GetVolumeLabel((PDWORD) &pir->ir_aux2.aux_ul,
                (char*) pir->ir_data);
            return -1;
            }                          // CLocalFileSystem::VerifyVolume

      BOOL CLpfs::SameVolume(CLocalFileSystem* fs)
            {                          // CLpfs::SameVolume
            return TRUE;
            }                          // CLpfs::SameVolume

      void CLpfs::GetVolumeLabel(PDWORD pVolSer, char* pVolLabel)
            {                              // CLpfs::GetVolumeLabel
            PBYTE bootsec = ReadBootSector();
            if (!bootsec)
                return;
            *pVolSer = *(PDWORD) (bootsec + 0x39);
            memcpy(pVolLabel, bootsec + 0x43, 11);
            pVolLabel[11] = 0;
            _HeapFree(bootsec, 0);
            }                              // CLpfs::GetVolumeLabel
```

Within *MountVolumeThunk*, I create an extra file system object simply to make it easy to perform I/O against the volume; we'll always discard this object before returning. I then call a member function named *VerifyVolume* to perform the actual request. *VerifyVolume* in turn calls a virtual function named *SameVolume* to compare whatever is important about the new volume with similar information remembered about the old volume. VFAT makes a number of checks, for example, including whether the vendor ID, serial number, label, and disk format all match. (VFAT will rewrite the vendor ID of a removable volume so that it can distinguish between mass-produced volumes. I discussed this somewhat questionable operation in a note in Chapter 15.) The last two of these functions—*CLpfs::SameVolume* and *CLpfs::GetVolumeLabel*—are essentially dummies that I wrote just to have this functionality work if it's ever called. (It isn't called, by the way, because the RAM disk against which I tested LPFS doesn't have removable media.)

Volume-Oriented I/O Requests

To implement an I/O request that pertains to your volume, the IFS Manager calls one of the functions whose addresses you provided in the *ir_vfunc* table when your driver returned from *IR_FSD_MOUNT*. The DDK documentation describes these functions with names like *FS_DeleteFile*, and so forth, so I'll follow the same convention. The functions are as follows:

FS_DeleteFile *FS_DeleteFile* deletes the files whose parsed pathname appears in *ir_ppath*. Since LPFS doesn't allow you to delete its one-and-only file, I don't have a sample to show you for this function. This function isn't simple to implement because you might have to search the lowest-level directory for wildcard matches to select files for deletion. When we discuss the *FS_FindFirstFile* function on page 618, I'll show an example of how to do a wildcard search in an FSD.

FS_Dir *FS_Dir* performs a function on a directory, such as creating or deleting a directory, checking for the existence of a directory, or converting a directory name between its long-name form and its 8.3 form.

FS_DirectDiskIO The IFS Manager calls *FS_DirectDiskIO* to handle MS-DOS INT 25h (absolute disk read) and INT 26h (absolute disk write) requests. Your FSD should implement the call in three steps:

1. Lock the memory pages involved in the request. If it's not possible to lock the pages, set the *IORF_DOUBLE_BUFFER* flag so that the IOS will perform the I/O into locked buffers it owns.

2. Build and execute an IOS request to read or write sectors.

3. Unlock the pages you locked earlier.

   For example:

```
int CLocalFileSystem::DirectDiskIO(pioreq pir)
    {                           // CLocalFileSystem::DirectDiskIO
    DWORD opcode;
    DWORD pageflags = PAGEMAPGLOBAL;
    DWORD iorflags = IORF_BYPASS_VOLTRK | IORF_HIGH_PRIORITY
        | IORF_SYNC_COMMAND;

    switch (pir->ir_flags)
        {                           // switch on function code
    case DIO_ABS_READ_SECTORS:
        opcode = IOR_READ;
        pageflags |= PAGEMARKDIRTY;
        break;
```

```
    case DIO_ABS_WRITE_SECTORS:
        opcode = IOR_WRITE;
        break;
    case DIO_SET_LOCK_CACHE_STATE:
        return pir->ir_error = 0;
        }                            // switch on function code

    DWORD nbytes = pir->ir_length * m_vrp->VRP_block_size;
    if (!nbytes)
        return pir->ir_error = 0;
    DWORD buffer = (DWORD) pir->ir_data;
    DWORD firstpage = buffer >> 12;
    DWORD npages = ((buffer + nbytes - 1) >> 12) - firstpage
        + 1;
    DWORD locked = _LinPageLock(firstpage, npages, pageflags);
    if (locked)
        pir->ir_data = (ubuffer_t) ((locked & ~4095)
            | (buffer & 4095));
    else
        iorflags |= IORF_DOUBLE_BUFFER;

    PIOR ior = CreateIOR(opcode, iorflags);
    ior->IOR_xfer_count = pir->ir_length;
    ior->IOR_start_addr[0] = pir->ir_pos;
    ior->IOR_buffer_ptr = (DWORD) pir->ir_data;
    SatisfyCriteria(ior);
    SendCommandAndWait(ior);
    pir->ir_error = (short)
        ((ior->IOR_status >= IORS_ERROR_DESIGNTR)
        ? IOSMapIORSToI24(ior->IOR_status, opcode) : 0);
    DestroyIOR(ior);

    if (locked)
        _LinPageUnlock(locked >> 12, npages, PAGEMAPGLOBAL);

    return pir->ir_error;
    }                            // CLocalFileSystem::DirectDiskIO
```

The *ir_flags* parameter indicates which direct disk function we're supposed to perform. (Here and on page 617, I've omitted the default case in the switch statement. A production system should include one.) Since LPFS doesn't maintain any caches, it ignores *DIO_SET_LOCK_CACHE_STATE*. In order to lock the I/O buffer, the function first determines the buffer's length (*nbytes*) by multiplying the transfer count in *ir_length* by the block size recorded in the VRP. It then determines the starting linear page number (*firstpage*) and the number of pages (*npages*) containing the buffer. *_LinPageLock* will lock those pages into physical memory. You use the *PAGEMAPGLOBAL* flag so that the locked buffer will be available in all address contexts, a necessary prerequisite for calling the IOS. If you're performing a read operation, you also supply the *PAGEMARKDIRTY* flag so that the paging supervisor will realize that data in the memory pages has changed.

If *_LinPageLock* succeeds, you compute a new address for the actual I/O operation using the locked address. If *_LinPageLock* fails, you simply set the *IORF_DOUBLE_BUFFER* flag to force the IOS to do its own data copying in and out of its own locked page buffers.

The code that performs the I/O operation is similar to many other examples we've already considered. If an error occurs, you need to map the IOS error code to an MS-DOS critical error code by using *IOSMapIORSToI24*.

The last step in a direct disk I/O operation is to unlock the pages you locked earlier. It's important to pass the *locked* page number to *_LinPageUnlock*. It's also important to supply the *PAGEMAPGLOBAL* flag as well. Since you used that flag in the call to *_LinPageLock*, the VMM will leak memory if you don't also supply the flag when you unlock the pages.

FS_DisconnectResource *FS_DisconnectResource* is the function you use to take the actions required when one of your volumes is unloaded or deleted. You would discard any caches and release all resources associated with the volume, including your own internal data structures. For example:

```
int CLocalFileSystem::DisconnectResource(pioreq pir)
    {                       // CLocalFileSystem::DisconnectResource
    delete this;
    return pir->ir_error = 0;
    }                       // CLocalFileSystem::DisconnectResource
```

FS_FileAttributes *FS_FileAttributes* gets or sets the attributes of a file. The first step in implementing this function would undoubtedly be to find the directory entry that describes the specified file. LPFS uses a particularly stupid directory format in which a single entry occupies an entire disk sector. Even though there's not much of a directory structure on an LPFS disk (just one entry, in fact), I wrote a utility function to perform the directory lookup function:

```
BOOL CLpfs::FindDirectoryEntry(ParsedPath* path,
    DirectoryEntry* ep, ULONG& sector,
    BOOL wantfile /* = TRUE */)
    {                       // CLpfs::FindDirectoryEntry
    CPosition pos(path, wantfile);
    GetRootDirectoryEntry(ep, sector);
    while (!pos.AtEnd()
        && FindNextDirectoryEntry(pos, ep, sector))
        pos.Step();                 // descend through pathname
    return pos.AtEnd();
    }                       // CLpfs::FindDirectoryEntry
```

This function attempts to fill the caller's *ep* structure with a directory entry representing either the file named by the *path* pathname (*wantfile* set to *TRUE*) or the directory containing that file (*wantfile* set to *FALSE*). It uses some machinery that probably doesn't have any general utility, but I can't explain how the example works without delving into that machinery. *CPosition* is an iterator class I wrote to help move through a parsed pathname. Its entire declaration is as follows:

```
class CPosition
{
public:

CPosition(ParsedPath* path, BOOL wantfile) {
    m_path = path;
    m_pos = 4;
    m_last = wantfile
        ? path->pp_totalLength
        : path->pp_prefixLength;}

ParsedPath*     m_path;
int             m_pos;
int             m_last;

BOOL            AtEnd() const {return m_pos >= m_last;}
PathElement*    Current() const {
                    return (PathElement*)
                        ((PBYTE) m_path + m_pos);}
void            Step(){m_pos += Current()->pe_length;}
};
```

The constructor records a pointer to the parsed pathname and a current position just past the header. It also records a stopping position based on whether the iterator's user will be descending all the way to the last element in the pathname (*wantfile* set to *TRUE*) or will stop at the lowest directory level instead (*wantfile* set to *FALSE*). *AtEnd* returns *TRUE* if you've stepped all the way to the place you said you wanted to end up, and *Step* advances you to the next path element. *Current* returns a pointer to the current path element.

Returning to the discussion of *FindDirectoryEntry*, we create an iterator to help descend through the parsed pathname and call *GetRootDirectoryEntry* to obtain the starting point for a traversal of the directory tree. Successive calls to *FindNextDirectoryEntry* then traverse the pathname and the directory tree together in order to locate the desired entry.

FindNextDirectoryEntry contains some sample code that you probably *do* want to know about. Basically, you'll compare the name for which you're searching with both the long name and the 8.3 name in each entry in the current directory (assuming, that is, that you keep both a long name and a short name). To prepare for these tests, you first check to see whether the current path element is a short name. If so, you use *ShortToLossyFcb* to construct an FCB-format name for later comparisons to use:

```
PathElement* element = pos.Current();
int elsize = element->pe_length;

BOOL islong = elsize > 12;
USHORT basename[11];
if (!islong)
    ShortToLossyFcb(basename, element-pe_unichars, elsize);
```

(*ShortToLossyFcb* deals gracefully—by substituting an underscore—with Unicode characters that have no OEM code page equivalents. Since you typically store names on disk using the OEM code page, you use this function instead of *ShortToFcb*.) Then you loop over all the entries in the current directory. If an entry's long name is the same length as the one you're searching for, you convert it to uppercase and do a straight word-for-word comparison:

```
USHORT ucname[LFNMAXNAMELEN];
UniToUpper(ucname, e.longname, e.namelen*2);
if (memcmp(ucname, element->pe_unichars, elsize-2) == 0)
    break; // i.e., leave the loop over directory entries
```

If the long name doesn't match, you do a word-for-word comparison of the short name (which you've presumably kept in the FCB format) with the result of the earlier *ShortToLossyFcb* call:

```
if (!islong
    && memcmp(ep->basename, basename, sizeof(basename)) == 0)
    break;                  // short names match
```

Once *FindDirectoryEntry* has found the directory entry for the file in question, your *FS_FileAttributes* function would then examine the subfunction code in *ir_flags*. For example:

```
int CLpfs::FileAttributes(pioreq pir)
    {                                // CLpfs::FileAttributes
    DirectoryEntry e;
    ULONG sector;

    if (!FindDirectoryEntry(pir->ir_ppath, &e, sector))
        return pir->ir_error = m_error;

    switch (pir->ir_flags)
        {                            // select subfunction
    case GET_ATTRIBUTES:
        pir->ir_attr = e.attr;
```

```
        break;
        ...
        }                               // select subfunction

    return pir->ir_error = 0;
    }                                   // CLpfs::FileAttributes
```

FS_FindFirstFile, FS_FindNextFile, and FS_FindClose Three functions go together to implement a normal file search with Win32 API calls. *FS_FindFirstFile*
initiates a file search that can include wildcards and creates a context handle.
FS_FindNextFile continues the search with the context handle until no more matches
are possible. *FS_FindClose* closes the context handle.

The basic algorithm for doing a wildcard search of a directory is to compare
the search pattern with the long and short names of each directory entry. The
semantics of a Windows 95 search are somewhat more complicated than the ones
MS-DOS uses, however. Windows 95 adds the concept of a set of "must-match"
attributes to the search, as follows: not only must the name of a candidate file match
the pattern, and not only must the attributes of the candidate be included in the
regular attribute mask passed to *FS_FindFirstFile*, but all of the attributes in the
must-match mask must be present.

As an example of how the must-match mask influences a search, consider a
search for *.* that specifies an attribute mask of 12h, (*FILE_ATTRIBUTE_DIRECTORY*
and *FILE_ATTRIBUTE_HIDDEN*) and no must-match mask. This search would pick
up every normal file plus every directory and every hidden directory or file, as would
a file search using the original MS-DOS semantics. If the search also includes a
must-match mask of 10h (*FILE_ATTRIBUTE_DIRECTORY*), only directory entries
(hidden or not) will be picked up.

The file search in Windows 95 is also complicated by rules about how to handle
long and short filenames. I can best explain the rules by showing you the code that
implements them. First comes a bit of setup based on the examination of some flag
bits that the IFS Manager passes you in the high-order byte of *ir_attr*:

```
int matchsemantics = 0;
if (pir->ir_attr & (FILE_FLAG_KEEP_CASE | FILE_FLAG_IS_LFN))
    matchsemantics |= UFLG_NT;
else
    matchsemantics |= UFLG_DOS;
if (pir->ir_attr & FILE_FLAG_WILDCARDS)
    matchsemantics |= UFLG_META;
BOOL hasdot = (pir->ir_attr & FILE_FLAG_HAS_DOT) != 0;

BYTE excludemask = (~pir->ir_attr) & (FILE_ATTRIBUTE_HIDDEN
    | FILE_ATTRIBUTE_SYSTEM | FILE_ATTRIBUTE_DIRECTORY);
```

This code creates a *matchsemantics* value that you'll use as an argument to the IFS pattern matcher, a *hasdot* value indicating whether the pattern contains a dot or not, and an *excludemask* value that contains attribute bits that can't be present in a matching directory entry.

Within a loop over directory entries, you first verify that the current entry has the right set of attributes:

```
if ((e.attr & excludemask) || !TestMustMatch(pir, e.attr))
    continue;
```

TestMustMatch is a macro Microsoft provided in IFS.H to implement the rules about must-match attributes; you and I don't have to actually understand those rules in order to honor them. Then you compare the long and short names to the pattern, as follows:

```
USHORT thisname[LFNMAXNAMELEN+1];
thisname[UniToUpper(thisname, e.longname, e.namelen*2)/2] = 0;

if (IFSMgr_MetaMatch(pattern, thisname, matchsemantics))
    break;          // found match

thisname[FcbToShort(thisname, e.basename, hasdot)/2] = 0;
if (IFSMgr_MetaMatch(pattern, thisname, matchsemantics))
    break;          // found match
```

IFSMgr_MetaMatch is the pattern matching program. It takes two null-terminated, uppercase Unicode strings and an indicator (*matchsemantics*) for what comparison semantics to employ. *UFLG_NT* indicates that the program should use the Win32 method of matching names, wherein * is a regular-expression operator and . is just another character in a name. *UFLG_DOS* (which we're not using in this function but which we will use in the *FS_SearchFile* function) indicates the MS-DOS method of matching, wherein ? matches a single character and . separates the name and extension components of a name. *UFLG_META* indicates that the pattern contains wildcard characters, which necessitates more work than a simple string comparison.

Here, then, is the set of search rules the code shown on this page and on the previous page implements:

- If the pattern contains wildcard characters (if *FILE_FLAG_WILDCARDS* is set), we will pass the *UFLG_META* flag to *IFSMgr_MetaMatch* so it will interpret them.

- If the last component of the pattern is a long name (if either *FILE_FLAG_-KEEP_CASE* or *FILE_FLAG_IS_LFN* is set), we will use Win32 semantics for the pattern matching. Otherwise, we are starting with a name that is 8.3-compatible, and we will use MS-DOS semantics.

■ If the pattern has a dot in it (if *FILE_FLAG_HAS_DOT* is set), whenever we compare a directory entry that doesn't have a file extension, we'll artificially add a trailing dot to the short name (by setting the last argument to *FcbToShort* to *TRUE*). The reason for this curious activity is that MS-DOS considers the pattern *x.* (with a trailing dot) to match files whose names match *x* and have no extension, but considers the pattern *x* (without a dot) to match files whose name matches *x* whether or not they have an extension. It's harder to explain than to code.

If the initial *FS_FindFirstFile* call succeeds, you will want to create a control block of some sort within which to record the ongoing context of the search. You set *ir_fh* equal to a handle (probably the address of your structure) that will let you find the block later on. Your *FS_FindNextFile* function will use the context information to resume the search from the most recent point. The IFS Manager will eventually call your *FS_FindClose* function to release the control block.

You also need to complete a *hndlfunc* structure whose address the IFS Manager gives you in *ir_hfunc*. There's a macro named *SetHandleFunc* in IFS.H to help you fill in the structure:

```
#undef vt
#define vt(f) f##Thunk,

static hndlmisc findmisc = {
    IFS_VERSION,
    IFS_REVISION,
    NUM_HNDLMISC, {
    vt(EmptyFunc)            // HM_SEEK
    vt(FindClose)            // HM_CLOSE
    vt(EmptyFunc)            // HM_COMMIT
    vt(EmptyFunc)            // HM_FILELOCKS
    vt(EmptyFunc)            // HM_FILETIMES
    vt(EmptyFunc)            // HM_PIPEREQUEST
    vt(EmptyFunc)            // HM_HANDLEINFO
    vt(EnumerateHandle)      // HM_ENUMHANDLE
    }};

SetHandleFunc(pir, FindNextFileThunk,
    EmptyFuncThunk, &findmisc);
```

The *findmisc* structure provides the addresses of some of the functions that the IFS Manager might need to call during the search loop. You supply the address of your *FS_FindNextFile* function in the *SetHandleFunc* macro itself. (The way I implemented LPFS, I actually need to give the IFS Manager the address of a thunk procedure in all cases. The thunk extracts a *this* pointer from *ir_rh* and then calls the corresponding member function associated with a *CLpfs* object.)

FS_FlushVolume *FS_FlushVolume* flushes any pending output data to the device. *ir_options* can contain two flag bits to control additional behavior. If the *VOL_RE-MOUNT* flag is set, you should discard all the information you've built up about the device and act as though you have just mounted the volume. You might, for example, receive a *VOL_REMOUNT* request after someone reformats your volume, meaning that the disk geometry might have changed.

If the *VOL_DISCARD_CACHE* flag is set, you should discard any cached data buffers you've been maintaining *instead of* letting them get written to the device.

Finally, you should send either an *IOR_FLUSH_DRIVE* or an *IOR_FLUSH_-DRIVE_AND_DISCARD* request to the device. For example:

```
int CLpfs::FlushVolume(pioreq pir)
    {                               // CLpfs::FlushVolume
    PIOR ior = CreateIOR((pir->ir_options & VOL_DISCARD_CACHE)
        ? IOR_FLUSH_DRIVE_AND_DISCARD : IOR_FLUSH_DRIVE, 0);
    if (!ior)
        return pir->ir_error = ERROR_NOT_ENOUGH_MEMORY;
    SendCommandAndWait(ior);
    DestroyIOR(ior);                // ignore any error

    return pir->ir_error = 0;
    }                               // CLpfs::FlushVolume
```

FS_GetDiskInfo *FS_GetDiskInfo* retrieves information about the free space on a disk drive. In real life, you would have a way of determining this information. LPFS just makes the information up:

```
int CLpfs::GetDiskInfo(pioreq pir)
    {                               // CLpfs::GetDiskInfo
    pir->ir_length = 512;   // bytes per sector
    pir->ir_size = 4096;    // total allocation units
    pir->ir_sectors = 1;    // number of sectors per alloc unit
    pir->ir_numfree = 42;   // number of free alloc units (a lie)
    return pir->ir_error = 0;
    }                               // CLpfs::GetDiskInfo
```

The documentation for this function also says (incorrectly) that a FAT-compatible file system should return a pointer to something called the FAT allocation byte in *ir_data*. The FSD should instead return the byte directly in *ir_flags*.

FS_GetDiskParms This function returns the real-mode address of the MS-DOS DPB. If your FSD doesn't maintain a DPB, you can fail this call. If you *do* maintain a DPB, you find it during the processing of *IR_FSD_MOUNT* by searching through the list of DPBs starting with the address you receive in *ir_rh*.

FS_Ioctl16Drive The *FS_Ioctl16Drive* function performs an I/O control (IOCTL) operation on the volume. Most FSDs pass this request through to the disk device. For example:

```
int CLocalFileSystem::Ioctl16Drive(pioreq pir)
{                              // CLocalFileSystem::Ioctl16Drive
PIOR ior = CreateIOR(IOR_GEN_IOCTL, IORF_SYNC_COMMAND);
if (!ior)
    return pir->ir_error = ERROR_NOT_ENOUGH_MEMORY;

// macro to simplify grossly long field name access:
#define ioctl(f) ior->_ureq.sdeffsd_req_usage._IOR_ioctl_##f

CLIENT_STRUCT* pRegs = (CLIENT_STRUCT*) pir->ir_cregptr;
ioctl(client_params) = (ULONG) pRegs;
ioctl(function) = _ClientAX;
ASSERT(_ClientBL-1 == m_drive);
ioctl(drive) = m_drive;
ioctl(control_param) = _ClientCX;

if (pir->ir_options & IOCTL_PKT_LINEAR_ADDRESS)
    ioctl(buffer_ptr) = (ULONG) pir->ir_data;
else
    {                          // 16-bit IOCTL
    ior->IOR_flags |= IORF_16BIT_IOCTL;
    ioctl(buffer_ptr) = (ULONG) Client_Ptr_Flat(DS, DX);
    }                          // 16-bit IOCTL

SendCommandAndWait(ior);
USHORT status = ior->IOR_status;
_ClientAX = (USHORT) ioctl(return);
DestroyIOR(ior);

if (status >= IORS_ERROR_DESIGNTR)
    status = (USHORT) IOSMapIORSToI21(status);
else
    status = 0;     // success after error is still success

return pir->ir_error = (int) status;
}                              // CLocalFileSystem::Ioctl16Drive
```

This example closely mirrors the way the VDEF sample in the DDK handles the IOCTL request. It first creates and initializes an IOS I/O request descriptor to perform an *IOR_GEN_IOCTL* request. The format of the IOCTL request isn't documented anywhere else, but you can deduce it from the sample:

- *_IOR_ioctl_client_params* points to the client register structure for the VM that's issuing the IOCTL request. You find a pointer to this structure in the *ir_cregptr* field of the *ioreq* structure.

- *_IOR_ioctl_function* contains the IOCTL function request from the client's AX register.

- *_IOR_ioctl_drive* contains the 0-based drive index for the request.

- *_IOR_ioctl_control_param* contains the control parameter from the client's CX register.

- *_IOR_ioctl_buffer_ptr* points to the client's data buffer. If a 16-bit client has requested the function, you generate this address from the client DS:DX register pair by calling *Map_Flat* (this is done inside my *Client_Ptr_Flat* macro). If a 32-bit client has requested the function, you receive the buffer address as a parameter.

- *_IOR_ioctl_return* will hold the IOCTL completion code on return.

Since you're dealing with the IOS, you have to type hundreds of extra characters to express these ideas. After about three lines, I gave up and wrote the little *ioctl* macro you see in this code sample. Without the macro, I know I would have had at least two compilation errors per line of code, and I wouldn't have been able to follow the logic either.

You might have noticed that the *Ioctl16Drive* function uses the *IORF_SYNC_COMMAND* flag, even though I said earlier that most FSDs use their own logic for awaiting a request. Since the command-waiting logic I'm using elsewhere relies on a field of the *_ureq* structure that's also needed by the IOCTL request itself, it's essential not to use that logic here!

FS_OpenFile *FS_OpenFile* is the basic function for opening files. I'll discuss it in detail in the next section of this chapter.

FS_QueryResourceInfo *FS_QueryResourceInfo* provides basic information about your file system to the IFS Manager. The *ir_options* value is a "level" indicator. Local file systems need to respond only to a level 2 inquiry. For example:

```
int CLpfs::QueryResourceInfo(pioreq pir)
    {                               // CLpfs::QueryResourceInfo
    if (pir->ir_options == 2)
        {                           // answer level 2 query
        pir->ir_length =
            sizeof(((DirectoryEntry*) NULL)->longname);
        pir->ir_options = FS_CASE_IS_PRESERVED
```

```
              | FS_UNICODE_STORED_ON_DISK
              | FS_VOL_SUPPORTS_LONG_NAMES;
        return pir->ir_error = 0;
        }                               // answer level 2 query
    return pir->ir_error = ERROR_INVALID_FUNCTION;
    }                                   // CLpfs::QueryResourceInfo
```

You set *ir_length* equal to the longest filename your file system supports. VFAT, for example, supports a 255-character filename, while LPFS supports only a 234-character filename. You set *ir_options* using flag bits that denote the capabilities of your file system. LPFS reports that it stores long filenames in Unicode and that it preserves the case of names. You could also report *FS_VOL_IS_COMPRESSED* if your file system compresses the data on the volume.

FS_RenameFile *FS_RenameFile* renames one or more files. If the user specifies wildcards in the source name for an MS-DOS RENAME command based on long filenames, MS-DOS will enumerate the source files and cause your driver to be called repeatedly to rename each one. The IFS Manager sometimes expects you to do the enumeration to satisfy a rename based on 8.3 names (such as when an ancient MS-DOS program uses INT 21h, function 17h—the FCB rename function). Consequently, you implement this function by first coding a loop to find all the source files. Within the body of the loop, you need to do four basic things:

1. Construct the new name of the file. If you've been doing wildcard matches on an 8.3 name, you need to use the search pattern to build the new name. If you're renaming a file with a long name, the IFS Manager will give you the new name.

2. Verify that no file currently exists with the same name.

3. Construct a new directory entry with new long and short names.

4. Either rewrite the directory entry back to the directory where the file started out or move it to a new directory.

I only want to discuss two of these tasks here: how you construct a short name for a file that also has a long name and how you choose the destination long name from the fields in the *ioreq* structure. You're already familiar with the results of this process: when you rename a file on a FAT volume, the VFAT constructs a new short named by appending a tilde (~) and a unique integer to the first several characters of the long name. Just like the long name, the short name has to be unique. The IFS Manager provides a service named *MatchBasisName* whose sole purpose is to make it easy for you to pick a unique short name.

To use *MatchBasisName*, you do some initial setup:

```
USHORT basename[11];
int maxtail = 0;
CreateBasis(basename, newname->pe_unichars, elsize-2);
```

Here, *newname* points to a *PathElement* item containing the long destination name. *CreateBasis*, as you already know, takes the first eight characters of a filename (padding with blanks if necessary) and appends the first three characters of a file extension (also padding with blanks if necessary) to create an 11-character "basis" name that will be the starting point for the final short name. For example, if the destination name were *HelloWorld.txt*, its basis name would be *HELLOWORTXT*. The variable *maxtail* will end up holding the largest name "tail" found. For example, if the destination directory already contains files named HELLOW~1.TXT and HEL-LOW~3.TXT, *maxtail* will end up equaling 3.

In order to verify that the destination name doesn't already exist, you'll loop over the destination directory comparing the uppercased names of files already in the directory to the *ir_ppath2* name. (*ir_ppath2* is the uppercased destination name. You do a case-insensitive comparison because Windows 95 doesn't distinguish between files whose names are the same apart from case.) Within that loop, include the following code:

```
int tail = MatchBasisName(basename, dup.basename);
if (tail > maxtail)
    maxtail = tail;
if (tail == -1 && !newlong)
    return pir->ir_error = ERROR_ACCESS_DENIED;
```

MatchBasisName compares a basis name (*basename*) to an FCB-format name (which might have a numeric tail preceded by a ~) in a special way:

■ If the directory name has a numeric tail (as in HELLOW~1TXT), *Match-BasisName* compares the characters before the tail to the basis name. If only those characters are the same, it returns the value of the tail as an integer. HELLOWORTXT would match HELLOW~1TXT under this rule, and *MatchBasisName* would return 1.

■ If the directory name lacks a numeric tail but matches the basis name, *MatchBasisName* returns -1. If you were dealing with an 8.3 rename, this return would signal a duplicate name.

■ Otherwise, *MatchBasisName* returns 0 to indicate a mismatch.

If you exit the loop without finding a duplicate long name, you'll end up renaming the file. You construct the short destination name by calling *AppendBasisTail*:

```
AppendBasisTail(basename, maxtail+1);
```

So if you already had HELLOW~1.TXT and HELLOW~3.TXT, you'd end up constructing HELLOW~4.TXT as the short name of the renamed file.

You find the new long name of the file in one of two places. Usually, you'll be asked to preserve case in the new name, so you'll use the Unicode string at *ir_uFName*. Otherwise, you just use *ir_ppath*'s last element (which is uppercase):

```
string_t newname;
if (pir->ir_attr2 & FILE_FLAG_KEEP_CASE)
    newname = pir->ir_uFName;
else
    newname = IFSLastElement(pir->ir_ppath2)->pe_unichars;
```

FS_SearchFile *FS_SearchFile* is the MS-DOS equivalent of the *FS_FindFirstFile* family of functions. The *ir_flags* field tells you whether you're doing a find-first operation (if *ir_flags* is equal to *SEARCH_FIRST*) or a find-next operation (if *ir_flags* is equal to *SEARCH_NEXT*). In addition to using an MS-DOS–style structure to report results, you use a slightly different algorithm for matching the search pattern to your directory entries than with *FS_FindFirstFile*. You can count on receiving an 8.3-compatible search pattern, so you can build an FCB-style version of the search pattern for use in the comparison loop:

```
PathElement* name = (PathElement*)((PBYTE) pir->ir_ppath
    + pir->ir_ppath->pp_prefixLength);
USHORT basename[11];
ShortToLossyFcb(basename, name->pe_unichars, name->pe_length);
int matchsemantics = UFLG_DOS;
if (pir->ir_attr & FILE_FLAG_WILDCARDS)
    matchsemantics |= UFLG_META;
```

Assuming that your directory entry records a short name in the FCB format, you can match names in this way:

```
if (IFSMgr_MetaMatch(basename, e.basename, matchsemantics))
    break;          // found match
```

That is, you call *IFSMgr_MetaMatch* with two FCB-format names and a semantics indicator that includes *UFLG_DOS*. (Since *UFLG_DOS* equals 0, it would be more accurate but less revealing to say that you *don't* include *UFLG_NT* in the semantics indicator.)

TUNNELING

In quantum physics, *tunneling* is a process whereby a particle can move from one place to another despite an intervening, apparently insurmountable energy barrier. The IFS Manager provides a similar feature to help long file-names tunnel through obstinate legacy applications.

Suppose a 16-bit application that isn't long-filename aware wants to rewrite HelloWorld.txt in such a way that no data loss can occur. The normal way to accomplish a safe rewrite is to create a temporary file, delete the original file, and then rename the temporary to have the same name as the original file. Since the 16-bit application only knows about short names, it will follow these steps:

1. Create a temporary file (such as FOO.BAR).

2. Delete the original file, which it only knows by the name HEL-LOW~1.TXT. Normally, deleting the file also deletes the long name of the file.

3. Rename the temporary file to HELLOW~1.TXT.

You'll notice that the long name of the file disappears in this process. Or it would if the long name couldn't tunnel through the energy barrier.

To prevent loss of long names in situations like the one I just described, the IFS Manager remembers the long and short names of a deleted file for about 15 seconds. A file create or rename that occurs within that 15-second window using the original short name causes the IFS Manager to pass a tunneling structure to *FS_OpenFile* or *FS_RenameFile*, as the case may be. The FSD is supposed to honor the name hints in the tunneling structure so that the recreated or renamed file ends up with the same long and short names as the original file. Of course, in the interim someone might sneak up and create a completely different file whose long filename duplicates the one in the hint, in which case the tunneling attempt fails because it can't create a duplicate long filename. (Tunneling is a probabalistic phenomenon in quantum physics, too.)

Needless to say, I thought tunneling was too complex to show in the sample, thereby further justifying my decision to prevent you from deleting any files in LPFS.

Operations on Files

The IFS Manager opens a file on one of your volumes by calling your *FS_OpenFile* routine. The *ir_ppath* field points to the parsed pathname of the file to be opened, *ir_flags* contains mode and sharing options, *ir_options* contains flags indicating what action to take if the specified file either exists or doesn't exist, and *ir_attr* contains flags that describe the parsed pathname as well as the attributes a newly created file should possess. In general, opening a file is a complex process. Since LPFS only allows you to open a file that can't be deleted or renamed, I dummied up an open function as follows:

```
int CLpfs::OpenFile(pioreq pir)
    {                               // CLpfs::OpenFile
    int mode = pir->ir_flags & ACCESS_MODE_MASK;
    int options = pir->ir_options;
    DirectoryEntry e;
    ULONG sector;
    WORD action = 0;
    if (!FindDirectoryEntry(pir->ir_ppath, &e, sector))
        {                               // file not found
        if (options & ACTION_NEXISTS_CREATE)
            m_error = ERROR_ACCESS_DENIED;
        return pir->ir_error = m_error;
        }                               // file not found

    if (!(options & (ACTION_EXISTS_OPEN | ACTION_TRUNCATE)))
        return pir->ir_error = ERROR_FILE_EXISTS;

    action = ACTION_OPENED;
    e.accessed = IFSMgr_Get_DOSTime();
    if (mode == ACCESS_WRITEONLY || mode == ACCESS_READWRITE)
        e.modified = e.accessed;
    WriteSectorNow(sector, (PBYTE) &e);

    #undef vt
    #define vt(f) f##Thunk,

    static hndlmisc openmisc = {
        IFS_VERSION,
        IFS_REVISION,
        NUM_HNDLMISC, {
        vt(FileSeek)
        vt(CloseFile)
        vt(CommitFile)
        vt(LockFile)
        vt(FileDateTime)
        vt(EmptyFunc)               // NamedPipeUNCRequest
        vt(EmptyFunc)               // NamedPipeHandleInfo
        vt(EnumerateHandle)
        }};

    CFile* fp = new CFile(this, &e, sector);
    if (mode == ACCESS_WRITEONLY || mode == ACCESS_READWRITE)
```

```
{                           // open for writing
    fp->m_flags |= CFile::FF_OUTPUT;
    if (options & ACTION_TRUNCATE)
        TruncateFile(fp);
    action = ACTION_REPLACED;
    fp->m_pos = fp->m_size; // append from here
}                           // open for writing

pir->ir_fh = (fh_t) fp;
pir->ir_dostime = e.modified;
pir->ir_size = e.size;
pir->ir_attr = e.attr;
pir->ir_options = action;
SetHandleFunc(pir, ReadFileThunk, WriteFileThunk,
    &openmisc);

return pir->ir_error = 0;
}                           // CLpfs::OpenFile
```

FindDirectoryEntry tries to find the directory entry describing the file we're opening. If the directory search fails, a real file system would create a new file if the *ACTION_NEXISTS_CREATE* action flag were set. LPFS punts at this point, though. Finding the file might be an error unless the caller wants to open an existing file. There are two different action flags that indicate that it will be okay to open an existing file: *ACTION_EXISTS_OPEN* means that the caller wants to read or append an existing file, and *ACTION_TRUNCATE* means that the caller wants to rewrite an existing output file from the beginning.

If your file system records a timestamp for each access to the file, you could capture the current time by calling *IFSMgr_GetDOSTime* and rewriting the directory entry. You could similarly capture and record a last-modification timestamp as well.

You probably need a structure to keep track of each open file on the volume. I defined the following rather minimal class to fulfill this purpose:

```
class CFile
    {                       // CFile
    public:
        CFile(CLpfs* fs, DirectoryEntry* ep, ULONG dirsector);
        ~CFile();

        CFile*  m_next;     // next open file
        CFile*  m_prev;     // previous open file
        CLpfs*  m_fs;       // owning file system object
        ULONG   m_direntry; // sector where directory entry is
        ULONG   m_size;     // current size of file
        ULONG   m_pos;      // current position in file
        ULONG   m_sector;   // sector where file is located
        BYTE    m_flags;    // flags
```

```
        enum FILEFLAGS {
            FF_OUTPUT = 0x01,   // opened for output
            };
    };                          // CFile
```

Opening a file includes creating one of these *CFile* objects. If so directed, you must also truncate an output file to a length of 0.

Finally, you fill in several fields of the *ioreq* structure with information about the file: *ir_fh* holds your handle for the file (probably the address of your internal data structure), *ir_dostime* holds the last-modified time for the file, *ir_size* holds the current size of the file, *ir_options* holds a code describing how you opened the file, and *ir_attr* holds the actual attributes of the file. You also fill in a *hndlfunc* structure belonging to the IFS Manager with the addresses of functions for performing operations on the open file.

By the way, a production file system needs to make a number of additional checks to implement *FS_OpenFile* correctly. For example, *ir_ppath* can be NULL if the file system is taking over a file that was opened in real mode before Windows 95 started up. The Windows 95 DDK documentation explains a number of other checks that are needed, too, in the section titled "FS_OpenFile," under "File System Driver Reference," in the "MS-DOS/Win32" section of the "Design and Implementation Guide."

Operations on Open Files

Your local FSD will supply eight functions for performing operations on open files. I'll discuss the most important of them here to wrap up the discussion of IFS. Refer to the DDK for information about *FS_CommitFile*, *FS_EnumerateHandle*, and *FS_LockFile*, which I won't discuss.

FS_CloseFile *FS_CloseFile* flushes any output buffers to disk, deletes internal structures related to the file, and generally cleans up after a series of operations on an open file. Since LPFS doesn't buffer or cache data, its implementation of this function is relatively simple:

```
int CLpfs::CloseFile(pioreq pir)
    {                               // CLpfs::CloseFile
    CFile* fp = (CFile*) pir->ir_fh;
    m_error = 0;
    if (fp->m_flags & CFile::FF_OUTPUT)
        {                           // file was open for output
        DirectoryEntry e;
        ReadSectorNow(fp->m_direntry, (PBYTE) &e);
        e.size = fp->m_size;
        m_error = WriteSectorNow(fp->m_direntry, (PBYTE) &e);
        }                           // file was open for output
```

```
delete fp;
pir->ir_pos = 0;                   // no file locks to remember
return pir->ir_error = m_error;
}                                  // CLpfs::CloseFile
```

This function rewrites the directory entry to capture any change in the size of an output file and deletes the *CFile* object LPFS has been using to keep track of the file.

The IFS Manager provides a way for file-level locks to be remembered while the entire volume is locked. The mechanism includes having *FS_CloseFile* return a structure in *ir_pos* that details any locks that are currently outstanding. Explaining the mechanism is beyond the scope of this book.

FS_FileSeek *FS_FileSeek* is an advisory service that allows an FSD to optimize its pre-fetches of a file. The function is advisory because the read and write functions both supply a file position that overrides anything recorded by the FSD. I elected to keep track of a current position in LPFS anyway, even though it never ends up being used for anything:

```
int CLpfs::FileSeek(pioreq pir)
    {                              // CLpfs::FileSeek
    CFile* fp = (CFile*) pir->ir_fh;
    ULONG pos = pir->ir_pos;
    switch (pir->ir_flags)
        {                          // select on seek origin option
    case FILE_BEGIN:
        break;                     // relative to beginning
    case FILE_END:
        pos += fp->m_size;         // relative to file size
        break;
    default:
        ASSERT(FALSE);
        break;
        }                          // select on seek origin option
    fp->m_pos = pos;
    pir->ir_pos = pos;
    return pir->ir_error = 0;
    }                              // CLpfs::FileSeek
```

I wondered, like you're probably wondering right now, what happened to the third case that you usually see in a file seek operation, positioning relative to the current position. Since the IFS Manager knows the current position of the file at all times, there's no need for the third variation. The IFS Manager doesn't necessarily know the size of the file, however (it could be changing constantly as people write new data); hence the provision of two variants named *FILE_BEGIN* and *FILE_END*.

FS_FileDateTime *FS_FileDateTime* sets or retrieves one of the three timestamps that you might associate with an open file. You *must* implement a last-modified time. You can implement created and last-accessed times too. Local file operations don't trigger calls to this routine, but I found that writing a file over the network did call it. LPFS implements this function as follows:

```
int CLpfs::FileDateTime(pioreq pir)
    {                               // CLpfs::FileDateTime
    CFile* fp = (CFile*) pir->ir_fh;
    DirectoryEntry e;
    ReadSectorNow(fp->m_direntry, (PBYTE) &e);
    BOOL changed = FALSE;
    switch (pir->ir_flags)
        {                           // perform requested operation
    case GET_MODIFY_DATETIME:
        pir->ir_dostime = e.modified;
        pir->ir_options = 0;
        break;

    case SET_MODIFY_DATETIME:
        if (!(fp->m_flags & CFile::FF_OUTPUT))
            return pir->ir_error = ERROR_ACCESS_DENIED;
        e.modified = pir->ir_dostime;
        changed = TRUE;
        break;
    ...
    }                               // perform requested operation

    if (changed)
        WriteSectorNow(fp->m_direntry, (PBYTE) &e);
    return pir->ir_error = 0;
    }                               // CLpfs::FileDateTime
```

I don't think that there's anything particularly noteworthy about this implementation.

FS_ReadFile *FS_ReadFile* transfers data from the file to a memory buffer. Implementing this function correctly takes a lot of work, in large part because you should perform any I/O operations asynchronously to maximize the overlap between CPU activity and peripheral activity and because you should work with the VCACHE driver to manage a cache of data. LPFS implements the function in a particularly facile way:

```
int CLpfs::ReadFile(pioreq pir)
    {                               // CLpfs::ReadFile
    CFile* fp = (CFile*) pir->ir_fh;
    PBYTE dp = (PBYTE) pir->ir_data;
```

```
    ULONG nbytes = (ULONG) pir->ir_length;
    ULONG pos = (ULONG) pir->ir_pos;

    if (pos > fp->m_size)
        pos = fp->m_size;
    if (pos + nbytes > fp->m_size)
        nbytes = fp->m_size - pos;

    BYTE data[512];
    ReadSectorNow(fp->m_sector, data);
    memcpy(dp, data + pos, nbytes);

    pos += nbytes;
    fp->m_pos = pos;

    pir->ir_pos = pos;
    pir->ir_length = nbytes;
    return pir->ir_error = 0;
    }                           // CLpfs::ReadFile
```

If you wanted to implement this function correctly, you would arrange to use a set of sector-sized buffers that you'd fill asynchronously by using one or more *IOR_READ* requests. You'd also use VCACHE facilities to maintain a cache of disk records to minimize physical I/O. Your *FS_ReadFile* routine would return the status *ERROR_IO_PENDING* to alert the IFS Manager that processing is ongoing. After you have read the sectors required to satisfy a particular request, you'd copy data from the sector buffers and call *IFSMgr_CompleteAsync* to signal completion.

FS_WriteFile *FS_WriteFile* is the last of the important handle-based requests. It transfers data from a memory buffer to the file. Implementing this function correctly is a lot of work because, as with *FS_ReadFile*, you really need to maintain a cache of sector-sized buffers containing the data and do physical write operations asynchronously. LPFS implements the function in a pretty dumb way:

```
    int CLpfs::WriteFile(pioreq pir)
        {                               // CLpfs::WriteFile
        if (ReadOnly())
            return pir->ir_error = ERROR_WRITE_PROTECT;

        CFile* fp = (CFile*) pir->ir_fh;
        ASSERT(fp->m_flags & CFile::FF_OUTPUT);
        PBYTE dp = (PBYTE) pir->ir_data;
        ULONG nbytes = (ULONG) pir->ir_length;
        ULONG pos = (ULONG) pir->ir_pos;
```

```
if (pos > 512)                    // maximum allowed file size for LPFS
    pos = 512;
if (pos + nbytes > 512)
    nbytes = 512-pos;

if (nbytes == 0)
    {                             // truncate file
    fp->m_pos = pos;
    TruncateFile(fp);
    }                             // truncate file
else
    {                             // write some data
    BYTE data[512];
    ReadSectorNow(fp->m_sector, data);
    memcpy(data + pos, dp, nbytes);
    WriteSectorNow(fp->m_sector, data);
    }                             // write some data

pos += nbytes;
fp->m_pos = pos;
if (pos > fp->m_size)
    fp->m_size = pos;

pir->ir_length = nbytes;
pir->ir_pos = pos;
return pir->ir_error = 0;
}                                 // CLpfs::WriteFile
```

ReadOnly is a helper function that checks to see whether the volume is read-only:

```
BOOL CLocalFileSystem::ReadOnly()
{                                 // CLocalFileSystem::ReadOnly
return (m_vrp->VRP_event_flags & VRP_ef_write_protected) != 0;
}                                 // CLocalFileSystem::ReadOnly
```

This implementation doesn't even allow the file to grow beyond 512 bytes, so I know you won't be using it to implement a real file system.

Chapter 17

The DOS Protected Mode Interface

I decided to end this book with a discussion about the point at which many people used to start when they began systems programming in Windows. In Windows 3.0 and 3.1, ring-three programs often needed to rely heavily on the DOS Protected Mode Interface (DPMI). DPMI provides an interface to the Virtual Machine Manager (VMM) for doing systemy kinds of things such as allocating memory and selectors, programming the debug registers, and whatnot. DPMI is still present in Windows 95, and 16-bit programs must continue to use it for limited purposes.

DPMI is a register-oriented API built on software interrupt 31h that allows ring-three protected-mode programs to obtain system services from a "DPMI host" such as Windows 95. DPMI was "invented," if you will, in 1989 and 1990 as part of the Windows 3.0 launch. Microsoft had developed an INT 31h interface between the Windows KRNL386 module and the Windows 3.0 VMM. At the same time, third-party vendors of commercially important applications—notably Lotus 1-2-3 version 3—were relying on DOS extender technology to gain access to protected mode and extended memory. The DOS extenders in turn needed either to be in charge of the whole machine (and thereby able to issue privileged instructions such as LGDT and MOV into CR0) or to be running under the umbrella of a memory manager compliant with the Virtual Control Program Interface (VCPI) standard. Enhanced-mode Windows 3.0 took over the machine and negated both infrastructure alternatives.

To avoid the fiasco of a Windows release that was incompatible with the most popular desktop applications, Microsoft wisely decided to make the INT 31h interface public. As I mentioned in Chapter 4, Microsoft and other interested parties formed the DPMI Standards Committee, which drafted and published a document[1] to describe the interface. Assuming that more work would result in a more fully featured interface, the committee dubbed the standard "version 0.9." It subsequently drafted a 1.0 standard, but Microsoft only implemented one small feature of the new standard. Like Windows 3.x, Windows 95 and all releases of Windows NT have adhered to the DPMI 0.9 specification. Independent vendors such as Qualitas and Quarterdeck Office Systems have embellished their memory managers to include additional features of DPMI, but DPMI 0.9 remains the standard to which you must code if you want Windows compatibility.

DPMI encompasses both a method whereby an application can switch from real mode to protected mode and a collection of functions for the application to use once it is in protected mode. The API allows an application to call on the host for memory and selector management, for mode switching (that is, for moving back and forth between real mode and protected mode), and for accessing shared resources such as the debug registers and the math coprocessor. Sixteen-bit Windows programs sometimes need to use a few of these services to perform system-oriented tasks.

SWITCHING TO PROTECTED MODE

All applications in a DPMI environment begin life in real mode. (In fact, it's probably V86 mode, but the distinction is without practical import for the application.) The application can test for the presence of a DPMI host and simultaneously learn the address of a *mode switch routine* by issuing INT 2Fh, function 1687h:

```
toprot   dd 0
hostsize dw 0

mov  ax, 1687h          ; get DPMI switch routine address
int  2Fh                ;  ..
test ax, ax             ; AX unchanged if no DPMI host,
jnz  nodpmi             ;  so skip if not 0

mov  word ptr toprot, di    ; ES:DI -> mode switch routine
mov  word ptr toprot+2, es  ;  ..
mov  hostsize, si           ; SI = size of host's memory block
```

---

1. DPMI Committee, *DOS Protected Mode Interface (DPMI) Specification, Version 0.9* (1990). This version of the spec is now out of print, but you can obtain the version 1.0 spec from Intel Corporation under the part numbr 240977-001.

INT 2Fh, function 1687h, tests for the presence of a DPMI host. If no host is present, none of the programs that have hooked INT 2Fh will alter the AX register, which will therefore still contain 1687h when the interrupt returns. A DPMI host will set register AX equal to 0, however, which is how the application can tell that a host is present. The host will return the address of a mode switch routine in the ES:DI register pair, and it will also set register SI equal to the number of paragraphs of MS-DOS memory it expects the application to allocate before calling the mode switch routine. Table 17-1 describes the contents of these and other registers in which the DPMI host returns values.

Register	Contents
AX	Zero to indicate success. A nonzero value means that there's no DPMI host present.
BX	Flags, in which only bit 0 has any meaning. If this flag is set, the DPMI host supports 32-bit programs. Windows 95 always sets this flag, of course.
CL	Processor type (2 = 80286, and so on).
DH	DPMI major version number (00h).
DL	DPMI minor version number (5Ah).
SI	Number of paragraphs required for DPMI host private data area.
ES:DI	Address of mode switch routine.

Table 17-1. *Register contents returned by a successful INT 2Fh, function 1687h, call.*

When ready, the application can call the mode switch routine after setting the ES register to the paragraph address of the required host data area. For example:

```
        mov   bx, hostsize          ; size of host data area
        test  bx, bx                ; any data area needed?
        jz    @F                    ; if not, okay
        mov   ah, 48h               ; if so, allocate DOS memory
        int   21h                   ;   ..
        jc    error                 ; skip if error
        mov   es, ax                ; ES -> host data area
@@:
        xor   ax, ax                ; bit 0 == 0 => 16-bit app
        call  [toprot]              ; switch to protected mode
        jc    error                 ; skip if error
```

This fragment of code uses MS-DOS INT 21h, function 48h, to allocate a block of memory for use by the DPMI host, and it sets the ES register equal to the paragraph address of the resulting memory block. It then calls the mode switch routine. If an error prevents the DPMI host from switching the application to protected mode, the carry flag will be set on return and the processor will still be in real mode. Otherwise, the processor will be in protected mode. In that case, because protected-mode programs use segment selectors instead of paragraph numbers, the DPMI host necessarily will have altered the segment registers before returning to the application. The new contents of the segment registers are especially convenient for programs that are used to receiving control from MS-DOS:

- The CS register holds a code selector that begins at the same linear address as the original real-mode CS segment did and has a limit of 64 KB. If your call to the mode switch routine came from real-mode address 2DF0h:908h, for example, the base address of the CS selector will be 0002DF00h.

- The DS register holds a data selector that begins at the same linear address as the original real-mode DS segment did and has a segment limit of 64 KB.

- The SS register holds a data selector that begins at the same linear address as the original real-mode SS segment did and has a segment limit of 64 KB. If SS and DS had the same paragraph number prior to the mode switch call, they will hold the same selector on return.

- The ES register holds a data selector whose base address is the same as the Program Segment Prefix (PSP) for the application and has a segment limit of 256 bytes (the size of a standard PSP). Furthermore, the DPMI host will have replaced the environment pointer at offset 2Ch in the PSP with a protected-mode selector.

- The FS and GS registers (if they exist on the computer) will be 0.

- All the general registers will be unchanged, except that the high half of the ESP register will be 0 if you set the AX register to 1 to indicate that yours is a 32-bit application.

Once an application is in protected mode, it can draw on the DPMI services I'll describe in subsequent sections. If your application is a DOS extender, it uses those services to load and execute an application. If all you want to do is run a program that needs a lot of memory, however, that program doesn't necessarily need to run under the supervision of a DOS extender because Windows (and perhaps other DPMI hosts) provides considerable support for standard MS-DOS and BIOS interrupts. See "Testing the Windows DOS Extender" (Walter Oney, *Windows/DOS Developer's Journal*, February 1994) for more details about this support than you're ever likely to want. In fact, I built the DPMI samples in this chapter using a short bootstrap program that invisibly turns an ordinary real-mode C program into a DPMI client—no commercial DOS extender needed!

You exit from a DPMI protected-mode program by executing INT 21h, function 4Ch—the normal way of exiting an MS-DOS application. Don't try to be cute and issue other interrupts that MS-DOS supports for compatibility: they don't work under DPMI unless your DOS extender happens to intercept them and turn them into INT 21h, function 4Ch, calls.

DPMI FUNCTIONS

Protected-mode programs issue DPMI function requests by loading parameters into the general and segment registers, including a function code in the AX register, and issuing software interrupt 31h. (The memory at location 000C4h, which would otherwise contain the real-mode interrupt vector for INT 31h, instead contains part of a JMP instruction whose only purpose is to maintain compatibility with the obsolete CP/M operating system. Since this memory doesn't contain the address of an interrupt service routine, no real-mode software should have depended on issuing INT 31h instructions at the time DPMI was invented. The protected-mode IDT can perfectly well contain a gate pointing to the DPMI host without impacting real-mode programs that used the real-mode vector for its traditional purpose.) Some DPMI functions require pointers for one or more of their parameters. If you declared your program to be a 16-bit client in the mode switch call, you must supply 16:16 far pointers (that is, pointers with a 16-bit selector and a 16-bit offset) for such parameters. If you declared your program to be a 32-bit client, you must supply 16:32 far pointers (that is, pointers with a 16-bit selector and a 32-bit offset). I'll follow the same convention as the DPMI specification and denote pointer arguments that can be either 16:16 or 16:32 with syntax like ES:[E]DI. The bracketed *E* indicates that you use the extended register (EDI, in this example) in a 32-bit program and the 16-bit register (DI, in this example) in a 16-bit program.

Thirty-two–bit DPMI Clients   It bears repeating that the Windows kernel is a 16-bit DPMI client even though Windows 95 supports Win16 and Win32 applications equally well. The only 32-bit DPMI clients are programs running under a 32-bit DOS extender such as Phar Lap Software's TNT. There's not much reason to use a 32-bit DOS extender in Windows 95 because you can just write a Win32 console application instead. If you need backward compatibility to Windows 3.1, though, or if your customers are demanding standalone MS-DOS applications, you need to use one. If you decide to go this route, be sure that your DOS extender supports at least the non-GUI portions of the Win32 API; otherwise you'll face an unnecessary portability problem.

The DPMI host returns with the carry flag set to indicate an error or clear to indicate success. With few exceptions, the host preserves all registers that aren't explicitly used for output parameters. The only exceptions occur with functions that invalidate selectors, in which the host normally zeros any segment register that it finds holding a newly invalid value.

DPMI organizes function codes by group. The high-order 8 bits of the function code (corresponding to the contents of the AH register) indicate a functional group (see Table 4-4 on page 55). The low-order 8 bits indicate a function within that group. For example, function group 03h contains functions that call real-mode software, and function 0301h is Call Real Mode Procedure With Far Return Frame. Although the 0Exxh services for coprocessor management are, strictly speaking, part of DPMI 1.0, all 0.9 hosts implement them because they are necessary for proper implementation of floating-point support in protected-mode applications.

I don't want to redundantly document all of the DPMI functions here. See the DPMI 0.9 spec and Ralf Brown and Jim Kyle's *PC Interrupts* (Addison-Wesley, 1991) instead, for example. I think it's helpful to see the vocabulary of DPMI used in complete sentences, however, so I want to give a few examples showing how to use the major functions. Along the way, I'll discuss the situations in which Windows 95 applications might still use DPMI.

Using Selector Management Functions

One of the most important groups of DPMI functions is the 00xxh set for selector management. You use function 0000h to allocate one or more descriptors. For example:

```
mov   ax, 0000h        ; function 0000: allocate descriptor
mov   cx, 2            ; we want two descriptors
int   31h             ; get descriptor (return in AX)
jc    initfail        ; die if can't
```

This fragment loads the AX register with the code for the DPMI Allocate LDT Descriptors function. Setting the CX register to 2 indicates that we want to allocate two descriptors. We then issue software interrupt 31h to communicate with the DPMI host. On return, the carry flag will be set if the host was unable to allocate the descriptors. Otherwise, the carry flag will be clear and the AX register will hold the first of the two allocated selectors. The selectors will be ring-three LDT data selectors, which you can confirm by the fact that they match the numeric pattern xxx7h or xxxFh. They will be marked as present but will have a base address and limit of 0. Without more work, all you can do with one of these selectors is read or write the single byte at linear address 0 in the current VM.

Setting Base and Limit

The next step after allocating a selector would probably be setting its base and limit to more useful values. Function 0008h sets the limit. To set a 64-KB limit for a segment, for example, you could use the following code:

```
mov    ax, 0008h      ; function 0008h: set segment limit
mov    bx, es         ; BX = selector
xor    cx, cx         ; CX:DX = new limit
xor    dx, dx         ;   ..
dec    dx             ;     (namely, 64 KB)
int    31h            ; call DPMI to set limit
jc     initfail       ; die if can't
```

When you call function 0008h, you first set the BX register to the selector whose limit you want to change, and you set the CX:DX register pair equal to the new limit. A segment limit is 1 byte less than the length of the segment, which is why I supply the value 0000h:FFFFh in this example. Even if your program is a 32-bit DPMI client, you must still break the limit into pieces in the CX:DX register pair, by the way.

How Long Is My Segment? Although DPMI function 0008h lets you *change* the limit for a segment, there's no DPMI function that lets you *query* the limit. That's because you can simply use the LSL (Load Segment Limit) instruction to find out how long your segment is.

Function 0007h sets the base address for a segment:

```
mov    ax, 0007h      ; function 0007h: set segment base
mov    bx, es         ; BX = selector
mov    ecx, edx       ; CX:DX = base address to set
shr    ecx, 16        ;   ..
int    31h            ; set base address for target segment
jc     initfail       ; die if error setting base
```

In this fragment, we start with the ES register holding the selector whose base address we want to change and with the EDX register holding the desired new base address. We load the BX register with the selector and the CX:DX register pair with the base address, and we then issue INT 31h, function 0007h, to set the base address. Once again, even a 32-bit client uses the CX:DX register pair for the base address.

Allocating Multiple Selectors

Function 0000h returns a selector pointing to only the first of a series of contiguous selectors that it allocates on your behalf. To find successive selectors, you need to add to the initial selector a value that can vary among DPMI hosts. You learn the *interselector increment value* by calling DPMI function 0003h:

```
mov    ax, 0003h      ; function 0003h: get selector increment value
int    31h            ;   (return in AX)
mov    selincr, ax    ; save for later use
```

In Windows 95, the return value is always 8. If you're devoted to portability, you'll always use the return value from function 0003h to get from one selector to the next. In normal practice, the main reason you'd allocate more than one selector is to manage a *huge* array. The *huge* attribute tells a 16-bit C compiler that your array might span more than one 64-KB segment. The Microsoft compiler generates array addressing code assuming that adjacent segments differ by the constant *_AHINCR*, which must equal 2 raised to the *_AHSHIFT* power. *_AHINCR* and *_AHSHIFT* are external constants. In a real-mode module, they equal 4096 and 12, respectively. In Windows programs, these two symbols are imported from the Windows KERNEL module and equal 8 and 3, respectively.

A little-known fact about the Windows memory manager is that it will allocate multiple segments to satisfy requests bigger than 64 KB. GDI bitmaps, for example, are frequently bigger than 64 KB but need to be treated as a unit. When you call *GlobalAlloc*, Windows uses code equivalent to DPMI function 0000h to allocate enough adjacent descriptors to let a 16-bit program access the whole block. It gives the first descriptor a limit equal to the entire length of the block (the length minus 1, that is, because segment limits are always 1 less than the segment size). It gives the last selector a limit equal to the length of the block modulo 64 KB; the intermediate segments all have 64-KB limits. Thus, a program that knows how to use 32-bit addressing can access the whole block using just the first descriptor, while 16-bit programs can use *huge* array arithmetic instead.

Canceling Selectors

When you're done using a selector, you should *cancel* it by calling DPMI function 0001h. For example:

```
mov    ax, 0001h      ; function 0001h: cancel selector
mov    bx, selector   ; BX ==> selector to cancel
int    31h            ; call DPMI
```

If you don't cancel the selectors you're through with, you might run out: there are only 8192 descriptors in one LDT. Windows applications programmers have to keep this point constantly in mind. It's not so much of a problem with DOS-extended applications.

Even though you can allocate more than one selector by a single call to function 0000h, you must make separate calls to function 0001h to cancel one selector at a time.

Alias Selectors

As you know, part of the reason that protected mode is called "protected" is that you can't store data into a code segment and you can't execute code from a data segment. There are times when you need to work around this rule. The standard *int86* function in the runtime library is an example: this function must modify an INT instruction to insert the interrupt number it receives as an argument. In real mode, there's no problem:

```
        mov    al, intno
        mov    byte ptr intinstr+1, al ; okay in real mode
        jmp    short $+2
intinstr:
        int    00h
```

This fragment stores the interrupt number in the second byte of the INT instruction at *intinstr*, executes a JMP instruction to empty the instruction pipeline of the microprocessor (something you need to do unless you're running on a Pentium), and then executes the just-modified INT instruction. As the comment indicates, modifying an instruction is just fine in real mode. In protected mode, however, the MOV into the code segment would cause a general protection fault.

To get around the prohibition against modifying code, you create a data alias for the code selector. For example:

```
        mov    ax, 000Ah                ; function 000Ah: create alias
        mov    bx, cs                   ; BX ==> selector to be aliased
        int    31h                      ; get alias, return in AX
        jc     error                    ; skip if error
        mov    es, ax                   ; access code as data via ES
        mov    al, intno                ; interrupt # from parameter
        mov    byte ptr es:intinstr+1, al; modify program using alias
        jmp    short $+2                ; drain pre-fetch queue
intinstr:
        int    00h                      ; execute modified instruction
        mov    ax, 0001h                ; function 0001h: cancel selector
        mov    bx, es                   ; BX ==> selector to cancel
        int    31h                      ; go cancel the selector
```

Commercial 16-bit DOS extenders contain modified versions of the runtime library *int86* function that do essentially what this fragment illustrates. In real life, of course, you'd create the alias descriptor the first time you execute the function and save it for later use, because the two DPMI calls in this sequence are relatively expensive.

A Problem Avoided   The DPMI host *should* prevent a problem that's not apparent in the preceding code. You can be pretty sure that the INT 31h handler saves and restores all of your registers when it handles the 0001h function. So there's a PUSH ES instruction somewhere near the beginning and a POP ES instruction somewhere near the end. But the selector in the ES register contains the selector you're canceling, and it will be invalid by the time the POP instruction occurs. So it looks like the DPMI host will generate a general protection fault on its way back to you. A well-written DPMI 0.9 host such as Windows will check the saved segment register images before restoring them, however, and will zero any of them that contain invalid selectors. A DPMI 1.0 host is *required* by the specification to do so. So don't be surprised if you find one or more of your segment registers 0 after you cancel a selector.

The BIOS Data Area

The BIOS data area at linear address 400h has a special status in Windows: it's the one memory area whose protected-mode and real-mode addresses are the same—namely 0040h:0000h. Selector 40h appears, of course, to be a ring-zero GDT selector. Indeed, it is located in the GDT, but the DPL in its descriptor is 3, meaning that ring-three programs can use it for data referencing. Accordingly, if you want to access the BIOS data area from a real-mode or protected-mode program in Windows, just load 40h into a segment register and blast away.

The reason selector 40h has these characteristics, by the way, is historical. It seems that Lotus 1-2-3 version 3 (and many popular extended-DOS applications) had 40h built into it in several places as a nonrelocatable constant. Rather than break these vital applications, Microsoft did the right thing and made this one exception to the normal rule that ring-three programs can use only those ring-three LDT selectors that they specifically allocate via DPMI function 0000h.

Other Special Addresses

PCs have other special memory addresses besides 400h. The text buffer for a standard VGA system is at linear address B8000h, for example. Although DPMI hosts needn't (and usually don't) provide the same sort of transparent access to these locations as you have to the BIOS data area, they do support one function—0002h—to simplify access. Function 0002h takes a real-mode paragraph address as an argument and returns a 64-KB data selector. Besides being easier to use than a combination of 0000h, 0007h, and 0008h, this function has the advantage of always returning the same selector for a given real-mode address each time you call it.

For example, the following code (included on the companion disc in the \CHAP17\DPMIDEMO directory) displays the string "Hello, World!" in blue against a cyan background on the sixteenth row of a VGA screen:

```
unsigned int b800;
unsigned short _far *video;
static unsigned char msg[] =
    {'H', 0xB5
    ,'e', 0xB5
    ,'l', 0xB5
    ,'l', 0xB5
    ,'o', 0xB5
    ,',', 0xB5
    ,' ', 0xB5
    ,'W', 0xB5
    ,'o', 0xB5
    ,'r', 0xB5
    ,'l', 0xB5
    ,'d', 0xB5
    ,'!', 0xB5};

pause();
_asm
    {                                   // get selector for video memory
    mov     ax, 0002h                   ; function 0002h: segment to descriptor
    mov     bx, 0B800h                  ; BX = real-mode segment
    int     31h                         ; get selector (return in AX)
    mov     b800, ax                    ; save selector
    }                                   // get selector for video memory
video = MAKELP(b800, 15*2*80);
_fmemcpy(video, msg, sizeof(msg));
```

In the call to DPMI function 0002h, you set the BX register equal to the real-mode paragraph you're trying to access. A successful call returns the selector in the AX register.

You never cancel a selector you obtain using function 0002h, and you don't change its base address or limit either. Because a selector allocated in this manner can never go away, you should use function 0002h sparingly.

Within a Windows program, you can use some predefined selectors that the Windows kernel creates and exports. For example, the symbol _B800H is defined in such a way that its address is linear 000B8000h. Other symbols whose addresses match frequently referenced low-memory locations include _0000H, _0040H, _A000H, _B000H, _C000H, _D000H, _E000H, and _ROMBIOS (instead of _F000H).

Selector Allocation in Windows Applications

Sixteen-bit Windows applications shouldn't usually use DPMI functions for selector allocation and maintenance. There are documented API functions (*AllocSelector, SetSelectorBase*, and *SetSelectorLimit*) that do the same job faster. They are faster because they implicitly use Windows KERNEL code that bypasses DPMI and manipulates the System VM's LDT directly. Even those functions won't work for all purposes, however, and you sometimes need to use the plain old *GlobalAlloc* function to simultaneously reserve a memory block and create a selector by which to address it. Windows hook functions, for example, must be in segments for which the Windows kernel has an arena header (allocated via *GlobalAlloc*, in other words), or else Windows will cancel them on the assumption that they belong to an application that exited without unhooking.

---

arena header The control block used by Windows to describe a global memory object.

Using Memory Management Services

DPMI provides services for managing extended and V86 memory. The main reason why people needed DOS extenders in the first place was to gain access to extended memory. To allocate an extended memory block, use DPMI function 0501h:

```
mov   ax, 0501h            ; function 0501h: allocate memory
xor   cx, cx               ; BX:CX = length (128 KB)
mov   bx, 2                ;  ..
int   31h                  ; (returns linaddr in BX:CX)
jc    err501               ; skip if error
mov   word ptr hmem, di    ; SI:DI = memory block handle
mov   word ptr hmem+2, si  ;  ..
```

Function 0501h expects the byte length of the memory block you want to allocate in the BX:CX register pair (even if your program is a 32-bit client) and returns two values: a memory handle in the SI:DI register pair and a linear base address in the BX:CX register pair. You use the linear base address to set the base address of the selector through which you'll access the memory. You must remember the handle so that you can release the memory block with function 0502h:

```
mov   ax, 0502h            ; function 0502: free memory block
mov   di, word ptr hmem    ; SI:DI = memory block handle
mov   si, word ptr hmem+2
int   31h                  ; release memory
```

As you might guess, function 0501h is a thin wrapper for a VxD call to *PageAllocate*, whereas 0502h is a wrapper for a call to *PageFree*. At the VxD level, some VxD is also watching for the End_PM_App system control message that signifies the end of the protected-mode application. If any DPMI memory blocks still exist, the VMM automatically releases them. Therefore, it's common practice for DPMI clients to just forget about releasing memory blocks allocated by function 0501h.

Another way of allocating extended memory in Windows is to simply issue an INT 21h, function 48h, call from within the DPMI client program. Windows' built-in DOS extender satisfies the request from extended memory instead of passing it down to MS-DOS. As you'd hope, the return value in the AX register is a selector for the memory block. You can also resize and release the memory block by using MS-DOS functions 4Ah and 49h, respectively.

Since Windows interprets INT 21h, function 48h, as a request for extended memory, it would be helpful if there were an easy way to allocate V86-mode memory. Functions 0100h (allocate), 0101h (free), and 0102h (resize) satisfy this need. Don't bother using these functions in a Windows application, however, because they always fail. The reason they fail is that the Windows kernel allocates all of the first megabyte of memory in order to take over its management. A Windows application should use *GlobalDosAlloc* to allocate V86-mode memory in the System VM.

The Visibility of V86 Memory   V86 memory that you allocate in one virtual machine isn't readily visible in another virtual machine. For example, if a Windows application calls *GlobalDosAlloc* to allocate a block of low memory (memory in the first megabyte), the only programs that can easily access that block are ones running in the System VM. Conversely, if an extended DOS program allocates a low memory block using DPMI function 0100h, usually only programs in the same VM as that program can see it. It's always possible for VxDs to look at memory in any VM's V86 area by using the "high linear" address you obtain by adding the *CB_High_Linear* value from that VM's control block to the desired V86 address.

Using Interrupt Hooking Services

DPMI provides services analogous to the MS-DOS *Get* and *Set Vector* services (INT 21h, functions 35h and 25h, respectively) that allow a protected-mode program to hook interrupts. Hooking an interrupt in protected mode means altering the interrupt descriptor table (IDT) entry for the interrupt. Since the host hides the IDT from casual view, you need help from the operating system if you want to inspect or change it.

The following discussion will clear up a few of the confusing details that surround interrupt hooking in a DPMI environment.

Protected-Mode and V86-Mode Interrupts

The first detail to consider is that software interrupts can occur either in protected mode or in V86 mode. A protected-mode INT instruction vectors through IDT entries that you can inspect and modify using DPMI functions 0204h and 0205h. A V86-mode interrupt appears to vector through the interrupt vector table at 0000h:0000h. (In actuality, the interrupt vectors through a special V86-mode IDT, but the DPMI host normally turns around and redispatches the V86-mode program at the address contained in the real-mode vector table.) You can inspect and modify the real-mode interrupt vector table using DPMI functions 0200h and 0201h.

Interrupt Reflection

Adding to the confusion generated by having both protected-mode and V86-mode interrupts to worry about is the fact that the DPMI host *reflects* a protected-mode software interrupt to V86 mode if no one has hooked it. Let's consider INT 5Ch, which is the interrupt interface to NetBIOS. Suppose a protected-mode program uses this interrupt to request a NetBIOS function in a system in which no one ever loaded the VNETBIOS VxD. Unless some support program has hooked the protected-mode 5Ch interrupt, the DPMI host will simply switch the processor to V86 mode and dispatch the real-mode NetBIOS handler. This particular interrupt uses the ES:BX register pair to point to a well-known control block (a network control block, or NCB for short) containing request parameters, one or more buffer addresses, and perhaps the address of a callback function. Since a protected-mode client thinks in terms of selectors, and since the real-mode NetBIOS provider thinks in terms of paragraphs, you can pretty much guarantee that the request will fail due to the unintelligibility of the NCB to the real-mode handler.

Hooking a Protected-Mode Interrupt

In Windows, you'd normally have either VNETBIOS or some 32-bit NetBIOS provider in the picture, and one of them would have used the *Set_PM_Int_Vector* VxD service to hook INT 5Ch. VNETBIOS goes on to translate all the pointers in the NCB to real-mode addresses and to reflect the interrupt down to the real-mode provider. You could accomplish exactly the same thing by hooking the interrupt yourself:

```
mov   ax, 0205h              ; function 0205h: set PM int vector
mov   bl, 5Ch                ; BL = interrupt number
mov   cx, cs                 ; CX:[E]DX -> new handler
mov   dx, offset int5c       ;  ..
int   31h                    ; go hook interrupt
```

(It's customary to also use function 0204h to get the previous handler's address first so you can restore it later, but I omitted this detail from the example.)

When your program later issues INT 5Ch requests, you get control in your own service routine (*int5c* in this example). The transfer of control from the INT instruction to your code isn't immediate, however:

■   Software interrupts in the range 50h through 5Fh actually cause general protection faults when issued in ring three because the IDT gate entries have a Descriptor Privilege Level of 0. Windows traps these interrupts because they are also used for hardware interrupts. Rather than have the interrupt handler inside the VPICD figure out that a hardware interrupt has occurred instead of a ring-three INT instruction, the designers of the VMM elected to just trap the INT instructions. Note that the GP fault results from the DPL stored in the gate entry rather than from any sort of general trap of the INT instruction. It's possible for a control program to trap all V86-mode INT instructions by setting the IOPL to 2 or less, but there's no way to trap all protected-mode INT instructions except by setting all the gate DPLs.

■ Software interrupts in the range 60h through FFh also cause general protection faults, but for a different reason. To save space, Windows allocates IDTs that are only 180h bytes long—long enough to cover interrupts 00h through 5Fh. Interrupts 60h and above are rare enough that saving space is more important than losing time in handling those interrupts.

■ Many other software interrupts vector directly to wherever the IDT points, which is wherever you direct with DPMI function 0205h. To know for sure that your program is going to get control directly, without any intervention from the VMM, you need to inspect the IDT from within a debugger immediately after hooking the interrupt. If the gate has a DPL of 3 and points to your service routine, you know that the interrupt will take the fastest possible path to your code. Otherwise, you know that the VMM will fiddle and diddle with the interrupt before giving you control.

Incidentally, when you hook one of the interrupts that corresponds to a regular real-mode IRQ (such as 08h through 0Fh or 70h through 77h), you establish the virtual-machine handler for a hardware interrupt. In the absence of a ring-zero interrupt routine, the VPICD will call your program to handle the actual hardware interrupt. This mechanism is how COMM.DRV worked in previous versions of Windows, for example.

Another way of hooking a protected-mode interrupt in Windows is to simply issue MS-DOS function 35h. The built-in DOS extender interprets this function as a request to hook the protected-mode vector and doesn't reflect it down to V86 mode.

Processor Exceptions

The single most confusing aspect of DPMI interrupt management arises from the distinction between regular interrupts and processor-generated exceptions. The difference between the two kinds of interrupts is easily described: a general protection fault is an exception that the processor recognizes when your program does something bad (and also when it does some perfectly normal things like clearing interrupts or calling NetBIOS). A regular interrupt occurs when a program issues the INT instruction or when a hardware device interrupts the processor. But how can you tell the difference between a hardware interrupt on IRQ 5 (which appears in the virtual machine as INT 0Dh), a general protection fault (also INT 0Dh), and a software-generated INT 0Dh instruction? You could inspect the in-service register of the interrupt controller and look at the instruction whose address was saved on the stack, I suppose, but those heuristics aren't guaranteed to always work.

DPMI tries to help you disambiguate interrupts by having you hook exceptions separately from interrupts. You use the DPMI functions 0202h and 0203h to get and set a protected-mode exception vector, respectively. So in the hypothetical problem posed in the previous paragraph, GP faults come to your 0203h exception handler, while IRQ 5 and software INT 0Ds come to your 0205h interrupt handler. (If someone deliberately issues an INT 0Dh instruction, they probably deserve the confusion that results because you think that the network card, or some other hardware on IRQ 5, has interrupted.)

The handler for a DPMI processor exception is very different from an ordinary interrupt handler. When you hook an ordinary interrupt, you get control with the stack nicely set up for you to do an IRET or an IRETD to return to the point of interrupt, and the registers (apart from CS:[E]IP and [E]SP, that is) are the same as they were at the time of the interrupt. When you hook an exception, however, DPMI *calls* you on a special 4-KB locked stack rather than on the stack in use at the time of the interrupt. The stack contains information about the exception that is aimed at helping you repair the damage and return to the point of interrupt (see Figure 17-1).

SS	0Eh
SP	0Ch
Flags	0Ah
CS	08h
IP	06h
Error code	04h
Return address	00h

Figure 17-1. *The stack layout at entry to a 16-bit DPMI exception handler.*

The "return address" at offset 00h in the exception frame is the far address to which your exception handler should return. The remaining fields are images of registers as they appeared when the exception occurred. (Sixteen-bit and 32-bit DPMI clients receive information in slightly different formats to reflect the fact that pointers are wider in a 32-bit application. I'm showing and describing only the 16-bit form here.)

Your handler will want to do one of two things in response to an exception: patch things up so the program can continue execution, or terminate the program. In nearly every case I've encountered, I've really wanted my handler to be running on the original stack in the context of the program that interrupted. For example, in some cases I've wanted to print an error message and then perform a *longjmp* around some problem, or I've wanted to invoke something like a floating-point emulator that needs to have all of the original registers easily accessible. Consequently, I've nearly always ended up writing exception handlers that arrange to transfer control to a program that looks like a regular interrupt handler.

For example, the following code fragment hooks the Coprocessor Not Present exception (interrupt 07h) under DPMI:

```
mov    ax, 0202h          ; function 0202h: get exception vector
mov    bl, 7              ; BL = interrupt number
int    31h                ; (return in CX:DX)
mov    word ptr org07, dx ; save current int 07h handler address
mov    word ptr org07+2, cx ;  ..

mov    ax, 0203h          ; function 0203h: set exception vector
mov    bl, 7              ; BL = interrupt number
mov    cx, cs             ; CX:DX -> exception handler
mov    dx, offset int07   ;  ..
int    31h                ;  ..
```

The first series of instructions uses function 0202h to obtain the current exception 07h vector. The second series uses function 0203h to establish *int07* as the exception handler. That function doesn't do anything except arrange to transfer control to a regular interrupt handler:

```
static void _far _loadds int07
    (unsigned int code,            // exception error code
    unsigned int oldip,            // interrupt-old IP
    unsigned int oldcs,            // interrupt-old CS
    unsigned int oldflags,         // interrupt-old flags
    unsigned int oldsp,            // interrupt-old SP
    unsigned int oldss)            // interrupt-old SS
    {                              // int07
    unsigned short _far *stack = MAKELP(oldss, oldsp -= 6);
    stack[0] = oldip;
    stack[1] = oldcs;
    stack[2] = oldflags;
```

```
        _asm
            {                                   // redirect restart address
            mov     oldcs, cs
            mov     ax, offset emulate
            mov     oldip, ax
            }                                   // redirect restart address
        }                                       // int07
```

The operation of this short program is anything but obvious. The argument declarations reflect the contents of the stack at entry to the exception handler, as shown in Figure 17-1 on page 650. The first thing you need to know is that DPMI will redispatch the interrupting program at whatever address, and with whatever flags and stack, it finds in the argument locations when we return. In other words, DPMI is passing arguments to us by location rather than by value, which is similar

---

A NOTE ON COPROCESSOR EMULATION

DPMI 0.9 hosts implement the 0E*xx*h functions from the 1.0 specification in order to provide for access to the math coprocessor. Suppose, for example, that I want to test a floating-point emulator on a machine that has a real coprocessor, and suppose that the emulator relies on trapping not-present exceptions. (The emulator for 16-bit Windows programs fields software interrupts 30h through 3Ah instead. The compiler, linker, and runtime loader all conspire to put either the interrupts or regular 80x87 instructions into your program, depending on whether you have a coprocessor.) I will need to set the EM-bit in register CR0 to enable the not-present exception, but CR0 is protected against ring-three access.

Overcoming the protection on CR0 is one of the main purposes of DPMI function 0E01h. Calling this function with the BX register equal to 2 enables emulation by setting the EM-bit while my virtual machine is in control. (The VCPD, the VxD that manages the coprocessor, has done a *Call_When_Task_Switched* call just so it can virtualize the EM-bit.) Calling it with the BX register equal to 0 disables emulation by clearing the EM-bit.

Real-mode programs can't, of course, call DPMI functions at all; they simply smash CR0 as if they hadn't a care in the world. Windows and most other V86 monitor programs notice that the only change to CR0 is in the EM-bit and virtualize the change. I once wrote a TSR utility to patch around the Pentium divide problem. The utility depended on trapping instructions to emulate divides and a few other problematic instructions. Although it worked fine under VCPI memory managers such as EMM386 and QEMM, it ran dreadfully slowly because of the high cost of virtualizing changes to the EM-bit.

to what happens when you use reference variables in C++. We first compute a far pointer (*stack*) to a location 6 bytes below the program's stack at the time of the interrupt. We then fill in a standard 16-bit interrupt frame with the flags, code selector, and instruction pointer. These steps simulate what the processor normally does when an interrupt occurs. We then alter the instruction address recorded in our arguments (*oldcs:oldip*) to point to a function named *emulate*.

The net effect of the exception handler shown above is that our *emulate* routine will end up getting control like a normal interrupt handler following a not-present exception. In the DPMIDEMO.C program (in the \CHAP17\DPMIDEMO directory on the companion disc), I execute an FNOP instruction after ensuring that a not-present exception will occur. The following simple handler then gains control:

```
typedef struct tagIFRAME
    {                                   // interrupt frame
    unsigned short es, ds;
    unsigned short di, si, bp, sp, bx, dx, cx, ax;
    unsigned short ip, cs, flags;
    } IFRAME;                           // interrupt frame

static void (interrupt _far emulate)(IFRAME f)
    {                                   // emulate
    _asm sti                            // enable virtual interrupts
    printf("Coprocessor not-present exception occurred"
        " at %4.4X:%4.4X\n", f.cs, f.ip);
    f.ip += 2;                          // skip "emulated" instruction
    }                                   // emulate
```

The differing treatment of interrupts and exceptions under DPMI mirrors the fact that VxDs use two different services to hook them: *Set_PM_Int_Vector* for interrupts and *Hook_PM_Fault* for exceptions. But the distinction ends up annoying systems programmers who try to use the different DPMI services, as you can see from the complexity of the preceding example. But there's more confusion yet, because some exceptions (namely 0 through 5 and 7) will be signaled as interrupts if you don't hook them as exceptions. Thus, it wasn't strictly necessary in the example to hook the not-present exception: I could have just hooked INT 7 as a regular interrupt (but then I wouldn't have had an example of exception handling to show you). The other processor exceptions (6 and 8 through 1Fh) cause DPMI to terminate your application if you don't handle them.

Calling Real Mode

DPMI function 0300h (Simulate Real Mode Interrupt) is potentially important to Windows programs, even in Windows 95. This function allows you to invoke a real-mode interrupt handler in the current VM and provides the basic mechanism to allow an application to perform functions that Windows' built-in DOS extender doesn't already handle. To execute this function, you first prepare a *real-mode register structure* (see Figure 17-2) containing images of the registers (*especially* the segment registers) that you want the real-mode interrupt handler to use. Then you set the ES:[E]DI register pair to the address of that structure, the BX register to the interrupt you want to issue, and the CX register to 0. Issuing INT 31h with the AX register equal to 0300h performs the real-mode interrupt you designated. You can inspect the resulting register values in the real-mode register structure.

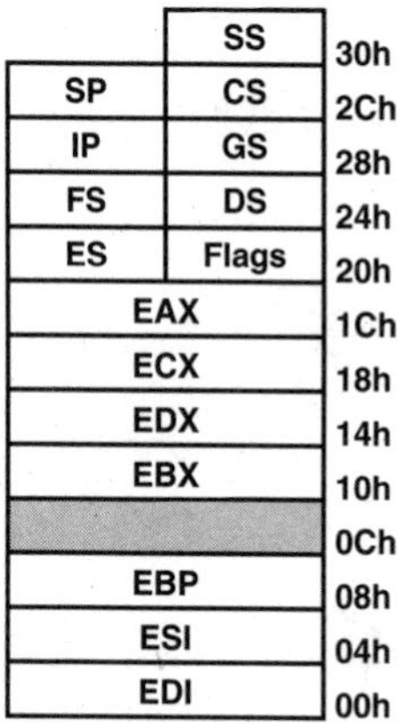

Figure 17-2. *A DPMI real-mode register structure.*

Part of the real-mode register structure depicted in the figure matches the way the PUSHAD instruction places registers on the stack. The missing field at offset 0Ch corresponds to the image of the ESP register, which the POPAD instruction skips over when restoring registers. There's no particular rhyme or reason to the order of the other fields. You should note that you can pass 32-bit general register values to and from real-mode code using this structure, even though most 16-bit programs are never even aware that the general registers have a high-order half.

For example, I needed to release an MS-DOS memory block in the bootstrap loader I used to build the examples for this section. Since DPMI function 0101h works only for memory blocks you allocate with function 0100h, I needed to issue an INT 21h, function 49h. But, since Windows interprets INT 21h, function 49h, as an extended memory management call, I needed to use DPMI function 0300h to execute the function in real mode. The code to do so is as follows:

```
mov     bp, sp          ; save stack pointer
xor     eax, eax        ; get DWORD of zeros
push    eax             ; build real-mode register structure: ss:sp
push    eax             ; cs:ip
```

```
push    eax                 ; fs, gs
push    ax                  ; ds
push    fixseg              ; es (segment to release)
pushf                       ; flags
mov     ecx, 4900h          ; eax = DOS function 49h
push    ecx                 ; ..
push    eax                 ; ecx
push    eax                 ; edx
push    eax                 ; ebx
push    eax                 ; reserved (ESP slot in PUSHAD)
push    eax                 ; ebp
push    eax                 ; esi
push    eax                 ; edi

mov     ax, ss              ; ES:DI -> real-mode register structure
mov     es, ax              ; ..
mov     di, sp              ; ..
mov     ax, 0300h           ; function 0300: simulate real-mode interrupt
mov     bx, 21h             ; BX = interrupt number (21)
xor     cx, cx              ; CX = number of bytes of stack to copy
int     31h                 ; release memory

mov     sp, bp              ; restore stack past register structure
```

Most of this code builds a real-mode register structure that contains lots of zeros on the stack. One fine point I didn't mention is that if you leave the SS:SP fields of the real-mode register structure at 0, DPMI will find a stack on which to execute the real-mode program. That service is very convenient, since it saves you the trouble of allocating and keeping track of a piece of real-mode memory and of filling in the SS:SP values every time you reflect an interrupt.

A Note on Generality The 03*xx*h series of DPMI functions are even more powerful than I described. In addition to using 0300h for simulating a real-mode interrupt, you can use 0301h to perform a far call to a real-mode procedure and 0302h to call a real-mode procedure that will exit using an IRET instruction. All three functions allow you to specify a flag bit in the BX register that causes the (virtual) A20 line to be reset, just in case you're dealing with software that expects addresses to wrap around the megabyte line back to 0. Ugh! In addition, all three services allow you to specify in the CX register the number of 16-bit parameters that you want to have copied from the protected-mode stack to the real-mode stack. This feature makes it relatively simple to call real-mode programs from protected mode.

Handling Calls from Real Mode

Another powerful DPMI function is 0303h (Allocate Real Mode Callback Address). A real-mode callback is a 16:16 pointer that a real-mode program can call in order to reach a protected-mode program you've written. If you wanted to provide a protected-mode handler for a real-mode interrupt, for example, you'd generate the address using function 0303h and then install the resulting callback address as the real-mode interrupt vector using function 0201h. To use function 0303h, first allocate a persistent real-mode register structure:

```
RMREGS rmregs;
```

You supply the address of this structure when you call function 0303h, but no one actually uses it until DPMI invokes the protected-mode callback routine. It needs to persist for the life of the real-mode callback. Therefore, you often need to reserve static storage for the structure, but you can allocate it on the stack if you know you'll free the callback address before the structure passes out of scope. Next, issue the 0303h function with the DS:SI register pair pointing to the protected-mode procedure you've written and with the ES:DI register pair pointing to the real-mode register structure you set aside. In my sample program, I wanted to trap Ctrl-Break signals. In real mode, you do this by hooking INT 1Bh. The first step is to establish a real-mode callback function with an *int1b* subroutine:

```
mov   ax, 0303h       ; function 0303h: allocate real-mode callback
mov   si, cs          ; DS:SI -> protected-mode procedure to call
mov   ds, si          ;  ..
mov   si, offset int1b
mov   di, ss          ; ES:DI -> real-mode register structure
mov   es, di          ;  ..
lea   di, rmregs      ;  ..
int   31h             ; call DPMI, return in CX:DX
mov   word ptr callback, dx    ; save callback address for 0304h
mov   word ptr callback+2, cx ;  ..
```

The return value from function 0303h is in the CS:DX register pair. (Since the high-order half of this far pointer is a real-mode paragraph number, it just won't work to put it into a segment register, which is why DPMI returns it to you in a general register.)

Continuing with the example of a Ctrl-Break handler, you could hook the real-mode INT 1Bh vector as follows:

```
mov   ax, 0200h          ; function 0200h: get real-mode vector
mov   bl, 1Bh            ; BL = interrupt number
int   31h               ; call DPMI, return in CX:DX
mov   word ptr org1b, dx ; save old 1B vector
mov   word ptr org1b+2, cx ;  ..
```

```
mov    ax, 0201h              ; function 0201h: set real-mode vector
mov    bl, 1Bh                ; BL = interrupt number
mov    dx, word ptr callback; CX:DX = new handler address
mov    cx, word ptr callback+2 ;  ..
int    31h                    ; (always succeeds)
```

The call to function 0200h retrieves the current vector so we can restore it later. The call to 0201h installs a new vector whose address is in the CX:DX register pair.

You could now launch a time-consuming process that you want to be able to interrupt. For example:

```
static volatile int breakflag;
...
    breakflag = 0;
    puts("INT 1Bh hooked. Press Ctrl-Break to test it . . .");
    for (i = 0; i < 10000000 && !breakflag; ++i)
        ;
    if (breakflag)
        printf("Loop terminated due to Ctrl-Break"
            " with counter = %ld\n", i);
    else
        printf("Loop terminated by itself after %ld iterations\n", i);
...
```

When you execute this long loop and press Ctrl-Break, Windows passes the resulting keyboard interrupt to the BIOS, which recognizes the sequence as denoting a break and signals INT 1Bh in real mode. Because you've hooked the real-mode vector, control passes initially to the real-mode callback address and eventually to your protected-mode *int1b* routine. That routine receives control on the 4-KB locked DPMI stack and should exit via an IRET instruction after altering the real-mode registers appropriately. For example:

```
static void (interrupt _far int1b)(IFRAME f)
    {                                  // int1b
    unsigned short _far *stack;        // pointer to real-mode stack
    RMREGS _far *rp;                   // pointer to real-mode registers

    breakflag = 1;

    stack = MAKELP(f.ds, f.si);
    rp = MAKELP(f.es, f.di);
    rp->ip = stack[0];
    rp->cs = stack[1];
    rp->flags = stack[2];
    rp->sp += 6;
    }                                  // int1b
```

The only substantive operation this function performs is to set a global variable (*breakflag*) to terminate the loop in the main program. The remaining statements are administrative overhead needed to properly unwind the real-mode INT 1Bh call. We first create a far pointer (*stack*) to the stack on which the real-mode program was running. DPMI gives us the protected-mode version of this stack in the DS:SI register pair. The sample shows how to extract the original contents of DS:SI from the location at which a Microsoft C *interrupt* function prolog saves them. DPMI also gives us the address of a real-mode register structure in the ES:DI register pair. This structure initially contains the registers at the time the INT 1Bh occurred, and after we return DPMI will restart the real-mode program with whatever register images we leave in this structure. In this case, we simulate a real-mode IRET instruction by popping the CS, IP, and Flags registers from the real-mode stack.

I couldn't help but notice, the first time I needed to handle Ctrl-Break in a protected-mode program, what a pain in the neck it was to jump through all of these DPMI hoops. Ah well, such is the price of progress.

Some Other DPMI Functions

Before wrapping up this discussion of DPMI, I want to mention a few more miscellaneous functions. First of all, it's worth it to know about the quirky behavior of function 0400h (Get Version). In all enhanced-mode versions of Windows, this function has returned the value 005Ah. The value 005Ah is 0.90 expressed as a fixed-point binary integer. Standard-mode implementations of Windows always returned 0090h instead, which is 0.90 expressed using binary-coded decimal notation. This value is a mistake, but even Windows NT version 3.1 made the same mistake. (Version 3.51 does not: it returns 005Ah as it's supposed to.) So if you ever find code claiming that you're using DPMI version 0.144, you can guess that you're running in standard-mode Windows 3.0 or 3.1.

Perhaps the most useless of the DPMI 0.9 functions is 0604h (Get Page Size). Windows has always used 4096-byte pages and probably always will, so this service always returns 4096. In fact, a delegate to the DPMI Standards Committee proposed renaming it "Function Which Returns 4096."

At almost the other end of the utility spectrum from 0604h is 0800h (Map Physical Address). This function takes a physical address in the BX:CX register pair and a byte count in the SI:DI register pair and returns (in the BX:CX register pair) a linear address by which the specified physical region can be addressed. Function 0800h is therefore invaluable for ring-three drivers that need to access the physical memory for a device. As you can imagine, this function is just a thin wrapper around the *_MapPhysToLinear* service we discussed in connection with I/O programming.

Finally, I want to mention the curious 09*xx*h functions, which help you manage the virtual interrupt state of your virtual machine. Real-mode code, especially real-mode interrupt handlers, often contains a sequence like the following:

```
pushf              ; save flags
cli                ; disable interrupts
...
popf               ; restore flags, including interrupt state
```

The PUSHF instruction saves the Flags register, which includes the *Interrupt Enable* flag, on the stack. The CLI instruction disables the processor so that some sensitive work or other can proceed undisturbed. The final POPF instruction restores the Flags register as it was before the CLI instruction was executed, thereby preserving whatever state the interrupt flag happened to be in. In general, you want to use a code sequence like this rather than just assuming it will be okay to execute an STI instruction when you leave the sensitive section of code. We used similar code (but with PUSHFD and POPFD so that we'd save and restore all 32 bits of the EFlags register) a few times in VxDs, too, for the same reason.

If you execute these three instructions in a ring-three protected mode program, an unexpected thing happens. The Intel chip is perfectly happy to save the Flags register when you execute PUSHF, and the saved flags indicate the enable state of the real machine. The CLI instruction causes a general protection fault because Windows sets the IOPL (the I/O Privilege Level in the Flags register) to 0 when it is running protected-mode applications. (You might recall that the IOPL is usually 3 for *V86-mode* applications, which avoids a sizable performance penalty.) Windows therefore traps the CLI instruction and clears only the *virtual* interrupt flag for the current VM. It leaves the real interrupt flag alone (it's probably enabled, in fact). Even though the real machine can take interrupts during execution of the sensitive section of application code, the VMM won't reflect any interrupts into the VM while the virtual interrupt flag is off. The VMM thereby honors the spirit of the request implicit in the CLI instruction.

But the POPF instruction doesn't do what you'd expect at all. It doesn't cause a fault, but it doesn't result in any change to the interrupt flag, either! So the processor stays enabled as it always was and the virtual machine stays disabled. This behavior isn't exactly a bug, but Intel rethought it for the Pentium and provided for more robust maintenance of a virtual enable state.

Avoiding this problem with the virtual interrupt flag is the purpose of the 09*xx*h series of DPMI functions. Instead of the three instructions I showed, you should use the following DPMI calls:

```
mov  ax, 0900h        ; get, then disable virtual interrupt flag
int  31h              ; returns 0900h or 0901h in AX
push ax               ; save result
...
pop  ax               ; restore 0900h or 0901h
int  31h              ; restore virtual interrupt flag
```

The initial call to 0900h disables virtual interrupts and returns either 0900h (if virtual interrupts were already disabled) or 0901h (if virtual interrupts were previously enabled). We save the return value on the stack until after the processing of the sensitive area of code. Then we set the AX register to whatever we saved and call DPMI again. If virtual interrupts were originally disabled, we'll execute function 0900h and leave them disabled. If virtual interrupts were originally enabled, we'll execute function 0901h and re-enable them.

Appendix

Plug and Play Device Identifiers

This appendix presents the information (including errors and omissions) that is found in DEVIDS.TXT, which is the ultimate source for Windows generic device IDs and Plug and Play BIOS device type codes. Part I lists the generic device IDs, while Part II lists the device type codes. You can obtain an up-to-date copy of this document by downloading DEVIDS.ZIP from the CompuServe PLUGPLAY forum. This document is also available from Microsoft's Web site. Use the URL *http://www.microsoft.com/windows/download/devids.txt*.

PART I: WINDOWS GENERIC DEVICE IDS

Many devices, such as the interrupt controller and the keyboard controller, have no standard EISA ID. There are also generic device classes (such as the class for VGA display adapters) that don't have EISA identifiers because they are *classes* of devices instead of single devices from single manufacturers. Yet another set of IDs is used to identify buses. To allow programs to identify various devices that do not have existing EISA IDs, as well as to define compatibility devices, Microsoft has reserved an EISA prefix of *PNP*. The IDs are defined below.

SYSTEM DEVICES - PNP0*xxx*

Device ID	Description
Interrupt Controllers	
PNP0000	AT interrupt controller
PNP0001	EISA interrupt controller
PNP0002	MCA interrupt controller
PNP0003	Advanced Program Interrupt Controller (APIC)
PNP0004	Cyrix SLiC MP interrupt controller
Timers	
PNP0100	AT timer
PNP0101	EISA timer
PNP0102	MCA timer
DMA Controllers	
PNP0200	AT DMA controller
PNP0201	EISA DMA controller
PNP0202	MCA DMA controller
Keyboards	
PNP0300	IBM PC/XT keyboard controller (83-key)
PNP0301	IBM PC/AT keyboard controller (86-key)
PNP0302	IBM PC/XT keyboard controller (84-key)
PNP0303	IBM enhanced keyboard (101/102-key, PS/2 mouse support)
PNP0304	Olivetti keyboard (83-key)
PNP0305	Olivetti keyboard (102-key)
PNP0306	Olivetti keyboard (86-key)
PNP0307	Microsoft Windows keyboard
PNP0308	General Input Device Emulation Interface (GIDEI) legacy
PNP0309	Olivetti keyboard (A101/102-key)
PNP030A	AT&T 302 keyboard
Parallel Devices	
PNP0400	Standard LPT printer port
PNP0401	ECP printer port
Serial Devices	
PNP0500	Standard PC COM port
PNP0501	16550A-compatible COM port

(continued)

SYSTEM DEVICES - PNP0XXX *continued*

Device ID	*Description*
Disk Controllers	
PNP0600	Generic ESDI/IDE/ATA-compatible hard disk controller
PNP0601	Plus Hardcard II
PNP0602	Plus Hardcard IIXL/EZ
PNP0603	HP Omnibook IDE controller
PNP0700	PC standard floppy disk controller
PNP0701	HP Omnibook floppy disk controller
ID Included for Compatibility with Early Device ID List	
PNP0802	Microsoft Sound System–compatible device (obsolete; use PNPB0*xx* instead)
Display Adapters	
PNP0900	VGA-compatible
PNP0901	Video Seven VRAM/VRAM II/1024i
PNP0902	8514/A-compatible
PNP0903	Trident VGA
PNP0904	Cirrus Logic laptop VGA
PNP0905	Cirrus Logic VGA
PNP0906	Tseng Labs ET4000
PNP0907	Western Digital VGA
PNP0908	Western Digital laptop VGA
PNP0909	S3 Inc. 911/924
PNP090A	ATI Ultra Pro/Plus (Mach 32)
PNP090B	ATI Ultra (Mach 8)
PNP090C	XGA-compatible
PNP090D	ATI VGA Wonder
PNP090E	Weitek P9000 graphics adapter
PNP090F	Oak Technology VGA
PNP0910	Compaq Qvision
PNP0911	XGA/2
PNP0912	Tseng Labs W32/W32i/W32p
PNP0913	S3 Inc. 801/928/964
PNP0914	Cirrus Logic 5429/5434 (memory mapped)
PNP0915	Compaq Advanced VGA (AVGA)

(continued)

SYSTEM DEVICES - PNP0*XXX* *continued*

Device ID	Description
Display Adapters *continued*	
PNP0916	ATI Ultra Pro Turbo (Mach 64)
PNP0917	Reserved by Microsoft
PNP0930	Chips & Technologies Super VGA
PNP0931	Chips & Technologies Accelerator
PNP0940	NCR 77c22e Super VGA
PNP0941	NCR 77c32blt
PNP09FF	Plug and Play monitors (VESA DDC)
Peripheral Buses	
PNP0A00	ISA bus
PNP0A01	EISA bus
PNP0A02	MCA bus
PNP0A03	PCI bus
PNP0A04	VESA/VL bus
Real Time Clock, BIOS, and System Board Devices	
PNP0800	AT-style speaker sound
PNP0B00	AT real time clock
PNP0C00	Plug and Play BIOS (only created by the root enumerator)
PNP0C01	System board
PNP0C02	ID for reserving resources required by Plug and Play motherboard registers (not specific to a particular device)
PNP0C03	Plug and Play BIOS event notification interrupt
PNP0C04	Math coprocessor
PNP0C05	APM BIOS (version-independent)
PNP0C06	Reserved for identification of early PnPBIOS implementation
PNP0C07	Reserved for identification of early PnPBIOS implementation
PCMCIA Controller Chipsets	
PNP0E00	Intel 82365-compatible PCMCIA controller
PNP0E01	Cirrus Logic CL-PD6720 PCMCIA controller
PNP0E02	VLSI VL82C146 PCMCIA controller

(continued)

SYSTEM DEVICES - PNP0*xxx* *continued*

Device ID	Description
Mice	
PNP0F00	Microsoft bus mouse
PNP0F01	Microsoft serial mouse
PNP0F02	Microsoft InPort mouse
PNP0F03	Microsoft PS/2 mouse
PNP0F04	MouseSystems mouse
PNP0F05	MouseSystems 3-Button mouse (COM2)
PNP0F06	Genius mouse (COM1)
PNP0F07	Genius mouse (COM2)
PNP0F08	Logitech serial mouse
PNP0F09	Microsoft BallPoint serial mouse
PNP0F0A	Microsoft Plug and Play mouse
PNP0F0B	Microsoft Plug and Play BallPoint mouse
PNP0F0C	Microsoft-compatible serial mouse
PNP0F0D	Microsoft-compatible InPort mouse
PNP0F0E	Microsoft-compatible PS/2 mouse
PNP0F0F	Microsoft-compatible BallPoint serial mouse
PNP0F10	Texas Instruments Quick Port mouse
PNP0F11	Microsoft-compatible bus mouse
PNP0F12	Logitech PS/2 mouse
PNP0F13	PS/2 port for PS/2 mice
PNP0F14	Microsoft Kids mouse
PNP0F15	Logitech bus mouse
PNP0F16	Logitech SWIFT device
PNP0F17	Logitech-compatible serial mouse
PNP0F18	Logitech-compatible bus mouse
PNP0F19	Logitech-compatible PS/2 mouse
PNP0F1A	Logitech-compatible SWIFT device
PNP0F1B	HP Omnibook mouse
PNP0F1C	Compaq LTE trackball PS/2 mouse
PNP0F1D	Compaq LTE trackball serial mouse

(continued)

SYSTEM DEVICES - PNP0*xxx* *continued*

Device ID	Description
Mice *continued*	
PNP0F1E	Microsoft Kids trackball mouse
PNP0F1F	Reserved by Microsoft Input Device Group
PNP0F20	Reserved by Microsoft Input Device Group
PNP0F21	Reserved by Microsoft Input Device Group
PNP0F22	Reserved by Microsoft Input Device Group
PNP0FFF	Reserved by Microsoft Systems

NETWORK ADAPTERS - PNP8*xxx*

Device ID	Description
PNP8001	Novell/Anthem NE3200
PNP8004	Compaq NE3200
PNP8006	Intel EtherExpress/32
PNP8008	HP Ethertwist EISA LAN Adapter/32 (HP27248A)
PNP8065	Ungermann-Bass NIUps or NIUps/EOTP
PNP8072	DEC (DE211) Etherworks MC/TP
PNP8073	DEC (DE212) Etherworks MC/TP_BNC
PNP8078	DCA 10-MB MCA
PNP8074	HP MC LAN Adapter/16 TP (PC27246)
PNP80c9	IBM Token Ring
PNP80ca	IBM Token Ring II
PNP80cb	IBM Token Ring II/Short
PNP80cc	IBM Token Ring 4/16 MB
PNP80d3	Novell/Anthem NE1000
PNP80d4	Novell/Anthem NE2000
PNP80d5	NE1000-compatible
PNP80d6	NE2000-compatible
PNP80d7	Novell/Anthem NE1500T
PNP80d8	Novell/Anthem NE2100
PNP80dd	SMC ArcNetPC
PNP80de	SMC ArcNet PC100, PC200

(continued)

NETWORK ADAPTERS - PNP8xxx *continued*

Device ID	Description
PNP80df	SMC ArcNet PC110, PC210, PC250
PNP80e0	SMC ArcNet PC130/E
PNP80e1	SMC ArcNet PC120, PC220, PC260
PNP80e2	SMC ArcNet PC270/E
PNP80e5	SMC ArcNet PC600W, PC650W
PNP80e7	DEC DEPCA
PNP80e8	DEC (DE100) Etherworks LC
PNP80e9	DEC (DE200) Etherworks Turbo
PNP80ea	DEC (DE101) Etherworks LC/TP
PNP80eb	DEC (DE201) Etherworks Turbo/TP
PNP80ec	DEC (DE202) Etherworks Turbo/TP_BNC
PNP80ed	DEC (DE102) Etherworks LC/TP_BNC
PNP80ee	DEC EE101 (built-in)
PNP80ef	DECpc 433 WS (built-in)
PNP80f1	3Com EtherLink Plus
PNP80f3	3Com EtherLink II or IITP (8-bit or 16-bit)
PNP80f4	3Com TokenLink
PNP80f6	3Com EtherLink 16
PNP80f7	3Com EtherLink III
PNP80fb	Thomas Conrad TC6045
PNP80fc	Thomas Conrad TC6042
PNP80fd	Thomas Conrad TC6142
PNP80fe	Thomas Conrad TC6145
PNP80ff	Thomas Conrad TC6242
PNP8100	Thomas Conrad TC6245
PNP8105	DCA 10 MB
PNP8106	DCA 10 MB fiber optic
PNP8107	DCA 10 MB twisted pair
PNP8113	Racal NI6510
PNP811C	Ungermann-Bass NIUpc
PNP8120	Ungermann-Bass NIUpc/EOTP
PNP8123	SMC StarCard Plus (WD/8003S)

(continued)

NETWORK ADAPTERS - PNP8*xxx* *continued*

Device ID	Description
PNP8124	SMC StarCard Plus with on-board hub (WD/8003SH)
PNP8125	SMC EtherCard Plus (WD/8003E)
PNP8126	SMC EtherCard Plus with boot ROM socket (WD/8003EBT)
PNP8127	SMC EtherCard Plus with boot ROM socket (WD/8003EB)
PNP8128	SMC EtherCard Plus TP (WD/8003WT)
PNP812a	SMC EtherCard Plus 16 with boot ROM socket (WD/8013EBT)
PNP812d	Intel EtherExpress 16 or 16TP
PNP812f	Intel TokenExpress 16/4
PNP8130	Intel TokenExpress MCA 16/4
PNP8132	Intel EtherExpress 16 (MCA)
PNP8137	Artisoft AE-1
PNP8138	Artisoft AE-2 or AE-3
PNP8141	Amplicard AC 210/XT
PNP8142	Amplicard AC 210/AT
PNP814b	Everex SpeedLink /PC16 (EV2027)
PNP8155	HP PC LAN Adapter/8 TP (HP27245)
PNP8156	HP PC LAN Adapter/16 TP (HP27247A)
PNP8157	HP PC LAN Adapter/8 TL (HP27250)
PNP8158	HP PC LAN Adapter/16 TP Plus (HP27247B)
PNP8159	HP PC LAN Adapter/16 TL Plus (HP27252)
PNP815f	National Semiconductor Ethernode *16AT
PNP8160	National Semiconductor AT/LANTIC Ethernode 16-AT3
PNP816a	NCR Token-Ring 4 MB ISA
PNP816d	NCR Token-Ring 16/4 MB ISA
PNP8191	Olicom 16/4 Token-Ring adapter
PNP81c3	SMC EtherCard PLUS Elite (WD/8003EP)
PNP81c4	SMC EtherCard PLUS 10T (WD/8003W)
PNP81c5	SMC EtherCard PLUS Elite 16 (WD/8013EP)
PNP81c6	SMC EtherCard PLUS Elite 16T (WD/8013W)
PNP81c7	SMC EtherCard PLUS Elite 16 Combo (WD/8013EW or 8013EWC)
PNP81c8	SMC EtherElite Ultra 16
PNP81e4	Pure Data PDI9025-32 (Token Ring)

(continued)

NETWORK ADAPTERS - PNP8xxx *continued*

Device ID	Description
PNP81e6	Pure Data PDI508+ (ArcNet)
PNP81e7	Pure Data PDI516+ (ArcNet)
PNP81eb	Proteon Token Ring (P1390)
PNP81ec	Proteon Token Ring (P1392)
PNP81ed	Proteon ISA Token Ring (1340)
PNP81ee	Proteon ISA Token Ring (1342)
PNP81ef	Proteon ISA Token Ring (1346)
PNP81f0	Proteon ISA Token Ring (1347)
PNP81ff	Cabletron E2000 Series DNI
PNP8200	Cabletron E2100 Series DNI
PNP8209	Zenith Data Systems Z-Note
PNP820a	Zenith Data Systems NE2000-compatible
PNP8213	Xircom Pocket Ethernet II
PNP8214	Xircom Pocket Ethernet I
PNP821d	RadiSys EXM-10
PNP8227	SMC 3000 Series
PNP8231	Advanced Micro Devices AM2100/AM1500T
PNP8263	Tulip NCC-16
PNP8277	EXOS 105
PNP828A	Intel '595-based Ethernet
PNP828B	TI2000-style Token Ring
PNP828C	AMD PCNet Family cards
PNP828D	AMD PCNet32 (VL version)
PNP82bd	IBM PCMCIA-NIC
PNP8321	DEC Ethernet (all types)
PNP8323	SMC EtherCard (all types except 8013/A)
PNP8324	ArcNet-compatible
PNP8326	Thomas Conrad (all ArcNet types)
PNP8327	IBM Token Ring (all types)
PNP8385	Remote network access (RNA) driver
PNP8387	RNA point-to-point protocol driver

SCSI AND PROPRIETARY CD ADAPTERS - PNPAxxx

Device ID	Description
PNPA000	Adaptec 154x-compatible SCSI controller
PNPA001	Adaptec 174x-compatible SCSI controller
PNPA002	Future Domain 16-700-compatible controller
PNPA003	Panasonic proprietary CD-ROM adapter (SBPro/SB16)
PNPA01B	Trantor 128 SCSI controller
PNPA01D	Trantor T160 SCSI controller
PNPA01E	Trantor T338 parallel SCSI controller
PNPA01F	Trantor T348 parallel SCSI controller
PNPA020	Trantor Media Vision SCSI controller
PNPA022	Always IN-2000 SCSI controller
PNPA02B	Sony proprietary CD-ROM controller
PNPA02D	Trantor T13b 8-bit SCSI controller
PNPA02F	Trantor T358 parallel SCSI controller
PNPA030	Mitsumi LU-005 single-speed CD-ROM controller + drive
PNPA031	Mitsumi FX-001 single-speed CD-ROM controller + drive
PNPA032	Mitsumi FX-001 double-speed CD-ROM controller + drive

SOUND/VIDEO CAPTURE AND MULTIMEDIA ADAPTERS - PNPBxxx

Device ID	Description
PNPB000	Sound Blaster 1.5–compatible sound device
PNPB001	Sound Blaster 2.0–compatible sound device
PNPB002	Sound Blaster Pro–compatible sound device
PNPB003	Sound Blaster 16–compatible sound device
PNPB004	Thunderboard-compatible sound device
PNPB005	Adlib-compatible FM synthesizer device
PNPB006	MPU401-compatible
PNPB007	Microsoft Windows Sound System–compatible sound device
PNPB008	Compaq Business audio device
PNPB009	Plug and Play Microsoft Windows Sound System device
PNPB00A	Media Vision Pro Audio Spectrum device (Trantor SCSI enabled, Thunder Chip disabled)
PNPB00B	Media Vision Pro Audio 3D device
PNPB00C	MusicQuest MQX-32M

(continued)

SOUND/VIDEO CAPTURE AND
MULTIMEDIA ADAPTERS - PNPBxxx *continued*

Device ID	Description
PNPB00D	Media Vision Pro Audio Spectrum Basic device (no Trantor SCSI, Thunder Chip enabled)
PNPB00E	Media Vision Pro Audio Spectrum device (Trantor SCSI enabled, Thunder Chip enabled)
PNPB00F	Media Vision Jazz-16 chipset (OEM versions)
PNPB010	Auravision VxP500 chipset - Orchid Videola
PNPB018	Media Vision Pro Audio Spectrum 8-bit device
PNPB019	Media Vision Pro Audio Spectrum Basic device (no Trantor SCSI, Thunder Chip disabled)
PNPB020	Yamaha OPL3-compatible FM synthesizer device
PNPB02F	Joystick/game port

MODEMS - PNPCxxx-PNPDxxx

Device ID	Description
PNPC000	Compaq 14400 modem (TBD)
PNPC001	Compaq 2400/9600 modem (TBD)

PART II: DEVICE TYPE CODES

Base Type	Subtype	Interface Type
0: Reserved		
1: Mass storage device	0: SCSI controller	
	1: IDE controller (standard ATA-compatible)	0: Generic IDE
	2: Floppy controller (standard 765-compatible)	0: Generic floppy
	3: IPI controller	0: General IPI
	80h: Other mass storage controller	

(continued)

continued

Base Type	Subtype	Interface Type
2: Network interface controller	0: Ethernet	0: General Ethernet
	1: Token Ring controller	0: General Token Ring
	2: FDDI controller	0: General FDDI
	80h: Other network interface controller	
3: Display controller	0: VGA controller (standard VGA-compatible)	0: Generic VGA-compatible
		1: VESA SVGA-compatible controller
	1: XGA-compatible controller	0: General XGA-compatible controller
	80h: other display controller	
4: Multimedia controller	0: Video controller	0: General video controller
	1: Audio controller	0: General audio controller
	80h: Other multimedia controller	
5: Memory	0: RAM	0: General RAM
	1: FLASH memory	0: General FLASH memory
	80h: Other memory device	
6: Bridge controller	0: Host processor bridge	0: General host processor bridge
	1: ISA bridge	0: General ISA bridge
	2: EISA bridge	0: General EISA bridge
	3: Micro Channel bridge	0: General Micro Channel bridge
	4: PCI bridge	0: General PCI bridge
	5: PCMCIA bridge	0: General PCMCIA bridge
	80h: Other bridge device	

(continued)

continued

Base Type	Subtype	Interface Type
7: Communications device	0: RS-232 device (XT-compatible COM)	0: Generic XT-compatible
		1: 16450-compatible
		2: 16550-compatible
	1: AT-compatible parallel port	0: Generic AT parallel port
		1: Model-30 bidirectional port
		2: ECP 1.*x*-compliant port
	80h: Other communications device	
8: System Peripherals	0: Programmable Interrupt Controller (8259-compatible)	0: Generic 8259 PIC
		1: ISA PIC (8259-compatible)
		2: EISA PIC (8259-compatible)
	1: DMA controller (8237-compatible)	0: Generic DMA controller
		1: ISA DMA controller
		2: EISA DMA controller
	2: System timer (8254-compatible)	0: Generic system timer
		1: ISA system timer
		2: EISA system timers (two timers)
	3: Real time clock	0: Generic RTC controller
		1: ISA RTC controller
	80h: Other system peripheral	

(continued)

continued

Base Type	Subtype	Interface Type
9: Input device	0: Keyboard controller	0: Not applicable
	1: Digitizer (Pen)	0: Not applicable
	2: Mouse controller	0: Not applicable
	80h: Other input controller	
0Ah: Docking station	0: Generic docking station	0: Not applicable
	80h: Other type of docking station	
0Bh: CPU type	0: 386-based processor	0: Not applicable
	1: 486-based processor	0: Not applicable
	2: Pentium-based processor	0: Not applicable

Index

Note: An *italic* page-number reference indicates a figure, a table, or a program listing.

WALTER ONEY

Walter Oney has been a professional systems programmer since he graduated from MIT in 1968. He has specialized in low-level Windows programming since 1990. While working for a major vendor of DOS extenders, he helped draft the DPMI standard. He wrote one of the first Windows extenders to run 32-bit Windows applications under Windows 3.1. As an independent consultant, he has helped many companies and individuals learn systems programming in the Windows arena.

The manuscript for this book was prepared and submitted to Microsoft Press in electronic form. Text files were prepared using Microsoft Word for Windows 95. Pages were composed by Labrecque Publishing Services using Ventura Publisher 4.2 for Windows, with text in Garamond and display type in Helvetica Black. Composed pages were delivered to the printer as electronic prepress files.

Cover Graphic Designers
Greg Erickson, Robin Hjellen

Cover Illustrator
Glenn Mitsui

Interior Graphic Designer
Kim Eggleston

Interior Graphic Artist
Travis Beaven

Principal Compositor
Lisa Bravo

Principal Proofreader
Andrea Fox

Indexer
Foxon-Maddocks Associates

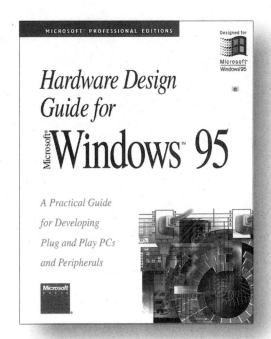

IMPORTANT—READ CAREFULLY BEFORE OPENING SOFTWARE PACKET(S). By opening the sealed packet(s) containing the software, you indicate your acceptance of the following Microsoft License Agreement.

MICROSOFT LICENSE AGREEMENT

(Book Companion Disk)

This is a legal agreement between you (either an individual or an entity) and Microsoft Corporation. By opening the sealed software packet(s) you are agreeing to be bound by the terms of this agreement. If you do not agree to the terms of this agreement, promptly return the unopened software packet(s) and any accompanying written materials to the place you obtained them for a full refund.

MICROSOFT SOFTWARE LICENSE

1. GRANT OF LICENSE. Microsoft grants to you the right to use one copy of the Microsoft software program included with this book (the "SOFTWARE") on a single terminal connected to a single computer. The SOFTWARE is in "use" on a computer when it is loaded into the temporary memory (i.e., RAM) or installed into the permanent memory (e.g., hard disk, CD-ROM, or other storage device) of that computer. You may not network the SOFTWARE or otherwise use it on more than one computer or computer terminal at the same time.

2. COPYRIGHT. The SOFTWARE is owned by Microsoft or its suppliers and is protected by United States copyright laws and international treaty provisions. Therefore, you must treat the SOFTWARE like any other copyrighted material (e.g., a book or musical recording) except that you may either (a) make one copy of the SOFTWARE solely for backup or archival purposes, or (b) transfer the SOFTWARE to a single hard disk provided you keep the original solely for backup or archival purposes. You may not copy the written materials accompanying the SOFTWARE.

3. OTHER RESTRICTIONS. You may not rent or lease the SOFTWARE, but you may transfer the SOFTWARE and accompanying written materials on a permanent basis provided you retain no copies and the recipient agrees to the terms of this Agreement. You may not reverse engineer, decompile, or disassemble the SOFTWARE. If the SOFTWARE is an update or has been updated, any transfer must include the most recent update and all prior versions.

4. DUAL MEDIA SOFTWARE. If the SOFTWARE package contains both 3.5" and 5.25" disks, then you may use only the disks appropriate for your single-user computer. You may not use the other disks on another computer or loan, rent, lease, or transfer them to another user except as part of the permanent transfer (as provided above) of all SOFTWARE and written materials.

5. SAMPLE CODE. If the SOFTWARE includes Sample Code, then Microsoft grants you a royalty-free right to reproduce and distribute the sample code of the SOFTWARE provided that you: (a) distribute the sample code only in conjunction with and as a part of your software product; (b) do not use Microsoft's or its authors' names, logos, or trademarks to market your software product; (c) include the copyright notice that appears on the SOFTWARE on your product label and as a part of the sign-on message for your software product; and (d) agree to indemnify, hold harmless, and defend Microsoft and its authors from and against any claims or lawsuits, including attorneys' fees, that arise or result from the use or distribution of your software product.

DISCLAIMER OF WARRANTY

The SOFTWARE (including instructions for its use) is provided "AS IS" WITHOUT WARRANTY OF ANY KIND. MICROSOFT FURTHER DISCLAIMS ALL IMPLIED WARRANTIES INCLUDING WITHOUT LIMITATION ANY IMPLIED WARRANTIES OF MERCHANTABILITY OR OF FITNESS FOR A PARTICULAR PURPOSE. THE ENTIRE RISK ARISING OUT OF THE USE OR PERFORMANCE OF THE SOFTWARE AND DOCUMENTATION REMAINS WITH YOU.

IN NO EVENT SHALL MICROSOFT, ITS AUTHORS, OR ANYONE ELSE INVOLVED IN THE CREATION, PRODUCTION, OR DELIVERY OF THE SOFTWARE BE LIABLE FOR ANY DAMAGES WHATSOEVER (INCLUDING, WITHOUT LIMITATION, DAMAGES FOR LOSS OF BUSINESS PROFITS, BUSINESS INTERRUPTION, LOSS OF BUSINESS INFORMATION, OR OTHER PECUNIARY LOSS) ARISING OUT OF THE USE OF OR INABILITY TO USE THE SOFTWARE OR DOCUMENTATION, EVEN IF MICROSOFT HAS BEEN ADVISED OF THE POSSIBILITY OF SUCH DAMAGES. BECAUSE SOME STATES/COUNTRIES DO NOT ALLOW THE EXCLUSION OR LIMITATION OF LIABILITY FOR CONSEQUENTIAL OR INCIDENTAL DAMAGES, THE ABOVE LIMITATION MAY NOT APPLY TO YOU.

U.S. GOVERNMENT RESTRICTED RIGHTS

The SOFTWARE and documentation are provided with RESTRICTED RIGHTS. Use, duplication, or disclosure by the Government is subject to restrictions as set forth in subparagraph (c)(1)(ii) of The Rights in Technical Data and Computer Software clause at DFARS 252.227-7013 or subparagraphs (c)(1) and (2) of the Commercial Computer Software — Restricted Rights 48 CFR 52.227-19, as applicable. Manufacturer is Microsoft Corporation, One Microsoft Way, Redmond, WA 98052-6399.

If you acquired this product in the United States, this Agreement is governed by the laws of the State of Washington.

Should you have any questions concerning this Agreement, or if you desire to contact Microsoft Press for any reason, please write: Microsoft Press, One Microsoft Way, Redmond, WA 98052-6399.